The Dealey Plaza UK 50th Anniversary Commemorative Book

JFK
Echoes From Elm Street

A Search for Historical Accuracy on the Assassination of President John F. Kennedy

Edited by Mark Bridger and Barry Keane

© 2013 DPUK, edited by Mark Bridger and Barry Keane

First edition published by Cambridge Academic, The Studio, High Green, Gt. Shelford, Cambridge CB22 5EG.

The rights of DPUK's authors to be identified as the authors of this work have been asserted by them in accordance with the Copyright, Designs and Patents Act 1988.

All rights reserved. No part of this publication may be reproduced, stored in a retrieval system, or transmitted in any form or by any means, electronic, mechanical, photocopying, recording, or otherwise without prior permission of Cambridge Academic at:
The Studio, High Green, Gt. Shelford, Cambridge. CB22 5EG

ISBN 1-903-499-73-9
978-1-903499-73-3

The contents of this publication are provided in good faith and neither The Authors nor The Publisher can be held responsible for any errors or omissions contained herein. Any person relying upon the information must independently satisfy himself or herself as to the safety or any other implications of acting upon such information and no liability shall be accepted either by The Author or The Publisher in the event of reliance upon such information nor for any damage or injury arising from any interpretation of its contents. This publication may not be used in any process of risk assessment.

Printed and bound in the United Kingdom by
4edge Ltd, 7a Eldon Way Industrial Estate, Hockley, Essex, SS5 4AD.

Cover images:
Bettmann Archive/Corbis Images
Kennedy Bust, London/Getty Images

The Editors and authors of this book would like to pay special thanks to Peter Antill for his invaluable contribution to the realisation of this tribute to the memory of John Fitzgerald Kennedy.

For information on Dealey Plaza UK, visit:
www.dealeyplazauk.org.uk

CONTENTS

INTRODUCTION i

ONE// The Lead up to the Assassination 1
Mark Bridger

TWO// The Dealey Plaza Witnesses 5
Bill Robertson

THREE// A Flurry of Shells Come Into the Car 29
Matt Mills

FOUR// Dallas Police and the Hunt for Oswald 41
Mark Bridger

FIVE// The Medical Evidence 55
Russell Kent

SIX// Unsound Acoustics? 101
Chris Scally

SEVEN// The Single Bullet Theory 173
Russell Kent

EIGHT// JFK at Risk 223
Larry Hancock

NINE// J.D. Tippit – a Troubled Officer 233
Stuart Galloway

TEN// A Man of Unusual Training 269
Alaric Rosman

ELEVEN// The Autopsy of John. F. Kennedy 345
Russell Kent

TWELVE// Jack Ruby 383
Tony Austin

THIRTEEN// The Authenticity of the Zapruder Film 441
Chris Scally

FOURTEEN// The Other Side of the Mirror 493
Adrian Morris

FIFTEEN// Why We Don't Know 501
Larry Hancock

SIXTEEN// JFK – Relevant Today? 517
Barry Keane

INDEX // 523

Introduction

It has been 50 years since the appalling murder of President John F. Kennedy in Dallas Texas, on the 22nd November 1963, with large numbers of interested individuals still seeking the truth of what transpired that day. Dealey Plaza UK is a group that research the assassination with a view to finding that truth - a truth the American Government and mainstream media have deliberately avoided for the past 50 years. This book is the result of that search, incorporating the work and endeavours of many group members from the UK, Ireland and the USA including such leaders in their field of research as Larry Hancock, Russell Kent, Alaric Rosman and Chris Scally.

When President John F. Kennedy was assassinated in Dallas his removal had a major effect on numerous disparate factions. A war that may never have taken place occurred, while corrupt officials that faced dismissal and possibly worse found instant job security. Government agencies that faced massive regulation or worse breathed easily again, while major corporations and oil magnates enjoyed monstrous profits that war and Kennedy's death ensured. The lives of organised criminals became easier overnight while in Dallas two days later an innocent man was murdered in police custody. Life changed for many powerful people with the firing of those few bullets that weekend.

The removal of President Kennedy was a tragedy for the USA and the majority of its citizens, but for a number of powerful individuals and vested interests it was crucial for their very survival. On reading this book you will see the murder of John F. Kennedy was a godsend for these powerful interests and of no consequence to an individual named Lee Harvey Oswald, who was posthumously and incorrectly labelled as his assassin.

The US Government produced a report in 1964 (known as the Warren Report) which laid the sole blame on Oswald, and US mainstream media has maintained this position for the past 50 years. This despite a subsequent 1979 U.S government HSCA finding of probable conspiracy in the murder, and the lack of any credible evidence supporting the claim that Oswald was the assassin. The Warren Report was a conscious pack of lies foisted on the world by a corrupt committee and a culpable media. It was straight out of George Orwell and a portent of things to come. It was a victory for power over honesty, for bullet over ballot, for brute force over justice – an ugly charade that has become the norm for Western Governments as we head into the 14th year of the 21st century. Fear and corruption rules and on the main we sit by and watch as criminals in Wall Street and other financial centres steal our wealth from under our noses. The Kennedy assassination was a wrestling of power from the American people by vested interests in the business, espionage and criminal communities. They maintain this power to this day with malleable puppets posing as leaders whilst in reality working for their corporate masters.

For a newcomer to the case this book will hopefully be a stark eye-opener to the real world of money, espionage, murder and corrupt power. To the seasoned researcher we hope the information within will be valuable additions to their understanding of the case. For all it should be clear the mainstream media's portrayal of those who believe in conspiracies as misguided or foolish is more an indication of their own culpability in a failure to question official edicts than anything else. It is they, the mouthpieces of those who perpetuate the "lone-nut" myth that are misguided and foolish. They follow agendas that have nothing to do with disseminating the truth and everything to do with concealing it from the people.

Think for yourself, and judge the evidence for yourself. When a President is shot almost simultaneously in the back from behind, and in the throat and head from in front, it is clear multiple shooters were involved. This book will help you towards the truth the American Government never wants you to discover. Enjoy the journey.

ONE
THE LEAD UP TO THE ASSASSINATION

Mark Bridger

> *"They don't care about you at all, at all, at all ..."* – George Carlin

John F. Kennedy had a proud Irish ancestry, the son of Joseph P. Kennedy, former U.S Ambassador to Great Britain and a multi-millionaire businessman. One of nine children he was born in Brookline Massachusetts on 29th May 1917. After serving in the US Navy during the war, he entered politics serving as a Congressman from 1947 to 1953, and as a Senator from 1953 to December 1960.

He defeated Richard Nixon, then Vice-President of the United States, in the 1960 US Presidential election by the smallest of margins. He was inaugurated on 20th January 1961 as the 35th President of the United States, aged just 43 years old. Less than three years later he would be dead – brutally murdered on the streets of Dallas. His murder has been debated and studied ever since.

In order to gauge what truly happened, and how or why JFK was murdered, it is vital to take a quick look at the important events within his 1,000 or so days in office and ascertain which powerful forces became disenchanted with him and were opposed to him or his policies. In any crime it is usual practice to evaluate which individuals or groups would have had strong enough motive to commit the act, and furthermore who had the capability to do so. Murder is the ultimate crime, and not usually one carried out lightly or without good reason. Where the victim is a man with professional protection the criteria of motive and means would presumably need to be even greater. The final criteria of opportunity would suggest such an assassination would also require meticulous planning.

Unfortunately the entire story of who opposed JFK by the end of 1963 and why would require miles of print and the following condensed précis merely gives an outline, and were the reader so inclined there are numerous books already written showing in minute detail the case for each faction's inclusion. Suffice to say a vast array of powerful and corrupt entities and individuals were manning the proverbial barricades which they calmly left soon after the 22nd November 1963.

Within months of Kennedy's inauguration, in April 1961 he faced his first major problem with what became known as The Bay of Pigs crisis. After Fidel Castro had seized power in Cuba in 1959 his move towards leftist ideals coupled with the expulsion of American criminal elements involved in gambling and prostitution led to a slow but steady deterioration in relations with the U.S., not least with the C.I.A. and the mafia, who increasingly worked together on plans to oust him. These plans were all but finalised by the time Kennedy came to power, culminating in the debacle of the C.I.A./Cuban exile Bay of Pigs invasion that was a complete disaster. Kennedy's refusal to be bullied by the C.I.A and U.S military into using American firepower to save the day incurred the wrath of both these factions as well as the Mafia and Cuban exiles, and this hatred for him would last until the day he died. The C.I.A and the Mafia would subsequently work together secretly on attempts to kill Castro by clandestine means without President Kennedy's authorisation. Many informed researchers feel individuals among these four groups were involved to some degree in facilitating his untimely demise.

Kennedy would also incur the wrath of the military and its intelligence cronies during the Cuban missile crisis in October 1962 with Soviet nuclear missiles stationed in Cuba less than 100 miles from the U.S coast, and the subsequent removal of U.S. missiles in Turkey and Italy was seen by military hawks as a capitulation. His famous speech at the American University in June 1963 spoke of peace and a test-ban treaty with the Soviet Union – ideas that put him at odds with the generals and other military leaders within the U.S. whose raison d'être appeared to be conflict and conquest. Kennedy was also moving towards a détente with Cuba and the Soviet Union before his death with the installation of a "hot line" to Moscow and the mooted closure of overseas military bases.

Through his brother Attorney General Robert Kennedy he was also tackling the problem of organised crime, which pitted him against powerful Mafia bosses such as Santos Trafficante, Sam Giancana, Carlos Marcello and the President of the Teamster's Union Jimmy Hoffa. Incredibly these crime bosses, who had friendly links to the C.I.A through the plots to kill Fidel Castro, were also the beneficiaries of a laissez-faire policy from F.B.I Director J.Edgar Hoover. Both the Mafia and Hoover had a hatred for Bobby Kennedy and no love for his brother who employed him. J.Edgar Hoover was also staring at retirement from his beloved Bureau on 1st January 1965 were Kennedy to remain in power. Lyndon Johnson's elevation to President on 22nd November 1963 ended that little worry for Hoover however.

ONE | THE LEAD UP TO THE ASSASSINATION

In Lyndon Baines Johnson, JFK had a Vice President who was a political liability by the autumn of 1963, an unscrupulous operator who had become implicated in potential scandals involving Billy Sol Estes and Bobby Baker, not to mention the mutual loathing between him and the President's brother Bobby Kennedy. 1964 may well have been an extremely embarrassing and difficult year for L.B.J had John F. Kennedy not been killed 40 days before it began.

As previously mentioned the military hawks in the United States, then as now, viewed an American military hegemony over the world as their right and were increasingly disillusioned at Kennedy's tentative steps towards peace and co-existence with others especially the Soviet Union and China. The situation in Vietnam and Laos in the far east looked increasingly unstable since French withdrawal, and the military along with the powerful arms manufacturers viewed a potential conflict there as a veritable gravy train of enormous proportions. Kennedy's dialogue however of moving towards peace did not augur well for those members of the arms industry and a mooted withdrawal of U.S elements from the region by 1965 spelled complete disaster for their expected windfall. History will show however that the events of 22nd November 1963 and a fortuitous incident at the Gulf of Tonkin ensured the generals got their war and the arms industry sucked well over $100 Billion out of the U.S taxpayer.

The oil industry was and remains an extremely powerful force in America and the oil magnates of the 1960s enjoyed major tax concessions including the oil depletion allowance, a loophole that benefitted a few very wealthy men, especially in oil rich Texas, the scene of J.F.K's murder. In late 1962 Kennedy announced he planned to do away with the oil depletion allowance, thus threatening to dent at least the enormous profits made by the oil industry. This attack on the oil barons however was dropped after the assassination on 22nd November 1963 placed Texan Lyndon B. Johnson in the White House.

Kennedy's policies were viewed as liberal or even "communist" by the rabid right wing elements in America; however groups such as the Ku Klux Klan or the John Birch Society were often difficult to distinguish from certain police or other law enforcement elements in the south, never more so than in Dallas where the assassination occurred. A general feeling of dislike for him in such environs may have ensured the conspiracy that eventually murdered him chose such a location for his public execution.

In 1962 Kennedy also enraged powerful steel industry bosses by pressuring them into reversing price increases in the "public interest" – another example of placing community before the free market, unpopular and exactly the sort of action that ensured big business and the unscrupulous dealers who ruled such enterprises viewed him as a threat to their cosy way of life.

In short Kennedy behaved in his three years in office as if he felt *he* was in charge and not the military and business interests who equally felt they ruled the nation. As we have seen since his death this kudos cannot be levelled at his successors. A rich man himself, Kennedy had embarked on a crusade which would not exactly remove all barriers to a fairer society, but one that may have gone some small way towards a more even distribution of wealth in America. That desire coupled with a move away from constant war meant he was too grave a threat to those violent elements hell bent on maintaining the status quo. Educated observers feel factions within the above named groups were responsible for the events of 22nd November 1963.

Despite all these powerful and sinister enemies however the U.S government would later find a lone stock filler "guilty" of the crime of the century. This finding may well be the lie of the century.

Two
The Dealey Plaza Witnesses

Bill Robertson

"Newsweek", 12/2/63, p. 2: "For a chaotic moment, the motorcade ground to an uncertain halt."
"Time", 11/29/63, p. 23: "There was a shocking momentary stillness, a frozen tableau."

Introduction
Dealey Plaza is a park, completed in 1940 on the western edge of downtown Dallas, where three streets converge (Main Street , Elm Street, and Commerce Street) to pass under a railway bridge known locally as the triple underpass. Dealey Plaza is bounded on south, east, and north sides by 100 foot plus tall buildings. One of these is the former Texas School Book Depository building (TSBD) from which, both the Warren Commission and the House Select Committee on Assassinations concluded, Lee Harvey Oswald fired a rifle that killed President John F. Kennedy.

There is a grassy knoll on the northwest side of the plaza, from which, the House Select Committee on Assassinations determined, there was a "high probability" that a second gunman also fired at President Kennedy, but missed. Things happened in Dealey Plaza before, during and after the assassination of John F Kennedy that prove there was a conspiracy involved in the murder of the President. This chapter concentrates on the evidence that proves the Warren Commission was wrong to conclude Lee Harvey Oswald, acting alone assassinated John F Kennedy and seriously wounded Governor John Connally.

We need to be clear from the outset that there were at least two men in the TSBD on 22 November 1963 using the name 'Lee Harvey Oswald'; the one who was later murdered by Jack Ruby shall be referred to as '**Harvey** Oswald'. The real **Lee** Harvey Oswald was elsewhere in the building and it may well have been he that was seen on the 6th floor of the TSBD. Therefore although the Warren

JFK | ECHOES FROM ELM STREET
A SEARCH FOR HISTORICAL ACCURACY ON THE
ASSASSINATION OF PRESIDENT JOHN F. KENNEDY

Commission was wrong on many things ironically it may have been correct to say that Lee Harvey Oswald was involved in the assassination of John F Kennedy – they just didn't identify the real Lee Harvey Oswald. For a clear explanation regarding the two men the reader should refer to the work of John Armstrong who wrote the excellent book 'Harvey and Lee: How the CIA framed Oswald'.

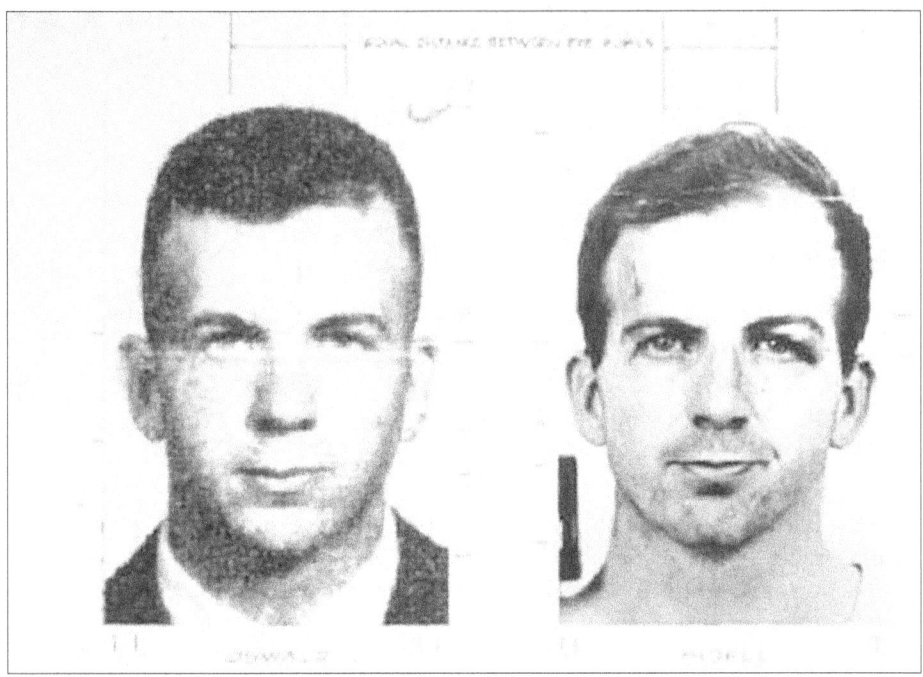

Both of the above men are said to be 'Lee Harvey Oswald'. The one on the right is Harvey, shot by Jack Ruby. Another Oswald look-alike and Dealey Plaza witness who played a major role in obstructing justice was TSBD employee Billy Lovelady; we shall explore his role in the assassination cover-up in more detail below.

November 20 1963
Perhaps the most significant pre-assassination event in Dealey Plaza occurred two days day prior to the assassination and it involved the shocking experience of an innocent 'bystander' who paid for his innocuous actions with 11 years of imprisonment in mental institutions.

Ralph Leon Yates picked up a young man hitchhiking in Oak Cliff, near the Beckley Avenue entrance to the R.L. Thornton Expressway on 20th November 1963 (near Lee Harvey Oswald's rooming house) The young man was carrying a brown wrapping paper package about 4 feet to 4.5 feet long[1]. The young man said that the package contained *'curtain rods'*. The young man was either Lee

TWO | THE DEALEY PLAZA WITNESSES

Harvey Oswald, or his double. During the journey the young man talked about the upcoming visit of John Kennedy and started to ask questions such as *"Do you think someone could assassinate the President from the top of a building or out of a window, high up"*. He chatted about other assassination related topics, clearly with the intention of making an indelible impression upon Ralph Yates.

The young hitchhiker asked to be dropped off in Dealey Plaza, along Houston Street. Yates dropped him off at the stoplight by the Texas School Book Depository building and watched the man carrying the package of *'curtain rods'* across Elm Street. From there he could have entered the TSBD.[2]

After the assassination and having seen Lee Oswald's photograph Ralph Yates did what any conscientious citizen would do; he contacted the authorities. As a result he was interviewed by the FBI several times. Unfortunately for Yates during the evolving 'investigation' into the assassination the authorities found his evidence 'not useful' in the sense that it placed Oswald in the wrong place, hitching a lift, when he was ostensibly at work in the TSBD. Additionally, it was one 'curtain-rods' story too many[3]. For whatever reason, the FBI wanted to bury the evidence of Ralph Yates so they told him to report to Woodlawn Hospital, a Dallas institution for the mentally ill. Yates obeyed the FBI directive and reported to the hospital. There he was subjected to polygraph testing that indicated that he was telling the truth; unfortunately for Ralph Yates this was not what the FBI wished to hear.

In one of the most appalling stories of injustice related to the JFK assassination Ralph Yates was then subjected to incarceration for 11 years in 3 different psychiatric hospitals. He was drugged to a zombie-like state and received over 40 electric shock treatments, apparently in an effort to erase his memory; but to the end he remembered the hitch-hiker he picked up on 20th November 1963. Ralph died at the age of 39 years of congestive heart failure. Ralph Yates had no inkling of the existence of an 'Oswald double'; he died without understanding fully why the FBI deemed it so necessary to silence him. Ralph Yates was a Dealey Plaza witness who found himself in the Plaza at the wrong time, in the company of the 'wrong man'. What are the odds that two young men, two days apart, both just happened to be carrying packages allegedly containing curtain rods in the vicinity of Dealey Plaza? Evidence of conspiracy?

November 22 1963
It is estimated that 600 people were in Dealey Plaza, Dallas at 12.30 on Friday 22nd November 1963 to witness the assassination of John F Kennedy.[4] However, the Warren Commission failed to take testimony from the majority of witnesses; indeed the Dallas Police made such a poor attempt to preserve the crime scene that little effort was made to even note down the details of people in Dealey Plaza. Eye-witnesses to the assassination who did not feel inclined to linger at the scene were allowed to just drift away. Eye-witnesses

who sought out the police to volunteer evidence were also dismissed, their evidence ignored. The Warren Commission had testimony from just 178 people who could be regarded as eye-witnesses. Some eye-witnesses, such as Beverly Oliver had their films confiscated, never to be returned.

However, those who have provided eye-witness testimony give a fairly consistent account of events. Around **sixty** people have described the following sequence of happenings and stated that: JFK's limousine proceeded slowly down Elm Street, at a leisurely speed of around 11mph (far slower than it should have been travelling). There was a sound 'like a firecracker' then two louder explosive sounds in rapid succession (too close together to have been fired by anyone using a bolt-action rifle). During the shooting sequence the car came to a halt momentarily, for maybe 2-3 seconds. Only after the last fatal headshot did the car accelerate. (During the short stop on Elm Street a police motorcyclist drove up to the car, the policeman looked inside, saw the dead President and he then rode ahead to confer with the lead car in the motorcade – see below).

Anyone reading just the eye-witness testimony would have little difficulty in accepting that the above account indicated accurately what happened during the assassination. The problem is of course that the Zapruder film shows something quite different, suggesting that the film has been transformed.

The value of eye-witness testimony
Defenders of the Warren Commission Report (WCR) and many lawyers try to devalue and even completely denigrate eye-witness testimony as being of little or no evidentiary value. Lawyers particularly favour data and documents as they can't talk back or protest that they are being misinterpreted. However, in the case of the WCR, documents can be and clearly were forged, e.g. the autopsy report. Many people who testified before the Warren Commission later complained that their evidence had been misreported and fabricated (see below).

For direction on the value of eye-witness testimony we can be guided by a British Home Office research document, titled, Face Value? Evaluating the Accuracy of Eyewitness Information. Authors *Mark R. Kebbell and Graham F. Wagstaff.* Police Research Series Paper 102.

Their conclusions are – Eyewitnesses play an important part in many crime investigations. Hence it is important that the police understand how to assess the reliability of the information that witnesses provide. Various factors have been identified that influence the quality of eyewitness statements, in particular:

- the nature of the offence and the situation in which it is observed;
- the characteristics of the witness; and

TWO | THE DEALEY PLAZA WITNESSES

- the way in which information is retrieved.

Of particular relevance to the JFK assassination they also state, *"Victims of serious crimes can sometimes maintain accurate memories of an offence over a long period of time as they tend repeatedly to go over the event in their minds, thus aiding storage in memory. Also, the presence of a weapon or threat of violence will increase the intensity of a witness's experience, and raise stress levels. Stress will lead to a narrowing of witness focus and this is likely to concentrate attention towards the incident itself and away from 'peripheral information'.* They also state *"We are more likely to remember something accurately if there was something that made it particularly salient or 'memorable'. For example, we are more likely to observe and encode details of an event if the components of the event are intense or unusual in some way".*

Finally, of relevance to us is their conclusion that *"Memory for actions is better than memory for descriptions. So, for example, if witnesses cannot accurately describe details of the participants in an event, this does not mean they cannot describe what happened".*

There can be little doubt that the persons who witnessed the JFK assassination would have repeatedly gone over the event in their minds, probably for many months if not years, thus their memory of the event would have been **improved** by the uniquely stressful and horrific nature of seeing a President have his head blown apart by bullet(s). There can be no more salient or memorable experience imaginable than what confronted the Dealey Plaza witnesses.

Thus we should not accept the argument put forward by the likes of Vincent Bugliosi, Arlen Specter and other WCR defenders that eye-witnesses were universally 'wrong' because they saw and heard things unhelpful to the Warren Commission. We should instead accept that many of the eye-witnesses were likely to be correct and their evidence has great value.

Mid-morning November 22 1963 – Julia Ann Mercer

A little before 11:00 a.m. on the day of the assassination, Julia Ann Mercer, who was twenty-three years old, was driving west on Elm Street, just beyond the spot where the President would be killed less than two hours later. A few yards beyond the triple underpass, Miss Mercer brought her car to a stop. A green truck was blocking her lane, sitting partly on the curb.

As Julia Mercer waited a young man got out of the passenger's side of the truck and went around to the rear. He opened the long tool compartment on the side of the truck. According to Miss Mercer, he removed a package that she believed was a rifle wrapped in paper. The young man walked up the embankment in the direction of the grassy knoll area with the package. That was the last time Miss Mercer saw him.

However, as she waited and then tried to move her car around the truck, Miss Mercer's eyes locked with those of the man behind the wheel. She was able to look at him clearly. He was heavily built with a round face. Miss Mercer edged her car by the truck and continued toward Fort Worth, where she was employed. (A Warren Commission document, disclosed later, showed that a police officer on the scene had observed apparently the same truck and believed it to be a legitimate breakdown.)

On Sunday morning she was watching the assassination coverage on television with friends and saw Ruby shoot Oswald. Instantly, she shouted that they were the two men she had seen on Friday. Ruby, she said, was the driver and Oswald the man with the rifle. If true, Julia Mercer's identification of Jack Ruby preceding his murder of Oswald would have introduced a new and unwelcome complication into the official FBI version of the assassination. The revelation not only would have suggested a rifleman on the grassy knoll, but would have shown a conspiracy in connection with the killing of Kennedy.

Some years later, when Miss Mercer saw the official reports, she was aghast. The FBI, in its report of the Mercer interview, omitted her identification of Jack Ruby as the driver of the truck. It also reported that even though Julia Mercer was shown pictures of Oswald, she was unable to identify him. The sheriff's department report included a statement attributed to Mercer to the effect that she did not see the driver clearly enough to be able to identify him. Julia Mercer adamantly denounces the reports as corruptions and fabrications by the FBI and the sheriff's department of her actual experiences. Julia Mercer is one of many other witnesses who claim discrepancies between what was told to the authorities and what later appeared in the official reports.

Bearing in mind what Julia Mercer says she saw, it makes Ed Hoffman's story (see below) of what he saw eminently believable; Ed Hoffman saw a gunman in the exact same spot that Julia Mercer saw 'Oswald' (or an impostor) carrying a gun earlier in the day.

The source of the noises or shots

People in Dealey Plaza heard noises, bangs or what they interpreted as firecrackers, motor-cycle back-fire or gun-shots. Seemingly the first noise heard by witnesses did not sound like a rifle shot, but was described as being like a backfire or fire-cracker. Maybe that is what it was; a distraction, something to cause people to look at the TSBD and make pigeons fly off the roof. Two of the noises, very close together, were apparently unmistakeable as gunfire.

Many people estimated that they heard three noises at the time of the shooting; one 'fire-cracker' sound followed by two explosive sounds very close together. This matches neatly with the Warren Commission's eventual determination that Oswald fired three shots. However, it does not take into account the

TWO | THE DEALEY PLAZA WITNESSES

distinct likelihood of rifles fitted with sound suppressors, commonly called 'silencers'. If the HSCA report is correct and there was a shot from the grassy knoll, then at least four shots had to have been fired. Thus we cannot place too much emphasis on how many sounds people heard for determining how many shots were fired.

Eye-witnesses in Dealey Plaza were divided about the source of the shots. A minority of 27.5% said they only heard noises or shots from the vicinity of the Texas School Book Depository (TSBD); 12% said they heard shots from the vicinity of the northern Grassy Knoll or railroad overpass, 44% said they could not determine where the shots came from. Some described hearing shots from both directions[5]. Evidence from the wounds inflicted on JFK and John Connally indicates that shots were fired from behind, at the side and in front of the motorcade (possibly some of the 'wounds' were not caused by bullets and may have been fabrications). So the eye-witnesses could all be correct when it comes to evaluating the evidence of sounds from multiple directions.

However, as the WCR said all three (and only three) shots came from the rear we shall examine evidence that this statement is wrong. Police officers know the value of a witness's first testimony, given while events are fresh in their mind and before they have had any opportunity to be influenced by other factors, such as a private briefing by Arlen Specter to inform them what he required them to say about what they witnessed. Thus we shall explore the ***first testimony*** given by some of the most important eye-witnesses.

Alan Smith – *"the car was ten feet from me when a bullet hit the President in the forehead; the car went about five feet and stopped."* ["Chicago Tribune", 11/23/63, p. 9; "Murder From Within" by Fred Newcomb & Perry Adams (1974), p. 71];

Dallas Morning News reporter **Mary Woodward** (Pillsworth) – *" Instead of speeding up the car came to a halt, she saw the President's car come to a halt after the first shot. Then, after hearing two more shots, close together, the car sped up"* [2 H 43 (Lane); DMN, 11/23/63; 24 H 520; "The Men Who Killed Kennedy" 1988].

Mrs. Earle ("Dearie") Cabell (who rode in Mayor Earle Cabell's car) said that the motorcade *"stopped dead still when the noise of the shot was heard."*[6] Mrs Cabell also reported smelling *'gunpowder'* **at street level (as did Senator Ralph Yarborough)**. Interestingly, Mr Leon Hubert of the WC who was questioning her did not try to correct her, indeed he said <u>"During the time that you were standing absolutely still for a few seconds...did you in fact look up at that window again"</u>. This was not the normal WC questioning technique where witnesses were often confronted by WC staff and told that they were mistaken. Hubert seemingly accepted that the motorcade came to a complete halt.

Former-Mayor Earl Cabell was equally unhelpful to the WC. Describing the shots he stated that, *"There was a longer pause between the first and second shots than there was between the second and third shots.* **They were in rather rapid succession.***"*

Police witnesses in Dealey Plaza
Statements made by police eye-witnesses were not helpful to the WC. In fact, virtually every Dallas police witness said something distinctly in variance to the conclusions of the WCR. For example:

DPD motorcycle Officer James W. Courson (one of two mid-motorcade motorcycles): *"The* **limousine came to a stop** *and Mrs. Kennedy was on the back. I noticed that as I came around the corner at Elm. Then the Secret Service agent [Clint Hill] helped push her back into the car, and the motorcade took off at a high rate of speed."* ["No More Silence" by Larry Sneed (1998), p. 129];

DPD motorcycle officer Bobby Joe Dale (one of two rear mid-motorcade motorcycles): *"After the shots were fired,* **the whole motorcade came to a stop***. I stood and looked through the plaza, noticed there was commotion, and saw people running around his [JFK's] car.* **It started to move, then it slowed again**; *that's when I saw Mrs. Kennedy coming back on the trunk and another guy [Clint Hill] pushing her back into the car."* ["No More Silence" p. 134];

DPD Earle Brown: *"The first I noticed the [JFK's] car* **was when it stopped**...*after it made the turn and* **when the shots were fired, it stopped***."* [6 H 233];

DPD motorcycle officer Bobby Hargis (one of the four Presidential motorcyclists): *"At that time [immediately before the head shot] the Presidential car slowed down. I heard somebody say 'Get going.'* **I felt blood hit me in the face and the Presidential car stopped almost immediately after that.***"* [6 H 294; "Murder From Within" p. 71; 6/26/95 videotaped interview with Mark Oakes & Ian Griggs: *"That guy (Greer) slowed down, maybe his orders was to slow down- slowed down almost to a stop."*

DPD D.V. Harkness: *"I saw the first shot and the President's car slow[ed] down to almost a stop* **I heard the first shot and saw the President's car almost come to a stop** *and some of the agents [were] piling on the car."* [6 H 309];

TWO | THE DEALEY PLAZA WITNESSES

DPD motorcycle officer B.J. Martin (one of the four Presidential motorcyclists) saw JFK's car stop *"just for a moment."* ["Murder From Within" p. 71];

DPD motorcycle officer Douglas L. Jackson (one of the four Presidential motorcyclists) stated: *"that the car just **all but stopped** just a moment."* ["Murder From Within" p. 71];

Texas Highway Patrolman Joe Henry Rich (drove LBJ's car) stated that: *"the motorcade **came to a stop** momentarily."* ["Murder From Within" p. 71];

DPD J.W. Foster stated that: *"immediately after President Kennedy was struck the car in which he was riding **pulled to the curb.**"* [CD 897, pp. 20, 21; "Murder From Within" p. 97];

Could so many policemen, trained to be observant, be wrong about the limousine stopping on Elm Street?

Eye-witness James Chaney and Zapruder film alteration

Startling evidence has emerged from research conducted by John P. Costella, Ph.D. What he discovered were multiple reports that James Chaney, a motorcycle patrolman who was to the right rear of the presidential limousine, rode forward to tell Jesse Curry[7], Dallas Chief of Police who was in the lead car with the head of the Secret Service in Dallas, Agent Forrest Sorrels, and a second Secret Service Agent, Winston Lawson—that the President had been shot. This led Chief Curry to issue instructions for the limousine to be escorted to Parkland Hospital. Bobby Hargis, a motorcycle patrolman riding on the left rear, confirmed Chaney's report. But this sequence of events is in neither the Zapruder film nor any other film.

James Chaney was one of two police motorcyclist located on the right-side of the motorcade. He stated that the Presidential limousine **stopped momentarily after the first shot** (according to the testimony of Mark Lane; corroborated by the testimony of fellow DPD motorcycle officer Marrion Baker: Chaney told him that *"at the time, after the shooting, from the time the first shot rang out, the car stopped completely, pulled to the left and stopped. Now I have heard several of them say that; Mr. Truly was standing out there, he said it stopped. Several officers said it stopped completely."* [2 H 44-45 (Lane) – referring to Chaney's statement as reported in the "Houston Chronicle" dated 11/24/63; 3 H 266 (Baker)]

James Chaney also said, *"I went ahead of the President's car to inform Chief Curry that the President had been hit. And then he instructed us over the air to take him to Parkland Hospital and that Parkland was standing by."*

JFK | ECHOES FROM ELM STREET
A SEARCH FOR HISTORICAL ACCURACY ON THE
ASSASSINATION OF PRESIDENT JOHN F. KENNEDY

Bobby Hargis (motorcycle patrolman on left rear of the Presidential limousine): *"The motorcycle officer on the right side of the car was Jim Chaney. He immediately went forward and announced to the Chief that the President had been shot."*

DPD Sergeant Stavis Ellis: *"We came west on Main Street to Houston Street and took a right, facing right into that building. The building with the window was looking right at us as we came up to Elm Street and made a left, heading back toward the Triple Underpass.... About the time I started on a curve on Elm, I had turned to my right to give signals to open up the intervals since we were fixing to get on the freeway a short distance away. That's all I had on my mind. Just as I turned around, then the first shot went off. It hit back there. I hadn't been able to see back where Chaney was because Curry was there, but I could see where the shot came down into the south side of the curb. It looked like it hit the concrete or grass there in just a flash, and a bunch of junk flew up like a white or gray colour dust or smoke coming out of the concrete.*

Just seeing it in a split second like that I thought, "Oh, my God!" I thought there had been some people hit back there as people started falling. I thought either some crank had thrown a big "Baby John" firecracker and scared them causing them to jump down or else a fragmentation grenade had hit all those people. In any case, they went down!

Actually, I think they threw themselves down in anticipation of another shot. As soon as I saw that, I turned around and rode up beside the Chief's car and BANG! ... BANG! Two more shots went off: three shots in all! The sounds were clear and loud and sounded about the same. But all the time I was moving up, I still didn't know it was shots until Chaney rode up beside me and said, "Sarge, the President's hit!"

I asked him how bad, and he replied, "Hell, he's dead! Man, his head's blown off!" "All right, we're going to Parkland," I said. This had been the prearranged plan in the event that someone was shot or injured; it was normal procedure. Chaney and I then rode on up to Curry's car. Curry was driving with the Chief of the Secret Service, Forrest Sorells (sic), in the front seat with him. "Chief," I said, "That was a shot! The President was hit and he's in bad, bad shape! We're going to Parkland!" He said, "All right, let's go!"

Winston Lawson (Secret Service Agent in the lead car in front of the Presidential limousine): *"A motorcycle escort officer pulled alongside our Lead Car and said the President had been shot. Chief Curry gave a signal over the radio for police to converge on the area of the incident."*

Forrest Sorrels (Secret Service Agent in the lead car in front of the Presidential limousine): Speaking on November 28, 1963: *"I noted that the President's car had accelerated its speed and was closing fast the gap between us. A motorcycle pulled* up alongside of the car and Chief Curry yelled 'Is anybody hurt?' to which the officer replied in the affirmative and Chief Curry immediately broadcast to surround the building. By that time we had gotten just about under the underpass when the President's car pulled up alongside, and at that time Chief Curry's car had started to pick up speed and someone yelled to get to the nearest hospital, and Chief Curry broadcast for the hospital to be ready." [Statement: 21H548]

Chief Jesse Curry (in the lead car in front of the Presidential limousine): "As I turned the lead car right from the Main Street parade route onto Houston Street I was thinking how impressed I was with the size of the crowds along Main Street. The crowd was well under control and the security along the route had been excellent. The weather was perfect. The people of Dallas had turned out in overwhelming numbers and had given the President a vibrant and warm welcome.

For a brief moment I almost started to relax. I made the left turn (west) and proceeded at a speed of approximately eight to ten mph toward the triple underpass. I did see a few unauthorized people on the overpass and wondered how they had gotten up there. About halfway between Houston and the triple underpass I heard a sharp crack. Someone in the car said, "Is that a firecracker?" Two other sharp reports came almost directly after the first. All of the reports were fired fairly close together, but perhaps there was a longer pause between the first and second reports than between the second and the third.

The President's car was only about 100 feet behind our car at that moment. I glanced into my rear view mirror and could see the commotion in the President's car. Everyone was confused.

President John F. Kennedy had been shot and the motorcycle officers on each side of the rear of the Presidential car knew that he was hurt and hurt badly. No one knew any more forcefully than motorcycle Officer Bobby Hargis. He had been following close, just behind the left rear fender of the limousine. A red sheet of blood and brain tissue exploded backward from Kennedy's head into the face of Officer Hargis. **The trajectory must have appeared to Hargis to have come from just ahead and to the right of the motorcade**. He parked his motorcycle and started running in that direction.

A solo motorcycle officer (Chaney) pulled up behind my car and I asked, "What has happened in the Presidential car – has someone been hit?" He answered, "Yes," and I told him to head for Parkland Hospital which is the nearest hospital from that location. I immediately went on the air as the motorcycles formed an escort for our vehicles which were rapidly gaining speed."

Nowhere in the Zapruder film do we see Chaney ride forward to speak to Jesse Curry. Numerous Police and Secret Service witnesses have confirmed that Chaney did exactly as he said he did. The Zapruder film is therefore not an accurate record of what happened.

JFK | ECHOES FROM ELM STREET
A SEARCH FOR HISTORICAL ACCURACY ON THE
ASSASSINATION OF PRESIDENT JOHN F. KENNEDY

Shots that hit the sidewalk

Numerous people saw the effect of shots that missed the occupants of the limousine (or possibly passed through them):

Austin Miller (on top of the triple overpass), November 22, 1963: *"One shot apparently hit the street past the car."* [Sheriff's Department affidavit: 19H485]

Royce Skelton (on top of the triple overpass), November 22, 1963: *"I saw something hit the pavement at the left rear of the car ... I then heard another shot and saw the bullet hit the pavement. The concrete was knocked to the South away from the car. It hit the pavement in the left or middle lane."* [Sheriff's Department affidavit: 19H496]

Ed Johnson (press; on Houston Street at the time of the shots), November 22, 1963: *"Some of us saw little puffs of white smoke that seemed to hit the grassy area in the esplanade that divides Dallas' main downtown streets."* [Fort Worth Star-Telegram, November 23, 1963]

Virgie Baker (Rackley) (on the north side of Elm Street, in front of the Texas School Book Depository), November 24, 1963: *"It sounded as though these sounds were coming from the direction of the Triple Underpass, and looking in that direction after the first shot she saw something bounce from the roadway in front of the Presidential automobile and now presumes it was a bullet bouncing off the pavement."* [FBI interview: CD5]

Austin Miller (on top of the triple overpass), December 18, 1963: *"He heard three shots and also noticed a powder dust spray in the street directly to the driver's side and rear of the car."* [FBI report: CD205]

Royce Skelton (on top of the triple overpass), December 17, 1963: *"Mr. Skelton noticed that as an open limousine turned on Elm Street, it had moved approximately one hundred feet at which time he noticed dust spray up from the street in front of the car on the driver's side. This dust spray came from the direction of the Texas School Book Depository building."* [FBI report: CD205]

Virgie Baker (Rackley) (on the north side of Elm Street, in front of the Texas School Book Depository), March 22, 1964: *"Well, after he passed us, then we heard a noise and I thought it was firecrackers, because I saw a shot or something hit the pavement."*

TWO | THE DEALEY PLAZA WITNESSES

Mr. Liebeler: *"As you went down Elm Street [sic] that you saw this thing hit the street—what did it look like when you saw it?"*
Mrs. Baker: *"Well, as I said, I thought it was a firecracker. It looked just like you could see the sparks from it ..."*
Mr. Liebeler: *"You saw this thing hit the street before the second shot; is that correct?"*
Mrs. Baker: *"Yes, sir; yes."*
Mr. Liebeler: *"So, if what you saw hitting the street was, in fact, a bullet, it would have been the first shot?"*
Mrs. Baker: *"Yes."* [Warren Commission testimony, 7H508, 509, 510, 513]

Royce Skelton (on top of the triple overpass), April 8, 1964: *"... I thought that they were these dumbbells that they throw at the cement because I could see the smoke coming up off the cement."* Mr. Ball: *"You saw some smoke come off the cement?"*
Mr. Skelton: *"Yes."*
Mr. Ball: *"Tell me, now, about the smoke—did you see some smoke?"*
Mr. Skelton: *"After those two shots, and the car came on down closer to the triple underpass, well, there was another shot—two more shots I heard, but one of them—I saw a bullet, or I guess it was a bullet—I take for granted it was—hit in the left front of the President's car on the cement, and when it did, the smoke carried with it—away from the building."*
Mr. Ball: *"You mean there was some smoke in the building?"*
Mr. Skelton: *"No; on the pavement—you know, pavement when it is hit with a hard object it will scatter—it will spread."* [Warren Commission testimony: 7H508]

Shots from the Grassy Knoll
Bill Newman was standing on Elm Street closest to JFK as he was fatally shot in the right side of the head. Bill Newman was not called to testify by the Warren Commission, probably because he was adamant that the shots came from the grassy knoll. Bill Newman is the man seen in photographs lying on the grass protecting his son. Newman was a major problem for the WC because he said that his perception was that the shots came from behind him, from the direction of the grassy knoll. He even thought, at first, that Abraham Zapruder might have shot at the President, Zapruder being stood on a concrete pedestal behind the Newman family. Newman spoke to the Dallas Police, who compiled a 'Not under arrest witness form':

Today at about 12:45 pm I was standing in a group of people on Elm Street near the west end of the concrete standard when the President's car turned left off Houston Street onto Elm Street. We were standing at the edge of the

JFK | ECHOES FROM ELM STREET
A SEARCH FOR HISTORICAL ACCURACY ON THE ASSASSINATION OF PRESIDENT JOHN F. KENNEDY

curb looking at the car as it was coming toward us and all of a sudden there was a noise, apparently gunshot. The President jumped up in his seat, and it looked like what I thought was a firecracker had went off and I thought he had realized it. It was just like an explosion and he was standing up. By this time he was directly in front of us and I was looking directly at him when he was hit in the side of the head. Then he fell back and Governor Connally was holding his middle section. Then we fell down on the grass as it seemed we were in direct path of fire. It looked like Mrs Kennedy jumped on top of the President. He kinda fell back and it looked like she was holding him. Then the car sped away and everybody in that area had run up on top of that little mound. I thought the shot had come from the garden directly behind me, that it was on an elevation from where I was as I was right on the curb. I do not recall looking toward the Texas School Book Depository. I looked back in the vicinity of the garden.

Bill Newman saw a shot hit JFK in the right temple; on film he has described how the shot *"blew the President's ear off"* – which it did not, but it must have looked that way.

Abraham Zapruder was also a witness to shots from the grassy knoll. Zapruder consistently stated that shots came from behind him which indicated shots from the grassy knoll. Excerpt from his testimony to the WC:

Mr. Liebeler - *As you were standing on this abutment facing Elm street, you say the police ran over behind the concrete structure behind you and down the railroad track behind that, is that right?*

Mr. Zapruder - *after the shots?*

Mr. Liebeler - *yes.*

Mr. Zapruder - *yes - after the shots - yes, some of them were motorcycle cops - I guess they left their motorcycles running and they were running right behind me, of course,* **in the line of the shooting. I guess they thought it came from right behind me.**

Mr. Liebeler - *did you have any impression as to the direction from which these shots came?*

Mr. Zapruder - **no, I also thought it came from back of me.** *Of course, you can't tell when something is in line it could come from anywhere, but being I was here and he was hit on this line and he was hit right in the head – I saw it right around here, so it looked like it came from here and it could come from there.*

Mr. Liebeler - *all right, as you stood here on the abutment and looked down into Elm Street, you saw the president hit on the right side of the head and you thought perhaps the shots had come from behind you?*

Mr. Zapruder - **well, yes.**

Mr. Liebeler - *from the direction behind you?*

Mr. Zapruder - **yes, actually** *– I couldn't say what I thought at the moment, where they came from – after the impact of the tragedy was really what I saw and I started and I said – yelling, "They've killed him" – I assumed that they came*

TWO | THE DEALEY PLAZA WITNESSES

from there, because as the police started running back of me, it looked like it came from the back of me.

On the grassy knoll
Emmett J. Hudson was the groundskeeper at Dealey Plaza, he cut the grass on the grassy knoll and during the assassination he was located on steps that ran from the top of the knoll to the street. Abraham Zapruder was just to his left side filming the assassination. But were others also filming the assassination from that location? According to Emmett Hudson, yes, there were a number of other people filming. According to his Warren Commission testimony:
Mr. Liebeler - *do you see this little pedestal back up here?*
Mr. Hudson - *yes.*
Mr. Liebeler - *did you see anybody standing up there that you can remember, during the time the President went by?*
Mr. Hudson - **<u>oh, there was a bunch of people in there, you know, a whole bunch of them - a lot of people in there - a lot of people in here</u>**.
Mr. Liebeler - *did you see anybody standing up there taking motion pictures with a movie camera?*
Mr. Hudson - **<u>oh, yes; I seen people up there trying to get - taking pictures.</u>**

Who were these people? Is it possible that there was more than one 'Zapruder' film being filmed as the limousine progressed down Elm Street, thus enabling the kind of film alteration now being discussed by the likes of John Costella and others?

The man who saw the grassy knoll gunman and the policeman who passed up the chance to arrest one of the men who killed JFK
Ed Hoffman's testimony destroys the Warren Commission's lone-gunman conclusion.

Strictly speaking Ed was not a Dealey Plaza witness, as he was standing on an elevated position on the shoulder of the Stemmons Expressway, giving him a clear view of the railway yard and western side of the TSBD. He was able to see the entire length of the triple underpass. He could see in to Dealey Plaza and he could see the crowds lining Elm Street. He was about 230 yards from the picket fence. From his position he saw the shooter positioned behind the picket fence on the grassy knoll. In 1963 there were no trees or anything else obstructing his view.

Ed Hoffman was deaf and mute as a result of a childhood infection that destroyed his hearing. He communicated via American Sign Language. WCR defenders have accused Ed Hoffman of having changed his story over the years, in an attempt to destroy the credibility of his evidence. Hoffman in fact never changed his story; it was just interpreted and reported wrongly at various times (deliberately it seems).[8] There is a strong indication that the FBI calculatingly misreported Ed Hoffman's story by employing incompetent translators. After taking into account the various misrepresentations of what he said, Ed Hoffman emerged as a highly credible witness.

What did Ed Hoffman see?

- A man in a plaid shirt stepped around from the north end of the picket fence from a location nearby the top of the steps leading from Dealey Plaza to the car park area. This man approached another man in a business suit and spoke to him for a few seconds
- The man in the plaid shirt then walked around the east end of the fence, out of Ed's view
- A man dressed in police uniform followed the man in the plaid shirt
- The man dressed in the business suit then walked over to a 'yard man' who was standing by the middle switch box (adjacent to the car park)
  and spoke to the man for a few seconds then returned to his original position behind the picket fence
- The yard man bent over at the waist and appeared to be working on something near his feet
- Ed saw a puff of smoke near where the man in the business suit was standing
- The man in the business suit turned 90° to the fence and faced Hoffman; he was holding a rifle. He carried the rifle with both hands and held the weapon close to his chest and ran towards the yard man
- The man in the business suit stopped running and tossed the rifle underhand over a steam pipe towards the yard man, who caught the rifle with both hands, bent over and dissembled the rifle into two parts, placing them into a soft tool box or bag. The yard man then walked briskly north along the railroad tracks carrying the box/bag in his hand
- The man in the business suit then walked casually back towards the north end of the fence where a uniformed police officer Joe Marshall Smith came around the east end of the picket fence and confronted him.
- Ed saw the police officer point his pistol directly at the man
- The man in the business suit reached into his coat and showed something assumed to be ID to the officer. The officer put his gun away and both men mingled with the crowd that was now swarming round both sides of the fence
- The man in the business suit walked over to a green Rambler station

- wagon in the car park and got in the passenger side. The Rambler drove out of the car park, went along the north side of the TSBD and made a right turn on to Houston Street
- Ed then saw the President's limousine pass underneath where he stood atop the freeway; he recalled Mrs Kennedy kneeling on the floor, shaking JFK with her hand, trying to rouse him
- He saw a large bloody wound in the President's head *"behind the right ear, a fist sized hole with blood covering the back seat"*

Ed Hoffman tried without success to get the FBI to take him seriously; they refused to do so. Over the years they tried to discredit him as a witness and misreported his story. To some extent it suited Ed's father that the authorities dismissed Ed's account as his father feared greatly for Ed's life.

Corroboration for Ed Hoffman
Lee Bowers; saw activity behind the picket fence. Saw the businessman and the yard man as described by Hoffman. (WC testimony Vol 6 p.286)

Sam Holland, signal supervisor Union Terminal Railroad; saw a puff of smoke come from the trees on the knoll.

Richard Dodd, track supervisor Union Terminal Railroad; saw a puff of smoke near the bushes and trees at the corner of the wooden fence.

Walter Winborn, switchman Union Terminal Railroad; saw smoke come out from under the trees on the right-side of the motorcade (i.e. the north knoll), ten feet long and two-three feet wide.

Clem Johnson, Union Terminal Railroad, saw white smoke *'near the pavilion'.*

Austin Miller, Union Terminal Railroad, saw steam or smoke coming from the trees north of Elm off the railroad tracks.

James Simmons, Union Terminal Railroad, saw exhaust fumes or smoke *'near the embankment in front of the TSBD'.*

Nolan Potter, Union Terminal Railroad, saw smoke *'in front of the TSBD'.*

Joe Marshall Smith, Dallas police Department; Smith was the police officer who confronted the gunman in the business suit. Smith said *"A woman came up to me and she was in hysterics…she said 'They are shooting the President from the*

JFK | ECHOES FROM ELM STREET
A SEARCH FOR HISTORICAL ACCURACY ON THE
ASSASSINATION OF PRESIDENT JOHN F. KENNEDY

bushes'. I [encountered] one secret service man when I got there...I pulled my pistol from my holster, and I thought, 'this is silly, I don't know who I am looking for' and I put it back. Just as I did he showed me that he was a secret service agent...he saw me coming with my pistol and right away he showed me who he was' (WC testimony Volume 6, page 535) – Thus Smith encountered one of the mythical secret service agents on the grassy knoll (there were none assigned there) and in accepting the false ID shown he passed up on the chance to apprehend one of the grassy knoll gunmen.

Astonishingly, in his WC testimony, Smith was not asked by WC attorney Wesley Liebeler to describe the man that he encountered:

Mr. Smith. *This woman came up to me and she was just in hysterics. She told me, "they are shooting the president from the bushes." So i immediately proceeded up here.*

Mr. Liebeler. *You proceeded up to an area immediately behind the concrete structure here that is described by elm street and the street that runs immediately in front of the texas school book depository, is that right?*

Mr. Smith. *I was checking all the bushes and i checked all the cars in the parking lot.*

Mr. Liebeler. *There is a parking lot in behind this grassy area back from elm street toward the railroad tracks, and you went down to the parking lot and looked around?*

Mr. Smith. *Yes, sir; I checked all the cars. I looked into all the cars and checked around the bushes. Of course, I wasn't alone. There was some deputy sheriff with me, and I believe one secret service man when I got there. I got to make this statement, too. I felt awfully silly, but after the shot and this woman, I pulled my pistol from my holster, and I thought, this is silly, I don't know who I am looking for, and I put it back. Just as I did, he showed me that he was a secret service agent.*

Mr. Liebeler. *Did you accost this man?*

Mr. Smith. *Well, he saw me coming with my pistol and right away he showed me who he was.*

Mr. Liebeler. *Do you remember who it was?*

Mr. Smith. *No, sir; I don't – because then we started checking the cars. In fact, I was checking the bushes, and I went through the cars, and I started over here in this particular section.*

Liebeler failed to extract either any name that the man might have uttered or shown on his ID or any physical description of the obviously fraudulent secret service agent!

What can we conclude from Ed Hoffman's account? At least one grassy knoll gunman was located adjacent to the end of the railroad overpass, where the picket fence ends in a small cluster of bushes/trees. It seems that the gunman, dressed in a business suit, fired just one shot, before handing the rifle to an accomplice who disassembled the rifle. The 'businessman' then coolly walked away from an encounter with a police officer by showing fake secret service ID before making his getaway in a green Rambler station wagon.

Victoria Adams and the lies of Billy Lovelady
Victoria Elizabeth Adams' testimony exonerates 'Harvey Oswald' the man killed by Jack Ruby; it proves 100% that Harvey Oswald did not fire a rifle from the 6th floor of the TSBD. As Victoria Adams was one of the most important eye-witnesses we are going to explore her experiences in considerable detail.

23-year-old Victoria Adams worked on the 4th floor of the TSBD at the Scott Foresman Company offices. On November 22, 1963, she stood behind a fourth-floor window of the Texas School Book Depository in Dallas. While looking out of the window she happened to notice a portly man in a fedora hat standing on the corner of Houston and Elm Street. She later identified this man as Jack Ruby. She watched John Kennedy's car pass under the window and heard three sounds (from her right and from below her, not from above her and to her left). Then, accompanied by co-worker Sandra Styles, within about 20 seconds of the shooting she ran down the back stairs of the building in order to get outside and determine what had happened. (These were the only stairs; the stairs that a fLeeing assassin would have to use, as the electricity supply to the building was cut for a few minutes during the assassination and the lifts were not working).

Unknown to her then was the fact that if she was telling the truth, then she had descended those stairs at the same time 'Lee Harvey Oswald' would have been on them as he made his escape from the sixth floor, having allegedly just shot at John Kennedy. Yet Victoria Adams and Sandra Styles saw no one. Even though the stairs were old, wooden, and very creaky under any weight, she heard nobody on them and saw nobody either.

The Warren Commission Report insists that Harvey Oswald was seen in the second floor lunch room by Police Officer Marrion Baker and building superintendent Roy Truly some 90 seconds after the shooting ceased. He was calm and collected, not breathless; he appeared not to have just shot a President and hastened down the back stairs of the building. Victoria Adams could confirm that indeed was the case; he had not raced down any stairs.

Her evidence presented obvious and overwhelming problems for the Warren Commission's conclusion that Oswald was the sole assassin as the entire case against Oswald relied on him descending the same set of stairs at the same time as Victoria Adams and Sandra Styles, having hurriedly hidden the rifle used in the assassination.

Therefore the Warren Commission did what it routinely did in difficult circumstances. Lawyer David Belin set out deliberately to bully, discredit, humiliate, and eventually brand Victoria Adams a liar, in the full knowledge that she was telling the truth. He ignored Sandra Styles entirely, not calling her as a witness. In the course of neglecting to do his duty he (in association with colleagues) persuaded witness Billy Lovelady to commit perjury (more on Lovelady below).

There was virtually a standard methodology employed by the Warren Commission when it needed to extract testimony from witnesses; an extensive off-the-record briefing session where WC Counsel would go through every question that would be asked, then discuss with the witness what they would say in response. We can see how Billy Lovelady was treated in this fashion by his concluding remarks to Joseph P. Ball:

Mr. Ball. *Mr. Lovelady, your testimony will be written up and it can be submitted to you for your signature if you wish and you can make any changes, or you can waive signature and* **we will make this your final –**
Mr. Lovelady. ***I want this to be the final one.***

From Lovelady's remarks we can conclude that there had been previous sessions with ball and/or other wc counsel. During testimony Lovelady 'jumped the gun' when discussing untruthfully how he encountered Victoria Adams. Without waiting to be asked he volunteered that he saw someone called 'Vickie'.

Mr. Ball. *Who did you see in the first floor?*
Mr. Lovelady. ***I saw a girl but I wouldn't swear to it it's Vickie.***
Mr. Ball. *Who is Vickie?*
Mr. Lovelady. *The girl that works for scott, foresman.*
Mr. Ball. *What is her full name?*
Mr. Lovelady. ***I wouldn't know.***
Mr. Ball. *Vickie Adams?*
Mr. Lovelady. ***I believe so.***
Mr. Ball. *Would you say it was Vickie you saw?*
Mr. Lovelady. ***I couldn't swear.***
Mr. Ball. *Where was the girl?*
Mr. Lovelady. ***I don't remember what place she was,*** *but i remember seeing a girl as* ***she*** *was talking to Bill or saw Bill or something, then i went over and asked one of the guys what time it was and to see if we should continue working or what.*

Lovelady also denied that he knew oswald other than *'vaguely'*. How could this be the case when workmates said that they used to call Lovelady *'Lee'* in joking how much the two men resembled each other? Surely if Lovelady was regularly being referred to in fun as *'Lee'* he would have more than a passing interest in the man he strongly resembled?

TWO | THE DEALEY PLAZA WITNESSES

In typical warren commission fashion, Joseph P. Ball extracted just enough information from Lovelady to introduce 'doubt' as to the accuracy of Victoria Adams' testimony, without even obtaining positive 100% identification from Lovelady that he saw or knew Victoria Adams. Was Lovelady's reluctance to name Victoria Adams due to the fact that he was lying about the encounter? **Sandra Styles confirmed that they never saw Lovelady at the bottom of the stairs**.

Co-worker William Shelley (the Bill referred to by Lovelady above) was with billy Lovelady the whole time before and after the shooting. **<u>Shelley refused to verify what Lovelady claimed</u>**.

Mr. Ball. *When you came into the shipping room (after the assassination) did you see anybody?*
Mr. Shelley. ***I saw eddie piper.***
Mr. Ball. *What was he doing?*
Mr Shelley. *He was coming back from where he was watching the motorcade in the southwest corner of the shipping room.*
Mr. Ball. *Of the first floor of the building?*
Mr. Shelley. *Yes.*
Mr. Ball. *Who else did you see?*
Mr. Shelley. ***That's all we saw immediately.***
Mr. Ball. *Did you ever see Vickie Adams?*
Mr. Shelley. ***I saw her that day but i don't remember where i saw her.***
Mr. Ball. *You don't remember whether you saw her when you came back?*
Mr. Shelley. ***It was after we entered the building.***
Mr. Ball. *You think you did see her after you entered the building?*
Mr. Shelley. ***Yes, sir; i thought it was on the fourth floor awhile after that.***
Failing to receive the answer he hoped for, ball came back later in the testimony to ask again,
Mr. Ball. *Did you see Vickie Adams after you came into the building and did you see her on the first floor?*
Mr. Shelley. ***I sure don't remember.***
Mr. Ball. *You don't.* Mr. Shelley. ***No.***

Thus Victoria Adams, Sandra Styles and William Shelley all said that they did not meet at the bottom of the stairs just a minute or so after the shots were fired. The Warren Commission chose to accept the testimony of Billy Lovelady and dismiss the devastating testimony of Victoria Adams.

Realising that David Belin refused to believe her, Victoria Adams implored Belin to arrange time tests of her actions and she begged them to question her co-workers, particularly Sandra Styles who could confirm the truth. Belin ignored these requests (Sandra Styles was not called to testify). Knowing the truth of what she had witnessed and fearing for her life because of it, Victoria

JFK | ECHOES FROM ELM STREET
A SEARCH FOR HISTORICAL ACCURACY ON THE ASSASSINATION OF PRESIDENT JOHN F. KENNEDY

Adams went into hiding and disappeared for the best part of 35 years until she was found by author Barry Ernest (see The Girl on the Stairs – Amazon Kindle).

No Oswald on the stairs means Harvey Oswald innocent. Case Closed?

Billy Lovelady – the ubiquitous, ever-willing lying witness

It seems that whenever the Warren Commission had a problem around events in the TSBD Billy Lovelady popped up to help solve the difficulty. In relation to Victoria Adams/Sandra Styles testimony Lovelady obliged David Belin by saying that he saw a girl, described as *'Vickie'* at the bottom of the stairs in question after he returned to the TSBD **six or seven** minutes after the shooting, not **one minute** after the shooting. Thus, even though Lovelady did not even name Victoria Adams specifically it enabled Belin to ignore Adams' testimony and choose instead to accept the word of Lovelady. To reinforce the deception Belin then arranged for Adams' testimony to be forged, to insert into it that she acknowledged seeing Lovelady at the bottom of the stairs, when in fact she had never said that. Thus Victoria Adams could be dismissed as yet another 'mistaken' witness.

Roger Craig – the 'pesky' policeman

Roger Craig was a Deputy Sheriff in Dallas at the time of the assassination of President Kennedy. He was a member of Dallas County Sheriff James Eric "Bill" Decker's office that were directed to stand in front of the Sheriff's office on Main Street and *"take no part whatsoever in the security of that motorcade."* Once he heard the first shot, Roger Craig immediately bolted towards Houston Street. His participation in the investigation during the rest of that day and into the evening included experiences that should have single handedly destroyed the entire Warren Commission fairy tale. Among the most important events he witnessed:

Shortly after Kennedy was shot Marvin Robinson, Helen Forrest and Craig, independently of each other, reportedly saw two men leaving Dealey Plaza in a light-coloured Rambler station wagon. One of them entered the car on Elm Street after running from the direction of the Texas School Book Depository (TSBD). Craig and Forrest described this man as identical to Lee Harvey Oswald.

A few minutes before this incident Richard Randolph Carr saw two men who had come from behind the TSBD enter what was apparently the same Rambler, parked next to the building on Houston Street. He saw a third man enter the car seconds later on Record Street near the TSBD.

At approximately 12:40 p.m. Craig was standing on the south side of Elm Street when he heard a whistle and turned to see a man in faded blue trousers and long sLeeved shirt made of some type of grainy material come running down the knoll from the direction of the TSBD. He saw a Rambler station wagon coming west on Elm Street pull over to the curb and pick up the man coming down the hill.

Craig ran to the command post at Elm and Houston to report the incident. When he got there and asked who was involved in the investigation a man turned to him and *said "I'm with the Secret Service."* Craig recounted what he had just seen. This "Secret Service" man showed little interest in Craig's description of the people leaving, but seemed extremely interested in the description of the Rambler to the degree this was the only part of the story he wrote down.

Immediately after this Craig was told by Sheriff Decker to help police search the TSBD. He was present when the rifle was found and when an unknown Dallas police officer came running up the stairs and advised Capt. Fritz that a Dallas policeman had been shot in the Oak Cliff area. Craig looked at his watch. The time was 1:06 p.m.

Later in the afternoon Craig received word of Oswald's arrest and that he was suspected of being involved in Kennedy's murder. He immediately thought of the man running down the knoll and made a telephone call to Capt. Fritz to give him the description of the man he had seen. Fritz said Craig's description sounded like the man they had and asked him to come take a look. When he saw Oswald in Fritz's office Craig confirmed this was indeed the man that he had seen running down the knoll and into the Rambler. They went into the office together and Fritz told Oswald,

"This man saw you leave" to which he replied, *"I told you people I did."* Fritz, apparently trying to console Oswald said, *"Take it easy, son – we're just trying to find out what happened."* He then said, *"What about the car?"* to which Oswald replied *"That station wagon belongs to Mrs. Paine – don't try to drag her into this. Everybody will know who I am now."*

Junior counsel for the Warren Commission David Belin (who of course had a track-record of forging witness testimony) was the man who interviewed Roger Craig in April of 1964. After being questioned, Belin asked *"Do you want to follow or waive your signature or sign now?"* After Craig first saw the transcript in 1968 he discovered that the testimony he gave had been altered, i.e. falsified by Belin, in fourteen different places.

Deputy Sheriff Roger Craig never changed his account of what he witnessed and experienced on 22nd November 1963. He remained convinced that the man entering the Rambler station wagon was Lee Harvey Oswald. Assassination researcher Penn Jones described Roger Craig as a true American hero.

Endnotes
[1] JFK and the Unspeakable, James Douglass, p351
[2] JFK and the Unspeakable p352
[3] Buell Wesley Frazier also provided a 'curtain rods' story for the Warren Commission – seemingly they preferred to use his one even though it was deeply flawed – the package was too short to hold a rifle
[4] Source – History Matters website: history-matters.com

5. HSCA final Report page 87
6. [7 H 487; "Accessories After the Fact" by Sylvia Meagher (1967), p. 4; "Murder From Within" by Fred Newcomb & Perry Adams (1974), p. 71]
7. Confirmed by Curry in his book published in 1969 "Assassination File" page 30.
8. See Beyond the Fence Line. JFK Lancer publications 2008

Three
"A flurry of shells come into the car..."

Matt Mills

This chapter will explore the debate regarding the number of shots, the sources of each known and suspected shot and the accounts of numerous witnesses in relation to where the shots were fired from. Eyewitnesses' reports concerning suspicious men on the sixth floor of the Texas School Book Depository is also discussed together with the accounts of Ed Hoffman and J.C. Price, both of whom saw men behind the picket fence on the grassy knoll at the time of Kennedy's assassination. In particular, Ed Hoffman as an eyewitness was notable due to the fact that he alone saw a man with a rifle at the fence.

There is much evidence to prove that the Warren Commission's single bullet theory was not plausible. In order to establish the number of known shots, the most important photographic record of the Kennedy Assassination – the Zapruder Film - is also studied. In addition, evidence of bullets striking the pavement in Dealey Plaza is examined as there is hard photographic evidence that reveals as many as ten or more shots were fired at President Kennedy as his limousine headed into the kill zone in Elm Street.

The Warren Commission established that Lee Harvey Oswald fired three 6.5mm bullets from a Mannlicher-Carcano bolt action rifle, or, more accurately, carbine, in 6.5 seconds. The Commission, due to the three spent cartridges found on the sixth floor of the Texas School Book Depository, insisted that only three shots were fired. The obvious shot of these three caused Kennedy's fatal head wound. The Warren Commission would have believed that one of the other two bullets hit Kennedy in the back and exited from his throat, while the remaining shot struck Governor Connally in the back, exiting from his chest before shattering his right wrist bone and lodging in his left thigh. However, during the early stages of investigation, eyewitness James Tague who had stood close to the Triple Underpass revealed to the authorities that he had been slightly wounded by a bullet fragment. This new information forced the Warren Commission to create the now much-ridiculed single (or magic) bullet theory.

JFK | ECHOES FROM ELM STREET
A SEARCH FOR HISTORICAL ACCURACY ON THE ASSASSINATION OF PRESIDENT JOHN F. KENNEDY

The 8mm colour home movie filmed by Dallas Dress Manufacturer Abraham Zapruder is a key piece of visual evidence in determining the truth regarding the number of shots. By studying the 35mm optically enhanced version of the Zapruder Film, which was produced by assassination researcher Robert J. Groden, it can be clearly seen that as the Presidential limousine journeys along Elm Street, the President turns to his left, which evidently indicated that he has heard a sound at this point[1]. Kennedy now begins to wave again to the crowds until, as the car is beginning to disappear behind the Stemmons Freeway road sign, he is clearly struck by a shot and is pushed back. When the President appears from behind the sign he begins to hold his hands towards his throat.

Jacqueline Kennedy, at this stage, did not appear to notice that her husband was wounded. Governor Connally, meanwhile, is seen to be turning back after looking towards the President. As the Governor turns, he is thrown forward as a shot hits him in the back[2]. As soon as the Governor is hit, the President, who after receiving his first wound was still sat against the back seat, is again hit, and he begins to fall forward, slowly rather than rapidly. At this point, Connally begins to fall towards his wife Nellie. It can be established that by this point, four shots have been fired.

As the Presidential limousine continues down Elm Street, passing a group of bystanders who would later become well-known eyewitnesses to the shooting – Beverly Oliver, Charles Brehm, Jean Hill and Mary Ann Moorman - Governor Connally continues to slump while still holding his Stetson. President Kennedy is now falling further forward with his hands still at his throat. The First Lady is now looking anxiously at her husband. At this moment, the President is thrown violently back and to his left. His head explodes into a mass of blood and brain tissue. At almost the same time, Governor Connally is hit again, this time in his right wrist by a bullet that was almost certainly meant for Kennedy's head. While the Governor began to fall towards his wife after being struck in the back, it can be seen in the Zapruder Film that he is now thrown forward again before falling into her lap. A study of acoustics evidence during the House Select Committee on Assassinations in the late 1970s found that the last two shots were fired only one sixth of a second apart[3].

As the Zapruder film has established, six shots can clearly be identified – five bullets that hit human targets and the first shot that missed. These six shots were audible on the Dallas Police Department's dictabelt recording analysed by the House Select Committee on Assassinations. Further evidence of the first shot will be discussed later in the chapter. Importantly, when considering the seconds between the back shot and the fatal head shot, there would have evidently been time to fire at least three more bullets; it is known that three further shots, possibly a fourth, were fired at President Kennedy's limousine. As noted earlier, a bullet fragmented when it hit the south pavement of Main Street. Some of the fragments, together with fragmented concrete, hit bystander

THREE | "A FLURRY OF SHELLS COME INTO THE CAR"

James Tague, who stood between Main and Commerce Streets next to the triple underpass. These fragments caused a deep cut on Tague's right cheek.

An eighth bullet struck a concrete area near a manhole cover on the south side of Elm Street. A mark is clearly visible in a photograph[4] of the concrete and a second image shows police officers looking carefully at the ground near where the bullet struck[5]. A Dallas Deputy Sheriff, Buddy Walthers, found a bullet close to the mark. However, this particular piece of evidence was soon gone forever, as Walthers handed the bullet to a man who had stated that he was an FBI Agent.

Photographic evidence in the work assembled by Robert J. Groden[6] also provides direct evidence of a ninth shot that lodged in the windscreen frame of the Presidential car. Yet another mark on a Dealey Plaza pavement was also noted, this being evidence of a possible tenth shot. The possible strike was in the north pavement of Elm Street; however, unlike the mark near the drain cover, it is not known for definite whether the deep cut in the concrete came from a missed shot. Robert J. Groden points out that "when the section of sidewalk was removed and tested (by a non-federal agency approximately 15 years later), no traces of bullet metal were found"[7].

There is a possibility, however, that if any traces of metal were present in the area of the marking, they may have been removed at some point in the months immediately following the assassination. The bullet strike on the south kerb of Main Street was apparently eliminated within a fairly short time after the assassination. James Tague himself visited the location sixth months after the President's murder and was planning to obtain a photograph. But Tague's discovered, to his disbelief, that the bullet mark could hardly be seen – it was clear to him that the section of concrete where the projectile had struck had been re-cemented[8]. Was this an effort to hide signs of the mark resulting from the bullet strike that fragmented and injured Tague?

But what of the first shot that was fired – the shot that caused both President Kennedy and Governor Connally to turn around? No photographs of the mark created by this bullet appear to exist. However, eyewitness Virgie Baker, who stood near the Texas School Book Depository, stated to the Warren Commission that she heard the first shot and, importantly, she saw the bullet strike the concrete on Elm Street. Baker told the Commission that after Kennedy's limousine had driven past the Book Depository, she heard a sound that she believed "was a firecracker"[9]. Subsequently, she saw the shot hit the street "toward the middle of the lane"[10]. The position of this strike was described by Baker as being fairly close to the centre of the road, also in close vicinity to the Stemmons Freeway road sign.

Evidence of a further shot striking the street comes from the testimony of witness Royce Skelton, a mail clerk who was standing on the triple underpass. In his statement to the Warren Commission Skelton said "I saw a bullet, or I guess that it was a bullet – I take for granted that it was – hit the left front of the President's car on the cement"[11]. No references to a mark caused by this apparent bullet appear in many works on the assassination. It is clear that if Skelton did witness a projectile strike the concrete on Elm Street, there were a total of eleven shots, if the mark on the kerb on the north side of Elm Street did indeed come from a bullet. This evidence reveals that as many as six shots could have missed human targets in the President's limousine.

Some assassination researchers have suggested the possibility of yet another bullet. This unaccounted-for round has been believed to have struck President Kennedy in the back of the head within a fraction of a second before the fatal shot fired from in front. Jim Marrs, in his description of the Zapruder Film, notes "an almost imperceptible forward motion of his head"[12] at the moment before the fatal shot stuck President Kennedy, throwing him rearward and to the left. Analysis of frames from both the Zapruder Film and the 8mm film taken by eyewitness Orville Nix, who stood on Main Street, shows the "slight forward movement of the President's head"[13]; this motion being suggested as a possible reaction to a bullet hit from behind, fired almost simultaneously with the shot from in front. Robert J. Groden, who carried out the above study, mentioned that this possible bullet "could have been a tangential shot, striking somewhere on the right side of the head, rather than a direct hit to the back of the head"[14].

Although ten and, indeed, possibly twelve shots fired from within approximately nine seconds is a fairly large number, further evidence suggests that even more bullets could have been fired at President Kennedy. The large road sign which read "Stemmons Freeway Keep Right" was removed soon after the assassination. It is not known of the exact time the sign was removed, but photographs taken on 23rd November show that the sign had been taken away[15]. A number of witnesses believed that a shot had hit the sign, although no further evidence of a bullet strike, or of the true reason for the removal, has ever been revealed.

A Secret Service Agent named Warren Taylor, who rode in the same car as Agent Clint Hill, directly behind the President's car, believed he saw "something strike the street to the rear of Johnson's car"[16]. However, Taylor was not certain that this object he thought he saw hit the road was indeed a bullet. If the Agent genuinely saw a bullet hit the concrete, this would have to have been fired from a point that did not match any of the known or suspected firing locations within Dealey Plaza – possibly from the South Grassy Knoll on Commerce Street, which will be discussed later.

Eyewitness accounts
A number of witnesses in Dealey Plaza informed the Warren Commission that they saw men on the sixth floor of the Book Depository a short time before

THREE | "A FLURRY OF SHELLS COME INTO THE CAR"

President Kennedy was shot. One notable witness, Arnold Rowland, who was standing on Houston Street with his wife Barbara, noticed a man armed with a rifle in one of the windows. However, this man was not in the so-called "Oswald" window at the eastern end of the sixth floor, but in the far western window. Rowland described him to be in a position "such as port arms in military terms...not quite level with my shoulder, and the right hand being lower than the trigger of the stock"[17]. Arnold Rowland believed at the time that the man may have been a security guard.

When considering the man's position in the far western window of the Book Depository's sixth floor, it is important to note both of Governor Connally's wounds. Both shots that hit the Governor were fired at a steep angle; the trajectories of which match this particular window and, importantly, not the "sniper's" or "Oswald" window. Also, the possible shot that made the mark on the north pavement of Elm Street was shown by Robert J. Groden to be in a position which corresponds with the westernmost window[18]. Notably, the alleged bullet mark was also commented upon by assassination researcher Harold Weisberg – an early critic of the Warren Report, who made a clear point that the mark was not in line with the famous eastern window of the Book Depository[19].

Arnold Rowland the gunman as wearing "a light shirt, a very light blue of a colour such as that"[20]. Rowland's testimony is corroborated by a photograph taken by Tom Dillard, a photographer working for the *Dallas Morning News*. Enlargements of the image show a distinct human figure in the western sixth floor window fifteen seconds after the fatal head shot. The person is clearly male, and is wearing a light-coloured, possibly white, T-shirt.[21] Rowland also stated to the Warren Commission that he spotted a second man this time in the "sniper's" window. He described the other person as an elderly black man who "had on a plaid shirt"[22]. It is highly possible that the man in the eastern window was of black Cuban ethnicity.

Another man with a firearm was seen on the sixth floor, but this gunman was located in the same window as the black man. Carolyn Walther, who worked at the Dal-Tex building, was also in Houston Street as the Presidential motorcade approached. She did not see the elderly black man, but instead witnessed a man "wearing a white shirt" who had blond or light brown hair[23]. Walther also mentioned that "the rifle had a short barrel"[24]. Another man was standing next to the armed man and he appeared to be dressed in a brown suit jacket.

A man of the same description was seen on the Book Depository's sixth floor by construction worker Richard Randolph Carr. Carr testified at the Clay Shaw trial that he witnessed the same man quickly walking down Houston Street, before heading into Commerce Street, anxiously looking back towards Elm Street.[25]. James Worrell stated to the Warren Commission that he also saw a man in a dark jacket walking in the same direction. As well as sighting of this individual, the man wearing a light shirt who Carolyn Walther observed was also spotted by Ronald B. Fischer and Robert Edwards, who stood together at the corner of Elm and Houston Streets.

Fischer told the Warren Commission that he saw a man in the easternmost sixth floor window who "had on an open necked shirt...it could have been a sport shirt of a T-shirt. It was light in colour, possibly white"[26]. The man's hair was described as being a shade of brown by Fischer, but Robert Edwards was able to give a detailed description in his statement to the Warren Commission, noting that the hair of this individual was "light brown"[27]. Edwards also informed the Commission that the man in the sixth floor window was wearing shirt that was of a light colour, thus supporting the statement of both his colleague Ronald Fischer and that of Carolyn Walther. However, the two colleagues did not notice the rifle that was observed by Walther.

It has been suggested by assassination researcher Craig Roberts that the men located on the sixth floor were in fact in "diversionary positions"[28]. As the Texas School Book Depository's location on the corner of Elm Street leads to the conclusion that that the building is not the prime location for gunmen in Dealey Plaza – and that, importantly, the view from the "Oswald" window to the upper area of Elm Street is blocked by a large oak tree . In comparison, the other buildings in Dealey Plaza offer an unbroken line of sight. Roberts has also commented that the position of the gunmen and spotters on the sixth floor "would be a good place for red herrings to be observed by witnesses."[29]

As well as Arnold Rowland seeing both a gunman in the far western window on the Book Depository's sixth floor and a man looking from the familiar "sniper's" window, and Carolyn Walther witnessing a second armed man in the same window, a sixteen year old High School student, Amos Euins, also spotted activity on the sixth floor. Euins saw a long object resembling a pipe protruding from the eastern "snipers" window. Due to all the above evidence of people in Dealey Plaza seeing men with guns in positions where they were easily seen, a person leaning from the easternmost window and the barrel of a gun pointing out of the window, it appears highly possible that these men were making their weapons seen in order to focus upon the Texas School Book Depository's sixth floor. The actions of these members of the assassination team being a key factor in the Warren Commission's belief that the shots came from no other location.

Although primarily employed for diversionary purposes, it has already been established that the two shots that struck Governor Connally were fired from an angle that matches the westernmost window of the sixth floor. However, it is also possible that the second gunman in the eastern window may have fired. The bullet that Royce Skelton saw hit Elm Street could possibly have originated from the "sniper's" or "Oswald" window. If a shot has also hit Kennedy in the back of the head a split-second before the frontal head shot, as has been suggested by some researchers, it would have almost definitely been fired from this window.

Witnesses to the Grass Knoll Gunmen
The most striking eyewitness account of shots being fired from behind the picket fence on the Grassy Knoll is that of Ed Hoffman. Despite the numerous witnesses who heard shots or saw smoke in the vicinity of the fence, only one witness actually saw a gunman fire from what was possibly the best position for an assassin to shoot at the President. Ed Hoffman, who worked at Texas Instruments, had not intended to watch the Presidential motorcade; the only reason he was near Dealey Plaza at the time of the shooting was due to an emergency visit to his dentist after he broke a tooth on an ice cube in a soft drink[30]. Hoffman recalled, while on his way across Stemmons Freeway, that President Kennedy was visiting Dallas. Hoffman decided to park his car near a bridge running over the freeway and walked to the area where the road ran above Elm Street.

Ed Hoffman had a clear view into the car park from his position. Hoffman was deaf-mute and was obviously unable to hear what was happening behind the fence. However, he spotted a man behaving in a suspicious manner near the corner of the fence, in the exact area where the House Select Committee for Assassinations established that a gunman stood. In an interview for a 1988 British television documentary, Hoffman described that he "saw a man standing here (indicating the area of the picket fence) wearing a black hat and a blue jacket. I saw a puff of smoke and I thought it was a cigarette, but it wasn't. He had a gun and walked toward the railroad"[31]. Ed Hoffman went on to describe how the shooter "tossed the gun to the other man"[32] after walking the whole length of the fence to the area where it joined the triple overpass. The second man, who, as Hoffman stated wore a "striped shirt, (a) railroad shirt...walked over to the electrical box...he took the gun apart and put it in a toolbox"[33].

Despite seeing one of the assassins fire and an accomplice dismantling the weapon that caused Kennedy's massive head wound, Ed Hoffman was not the only eyewitness to see suspicious individuals in the car park behind the stockade fence. J.C. Price, who worked as the engineer for the Union Terminal Annex on the corner of Houston and Commerce Streets, was seated on the roof of the building to obtain a good view of the President's visit. As well as hearing shots, Price also saw a man running towards the direction of the railway sidings behind the fence. Price stated to the Dallas Sheriff's Department that "this man had a white dress shirt, no tie and Khaki coloured trousers...he has something in his hand. I couldn't be sure, but it many have been a head piece"[34] - "head piece" being a dialect term for hat.

It is possible that Price saw a man who was carrying a gun. This means that there may well have been two shooters at the picket fence. A notable point

JFK | ECHOES FROM ELM STREET
A SEARCH FOR HISTORICAL ACCURACY ON THE
ASSASSINATION OF PRESIDENT JOHN F. KENNEDY

in the debate as to whether more than one man fired from the fence is that Dallas doctor Malcolm Perry, one of the first to examine President Kennedy at Parkland Hospital, noted that the throat wound was a small injury up to 5mm in diameter. A smaller calibre rifle could have been used to inflict the President's first wound. This fact was noted by Craig Roberts, who suggested that the weapon was "probably a CIA-issued .22 calibre Winchester"[35]. In contrast, as has often been commented upon, the round fired at Kennedy's head was not only high-powered, but was the type of bullet which explodes on impact, creating the massive volcano-shaped wound which is so clearly visible in the Zapruder film.

Locations of other gunmen
As well as the two known locations from which the shots were fired at President Kennedy, there is clear evidence that at least two more buildings in Dealey Plaza were the sources of at least some of the gunshots on that warm November afternoon. Robert J. Groden notes, in his 1993 Documentary *JFK: The Case For Conspiracy* that during the House Select Committee on Assassinations investigation, "the acoustics panel found echo correlations, or acoustic matches, for only four of the seven shots"[36] when analysing the Dallas Police Department's Dictabelt recording of the gunfire. Although the HSCA stated that one shot was indeed fired from the stockade fence, they ignored any other additional locations. Despite the Committee establishing from their findings that three shots were fired from the Texas School Book Depository and one shot was fired from behind the fence on the Grassy Knoll, the remaining three shots were found to originate from a different location behind the President's car. Groden comments that "the echo patterns did not match the patterns of the test shots"[37] that were fired only from the Book Depository and the Grassy Knoll.

A third location where some of the shots almost definitely originated from is the Dal-Tex Building on the corners of Elm and Houston Streets and across the road from the Book Depository. The building is now known by a different name, and has been for a considerable time. Although no witness is on record stating that they heard gunshots from the building, ballistics evidence does suggest that at least three shots were fired from there. The first shot, noticed by witness Virgie Baker to hit the concrete as the car passed by the Book Depository, being an obvious contender. The President's back wound, due to its position, almost definitely came from the Dal-Tex building, as well as the bullet that fragmented on the south kerb of Main Street, injuring James Tague on the cheek. A fourth bullet that lodged in the windscreen frame of the limousine is another shot that is likely to have originated from the same building.

The other location to be considered is the Dallas Country Records Building, directly opposite the Dal-Tex Building. In the present day, this building still

THREE | "A FLURRY OF SHELLS COME INTO THE CAR"

serves the same purpose as in 1963, unlike the Texas School Book Depository and the Dal-Tex Building.

A shocking discovery was made on the roof of the County Records Building in the 1970s.

A maintenance worker found an empty cartridge case under roofing tar in the area at the bottom of a parapet.[38] The shell was found to be 30.06 calibre and it was also noticed, importantly, that this wasn't a regular bullet, for the case had a crimping indentation at the point where the slug would have protruded. This prominent marking suggests that the cartridge may have been used as a Sabot round.

A Sabot is a firearm cartridge which has a plastic attachment allowing a slug of a different calibre to be fired. For example, a Sabot could have been used to fire a 6.5mm bullet from a 30.06 cartridge – a calibre of a higher velocity. Also, by using a 6.5mm round loaded into a Sabot shell, the gunmen were able to fire a shot that could be linked to the "Oswald" Mannlicher-Carcano. The bullet that hit the concrete area near a drain cover on Elm Street's south side - and was later found near the mark – was in fact fired in a trajectory that corresponded with the Dallas Country Records Building, for the mark is clearly in line with the building's roof.

Although no eyewitness to the assassination stated that they heard gunshots originating from the Dal-Tex Building or the Dallas County Records Building, one notable witness, a Dallas Assistant District Attorney named Samuel Paternostro stated that he heard shots that may have come from the Dallas Criminal Courts Building to the right of the County Records Building[39]. However, Paternostro was uncertain with regards to the exact location, also thinking that the shots could have been fired from the direction of the Book Depository as well as from in front. Samuel Paternostro may have been mistaken, as there is no evidence of any shots originating from the Dallas Courts Building, although it is possible that he could have heard the shot from the County Records Building, the building in which his own office was situated.

There has in fact been some debate for many years regarding the origins of at least one of the missed shots. The bullet which caused the damage to the limousine's windscreen is believed by some researchers to have possibly been fired from in front. Although as noted, it was highly possible that the round was fired from the Dal-Tex building. It has been argued by Craig Roberts, [40] among other researchers that the shot actually came from a frontal direction. If this bullet was fired from in front of the President, the trajectory does not match the area of the picket fence on the Grassy Knoll where two of the shots are known to have originated from.

A possible location for another frontal shooter has been suggested as the southern Grassy Knoll area in Commerce Street, which is identical to the more famous Knoll in Elm Street. It must be considered, though, that no witness ever came forward to say that they heard shots coming from any other directions in front of the President's car. Despite the fact that no-one specifically said that they heard gunfire coming from the direction of the Dal-Tex Building or the Dallas County Records Building, there is still evidence in terms of trajectories which are clearly supported by descriptions of President Kennedy's back wound, the trajectory of the shot that fragmented on the pavement of Main Street and the location of the bullet mark near the Elm Street drain cover. Further evidence, of course, comes from the discovery of the Sabot cartridge on the roof of the County Records Building.

However, despite the debate as to whether the bullet damage to the Presidential limousine's windscreen frame was the result of a shot that came from in front or behind, there has been no distinct evidence to prove another frontal shooter on the opposite side – or indeed any other part of – Dealey Plaza. The opinions of some assassination researchers does suggest, though, that there may be a possibility that this particular shot could have been fired from a location in front of the President. The Triple Overpass was guarded by policemen, so the only plausible position for an assassin would be the area behind the Grassy Knoll on the southern side of the Plaza. At the time of Kennedy's assassination, the South Knoll also had a car park situated to its rear. The possible firing position could possibly have been at the far end of the car park, behind bushes, as there was no fence on the South Grassy Knoll. The area as a suggested location for a shooter has been mentioned, as well as all other known and suggested positions of gunmen by Assassination researcher Don Roberdeau[41].

This chapter has aimed to cover all of the relevant evidence regarding eyewitness and ballistics evidence in the murder of President John F. Kennedy. Studies of available sources have confirmed evidence of at least three gunmen and possibly more. Visual evidence of the assassination clearly shows that more than one person was involved and that accounts of certain people present at the scene of the crime clearly support the Zapruder and Nix Films. It cannot be proven for definite how many shots were fired at President Kennedy's limousine, or the exact locations of certain shooters, but all of the evidence relating to witnesses' testimonies and statements obviously point to the fact that more than one gunman fired at President Kennedy in Dallas on 22nd November 1963. Further evidence in terms of bullet marks also proves the existence of multiple shooters in Dealey Plaza, thus giving evidence of conspiracy and proving that the Warren Commission's investigation resulted in the wrong conclusion – also evidently proving a cover-up in the assassination of the 35th President of the United States.

THREE | "A FLURRY OF SHELLS COME INTO THE CAR"

Endnotes

1. Robert J. Groden, JFK Assassination Films: The Case for Conspiracy, Grodenfilms, 1995
2. Robert J. Groden, The Killing of a President, pp.26-27. Penguin Books USA, New York City, 1993
3. The Day The Dream Died, Channel Four, 1988 Dir. Godley & Creme
4. Robert J. Groden, The Killing of A President, p.41
5. Ibid, p.68
6. Ibid, p.41
7. Ibid, p.41
8. Jim Marrs, Crossfire: The Plot That Killed Kennedy, p.62 Carrol and Graff Publishers, New York City, 1989
9. Warren Commission, Vol. VII, p.510
10. Ibid, p.510
11. Warren Commission, Vol. VI, p.238
12. Marrs, *Crossfire: The Plot That Killed Kennedy*, p.65
13. Groden, *The Killing of A President*, p.40
14. Ibid, p.40
15. Marrs, *Crossfire: The Plot That Killed Kennedy*, p.317
16. Vince Palamara, *The Third Alternative* in Livingstone, p.163
17. Warren Commission, Vol. II, p.170
18. Groden, The Killing of A President, p.40
19. Weisberg, Harold, *Whitewash II: The FBI, Secret Service Cover-up, Volume I*. Hyattstown, Maryland, 1966
20. Warren Commission, Vol. II, p.171
21. Groden, The Killing of A President, pp. 208-209
22. Warren Commission, Vol. II, p.188
23. FBI Statement of Carolyn Walther, Warren Commission Exhibit 2086, p.24
24. Ibid, p.24
25. Testimony of Richard Randolph Carr, State of Louisiana, February 19, 1969
http://www.jfk-online.com/carrshaw.html
26. Warren Commission, Vol. VI, p.194
27. Warren Commission, Vol. VI, p.204
28. Craig Roberts, Kill Zone: A Sniper Looks At Dealey Plaza, Tulsa, Oklahoma, Consolidated Press International, 1994, p.55
29. Ibid, p.14
30. Ian Griggs, *The Better-Known Witnesses,* 1997 in Ian Griggs, *No Case To Answer*, pp.17-24. p.17
31. The Men Who Killed Kennedy, Dir., Nigel Turner, Central Independent Television, 1988
32. The Men Who Killed Kennedy, 1988
33. The Men Who Killed Kennedy, 1988
34. Voluntary Statement of J.C. Price, Sheriff's Department, Country of Dallas, Texas, 22nd November 1963
35. Roberts, *Kill Zone*, p.60
36. JFK: The Case For Conspiracy, Dir. Robert J, Groden, 1993
37. JFK: The Case For Conspiracy, 1993
38. Marrs, *Crossfire*, p.317
39. Warren Commission, Vol. XXIV, Commission Exhibit No. 2015
40. Craig Roberts, *Kill Zone*, p.84
41. Don Roberdeau, *Theorized Trajectories to President Kennedy at Z-313*
http://droberdeau.blogspot.co.uk/2011/05/page-8.html

JFK | ECHOES FROM ELM STREET
A SEARCH FOR HISTORICAL ACCURACY ON THE
ASSASSINATION OF PRESIDENT JOHN F. KENNEDY

Four
Dallas police and the hunt for Oswald

Mark Bridger

President Kennedy was murdered at 12.30pm CST and Lee Harvey Oswald – the official perpetrator[1] – was in their custody a short while later. The speed with which the Dallas Police "solved" the case was nothing short of a miracle and has led, amongst numerous other anomalies in the case, to the question of whether Oswald was guilty or set-up. It all seemed just too pat to many, too good to be true.

In any police investigation a rational and objective appraisal of the evidence should direct the officers on the ground towards their suspect. Physical evidence and eyewitness testimony comprise the initial leads to be followed with no credence attached to clairvoyance or leaps of faith. The path that led to the police capture of Oswald approximately 75 minutes after Kennedy was murdered was not as straightforward as one might imagine, or the case against him as clear cut as the U.S authorities and national media have led us to believe for the last 50 years.

One problem with this study is that 50 years on we have all heard of Lee Harvey Oswald and the official proclamation of his guilt. For a rational appraisal of the assassination however and of how he came to be arrested we need to suspend reality and proceed as if we had never heard of him. In that way we can assess the actions and activities of the Dallas law enforcement personnel involved.

The U.S Secret Service were responsible for Kennedy's protection so when the barrage of shots rained down on the motorcade the Dallas police and Sheriff's Department were only in the area as motorcycle escorts or crowd control. The immediate job of protecting the President and apprehending any perpetrators initially fell on the Secret Service, a role they failed in with spectacular aplomb.

Whilst the protection of the President was primarily the Secret Service's domain the hunt for those responsible immediately fell into the hands of the

JFK | ECHOES FROM ELM STREET
A SEARCH FOR HISTORICAL ACCURACY ON THE ASSASSINATION OF PRESIDENT JOHN F. KENNEDY

local forces, ostensibly the Dallas Police Department. As the shots rang out local officers were on the scene and set about ascertaining what exactly had occurred.

Multiple shots from 2 directions – most witnesses head for knoll
Witnesses in Dealey Plaza quickly charged the knoll to the right front of Kennedy and it soon became apparent many believed shots had come from that direction, in complete disagreement with the later official version.[2] Police officers in the plaza began to get reports of shots from multiple directions, especially the knoll area, and as Oswald was behind the Kennedy limousine during the shooting he could not have been responsible for any from the front. Police and Secret Service agents on the scene also had first hand experience of shots emanating from in front of the motorcade.

In an ABC interview on 22nd November, Dallas motorcycle officer James Chaney told of riding behind the limousine's right rear bumper and of seeing *"The President struck in the face..."* indicating a shot from the knoll or the overpass ahead.

Dallas motorcyclist Bobby Hargis riding behind Kennedy reported being hit with blood and brain matter as Kennedy's head exploded, indicating a shot from the front.[3] Dallas motorcyclist B.J.Martin riding to the left and rear of the limousine reported blood and flesh matter on him and his motorbike, reinforcing the notion of shots from the front and right.[4]

Motorcade Secret Service agent Clint Hill saw the *"rear portion"* of Kennedy's head missing and *"...blood and bits of brain all over the entire rear portion of the car"*.[5]

DPD officer Joe Marshall Smith thought the shots came from the *"bushes of the overpass"* to the front of the motorcade[6] Smith would rush into the car park behind the knoll within seconds and encounter a *"Secret Service man"* despite no official Secret Service presence being there[7], a fact supported by Deputy Sheriff Seymour Weitzman.[8]

Witness William Newman watching from the north side of Elm Street was just feet away when President Kennedy was shot, and he stated *"I thought the shot had come from the garden directly behind me, that was on an elevation from where I was ...I do not recall looking towards the Texas School Book Depository"*.[9]

Sam Holland was among a group of railway employees watching the parade from atop the triple underpass and during the shooting he witnessed a puff of smoke coming from out of the trees on the knoll.[10]

Dallas police chief Jesse Curry and Dallas County Sheriff Bill Decker both rode in the Presidential motorcade and on hearing the shots both immediately issued orders to their men to get on the triple underpass and into the rail yards to ascertain what had happened[11] – no mention of the T.S.B.D. behind them.

Deputy Sheriff Harry Weatherford heard a loud report that he thought *"...*

FOUR | DALLAS POLICE AND THE HUNT FOR OSWALD

sounded as if it came from the railroad yard" behind the knoll.[12]

Secret Service agents Forrest Sorrels and Paul Landis, both riding in the motorcade thought shots came from the right front or up on *"that terrace up there".*[13]

Of the twenty five known affidavits or statements given in the immediate 24 hours after the assassination, concerning direction of the shots in Dealey Plaza twenty two said they believed they came from the grassy knoll.[14]

Witnesses also spoke of shots from the Texas School Book Depository (T.S.B.D) yet save one officer, Marrion Baker, police interest in the immediate aftermath centred on Elm Street, the knoll and the car park and rail tracks behind it. With all the confusion and differing eyewitness and ear witness reports flooding in individual officers would have struggled to evaluate the assassination and who or what was responsible from the information each received amid the chaos. Reports of different shooter locations would have alerted them very rapidly to the probability that President Kennedy had been the victim of a professional ambush involving multiple assassins. This probability would soon be reinforced by details of the wounds inflicted on the mortally wounded President.

JFK wounds indicate frontal shots

Witnesses in the plaza close enough to see the impact of the bullets on the President's body were aware that his injuries were fatal. A devastating shot that appeared to strike him in the right temple literally blew the back of his head off and was an immediate life ending round. In addition to this shot Kennedy was hit in the throat and the back by non-fatal shots.

The reports of motorcycle officers Chaney, Hargis, Martin and Secret Service Agent Clint Hill all indicated a vast wound in the back of Kennedy's head, the result of a shot fired from the front. The film taken by Abraham Zapruder of the assassination showed the violent rearward recoil of the President as this frontal shot exploded into him.

Further confirmation, if any were needed of the fatal shot coming from the front were the findings of the doctors at Dallas' Parkland Memorial Hospital where Kennedy was rushed to after the shooting[15] A large hole of exit was observed in the rear of his head consistent with a shot from the front.

At an impromptu press conference at Parkland Hospital, at approximately 1.30 p.m Assistant White House press secretary Malcolm Kilduff officially confirmed Kennedy's passing, adding the cause of death as *"...it's a simple matter of a bullet right through the head"* and pointed at his right temple.

The Dallas doctors would also locate two further wounds on Kennedy's body, as well as five to Texas Governor John Connally. Kennedy was hit by a non-exiting shot in the back approximately 5 ¾ inches below the neckline[16] and a frontal shot into his throat[17] confirming he was shot from more than one direction. Witnesses back in Dealey Plaza of course already knew this.

JFK | ECHOES FROM ELM STREET
A SEARCH FOR HISTORICAL ACCURACY ON THE ASSASSINATION OF PRESIDENT JOHN F. KENNEDY

Suspicious activity

During and immediately after the shooting various witnesses reported strange goings-on behind the picket fence atop the knoll. Lee Bowers situated in a 14 foot rail control tower behind the knoll saw three cars enter and circle the car park in front of him, in the minutes leading up to the assassination. At the time of the shooting he saw two men behind the fence and a *"commotion"*. He later told researcher Mark Lane *"At the time of the shooting, in the vicinity of where the two men I have described were, there was a flash of light...a flash of light or smoke or something which caused me to feel like something out of the ordinary had occurred there"*.[18]

Deaf mute Ed Hoffman stated he saw two men behind the fence, one of whom he said, dressed in a business suit shot at President Kennedy with a rifle, before tossing the gun to an accomplice dressed as a railway employee who broke it apart and placed it in a box or a bag.[19]

Dallas policeman Joe Marshall Smith ran to the area and encountered a fake Secret Service man after a lady had alerted him *"They are shooting the President from the bushes"* Smith also spoke of smelling gunpowder behind the fence at that time.[20]

The imposter flashed credentials when Smith drew his pistol. This man however, who was not Lee Harvey Oswald was almost certainly part of the assassination team that murdered President Kennedy, and Smith may go down in history as the man who got about as close as anyone that fateful day in capturing one of them.

J.C.Price overlooking the entire scene from atop the Terminal Annexe Building saw *"...one man run towards the passenger cars on the railroad siding after the volley of shots"* The bareheaded man *"was running very fast ...carrying something in his right hand... which could have been a gun"*.[21]

Other witnesses saw suspicious activity in the Texas School Book Depository concerning two men on a high floor; one of them possibly a Negro. They saw a rifle-like object protruding from an upper floor window. Arnold Rowland and Carolyn Walther saw two men with a gun, Rowland also claimed one of the men to be an elderly Negro.[22]

15 year old Amos Euins told a reporter immediately after the shooting that he had seen a black man fire from the window, and Euins and witness James Worrell told of a man running out the back of the Depository immediately after the assassination, a man the authorities have never claimed to be Lee Harvey Oswald.[23]

Deputy Sheriff Roger Craig claimed Lee Harvey Oswald was however picked up in front of the Depository building about 10 minutes after the assassination by a husky Latin man in a Rambler station wagon[24] and Dallas police Chief Jesse Curry would later tell reporters Oswald *"was picked up by a negro in a car"* – a scenario later dismissed by the official Government report into the assassination.

FOUR | DALLAS POLICE AND THE HUNT FOR OSWALD

Anyway police interest in Oswald would not begin, officially at least for another hour or so and he would leave the plaza amid all the chaos and confusion therein.

TSBD ignored for 30 mins

With the police focusing on the grassy knoll area interest in the T.S.B.D. would remain lackadaisical, certainly in respect to sealing it quickly enough to trap any fleeing assassin. Lee Bowers witnessed over 50 officers in the area behind the knoll *"...within a maximum of five minutes"*[25] while concerning the T.S.B.D, witness James Tague commented *"If Oswald was in that building, he had all the time in the world to calmly walk out of there"*.[26]

Officers did eventually start a search of the building but failed to stumble across the "sniper's nest" located on the sixth floor until 1.12 p.m despite witnesses alerting them to the high floors of the building in the minutes after the shooting. Why?[27]

Other suspects

The initial short but sweet hiatus before the myopic but seemingly "official" focus on Oswald saw attention in the plaza fall on more than one suspicious individual. Larry Florer was voluntarily detained by officers in the Dal-Tex building opposite the T.S.B.D. (footage shows he was being held so how voluntary it was is open to question) as was Jim Braden, both arrested after being spotted as strangers in the building. Both were later released before the Dallas authorities realised Braden's true name was Eugene Hale Brading, a career criminal from California with mafia connections. Their statements given that day are strikingly similar and have aroused suspicion over what exactly they were doing in the Dal-Tex building that day.[28]

Even more of a coincidence, apparently, was the reported arrest of a William Sharp who was in the same building *"without a good excuse"*[29] Either the Dal-Tex building, yards from the T.S.B.D. and with a perfect view of the motorcade was a subconscious vantage point of choice for random spectators that day or else there is some other explanation. Researchers have since suspected the building as a location for one or more of the snipers in Dealey Plaza that day, who again were not Lee Harvey Oswald.

In Fort Worth an Oswald lookalike Donald Wayne House was arrested in connection with the assassination but later released.[30]

At approximately 2p.m three individuals dubbed the "three tramps" were also arrested in the rail yards behind the knoll and escorted to the Sheriff's office nearby. Like the men arrested in the Dal-Tex these suspects would all be released without further delay once Oswald was apprehended in Oak Cliff, a Dallas suburb nearby. For that to happen however police interest needed to shift from the knoll and on to Oswald. That this happened is confirmed by his apprehension in Oak Cliff at 1.51p.m; the rationale for his arrest is not so obvious however.

Attention focus switches to LHO alone
With shots coming from the knoll and suspicious individuals being arrested in the Dal-Tex building how did police (and later the F.B.I. and Warren Commission) within an hour or so shift ALL attention and blame onto Oswald? Even if the evidence pointed to his involvement it would surely have been in addition to that initially suspected as coming from the other locations – especially as Kennedy's wounds being observed a few short miles away at Parkland Hospital confirmed shots from multiple directions.

The official conclusion offered in 1964 claimed that Oswald became a suspect when his supervisor Roy Truly alerted the police to his disappearance from the T.S.B.D. *"...the only one that I could be certain right then that was missing"*[31] however the time of this alert and the fact that Oswald was one of many missing employees showed the official version to be incorrect.[32] Dallas police however seemed to take far more interest in the "Oswald" information than any other previous or subsequent in their possession. What prompted this clairvoyance on their part?

At 12.45 Dallas police issued a description of the suspect *"...slender white male about thirty, five feet ten, one sixty five; carrying what looked to be a 30-30 or some type of Winchester"*.[33]

The Warren Commission guessed witness Howard Brennan was the source of this description but this was unlikely[34]. Anyhow it no more fitted Lee Harvey Oswald than it did a thousand other men in Dallas that day.

Officially Oswald made his departure from the building by merely walking out the front door and then boarding a bus a short distance away[35] which he then left after it got bogged down in traffic. He then took a taxi to North Beckley near his lodgings, the driver of which stated he was calm and *"...wasn't in any hurry. He wasn't nervous or anything."*[36] Obviously this scenario and the Roger Craig Rambler sighting contradict each other, and the evidence is strong that Oswald was impersonated, incriminatingly so, in the weeks leading up to the assassination. The work of John Armstrong also makes a case for there actually being two Oswalds – Harvey and Lee, with Harvey being the fall-guy (the patsy) murdered by Jack Ruby two days after his arrest, whilst in police "protective" custody.

For the benefit of this chapter however and the question of Dallas police advance sinister knowledge of Oswald it is not imperative to know which of the escape routes was used. Oswald left Dealey Plaza shortly after 12.30 and was Oak Cliff bound long before anyone in authority had a valid reason to suspect him or be hunting him.

Oswald entered his lodgings at 1026 North Beckley at approximately 1pm,

FOUR | DALLAS POLICE AND THE HUNT FOR OSWALD

staying a matter of minutes before leaving again 3 or 4 minutes later, as seen by his housekeeper Earlene Roberts.[37]

About a mile away a few short minutes later Dallas policeman J.D.Tippit was killed. The official version would later state Oswald was the perpetrator of this heinous crime but he did not have time to make the scene at Tenth and Patton in Oak Cliff on foot, and as he would always be labelled a loner with no assistance whatsoever, the concept that he had a lift there could not be contemplated. The official version still states he was Tippit's killer however. Tippit's murder did though prove the catalyst for dozens of officers to converge on the area and eventually to the Texas Theatre on West Jefferson Boulevard where Oswald was arrested.

And the rest is history – unfortunately hindsight provides the only validity for the cop-chase around Oak Cliff that culminated in his arrest; common sense does not. From Kennedy's murder to Oswald's arrest it took a mere 81 minutes – not bad work in solving the crime of the century. The problem is 50 years on few people buy it.

With Roy Truly's "roll call" that never happened and the loose 12.45 police alert, followed by the finding of incriminating (planted) evidence at both the T.S.B.D. and the Tippit murder site what very quickly became the "Oswald Show" relied on a presumption, for it to be true, of Oswald as the biggest fool in history. The reality is that persons unknown had set him up with incriminating titbits too blatant to be anything other than plants.

At approximately 1.12p.m Deputy Sheriff Luke Mooney had, according to the Warren Commission, found three rifle shells in the 6th floor "sniper's nest" and at 1.22 p.m a rifle was found on the same floor[38] Despite a rifle order later being traced to Oswald's alias A.Hidell (but no evidence of any ammunition ever purchased) at that time (1.22p.m, 22/11/63) and for many hours to come, no link to Lee Harvey Oswald was possible. Indeed for the first 24 hours or more confusion reigned as to whether the rifle was even a Mannlicher-Carcano at all, or a Mauser.[39]

So despite a questionable link being eventually made to Oswald, and ignoring the fact that anyone could have purchased a rifle in Texas in 1963 without leaving any such paper trail, no link was made or could have been made prior to his 1.51 p.m arrest.

At the Tippit murder site a wallet and shells were also conveniently left by the publicity hungry culprit, though no mention of the wallet was made in the official report back in 1964.

Although the wallet and shells, dependant of course on whose wallet and which shells were actually there, may have been incriminating once Oswald was arrested, they did not lead the DPD to him in the Texas Theatre a few blocks away. Officially a shoe store manager Johnny Calvin Brewer saw someone acting suspiciously who he followed to the theatre, where he conferred with the cashier Julia Postal who called the police, answering their reason for suspecting him as *"Well I didn't know"*.[40]

The actions of Brewer and Postal following Oswald, if it were indeed he, doing little more than entering a theatre possibly without a ticket, were the fortuitous catalyst for a fleet of patrol cars and assorted officers to finally get their man with little justification. Initially the capture of Oswald was only for the murder of Officer Tippit yet comments made by some of the policemen at the theatre betray yet again a clairvoyance human logic cannot explain.

According to Postal a policeman at the theatre stated *"I think we have got our man on both accounts"*[41] and Johnny Brewer heard one say *"Kill the president will you"*[42]. These corroborating claims by two separate witnesses at Oswald's arrest confirm at least some of the Dallas police interpreted entrance to a theatre possibly without a ticket as firm evidence of a double-murder some distance away. Such ability makes it a puzzle as to how any crime could ever go unsolved in the great city of Dallas.

With little justification Dallas police had their man, officially for the murder of Tippit yet this would soon extend to the assassination of Kennedy also.

Let us now look at the indications that Dallas police did not arrest Oswald through some telepathic ability and rather how their actions betray a foreknowledge that confirms the assumption of many researchers that Oswald had been set up and the police, some of them at least, knew who their man was in advance.

Oswald was either on, or believed to be on Cecil McWatter's Marsalis bus at approximately 12.40 p.m but exited this mode of transport when it became snarled in traffic. Moments later two Dallas police officers entered the bus and started searching it.[43] Of all the buses in Dallas that day why did the police pick that one alone to search in the immediate minutes after the shooting? Were the police hunting him within ten minutes or was this just a coincidence?

Officer Tippit, who would be killed in Oak Cliff soon after (probably between 1.06 – 1.10 p.m) was apparently acting strangely in the period up to his murder, not least his being in Oak Cliff itself in an area outside his own patch. At approximately 12.40 p.m he was parked up at the GLOCO station at the end of the Houston Street viaduct observing the traffic pass by, at a position Oswald would have to pass were he on the Marsalis bus.[44] At approximately 12.50 p.m he left and soon after made a phone call at the Top Ten Record store on Jefferson Boulevard.[45] Who was he attempting to contact – presumably not a fellow officer but a civilian?

A few minutes after 1 p.m a witness James Andrews claimed he had been stopped by Tippit who cut his patrol car in front of him as he was driving along West 10th Street. Andrews stated Tippit jumped out of his car and ran to Andrews' car and looked inside for somebody/something.[46] Without uttering a word Tippit then returned to his car and departed.

FOUR | DALLAS POLICE AND THE HUNT FOR OSWALD

Elsewhere at approximately 1 p.m Oswald's lodging housekeeper Earlene Roberts stated a Dallas police car with two men in sounded their horn outside 1026 North Beckley while Oswald was inside.[47] If true this was the second time in a short space of time two Dallas policemen had shown an interest in the apparently unknown Lee Harvey Oswald.

At 1.30 p.m a police broadcast stated the Tippit murder suspect had been seen entering the Jefferson Library a couple of blocks away from 10th & Patton.[48] As a result a fleet of patrol cars and officers headed that way, and rounded up patrons and staff alike. A young 19 year old man Adrian Hamby was grabbed and pushed against the wall. According to Detective Marvin Buhk a *"Secret Service"* man vouched for Hamby as *"not the suspect"*[49] despite there being no Secret Service agents in Oak Cliff at that time. Unfortunately Lee Harvey Oswald would not enjoy the protection of such a guardian angel a short while later. Buhk's agent was possibly a plain clothes police officer but the relevant point was how could anyone in a position of authority possibly know Adrian Hamby was not their man UNLESS they knew for sure who WAS their man. This question remains unanswered today.

While still in the area a call came over the police radio that a suspect *"just went in the Texas Theatre on West Jefferson"* apparently without purchasing a ticket. This minor offence caused a rush of police manpower to descend on the theatre, along with F.B.I agents and a news crew. Inside they found Oswald and he was arrested, finally, at 1.51 p.m.[50] Dallas police had their man and the overriding feeling when evaluating the Oak Cliff chase is one of a hunt for Oswald and for Oswald alone. Once caught no further suspects were sought for either murder, despite Oswald, officially anyhow, only being arrested for the Tippit case not the murder of the President. The past 50 years of hindsight has perhaps dulled the capacity to view the Oswald arrest with the incredulity it warrants. F.B.I agents and twenty officers do not routinely, or more precisely, EVER rush to a theatre to sniff out a man without a film ticket.

Back at 1026 North Beckley during this period further developments reinforced the notion that Oswald was wanted by police long before they had any legitimate reason to do so. Tenant Hugh Slough[51] returned home early from his employ as a Tab operator at the Republic National Life Insurance company on North Central Expressway to hear Earlene Roberts recall how Oswald had *"rushed in and out" "that the police had had been there looking for Oswald right after he left and shortly before I arrived. His room had not been searched yet".*

Slough recalled he had arrived at 1026 *"one to two hours after it was announced Kennedy was dead"* and *"as it was so early I was going to Waco to be with my parents"*[52]. This could have been as early as 1.45 p.m local time, even prior to Oswald's arrest and long before the official police arrival at 3 p.m.

Officially Dallas police officers Potts, Senkel and Cunningham arrived at 3 p.m; waited for a warrant to search, and stayed until 5.30 p.m to 6 p.m.[53]

JFK | ECHOES FROM ELM STREET
A SEARCH FOR HISTORICAL ACCURACY ON THE
ASSASSINATION OF PRESIDENT JOHN F. KENNEDY

suggesting Slough arrived and left for Waco before 3 p.m. *"...as it was so early".*

In an affidavit of 5thDecember 1963 Earlene Roberts described how she had seen Oswald enter and leave, then he stood outside 1026 at a bus stop and how *"About thirty minutes later three Dallas policemen came to the houselooking for Lee Harvey Oswald".*[54]

If these three officers were Potts, Senkel and Cunningham at 3 p.m they wouldn't have been looking for Oswald as he was safely (well not really) back in City Hall when they arrived at 1026.

The owner Mrs Johnson said the police arrived *"...and these officers were there 1.30 or 2..."*(55) and her husband Arthur Johnson confirmed *"Well it must've been around 1.30 or 2 o'clock".*[56]

Mr Johnson also stated *"...when the officers came looking for him ...after Tippit was shot ...they just came down there looking for – uh – Oswald"* with the police stating his full name *"Lee Harvey Oswald"* and *"...they searched him and found my address in his pocket".*[57]

None of this ties in with the official version in which they had already arrested Oswald before going anywhere near 1026 North Beckley, and at no time have the police ever claimed their knowledge of the address came from a slip of paper found in Oswald's pocket. Nor were they sure of his real identity immediately. Johnson's claims may tie in however with the wallet conveniently left at the Tippit murder that "disappeared" until the late 1990s, leading police to 1026 between 1.30 and 2 p.m.

Johnson's address "document" nor the search warrant have ever surfaced which defies belief in the investigation of the crime of the century. Additionally the official version of how Dallas police became aware of 1026 North Beckley is equally disturbing. Slough stated he was interviewed by the F.B.I. in the days shortly after the assassination also but this report has yet to surface.

Officially Oswald did not volunteer the information, nor were his employers at the T.S.B.D. aware of it He was registered there under the address of Ruth Paine at 2515 West 5thStreet, Irving. Captain Will Fritz who led the investigation sent officers Adamcik, Stovall and Rose to this Irving address at approximately 2.30 p.m, arriving around 2.55 p.m[58] where they waited for 35 to 40 minutes for Deputy Sheriffs with jurisdiction, to arrive. They entered the Irving address at 3.30 p.m. where Ruth Paine gave them a telephone number for Oswald that was criss-crossed and came up with the North Beckley address.[59]

At 2.40 p.m however Dallas police officers Potts, Senkel and Cunningham had been dispatched to 1026 North Beckley by Fritz a full fifty minutes before the commencement of the Irving address search. According to Fritz this foreknowledge of the rooming house address was via *"...some officer"* who told him this outside his office.[60] Fritz declared amnesia as to the identity of this officer who gave him one of the most important tips in the history of Dallas law enforcement.

FOUR | DALLAS POLICE AND THE HUNT FOR OSWALD

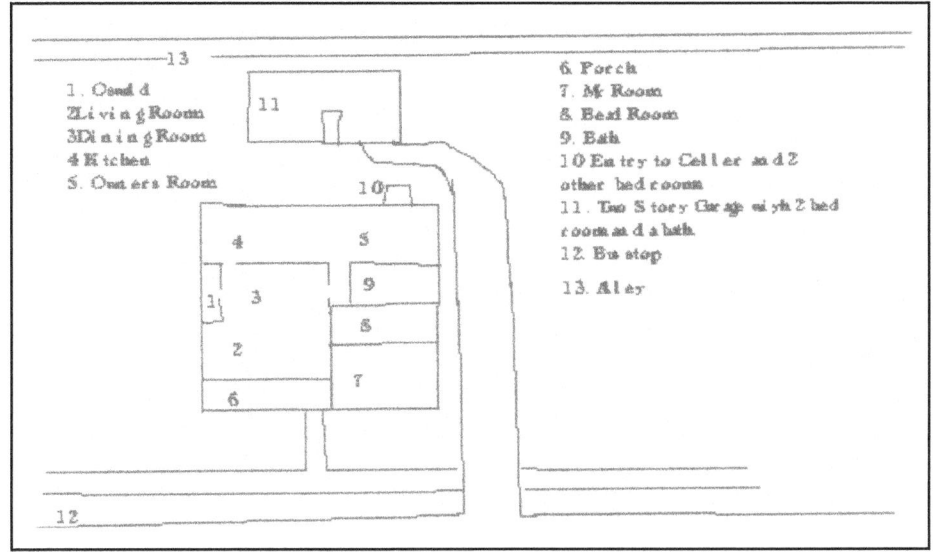

Slough's picture of 1026 showing his room (7) and Oswald's room (1)

The U.S government House Select Committee on Assassinations report (page 221) stated local military intelligence had a file on Oswald prior to 22ndNovember 1963 and had contacted the F.B.I. on that date regarding Oswald. Did Dallas police intelligence have files on Oswald prior to that date also, files that were subsequently destroyed? Or does it make more sense that Fritz himself, Captain and head of the Homicide and Robbery Bureau was one of the Dallas officers with foreknowledge of Oswald.

The fact remains Dallas police had foreknowledge of Oswald's address as proven by Fritz's testimony, and the residents' claims appear to suggest they used this foreknowledge in advance. Dallas researcher Mary Ferrell would tell the H.S.C.A. years later that five boarders at 1026 would coincidentally bear the same names as serving Dallas police officers.[61]

History shows that whatever the truth is concerning the arrest of Lee Harvey Oswald his brutal death occurred whilst in Dallas police protective custody. That fact alone condemns the Department and permits us to wonder what other violations of his rights occurred at that time.

Captain Fritz upon being informed by Roy Truly that Oswald was one (of many) missing employees stated "*...I felt it important to hold that man...*"[62] in an act of unparalleled clairvoyance.

Police chief Jesse Curry and Dallas District Attorney both told news reporters that a paraffin test administered to Oswald were positive and that he had fired a gun despite the tests confirming nothing of the sort. Why the lies and disinformation unless Oswald was the pre-designated fall-guy? The leaking of such information to the press implicating Oswald in advance of the evidence suggests purely that.

Conclusion

Senior personnel in the Dallas police Department denied any knowledge of Oswald prior to the assassination; yet it seems apparent they were not only aware of his presence they were also hunting him for the murder of the President long before having any reasonable grounds to do so. Although officers on the ground, most of whom initially were unaware of the set-up, were gathering evidence pointing to a conspiracy any such activity following these leads were cut off almost immediately. Arrests made in Dealey Plaza were dealt with in a near nonchalant manner, and the hunt for a suspect in Oak Cliff met with "he's not the one" shortly before an over the top arrest of Oswald for not buying a theatre ticket.

Witnesses at 1026 North Beckley testified that police officers arrived there at approximately 1.30 p.m to 2 p.m searching for him. If correct this confirms that Oswald was not arrested as a result of a natural progression of events but rather his capture had a pre-ordained nature to it and that he was the victim of a set-up. An officer shouting *"Kill the President will you"* at his arrest for the murder of officer Tippit bolsters this assumption.

Someone high up had to steer the focus onto him or else the case might have stopped with the three tramps, Larry Florer, Eugene Hale Brading, the man in the plaza who "didn't speak English", Adrian Hamby and so forth. The fact is it stopped with Oswald. The presence of officers at his bedsit earlier than they should have been is entirely consistent with his being set-up. Kennedy was killed by a conspiracy of powerful interests and those responsible were not going to take the blame.

Once we accept and recognise this it is also clear the police would have had to be directed to the person set to take the rap, either by a series of incriminating plants or through the foreknowledge of a few key individuals in the murder location. It appears both of these scenarios happened and were an essential part of the plot. The fall guy's own murder was unfortunately (for Oswald) also a key part of the plan, and that is exactly what happened 46 hours later, thanks largely to the Dallas police force. Had the police encountered Oswald at 1026 shortly after Tippit's murder would he have been killed there "resisting arrest" one wonders?

Oswald's 46 hours in police custody was a brief interlude of course but he was thus allowed a short but succinct soliloquy to his actual involvement *"I don't know what dispatches you people have been getting but I emphatically deny these charges...I'm just a patsy"*.

You better believe it.

FOUR | DALLAS POLICE AND THE HUNT FOR OSWALD

Endnotes

1. WR 19
2. 3H 283; 7H 535, 568, 18H 759; 19H 471, 472, 480, 481, 485, 486, 489, 490, 502, 511, 514, 516; 21H 548; 22H 600; 24H 228; WCD 87; WCD 205, P39.
3. 6H 294
4. 6H 292
5. 2H 141
6. 22H 600
7. 7H 535
8. 7H 107
9. CE 2003, P45
10. 6H 243-4; 24H 212
11. 17H 461
12. 19H 498
13. 7H 346; 18H 759
14. Mark Lane, Rush to Judgment, page 30 (Fawcett Publications 1967)
15. 6H 3, 11, 20, 33, 71.
16. WR 87-88
17. Malcolm Perry, Parkland Hospital press conference, 2.16pm 22/11/63; Dr Caricco WCE 392
18. 6H 285-6; Lane page 24
19. Eyewitness, Ed Hoffman & Ron Friedrich (Lancer publications 1995)
20. 7H 535; Ronnie Dugger, The Texas Observer 13/12/1963
21. 19H 492; Lane page 25
22. WR 64-5, 251; 24H 522
23. 2H 194-6, 205; 6H 170; 16H 959
24. When They Kill a President, Roger Craig (unpublished, 1971)
25. 6H 288
26. 7H 558
27. See Accessories after The Fact, pp 10-15, Sylvia Meagher (Vintage books 1992)
28. 19H 469, 476
29. 20H 499
30. See "Under House Arrest", Dealey Plaza Echo volume 6, no: 2; July 2002.
31. 3H 230, 4H 206
32. See "The Myth of the Depository Roll Call", Dealey Plaza Echo volume 11, no: 2, July 2007
33. WR 144
34. Lane, pp 68-83
35. CE2168
36. 2H 261
37. 6H 440
38. WR79
39. Meagher, pp 94-100
40. 7H 11
41. 7H 12
42. 7H 6
43. 25H 900
44. Car #10 where are you? - Bill Drenas, October 1998
45. The Top Ten Record Store, Bill Drenas, 1999
46. See Drenas, footnote 44
47. 6H 443
48. 7H 36
49. Dallas P.D Archives Box 2, folder #7, item #8, (report 3/12/1963)
50. WR 179
51. All information on Slough from series of emails with the author, 2006. Slough indicated his name is

an Anglicised version of the German name Slouach. Slough made some very interesting observations regarding the rooming house in November 1963, including never seeing a gun there and believing the house could only accommodate 14 people maximum. He also stated J.D.Tippit was a very strict law enforcer.

52. Jay Watson, WFAA *"...have been cut down by assassin's bullets"* at 12.45 p.m, CST, initial broadcast.
53. Dallas police Archives, Box 2, folder #9, item #32; Box 3, folder #3, item #1.
54. 7H 439
55. 10H 295
56. 10H 304
57. 10H 303-4
58. 4H 207; 7H 204
59. 19 H 503, 520, 530
60. 4H 207
61. HSCA Critics' Conference, 17 Sept. 1977
62. 4H 206

Five
The Medical Evidence
Russell Kent

> *"The men who create power make an indispensable contribution to the nation's greatness, but the men who question power make a contribution just as indispensable, especially when that questioning is disinterested, for they determine whether we use power or power uses us."* John F. Kennedy

The official, US Government description of the wounds to President John F Kennedy and Governor John Connally can be read in the Warren Commission Report. Essentially, the Warren Report's description of this evidence is that:

1) JFK suffered two perforating gunshot wounds from behind. The first entered "the back of his neck"[1] and left the body through his throat, just beneath the Adam's apple. The second entered the centre of the back of his head and came out through the upper right of his head. The Warren Report did not specify exactly where the bullet came out. Instead, it described a "large opening on the right side of his head"[2].

2) John Connally was hit in the back by the first bullet which hit Kennedy, the one that came out through JFK's throat. This bullet went into the back of Connally's right armpit came out through his chest, just below his right nipple, perforated his right wrist and ended up embedded in his left thigh.

A later US Government investigation by the House Select Committee on Assassinations (HSCA) drew the same conclusions regarding the medical evidence, but with one major difference. The HSCA concluded that the second bullet hit JFK's head 10cm (almost 4 inches) higher in the back of the head in "the cowlick area" (the area on the crown of the head where most peoples' hair swirls)[3].

JFK | ECHOES FROM ELM STREET
A SEARCH FOR HISTORICAL ACCURACY ON THE ASSASSINATION OF PRESIDENT JOHN F. KENNEDY

The official position is that all the shots which wounded the two men were fired by Lee Harvey Oswald from above and behind the limousine. But does the medical evidence support this conclusion?

Recently, on hearing that I was interested in the medical aspects of the JFK assassination, a colleague expressed surprise that there could be anything but a straightforward story to relate. Quite so. Anybody unfamiliar with the evidence would reasonably assume that there could be little doubt about the nature of the President's wounds, the treatment he received or his autopsy.

Moreover, as the injuries to the Governor of Texas could only have occurred one way, the nature of Connally's injuries should mesh with the evidence arising from Kennedy's injuries, producing a singular account of what happened to both men.

But in response to these utterly reasonable assumptions, those of us familiar with the medical evidence respond, "*If only*". For the truth is that the medical evidence is riddled with ambiguity, complexity, uncertainty and doubt. It is a multi-dimensional nightmare.

For many years I have steered clear of writing anything about several parts of the medical data for fear of disappearing into an abyss of data from which I might fail to return. The abyss is immense. There are many thousands of pages of information to read in doctors' reports and official government records on the assassination, before one gets to the medical evidence in some of the most remarkable books that have been written about the case. Beyond that lies the vast number of papers by well-qualified and respected private researchers.

This gargantuan body of work has recently been supplemented by Doug Horne's [4] five volume book on his experiences at the Assassination Records Review Board, parts of which I have had to read several times.

But reading is only a part of historical medical research. Other researchers must be consulted, copious notes taken and cross-checked, diagrams and tables drawn up, mathematical calculations made and logic applied through sleepless nights.

This, though, is only the start of the process. Within the millions of pages of information that need to be digested are highly specialised areas like ballistics, micrographics, neutron activation analysis and trigonometry which generate a further problem: a medical researcher is either a generalist or a specialist – it is impossible to be both – and inevitably, both approaches have strengths and weaknesses.

The generalist tends to have good overview knowledge of most aspects, but cannot be fully conversant with the minutia of, for example, X-ray lacquers, 1960s trauma techniques or neuro-surgical tools.

Meanwhile, the specialist takes the more blinkered approach of concentrating on one part of the evidence. This requires highly detailed

FIVE | THE MEDICAL EVIDENCE

analysis that is often responsible for some of the most dramatic revelations in medical research. But, by definition, a specialist is almost bound to miss the implications of other specialist work either because he doesn't have time to read it or he doesn't have the knowledge to understand it.

Compounding the problem still further is the fact that the physical evidence in the assassination has, almost without exception, been poorly handled, lost, substituted or altered and this is particularly true of the medical evidence. If anybody had been brought to trial for the murder of Kennedy and the attempted murder of Connally the trial would have been undermined from the beginning by the obvious flaws in the preparation of the medical evidence.

The straightforward question that the layman always asks – "Who did it?" – cannot be answered to a morality certainty based on the evidence the evidence itself is unreliable. This unreliability can be traced to four specific areas.

Firstly the wounds suffered by Kennedy and Connally were, incredibly, measured differently. This almost beggars belief, not least because the wounds were measured by medically-qualified personnel. But before there was any dispute about entrance and exit wounds, different methods had been used to measure the size, shape, position on the body and other routine and straightforwardly quantifiable characteristics of the two men's wounds. This makes it extremely difficult to compare the wounds and yet they are the central aspect of the whole case.

Secondly, the wounds have been illustrated differently. Many different drawings, figures and diagrams have been used by medical staff involved in the case and by official investigators. These range from the – probably authentic – drawings made by the Dallas doctors, to some peculiar medical illustrations and diagrams commissioned by the various US government agencies that subsequently became involved in the case.

Thirdly, the autopsy report, which should be utterly dependable as a legal document describing the wounds and cause of death, is bereft of reliability. A layman might expect a military autopsy performed by a high-ranking doctor to be of the best quality. But the autopsy report turns out to be an extraordinarily poor document with, at best, a dubious provenance.

Fourthly, the photographs and X-rays of the wounds are, at the very least, of questionable origin. In the opinion of many qualified experts who have seen them, the autopsy photographs and X-rays are flawed, amateurish and may indeed be bogus. Even the photographs of bullet wounds to goats used by the Warren Commission in an attempt to reproduce JFK's wounds are of better quality[5] than are the official pictures of the President's wounds (overleaf).

JFK | Echoes From Elm Street
A Search for Historical Accuracy on the
Assassination of President John F. Kennedy

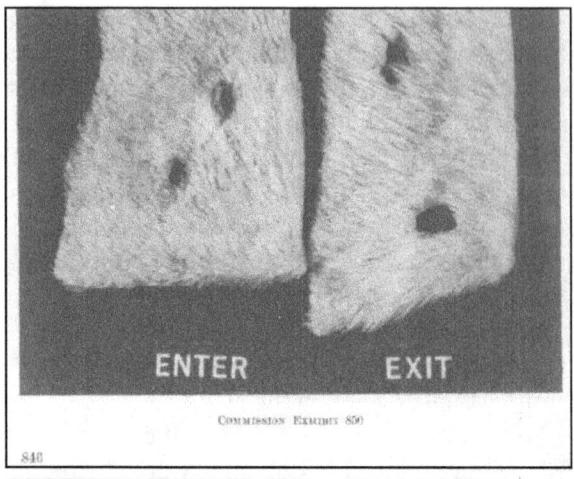

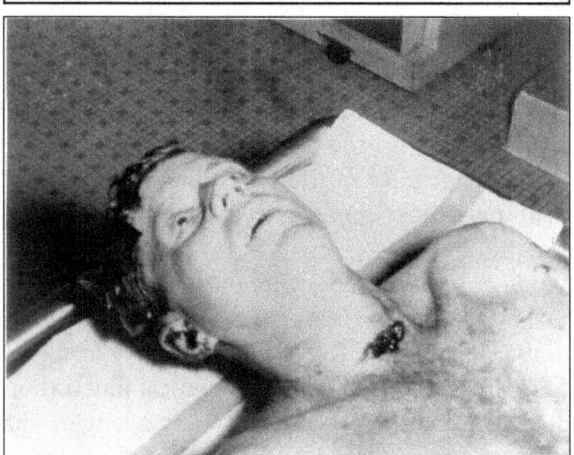

CE850 Photographs of Bullet Wounds to Goat Skin Compared with JFK Autopsy Photograph

The Kennedy family donated the autopsy photographs and X-rays of JFK to the US National Archives in 1966. An agreement made with the Archives limits access to these materials to the following:

- People authorised to act for an official agency of the US government with authority to investigate the assassination
- Experts in pathology or related areas whose applications are approved by Paul Kirk who acts on behalf of the Kennedy family[6]

The autopsy photographs and X-rays have never, officially, been unavailable for publication. However, a subset of them has leaked into the public arena. In November 1963, James K. Fox, a US Secret Service photographer, made

FIVE | THE MEDICAL EVIDENCE

several sets of black and white autopsy photo prints at the Secret Service lab. He kept at least one set for himself and these became known as "the Fox photos". In 1981, some were sold to JFK researcher Mark Crouch who shared them with several others. In 1993, Crouch sold his JFK assassination collection, including negatives made from the photos, to Walt Brown, a highly-respected assassination researcher, who continues to make them available to researchers. I own a set myself.

Researchers who have spent many hours in the National Archives studying the original photographs have confirmed that the Fox photos are authentic copies of the originals. Although they may be cropped differently and are not quite as clear as the originals in the National Archives, they are basically the same. There is a problem though: the photographs and X-rays of Kennedy's wounds in the National Archives – and therefore, the Fox photos – are so vague, poor in quality and at serious variance with the descriptions of Kennedy's wound by all of the doctors who worked on Kennedy that it is actually possible that they are false.

The first indication that the photographs and X-rays may be false is their extraordinarily sloppy presentation. Autopsy photography is an exact science. In the early 1960s, as now, each item of interest at an autopsy was routinely photographed at least three times: close up, mid-range and at a wide-angle. Autopsy pictures, then as now, were usually in colour, expertly lit and fully identified with proper tags. These were all standard autopsy procedures in 1963, but none of them were followed in the case of President Kennedy's autopsy.

Oswald's autopsy, performed by Dr Earl F Rose just days after JFK's, however, was expertly done in the standard way with the photographs in colour, expertly lit and fully identified as in the picture below. Equally, J D Tippit, the Dallas policeman that Oswald was also accused of murdering on 22 November 1963, received an exemplary autopsy at the hands of Dr Rose.

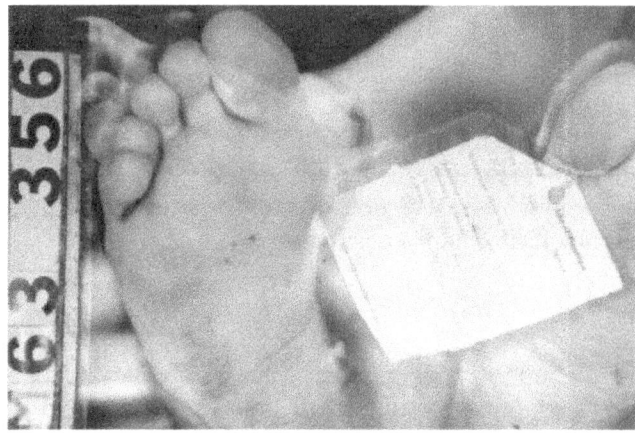

Autopsy Photograph of Oswald's Feet

Wouldn't you expect the remains of the President to have been treated at the top level of contemporary expertise? Wouldn't you further expect all the medical evidence gathered from the President and John Connally to have been treated with exaggerated caution and with an extremely careful eye to legal procedure? Well, none of these things happened. Far from it.

Nonetheless, the medical evidence is the basis of the official US Government position that a single bullet caused all the wounds to JFK and Connally except for JFK's fatal head wound. This is widely known as the "Single Bullet Theory" (SBT) and has to account for at least seven wounds in the two men (JFK's back and throat wound, Connally's thorax entry and exit, wrist entry and exit and thigh entry) wounds.

There is another chapter in this book focussing on the SBT, but it is impossible for me to give a lucid account of either the medical evidence or the SBT without some cross-reference. Please forgive any repetition.

I believe that the true nature of JFK's wounds cannot be established beyond a reasonable doubt. Given the way the evidence was handled, it is hard to escape the conclusion that this was intentional. The reason that the nature of the wounds cannot be known began with official persuasion of doctors (who actually had the body in their hands) to change their descriptions of the wounds. It continued with a dishonest autopsy. It ended with corruption in the US Government investigations.

Dallas: First Reports & Medical Testimony
The first descriptions of the wounds were provided by eye witnesses in Dealey Plaza. These can be found in several books, articles and videos on the case and include, for example, Charles Brehm, Mary Moorman and the Newmans. I don't wish to dwell on this information, firstly because other accounts have covered it well and secondly because the doctors who described the wounds later were closer to them and more precise in their accounts.

Later descriptions were offered to the Warren Commission in testimony from Clint Hill and Jacqueline Kennedy. Once again, I do not want to be diverted into a long discussion about their evidence as the descriptions were given months after the event and because the Warren Commission transcripts are not wholly reliable. This may be quite a surprise to some readers, but it's easy to prove. In one instance among many, when the Warren Commission took the testimony of Jacqueline Kennedy, the following exchange occurred:

Mr RANKIN: Do you remember Mr Hill coming to try to help on the car?

Mrs KENNEDY: I don't remember anything. I was just down like that. And finally I remember a voice behind me, or something and then I remember the people in the front seat, or somebody, finally knew something was wrong and

FIVE | THE MEDICAL EVIDENCE

a voice yelling, which must have been Mr Hill, "Get to the hospital," or maybe it was Mr Kellerman, in the front seat. But someone yelling. I was just down and holding him. **[Reference to wounds deleted.]**

Mr RANKIN: Do you have any recollection of whether there were one or more shots?[7]

[Reference to wounds deleted.] is a clear indication that the Warren Commission transcripts do not contain the whole truth.

There is potent evidence of further medical evidence that was given during the hearings being omitted from the transcripts. This evidence was contained in the many off-the-record discussions noted as occurring by the Warren Commission stenographers, but not recorded. All of these discussions of the Kennedy and Connolly wounds are lost to posterity.

The first *reliable* descriptions of the wounds were written the same day they occurred by the doctors that attended both JFK and Connally in the trauma rooms of Parkland Memorial Hospital (Parkland) in Dallas. There is also a statement to the press given by Dr Perry before any report had been written.

JFK's Throat Wound

For the official solution to the JFK assassination to be correct – that is, for all the shots to have been fired from behind and by Lee Harvey Oswald – all the entrance wounds on Kennedy's body had to be in the back of his body and all the exit wounds had to be in the front. But the wound in the front of Kennedy's throat was described at Parkland as an *entrance* wound.

JOURNALIST: "Where was the entrance wound?"

Dr PERRY: "There was an entrance wound in the neck. As regards the one on the head, I cannot say."

JOURNALIST: "Which way was the bullet coming on the neck wound? At him?"

Dr PERRY: "It appeared to be coming at him."

Later in the press conference, the following exchange took place:

JOURNALIST: "Doctor, describe the entrance wound. You think from the front in the throat?"

Dr PERRY: "The wound appeared to be an entrance wound in the front of the throat: yes, that is correct. The exit wound, I don't know. It could have been the head or there could have been a second wound of the head. There was not time to determine this at the particular instant."[8]

Perry performed a tracheotomy on JFK. This was and remains a standard emergency procedure for patients who are unable to breathe properly and a procedure that Perry had performed many times. It involved Perry making a small incision into Kennedy's windpipe and inserting a tube. Kennedy would then have been able to breathe through the tube.

By pure chance, the throat wound was at the correct place for a tracheotomy incision and Perry simply extended the hole by 2-3mm each side and inserted a cuffed endotracheal tube. This coincidence of wound and tracheotomy was to have a devastating effect on the clarity of the medical evidence. If I had to choose a single pivotal moment within Kennedy's treatment that created the years of controversy that followed, this was it. Perry's tracheotomy incision obscured what he and the other Parkland staff described as a straightforward entrance wound. By enlarging this wound into a tracheotomy incision, its original nature was distorted and what would have been irrefutable evidence of Kennedy being shot from in front as well from behind was lost.

When talking to the press, just over an hour after JFK had been pronounced dead at Parkland, Dr Perry, the doctor who had the best look at his throat wound believed it to be an entrance wound. Remember, Oswald, the alleged assassin, was only ever accused of firing from behind. So, at this point Dr Perry was, unwittingly, saying that there was probably a conspiracy. For the official case to be supported, however, Perry had to come down thoroughly on the side of there being a single gunman shooting from behind Kennedy. That is, the throat wound needed to be an exit wound in order for the single bullet explanation of Kennedy's death to be true and Perry had to be made to change his mind.

By the time Dr Perry gave testimony to the Warren Commission, he had indeed changed his mind. Over the years, the way that Dr Perry was coerced into reversing his opinion on the throat wound from entrance to exit has been revealed. There is considerable evidence that he was harassed all night from the 22nd to 23rd November 1963 by someone from Bethesda Naval Hospital[9] and by the Secret Service before giving evidence to the Warren Commission[10].

In the 1990s, in his book *Case Closed*, Gerald Posner quoted Dr Perry thus:

"As the press is wont to do, they took my statement at the press conference out of context. I did say it looked like an entrance wound since it was small, but I qualified it by saying that I did not know where the bullets came from. I wish now that I had not speculated. Everyone ignored my qualification. It was a small wound, slightly ragged at the edges and could have been an exit or entrance. By Sunday, after working on Oswald, I had learnt my lesson and I handed out a written statement to the press and took no questions. I had got a lot smarter in two days."[11]

Five | The medical evidence

The best way to treat Perry's apparent about-turn is to see whether the other Parkland staff that saw Kennedy's throat wound before the tracheotomy also defined it as an entrance wound.

In his first testimony to the Warren Commission, Dr Charles J Carrico described the throat wound as "rather round and there were no jagged edges or stellate lacerations."[12] These characteristics are standard indications of an entrance wound and Carrico would have known this.

In his Admission Note, Carrico described this hole as a "small penetrating wound"[13]. Carrico's use of the word "penetrating" is crucial. It means that he thought that the bullet which had caused Kennedy's throat wound had gone into his body at that point and, with no reliable indication of its leaving the body, the bullet had stayed there. When used as a medical term, "penetrating" means that an object has gone into a body and not through the body. In contrast, a through-and-through wound is described as "perforating". In layman's terms, Carrico was saying that the throat wound was an entry wound and that either the bullet was still in Kennedy's body or he didn't know where it came out – but that it had entered from the front.

Further evidence that Carrico considered the throat wound to be an entrance is contained in this answer that he gave to the Warren Commission:

> "As I recall, Dr. Perry, and I talked and tried after - later in the afternoon to determine what exactly had happened, and we were not aware of the missile wound to the back, and postulated that this [the throat wound] was either a tangential wound from a fragment, possibly another entrance wound. It could have been an exit wound, but we knew of no other entrance wound."[14]

In other words, when they talked about the throat wound, Carrico and Perry had only considered *how* this entrance wound had come about, not *whether* it was an entrance wound. The importance of this cannot be overstated. Everything they saw told Carrico and Perry that the throat wound was an entrance wound. Whether they might have thought it could have been an entrance wound if they had turned Kennedy over and seen the wound in his back is an extraordinarily complex matter which takes up an entire chapter in this book – see the chapter on the Single Bullet Theory.

My own belief is that it would have made no difference. That is, if the doctors had turned Kennedy over and seen his back wound, I believe they would still have judged the throat wound to have been an entrance wound. Indeed, this chapter will shortly present what I consider to be overwhelming evidence that the back wound had nothing whatsoever to do with Kennedy's throat wound. Again, for the sake of simplicity in this complex matter, it has to be stated that if the wounds to Kennedy's back and throat were not connected then there must have been two gunmen – one behind him and one in front of him – and therefore a conspiracy.

But before presenting that evidence, it is necessary to examine further evidence from Parkland staff who saw Kennedy's throat wound before its shape was distorted by the tracheotomy.

Registered Nurse Margaret M Henchliffe saw Kennedy's throat wound before the tracheotomy incision in to his throat and described it as an entrance wound. This is an extract from her Warren Commission evidence. Arlen Specter, who was questioning Henchliffe, was the Commission's Assistant Counsel.

Mr. SPECTER: Have you ever had any experience with bullet holes?

Miss HENCHLIFFE: Yes.

Mr. SPECTER: And what did that appear to you to be?

Miss HENCHLIFFE: An entrance bullet hole – it looked to me like.

Mr. SPECTER: Could it have been an exit bullet hole?

Miss HENCHLIFFE: I have never seen an exit bullet hole – I don't remember seeing one that looked like that.

Nurse Henchcliffe's last answer may, at first, appear to be contradictory. It is not. She began to say "I have never seen an exit bullet hole *which looked like that*" but appears to have stopped herself, possibly because she thought that answer to be somewhat blunt. She changed herself, mid-sentence to say, "I don't remember seeing one that looked like that."

The abiding point is that two medically-qualified people, in addition to Perry, described Kennedy's throat wound as being an entrance wound and these three people – Carrico, Henchliffe and Perry – were the first to see Kennedy's throat wound when he was brought in the emergency room and before Perry performed a tracheotomy on his throat. A reasoned appreciation of the first day evidence can only come to the conclusion that the Parkland staff had no reason to lie and were correct in saying that the throat wound was an entrance wound.

This, though, was not the end of the phenomenon of wounds changing their nature between Parkland and Bethesda. While one wound changed from an entrance wound into an exit wound when it reached Bethesda, another wound changed its location. A wound that the Parkland doctors clearly described as being in the back of JFK's head moved to the top and slightly to the side of his head when Kennedy's body was examined at Bethesda. This was not a trivial change or one that could have been brought about by misunderstanding.

FIVE | THE MEDICAL EVIDENCE

To appreciate what is involved here, readers need to understand a combination of gunshot and medical terminology. Gunshot terminology first. At the risk of spelling out the obvious, when somebody is shot the bullet creates an entrance wound and this is most often a small wound simply because bullets are small. Thereafter, the bullet either lodges in the body, as a whole or in parts, or it leaves the body. If it leaves the body, it creates an exit wound, which is nearly always larger than the entrance wound and generally *much* larger. Bullets tend to blast their way out of bodies and to create large holes at the point they blast their way out.

In the case of Kennedy's exit wounds, though, there is an elementary problem: the Parkland staff saw a large exit wound in one place but the Bethesda staff saw it in a quite different place. Since the Bethesda staff were writing the President's autopsy report, their version became the official version and at this point, politics become relevant. The Bethesda version supported the conclusion that Lee Harvey Oswald, who had been arrested six hours before the autopsy, was Kennedy's lone killer. But the Parkland version meant that either Oswald had an accomplice in front of Kennedy or that Oswald was innocent. The two versions of where the shot to Kennedy's head left his body were utterly incompatible.

Which brings us to the medical terminology involved in these conflicting versions of the same wound.

In medical language, an exit wound to the occipital area (see diagram below) that extended up into the parietal area would strongly indicate a shot from the front of the President, with the entrance wound being on the front of the skull.

But an exit wound in the parietal area that extended down into the temporal area could result from a shot coming from behind the President. In that case, we would expect to find an entrance wound on the back of the skull.

The diagram below shows the bones of the human skull. From it, you can see that a wound to the back of the head would chiefly involve the occipital and parietal bones whereas one to the side and top would involve the parietal and temporal bones.

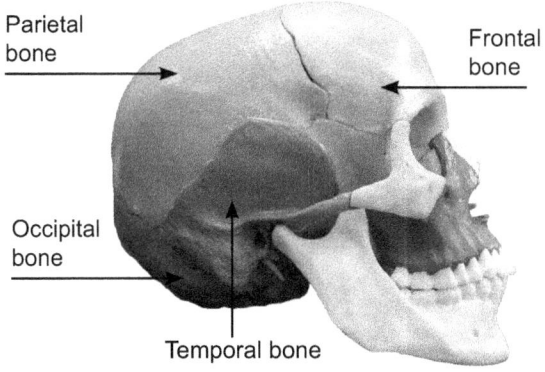

Human Skull Bones – Right Side View

Parkland Doctors' Testimony

The next diagram shows a side view of the human brain. Brain anatomy is very complex, but you only need to understand the difference between cerebrum (cerebral tissue) and cerebellum (cerebellar tissue).

Cerebrum makes up most of the brain. The gaps between its folds (called sulci) are broad. The cerebellum sits below the cerebrum. Its sulci are much narrower and the tissue appears to be tightly folded. This is the typical way anatomy teachers distinguish between the two brain tissue types.

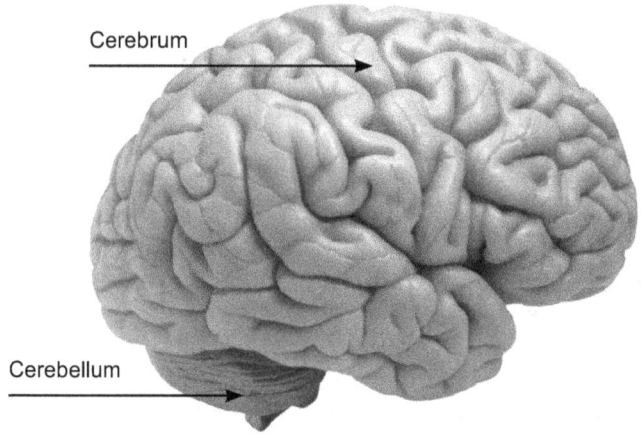

Human Brain – Right Side View and Top View

The next diagram shows the brain within the skull. This is a section as if the skull had been cut in half like an apple. Here you can see that the cerebellum is protected inside the skull by the occipital bone.

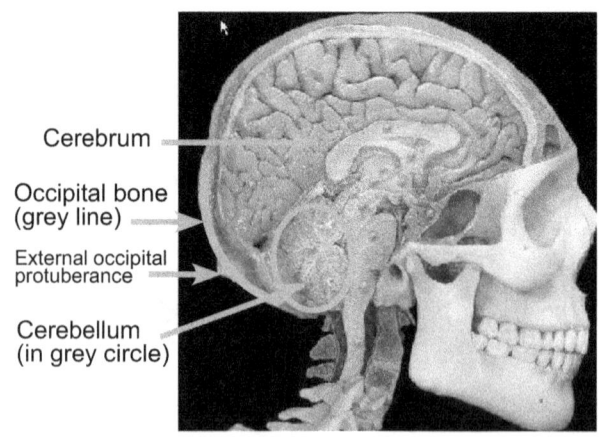

Human Brain within Skull – Right Side Section

FIVE | THE MEDICAL EVIDENCE

I have digressed into anatomy so that you can appreciate that cerebrum and cerebellum are easily identified. First-term medical students, when sober, are quite capable of distinguishing them. In addition, you can now see that if the cerebellum is seen in a wound, the wound must be in the rear of the skull and involve damage to the occipital bone.

For the official description of the JFK assassination to be correct (that is, all the shooting was done from behind by Lee Harvey Oswald), all the entrance wounds on JFK's body had to be in the back of his body and all the exit wounds had to be in the front. However, an exit wound in the occipital region involving damage to the cerebellum strongly indicates a shot from the front for which Oswald could not have been responsible.

Several doctors who attended JFK in Trauma Room 1 have modified the descriptions they gave of JFK's head injuries after they had treated him, especially in interviews allegedly conducted by author Gerald Posner in 1993. Posner's book has been widely quoted and positively evaluated by the mainstream media. He believes that the Warren Commission got it right. But, the statements attributed to the Parkland doctors by Posner need to be compared to what they have said previously and particularly what they said under oath in 1964 just a few months after they had treated Kennedy.

Some Parkland doctors have hinted that maintaining their original statements and speaking out against the official Warren Commission conclusions would have been detrimental to their careers. It is possible that strong pressure was brought to bear.

There can be little doubt that the earliest evidence and testimony is usually the most reliable. So there is no better source for a description of the wounds than those recorded in the Parkland doctors' own Admission Notes, before the doctors were visited by the Secret Service, coached and cross examined by Arlen Specter and interviewed by Posner. It should always be borne in mind that the Dallas doctors were extremely familiar with gunshot wounds – several of them testified to treating hundreds.[15]

Dr Carrico
Dr Charles Carrico's original Parkland Admission Note states that the Parkland doctors attempted "...to control slow oozing from cerebral and cerebellar tissue via pads instituted."[16] In his Warren Commission testimony, he stated, "I believe there was shredded and macerated cerebral and cerebellar tissues both in the wounds and on the fragments of skull."[17] Describing the damage to JFK's skull, Carrico testified again to the Warren Commission, "This [wound] was a 5cm by 17cm defect in the posterior skull, the occipital region. There was an absence of the calvarium or skull in this area."[18] [He probably meant 5cm by 7cm]. "Posterior" means the back of the head.

JFK | ECHOES FROM ELM STREET
A SEARCH FOR HISTORICAL ACCURACY ON THE ASSASSINATION OF PRESIDENT JOHN F. KENNEDY

So, as you can see from the diagrams above, Carrico's earliest and sworn accounts describe damage to be low on the back of JFK's head (occipital) and he said that cerebellar tissue was present.

According to Posner though, Dr Charles Carrico said to him in an interview: "We saw a large hole on the right side of his head. I don't believe we saw any occipital bone. It was not there. It was parietal bone."[19] This cannot be right though, because if only parietal bone was involved there would have been no cerebellar tissue.

Dr Peters

Dr Paul Peters told David Lifton a number of years before Posner interviewed him: "I could see the occipital lobes clearly . . . I thought it looked like the cerebellum was injured, or missing, because the occipital lobes seemed to rest almost on the foramen magnum."[20]

This statement is especially revealing. To describe damage to JFK's brain in such detail, Peters must have had an excellent view of the head wound. The occipital lobes are an area of the cerebrum at the very rear of the brain and would not have been visible if the wound was on the side of JFK's skull.

Furthermore, if Peters' description is accurate, the bulk of the cerebellum must have been missing as the foramen magnum is the hole in the skull where the brainstem continues into the spinal column and is *below* the cerebellum. Peters may have realised in later years how damaging to the official case his comments might be as he gave Posner a far less sensational account.

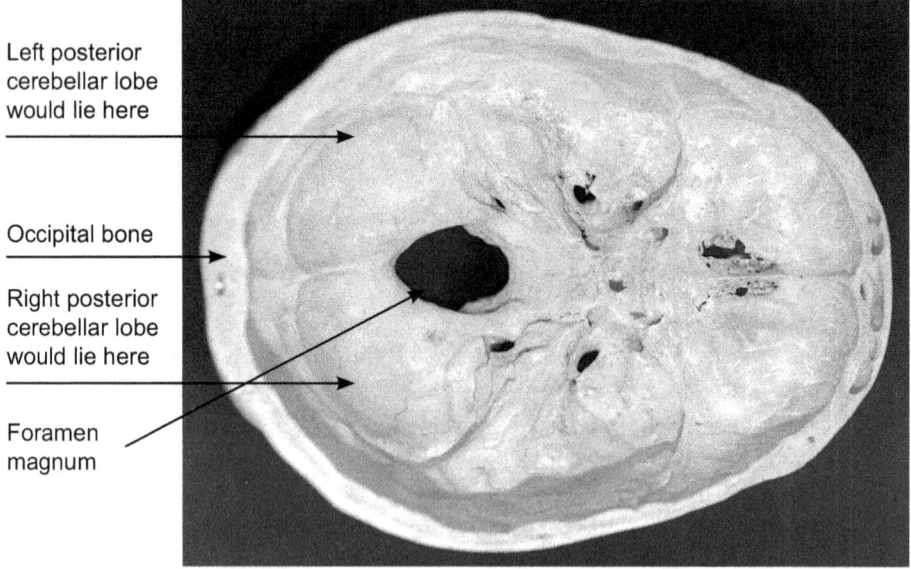

Base of Skull (Inside) Showing Foramen Magnum

FIVE | THE MEDICAL EVIDENCE

Dr Jenkins
Dr Marion Jenkins apparently told Posner: "...there could not be any cerebellum. The autopsy photo, with the rear of the head intact and a protrusion in the parietal region, is the way I remember it. I never did say occipital."[21]

But contrary to this, in his Admission Note Jenkins had written "occipital": "There was a great laceration on the right side of the head (temporal and occipital)...even to the extent that the cerebellum had protruded from the wound."[22] Also, in his testimony to the Warren Commission, Jenkins discussed seeing cerebellum: "I really think part of the cerebellum, as I recognized it, was herniated from the wound".

Jenkins testimony involved one of the strangest of the very odd questions Specter asked in the course of the Warren Commission. After describing the damage to JFK's brain, Specter asked: "Did you observe any wounds immediately below the massive loss of skull which you have described?"[23]

But Jenkins had not described massive skull damage. We will see later that the autopsy report describes an extensive loss of skull which was not seen at Parkland. Perhaps Specter had already noticed what many researchers have noticed down the years – that Kennedy's head wound was much smaller at Parkland than it was said to be at Bethesda. So was this Specter's way of closing the apparent gap between the Parkland and Bethesda observations – that is, by getting the comment "massive loss of skull" accepted by a Parkland doctor?

Dr Perry
According to Posner, Dr Malcolm Perry said to him in an interview which Posner says he conducted on April 2nd, 1992: "I did not see any cerebellum."[24] Fifteen years earlier, however, Perry told the House Select Committee on Assassinations: "...the parietal occipital head wound was largely evulsive and there was visible brain tissue...and some cerebellum."[25] Perry is very particular about cerebellar tissue being present, otherwise he could have stuck with the general description "brain tissue".

Dr Clark
Despite the alleged statements made to Posner, the doctors did identify JFK's head wound to be both occipital and cerebellar. The Parkland doctor most qualified to report on a head wound and who apparently had a clear view of JFK's head injuries was Dr Kemp Clark, Associate Professor and Chairman of Neurosurgery: What did Clark's Admission Note say at the time?

"There was a large wound in the right occipito-parietal region ...", "Both cerebral and cerebellar tissues were extruding from the wound."[26]

If the Parkland doctors made the statements attributed to them by Posner, then they have significantly altered their initial views. Why would medical professionals so alter their testimony that their credibility is called in to question, unless they were pressurised to do so?

JFK | Echoes From Elm Street
A Search for Historical Accuracy on the
Assassination of President John F. Kennedy

As you continue reading, please remember that the Parkland observations were that JFK died with a small hole in his throat (probably an entrance wound) and a 5 to 7cm oval exit wound in the back of his head involving mainly the occipital bone, but with some damage to the parietal bone – an occipito-parietal wound.

Wounds in the Left Temple

A throat wound that changed from entrance to exit and a head wound that changed location are freakish enough, but they pale besides the wound that disappeared altogether.

Two Parkland, Doctors Marion T Jenkins and Robert N McClelland had both reported a wound in the left temple that does not appear in the Bethesda autopsy. This was a wound that could not have been caused by somebody shooting Kennedy from his right rear (the Texas School Book Depository – Oswald's alleged location) and could only have been caused by somebody shooting Kennedy from in front.

Yet again, it must be emphasised that if there was also a gunman in front of Kennedy conspiracy is proved. And it has to be said that the two Parkland doctors, Jenkins and McClelland, who saw a left temple wound that could only have been caused by shots from in front, really knew their stuff.

Dr Jenkins was Professor and Chairman of Anaesthetics, a very senior position in any hospital and especially so in a teaching hospital, which Parkland was. He had been a doctor since 1940, had spent three years on active duty in the US Navy during the Second World War and had been a professor in Parkland for 12 years. His natural position in the trauma room was at the head of the patient monitoring and administering anaesthetics or, as with JFK, oxygen. So he would have been in the best possible position to study the head wounds and would not have been treating his patient with due care and attention had he not given the head his full attention.

Bearing in mind Jenkins' level of expertise, some of his treatment by the Warren Commission is extraordinary:

Dr JENKINS: "... I do not know whether this is right or not, but I thought there was a wound on the left temporal area, right in the hairline and right above the zygomatic process."

At this point, one needs to understand that in medicine, left and right always refer to the perspective of the body being described. So when Jenkins referred to the left temporal area, he meant the left side of Kennedy's head. He was describing Kennedy's left temple. The problem for the Warren Commission was that it was already committed to Oswald being Kennedy's lone assassin and the wound Jenkins was describing in the left temporal area could only have been caused by a gunman in front of Kennedy.

FIVE | THE MEDICAL EVIDENCE

Had Jenkins been referring to Kennedy's *right* temple such a wound could – just about – have been traced back to a gunman behind Kennedy. But Jenkins was referring to Kennedy's *left* temple, the part of Kennedy's head that was furthest away from – and out of sight of – any gunmen behind him. The only way that area could have been wounded by a bullet from behind Kennedy was if a shot from behind him had blasted its way out of Kennedy's skull at that point, making the left temple wound an exit wound. But the Warren Commission never suggested that this was an exit wound and neither did any of the subsequent government reviews of the evidence.

So as nobody claimed this was an exit wound and as this wound could only have been caused by a gunman in front of Kennedy, the Warren Commission had to make it legally void. For the Warren Commission to maintain its conclusion, the wound Jenkins thought he had found in the left temple had to become a non-wound. As indeed it did. Specter's response to Jenkins hesitant description of a wound in Kennedy's left temple was this:

Mr SPECTER: "The autopsy Report discloses no such development, Dr Jenkins."

Dr JENKINS: "Well, I was feeling for - I was palpating here for a pulse to see whether the closed chest cardiac massage was effective or not and this probably was some blood that had come from the other point and so I thought there was a wound there also."[27]

In layman's terms, Jenkins was saying that he had been feeling for a pulse in the left temple and while doing so had come across a wound there. But he was now saying that the blood he had seen in the left temple might have come from somewhere else and that could have deceived him into believing there was a wound in the left temple.

This beggars belief. No doctor would assume that blood on the surface of any area of a body meant there was a wound there too. Blood on the surface of a patient with several wounds could have come from any of those wounds. This point is so basic that it is really a matter of first aid and it is inconceivable that an experienced doctor like Jenkins would get it wrong.

In fact, any doctor treating Kennedy would have been particularly unlikely to assume that surface blood at any location on the body indicated a wound there because Kennedy was losing litres of blood. He was covered in blood and more was constantly pouring out of him. So the medical truism that blood at any point on a body does not mean there is a wound at that point was particularly so in Kennedy's case.

Therefore, for Jenkins to have believed there was a wound in the left temple there must have been another indication of a wound in addition to blood. A hint of a further factor lies in Jenkins' opening words in the testimony quoted above: "Well, I was feeling for - I was palpating here for a pulse to see whether the closed chest cardiac massage was effective or not...." This suggests that he may have *felt* a hole in the left temple.

To the layman, this short Jenkins- Specter exchange may seem innocuous, but to anybody familiar with both legal and medical matters, it sends out warning signs. There was something disingenuous to the point of disturbing in Specter's wording during this exchange with Jenkins. Note that Specter was careful to not deny that there had been a wound in the left temporal area. Rather, he said that the autopsy report didn't disclose such a wound. But the autopsy report didn't disclose other things which would have been obvious to medical personnel, like Kennedy's disintegrated adrenal glands[28].

If something as basic as the absence of adrenal glands could be left out of his autopsy report, then other equally basic facts such as a wound to the left side of Kennedy's head could have been left out. It must be emphasized again that a wound to the front of Kennedy's head was irrefutable proof that there had been a gunman in front of him and therefore a conspiracy. If this wound, seen and described at Parkland Hospital immediately after the assassination, had been confirmed by Kennedy's autopsy later in the evening at Bethesda, the Warren Commission would have been obliged to say Kennedy was killed by a conspiracy.

A further indication that something was seriously amiss in Jenkins' evidence to the Warren Commission was its tone. Although Jenkins was a medical expert and had treated Kennedy, he constantly deferred to Specter, who was a lawyer with no medical expertise. This made no sense. Jenkins deferring to Specter on a medical matter was equivalent to an experienced airline pilot taking the word of somebody who had never flown that he was on the wrong route.

Look again at the tone of Jenkins' replies to Specter. They are hesitant and stumbling, almost to the point of apologetic. But in my experience, surgeons and anaesthetists are not in the least hesitant or unsure when it comes to describing their work and Jenkins had been both a surgeon and an anaesthetist. The tone of Jenkins' exchanges with Specter is highly indicative that he was coached by Specter before he gave his testimony. Evidence for this can be readily seen in Jenkins' Warren Commission testimony:

Mr SPECTER: And did you and I have a very brief conversation before the deposition started today, when you gave me some of your views which you expounded and expanded upon during the course of the deposition on the record?

Dr JENKINS: Yes.[29]

Jenkins' testimony at this point reads to me as if he had already discussed a

Five | The medical evidence

left temporal wound with Specter away from the formal hearing and been told to downplay it.

Two pages after this remarkable testimony, Jenkins asked to go off-the-record for a discussion with Specter. One page later, after they had held their off-record discussion, the questioning continued:

Mr SPECTER: "Aside from that opinion [that one bullet must have damaged the sac containing the lungs], have any of your other opinions about the nature of his wounds or the sources of the wounds been changed in any way?"

Dr JENKINS: "No: one other. I asked you a little bit ago if there was a wound in the left temporal area, right above the zygomatic bone in the hairline, because there was blood there and I thought there might have been a wound there (indicating)."

Mr SPECTER: "Indicating the left temporal area?"

Dr JENKINS: "Yes: the left temporal, which could have been a point of entrance and exit here (indicating), but you have answered that for me. This was my only other question about it."[30]

Jenkins returning to the issue of a left temple wound so quickly after Specter had said that the autopsy report did not disclose it and the fact that the two men had had talked off the record, suggests that Specter wanted Jenkins to refute the possibility of Kennedy having such a wound. In other words, to deny his own evidence.

The very specific location that Jenkins gives to a wound now deemed to not have existed suggests to me that he was troubled by having to retract his initial findings about there being such a wound. It is particularly suspicious that Specter seemed to have "answered that" after an off-the-record discussion and quite odd that Jenkins referred to a conversation with Specter where he, Jenkins, had asked if there had been a wound in the left temporal area. A doctor asking a lawyer about the location of a wound? Again, this was equivalent to an experienced airline pilot asking a civilian who had never been inside a cockpit if he thought the pilot was doing his job properly.

Off-the-record discussions were to be a distinct feature during the taking of medical testimony by the Warren Commission as we will also see later with John Connally. The frequency of unrecorded discussion in such key evidence is particularly suspicious as it often occurred at points when information damaging to the official story of a single gunman shooting from behind was starting to emerge.

Sometimes, less subtle methods were used to deflect attention from unwelcome evidence. When Dr McClelland, who had worked on Kennedy at Parkland testified to the Warren Commission, Specter reproduced McClelland's Admission Note for JFK. It was written at 16:45 on November 22 shortly after McClelland had treated Kennedy and part of the note read: "The cause of death was due to massive head and brain injury from a gunshot wound of the left temple"[31].

This was clear written, authoritative and unambiguous evidence of Kennedy being shot from the front from somebody well qualified to pronounce on such matters. McClelland was Parkland Hospital's Assistant Professor of Surgery, a senior role in any hospital's hierarchy and would not be expected to mistake the site of a wound in any patient, let alone the President. I suggest that McClelland would have written a very carefully considered Admission Note for this patient.

In an Admission Note – always a short, succinct document – such a major divergence from what became the official line is easily spotted. But Specter effectively changed the subject. He did not ask McClelland to clarify this statement and directed McClelland away from re-reading his Admission Note by asking him to check his signature. Specter then asked whether McClelland would stand by his Admission Note before bringing questioning to a speedy halt[32].

In 1993, Jenkins claimed that McClelland's impression of a wound to the left temple was mistaken and stemmed from a short exchange between the pair when McClelland entered Trauma Room 1. Jenkins claims that McClelland asked where JFK was hit. Jenkins said that he was searching for a temporal pulse at this time and that McClelland assumed Jenkins was pointing out a wound[33].

But as we have seen from Jenkins' sworn 1964 testimony, it is quite likely that Jenkins was indeed pointing to an area he thought was wounded.

Parkland and the Back Wound

The Parkland doctors did not mention any back wound in their reports. But this does not mean that there was not a back wound. It means that Kennedy died while the Parkland doctors were still treating him with the standard emergency procedures and those procedures did not involve or necessitate turning over his body. For that simple reason, the Parkland doctors did not see any wounds to Kennedy's back.

In reality, as the Parkland doctors realised from the moment they saw him, Kennedy had been killed by the shot or shots which hit his head. But some of the processes in his body, including his heart, were still functioning and while that was the case, the Parkland staff did all they could to treat him. This involved the standard emergency procedures used in extreme situations the world over and known in medical circles as ABC.

The ABC of trauma medicine is the order of measures that must be taken when treating a patient in an emergency.

A is for "airway", the most important thing to do is to stabilise the patient's airway (trachea).

FIVE | THE MEDICAL EVIDENCE

B is for breathing, once the airway is stable, doctors can help the patient to breathe.

C is for circulation, once the patient can breathe, the next thing to do is try to control bleeding and replace blood loss.

An experienced team of doctors will do the ABCs almost simultaneously, as did the Parkland team. Dr Carrico made a brief examination of JFK, noted the wounds he could see from the front and quickly ran his hands underneath Kennedy's back to see if he could feel any obvious large, sucking wounds. There was no need and no time to turn the President over because his airway – his throat – needed immediate attention. Everything else was academic until Kennedy was able to breathe.

So, Carrico immediately tried to stabilise the President's airway by inserting a tube into his trachea and connecting it to an automatic breathing machine [34]. When this did not appear to be helping, the doctors suspected that his lung had collapsed (meaning that Kennedy had suffered a pneumothorax, in medical terms) and the team began inserting tubes into his chest and to administer blood and other fluids.

If this sounds like an orderly "first this was done, then that was done" type of sequence, that is not how it was at all. You have to imagine a large team of experienced doctors and nurses moving quickly but competently around the most important patient they had ever treated, urgently trying to save his life. They followed the ABCs, but more in parallel than in sequence and by the time the team had completed the airway and breathing stabilisation, it was clear that the major bleeding was coming from the President's head wound and that whatever chance there had been of restoring his life had gone.

There was no point in working on Kennedy's circulation or turning his body over to check for back wounds. The Parkland staff had tried to work with all the functions in Kennedy's body that had – technically – survived his shooting, but they had been unable to save his life. They knew that this would be the case as soon as they had seen his wounds but they still made the effort. JFK was pronounced dead in Parkland at 1pm by Dr Kemp Clark.

The next time the President's wounds should have been described was in an autopsy report by the Dallas County Medical Examiner, Dr Earl Forrest Rose, who was on hand as he had an office in Parkland. Texas law stated that a violent death required a local post-mortem examination by a medical examiner and Rose practically had his surgical gloves snapped on, but he never got to examine the President's body.

Instead, a combination of Kennedy's aides and the Secret Service surrounded the trolley on which the coffin was perched and physically forced their way past Dr Rose and out to a waiting ambulance[35] which took it to the Presidential plane at Love Field airport and on to Washington DC. In the agitated stand-off between local and Federal officials over the coffin in the corridor, a Dallas

Justice of the Peace, Theron Ward, who had the authority to overrule Dr Rose, added little to the gravitas of the occasion by saying, "It's just another homicide case as far as I'm concerned".

Washington DC – The Autopsy
The next time JFK's wounds were actually described by a doctor was by Dr James Joseph Humes, Director of Laboratories of the Naval Medical School at Bethesda Naval Hospital.

Kennedy's autopsy was witnessed by a large audience of military and intelligence service personnel. As was standard procedure Humes gave a narration as he and the other autopsy staff worked. At that time, the narration was usually recorded and the autopsy room had closed-circuit TV equipment[36] but no verbal or visual recording of the Kennedy autopsy is known to exist.

Humes's descriptions were, however, quoted by two FBI agents, James W Sibert and Francis X O'Neill in their field report[37] and used in the FBI five-volume report "Investigation of Assassination of President John F. Kennedy November 22, 1963"[38] issued on December 9, 1963 (hereafter referred to as "the FBI Report"). Dr Humes wrote the official autopsy report[39].

Controversy surrounds both the FBI Report and the official autopsy report. But it should not. If JFK's body left Parkland with a large occipito-parietal wound and a small throat wound (admittedly modified by a short tracheotomy incision), that's how it should have appeared on arrival at Bethesda Naval Hospital (Bethesda). That it did not is troubling and has led to massive research by many medical and non-medical experts from shortly after the assassination to this day.

If you thought that things were already complex, we're about to enter a whole world of complexity. The reason for this is that the wounds as reported in Parkland do not seem to be the same as when they were next described in Washington DC at Bethesda. The differences were substantial. There are the following explanations for this:

1) The Parkland doctors described the wounds they saw incorrectly.
2) The Parkland doctors lied in their descriptions of the wounds.
3) The Bethesda doctors described the wounds they saw incorrectly.
4) The Bethesda doctors lied in their descriptions of the wounds.
5) The wounds seen at Parkland were different to those seen at Bethesda.

The first two possibilities are easy to dismiss. The Parkland doctors were used to receiving and treating trauma patients. They saw many gunshot wounds each week and had treated thousands. Their descriptions, on the whole, have an internal consistency, that is they agree with each other. There are some minor differences but, no significant ones and the probability is that

FIVE | THE MEDICAL EVIDENCE

the Parkland evidence was and remains accurate. On the day that JFK was shot, the Parkland medical team had no reason to lie. Quite the opposite. They had just treated their head of state, their reports were contemporaneous and they would have taken the greatest care over what they wrote.

But whether the Bethesda doctors were inaccurate or lied is less easy to dismiss – in fact, it may be possible to prove that they were both inaccurate *and* lied. Furthermore, it is at least a possibility that the wounds seen at Parkland actually *were* different to those seen at Bethesda.

Two FBI agents, James W Sibert and Francis X O'Neill, were sent to Andrews Airforce Base to meet Air Force 1, which was bringing Kennedy's body back from Dallas. They were instructed to go with the President's body to Bethesda and "to obtain bullets reportedly in the President's body."[40] In effect, they became the FBI's eyes and ears at the President's autopsy. Their job was to note down the deductions of the pathologists and produce a field report. That is exactly what they did. I believe that they wrote a truthful field report and that it was an accurate record of what they witnessed at the autopsy.

So far, so good. But one particular phrase, entered in the Sibert and O'Neill report and almost certainly uttered by Dr Humes[41] along with the autopsy conclusions arrived at before the FBI agents left late in the night of November 22nd 1963 have resulted in much speculation over what actually happened during the autopsy and *before it began*.

The phrase in the Sibert and O'Neill report that has generated so much research is "surgery of the head area"[42]. David Lifton noticed this in 1968 and began to look into what it could mean. He knew that the doctors at Parkland had never said that they had performed any surgery to the head. So, to Lifton, it seemed to suggest that another doctor had worked on the President before he arrived at Bethesda.

Lifton began to look for other examples of changes to the wound descriptions reported in Parkland to those described in the official autopsy report. He found many. The theory he developed from his observations has become known as "The Body Alteration Theory". Central to Lifton's theory and his book, "Best Evidence", is his belief that JFK's body was intercepted before it reached Bethesda and the wounds were changed from indicating shooting from the front to indicating shooting only from behind. A quick and furtive alteration of the wounds before Kennedy's body reached the autopsy also created an opportunity to remove ballistics evidence from his body.

Critics of Lifton point out that there was scant time to perform any pre-autopsy surgery and that there are no recorded witnesses to it. His theory does, however, offer an explanation to why the wounds described at Parkland appear to have grown larger post-mortem and why there is a remarkable lack of ballistics evidence in JFK's body.

> and it was also apparent that a tracheotomy had been performed, as well as surgery of the head area, namely, in the top of the skull. All personnel with the exception of medical

Extract from Sibert & O'Neill FD302 Report

Lifton's theory has stimulated ferocious and often acrimonious debate amongst people who study the assassination from the time of *Best Evidence*'s publication in 1981 to the present day.

Recently, Lifton gained an important ally. Doug Horne was the Chief Analyst for Military Records on the staff of the Assassination Records Review Board, a body set up by Congress in 1992 to review all US government records of the Kennedy assassination. Horne also argued that there were alterations made to JFK's body, but Horne believes that they were made by the Bethesda pathologists *themselves* before beginning the official autopsy.

I am not persuaded by this. I can't imagine why Humes would have referred to "surgery of the head area", thereby drawing attention to distortion of the body and fraud in the medical evidence that had been perpetrated by himself. That is just irrational. Moreover, an excellent and thorough review of Horne's book *Inside the ARRB* by a leading JFK assassination writer, James Diegueno, has shown that Horne placed far too much reliance on witnesses who have changed their testimony over the years and whose recollections on some aspects are provably wrong[43].

But whether the body was altered or not, it is crucial to understand that the two official records of JFK's autopsy – those in the FBI Report and those in the Warren Commission Report – *are different*.

The FBI investigation concluded that JFK was hit twice from behind: once in his head and once in his back. The FBI Report said that the wound in Kennedy's back did not go through his body. Instead, it said that the bullet dropped back out of the entrance wound. It makes no mention of a bullet wound in JFK's throat, only the tracheotomy incision. The FBI Report comes to this conclusion because it is based on the Sibert and O'Neill field report which the two agents wrote as soon as the autopsy finished. In other words, the Sibert and O'Neill report contains the autopsy doctors' conclusions at the close of the autopsy early in the morning of 23rd November 1963.

But the Warren Commission Report said that the back wound did perforate (go right through) Kennedy's body and that it came out of his throat at the site of the tracheotomy incision. This radically different conclusion was reached by the Bethesda doctors many hours after they had finished the autopsy and was then incorporated in to the official autopsy report and endorsed by the Warren Commission.

Crucially, the conclusion was reached at a time when the Bethesda doctors no longer had the body in front of them and without the body in front of them, the

FIVE | THE MEDICAL EVIDENCE

autopsy doctors could not have assessed any of the bullets trajectories. It was impossible to do so at that point. This type of autopsy conclusion, then as now, is not reached by reflective discussion over coffee in the hospital canteen after the autopsy staff have finished looking at the body. Such a conclusion can only be reached when the body is in front of the doctors concerned. That is how the first autopsy conclusion, the one reported by Sibert and O'Neill and contained in the FBI's report of the autopsy, was reached.

Here lay a complication. Sibert and O'Neill had reported a misunderstanding on the part of the autopsy staff, namely that the throat wound was purely a tracheotomy incision in JFK's throat to help him breathe. When, some hours later, Humes learnt that there had been a wound in JFK's throat before the tracheotomy had been made, standard autopsy procedure required him to get the body recalled and re-assessed.

That too, was next to impossible. Nobody knows exactly when Humes learnt, as he did, in a phone call with Dr Perry in Dallas that the Parkland doctors had found a wound in Kennedy's throat before they had made the tracheotomy incision there. But this discovery seems to have been made in the morning of November 23, the day after the assassination and by that time, Kennedy's body was lying in state in the White House. It would have been extremely difficult for Humes to have had the President's body brought back to Bethesda for re-examination.

So, what appeared in Dallas to be a bullet entrance wound was morphed, after the autopsy, into a bullet exit wound with no medical explanation for the change. The question would have been resolved had the autopsy doctors performed one of the most routine autopsy procedures and dissected the back wound. That they did not, is inexplicable. For doctors in an autopsy not to dissect a wound is equivalent to a policeman arresting a suspect but not investigating them. It is inconceivable. But not for the first time in the Kennedy case, the inexplicable and the inconceivable prevailed. The Bethesda doctors did not dissect the back wound.

The reason that they didn't do this was revealed by Dr Pierre Fink (the third of JFK's autopsy doctors) in his testimony at the Clay Shaw trial, "As I recall I was told not to, but I don't remember by whom."[44]

Later in his testimony, Finck said that a general or an admiral – Finck was not sure which – was in charge of the autopsy. Incredibly, the autopsy doctors were told not to dissect the track of the bullet wound.

Perhaps the only thing more outlandish than the back wound not being dissected was that the autopsy was being controlled by an unqualified General or Admiral instead of by the chief autopsy pathologist. There is no good reason for this to have occurred and the only possible explanation is that the evidence was being directed in a pre-determined direction.

We should expect nothing but straightforward procedures performed in the most transparent way so that the accused assassin(s) would get the fairest trial.

JFK | ECHOES FROM ELM STREET
A SEARCH FOR HISTORICAL ACCURACY ON THE
ASSASSINATION OF PRESIDENT JOHN F. KENNEDY

The Problem with Autopsy Report Drafts

There is much valid criticism of the published autopsy report [see my own critique elsewhere in this book]. But there is yet more. It would appear that the content of the report changed as the doctors were constantly confronted with new so-called facts about the assassination[45]. An autopsy report on a murder victim is central to any murder trial. It is a crucial document and it must only contain data that has been directly observed by the doctors. In other words, the autopsy data must be *independent* of other evidence.

Prior to knowing about the wound to JFK's throat, Humes assumed it was only a tracheotomy incision. But once Humes knew, from speaking with Dr Perry at Parkland, that there was a small throat wound, he simply incorporated this into the autopsy report. There is some evidence that this version concluded that the throat wound was an exit for a fragment of bone[46].

Whatever the truth of this, Humes testified that he later rewrote the report and then burned the first draft. The final version of the autopsy concluded that the throat wound was a bullet exit wound. But Humes reached this conclusion without the body in front of him. He had been told that all the shots came from behind the President, so this solution seemed to fit but, he had not proven this scientifically by dissection.

All versions of the autopsy report should have been retained and any reason for redrafting them explained. This is normal procedure for a medicolegal autopsy (a forensic autopsy which concerns the gathering of information to be used in court). As this was not done, if ever Oswald or anybody else for that matter had been bought to court, it would have been very simple for their defence to mount a legal challenge to the autopsy report.

In court, the autopsy notes written by the doctors would be subject to disclosure. That is, the defence would have the right to see the autopsy notes which, presumably, held all the relevant measurements. That these would not be available would appear highly suspicious to the court. Furthermore, any prior autopsy report drafts would be subject to disclosure. If *they* could not be presented either, the prosecution's case would be seriously weakened. I believe, however, that the powerful people involved in the conspiracy to kill JFK and cover up the deed afterwards knew that this would never matter. They knew nobody would ever be brought to trial.

The nearest Oswald ever got to court was the Warren Commission. They knew that the absence of the notes and earlier drafts of the autopsy weakened the case against Oswald, but never acknowledged the absence of these basic documents.

A reliable autopsy report really is one of the keys to understanding any murder case. In this instance, an unscrupulous autopsy report raises more questions than it answers. Destroying a version of an autopsy report is so rare as to be virtually unknown.

FIVE | THE MEDICAL EVIDENCE

The result is that we can never know the true nature of JFK's wounds and for that reason alone, working out who killed him has become extremely difficult.

The Poor Autopsy Photographs and X-rays

Many researchers have already done excellent work describing the autopsy photographs and X-rays, discussing their provenance and questioning their veracity. The debate about these two areas has long since become, of necessity, extremely technical and readers interested in pursuing the debate about either the autopsy photographs or X-rays should look to the works of Robert Groden, David Lifton, Harrison Livingstone and Dr David Mantik.

I am not a photography expert and neither do I know about making X-rays. I do, however, know how to count. There is no doubt that the number of JFK autopsy photographs and X-rays (not to mention microscope slides and tissue samples) has decreased since the night they were made. The curious reader can pursue this in several places including Harold Weisberg's books.

That said, I do have a few words to add to the considerable volume of work already published on the autopsy photographs. These are represented as having been taken by John T Stringer, Director of Medical Photography at Bethesda. In 1963, Stringer already had over 20 years experience in medical photography.

Given that the photographs were allegedly taken by such an expert, it is astounding that those which are still in existence are extremely poor quality. Although I have yet to see the originals, the multi-generational set that I own, known at the "Fox Set", have been confirmed as true copies of those in the National Archives. But they are so poor that, quite apart from any deterioration caused by repeated copying, it is doubtful that they were taken by a qualified medical photographer[47] in the first place.

There are major problems with the original set of photographs of which the Fox Set is said to be a copy:

- There are too few views – each item of interest should have a wide-angle shot, medium range shot and close up. This is standard medical photography procedure, but the JFK autopsy photographs only ever contain one of these views per item (although there are often several photographs *of the same view*).

- The lighting is poor and detail is frequently hidden in shadow.

- Exposure settings appear to be random – sometimes the pictures are too dark, sometimes they are too light.

- The centre of focus in some is not on the feature being illustrated.

- There are no medical photographer's notes. These should correspond to the photographs and describe which views were taken and what was being illustrated. Yet again, this is standard autopsy procedure, but was not followed.

- There are no identifying tags. There should be, at least, a reference number to identify the body. The leaked photographs of Lee Harvey Oswald's autopsy are of far superior quality to those of JFK, not least because they have identification tags:

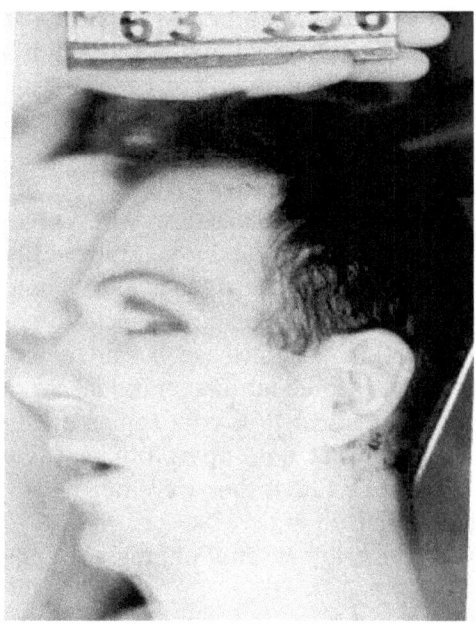

Profile Photograph from Autopsy of Lee Harvey Oswald

These major breaks of standards autopsy procedure are the least of the problems with JFK's pictures. The fact is that the President's autopsy pictures do not corroborate the conclusions of his autopsy report. In fact, they quite spectacularly contradict it.

FIVE | THE MEDICAL EVIDENCE

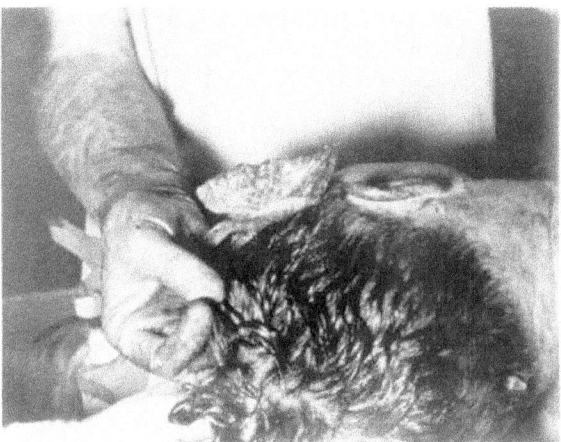

Fox 3 Photograph

The Fox 3 photograph (above), does not show the damage reported by Dr Humes, *"There is a large irregular defect of the scalp and skull on the right involving chiefly the parietal bone but extending somewhat into the temporal and occipital regions."* **No such damage appears in this photograph:**

The flap of what appears to be skull near the doctor's wrist is forward of the ear. If you look at the skull diagram above, this wound can only be described as temporal extending a little into the parietal and frontal bones. It absolutely does not show damage of any type in the occipital region.

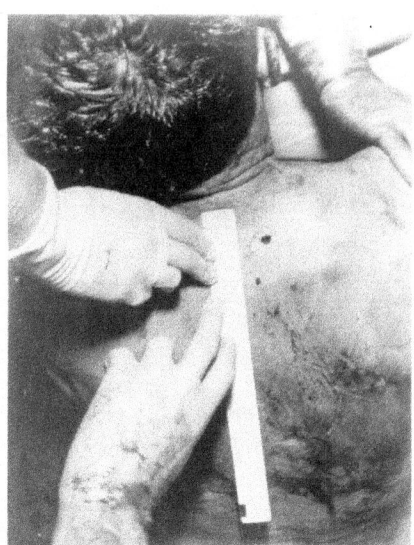

Fox 5 Photograph

The Fox 5 photograph (previous page) might or might not be an attempt to illustrate a back wound. It is too difficult to tell:

- The body is being lifted, so it is distorted
- There are several spots which may be wounds.

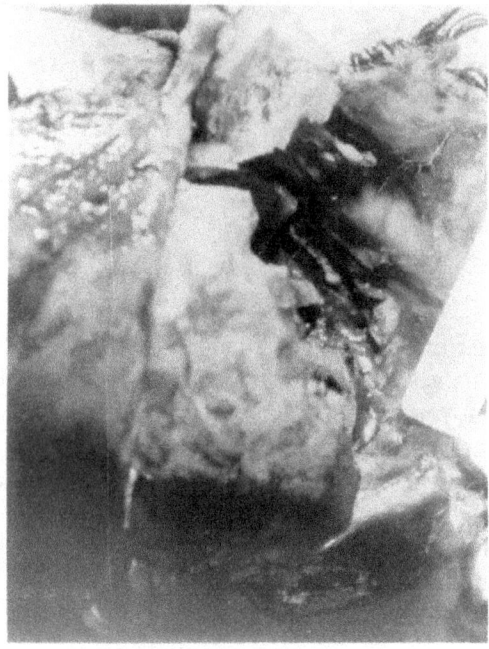

Fox 8 Photograph

The problems with the Fox 8 photograph, above, almost defy belief:

- Nobody really knows what it is attempting to illustrate

- It is difficult, if not impossible, to orientate

- The focus seems to be on the interior of the head, but there is no guidance as to what it is meant to be showing

- The ruler does not appear to be anywhere near anything worth measuring

- As with the other photographs, it is by no means clear that the picture actually is of Kennedy.

FIVE | THE MEDICAL EVIDENCE

The Warren Commission avoided all discussion of the autopsy photographs and X-rays by not including them in their Report. They did this by not admitting them as evidence, although there are some indications that one or two photographs were seen by members of the Commission and their staff.

The HSCA, however, did admit the photographs and X-rays and they were used by their medical panel. The HSCA also commissioned some experts to examine the autopsy materials for fakery. They seem to have done this largely by comparing stereoscopic pairs. A stereoscopic pair of photographs is deliberately made by taking two shots of the same thing, but moving the camera slightly between shots. This constituted yet another major breach of standard autopsy procedure – stereo pairs were not standard and none of the autopsy photographers ever said they took any.

Look at Fox 6 and Fox 7 (most likely a pair from the HSCA set numbered 32, 33, 34 and 37 all four are similar) below. What medical justification is there for taking both of these? They have the same focal point, similar lighting and are taken from mid-range.

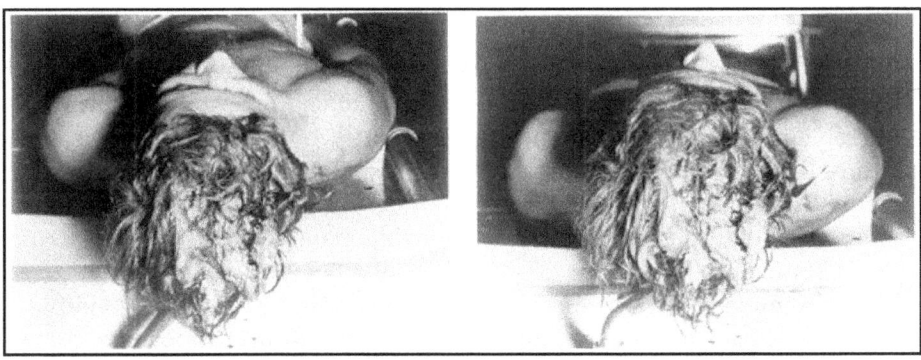

Fox 6 & 7

In trying to work out JFK's wounds would you rather have these two photographs or one closer to his head (mid-range) followed by a close-up?

The Poor Medical illustrations

Before we start to examine the drawings of Kennedy's wounds that were adopted by the official investigations, we need to ask why illustrations were necessary in the first place. There were photographs taken at the autopsy and illustrations can never be a substitute for photographs. At best, illustrations are approximations and, even when honestly produced, they can easily contain unintentional inaccuracies. Nonetheless, both the Warren Commission and the HSCA, relied heavily on drawings.

In both cases, the medical illustrations were hugely inaccurate and misleading when compared to other evidence. Was this intentional? It was certainly easy to achieve.

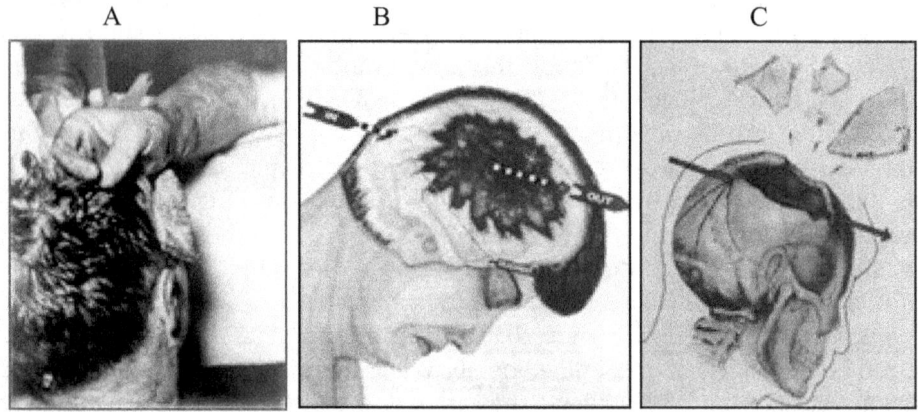

Comparison of Alleged Autopsy Photograph, Ryberg Diagram and Dox Drawing

The three pictures above show how misleading the drawings were. Picture A is an alleged autopsy photograph – all the official investigations since the Warren Commission (who did not use the photographs) have authenticated it. Picture B is a drawing made for the Warren Commission by medical illustrator Harold Ryberg[48] from the autopsy doctors descriptions (without access to the autopsy photographs). Picture C is a drawing made for the HSCA by medical illustrator Ida Dox[49].

What is immediately obvious is that they do not show the same wounds.

Picture A, said to be a photograph from the autopsy, appears to show a possible entrance wound low on the back of his head. The picture is difficult to compare to the two drawings as it shows less of Kennedy's head, is taken from a different angle than the perspective of the two drawings and is appallingly lit. Nonetheless, two things are clear – that there is no large-scale damage to the back of his head, contrary to both the Parkland and Bethesda doctors, and that the exit wound is apparently the small flap of skull bone standing up some way forward of JFK's right ear. Again, this is not an area in which the Parkland doctors reported any wounds.

Picture B shows an entrance wound in the middle of the back of JFK's head. The exit wound is illustrated as a huge jagged hole – almost half of JFK's skull is shown as missing with extensive damage to the side of his head including behind the right ear. A "neat" flap of skull bone is not shown. The position of the head in this drawing – drastically dropped forward – is unnatural and confuses the perspective. No photograph or film of the assassination shows Kennedy's to have ever been in this position.

Five | The Medical Evidence

Picture C shows an entrance wound high up on the back of the head. The exit wound is drawn as a smaller, less jagged hole involving mostly the top of the head behind the ear. Again, the bone flap seen in picture A is not illustrated.

Of course, any misrepresentation was not the intention of the illustrators themselves. Two recent authors, William Law and Doug Horne, have discovered how the illustrations were commissioned and have discussed why they might show what they do.

Illustrations of Connally's Wounds

The Warren Commission was not content with leaving the description of JFK's wounds to poorly conceived drawings. It did the same thing with the wounds to Texas Governor John B Connally who was sitting in front of JFK during the November 22nd 1963 Dallas motorcade. During the shooting in Dealey Plaza, he too was seriously injured. Connally, however, survived and became key to the Warren Commission's single bullet theory (SBT). All subsequent official investigations have given their backing to the SBT even though it is provably wrong [see my chapter in this book].

To support their conclusions regarding the SBT, the Warren Commission used two sets of body diagrams during the testimony of Drs Shaw and Gregory who treated Connally at Parkland. They were not drawn by the doctors at the time of treating Connally. They were copies of drawings in a Secret Service file and seem to have been used by the Warren Commission in an effort to confuse and deceive rather than to aid testimony.

To put it mildly, these two sets of diagrams went through a dizzying process of being labelled and re-labelled. This process may initially have been just a matter of American bureaucracy. Few organisations are as fanatical about labelling and re-labelling their documents as are the two bureaucracies involved here, the American legal system and national security agencies. But as the process wore on, the re-labelling seems to have taken a more sinister turn.

Shaw and Gregory's testimony was taken by the Commission's Assistant Counsel Arlen Specter, the man most closely associated with the SBT. I believe that the diagrams and the doctors' testimony were deliberately guided by Specter's need to legitimise the SBT rather than get to the truth.

The Provenance of the Connally Body Diagrams

The truth about these diagrams is devastating to the Warren Commission.
On January 27th 1964, Inspector T. J. Kelley of the Secret Service requested diagrams be made of the wounds suffered by Connally. What they were needed for is not revealed in their file (Secret Service 969).

Special Agent Roger C Warner got some blank body diagrams from the Dallas County Pathologist, Dr Rose. These are the body diagrams Dr Rose would markup when noting features during an autopsy.

Warner then interviewed Connally's three doctors Shaw, Gregory and Shires. He showed them two body diagrams which they marked to show Connally's wounds. These were diagrams 3 and 4 as shown below.

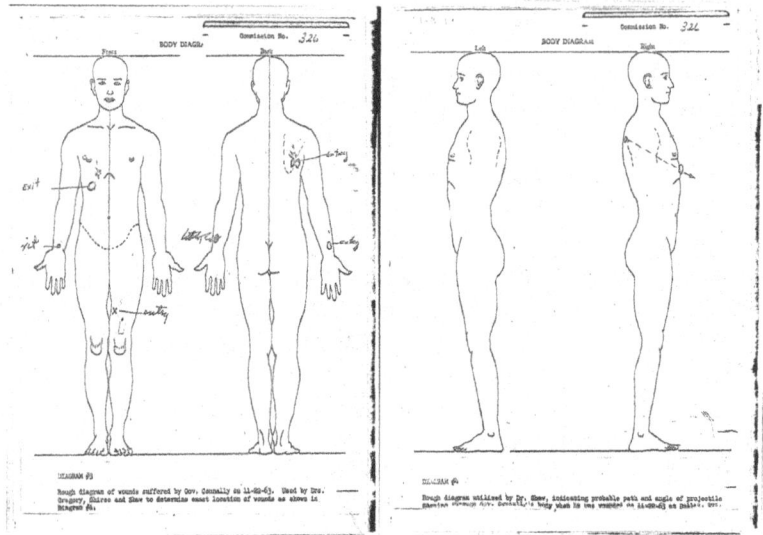

Diagrams 3 & 4 – Rough Drafts

Warner took these diagrams (described as "rough drafts" as they were marked up by hand) and traced them. On these traced copies, the wound's identifications were typed rather than hand-written. These were diagrams 1 and 2 shown below.

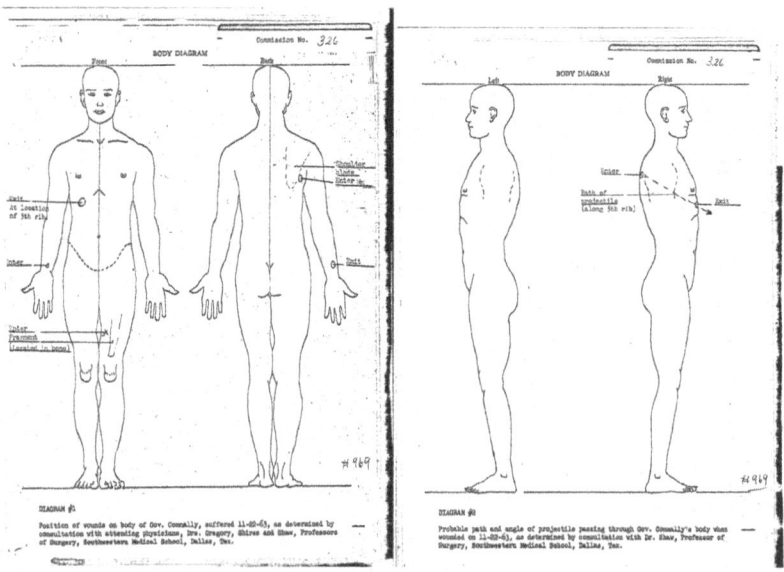

Diagrams 1 & 2 – Typed Drafts

FIVE | THE MEDICAL EVIDENCE

When transcribing the wounds, Warner made an error and labelled the wrist entry as an *exit*. He also labelled the wrist exit as an *entry*. The effect of this was that a wound determined by Dr Gregory as entering on the top side of the wrist and exiting on the underside of the wrist (where your veins are) was reversed. Warner perpetuated this error by producing a fifth diagram also showing the wrong trajectory through the wrist:

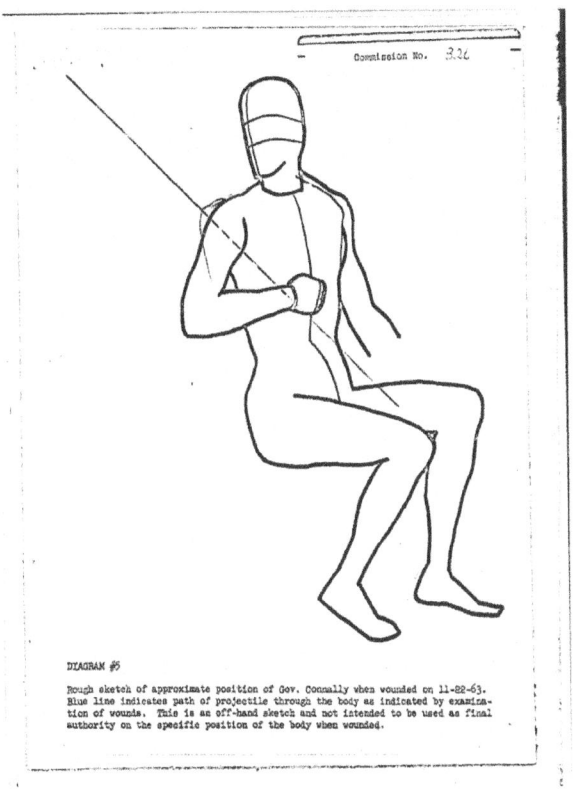

Diagram 5 Attempting to Show Path of Projectile

To summarise, Secret Service file 969 contained five diagrams:

#1 – Front and back drawings with typed wound labels. The wrist entry and exit are *incorrect*.
#2 – Side drawings with typed labels.
#3 – Front and back drawings with hand-written wound labels. The wrist entry and exit are correct.
#4 – Side drawings with hand-written labels.
#5 – A Secret Service sketch showing position of Connally when wounded and the path of a projectile. The trajectory through the wrist is *incorrect*.

JFK | ECHOES FROM ELM STREET
A SEARCH FOR HISTORICAL ACCURACY ON THE
ASSASSINATION OF PRESIDENT JOHN F. KENNEDY

A copy of the Secret Service file 969 containing the five diagrams was provided almost immediately to the Warren Commission and became Commission Document 326 on 28th January 1964.

Two weeks later, David W Belin, an Assistant Counsel for the Warren Commission, noted the error in diagrams 1 and 5 when he compared Dr Gregory's written account of operating on Connally's wrist with the Secret Service diagrams. He wrote to Inspector Kelley on February 12th 1964 to ask for the "entire matter [to be] reviewed" and for the Secret Service to make "a further report of your findings".

Warner got right onto it. He spoke with Dr Gregory again, discovered that his previous diagrams 1 and 5 were wrong and made two corrected diagrams (6 and 7) as shown below.

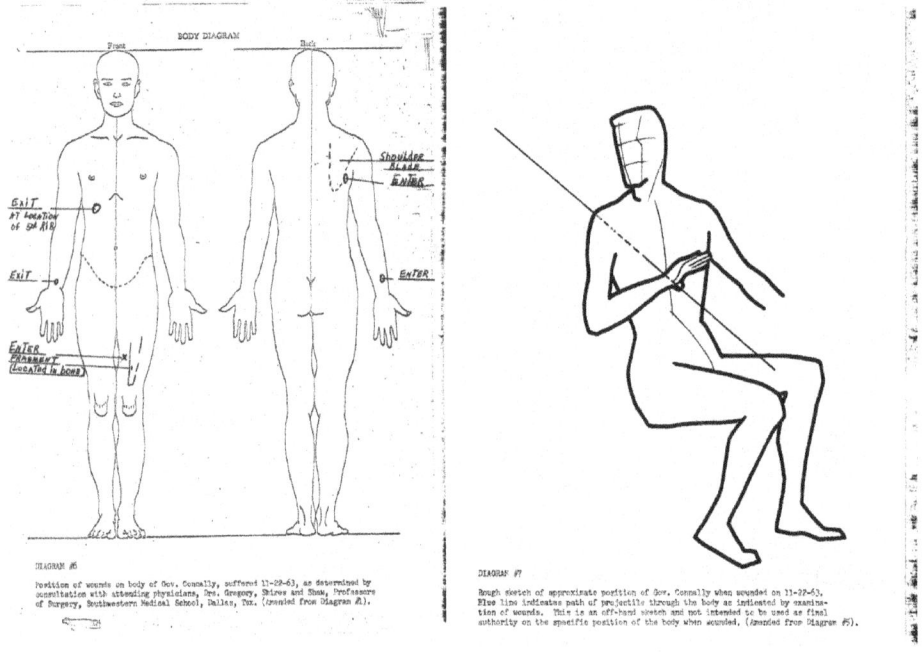

Diagrams 6 & 7 Corrected Trajectory

To summarize, two more diagrams were added to Secret Service file 969:

#6 – Front and back drawings with typed wound labels. The wrist entry and exit are now correct.
#7 – A Secret Service sketch showing position of Connally when wounded and the path of a projectile. The trajectory through the wrist is correct, but the position is highly unnatural.

FIVE | THE MEDICAL EVIDENCE

A copy of the corrected diagrams was provided almost immediately to the Warren Commission and became Commission Document 381 on 14th February 1964.

Just over a month later, on March 22nd 1964, Specter took the first testimony from Connally's doctors. Specter was renowned for thorough preparation that bordered on the fastidious and it is inconceivable that what he did next was a mistake. When cross-examining first Shaw and then Gregory, Specter used the wrong diagrams. That is, instead of using those that agent Warner had taken back to Gregory for correction after Warner's original mistake had been spotted (6 and 7), Specter used the diagrams on which Warner had got the trajectory wrong (1 and 5).

This may have been a major blunder, but I don't think so. I believe that Specter used the incorrect diagrams published because they better supported the SBT.

The Medical Evidence and John Connally

If you thought that the anomalies in the Warren Commission's handling of the medical evidence were confined to wounds that changed in nature or location, wounds that disappeared between two diagnoses made on the same day, conflicting measurements of the same wounds, photographs that contradicted the autopsy report, grotesque illustrations which contradicted inadequate photographs, doctors asking lawyers to pronounce on medical matters, military personnel directing medical staff on how to conduct an autopsy, evidence that was given but not recorded and evidence which was revised to say its opposite, you would be wrong. For none of this touches the breathtaking audacity of how the Commission treated the evidence of Governor Connally's wounds.

John Connally would have died in the assassination were it not for the reactions of his wife. When Nellie Connally pulled her husband onto her lap and covered him with her body, she inadvertently followed the correct medical procedure for saving his life by pressing herself against him. This pressure helped seal the sucking wound in his chest and prevented Governor Connally from suffocating.

Connally's wounds ought to clarify all of the assassination's medical issues. Since the core of the Warren Report was that both men had been wounded by the same bullet, Connally effectively had a casting vote on the medical evidence. Unfortunately, Connally's stance was totally ambiguous. From the time of the assassination until he died in 1993, Connally insisted that he was hit by a different bullet from that which first hit Kennedy – but was equally vocal in saying that he believed Oswald shot Kennedy and that nobody else was involved. The two statements are irreconcilable, but the American media barely alluded to the discrepancy.

This is unfortunate because the evidence regarding Connally's wounds and how the Warren Commission handled it probably sheds more light on both the assassination and the Commission's work than does anything else. The evidence about Governor Connally's wounds has received less scrutiny because the attention, not surprisingly, has always been on President Kennedy's wounds. But Connally's wounds are the weak link in the Warren Commission's case and looking at this aspect sheds extraordinary light on the medical evidence and how the Commission treated it.

The Warren Commission argument was that Connally was only hit by one bullet and this bullet caused three wounds. These wounds were:

- A perforating wound of the chest which had shattered a rib and damaged the pleural sac covering his right lung

- A perforating wound of the right wrist which had shattered his radius

- A penetrating wound of the left thigh.

According to the Warren Commission, the bullet that caused these wounds first went into the President's neck and out through his throat before ploughing into Connally's chest, going through his right wrist and finishing up in his left thigh. This bullet, in the Commission's version of events, then dropped out of Connally's thigh and was found – virtually intact – on a stretcher at Parkland.

Connally was in surgery for over three hours. The doctors divided into three teams, each concentrating on one wound. Each team was led by a senior doctor, a professor in his field of medicine who taught at the University of Texas Medical School and unquestionably the best man for the job in the Dallas area. Connally got the best medical attention available. There is no doubt about that. An examination of their testimony and how it was received is extremely revealing.

The Doctors' Testimony
Given their seniority, their obvious intelligence and their ability to teach – each of these three professors taught at the University of Texas Medical School – the testimony of Dr Robert Shaw, Dr Charles Gregory and Dr George Shires, should have been crystal clear. The Warren Commission, however, seem to have done everything possible to make it unclear:

The doctors' testimony is spread over volumes 4 and 6 of the Warren Commission Hearings with the later testimony from April 1964 presented in the earlier volume[58] The exhibits are treated in the same way.

On some occasions, only one doctor was questioned by one counsel[59].

On other occasions, several doctors were questioned by several counselors and other witnesses were present[60]. Connally himself was there on one occasion and even took his shirt and trousers off[61].

Hypothetical questions were mixed with specific questions about the case

FIVE | THE MEDICAL EVIDENCE

until the doctors may have been unsure which type they were answering.

Questions were often asked about wounds that the doctors had not seen well or not treated[62]. The doctors were asked complete nonsense questions[63].

I am not the first to notice that presentation of data in this way seems almost a deliberate ploy to confuse anyone checking up on the facts behind the Warren Commission Report.

Dr Robert Roeder Shaw

Dr Shaw was Professor of Thoracic Surgery at the University of Texas Medical School at the time of the assassination[64]. He worked on Connally's chest wound and was assisted in surgery by Drs. Boland, Duke, Fueishier, Giesecke, Hunt and Mebane[65].

In his operative record (his written description of the surgical procedures carried out on his patient), Dr Shaw said that the bullet which caused Connally's chest wound entered his back at the right armpit and came out near Connally's right nipple [66]. Shaw later measured the angle of perforation as being about 25 degrees downward (a much steeper angle than the Warren Commission had for the bullet path they claimed went through JFK's neck) with the bullet travelling very slightly right to left[67].

Shaw gave evidence to the Warren Commission in March 1964 (6H 83) and a month later, in April 1964 (4H 101). On the first occasion, Dr Shaw was willing to speculate that one bullet did all the damage to Connally. But when he returned to give more testimony a month later, Shaw's views had gone through an extraordinary about-turn.

What made the difference was that between his two Warren Commission appearances, Dr Shaw had been allowed to view the Zapruder film, CE399 (the alleged single bullet) and the Governor's clothes. His testimony was markedly different after viewing the physical evidence.

In March 1964, Dr Shaw was willing to speculate that one bullet did all the damage to John Connally, but in April, he would not be held to that and even discusses the possibility of several bullets[68]. Dr Shaw said in April 1964:

> "Mr Dulles, I thought I knew just how the Governor was wounded [that is, with one bullet] until I saw the pictures today and it becomes a little bit harder to explain."[69] The extent to which the Warren Commission had already committed itself to the SBT is evident in Dulles' confusion when Shaw suggests the possibility of three bullets accounting for Connally's three wounds[70].

After seeing the Zapruder film and CE399, Dr Shaw would not agree to one bullet having caused all Connally's wounds. Furthermore, Dr Shaw said that even if one bullet had caused all of Connally's wounds, he doubted that it could have been CE399[71]. Given this and Connally's recollections, Shaw said: "I think it is hard to say that the first bullet hit both of these men almost simultaneously."[72]

Dr Charles Francis Gregory

Dr Gregory was Professor of Orthopaedic Surgery University of Texas Medical School in November 1963[73]. He worked on Connally's wrist wound and was assisted in surgery by Drs. Osborne and Parker[74]. Gregory described the wound on the upper (or dorsal) surface as 2cm round and ragged about 5 cm above the wrist joint. The wound on the underside (volar) he described as 1cm round and smooth cut, about 1.5cm above wrist joint[75]. Both were roughly in the midline of the wrist.

The upper side (dorsal) surface of the wrist has a typical bony lump. The underside (volar) surface is where you can see the veins in your wrist.

Gregory's descriptions alone destroy the SBT because he describes an entrance wound on the upper surface of the wrist where the SBT demands an exit wound. In fact, the shot that wounded Connally's wrist was more likely to have been fired from the front.

Gregory states in his Warren Commission testimony that the wrist wound goes from the upper (dorsal) surface to the under (volar) surface for five reasons:

- The general appearance of the upper side wound is typical of an entrance wound[76].
- Bits of thread and cloth were carried into the wound on the upper side and these correspond with a tear in the jacket sleeve[77].
- Two or three fragments were shed after the bullet had hit the radius, the major wrist bone. The three fragments taken from the wrist were closer to the underside and caused by the radius flaking them off[78].
- The distortion of the soft tissues shows the pathway to be upper side to lowerside[79].
- Air in the wound is more visible on the upper side of the x-ray which is typical of an entrance wound[80].

Please remember, Dr Gregory was a Professor of Orthopaedic Surgery. For such a senior and experienced surgeon to give five reasons that the wound in Connally's wrist was dorsal to volar – that is, from front to back – demolishes the SBT which relies on totally the opposite trajectory.

Specter and Gregory spent some time during testimony sessions discussing whether the bullet that injured Connally's wrist had already lost velocity by going through other tissues beforehand[81]. While Gregory's responses to Specter's questions seem to support the SBT, previous penetration is not the only thing that causes a bullet to be slow moving.

FIVE | THE MEDICAL EVIDENCE

I can think of at least three reasons which could explain a slower bullet hitting Connally:
- The bullet could have been fired from a lower-powered gun
- The bullet could have been fired from a longer range
- The bullet could have been deflected form an object in Dealey Plaza.

But all these other and standard explanations for Connally being hit by a slow bullet were ignored.

For Connally's wounds to conform to the SBT, we first have to accept that a bullet perforated JFK's neck and that as it did so, Connally had the upper – that is the top or outer – side of his right wrist, which was holding his Stetson, pressed against his right nipple. Try this manoeuvre – it is utterly unnatural, but there is more to come. For the SBT to work, Connally would then have had to move to his left and begin to stand up for a bullet leaving the midline of JFK's neck to hit the Governor in the back near his armpit. At the same instant, Connally would need to lift his left thigh so that it caught a bullet emerging from the underside of his wrist. There is no evidence that Connally performed this grotesque and anatomically near-impossible manoeuvre on November 22nd 1963.

Gregory testified that he doubted that the SBT was likely because the bullet would not have had sufficient energy to smash Connally's radius and then go on to penetrate his thigh[82]. He said that it was more likely for sharp and irregular-shaped bullet fragments to have remained after causing Connally's wrist injury[83]. Such fragments are in evidence[84], but the Warren Commission claimed these were the remains of the bullet which hit JFK in the head. Nevertheless, this is crucial testimony – the orthopaedic surgeon who treated Connally's wrist testifying that it was probably not CE399 that damaged Connally's wrist.

I have much sympathy for Gregory and his colleagues – Specter had boxed them in. The doctors were only allowed, by the Warren Commission, two bullets over which to speculate. Rather than this mental bondage, the probability of other shots and shooters should have been considered. That such alternative possibilities were not considered is unforgivable as it has probably allowed at least one assassin to go free and the accessories to the crime to have lived without fear of prosecution since.

Dr George T Shires

Dr Shires was Professor of Surgery at University of Texas Medical School at the time of the assassination[85]. He worked on Connally's thigh wound and was assisted in surgery by Drs. Baxter, McClelland, and Patman[86]. Dr Malcolm Perry was also asked to scrub up in readiness to assist with vascular surgery if it became necessary[87].

Dr Shires described how the entrance wound in the skin was larger than the path into the muscle below[88]. The thigh wound looked to Dr Shires like a tangential hit[89] meaning that a missile had struck a glancing blow at a sharp angle to Connally's leg.

Dr Shires was very insistent with Specter that the wound had to have been caused by a tangential hit[90]. That means that it could not have been CE399 which, for the SBT to work, had to penetrate the Governor's thigh and fall out later on his stretcher. A Professor of Surgery testified that this could not be what happened, but the Commission ignored him.

The Warren Commission was sent more evidence about the wound to Connally's thigh by the FBI. Parkland doctor, Dr Jack Reynolds, sent a note to the FBI describing the wound and with an X-ray of Connally's left thigh attached[91]. He described the thigh wound as round, 1cm diameter and containing a roughly oval fragment, 3.5mm long, 1.3 mm wide lying on the axis of the thigh. The note and X-ray were forwarded to the Warren Commission, but they chose not to use this information.

With the testimony of Dr Shires and the FBI note from Dr Reynolds, the Warren Commission was well aware that a whole bullet did not penetrate Connally's thigh, only a fragment. Dr Shires said that the skin wound was either tangential or that a larger fragment (not a whole bullet) had penetrated or stopped in the skin and then fallen out.

Conclusion

The medical evidence should have been gathered by independent, well-qualified scientists, medical or otherwise. For the murder of a President of the United States of America, where the future of the whole world might be at stake, you would expect the very best scientists in their field to have been used to gather the evidence using the best of their skills, the latest techniques and the top equipment available.

This should have resulted in a clear record of the wounds suffered by President Kennedy and Governor Connally or, at the very least, something that would stand up in court. A clear record of the medical evidence would not, on its own, have solved the case as there are so many unanswered questions and complications with the non-medical evidence, motives and circumstances. But a straightforward account of the wounds suffered by Kennedy and Connally would have made a monumental inroad into those problems as it would have shown whether they were shot from behind or from behind and in front.

At the time the evidence was being gathered, this was critical to the man under arrest and facing trial for the shooting, Lee Harvey Oswald. If the evidence showed that shots came from two or more directions, then there was a conspiracy and the agencies of the US government had a duty to pursue that, wherever it may have led and to bring all the guilty parties to justice.

In my opinion, the medical evidence does show that JFK and John Connally were shot from more than one direction and, therefore, by more than one

FIVE | THE MEDICAL EVIDENCE

assassin. I believe that this evidence was deliberately unexplored, mishandled, distorted, lost and lied about to disguise the fact.

Acknowledgements

Chris Lightbown spent many hours questioning my logic, clarifying important points and helping me to rewrite some tortuous English. His patience appears to be limitless as he did this for two of my chapters in this book. I thank him wholeheartedly. There's a pint on the bar.

Endnotes

[1] Warren Commission Report page 19
[2] Warren Commission Report page 86
[3] HSCA Appendix to Hearings - Volume VII p103 (7HSCA 103)
[4] Douglas P Horne, *Inside the ARRB*
[5] Volume 17 Warren Commission Hearings page 846 (17H 846) Warren Commission Exhibit Number 850 (CE850)
[6] http://www.archives.gov/research/jfk/faqs.html#xray
[7] 5H 180
[8] Parkland Memorial Hospital November 22, 1963 press conference transcript http://mcadams.posc.mu.edu/press.htm
[9] Doug Horne re: Audrey Bell
http://insidethearrb.livejournal.com/2370.html
[10] Gary L Aguilar, "Malcolm Perry, MD Falls into the Kennedy Vortex" http://www.ctka.net/2010/mop_obit.html
[11] Gerald Posner, *Case Closed* (New York, Random House, 1993) p305
[12] 6H 3
[13] WCR 519
[14] 6H 5
[15] 6H 5, 6H 18, 6H 31
[16] CE392
[17] 6H 6
[18] 3H 361
[19] Gerald Posner, *Case Closed*, (London, Warner Books, 1994) p311
[20] David S Lifton, *Best Evidence*, (New York, Carroll & Graf, 1991) p324
[21] Gerald Posner, *Case Closed*, (London, Warner Books, 1994) p311-312
[22] CE392
[23] 6H 48
[24] Gerald Posner, Case Closed, (London, Warner Books, 1994) p312
[25] 7HSCA 268
[26] CE392
[27] 6H 48
[28] Harrison Livingstone, *High Treason 2*, (New York, Carroll & Graf, 1992) p179
[29] 6H 51
[30] 6H 51
[31] CE392
[32] 6H 35
[33] Gerald Posner, *Case Closed*, (London, Warner Books, 1994) p313
[34] 3H 360
[35] 7H 452
[36] Humes testimony to ARRB

37. ARRB Medical Document MD 44 - Sibert and O'Neill Report on the Autopsy (11/26/63)--"Gemberling Version"
38. Warren Commission Document 1 – FBI Report (Investigation of Assassination of President John F. Kennedy November 22, 1963)
39. Warren Commission Report Appendix IX
40. MD 44 - Sibert and O'Neill Report on the Autopsy (11/26/63)--"Gemberling Version"
41. Douglas P Horne, *Inside the Assassination Records Review Board*, Vol 3 p709
42. MD 44 - Sibert and O'Neill Report on the Autopsy (11/26/63)--"Gemberling Version"
43. http://www.ctka.net/reviews/horne_jd.html
44. http://www.jfk-online.com/finckshaw07.html Finck also reveals that Admiral Galloway had a hand in writing the autopsy report
45. Ibid Vol 3 p845
46. Ibid Vol 3 p865
47. Ibid Vol 1 p154-155
48. CE388 16H 983
49. JFK Exhibit F-66 HSCA1 p252
48. 6H 86
49. Ibid
50. 6H 97
51. 6H 103
52. Ibid
53. 6H 101
54. Ibid
55. 6H 87
56. 4H 103
57. 4H 126
58. Volume 4 of the Hearings contains testimony taken from the doctors in April 1964. Volume 6 of the Hearings contains testimony taken in March 1964.
59. For example, see Dr Shaw's testimony given to Arlen Specter in volume 6H
60. For example, see Dr Gregory's testimony in volume 4H
61. Connally takes his shirt off 4H 136. Connally takes his trousers off 4H 138.
62. 4H 109
63. McCloy's question in 4H 115 and Cooper's question in 4H 117
64. Testimony of Dr Robert Shaw, 4H 102
65. Testimony of Dr Robert Shaw, 4H102 and 6H 84
66. CE392
67. 4H 137
68. 4H 109
69. Ibid
70. Ibid
71. 4H 113-114
72. 4H 114
73. 6H 96
74. 6H 97
75. 6H 97-98
76. 4H 118
77. 4H 119
78. 4H 120
79. Ibid
80. Ibid
81. 6H 102
82. 4H 127
83. 4H 128

FIVE | THE MEDICAL EVIDENCE

84. CE567 and CE569
85. Testimony of Dr Shires, 6H 104
86. 6H 106
87. Perry scrub in 3H 383
88. 6H 106
89. Ibid
90. 6H 111
91. Harold Weisberg, *Post Mortem.*

JFK | Echoes From Elm Street
A Search for Historical Accuracy on the
Assassination of President John F. Kennedy

Six
Unsound Acoustics?

Chris Scally

> *"Let both sides seek to invoke the wonders of science instead of its terrors."*
> – President John F. Kennedy, Inaugural Address, 20 January 1961.

Introduction

The final report of the United States' House of Representatives Select Committee on Assassinations (the HSCA) was published on July 29, 1979. This second official investigation into the Kennedy assassination found that President Kennedy was "probably assassinated as a result of a conspiracy",[1] although Lee Harvey Oswald did fire three of the four shots, and he fired the shot that actually killed the President.[2] The HSCA's report stated that "scientific acoustical evidence establishes a high probability that two gunmen fired" at the President - Oswald from the Texas School Book Depository building above and behind the President, and a second, unidentified gunman from the grassy knoll in front and to the right of the motorcade.[3] The HSCA recommended that the U.S. Department of Justice review the Committee's findings and determine whether further official investigation was warranted.[4] The Justice Department's findings were to be reported to the House Judiciary Committee.[5]

The Justice Department turned to the National Research Council, the principal operating agency of the National Academy of Science (NAS), in order to obtain a private and independent review of the acoustics evidence. On October 1, 1980, the Justice Department asked the Council to perform a study of the methodology used by the HSCA's acoustics experts, and the validity of their conclusion of a shot from the grassy knoll.[6] The Council's Commission on Physical Sciences, Mathematics and Resources created a "Committee on Ballistic Acoustics" under the Chairmanship of Professor Norman Ramsey of Harvard University to perform the analysis.[7] The Ramsey Panel, as the NAS committee has become known, reported on May 14, 1982 that "the acoustic analyses do not demonstrate that there was a grassy knoll shot", and that "reliable acoustic data do not support a conclusion that there was a second gunman".[8]

In compliance with the HSCA's recommendation, the Ramsey Panel's report was submitted to the Justice Department for evaluation.[9] The Justice Department's conclusions, submitted nearly six years later to Hon. Peter W. Rodino Jr., Chairman of the House Judiciary Committee on March 28, 1988, stated that "no persuasive evidence can be identified to support the theory of a conspiracy", and "no further investigation appears to be warranted... unless new information which is sufficient to support additional investigative activity becomes available".[10] The Justice Department report noted that "all investigative leads which are known to the Department have been exhaustively pursued", and added that while further acoustical tests would not be cost justified at that time, "it is the Department's intention to continue to review all correspondence and to investigate, as appropriate, any potentially productive information".[11]

The acoustics evidence is central to the question of whether or not President Kennedy was killed as the result of a conspiracy, and its evolving history can be summarised as follows:

- **Warren Commission Report, published on September 24, 1964:**
  Lee Harvey Oswald was the lone assassin;[12] There was no evidence of conspiracy, and if one existed, it was "beyond the reach of all the investigative agencies and resources of the United States."[13]

- **House Select Committee on Assassinations Report, published on July 29, 1979:**
  The assassination was probably the result of a conspiracy;[14] Oswald fired three of the four shots, including the one that actually killed the President;[15] "Scientific acoustical evidence establishes a high probability that two gunmen fired".[16]

- **National Academy of Science Panel Report, published on May 14, 1982:**
  "The acoustic analyses (the panel's review of the HSCA scientists' methodology) do not demonstrate that there was a grassy knoll shot";[17] "The acoustic impulses attributed to gunshots were recorded about one minute after the President had been shot and the motorcade had been instructed to go to the hospital";[18] "Reliable acoustic data do not support a conclusion that there was a second gunman".[19]

The scientific experts engaged by the HSCA and the Ramsey Panel had clearly reached diametrically opposing conclusions. So which – if either – set of scientific conclusions was seriously in error? And what was this 'acoustics evidence', anyway?

Six | Unsound Acoustics?

The HSCA Evidence

On November 22, 1963, the Dallas Police Department (the DPD) utilised two radio channels, identified simply as Channel 1 and Channel 2. Channel 1, the more significant of the two in the context of this chapter, was the one ordinarily used to handle DPD radio communications, and was designated for the transmission of routine police radio messages on the day of the assassination.[20] Recording on both Channel 1 and Channel 2 was sound-activated.[21]

Transmissions on Channel 1 were recorded onto thin blue polyester dictabelts by means of a stylus embossing a continuous vertical groove onto a blank belt, using Dictaphone recording equipment.[22] The dictabelts themselves were approximately 90mm wide (3 1/2") and approximately 300mm long (11 3/4"), with a diameter of approximately 100mm (4").[23] The dictabelts being used on November 22, 1963 were from a batch of dictabelts manufactured in June 1963.[24]

Through the assistance of Dictaphone equipment historian Bob Swenson, and engineer Bill McWilliams, who worked on the actual DPD equipment in the 1960s, it has been possible to confirm the precise configuration of the Channel 1 recording configuration used by the DPD in November 1963. The equipment, initially purchased by the DPD in 1957,[25] consisted of two Model 5 Time Master recorders placed on top of, and electrically connected to, an A2TC Model 5 controller on the bottom.[26] The two recorders each contained a dictabelt; so that when one belt ended the second one would start recording automatically, thereby ensuring that there was no break in recording. Each belt was capable of recording for up to 30 minutes, and the way in which the A2TC device was configured resulted in a recording "overlap" of about 20 seconds at the start of each dictabelt, to ensure continuity of recording (i.e. about 20 seconds of the end of each belt was also recorded on the beginning of the next belt, so that nothing was lost as the machine switched from one belt to the next). The Model 5 controller box was also fitted with a "Belt Change Signal" light, which indicated when one or both of the dictabelts needed to be changed.[27]

Fig 1: The DPD Channel 1 Configuration, as of November 1963

Channel 2 was an auxiliary channel, used to handle the additional radio traffic generated by special events, and was designated for use by DPD officers in the motorcade on November 22, 1963.[28] The transmissions on Channel 2 were recorded onto 8 1/2-inch diameter flexible green plastic discs by means of a Gray Audograph recorder.[29]

The HSCA first became aware of the existence of the 'acoustics evidence' in late 1977, when their attention was drawn to research which had been carried out by the then Program Director at KFJZ-FM in Fort Worth, Gary Mack, indicating that the sounds of gunfire may have been recorded over the Dallas Police radio, which was routinely recording all radio traffic on the day of the assassination.[30] In mid-1978, the HSCA obtained a series of dictabelts purporting to contain those recorded radio transmissions from retired DPD Deputy Director of the Intelligence Division, Paul McCaghren.[31] The dictabelts were handed over to Bolt, Beranek and Newman (BBN), a Massachusetts-based firm that specialised in the field of acoustical consulting, in an effort to resolve the question of whether or not the shooting had been inadvertently recorded over the DPD radio system.[32]

BBN found that, from about 12:28 to 12:34,[33] precisely the time of the assassination, there was a 5 1/2 minute segment of interference consisting mainly of motorcycle engine noise on Channel 1, presumably caused by a police motorcycle radio being stuck in the 'open' or 'transmit' position.[34]

One of the first procedures applied by BBN to the DPD recording was an attempt to reduce the motorcycle engine noise, thereby making any other background noise more distinguishable. However, for reasons that are not clear, the engine noise was too irregular, and this clean-up process was unsuccessful.[35]

An additional complication arose due to the presence of in-built Automatic Gain Control (AGC) in the DPD radio system. AGC essentially amplifies weak signals, while at the same time dampening loud signals, thereby converting all sounds into a common 'range' of acceptable volumes, making them easier to hear over the radio system. As a result, a waveform produced from the DPD radio system will not visually match the waveform of the same sound, as it would appear in a recording made with high-fidelity equipment such as that used by BBN.[36] The impact of AGC was such that BBN specifically warned against such misinterpretations: "The time of the arrival of the impulses or echoes, in each sequence of impulses, was the characteristic being compared, not the shape, amplitude or any other characteristic of the impulses or sequence".[37]

These difficulties notwithstanding, BBN's initial study of the Channel 1 recording pinpointed seven impulse patterns for further study, at 136.20, 137.70, 139.27, 140.32, 145.15, 145.61 and 146.30 seconds respectively after the start of the period of radio interference.[38] These impulses were then

Six | Unsound Acoustics?

subjected to six screening tests designed to answer the following questions:

- Did the impulse patterns occur at the same time that the shots were actually fired?

- Were these impulse patterns unique?

- Did the time span between the patterns correspond to the other evidence of intervals between shots?

- Did in the shape of the impulse patterns resemble those generated by actual recordings of gunfire?

- Did the range of amplitude, or loudness, of the impulse patterns resemble that of the echo patterns produced when the sound of gunfire is recorded through a radio transmission system such as that used in November 1963 by the Dallas Police Department?

- Did the number of echoes for each impulse correspond with the number of echoes which might have been generated by gunfire in Dealey Plaza?[39]

If any of the patterns failed to pass these screening tests they could reasonably be discarded as being caused by something other than gunfire. Conversely, however, the fact that an impulse pattern passed all six tests did not prove that it was caused by a shot being recorded. It simply meant that further, more sophisticated tests would be required.[40]

BBN's preliminary report to the Committee indicated that the only way to determine whether or not the impulses were caused by the recording of gunfire in Dealey Plaza was to go back to the scene of the assassination and hold an acoustical reconstruction.

The purpose of the on-site test was to record the firing of shots at a number of locations along the motorcade route through the Plaza, and to then compare these recordings with the sounds on the Channel 1 recording.[41] The rationale behind this was that the sequence of impulses from a gunshot is caused by the noise of the shot followed by several echoes, and every combination of sound origin, target location and microphone location has a completely unique impulse pattern.[42] In an environment such as Dealey Plaza, surrounded as it is by high buildings, these unique patterns would be extremely useful in determining both the source of the jammed police radio transmitter and the source of the shots, if the acoustical "fingerprints" obtained during the reconstruction could be matched to the impulses on the Channel 1 recording.[43]

On August 17, 1978, just three days before the tests were to be conducted, the HSCA decided to call upon the additional expertise of Professors Mark Weiss and Ernest Aschkenasy, acoustic scientists at Queens College in New York.[44] These two men were asked to review Dr Barger's results to date, to examine the plan for the re-enactment, and to provide an independent opinion as to the need for such an apparently extraordinary step. Weiss and Aschkenasy concurred with the findings of their professional colleague, and agreed with his proposal to carry out a series of acoustical tests in Dealey Plaza.[45]

The four-block section of Dallas surrounding Dealey Plaza was cordoned off by a team of 50 police officers at 5:30 am on the morning of Sunday, August 20, 1978.[46] Two locations were chosen by the HSCA from which the test shots would be fired: the south-eastern window on the 6th floor of the Texas School Book Depository (the TSBD) from where the Warren Commission had concluded Lee Harvey Oswald had fired all the shots, and a point about 3 feet north of the corner of the picket fence which runs along the top of the grassy knoll. According to HSCA Chief Counsel Robert Blakey, "we took the two most likely places based on the testimony, and that's all we did."[47] Four sandbag targets were set up on Elm Street, corresponding with the position of the limousine at the times of the projected shots, along with an array of 36 microphones spaced at 18-foot intervals along Houston and Elm Streets.[48] When the tests concluded around noon, Dr. Barger and his colleagues were in possession of a veritable mountain of raw acoustical data which then had to be analysed.[49]

The matching technique consisted of two distinct parts. Each of the 432 acoustical "fingerprints" (12 shots, each recorded at 36 microphones) obtained during the test was compared with each of the questioned impulse patterns on the Channel 1 recording.[50] If a point representing the time of arrival of an echo on the Channel 1 recording from 1963 could be correlated within 6/1000th of a second to a point in an impulse pattern on the reconstruction recording, it was considered to be a "match".[51] This 6/1000th of a second "acceptance window" was chosen to allow for the fact that the motorcycle with the open microphone in 1963 could have been at a point between any two of the microphone positions used in the re-enactment, in which case an exact match would be impossible.[52] While it was possible that this margin of error could allow "false alarms", it was considered small enough to be reliable and accurate. Having thus obtained what they believed was a matching impulse, the BBN scientists then compared the number of echoes associated with each impulse, and where they matched with a correlation coefficient of 0.6 or better (a coefficient of unity indicating an absolutely perfect match), the impulses could be said to be from the same source.[53]

This mammoth task was completed only four days before Dr. Barger was due to testify before the HSCA at a public session on September 11, 1978.[54] Dr. Barger would testify that there was an 88% likelihood that a shot from the Book

SIX | UNSOUND ACOUSTICS?

Depository occurred at 137.70 seconds into the open microphone sequence, based on three matches; an 88% chance that a second shot from the TSBD was recorded at 139.27 seconds, again based on three matches; a 50% chance that a shot from the grassy knoll area was recorded at 145.15 seconds, based on a single match; and a 75% possibility that the two remaining matches at 145.61 seconds represented another shot from the Book Depository.[55]

The Committee now had scientific evidence which indicated that as many as four shots may have been fired at the President, that one of these shots may have come from the grassy knoll and that the President had therefore been the victim of a conspiracy. Dr Barger's testimony was a major cause of concern to the committee since he would only say that there was a 50-50 chance of a shot from the knoll. The Committee therefore decided to ask the experts at Queens College in New York with whom they had previously conferred, Mark Weiss and Ernest Aschkenasy, if they could go beyond what Dr. Barger had done, and determine with greater accuracy if in fact there had been a shot from the knoll.[56]

In addition to a high-fidelity tape recording of the original DPD dictabelt recording, a high-fidelity copy of the recording used by BBN in their initial study, and a high-fidelity copy of the sounds recorded during the re-enactment of August 20, Weiss and Aschkenasy were given very detailed maps of Dealey Plaza as well as a number of photographs of the area to assist them in their analysis. This task began on October 24, 1978.[57]

Weiss and Aschkenasy took a totally different approach to that used by Dr. Barger and his colleagues at BBN. Using the maps and photographs, they identified which structures in Dealey Plaza were most likely to have caused the echoes received by the microphone during the acoustical reconstruction that had recorded the match to the shot from the grassy knoll. Twenty-six such echo-producing objects were identified, a finding which Dr. Barger then confirmed after his own independent study.[58]

The HSCA's Report described the process then used by Weiss and Aschkenasy as follows: "Once they had identified the echo-generating sources for a shot from the vicinity of the grassy knoll and a microphone located near the point indicated by Barger's tests", Weiss and Aschkenasy were able to "predict precisely what impulse sequences (sound fingerprints) would have been created by various specific shooter and microphone locations" at the time of the assassination. They could then "compare acoustical fingerprints for numerous precise points in the grassy knoll area with the segment identified by Barger" on the Channel 1 radio recording as possibly reflecting a shot fired from the knoll.[59]

Armed with this data, "Weiss and Aschkenasy were able to look for a match to the 1963 DPD radio recording that correlated to within 1/1000 of a second, as opposed to 6/1000 of a second as Barger had done. By looking for a match with such precision they considerably reduced the possibility that any match they found could have been caused by random or other noise, thus substantially reducing the percentage probability of an invalid match."[60]

The HSCA Report explained that Weiss and Aschkenasy initially pinpointed a combination of shooter-microphone locations for which the early impulses in the 'grassy knoll shot' pattern matched quite well, although later impulses in the pattern did not. Similarly, they found other microphone locations for which later impulses matched those on the channel 1 recording, while the earlier ones did not. The HSCA Report continued: "They then realised that a microphone mounted on a motorcycle or other vehicle travelling in the motorcade would not have remained stationary during the period it was receiving the echoes. They computed that the entire impulse pattern or sequence of echoes they were analysing on the DPD radio recording occurred over approximately three tenths of a second, during which time the motorcycle or other vehicle would have, at 11 miles per hour, travelled about five feet. By taking this into account, Weiss and Aschkenasy were able to find a sequence of impulses representing a shot from the grassy knoll in the reconstruction that matched both the early and late impulses on the dictabelt recording.

Approximately 10 feet from the point on the grassy knoll that was picked as a shooter location in the 1978 reconstruction and four feet from a microphone location which, Barger found, recorded a shot that matched the Channel 1 recording within 6/1000 of a second, Weiss and Aschkenasy found a combination of shooter and microphone locations they needed to solve the problem. It represented the initial position of a microphone that would have received a series of impulses matching those on the DPD radio recording to within 1/1000 of a second. The microphone would have been mounted on a vehicle that was moving along the motorcade route at 11 miles per hour."[61]

The points at which the gunman and microphone were located are more specifically defined in Weiss and Aschkenasy's report to the HSCA. In that document, they located the gunman "about 8 feet to the left of the corner of the wooden stockade fence on the grassy knoll", and the initial location of the microphone "97 feet south of the TSBD and 27 feet east of the southwest corner of the TSBD".[62] Professor Weiss testified that there was only a margin of error of plus or minus 18 inches in the positioning of the microphone, and that flexibility of plus or minus 5 feet in the positioning of the gunman fell within that 1/1000 of a second tolerance.[63]

The HSCA's final report concludes: "Since Weiss and Aschkenasy were able to obtain a match to within 1/1000 of a second, the probability that such a match could occur by random chance was slight. Specifically, they mathematically computed that, with a certainty factor of 95% or better, there was a shot fired at the Presidential limousine from the grassy knoll. Barger independently reviewed the analysis performed by Weiss and Aschkenasy and concluded that their analytical procedure was correct. Barger and the staff at

Six | Unsound Acoustics?

BBN also confirmed that there was a 95 percent chance that at the time of the assassination a noise as loud as a rifle shot was produced at the grassy knoll."[64]

Additionally, examination of the Channel 1 recording indicated that the impulse pattern believed to indicate a shot from the knoll was preceded by a supersonic shock wave, or N-wave. This was a significant additional indication that the impulse on the recording represented gunfire and more precisely, a shot from a rifle, since very few pistols were known to fire supersonic rounds. This N-wave was also highly suggestive of the fact that the shot was fired in the direction of the President since, had the source been pointed upward or away from the limousine, the N-wave would not have been recorded by the open microphone.[65]

Weiss and Aschkenasy's review of the acoustics evidence was not completed until the end of November 1978. Because it established the fact that there was a second gunman in Dealey Plaza – and therefore the existence of a conspiracy "beyond a reasonable doubt", as Professor Weiss would later testify – the HSCA attempted to ascertain the identity of the police officer on whose motorcycle the stuck transmitter was located.[66] Examination of the Dallas Police Department assignment records for November 22, 1963 showed that four officers were assigned to travel in close proximity to the presidential limousine: Officers B.W. Hargis, B.J. Martin, D.L. Jackson, and J.M. Chaney.[67] However, the acoustics evidence indicated that the jammed transmitter was on a motorcycle located about 120 to 138 feet behind and to the left of the limousine, which would seem to eliminate the two left-hand side limousine outriders, Hargis and Martin.[68] The assignment logs showed that Officers H.B. McLain and J.W. Courson would have been the next pair of outriders on the left-hand side of the motorcade, and testimony from both officers indicated that McLain positioned himself between 2 and 7 car-lengths behind the President's limousine, with Courson several car-lengths further behind.[69] An 8-mm colour movie film taken by spectator Robert Hughes from a point near the intersection of Main and Houston Streets was then reviewed by the HSCA. The final frames of the film show the President's limousine as it makes the turn onto Elm from Houston Street, and they also show Officer McLain as he completes the turn from Main onto Houston.[70] According to BBN, these frames, depicting the scene some 4 to 5 seconds before the first shot was fired, show that McLain was then about 215 feet behind the President's limousine.[71]

On December 29, 1978, the day on which Weiss and Aschkenasy presented their own historic testimony, Officer McLain also testified in public at the Committee's request.[72] He said that he recognised himself as the officer in the Hughes film and acknowledged that other films showing earlier stages of the motorcade through Dallas confirmed his positioning.[73] McLain said that he did not use his microphone at any stage along the motorcade route, and said that it may have been switched – as it usually was – to Channel 1.[74] He also testified that the transmit button on his radio was known to stick, that it had done so on previous occasions, but that he did not know if it was stuck that day.[75] He recalled hearing only one shot, and he said he heard it when he was approximately halfway between Main and Elm Streets, on Houston Street.[76]

The HSCA's acoustics evidence can be summarised as follows:

> Four shots were fired at the President's limousine. Three of these shots came from the area surrounding the sixth floor at the south-eastern corner of the Texas School Book Depository, while the third shot in the sequence undoubtedly came from the grassy knoll;[77]

> The acoustics evidence, when considered in the light of other evidence available to the Committee, indicated that the first shot was fired from the Texas School Book Depository and reached the limousine at Zapruder frame 157-161; that the second shot, also from the Book Depository, reached the limousine 1.6 seconds later, at Z-188-191; that a third shot, fired from the grassy knoll, reached the limousine at Z-295-296 but missed its target; and a fourth and final shot – again fired from the Book Depository - struck the President between Zapruder frames 312 and 313;[78]

> The microphone which recorded the shots was located on the police motorcycle which was been ridden by Officer H.B. McLain;[79] McLain was about 215 feet behind the President's limousine as it turned into Elm Street, and he was about 140 feet behind the limousine at the time the shots were fired.[80]

The HSCA's acoustics evidence was further strengthened by the fact that it was supported by independent non-scientific evidence which did not depend on any statistical interpretation, and which would require a coincidence of enormous magnitude to have occurred simply by chance:

> The impulses found by the acoustics experts were unique – they existed around the time of the shooting, and nowhere else, on the DPD radio recording;

> The recorded impulses, and their relative timing, could be matched to the predicted time of arrival of the associated echoes off the surrounding buildings at the open microphone;

> The chronological order of the data was consistent. The matches were obtained in a logical sequence along Elm Street, namely, the first 'shot sound' matched a microphone location at the Elm/Houston intersection, the

Six | Unsound Acoustics?

second set of impulses matched at a point further down Elm Street, and the third and fourth patterns matched at points still further west on Elm Street;

The spacing of the projected shots matched other evidence of what had actually happened. The first and second shots were 1.6 seconds apart; there was then a 6 second gap before the third shot; and then just 7/10ths of a second elapsed between the third and fourth shot. Furthermore, the entire sequence took just 8.3 seconds;[81]

The speed of the motorcade and the open microphone were also consistent with the acoustical findings. The first and last shots were detected at microphones 130 feet apart, which would mean the open microphone was moving at 12 mph. Back in 1964, the FBI used the Zapruder film to calculate the limousine speed on Elm Street, and came up with an average speed of 11.3 mph;

The sequence of shots was supported by eyewitness testimony. Many eyewitnesses reported a noticeable "gap" between the second and third shots;

The spacing between the shots, as identified by the scientists, is in accord with the spacing of the shots apparent in the Zapruder film; and finally,

The acoustics findings are consistent with the Warren Commission findings. Shots 1, 2 and 4 as detected by the HSCA's acoustics experts are consistent with the Warren Commission's findings of three shots from the TSBD, and the order and spacing of the matches / shots also agree with the Commission. It is somewhat ironic, then, to find that rejection of the acoustics evidence is to also indirectly reject the Commission's conclusions.

The Ramsey/NAS Panel Evidence

In October 1980, over fourteen months after the publication of the HSCA Report, the Ramsey Panel was formed in order to provide the Justice Department with an independent appraisal of the methodology used by BBN and Weiss and Aschkenasy, and to confirm the validity of their conclusion of a shot from the grassy knoll.[82]

Unfortunately, it appears that that Ramsey Panel may have started out with a preconceived and negative approach to the work of the HSCA. Nobel Prize winning physicist Professor Luis Alvarez, who had initially been offered but declined the chairmanship of the committee, told reporters he was "simply amazed that anyone would take such evidence seriously".[83] Later, when Dr. Barger met with the Ramsey Panel to explain his analysis and conclusions,

Alvarez allegedly told him that "it didn't really matter" what he said, since he (Alvarez) was "going to vote against the HSCA findings anyway."[84]

Ultimately, the Ramsey Panel faulted BBN's finding that there were probabilities of 88%, 88%, 50% and 75% respectively that four shots were fired at the President. Using BBN's base data, they recalculated the probabilities for each of the four shots as 53%, 53%, 22% and 40%.[85] The Panel then suggested that their figures may have been somewhat over-conservative, and offered yet another set of probabilities of 70%, 70%, 33% and 55% respectively for each of the four shots.[86] Weiss and Aschkenasy's work in respect of the third shot – the one from the grassy knoll – was also criticised by the Panel. The calculation of a 95% probability that a shot was fired from the knoll was reduced to one of 78%, and Weiss, Aschkenasy and BBN were taken to task for their use of "subjective procedures" and a methodology which was "insufficiently tested and calibrated".[87]

While these criticisms undoubtedly reduced the strength of the HSCA's acoustics evidence in terms of its being the much-vaunted 'proof of conspiracy', the objections and criticisms raised by the Panel hardly seem sufficient to justify the total rejection of the HSCA's conclusions. Yet, on the basis of these points alone, the Ramsey Panel claimed that no member of the group was convinced of the validity of the acoustics evidence which indicated a shot from the knoll.

However, of far greater importance than the Ramsey Panel's criticism and differing interpretation of methodologies was evidence which the panel received from Ohio researcher Steve Barber on October 6, 1980, which constituted a serious obstacle to the conclusions of the HSCA.[88] The panel's report devoted considerable space to an examination of Barber's work, which indicated that a post-assassination statement made over Channel 2 of the police radio was simultaneously recorded on Channel 1 by an open microphone, but appears on Channel 1 at the time of the shooting.[89] According to the Ramsey Panel, the Channel 2 order from Sheriff Bill Decker to "hold everything secure" was actually given at least 30.9 seconds after DPD Chief Jesse Curry had instructed the motorcade to "go to the hospital" after the shots were fired.[90] However, since the Decker statement appears on Channel 1 at the same time as the impulses said by the HSCA's experts to represent the third and fourth shots, and since the panel established that the crosstalk from Channel 2 to Channel 1 occurred at the time the Channel 2 recording was made (and not as a result of subsequent re-recording), the panel was forced to conclude that the impulses studied by the HSCA's acoustics experts were not caused by the recording of shots on Channel 1.[91] Quite simply, the HSCA experts were looking at "shots" which were fired over half-a-minute after the assassination took place.

Subsequent research by researcher Michael O'Dell established that the "hold everything secure..." phrase from Channel 2 begins 0.84 seconds before the suspected grassy knoll pattern. It overlaps the impulses identified by Weiss

Six | Unsound Acoustics?

and Aschkenasy as a shot from the Grassy Knoll, and O'Dell has said that he got a better correlation with the second syllable of the word "secure" than the acoustics experts got against the dictabelt impulses.[92]

Arising from the work of the Ramsey Panel, therefore, a number of major inconsistencies became apparent:

The unique nature of the impulses, the chronological order of the detections, the consistency of the scientists' findings with the known speed of the limousine and the open microphone on Elm Street, and the elapsed time between the impulse patterns, all supported the HSCA's conclusions; The fact that a substantial body of evidence (which will be discussed shortly) disputed the conclusion that Officer H.B. McLain was the source of the "open mike"; the fact that the impulses were recorded on Channel 1 (the channel for routine, non-motorcade transmissions) while the stuck transmitter was allegedly on a motorcycle in the motorcade, and therefore on the "wrong" channel; and the absence of siren sounds for nearly two minutes after the shooting despite the fact that the open microphone was supposedly in the motorcade, all supported the view of the Ramsey Panel.

The HSCA experts, looking at echo patterns and acoustical fingerprints, said there were shot impulses on the recordings, while the NAS/Ramsey Panel, looking at the HSCA's methodology and the Sheriff Decker "hold everything secure..." crosstalk, said there were not. Essentially, these diametrically opposing conclusions meant that if the echo pattern evidence was correct, the crosstalk evidence was wrong, or the crosstalk evidence was correct, and the echo matching was wrong.

As we have already seen, a number of factors combined to prevent the HSCA's acoustics evidence from being dismissed out of hand, with the result that the contradictions and conflicts had to be explainable. While scientists and statisticians can (and probably will) argue forever about the validity of statistical probabilities and the methodologies employed by the HSCA's experts, there are a number of non-scientific issues which arose as a result of the conflicting conclusions of the HSCA and the Ramsey Panel, and which can be addressed without recourse to either statistics or science.

The Open Microphone
A basic requirement of the HSCA's acoustics evidence was that the shots were recorded over the DPD radio by an open transmitter which was located on a police vehicle (almost certainly a motorcycle ridden by DPD Officer H.B. McLain) which was travelling some 140 feet behind the presidential limousine and at a speed of about 12 miles per hour, when the shooting took place.

However, there were problems with this evidence from the outset. Shortly after Dr. Barger testified to the HSCA on September 11, 1978, HSCA photo consultant Richard E. Sprague told this author that "there was no motorcycle" where BBN said it was located, and that the open microphone was on a motorcycle in close proximity to the presidential limousine.[93] When Sprague spoke with Dr. Barger and asked if he had seen any of the relevant photographic evidence, Barger said, "No." Sprague then asked what difference it would make to the acoustics findings if the open microphone was on one of the four DPD motorcycles closest to the President, to which Barger replied that it could impact the identified points of origin of the shots. Barger told Sprague that he could re-examine the data produced in the reconstruction test, but said that it would require another re-enactment to be certain, an eventuality that was never likely to occur.[94]

Subsequently, on December 26, 1978, Sprague was asked by HSCA Deputy Chief Counsel Gary Cornwell to assist in identifying the motorcycle on which the stuck transmitter was located.[95]

On the following day, December 27, Sprague contacted Cornwell and told him: "Gary, I've got bad news for you. Not only did I not find any films or photos showing your motorcycle, I found two films showing that it wasn't there." Sprague had prepared a number of slides that documented his findings for the Committee, and these were collected within a few hours and hurriedly taken back to Washington for study by the HSCA staff.[96] Two days later, in the glare of publicity that surrounded the presentation of the evidence that proved conspiracy beyond a reasonable doubt, McLain would testify before the same staff that he could have been the officer with the stuck transmitter.[97]

Sprague continued to examine the photographic evidence, however, and in subsequent oral and written submissions to the Justice Department on March 11, March 18 and April 3, 1980, he reiterated his belief that McLain was not the officer with the open microphone.[98]

In his testimony before the HSCA on December 29, 1978, DPD Officer H.B. McLain admitted that his could have been the motorcycle with the open microphone. Within days of his HSCA testimony, however, he was telling a totally different story.[99]

On January 4, 1979, exactly one week after he testified in public before the HSCA, McLain told CBS television viewers that he was not the officer with the open microphone. He told interviewer Eric Enberg that, immediately after the shots were fired, he turned on his siren and sped after the limousine towards Parkland Hospital.[100]

McLain said that he turned on his siren in response to Dallas Police Chief Curry's order to proceed to Parkland Hospital, which was transmitted on Channel 2 less than one minute after the shooting.[101] If this were true, McLain could not have recorded the shooting, since no sirens are heard on the Channel 1 recording until minutes after the final shot was fired.[102] Furthermore, if McLain heard Curry's order over his own radio, it must have been switched to Channel 2 at the time, a further indication that he did not record the shooting.

Six | Unsound Acoustics?

The HSCA's response, presented in their final report issued on March 29, 1979, simply dismissed both McLain's statements and Sprague's research.[103] The Committee believed that McLain may have overhead Curry's order over the radio of another motorcycle nearby (as McLain had testified was possible), and stated that McLain was simply mistaken on the point of his use of his siren.[104] The report also suggested that McLain did not leave the area immediately, but remained behind at least momentarily.[105]

On April 14, 1982, former DPD Communications Supervisor Sergeant James C. Bowles told Dallas Morning News reporter Earl Golz that he had "known for several years about the possibility of the stuck microphone being that of [Officer Leslie] Beilharz or another policeman in the same area".[106] Bowles said that the other policeman, whom he thought was "more inclined toward being the person that had the open mike", was now retired, and in very poor health.[107] (As will be discussed shortly, this "other officer" could have been Officer Willie Price, who had suffered a heart attack, and whose wife had suffered a similar fate. Both of them were in poor health, and both sadly passed away in the 1990s.[108])

In the same article, Beilharz said he met with Bowles in 1979, after McLain's testimony before the HSCA, at which time he listened to the tapes for the first time.[109] Arising from this Earl Golz article, Beilharz, who was riding a three-wheel motorcycle on the day of the assassination, contacted Norman Ramsey, chairman of the Ramsey Panel.

The Ramsey Panel's report, published in May 1982, pays scant attention to Beilharz, merely stating that "As the present report was about to be printed, Officer Leslie Beilharz... told the Committee Chairman by telephone that there was a 'good possibility' that his microphone may have been the one stuck open".[110]

But could it really have been Beilharz?

The only public record of Beilharz' activities in the period of time surrounding the assassination is the above-referenced story by Earl Golz in the Dallas Morning News on April 14, 1982. In that article, Beilharz claimed not to remember any radio transmissions at the time of the shooting because, he said, his radio was malfunctioning and simply did not pick them up.[111] Beilharz added that he was unaware of the shooting while he was at his assigned location at the intersection of the Stemmons Freeway and Industrial Boulevard.[112]

According to Beilharz, he remained at the intersection for approximately five minutes after the motorcade passed by, before he decided to follow it to Parkland Hospital.[113] It was only on arrival there, he said, that he heard about the shooting in Dealey Plaza from other officers.[114] However, if Beilharz spoke to nobody until he arrived at the hospital, and his radio was failing to pick up transmissions, one must ask how he knew – especially as the motorcade had passed his location some five minutes earlier – where the motorcade had gone?

Despite this, Beilharz was continuing to claim that his was the open microphone until 1993, at least. During an interview with researcher Denis Morissette, Beilharz stated: "I think that was my button that was stuck on the motorcycle. I was riding the motorcycle."[115]

In 1996, H.B. McLain was being quoted as saying that he and Bowles had determined that Beilharz was the motorcycle officer who had the stuck microphone.[116] By 1997, however, McLain was saying that Bowles now believed that the motorcycle with the stuck microphone was a three-wheeler ridden by Sgt. D.V. Harkness,[117] although McLain himself continued to believe, until late November 2005 at least, that Beilharz was the officer with the open microphone.[118]

In a 66-page endnote to his book "Reclaiming History"[119], author Vincent Bugliosi dismisses the HSCA's acoustics evidence. Of the acoustic scientists whose work formed the basis of that acoustics evidence, Bugliosi said their "presumed expertise", "demonstrated incompetence" and "possible zeal to become famous" led them to "unintentionally" mislead the HSCA.[120]

However, hidden away in this important footnote, but not referenced in the book's Index, are three remarkable revelations:

- The identification of DPD Officer Willie Price as "the officer with the open mike"
- The claim that Price's identity was common knowledge in the immediate aftermath of the assassination;
- and the very serious allegation that his identity was made known to (but apparently ignored by) a HSCA investigator.[121]

Former DPD Sergeant Jim Bowles was clearly Bugliosi's primary source of information regarding the acoustics evidence. Indeed, in the course of the endnote under discussion, Bugliosi refers to an incredible twenty-one different telephone interviews he had with Bowles, in addition to three letters he received from Bowles, and a further sixteen references to Bowles' 1979 manuscript, "The Kennedy Assassination Tapes – A Rebuttal to the Acoustical Evidence".

On December 8, 2005, during one of those telephone interviews, Bowles "casually mentioned" to Bugliosi that it was "Willie Price's three-wheeler at the Trade Mart" that had the open mike. When Bugliosi asked Bowles how long he had been in possession of this "explosive information", Bowles told him it was "common knowledge in the traffic division", and that Price had admitted it to him personally.[122]

In an effort to verify Bowles' claim, Bugliosi spoke to a total of seven former DPD officers, including five whose names and phone numbers had been supplied by Bowles. The first (un-named) officer said he "may have heard it was Price, but this was just hearsay."[123] Officer B.J. Dale said he had not heard that Price was the officer with the open mike,[124] while Officer John Toney said,

Six | Unsound Acoustics?

""It was the belief [on the force] that it was Willie Price. That was the word in the department at the time."[125] Officer H.B. McLain, the man whom the HSCA had identified as the source of the open mike, told Bugliosi that "it wasn't Price... we (McLain and Bowles) concluded it was Leslie Beilharz".[126] Officer Paul Bentley told Bugliosi that he "heard it was Willie Price's cycle that had the stuck mike... within a week of the assassination",[127] while Officer J.W. Courson said he "heard Willie Price's name mentioned as being the one with the open mike."[128] Courson said he "heard other names too," although he was unable to remember whose they were.[129] Finally, Officer Leslie Beilharz, who Bowles and McLain had "concluded" was the open mike culprit, told Bugliosi, "The first time I heard Willie Price's name in connection with this is when Jim [Bowles] called me last week."[130] As an aside, one might reasonably ask why Bowles was making phone calls to these officers while Bugliosi was checking out his claims.

Armed with this conflicting evidence, Bugliosi went back to Bowles in an effort to clear up the matter. He pressed Bowles about when he had first heard about Officer Price. "I believe I first heard about it being Willie's mike by hearsay in the department back in 1963 and 1964. And it was probably in 1978, around the time of the HSCA, that Willie told me personally that it was his mike."[131] Bowles added that one of the officers to whom Bugliosi had spoken had told Bowles that Price had told him the stuck mike was his, and that the unnamed officer also knew that Price had taken his motorcycle into the repair shop after the assassination for some type of repair, which the officer assumed was to fix Price's microphone.[132]

Bowles explained the apparent reluctance of those to whom Bugliosi had spoken to speak openly about what they knew. "These men didn't want to go on the public record. They're weary and leery over the assassination and want to move on", he said.[133]

But could Price have been the officer with the open mike?

Price was using radio call number 295 on November 22, 1963. His first assignment that day was traffic control at McKinney and Harwood, and after the motorcade had passed that location, he was assigned to the Trade Mart.[134]

According to the radio transmissions aired on Channel 2 (the channel assigned to the motorcade), we can determine that the lead car in the motorcade passed Price's location at McKinney and Harwood at about 12:20.[135] According to Bowles' version of events,[136] this leaves only three minutes for the entire motorcade to pass Price's location, and for Price to set out on his journey to the Trade Mart. While it is unlikely that the entire motorcade could have passed Price's location – and normal traffic flow resumed – in such a short period of time, it is still possible that this could be considered consistent with Price's completion of his first assignment at approximately 12:23.

According to Bowles' manuscript, the officer with the open mike said something unintelligible over Channel 1 at 12:33, at a time when the motorcade would have been in the vicinity of the Trade Mart, en route to Parkland

Hospital.[137] Again, this is consistent with Price's projected movements, insofar as he was due to report to the Motor Pool at the Trade Mart at 12:30.[138]

Between 12:40 and 12:41, Price interrupted an exchange between the Channel 2 dispatcher and Asst. Chief Batchelor regarding the shooting, and said he believed the President's head was "practically blown off". When asked if he knew the extent of the injury, Price replied, "It's not for me to say" and asked for the comment to be disregarded. Asked where he got the information, Price said he was "at the car when they took him out".[139] Once again, this is consistent with Price's known movements. However, it appears to contradict Bowles' claim in 1979 that the officer with the open mike did not recall moving his motorcycle again after he arrived at the Trade Mart – and by 1994, Price still clearly remembered having been at Parkland Hospital as the President was being taken from the limousine, and not at the Trade Mart.[140] Furthermore, Bowles had also claimed in 1979 that the officer with the open microphone "was using a relief motorcycle that day, one which was not equipped with a Channel 2 radio, and one which had experienced frequent radio trouble" in the past.[141]

The personal recollection of Officer Roy Higgins, however, appears to at least partially contradict Price's version of events. According to Higgins, who was also riding a 3-wheel motorcycle that day, he was making his way towards the Trade Mart from his first assignment at the intersection of Cedar Springs and Maple when the call came to go to Parkland Hospital. Higgins continued: "I don't recall just where I was when I heard the chief order officers to go to Parkland, but I was fairly close and felt I should go. I arrived at the emergency dock shortly before the motorcade... I assisted in removing the victims from the limousine."[142] In his Sixth Floor Museum Oral History interview, however, Price claims to have been talking to Higgins at the Trade Mart before they both headed to the hospital, arriving there before the motorcade and assisting in removing the President and Governor Connolly from the limousine.[143]

Not for the first time, the idea that the open microphone was located at the Trade Mart was being put forward as recently as 2010, when former Ramsey Panel member Charles Rader gave an interview to IEEE.tv, the Internet-based television network of the Institute of Electrical and Electronics Engineers.[144] In that interview, Dr. Rader put forward the theory that the Dallas Police had a "staging area", or control post, in the basement of the Trade Mart. He suggested that there was a loudspeaker mounted on a pillar in this basement "staging area", over which all Channel 2 (what he calls "Channel M", the motorcade channel) radio traffic was being transmitted. Dr. Rader hypothesised that a police motorcycle with a stuck microphone transmitter was parked in the basement, and it had transmitted what was coming over the loudspeaker, as well as some of the other nearby sounds (such as the passing police sirens in the motorcade) over Channel 1.

Six | Unsound Acoustics?

Anxious to determine if there was any validity in this seemingly plausible theory, the author contacted the DPD Communications Supervisor at the time of the assassination, Jim Bowles, who responded: "No, there was no such station. The defective mike was on Willie Price's 3-wheeler in the Trade Mart parking area. It picked up transmissions from an outside speaker on a nearby car."[145]

And what of the very serious charge that the HSCA were aware of Officer Price, and the possibility that he had the open microphone, but chose to ignore the matter?

Bowles told Bugliosi that Jack Moriarty was the HSCA investigator to whom he had given the information concerning Price.[146] HSCA Chief Counsel G. Robert Blakey, however, denied any knowledge of such information. Blakey told Bugliosi, "I don't remember Moriarty telling me that Bowles thought he knew the identity of the cyclist with the open mike, and the name Willie Price rings no bell for me. Moriarty was a fine investigator, and if anything he always told me more than I needed to know. If Bowles had told Moriarty about this Price fellow, Moriarty would have told me and of course we would have contacted Price."[147] Similarly, Blakey's Deputy Chief Counsel, Gary Cornwell told Bugliosi that he had never heard of Price, or Bowles' alleged reporting of him to Moriarty.[148]

According to Bugliosi, Bowles is a good and honourable man, who admits to having a failing memory at 77 years of age.[149] Bugliosi believes that Bowles probably alluded to Price, but never actually gave Price's name to Moriarty.[150] Bowles, however, insists that he gave Price's name to Moriarty, saying he gave "Price's name to Mr. Moriarty because he and the committee were conducting a lawful investigation. It would have been misconduct for me to withhold his name or to misrepresent any fact".[151] Despite such determined insistence, however, Bowles' 1979 manuscript claims that information about the officer with the open microphone was "available to the (HSCA) investigators had they sought it",[152] suggesting that Bowles did not tell the HSCA investigators, for the simple reason that they never asked him. HSCA records failed to reveal any indication whatsoever of any contact with Officer Price.[153]

Subsequent studies have, to this author's satisfaction at least, clearly established that Officer H.B. McLain did not have the open microphone, as claimed by the HSCA.[154]

In addition, while the HSCA said that Officer McLain's two-wheel motorcycle was the source of the open microphone, many DPD officers thought the stuck radio was on a three-wheel motorcycle.[155] However, DPD Chief Dispatcher Jerry Henslee said he was "convinced" it was a two-wheeler,[156] and Bowles himself had admitted that at one point in the radio recording it sounds like a two-wheel motorcycle, although his overall view has always been that it was a three-wheeler.[157]

One of the most outspoken critics of the acoustics evidence is researcher and author Dale Myers. As a result of his study, Myers believes that the photographic evidence totally refutes the HSCA conclusion that the only police motorcycle that could have recorded the shots was that of DPD Officer H.B. McLain, who was some 140 feet to the left and rear of the presidential limousine at the time of the shooting. According to Myers (and others), the photographic evidence proves beyond all doubt that there was no motorcycle at the locations and times predicted by the acoustics evidence, and that for McLain to have been in the acoustically-predicted location at the time of the first shot, it would have been necessary for him to have travelled at relatively excessive speeds (46 to 56 mph respectively, according to researchers Michael Russ and Paul Seaton), if not indeed an unattainably high 198 mph (according to Myers) along Houston Street.[158] However, author Don Thomas claims that such assertions are based on "unsupported inferences and miscalculations" such as the timing of the first shot, the speed and position of the cars in the motorcade, and a "coaches in a train" model for the motorcade (i.e. all vehicles moved at the same speed).[159] Thomas has calculated that, if the cars were slowing and accelerating as the procession negotiated the sharp turn off Houston onto Elm Street, and if the assumption that the grassy knoll shot missed (instead of hitting the President in the head) was in error, then McLain could easily have reached the points where the open microphone was determined to be by the acoustics evidence, in the time available.[160]

The absence of any photographs or films showing McLain (or any other officer) in the required locations has also been offered as proof that McLain could not have been the motorcycle officer with the open microphone, and that the entire HSCA scenario is based on the falsehood that the impulses were recorded by any police motorcycle radio. However, this is a classic example of the maxim that "absence of proof is not proof of absence", and simply proves that no photographs of the precise locations at the precise times in question were taken, rather than proving that McLain was not there.

So what does the photographic evidence actually show?[161]

Let us first deal with McLain. He is seen in the Hughes film as he completes the turn from Main onto Houston, between 9 and 10 seconds before the head shot, or less than 2 seconds before the first shot was fired. McLain was, at that time, some 174 feet from the point where the first impulses were recorded by the open microphone.[162] The Hughes film shows that there was no police motorcycle officer between McLain and the limousine at that point.[163]

Now, let us look at what McLain himself says happened next.

On September 26, 1977, HSCA investigator Harold Rose interviewed McLain. According to that interview record, McLain "was coming down Main Street and made a right turn onto Houston. He was facing the depository. Just as he was completing his turn, he heard what he believes were two shots."[164]

On December 29, 1978, McLain testified before the HSCA that he could

Six | Unsound Acoustics?

"remember hearing only one" shot, and that he heard it when he was approximately halfway between Main and Elm Streets on Houston.[165]

In his 1979 manuscript, Jim Bowles states that McLain was "on Houston Street approximately 100 feet south of Elm" when the shots were fired. McLain "watched Secret Service Agent Clinton J. Hill mount the rear of President Kennedy's limousine, after the last shot had been fired. [He] observed that through an opening in an ornamental wall on Houston".[166]

In his own personal account of what happened, also published in Bowles' manuscript, McLain provided some further detail. He said he was "either stopped or stopping" at the time he heard a single shot. An unspecified period of time after he saw Secret Service agent Clint Hill jump onto the rear of the limousine, McLain heard Chief Curry issue an order for the motorcade to head for Parkland Hospital, and he responded immediately. As he made the turn onto Elm Street, McLain claims to have seen his fellow motorcycle escort rider Bobby Hargis on his hands and knees, with his motorcycle on its side. McLain's initial reaction was that Hargis had been hit, but by the time McLain reached him, Hargis was back on his feet and heading "up the hill to my right, the one they now refer to as the grassy knoll". McLain said he eventually caught up with the main vehicles in the motorcade as they reached the point "where Stemmons goes over Continental, and about even with the Cabana Motel [about 600 to 800' north]", and he remained with the motorcade for the remainder of the journey to Parkland.[167]

McLain was interviewed again sometime prior to 1998 by author Larry Sneed, at which time he reiterated everything he had already said, but added that he had caught up with the vehicles in front of him and was actually stopped "opposite to the entrance to the old jail" when he heard "one very clear shot".[168]

The incident described by McLain, whereby he saw Mrs. Kennedy crawling onto the rear of the limousine, is clearly visible in the Zapruder, Nix and Muchmore films, and occurred only moments after the final shot – Mrs. Kennedy starts to get up at Z-345, and has both hands on the trunk of the limousine at Z-360 (about 2 1/2 seconds after the headshot). She is getting back down into the back seat from about Z-390 onwards, approximately 4 seconds after the headshot. But if McLain were stopped, approximately 100 feet south of the Houston/Elm Street intersection, one to 2 seconds after the final shot, can we be certain that he got to the location identified in the Dorman film less than 2 seconds later?

In 1997, McLain marked and initialled a drawing of Dealey Plaza for researcher Greg Jaynes, to show exactly where he stopped on Houston Street:[169]

JFK | ECHOES FROM ELM STREET
A SEARCH FOR HISTORICAL ACCURACY ON THE ASSASSINATION OF PRESIDENT JOHN F. KENNEDY

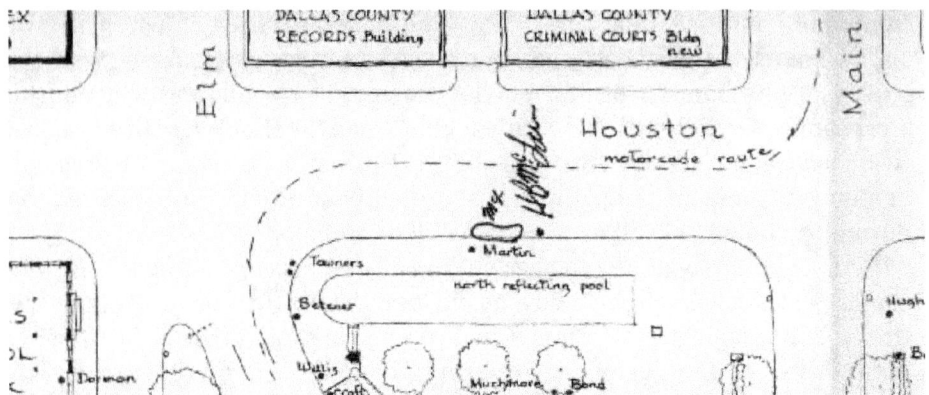

Fig 2: Drawing by R.B. Cutler, as marked and initialled by H.B. McLain (Photo Credit: Greg Jaynes)

In an article published around the same time, Jaynes further related that McLain told him that when he stopped on Houston, McLain "was in position to see Jackie Kennedy on the trunk of the Presidential limo through the square ornamental holes in the white wall that separates the Houston street reflecting pool from the infield grass between Elm and Main Streets".[170]

If McLain stopped, what subsequently prompted him to move off in pursuit of the motorcade, heading for Parkland? His HSCA testimony gives us the answer:

Q: At some point thereafter did you hear anything with respect to what was going on? Did you hear any radio broadcast?
A: Yes, sir. The chief came on across the radio and said head back for Parkland Hospital.[171]

McLain also told Larry Sneed that he set off in pursuit of the President's car in response to the order from Chief Curry to go to Parkland Hospital. He added that, as he sped down Elm Street towards the Stemmons Freeway, the only thing he noticed was Officer Hargis with his motorcycle lying on the ground, "crawling on his hands and knees across the grassy knoll".[172]

Additionally, McLain gave a videotaped interview to Mark Oakes, Greg Jaynes and Steve Barber around the same time, in which he again reiterated his claim that he was "sitting still" for a short time on Houston Street, and that from the time he stopped until he heard the order from Chief Curry was "maybe half a minute to a minute, something like that".[173]

So, in summary, McLain has consistently claimed that he stopped on Houston for between 30 seconds and one minute, during which time he saw Secret Service Agent Clint Hill getting onto the back of the presidential limousine. He further said that he saw Mrs. Kennedy on the trunk of the car, an incident that we have already established took place 2.5 to 4 seconds after the headshot.

Six | Unsound Acoustics?

Furthermore, all indications are that Officer McLain had his radio switched to Channel 2 throughout the period of the assassination and its immediate aftermath. We have seen above that he repeatedly claimed to have responded to a Channel 2 order from Chief Curry to proceed to Parkland Hospital, and a photograph of a DPD motorcycle at the hospital, which McLain identified as his motorcycle, appears to show that the radio channel selector switch was set to Channel 2.[174]

An 8-mm home movie film taken from the 4th floor of the Book Depository at the time of the assassination by TSBD employee Mrs. Elsie Dorman[175] shows an unidentified motorcycle officer moving slowly along Houston Street near the intersection of Houston and Elm, some 3 to 5 seconds after the fatal headshot. The motorcycle was travelling between Camera Car #3 and Dignitaries Car #1.[176] But if McLain was stopped approximately 100 feet south of the Elm and Houston intersection at that time, who was the officer in Mrs. Dorman's film?

The next police motorcycle behind McLain in the parade was that of Officer J. W. Courson, whose assigned location was approximately 100 to 120 feet behind McLain. He too, had an interesting story to tell.

In an interview with HSCA investigator Harold Rose in 1977, Courson said he was assigned to a position "in front of the Press Bus, approximately six or seven cars to the rear of the Presidential limousine.[177] As he turned onto Houston Street, his motorcycle would have been facing the TSBD. He heard three shots about a second apart. He could tell it was a high-powered weapon. There was an echo but he was sure there were three shots. He could not tell that anyone had been shot. He drove up to the left rear of the Presidential limousine and escorted the vehicle to Parkland Hospital."[178]

In his own personal recollection, published in Bowles 1979 manuscript, Officer Courson (identified only as Officer "F") said he was stopped on the west side of Houston Street, waiting for the press bus to complete the turn off Main Street, when he heard three shots. Courson said the motorcade was "backed up almost to a standstill" when the shots were fired, from a location which was "definitely...ahead of me". Courson could not see the President's car on Elm Street, so he immediately rode forward to see what had happened. He, like McLain, described seeing a motorcycle escort rider crawling on his hands and knees by the curb, with his motorcycle lying down. Courson added that the lead vehicles in the motorcade were already heading for the access road leading onto the Stemmons Freeway, but said that they slowed down on the access road, which allowed him to catch up with them "just about where the railroad goes over" the access ramp.[179]

In a 1986 interview with Todd Vaughan, Courson said he was positioned two cars in front of the White House Press Bus, which would place him between Congressman's Cars #2 and #3, some 100 to 120 feet behind McLain. Courson indicated that he was on Houston Street, 60 feet from the Elm/Houston intersection. He heard three shots. He turned onto Elm Street and saw Clint Hill jump onto the back of the limousine to assist Mrs. Kennedy, who was already on the trunk of the limousine. Courson said he and McLain moved down towards the limousine and got on either side of the rear of the car – himself on the left, and McLain on the right. Courson stated that he caught up with the limousine before they reached the Triple Underpass.[180]

Courson added further details to his account of events when interviewed by author Larry Sneed. He said that he heard three very distinct shots, all of which came from the same location. He said the first two shots were fired in close succession, with a longer delay between the second and third shot. In contradiction of his own personal recollection, which he gave Bowles in 1979, he told Sneed that he saw Mrs. Kennedy on the back of the limousine as he came around the corner onto Elm Street. He repeated his claim that he caught up with the lead vehicles on the Stemmons access ramp, and said that once they got onto the Freeway, he took up position on the left side of the limousine for the journey to Parkland.[181]

In summary, Courson said he was stopped on Houston Street, 60 feet from the Elm / Houston intersection, when he heard three shots. He could not see what was happening up ahead, so he "took off for the front of the motorcade". If we believe what he told both Vaughan and Sneed, he saw Mrs. Kennedy on the rear of the limousine as he came around the corner from Houston onto Elm, thereby implying that he had already gone past the location occupied by the unidentified officer seen in the Dorman film!

We next see McLain and Courson in the film taken by Malcolm Couch, a photographer/reporter for the local ABC affiliate WFAA, who was travelling in Camera Car #3, eight cars behind the President.[182] Couch's film shows McLain slightly ahead of Courson on Elm Street, approaching the parked motorcycle of Officer B.W. Hargis, who had dismounted his motorcycle and run across the street towards the grassy knoll immediately after the shots were fired. The segment of Couch's film showing this scene occurred approximately 25 seconds after the headshot.[183]

A few seconds later, eyewitness Wilma Bond snapped the fourth in a series of still photographs that she took that day. Bond's photo shows Hargis just as he reached his motorcycle on his return from the grassy knoll area, and McLain and Courson passing it. According to Dale Myers, the Bond #4 photograph "was actually exposed 31.3 seconds after the head shot".[184]

During his HSCA testimony, McLain confirmed that he and Courson are the two motorcycle officers visible in HSCA Exhibit F-675, a photograph taken by UPI photographer Frank Cancellare showing two DPD motorcycles alongside one another as they travelled along Elm Street, having passed Hargis' parked motorcycle, some 34-35 seconds after the headshot.[185]

Finally, a detailed examination of the DPD radio recordings for November

Six | Unsound Acoustics?

22, 1963 reveals an interesting (and possibly relevant) fact – of the motorcycle officers who were anywhere near the limousine at the time of the shooting, and who could possibly have recorded the sounds of gunfire in Dealey Plaza, only one used Channel 1 at any time that day – J.W. Courson, who spoke to the Channel 1 dispatcher while travelling on his motorcycle on Harry Hines Boulevard just after 2pm.[186]

There are conflicts in the accounts of both McLain and Courson, however. For example, the police motorcycle officer in the Dorman film is seen after Secret Service Agent Hill jumped onto the back of the limousine, making it virtually impossible for Courson to be the motorcycle officer in Dorman. Courson told Todd Vaughan that he caught up with the limousine before it reached the Triple Underpass – incorrect, as can be clearly seen from the Couch and Daniel films, and a still photograph taken by local professional photographer, Mel McIntire. Both McLain and Courson recall seeing a police motorcycle lying on the ground, and Officer Hargis scrambling on his hands and knees to stand up. However, the photographic evidence shows that Hargis' motorcycle was standing up at all times, and there is no indication that Hargis ever fell to his hands and knees.[187] The only police motorcycle shown to have been "lying on the ground" on Elm Street in the aftermath of the shooting was that of Officer Clyde Haygood, but he was behind both McLain and Courson at all times! It should be noted that Haygood, who was assigned to ride on the right-hand side of the motorcade level with Courson, is also visible in the segment of the Couch film mentioned above, also well forward of his assigned position.

Did McLain really stop on Houston Street, as he claimed? Officer Courson was initially some 100 to 120 feet behind McLain in the motorcade[188] – so if McLain did not stop on Houston, how did Courson catch up with him so quickly? Furthermore, McLain does not appear to have been in any great hurry to leave the Plaza – according to their own accounts, Courson caught up with the presidential limousine on the Stemmons Freeway access ramp, up to one minute or more after the headshot, but McLain said he did not catch up with limousine until it was on the Stemmons Freeway, 500 yards north of the access ramp from Elm Street onto the Freeway.

HSCA acoustics expert Ernest Aschkenasy was so convinced of the validity of his findings that he testified under oath that, if it could be proven that the impulses on the Channel 1 recording were recorded elsewhere, he would expect that place to be an exact replica of Dealey Plaza.[189] But was McLain the officer with the open microphone? Could it have been Courson? The photographic evidence alone strongly suggests that neither McLain nor Courson had sufficient time in which to reach the point at which the impulses were recorded, and were not the source of the open microphone.

To summarise briefly:

- If Dale Myers' synchronisation of the Hughes, Dorman and Zapruder films is correct, then Officer H.B. McLain could not have been in a position to record the shots;

- If McLain stopped on Houston, and saw Mrs. Kennedy and Secret Service Agent Hill on the back of the car, he could not have recorded the shooting;

- If McLain stopped on Houston, he could not be the officer on the motorcycle seen in the Dorman film;

- If McLain moved off only when he heard Chief Curry's "Go to the hospital" instruction, then his radio was switched to Channel 2, so he was not the source of the open microphone;

- If McLain responded only when Curry's order was issued, and if Curry's order was issued anything more than 30 seconds after the headshot, there is a serious conflict with McLain's photographically-proven presence on Elm Street within 30 seconds of the headshot;

- If Courson was stopped on Houston 60 feet from the intersection with Elm, and if he saw Mrs. Kennedy on the back of the limousine as he turned from Houston onto Elm, he could not have recorded the later shots, and particularly the headshot;

- If Courson saw the President's wife on the rear of the car as he turned onto Elm, and McLain saw her while he was still stopped opposite the County Records and Courts buildings, then Courson must have been ahead of McLain at that time, making him more likely to have been the motorcycle officer visible in the Dorman film;

- If McLain stopped on Houston, it would have given Courson time to catch up with (and possibly overtake) him, which is consistent with their accounts of when they saw Mrs. Kennedy on the rear of the limousine;

- If Courson caught up with and overtook McLain, why did he suddenly slow down to allow McLain to overtake him again by the time they both appear in the Couch film?

- If Courson caught up with the limousine on the Stemmons Freeway entrance ramp, but McLain did not catch up with the motorcade for

Six | Unsound Acoustics?

another 500-600 feet, what happened to McLain after he is last seen on Elm Street in the Cancellare photograph?

While the foregoing appears to cast serious doubt on the HSCA's findings, is it possible that the open microphone really was in Dealey Plaza at the time of the assassination, as concluded by the HSCA's acoustics experts? Could there possibly have been yet another police motorcycle officer in Dealey Plaza who might have recorded the shooting?

Can the Channel 1 Recording Sound help us?
Three independent assessments of the motorcycle engine noise have been made public – by Jim Bowles in 1979, by Steve Barber in February 1980 (and further refined by Todd Vaughan in December 1980), and – to a far lesser degree - by Dr. James Barger for the HSCA in 1978.[190] Unfortunately, the HSCA did not conduct any independent study of the noise generated by the engine of the motorcycle with the open microphone.

BBN's initial study of the Channel 1 recording indicated that about 133 seconds into the open microphone sequence, and five seconds before the first shot was apparently recorded, the noise level of the motorcycle engine dropped to about 25% of its previous level, indicating that the motorcycle slowed down. BBN concluded that this was due to the motorcycle officer slowing down to negotiate the sharp left-hand turn from Houston Street onto Elm Street and then continuing slowly down Elm Street.[191] The engine noise level stayed down for the next 30 to 40 seconds before it rose again to an even higher level than it had achieved earlier, and remained at this high level for at least two minutes.[192] Between 260 and 300 seconds into the open microphone sequence, the sounds of sirens coming and going in the vicinity of the open microphone (as opposed to being carried on a passing vehicle with a wailing siren) can be heard.[193]

In February 1979, Dr. Barger confirmed researcher Bob Cutler's suggestion that the motorcycle engine was, in fact, idling after the shots were fired, before apparently moving off at high speed.[194]

The analyses of the motorcycle engine noise carried out by Steve Barber and Jim Bowles were, however, considerably more detailed.

According to Bowles, the motorcycle was moving at 25-30 mph, which is about the average speed for a DPD three-wheeled motorcycle.[195] Barber's interpretation includes three gear changes in the 1.5 minutes prior to the final shot.

The Bowles analysis then indicates that, in the 4.5 minutes after the shooting in Dealey Plaza, which includes approximately 2 minutes after sirens passed its location, the open microphone moved short distances approximately 5 times. The longest of these trips was of no more than 45 seconds' duration, and the open microphone was always near other sound sources.[196]

Finally, according to Bowles, at just after 12:36, the officer with the open microphone started to move off to Parkland after the motorcade. He "checked his mike as he started to leave and discovered that his was the offending microphone. The problem of the open mike was corrected at that time, and the officer arrived at Parkland a couple of minutes later".[197]

Steve Barber's interpretation of the engine noise is not dissimilar to that of Jim Bowles, other than it contains only three periods of movement in the minutes after the shooting. The longest of these, however, was of 65 seconds duration, which is indicative of a journey of up to half a mile at "normal" three-wheeler speed.

What if there was a police motorcycle in Dealey Plaza, whose movements fitted the motorcycle engine sounds as interpreted by Steve Barber and Todd Vaughan? Was there a police motorcycle officer in Dealey Plaza who:

- Changed gear 3 times in the minute and a half prior to the shooting?

- Slowed down, and possibly stopped, seconds before the fatal head shot?

- Was overtaken by one or possibly two motorcycles within 10 or so seconds of the shooting?

- Snapped his kickstand into place as he possibly prepared to leave the scene a few seconds later?

- Moved off for about 16 seconds, may have passed through an underpass/tunnel or other such echo-generating area, and may have stopped again for 16 to 20 seconds?

- Moved off again for 18 seconds, and then stopped?

- Moved off again, and in the course of about 65 seconds, went through another echo-generating area, and was in the vicinity of a number of vehicles with their sirens "on"?

- Was then stopped for almost 5 minutes, possibly in the vicinity of people who may have been reacting to the news of the shooting?

- Moved off slowly again?

Is this consistent with the movements of a police motorcycle officer, in the motorcade in Dealey Plaza at the time the shots were fired, who told the Warren Commission:

Six | Unsound Acoustics?

"... and I stopped and got off my motorcycle and ran to the right-hand side of the street, behind the light pole... and I ran up to this kind of a little wall, brick wall up there to see if I could get a better look ... Then I got back on my motorcycle, which was still running, and rode underneath the first underpass to look on the opposite side in order to see if I could see anyone running away from the scene, and since I didn't see anyone coming from that direction I rode under the second underpass, which is Stemmons Expressway and went up around to see if I could see anyone coming from across Stemmons and back that way, and I couldn't see anything that was of a suspicious nature, so I came back to the Texas School Book Depository... and so, I went to a gap that had not been filled, which was at the southwest corner." [198]

If the answers to these questions are "Yes", then the officer with the open microphone could possibly be B.W. Hargis, who was riding approximately 10 feet behind and immediately to the left of the President, and whose Warren Commission testimony is quoted above.[199]

Hargis' known and projected movements are generally consistent with all the analyses of the motorcycle noise.[200] Were his activities to be in total agreement with these analyses, it might reasonably be argued that the two sets of data had been manipulated to fit a preconceived theory. However, Hargis' movements in the period of time surrounding the assassination and its aftermath answer most, if not all, of the outstanding questions about the identity of the motorcycle policeman with the jammed transmitter.

However, it must also be acknowledged that this scenario raises one new question: If Hargis was the source of the interference on Channel 1 between 12:28 and 12:33, how can one explain his Channel 2 conversation with the dispatcher at 12:34 in which he says: "A passer-by states the shots came from the Texas School Book Depository Building", in response to which the Dispatcher told Hargis to "Get all the information". While this seems to be prima facie evidence that Hargis' radio was (as it should have been) switched to Chanel 2, it is equally possible that Hargis simply transmitted this message over another police motorcycle or car radio, since Hargis undoubtedly parked his motorcycle near the TSBD and then moved around the area on foot. He could therefore easily have used another radio to make his transmission on Channel 2, a possibility reinforced in his HSCA interview of August 8, 1978, when Hargis said that "at no time" did he have reason to use his own radio. Indeed, if he used another radio to transmit the Channel 2 message, and his own motorcycle was parked nearby and was the source of the open microphone, it is quite possible that it caused the Hargis transmission to be heard over Channel 1.[201]

While the HSCA did take an active interest in Hargis, they seemed strangely anxious not to publicise the fact. In his 1981 book, HSCA Chief Counsel and

Staff Director G. Robert Blakey said that the Committee "did not contact Hargis, who was ill at the time of our investigation", a claim which was also made in the HSCA's final Report.[202] However, this claim is refuted by a footnote elsewhere in the HSCA's published evidence, which indicates that a HSCA staff interview with Hargis took place on October 26, 1977, and the same footnote shows a second HSCA staff interview with him was conducted on January 17, 1979.[203] Further searches of National Archives records established the existence of three contacts with Hargis: an "Outside Contact Report" dated October 26, 1977[204]; an interview report by Jack Moriarty dated August 8, 1978[205] (and not January 17, 1979), as incorrectly reported by the HSCA; and another interview with Hargis on December 29, 1978.[206]

HSCA investigators James Kelly and Harold Rose interviewed Hargis on October 26, 1977, and their interview report noted:

"Hargis said he pulled over to the curb at the grassy knoll. He got off the bike and went up the hill on the grass. He didn't see anyone with a gun, so he went over to the Texas School Book Depository and helped other police officers seal it off." There was no mention of his radio in this interview.

The August 8, 1978 interview report by investigator Jack Moriarty states in part:

"Hargis remained behind (in Dealey Plaza) parking his bike where it stood in the left side of Elm now about one half way down the hill. He ran to the grassy knoll and continued until he had reached the top section of the underpass. Finding nothing significant, he returned to his bike - still on the stand with the radio on (and working) and the engine off. He started the bike and drove back up Elm and parked just west of the front door where he joined Brewer as they became part of the effort to seal off this building... He remained there for 30 to 40 minutes... did overhear call for Tippit's shooting.... At no time did he have occasion to use his transmitter, nor the siren".

This implies that Hargis did not speak to the Dispatcher at 12:34, as indicated in the Channel 2 transcript. The reference to the Tippit shooting does not help to determine whether Hargis' radio was switched to Channel 1 or 2, since news of Tippit's shooting was broadcast on both channels at around 1:18 pm.

Finally, in his report of the December 29, 1978 interview, Jack Moriarty said that, to the best of Hargis' knowledge, "his radio was working OK – hadn't had trouble with his since they replaced the old tube-type with this new transistor model. Sticking transmitters were nothing new. Everyone had his problems at one time or another. (His radio and motor had been replaced about one year prior to the JFK visit)."

It is perhaps ironic that, on the same day that the crucial evidence of

Six | Unsound Acoustics?

Weiss, Aschkenasy and McLain was being presented to the HSCA, one of the Committee's investigators was interviewing Hargis about his radio, and his location at the time of each of the shots!

While there are discrepancies between Hargis' Warren Commission and HSCA interview accounts with regard to his exact movements both during and after his brief look for "anyone with a gun" on the grassy knoll area, these can possibly be explained by the passage of time (1964 to 1979) between the various accounts.

As the matter stands at the present time, the case for Hargis having the open microphone certainly seems to justify further investigation, which the Justice Department is committed to carrying out.

The similarity between Hargis' known movements and the sounds on the Channel 1 recording are obviously open to other interpretations. It may be argued that Officer Hargis, like Officer McLain, does not 'fit' the acoustical facts, since he was not in the locations where the sounds on the Channel 1 recording matched those from the 1978 reconstruction either. This fact, in addition to the fact that Hargis transmitted on Channel 2 between 12:34 and 13:35 (after he arrived at the Texas School Book Depository), cannot simply be dismissed. However, the following should be borne in mind before dismissing Hargis as the motorcyclist with the jammed transmitter:

- The detailed review by Professors Weiss and Aschkenasy of Dr. Barger's work for the HSCA was restricted to the third shot only;

- Unlike those of McLain, the actions of Officer Hargis correspond with those which must have occurred in order to generate the motorcycle engine noises found on the radio recording.

The foregoing notwithstanding, this author is anxious to emphasise that there is no suggestion whatsoever of any wrongdoing on the part of Officer Hargis, or that the open microphone was "jammed" deliberately. Indeed, the HSCA became aware that the very proximity of the microphone to the brake cable would occasionally activate the microphone button, simply by pulling the brake cable, which was located within a half-inch of the button.[207] The committee also heard how wear and tear on a gasket in the microphone could cause it to stick in the 'open' position.[208]

In an effort to resolve some of the questions surrounding the motorcycle engine noise, the author gave a copy of the open microphone recording to an acknowledged Harley-Davidson expert in May 2006.[209] The expert was told that it was a recording of what was believed to be one or more 2 and/or 3-wheel Harley Davidson police motorcycles from the 1960s, and he was asked to tell what (if anything) he could decipher from the recording. He was not given any details of what the recording was about until after he gave his opinion.

He reported that he could hear one motorcycle stopping, and then two or more motorcycles pulling away quickly; he was unable to tell whether it was a two or three-wheel Harley-Davidson that stopped, but – from the sound of the gear changes, which he said were on the older three-wheelers – he believed the ones pulling away were three-wheelers; and he said that, wherever the recording was made, there were a number of Harley-Davidsons in the vicinity of the recording device.

While no alternative scenarios involving any other motorcycles and (or) different shooter locations were ever officially identified, investigated or tested, there is evidence that the HSCA did consider some form of limited investigation.

On July 18, 1978, HSCA researcher Margo Jackson wrote a memo to Deputy Chief Counsel Gary Cornwell, in which she identified seven motorcycle officers who had taken part in the motorcade, but had not been contacted by the committee.[210] Seven days later, she followed this with another memo in which she specified a series of eleven questions relating to the officers' activities, their movements in the minutes prior to the shooting, and the use of their radios, which could be put to each of the seven officers.[211] It appears that only limited further action was taken, however.[212]

There is one serious problem with this tentative identification of Hargis as the officer with the open microphone. By comparing the impulse patterns on the Channel 1 recording with the patterns obtained during a test firing in Dealey Plaza on August 20, 1978, the HSCA acoustics experts were able to pinpoint the location of the motorcycle with the open microphone at the time each of the four shots were fired. These locations differ significantly from the known location of Hargis at each point. However, the HSCA carried out test firings from only two locations - the alleged "sniper's nest" on the sixth floor of the Book Depository, and a point behind the fence on the grassy knoll. It is therefore within the bounds of possibility that, if other firing points were used, the resulting impulse patterns might point to Hargis' known locations.

Alternatively, it should still be possible to perform the experiment in reverse. By plotting the known locations of Officer Hargis at the time of each shot, and using the impulse patterns on the DPD Channel 1 recording, the point of origin of each shot could be calculated. If the points of origin thus identified were reasonable (i.e. not the middle of Elm Street or some other such unlikely place), the possibility that the open microphone was on Hargis' motorcycle could not be ruled out, and would be strengthened by the similarity between the engine noises subsequently identified by Steve Barber in the recording, and Hargis' known movements after the shooting.

The timing of the crosstalk
Although the Ramsey Panel reported that the "Hold everything secure" phrase

occurred almost one minute after the actual shooting took place, there is evidence to suggest that it may actually have occurred significantly later, thereby implying that the acoustic "impulses" also occurred much later than even the Ramsey Panel believed.

Dallas professional photographer Mel McIntire took a still picture as the leading vehicles emerged on the west side of the Triple Underpass, which was located some 200 yards further west on Elm Street from the spot where the fatal shot hit the President.[213] Research by Dealey Plaza UK member John Hovland indicates that the photograph was taken between 19 and 20 seconds after the headshot.[214]

McIntire's photograph shows the presidential limousine just ahead of Curry's car. Behind them, Officer Martin has begun to emerge from the Underpass, and only then – 20 seconds after the shooting – is Officer Chaney seen for the first time. It should be remembered that Chief Curry said that he did not know what had happened until Chaney rode up to his car, and told him through the open window; and Chaney is still approximately 70 yards behind Curry at this time.

Unfortunately, this is also the last photograph (movie or still) of the motorcade that can assist in this context, so any timing reconstruction will have to depend on witness testimony and common sense.

It is this author's firm belief that the motorcade came to a halt somewhere in the area of the Stemmons access ramp, thereby allowing Chaney to catch up with Curry. Consider the following facts:

- DPD Officer Earle Brown, on the railway overpass above the Stemmons Freeway about 100 yards from the access ramp, told Dallas newsman Earl Golz in March 1980 that he saw the limousine and four other cars stop on the access ramp for at least 30 seconds. Brown later repeated the story for Gary Mack;[215]

- Officer Doug Jackson told Mack in October 1981 that he and Officer Jim Chaney raced after the lead car, caught up with it after about 30 seconds, and Chaney spoke through the car window to Curry;[216]

- Curry told yet another researcher in 1979 that Chaney caught up with him as they began climbing the Stemmons on-ramp;[217]

- Curry told Mack that he slowed down in order to find out if anyone had been hit, as he was unaware that anyone had been hit until Chaney told him. He said he then had to tell the limousine driver, Secret Service Agent Bill Greer, how to get to Parkland Hospital, before issuing his "Go to the hospital" order (the one to which McLain said he responded);[218]

- Greer said he had "no prior knowledge of the motorcade route, and was simply following the lead car up ahead".[219] As Greer had passed the lead car as they emerged from the Underpass, he would have had to stop to check where he was going; Curry told the Warren Commission that he did not transmit on Channel 2 until after he spoke to Chaney;[220]

- DPD Officer Courson said Curry, in the lead car, had slowed sufficiently for him to catch the lead car on the Stemmons access road.[221] Recall that Courson was 100-120 feet behind McLain in the motorcade, and McLain was himself about 140 feet behind the presidential limousine when the shots were fired. (Courson was approximately 80 yards behind the President at the time of the fatal headshot).

In summary:

It is generally agreed that it took the limousine 10 seconds to reach the Triple Underpass, and 4 or so seconds to go through it, and that McIntire's photo was taken about 20 seconds after the head shot.
- It is also generally agreed that it took about 30 seconds for Chaney to reach Curry, catching him somewhere on the Stemmons access ramp;

- Chaney (or Sgt. Ellis, who claimed Chaney told him, and he told Curry) then spoke to Curry through the right-hand window of the lead car;

- Curry then told Greer, the limousine driver, where they were going, and to follow the motorcycle escort riders;

- Curry then issued his "Go to the hospital, officers" order.

- Placing all this in context with the other known timings, the "Hold everything secure..." order from Sheriff Decker appears 67.5 seconds after Curry's order, putting it just over 2 minutes after the shooting – exactly when Decker said he gave the order.[222]

Based on this data, and accepting the validity of the "Hold everything..." crosstalk, the sequence of events would be as follows:

```
0 seconds    - Shots fired in Plaza
10 seconds   - Limousine reached Underpass
15 seconds   - Limousine emerges from Underpass
20 seconds   - McIntyre snaps his photo
30 seconds   - Chaney reaches Curry, tells him what happened
```
Delay of up to 30 seconds while Curry talks to Greer, etc.

Six | Unsound Acoustics?

1 minute   - Curry issues his "Go to the hospital, officers...." order
2 mins 1 sec - [HSCA impulses begin]
2 mins 7 secs - Decker's "Hold everything secure..." order

Sheriff Decker, who was riding in the lead car with Chief Curry and Secret Service Agents Lawson and Sorrels, told the Warren Commission that he did not transmit on Channel 2 until they were on the Stemmons Freeway, one-and-a-half to 2 minutes after the shooting. Decker's radio message, as our timeline establishes, was transmitted at least 2 minutes after the final shot was fired, if we accept the Ramsey Panel's timing of events. This is wholly consistent with what Decker told the Warren Commission.

On the face of it, this analysis clearly supports the Ramsey Panel's version of events rather than the HSCA's conclusions, since Curry's order to "Go to the hospital..." occurs before the HSCA impulses appear on the Channel 1 recording. If this were truly the case, then whatever caused the impulse patterns on the dictabelt recording, it certainly was not gunfire in Dealey Plaza.

So which version do we – or should we – believe? According to U.S. Navy physicist G. Paul Chambers, the high-profile composition of the Ramsey Panel "is no proof against being wrong", since even established Nobel-winning scientists are not always correct when they challenge the findings of a fellow scientist in his or her area of expertise, especially when that work is supported by other experts in the same field. According to Chambers, there is a one-in-sixteen-million chance that the acoustics analysis could match up the timing and shot sequence in the Zapruder film by chance. In addition, the chances of six microphones randomly matching up in the correct sequence with the journey along Elm Street is approximately 1 in 720, coupled with the very small probability that the timing of this sequence would randomly match the known speed of the motorcade on Elm Street, leads Chambers to conclude that there is only about one chance in eleven billion that the acoustical impulses found on the DPD radio recording could have been caused by random noise, rather than gunfire in Dealey Plaza at the time of the assassination.[223]

That still does not resolve our dilemma, however. On the basis of scientific studies and an acoustical reconstruction in Dealey Plaza, Dr. James Barger and his colleagues testified to finding evidence of four gunshots on the dictabelts in 1978. Three years later, Professor Norman Ramsey and his panel of experts verified that crosstalk from Channel 2 was found on Channel 1 at the point where Dr. Barger had found the shot impulses – but the Channel 2 transmission in question occurred more than 30 seconds after the assassination. Therefore, the Ramsey Panel's findings were in clear conflict with those of the HSCA's acoustics experts. As Ramsey Panel member Richard Garwin said, "Both sets of workers could not be correct."[224]

Or could they? Could experts like BBN or the NAS Panel really get it so wrong, or were one (or both) bodies looking at evidence which was somehow contaminated?

The belt overlap question

As mentioned earlier in this chapter, the configuration of the DPD Channel 1 radio equipment was designed to ensure that when one dictabelt ended, a second one would start recording automatically, thereby ensuring that there was no break in recording. In addition, to ensure continuity of recording, about 20 seconds of the end of each belt was also recorded on the beginning on the next belt, so that nothing was lost as the machine switched from one belt to the next. Finally, the equipment was also fitted with a "Belt Change Signal" light, which indicated when one or both of the dictabelts needed to be changed.

In April 2006, this author obtained digitised copies of Belts #11 and #12, which had been made in April 2004 by the National Archives (NARA) for former Ramsey Panel member Paul Horowitz. Belt #11 recorded the transmissions from 12:40 to 13:12, and Belt #12 covered the period between 13:12 and 13:44.

When researcher Mary Ferrell obtained a copy of the Channel 1 recording in 1969, she made it available to her fellow-researcher Arch Kimbrough, who began the unenviable task of preparing a verbatim transcript of the entire 2-hour recording, from 12:14 to 2:13 pm.[225] This task was completed in December 1969, and resulted in a 71-page typed transcript, which is without doubt the most complete transcript ever made of the DPD recordings.[226]

The FBI transcript, made from the original Dictabelts in 1964,[227] and Arch Kimbrough's 1969 transcript[228] both show Belt #12 starting with a call to the Dispatcher from "212", Officer Spradlin. Despite the poor quality of the April 2004 recording (due to the now poor quality of the sound on the ageing and physically deteriorating original Dictabelt), this author's transcript of this same period from the digital recordings of these two belts is as follows:

Dispatcher:	45, Signal 9, 4916 Live Oak, manager's office. 1:12.
45:	45.
Unknown:	... on 5.
Dispatcher:	Did you get it, 45?
45:	Repeat.
Dispatcher:	Signal 9, manager's office, 4916 Live..

------------------(End of Dictabelt #11 / Start of Dictabelt #12) -----------------

Unknown:	{Garbled} "Go Ahead" (?)
Dispatcher:	{Garbled}
Unknown:	10-4.
212:	212.

Six | Unsound Acoustics?

Dispatcher: {Garbled}
212: Have you got another squad that can meet that unit at the dead end of Laws? I'm blocked in over here and can't get out.

The first three transmissions at the beginning of Belt #12 do not appear in any of the transcripts (probably because they are so garbled), nor do those three transmissions appear on any versions of the recordings generally available to the research community. They clearly are not the last three transmissions from Belt #11, and there is no other evidence to suggest that Belt #12 began before Belt #11 ended.

Spectrograms made by the author of the last 3 transmissions on Belt #11 and the first 3 transmissions on Belt #12 are also clearly different – the combined auditory and digital analyses therefore seem to establish the absence of any overlap between the end of Belt #11 and the start of Belt #12.[229] So what happened to the inbuilt overlap between Belts #11 and #12? Is it possible that Belt #12 might not be an original dictabelt, created on November 22, 1963?

It has been suggested that, in the confusion that prevailed in DPD Headquarters on the afternoon of the assassination, no one re-loaded the recorders with fresh belts as Belts #10 and #11 became full. Then, someone realised what had happened, managed to perform the re-load of the Dictaphone machine in exactly 20 seconds, so that there was no overlap, and (presumably) no loss of data, either.

This explanation is certainly possible – but the Dictaphone A2TC controller had a 'Belt Change Signal' warning light, designed to prevent exactly such an eventuality, and the Communications Room was hardly at the centre of the mayhem in police headquarters that afternoon (although it was located on the third floor, where much of the activity took place).[230]

After Oswald was shot in police custody on November 24, and secure in the knowledge that no criminal trial relating to the assassination would therefore take place, the Dallas Police appear to have become very careless with the evidence, as a result of which much of it was allegedly taken and/or duplicated as souvenirs.

There have been suggestions that Belts #11 and 12, which were recording during the period of time encompassing the murder of Officer J.D. Tippit, may have been altered for reasons relating to Tippit's murder.

At 12:45 pm, the Channel 1 Dispatcher instructed Officers Nelson (87) and Tippit (78) to "move into Central Oak Cliff area".[231] Nine minutes later, at 12:54, the Dispatcher called Tippit, and asked: "You are in the Oak Cliff area, are you not?"[232] Tippit replied that he was at "Lancaster and Eighth", to which the Dispatcher responded, "You will be at large for any emergency that comes in".[233] However, Officer Nelson told Dallas researcher Larry Harris in 1978 that he was told by the Dispatcher at 12:45 to go to the Texas School Book Depository, and not Oak Cliff, as the dictabelt evidence shows.[234]

Another unidentified officer told author Henry Hurt in March 1984 that he believed Tippit was killed as a result of "a volatile personal situation" and felt that some evidence (such as the hulls from Oswald's gun) had been tampered with in the DPD property room, and that the dictabelts may have been altered as well to make the story fit together neatly.[235]

Finally, Prof. Murray Miron of Syracuse University, New York, a renowned linguist and frequent FBI consultant, examined the transmissions in question for researcher Paul Hoch in late 1984. In Professor Miron's opinion, "the communications directed to Officer Tippit are anomalously at variance with the other transmissions" on the DPD recordings, and "have the appearance of transmissions made more for an audience's benefit than those for which the intent is to convey instructions." Professor Miron did emphasise that his analysis did not preclude an innocent explanation, but said that the query regarding Tippit's location was "rhetorical rather than questioning", in his opinion.[236]

And if Belt #11 and/or Belt #12 are not originals, were other belts – including Belt #10, which was recording at the time of the assassination – also duplicated?

The history of the DPD recordings

In a HSCA executive session on August 3, 1978, Dr. Barger told the committee that while they had "the Dictabelt which is the recording medium of the police dispatch radio", they were "actually analyzing a tape recording" as the original dictabelt recording was very scratchy and noisy, and the needle skipped when it was played. He said that "the magnetic tape recording that we have was made of that dictabelt a long time ago before the Dictabelt was severely distorted and there are no needle jumps or anything on it. It is quite a good recording". He said that while they had the capability of verifying that the copy was a "faithful and non-tampered with" copy of the dictabelt, "we have not done that".[237]

Dr. Barger also expressed the view that "whoever took the precaution of (copying) the dictabelt early on was doing us a great favor. If we had to do this (acoustics study) from the dictabelt we would have found nothing, I am quite certain. I mean as it now exists. It has been played too often." Under further questioning, Barger admitted that he did not know when or by whom the tape recording was made, claiming that it was among material received from the Dallas Police Department.[238]

In order to validate the claim that the tape recording received from the HSCA was an "original dub made by the DPD", BBN made their own magnetic tape recording from the dictabelts provided to them.[239] The date on which this recording was created is not known, but the foregoing comments by Dr. Barger would suggest that it had not been done prior to August 1978. The whereabouts of that BBN recording is now unknown, although it does not appear to be among the HSCA records at NARA.[240] According to Dr. Barger, comparison of this recording with the DPD tape recording showed the two

SIX | UNSOUND ACOUSTICS?

tapes to be "virtually identical",[241] and Barger's report indicates that the DPD recording was subsequently used during the BBN study.[242]

When Weiss and Aschkenasy were asked to independently review Barger's work, they were given a comprehensive body of data, including BBN's own recording from the dictabelts and the "virtually identical" DPD tape recording. The dictabelts themselves, however, were not given to them.[243]

We therefore know that a tape-recorded copy of the key dictabelt was the foundation upon which the work of the HSCA's experts was based.

When the Ramsey Panel began their deliberations in 1981, they too did not have access to the original dictabelts. The Ramsey Panel report simply states that the panel "obtained access to the original Gray Audograph and Dictaphone recordings from the Department of Justice".[244] It now appears, however, that it was not until December 9, 1981 that the panel had access to the original recordings[245], weeks after they had begun to draft their final report.[246] Prior to December 9, the panel had been working from tape recordings provided by Jim Bowles and Dr. Barger.[247] Furthermore, their access to the original dictabelt material was apparently limited to its presence at a meeting organised by Professor Ramsey with the FBI for 9:15 on the morning of December 9. Among the issues to be addressed at the meeting were an examination of the "original Dallas Police Department Channel 1 Dictabelt" for "physical evidence of possible superposed recordings", and the creation of "a fresh copy of Channel 1 from 12:28... through 12:37".[248] The "original Dictabelt" was brought to the meeting by Roger Cubbage of the U.S. Justice Department (DOJ), and retained by him after the meeting.[249] According to information provided to this author by Michael O'Dell, a tape copy of the original dictabelt for the period 12:28 to 12:34 was made at FBI headquarters that day, given to Professor Ramsey, and returned by him on December 18.[250]

It is important to note therefore, that despite the claim that they had access to the original data, the panel "never worked with" the original recordings.[251] According to panel member Charles Rader, "nobody on our committee ever had custody of any of the dictabelts. There was always an official of the DOJ or FBI who controlled the belts and I was never alone with them".[252]

So what is known about the provenance of these tape-recorded copies which were used – and which were the basis on which vitally important conclusions were reached - by both the HSCA and the Ramsey Panel? And what of the provenance of the original dictabelts themselves?

In an interview with HSCA investigators Jim Kelly and Harold Rose on October 20, 1977, Channel 1 dispatcher Murray Jackson said that the dictabelts recorded by the DPD on the day of the assassination "were sequestered almost immediately after the shift ended".[253] Jackson's account is corroborated by that of his supervisor, Chief Dispatcher Gerald Henslee, who was interviewed by Jack Moriarty for the HSCA on August 12, 1978.[254] Sergeant Henslee told

Moriarty that, "about 5 pm" on the afternoon of the assassination, Deputy Chief George Lumpkin (who was in overall charge of the Service Division, of which the dispatcher's office was a part) told him to put all the Channel 1 and 2 recordings into sealed envelopes and bring them to Lumpkin's office.[255] According to Henslee, the recordings were then turned over to the FBI, who later returned them to Lumpkin.[256]

In March 2003, Dr. Bruce Ledford, formerly on the faculty of East Texas State University (now Texas A&M – Commerce), placed a three-CD set of DPD recordings for auction on the Internet. According to Dr. Ledford:

"In 1976... I consulted with a colleague from the Physics Department of the University. This colleague, who was a former FBI agent in the Dallas area, was asked, as I recall, by the DPD to transfer their transmissions... from dictabelt to audio tape. In 1963 the dictabelt was the storage medium. For some reason unknown to me, the signal was on the belt in reverse. As I understand it, because the special techniques required to make the transfer were within my colleague's area of expertise, he was asked to make the transfer... I have continued over the years to honor the request of my colleague to remain anonymous concerning this audio."[257]

There is one difficulty with this scenario. Dr. Ledford, who passed away at the age of 65 on July 3, 2007,[258] had always refused to divulge the identity of his source. This author's 2006 correspondence with Texas A&M produced a list of all those on the Physics Faculty from 1975 to 1977, but a comparison of the names on that list with those listed in the FBI's Field Office Personnel file for Dallas and ten other field offices in the Dallas/Fort Worth area at the time of the assassination shows no matches.[259] Was Dr. Ledford going to extreme lengths to protect his source? FBI Supervisor Richard Rogge, who was responsible for the initial FBI investigation in Dallas, told this author that the FBI made no copies of the dictabelts for the Dallas Police, nor did he know anything about an agent who subsequently worked at Texas A&M.[260]

If the FBI did have early access to the dictabelts, they must have returned them within a few days, because Secret Service records show that on or before November 29, 1963, Chief Lumpkin provided "the Police recordings" to Special Agents Roger C. Warner and Elmer W. Moore for "transcription".[261] Rather than transcribing the recordings himself, Warner copied them to tape. This is the first known tape-recorded copy of the dictabelts, apart from those mentioned by Ledford.

In 1970, researcher Paul Hoch asked both the Secret Service and the National Archives to search for this Secret Service tape-recording, but no trace of it could be found.[262] The HSCA also tried unsuccessfully to pursue the issue of Secret Service access to the dictabelts. Staff researcher Margo Jackson contacted

SIX | UNSOUND ACOUSTICS?

Tom Ferrell of the Secret Service on January 24, 1978 and "inquired about material regarding the filtering, rerecording, and transcription requested to be performed on the above tapes".[263] Ferrell replied that he "would have to check with the Assistant Director of the Washington Protective Research Section, whose name he would not disclose", and promised to call Ms. Jackson back.[264] Unfortunately, there is no record of any further communication with or from Ferrell. On September 23, 1981, Paul Hoch suggested to Professor Ramsey that a search for Warner's tape – requested by the Ramsey Panel rather than by an individual researcher – might be worthwhile.[265] There is, however, no evidence to suggest that the Ramsey Panel made such a request, or that any search was made on their behalf.

In late 1982, this author again requested both the Secret Service and the National Archives to renew their search for the tape made by Warner, and the further copy made by the Protective Research Section in Washington. However, no trace of either recording could be found.[266]

As previously noted, the FBI apparently obtained the Channel 1 and 2 recordings from Deputy Chief Lumpkin on the evening of the assassination, and when the recordings were returned by them to Lumpkin, he gave them back to Sergeant Henslee "for complete transcribing".[267] This exercise took 3 to 4 days to complete, and is undoubtedly the same edited transcript of the Channel 1 and 2 transmissions which Henslee prepared in the first few days of December 1963, and which his testimony before the Warren Commission on April 8, 1964 clearly states was made directly from the original recordings – "They were prepared from the tapes on the Channel 1. We have a tape on channel 1, and we have a record on channel 2. Two separate tape records, but they are prepared from those records and tapes".[268] When Henslee finished making the transcript, he returned the recordings to Lumpkin.[269] The record shows that Henslee's Channel 1 transcript was completed on December 3, and was given to Police Chief Jesse Curry on December 5, 1963. Curry gave the transcript to Secret Service Inspector Thomas Kelley, who forwarded it to his superior under date of December 6. The transcript was later entered into the records of the Warren Commission as Sawyer Exhibit B on April 8, 1964 at the time of Henslee's testimony.[270]

By December 19, 1963, the DPD internal investigation into the murder of Officer J.D. Tippit and the lack of security in police headquarters at the time of Oswald's murder by Jack Ruby was ended.[271] All materials gathered in the course of that investigation, including "tape recordings of the Dallas dispatcher tapes" which consisted of "a tape recording and a Dictabelt tape" was handed over to Chief Curry.[272] The origin of this tape recording is currently unknown, but it is not the "Bowles tape" which, by implication at least, was used by the HSCA and the Ramsey Panel as their 'control copy' of the dictabelts.

Former DPD Communications Supervisor, Sergeant Jim Bowles said he made copies of the dictabelts in March 1964 "with a nice reel to reel tape recorder which the FBI furnished to me" before making a transcript from the original dictabelts which "were in as good a condition as you would expect considering the fact that the FBI had tried to transcribe them using a single stylus...".[273]

On March 20, 1964, Dallas Police Inspector J. Herbert Sawyer provided the Dallas FBI with another transcript of the Channel 1 transmissions, which they forwarded to FBI Headquarters in Washington on March 23.[274] As already noted, it was prepared by Bowles following a request from the FBI on March 6,[275] and identified the police officers using Channel 1 by their radio "call number" rather than by name. On April 7, FBI Director J. Edgar Hoover sent the transcript to the Warren Commission,[276] and it subsequently became Warren Commission Exhibit (WCE) 705 on April 22, during the testimony of Dallas Police Chief Jesse Curry.[277] It is this March transcript to which Bowles was undoubtedly referring in his 1980 interviews with the FBI, when he said that he prepared a transcript for the FBI after they had experienced "difficulty in preparing a transcript of those recordings due to a lack of familiarity with the Dallas Police Department radio parlance and terminology".[278]

Bowles made four reel-to-reel tape-recorded copies of the dictabelts prior to making the above transcript in March 1964.[279] He recalls that the dictabelts were still in very good condition at that time, although "they were well worn when I finished".[280] This is hardly surprising, given the cumbersome process which he had to follow in making the transcript and his four tape copies of the dictabelts.

The DPD only had one Dictaphone machine, which used a switching mechanism to alternate between two drives so that a new belt could automatically begin recording just before the previous belt ended. Using that Dictaphone machine to make direct copies of the dictabelts would necessitate disabling the switching mechanism,[281] so Bowles obtained permission from Chief Lumpkin to rent a second Dictaphone machine, which handled only one belt at a time, and was strictly a playback machine.[282] Then, according to the FBI:

"It was necessary to stop and start the playback machine many times in order to prepare an accurate transcript. The stylus... was inserted into previously recorded track on many occasions and in many different locations. It is Captain Bowles' opinion that the playback process, including the numerous placings of the stylus on the previously recorded track, may have created degradations of the original recorded material, as well as actually adding new impulses to the track... Captain Bowles stated that he made a reel-to-reel tape recording of the original dictaphone belts using a Wollensak recorder provided him by the FBI."[283]

In his 1979 manuscript, Bowles again raised the intriguing possibility, hinted

Six | Unsound Acoustics?

at in the FBI report above, that he had inadvertently added "impulses" to the original dictabelts. He said that he had made reel-to-reel tapes of the original recordings before preparing a transcript for the Warren Commission. These copies, he said, were made to preserve the contents the dictabelts, which had already been played repeatedly. He pointed out that repeated playing considerably reduced the quality of the recorded sounds, and that "repeated lowering of the replay needle... added minute dimples" to the belts. Bowles suggested that it was possible that these dimples might have been detected as impulse patterns by the sensitive equipment used by the HSCA's acoustical scientists, but questioned whether these patterns were only identified as gunshots "where it was essential for gunshots to appear".[284]

Of the four reel-to-reel tape copies he made in March 1964, Bowles kept one for his own files, one was given to Chief Curry, and the other two (one "filtered" and the other "unfiltered") were given to the FBI.[285] One of the FBI's tapes, which became the Warren Commission's official copy of the dictabelts, was later deposited with the Commission's files at the National Archives, from where it was reported "mislaid" in 1976.[286] The whereabouts of the other FBI tape copy of the dictabelts is currently unknown, although Bowles told Gary Mack in 1982 – and this author in October 1983 – that he understood it was sent to a laboratory for analysis, and he heard that it was or might have been in Oklahoma.[287]

What do we know about those tape recordings, made by Bowles in March 1964?

In 2007, this author obtained details of the 10-inch reels of tape onto which Bowles had made copies of his own 1964 copies of the dictabelts for the Sixth Floor Museum in Dallas in 1988. A similar set of copies of Bowles' 1964 tapes was made available by Bowles to author Dale Myers when he was writing his 1998 book, "Without Malice".[288]

The recordings provided to the Sixth Floor Museum were "dubs made in 1988 from either his original tapes or his copies", and consisted of four reels of tape covering the period from 11:42 am to 01:57 pm on Channel 1, and four further reels, from 09:00 am to 01:33 pm, for Channel 2.[289] The recordings given to Myers, however, consisted of eight reels covering the period from 11:42 am to 02:13 pm on Channel 1, and a further ten reels, covering the period 09:15 am to 03:14 pm for Channel 2.[290] However, there is considerable redundancy and duplication in the reels provided to Myers, and Myers believes that what he received was "a second generation dub of the original reel-to-reel recordings (third generation removed from the dictabelts) and were probably made at the Dallas CBS affiliate in the mid-sixties."[291]

DPD Chief Curry retired on March 10, 1966, and was succeeded by Chief Charles Batchelor.[292] In a locked metal filing cabinet outside his new office, Batchelor found the evidence which had been turned over to Curry when the internal DPD review was concluded in December 1963.[293]

On some unspecified date in 1969, Batchelor called Paul McCaghren, then Director of the DPD's Intelligence Division and a former member of Curry's investigative team, into his office and told him to "take charge of the material. Make sure no unauthorized person comes in contact with the material."[294] McCaghren kept the evidence in a box, measuring 2.5 by 1.5 feet and 1 foot deep, in his office until 1971 or 1972, at which time he decided to remove the box to his home for safekeeping, where it remained until 1978.[295] According to McCaghren, he "had control of this property at all times, from 1969 until this year (1978). No one, no one tampered with that material."[296]

But what happened during the three-year period from 1966 to 1969?

Sometime prior to early 1967, a recording of the DPD Channel 1 and Channel 2 radio transmissions was given to author Judy Bonner who was, at the time, writing her book "Investigation Of A Homicide", apparently in association with DPD Sergeant Gerald Hill, himself a former news reporter.[297]

The recording given to Ms. Bonner originated from Sgt. Hill, but it is unclear as to whether it was a tape recording or the original dictabelts themselves. In an interview with HSCA investigator Jack Moriarty on August 12, 1978, retired DPD radio dispatcher Gerald Henslee said that "in the fall of 1968" he received a call from Judy Bonner, who wanted him to transcribe "the original tapes" for her. Henslee agreed to carry out the transcription, and Ms. Bonner subsequently delivered the "tapes" to his apartment. According to Henslee, he did not know where the recordings had been "between November, 1963 and Fall of 1968".[298] While it would appear logical to assume that Ms. Bonner only received a tape-recorded copy of the original dictabelts, Henslee's reference to the chain of possession of "the original tapes" might be indicative of the fact that Sgt. Hill somehow managed to provide Ms. Bonner with the original recordings. However, Henslee's failure to comment on the fact that original evidence was in the hands of a journalist, and the fact that he does not mention the return of the material to the DPD, leads one to believe that Ms. Bonner only had a tape-recording made from the dictabelts. [It should also be noted that Ms. Bonner's book was published in 1969, which might suggest that she had the transcript made in late 1967, rather than the fall of 1968, as Henslee believed].[299] Gerald Henslee subsequently made a taped copy of Ms. Bonner's recordings, along with a copy of his own typed transcript, available to Dallas researcher Mary Ferrell in June 1969.[300]

It was from that Mary Ferrell tape that most of those in the hands of researchers until the early 1980's originated.[301] According to Gary Mack, now the Curator at The Sixth Floor Museum at Dealey Plaza, the tape that Mary Ferrell received in June 1969 was, at best, a third-generation copy, and is probably fourth-generation.[302]

According to HSCA Chief Counsel G. Robert Blakey, HSCA investigator Jack Moriarty "located" Paul McCaghren on or about February 11, 1978.[303] McCaghren's story is slightly different, however. He said that he was sitting

Six | Unsound Acoustics?

in on an interview, which Moriarty was conducting with a former colleague, when he mentioned to Moriarty that he had some material which might be of interest to the HSCA.[304] The accuracy of this version is confirmed by Moriarty's interview notes, which also disclose that the interview in question took place on March 10, and not February 11, as recalled by Blakey.[305] Moriarty's notes indicate that McCaghren gave him "the three original tapes of channel 1 and 2", along with transcripts of those tapes.[306] The tapes were part of a large collection of material including reports, maps, photographs and films, which Moriarty inventoried in McCaghren's office on the following afternoon.[307]

The 2-page, 46-item inventory prepared by Jack Moriarty on March 11, 1978 shows that McCaghren provided six Channel 1 transcripts, five Channel 2 transcripts, and three "original" tapes, which were stored in a brown envelope.[308] Tape 1 was a copy of Channel 2 from 10 am to 5:12 pm, and tapes 2 and 3 consisted of a copy of Channel 1 from 9:45 am to 2:15 pm – the first part of the recording was on tape 3, and the remainder was on tape 2.[309]

Interestingly, the duration of these tape-recorded copies of the original Channel 1 dictabelts suggests that they are not the ones produced by Jim Bowles in March 1964. As previously noted, Bowles gave copies of his 1964 recordings to the Sixth Floor Museum and to author Dale Myers, and they covered the period 11:42 am to 2:13 pm. Furthermore, Bowles published a transcript of his 1964 recordings in his manuscript, and that transcript also begins at 11:42 am, although it ends at 12:36 pm.[310] Finally, Bowles provided a partial Channel 1 transcript to the Ramsey Panel, covering the period 12:29 to 12:36 pm.[311]

According to the records of the HSCA, two tape recordings of Channel 1, obtained by Jack Moriarty from Paul McCaghren, were placed in the HSCA's Security Office by staff researcher Margo Jackson on April 24, 1978.[312] A similar receipt for one Channel 2 tape recording also appears in the records of the HSCA, indicating that it, too, was placed in the Security Office on April 24, 1978.[313] The author's subsequent efforts to contact Ms. Jackson in an effort to elicit any further clarification have been unsuccessful.[314]

The Channel 1 tape recording, which McCaghren gave to the HSCA, was subsequently identified by BBN as an "original dub" made by the DPD.[315] McCaghren's HSCA testimony indicates that the tape was among the material given to Chief Curry in 1963 by his internal investigation team.[316] [Although not supported by the inventory listing, McCaghren has subsequently claimed that there were "several tape copies of the belts" among the material handed over to the HSCA[317]]. Either way, however, the recording given to the HSCA by McCaghren was made from the original dictabelts, according to BBN.[318]

The HSCA's final report says that in May 1978 the Committee contracted with BBN to perform the acoustical analysis.[319] The report further states:

"Prior to the BBN analysis of the original Dictabelt and tapes, the firm was given a tape that had been supplied to the Committee by a Warren Commission critic... BBN determined that this tape was a second generation copy... it was not used in the BBN work. The Dallas Police dispatch materials given to BBN to analyse in May 1978 were as follows: The original Dictabelt recordings made on November 22, 1963, of transmissions over channel 1; A tape recording of channel 1 Dictabelts; A tape recording of transmissions over channel 2."[320]

BBN's Chief Scientist, Dr. James Barger, tells a somewhat different story, however. Both during his public testimony in September and December 1978 as well as in his final report to the HSCA, Dr. Barger claimed to have received nothing from the HSCA prior to May 1978, and only received the McCaghren material two months later, in July. The following excerpts from his testimony serve to illustrate this anomaly:

"When were you first approached by this Committee with the Dallas Police dispatch tape? I believe it was in May of 1978";[321]

– "On May 12, 1978 (BBN received from the HSCA) the following material: Tape recordings reportedly made of the sounds in Dealey Plaza around 12:30 pm on November 22, 1963";[322]

– "The first tape we received on May 12... had a very scratchy overlay of needle noise, indicating that it was a very poor or multiple-generation dub of a recording."[323]

– "In July, the Committee gave us an electromagnetic tape recording that was identified as an original dub made by the DPD, as well as the original Dictabelt record."[324]

One might reasonably expect that the chain of possession of such vital material would be carefully analysed and documented by the HSCA. Not so, however. The only public record of any such study appears in the transcript of the public testimony of DPD motorcycle Officer H.B. McLain on December 29, 1978. During McLain's testimony, two Committee members asked a series of questions regarding the authenticity of the dictabelt evidence. The replies to these questions, by Chief Counsel Blakey and Deputy Chief Counsel Cornwell, were as follows:

– "Paul McCaghren – he was an officer in the Dallas Police Department, and he had custody of a large number of records relating to the Kennedy assassination, and he retained that custody in a large trunk, and when the material was turned over to one of our investigators, Jack Moriarty, it was taken from that same trunk. I might indicate that an effort was made to match the transcript that we have of channels 1 and 2 to the material appearing on both the Dictabelt and the tape belt that we have. Consequently, the authenticity of the tape appears to be adequate, appears to have been adequately established..."[325]

– "...the Dictabelt that was found among this material is the same kind of Dictabelt that the Dallas Police Department was using at that time..."[326]

– "What appears on the Dictabelt and the tape recording of the Dictabelt are indeed the same sounds, the same information that we have based on the transcripts that we had of channel 1 and channel 2 that go back to 1963-64..."[327]

– "The transmissions on the tapes do correspond with the Warren Commission testimony of various officers who described doing certain things and then reporting it over the radio, and therefore there is substantial corroboration of that nature, that the kinds of transmissions we have on these tapes were of the events that were actually happening on November 22."[328]

So, the HSCA's "chain of possession" began when Paul McCaghren took possession of the evidence in 1969, and was based on the fact that the existing recordings were consistent with the DPD and FBI transcripts of 1963 and 1964, insofar as those transcripts could be roughly reconciled with the testimony of police officers before the Warren Commission!

Not only was the chain-of-possession never properly established, however, but if one carefully examines the FBI's July 1964 "verbatim" transcript carefully, and compares it to the actual recorded radio transmissions, the accuracy and completeness of the transcript comes into serious question, as does the HSCA's claim that the recordings they received were consistent with the transcripts.

The FBI transcript suggests that dictabelt #4 began at 11:37 and ended at 11:51, with dictabelt #5 beginning at 11:51 and ending at 12:40.[329] However, a study by the author showed that of the last 144 actual transmissions on dictabelt #4, only 28 (19%) were transcribed by the FBI. Furthermore, the final transcribed transmission on dictabelt #4 occurred between 11:50 and 11:51, but the first transmission transcribed from dictabelt #5 does not actually occur until 12:06 – almost 180 transmissions later. Analysis of the number of actual transmissions and the number of transcribed entries reveals that only 15% of the transmissions on belt 5 (approximately 100 out of 600 transmissions) were transcribed, further emphasising the inadequacy of the FBI transcript.

Is it any wonder that the validity of the HSCA's acoustics evidence is still being questioned when that "scientific acoustical evidence" was based on such flimsy and unauthenticated tape recordings?

As previously noted, the Ramsey Panel was also working primarily from tape recordings provided to them by Jim Bowles and Dr. Barger.[330] It was not until December 9, 1981 that "a fresh copy of Channel 1 from 12:28... through 12:37" was made from the original dictabelt recording.[331] In February 1983, researcher Steve Barber made available a copy of that December 1981 copy, which he had obtained from a member of the panel.[332] The copy made available by Barber was described as a "copy of a high-quality copy of the original Channel 1 dictabelt", according to Professor Ramsey's narration at the beginning of the recording.[333] Furthermore, Professor Ramsey subsequently confirmed to this author that the high-quality copy used in making the recording given to Steve Barber "was made by the FBI at our request from the original Dictabelt."[334]

While all indications are that the Ramsey Panel saw – but never had direct and unrestricted access to – the original dictabelt recordings, one small and apparently innocuous event demonstrates the inaccuracy of the official records.

Dr. Barger testified before the HSCA that the crucial dictabelt was "a plastic continuous blue colored belt that was marked as 'Being recorded from Channel 1' in a white marking pencil".[335] He made no reference to any other handwriting on the belt.

The Ramsey Panel reported that there was "considerable writing with a china marking pencil on the surface of the Dictabelt. The markings give in one handwriting '11-22-63, PL2' and an encircled '10'. The times 12 5 and 12 40 in a different handwriting also appear as do the letters J and H. These markings were similar to those on the other Dictabelts made that day."[336] No mention is made of the "Being recorded from Channel 1" notation observed by Barger, nor did the panel explain the meaning of the observed handwriting. [The date 11-22-63 is self explanatory; PL2 could indicate Platoon 2, who worked the 7 am to 3 pm shift on the day of the assassination[337]; the number 10 denotes the tenth belt created during that shift; the times 12:05 and 12:40 represent the period of time encompassed by the belt; and the initials J and H refer to the DPD Dispatchers Jackson and Henslee].[338]

The Ramsey Panel addressed the question of the handwriting on the key dictabelt as follows: "A photograph of the Dictabelt has been submitted to Ms. Doris Schwartz, who serviced the recorder during the period in question and who now lives in Duncanville, Texas. Although Ms. Schwartz does not recognise the other handwriting, she does identify the "11-22-63, PL2, 10" as her own handwriting. She uses an unmistakable 2 and feels that the specimen is the original belt."[339]

The photograph of the belt was allegedly sent to Ms. Schwartz via Jim Bowles, and the panel's report does not address the fact that she did not recognise the other handwriting, which she obviously did not write, although one would assume that she would recognise the writing of colleagues with whom she regularly worked.[340] A partial identification, based on a photograph of some handwriting passed through a third party, is hardly a satisfactory basis for making a positive identification and conclusion regarding the authenticity of such vital evidence, yet it seems to have satisfied the Ramsey Panel.

SIX | UNSOUND ACOUSTICS?

But did the photograph allegedly sent by the Ramsey Panel to Ms. Schwartz ever really exist? In May 1999, when this author requested a copy of the photograph shown to Mrs. Schwartz, NARA were unable to find it (or any other photos of the dictabelts).[341] The Ramsey Panel also claimed that Ms. Schwartz had identified the "PL2" as her own handwriting – but "PL2" does not appear in any of the sixteen photographs of Belt #10 (or in any of the seven photographs of Belt #9) taken by NARA in April 2004, or in the NARA description of what appears on the belt identified as Belt #10 held by them on July 14, 2005.[342]

Jim Bowles had a slightly different recollection of Ms. Schwartz' identification of the dictabelts, however. He told author Larry Sneed that a visual inspection of the belts indicated that they were what they purported to be, but that he had gone further than that and physically showed them to Ms. Schwartz. According to Bowles, Ms. Schwartz confirmed that her signature was on the belts, (strange, as there has never been any suggestion that she signed or even initialled the belts) and that "the belts appeared to be the legitimate originals."[343]

So did Bowles show Ms Schwartz the actual belts, or just a photograph of them?

According to a 'Call Report' written by Ms. Anne Buttimer of the Assassination Records Review Board (the ARRB) on June 12, 1995, following a telephone conversation she had with Gary Mack, curator of the Sixth Floor Museum in Dealey Plaza, Jim Bowles had "recently" claimed that "at the conclusion of the Ramsey Panel inquiry he hand-delivered the belts to the FBI".[344] Is this confirmation that Bowles did, indeed, have possession of the original dictabelts in 1981, when he claims to have shown them to Doris Schwartz?

In June 2008, Bowles told this author that "Ms. Schwartz personally examined the belts and assured me they were her true and correct originals."[156] However, it must be remembered that this contradicts not only what the Ramsey Panel reported regarding Ms. Schwartz being shown a photograph for identification purposes, but also contradicts the claim by panel member Dr. Charles Rader that they were never allowed sole or unsupervised access to the original dictabelt recordings.[345]

Although their analyses were carried out primarily on recordings provided by Jim Bowles, the Ramsey Panel's records also show that the original Channel 1 dictabelts were also copied to tape on their behalf by the FBI in December 1981. With reference to these copies, the Ramsey Panel's report states that "no skips or repeats were apparent" on the dictabelts during the copying process, "nor are there indications of any on the resulting tapes".[346]

In August 2006, Ralph Linsker of the IBM Thomas Watson Research Centre told this author that, while working on a 'Science & Justice' article with members of the NAS/Ramsey Panel in 2004, he studied a recording (covering the period from 12:29 to about 12:35) made directly from the belt by the FBI in 1981, which we can reasonably assume is the copy originally made for the Ramsey

Panel. He said he found "No evidence of skips or repeats...during the work on this paper, which is the only history I can comment on. However, we did not do a systematic survey ... regarding this point." Linsker need not have looked too far, however.

By comparing a short segment - from just before 12:37 to shortly after 12:38 - of the Channel 1 recording with the corresponding period on the Ramsey Panel's copy of the Bowles recording, this author identified ten repeated transmissions, caused by the belt skipping backwards, and seven missing messages, caused by the belt skipping forward, as shown below:

Disp.   35, did you receive?
35   I got it.
Disp.   10-4.
61   61, clear
Disp.   61 clear. 12:37
4   4 to (11?), 1131
21   21.
Disp.   21... continue.
24   24.
93   93.
Disp.   Inwood and Stemmons and assist 24. 21 go on up there to Hines and cut that service road off there where the ambulance can go on to Parkland.
[24   24, 10-4.
93 or 21   10-4.
?   Unintelligible.
4   Yes, go ahead.]
Disp.   Did you call?
4   Yes, I don't know what happened to the traffic officers assigned to Cedar Springs and Mockingbird, but they're not there and the traffic is really snafued.
32   32, clear.
Disp.   32, on mark out, report to Cedar Springs and Mockingbird.
32   10-4.
Disp.   71, robbery of an individual...
      {...mark out, report to Cedar Springs and Mockingbird}
      {10-4}
      {71, robbery of an individual}
      ...2205 Cockrell. 12:38.
      {10-4}
      {71, robbery of an individ...}
[71   2205.]
51   51's clear.

Six | Unsound Acoustics?

Disp. 51, clear. 12:38.
       {51's clear}
80   80, clear.
Disp. 80, clear. 12:38.
24   24 (pronounced "Twenty. Four".)
Disp. 24
24   Ah, these ambulances must've **[gone]** past through Stemmons and Inwood.
       {4}
       {24}
       {Ah, these ambulances must've...}
[Disp. 10-4.
58   58]
24   Was an A…
Disp. It's unknown, 24.
       …PB car supposed to be following the ambulance?
       {…PB car supposed to be following the ambulance?}

The Bold Text [in square brackets] denotes transmissions, or parts thereof, which are missing, while Italic Text {in round brackets} denotes transmissions, or parts thereof, which are repeated in this copy of the dictabelt, obtained by Steve Barber from Professor Ramsey. Timing of the above segment on the dictabelt recording indicates that it is 2 minutes 1.07 seconds long, but timing of the Bowles' tape segment is 1 minute 59.09 seconds, a 1.66% difference.[348]

A comparison of a six-minute segment containing the entire 'open microphone' sequence, using the same two recordings as were used above, showed that the dictabelt recording was again longer than the corresponding segment of the Bowles tape recording, but this time the difference was 2.12%.[349] While this might be evidence of even more skips and/or repeats in the 'open microphone' sequence, this author was unable to positively identify any such specific skips or repeats.

The foregoing highlights the unreliability of tape recordings (and specifically, the FBI/Ramsey Panel recording made in December 1981) made directly from the now badly-deteriorated dictabelts. While the results are hardly surprising given the age and use to which the original belts have been exposed, they equally call into question the reliability and integrity of any findings based primarily on such tape recordings. The use of recordings, rather than the belts themselves, and the possibility that such tape recordings might not be totally faithful copies of the belts, is fraught with danger.

Are the original DPD Channel 1 dictabelt recordings themselves any more reliable?

The numbers game

The author's main area of research for many years has been the establishment of a detailed chain of possession of the dictabelts on which all radio transmissions over Channel 1 of the Dallas Police radio were recorded on the day on the assassination. This resulted in the author first raising the possibility of problems with belt authenticity with the Department of Justice on August 24, 1982.

As we have already seen, the original Channel 1 dictabelts were given to Deputy Chief George Lumpkin on the evening of the assassination, and were used in the creation of a number of transcripts which found their way via the Dallas police, the Secret Service and the FBI to the Warren Commission.[350] The dictabelts were then put into a filing cabinet belonging to Dallas Police Chief Jesse Curry, where they remained until his retirement in 1966.[351]

Deputy Director of the DPD Intelligence Division, Paul McCaghren took the dictabelts into safekeeping when they were discovered following Curry's retirement.[352] McCaghren stored the belts in his office until 1971 or 1972 when he took them home. The belts then remained in McCaghren's home until 1978, when he turned then over to investigators for the HSCA.[353] However, that was when the first problems came to light.

Back in 1964, when the FBI asked for the belts coving the period 10 am until 3 pm on the day of the assassination, Chief Curry handed over a total of ten belts.[354] There is no record of how many belts were placed in Chief Curry's filing cabinet in 1963, but Paul McCaghren testified to the HSCA that nobody had access to the belts after they came into his possession in 1966. However, McCaghren has told this author that he handed over two – or possibly three – dictabelts, which were in an envelope marked "Channel 1", and the records of the HSCA only show receipts for three belts received from him.[355]

After the HSCA received the dictabelts, they turned them over to BBN's Dr. James Barger. Dr. Barger subsequently provided a detailed inventory of the 14 belts he received from the HSCA – yes, fourteen, and not the "two or three" which McCaghren told this author he gave the HSCA, and which the HSCA receipted.[356]

At the conclusion of the HSCA's investigation, Chief Counsel G. Robert Blakey contacted the Justice Department and asked them to take possession of "the dictabelt" which had been used in the investigation.[357] When this author asked Professor Blakey how many belts the HSCA had handed over, he said that he had "no memory of numbers. I only remember that we had a tape and some dictabelts".[358] According to documentation provided to the author by NARA, the HSCA turned over three dictabelts to the DOJ on March 30, 1979 – the three obtained from Paul McCaghren in March 1978.[359] The belts then remained under the control (and presumably in the possession) of the Justice Department until 1988, when they were "found" in the safe of an unnamed senior attorney

Six | Unsound Acoustics?

in the DOJ Criminal Division.[360] The belts were subsequently handed over to NARA in March 1990, where they remain to this day under strict security and environmentally-controlled conditions. However, even that handover is clouded in mystery. According to the records of NARA, the Justice Department handed over 5 dictabelts – two more than the HSCA had apparently given to the Justice Department eleven years earlier![361]

Over a number of years, this author has invested a lot of time and effort in trying to unravel this "numbers game", which has turned into one of the great mysteries of the acoustics evidence. It is clear that while BBN got fourteen dictabelts from the HSCA in 1978, the HSCA apparently turned over only three belts to the DOJ in March 1979, yet five belts were turned over by the DOJ to NARA in 1990 – and it has never been possible to get to the bottom of this numeric puzzle. So where are the missing belts?

It was only recently that at least a partial answer came to light. It now appears that BBN did not return all the dictabelts received by them in 1978 to the HSCA in 1979, and therefore some of the dictabelts never found their way – via the Justice Department – to NARA.

This possible solution to the mystery came to light as a result of a conversation between researcher Todd Vaughan and Stephen Lyons, the Associate Producer / Senior Researcher for the 1988 Nova TV programme, "Who Shot President Kennedy?" In May 1988, Lyons told Vaughan that the Nova team had visited and interviewed Dr. Barger at BBN's offices. Lyons related how, at one point during the interview, Barger opened a file cabinet drawer and was "surprised to find an original Dictabelt from the HSCA investigation, though not the relevant one" (i.e. the one covering the period of the assassination, which is among those now stored securely in NARA).[362]

If this story is correct (and there is no reason whatsoever to believe otherwise), then it appears that Dr. Barger may have had (and might still have) some or all of the "missing" belts. Unfortunately, the author's attempts to obtain further clarification regarding this story from Dr. Barger himself were unsuccessful. According to a BBN representative, "Dr. Barger does not wish to comment on the Kennedy assassination".[363]

This author would not suggest for a single moment that there was anything underhand or untoward in this 1988 discovery of an original dictabelt in a filing cabinet in Dr. Barger's office. The author feels certain that Dr. Barger truly was "surprised" when he made the discovery, but it does serve to illustrate the vulnerability of the acoustics evidence to charges that it is inconclusive and incomplete.

The discrepancy between the number of belts given to the Justice Department by the HSCA, and the number given to NARA by the DOJ in 1990 remains unresolved to date, despite the author's best efforts. Is it possible that someone in the HSCA, the DOJ or NARA simply quoted the wrong number of belts, and the pertinent documentation is simply wrong as a result? There is no question whatsoever about the fact that five belts are stored in NARA today, but the provenance of those belts must unfortunately remain suspect until this mystery is satisfactorily resolved.

And what of the Channel 2 recordings, which have only been briefly referred to in this chapter?

Like their Channel 1 counterparts, the whereabouts of the Channel 2 recordings over the years is also rather vague. The recordings were in the possession of DPD Chief Curry in July 1964, when he made them available to the FBI for transcription.[364] The original Audograph recordings do not appear in the inventory of material given to the HSCA by Paul McCaghren in 1978, however.[365]

While BBN did not seem to have any particular interest in the Channel 2 recordings, the Ramsey Panel certainly did. As previously noted, the Panel were initially working with copies of the recordings of both channels which had been provided by Jim Bowles and Dr. Barger.[366] They subsequently used "high quality magnetic tape copies", but the origin of these is unclear.[367] They could also be the "tape copy (which) was prepared by members of the Committee directly from the original Audograph plastic disk itself",[368] or the copies of the Channel 2 recordings which were produced for them in December 1981 by the FBI.[369]

As with the Channel 1 recordings, transcripts were made by the Secret Service, the DPD and the FBI of the radio transmissions over Channel 2 on November 22, 1963. Once again, the FBI transcript of July 1964 is the only one which indicates when each Gray Audograph disc started and finished. However, as with the Channel 1 recordings, there are discrepancies between the start and end times documented by the FBI, and those now quoted by the National Archives.

The FBI transcript of Channel 2 shows that the discs' start and end times were as follows:[370]

Disc No.	Started	Ended
1	Just before 10:15 am	12:03 pm
2	12:03 pm	Between 12:45 and 12:48 pm
3	Between 12:45 and 12:48 pm	Between 1:44 and 1:50 pm
4	Between 1:44 and 1:50 pm	Between 2:38 and 2:41 pm
5	Between 2:38 and 2:41 pm	3 pm – transcript ends.

The start and end times of the Channel 2 discs which were handed over to the National Archives by the Justice Department in March 1990 are somewhat different.[371] According to the Inventory of material handed over to the Archives, the five corresponding discs' start and end times are:

Disc No.	Started	Ended
1	10:00 am	12:03 pm

Six | Unsound Acoustics?

2	12:03 pm	12:48 pm
3	12:48 pm	2:39 pm
4	2:39 pm	4:09 pm
5	4:09 pm	5:12 pm

If the FBI and National Archives data are to be believed, the only explanation for these differences would appear to be that, at some point between July 1964 and March 1990, somebody merged the FBI discs #3 and #4 (from 12:48 to 2:39) into a new, single disc #3. There is, however, some indication that this was done prior to December 1981, when the Ramsey Panel reviewed the physical evidence.

According to the File Note of December 10, 1981 by Roger Cubbage of the Justice Department, regarding the Ramsey Panel's examination of the Channel 1 and 2 recordings: "The audograph marked 4:09 p.m 5:12 11/22/6 (sic) was played to test the playing equipment and then viewed through a microscope. The audograph marked 12:02 p.m. 12? p.m. (sic) was played and copied. Then the audograph marked 1:40 p.m. 2:39 p.m. was also played and recorded."[372]

The 4:09 to 5:12 audograph is undoubtedly disc #5 of the Archives set. The audograph starting at 12:02 and ending during the same hour is obviously disc #2 of the same set, as it is disc #2 of the FBI set. The 1:40 to 2:39 audograph, however, is almost certainly disc #4 of the FBI set, but does not exist in the Archives set. Therefore, there are clear indications of the existence of two distinct sets of discs.

To ask why anybody would want to duplicate the original Dallas Police recordings is to possibly venture into the realm of pointless speculation. As is often the case, the correct answer may be a very simple one. Perhaps somebody decided to make copies, in order to preserve the recordings for posterity. However, whatever the answer, the possibility exists that the dictabelts and Audograph discs now in the Archives are not the true original items, and with that possibility, the inevitable questions about the authenticity and completeness of the material must also remain.

If, as this chapter suggests, the most fundamental aspect of the acoustics evidence - the authenticity of the police radio recordings - is questionable, then the very foundation upon which both the HSCA and the Ramsey Panel based their conclusions is unreliable. The authenticity of the currently existing radio recordings is primarily dependent on the establishment of an unbroken chain of possession for that evidence, from November 22, 1963 up to the present time. In the absence of such an unbroken chain of possession, it is surely unfair and unreasonable to accept one set of experts' conclusions and dismiss contradictory ones unless and until we are certain that we are dealing with the original evidence? And as Jim Bowles so correctly asked, "The question here is, "original" on whose authority?"[373]

If one - or even both - groups of acknowledged scientific experts were using tape recordings and dictabelts of questionable provenance....

Against the evidentiary background discussed here, what level of credibility can we afford to the conclusions of either the HSCA or the Ramsey Panel?

The Dictabelt restoration project

After they received the series of five dictabelts (officially described as "Dallas Police Department Channel I Dictaphone Belt Recordings Nos. 9, 10, 11, 12, 13. November 22, 1963"),[374] from Robert Keuch of the DOJ's Criminal Division in March 1990, NARA needed to make copies from the original belts in order to fulfil their preservation and access requirements.[375] The Cutting Corporation, a Bethesda, Maryland-based archival sound lab which has been involved in the preservation and restoration of archival audio materials since 1979, made the necessary copies of dictabelts 11, 12, and 13 in February 2004 on behalf of NARA. However, "inspection of belts 9 and 10 indicated they likely could not tolerate this procedure due to their poor condition", and efforts to play the belts "would likely have resulted in additional damage to the belts". Accordingly, belts 9 and 10 were not copied, and the decision was made to "consider further the optimum procedures for the preservation/conservation" of the belts.[376] In early August 2004, plans to produce a new "digital copy" of the Dallas Police Department (DPD) Channel 1 dictabelts were announced. [377]

Few people realise quite how deteriorated and inflexible the belts had become through improper handling and storage before they were eventually handed over to NARA in 1990.

Having been folded and stored flat for many years prior to its receipt by NARA, the crucial dictabelt (belt #10) had developed two severe creases.[378] The first of these was located approximately 40mm to the left of the manufacturer's edge printing and the second one was approximately 25mm to the right of the edge printing.[379]

Fig 3: A photograph of Belt 10, showing a major crack which has developed across the entire width of the belt and the many smaller cracks that have developed along the lower edge, all of which have encroached onto the recording surface. (Photo Credit: NARA)

Six | Unsound Acoustics?

The belt had also split along the crease lines. There were three splits, measuring 7mm, 23mm and 4mm in length respectively, along the first crease, and there was one 20mm split as well as three other smaller ones along the line of the second crease. A 75mm strip of clear pressure-sensitive tape had been applied to the inside surface of the belt behind the second crease.[380]

The lower edge of the belt was also quite severely damaged, containing as many as 29 edge cracks of between 5 and 10mm in length. Clear adhesive tape had been applied to about 240mm of the lower edge of the belt in an effort to prevent the cracks from opening further.[381]

A NARA Advisory Committee on Preservation meeting took place on June 15, 2004, as a result of which NARA commissioned a research project led by Carl Haber of the Physics Division at the Lawrence Berkeley National Laboratory in California, to determine whether a non-invasive, non-contact copy of the belts could be produced by means of optical scanning.[382]

The results of this evaluation project were contained in Carl Haber's final report, submitted to NARA in January 2007, which concluded that optical scanning was a viable approach for non-invasive transfers of audio from plastic dictation belts. The report further concluded that speech recovered optically from dictation belts was intelligible, and of roughly similar quality to that obtained by normal playback, and that optical scanning of historical dictabelts was likely to yield a useful and good quality copy, which would be comparable or better than the existing tape copies.[383]

In order to progress from this initial feasibility study to a full-blown implementation of the 3D optical scanning technology which Haber had concluded could transfer the information from the damaged dictabelts to another medium, however, required additional work and the inevitable associated costs.

The design and testing of special equipment capable of holding the fragile and damaged dictabelts during the scanning process, the upgrade of the required control and analysis software, and the modification of a Dictaphone model A2TC recording machine (identical to the one used by the DPD to create the belts in 1963) to allow accurate signal measurements, were among the tasks which remained outstanding before the belts could be copied.[384]

As of December 2008, Carl Haber was ready to proceed, but NARA still needed to complete the necessary paperwork to authorize funds to do the work. NARA was optimistic that the relevant contractual agreement could be in place within the financial year.[385]

Unfortunately, a year later, the necessary agreement had still not been finalised.[386] Furthermore, NARA's Motion Picture, Sound and Video Branch chief Les Waffen appears to have been the main driving force behind this project, so his retirement in 2010 – coupled with the obvious cutbacks in spending that have accompanied the current worldwide financial downturn – would unfortunately suggest that little or no progress will be made in the foreseeable future.

Irrespective of when the project is completed, however, it is worth remembering that the sole purpose of the project is to make digital copies of the damaged belts, 9 and 10. Any analytical work which might reflect on the accuracy or otherwise of the House Select Committee on Assassinations' acoustical conclusions is totally beyond the scope of the project.

However, the creation of such digital copies might yet enable resolution of at least some of the questions regarding the acoustics evidence.

An essential element in any scientific evidence is the ability of any test or experiment to be accurately reproduced, or replicated, by someone else working independently, and the absence of any such capability on the part of the BBN/HSCA acoustics evidence is yet another factor undermining the evidence.

The missing Raytheon/BBN material

Because the BBN matching process was a manual one, it seemed reasonable to assume that current technology might allow a faster and more accurate comparison of the impulse patterns on the original dictabelts and the 1978 reconstruction recordings to be performed. Accordingly, following the retirement of Les Waffen from NARA in June 2010, and the apparent cessation of all further work on the dictabelt restoration project,[387] a group of interested individuals came together in late 2010 in an effort to determine the whereabouts and availability of the necessary recordings.

Back in 1978, BBN made a digital copy of the Channel 1 dictabelt #10 on which the sounds of the shots in Dealey Plaza were allegedly recorded.[388] From that recording, they produced an oscilloscope printout, showing the impulses patterns believed to be the results of recorded gunfire. Unfortunately, the whereabouts of that digital recording are unknown – Dr. Barger claimed not to know, telling researcher Todd Vaughan in December 1980 that BBN had kept none of the material relating to their work for the HSCA,[389] and the recording is not listed among the JFK acoustics recordings stored in the National Archives. As previously noted, high-quality copies of the key dictabelt were made by the FBI in 1981, and copies of these are still available in the research community, although the quality of the original dictabelt would obviously have deteriorated even further between the HSCA's access in 1978 and that of the Ramsey Panel in 1981.

However, in a reversal of his original position regarding the disposition of the material, Dr. Barger acknowledged in 2002[390] and again in 2010[391] that BBN still had the original recordings made during the acoustical reconstruction carried out on Sunday, August 20, 1978. Indeed, Dr. Barger went further, and said that he would be willing to loan out the recordings (which are now believed to be badly deteriorated) for further testing, if permission were obtained from BBN's new owners, Raytheon, who had acquired BBN on October 29, 2009.[392]

An initial attempt was made to obtain the necessary permission from Barger's Raytheon boss in November 2010, but this only elicited the response that he was "not interested in trying to pursue this up the chain".[393] However, in August 2011, this author wrote directly to Robert G. ('Tad') Elmer, the CEO of Raytheon/BBN, asking for information on the current whereabouts of the reconstruction recordings. He replied: "Dr. Barger is retired and any materials associated with this work have either been destroyed or returned to the client. We have no information in our possession pertaining to this work".[394]

Dr. Barger said Raytheon/BBN had the reconstruction recordings in August 2010 – just twelve months later, however, Raytheon claimed to have either destroyed those recordings or returned them to the client, and were apparently uninterested in further discussion on the matter. As the HSCA (Raytheon/BBN's original client) went out of existence in 1979, and at least some of the original Dallas Police dictabelts to which BBN had access in 1978 were finally turned over to NARA by the Justice Department in March 1990, it was perhaps reasonable to surmise that Raytheon/BBN might have sent the reconstruction test-firing recordings either to the Office of the Clerk of the House or to NARA. Unfortunately, however, searches carried out on the author's behalf by both NARA and the Office of the Clerk failed to uncover any trace whatsoever of the recordings.[395] It would therefore appear likely that the recordings were most probably destroyed by Raytheon when Dr. Barger retired, early in 2011.

In view of the foregoing, and the problem of the unavailability of a certified digital copy of the original dictabelt which was recording Channel 1 radio traffic at the time of the assassination, any hopes of resolving the issue of the reproducibility of the BBN findings appear to have evaporated (at least for the present), given that the key dictabelt is now effectively beyond use.

Were it possible as some stage in the future to obtain a high-fidelity digital copy of the key dictabelt using optical scanning methods such as those proposed in the NARA Dictabelt Preservation Project, and also to find and digitise even a certified copy of the re-enactment recordings created by BBN, it would not be beyond the capability of modern computer software for the BBN impulse matching process to be automated, such that it could be repeated at will. Furthermore, a combination of such software with virtual modelling technology would allow the impulse patterns from any number of theoretical shots, from any number of theoretical gunman locations, to be generated and automatically compared with those on the dictabelt and on the BBN reconstruction recordings.

Conclusion

There have been a number of serious challenges to the acoustics evidence which was the basis for the HSCA's conclusion that there was "a high probability that two gunmen fired" at the President:

- some of the original dictabelts are undoubtedly missing from NARA, and have either been destroyed or are in private hands;

- the possibility that some of the belts now stored in NARA may be duplicates rather than the originals;

- the claims that the photographic evidence does not support the cornerstone of the acoustics evidence, which requires a motorcycle with an open microphone (and switched to Channel 1 of the police radio) to be in specific positions at specific times;

- the crosstalk issue, whereby an order given on Channel 2 by Sheriff Decker over one minute after the shooting appears on Channel 1 at the same time as the acoustical impulses claimed to have resulted from the shots fired at the President in Dealey Plaza.

If the HSCA's acoustics experts erred such that - instead of 100-120 feet – the open microphone was 10-12 feet behind the President (an error which could have been caused by nothing more sinister than a misplaced decimal point), could it explain the inconsistency between the photographic evidence and the projected location of the open microphone?

The Ramsey Panel's conclusion that a Channel 2 transmission which occurred more than 30 seconds after the shooting overlays the impulses said by the HSCA's acoustics experts to have been caused by the shots, seriously undermines the HSCA's conclusions, unless another realistic explanation can be produced – would the possibility of duplicate (i.e. non-original) radio recordings be that explanation?

There is compelling evidence on both sides of the acoustics debate, and powerful reasons on both sides to believe and disbelieve it. If nothing else, the acoustics evidence proves the impossibility of ever knowing or proving anything with absolute certainty. Indeed, the converse is true in this case, whereby the truth (and, indeed, the evidence) is becoming increasingly lost in a mist of ambiguity. However, if this environment of nagging doubt is allowed to continue indefinitely, and if the capabilities of modern technology cannot be fully utilised in the search for closure on this subject, then it would appear that the truth of the acoustics evidence may never be known, and it will suffer what was most aptly described by researcher Paul Seaton as "death by default".

Six | Unsound Acoustics?

Acknowledgments

I am particularly indebted to Les Waffen, former chief of the Motion Picture, Sound and Video Branch, NARA, and Gary Mack, Curator at the Sixth Floor Museum at Dealey Plaza, for their endless help over many years.

In addition, I would like to record my sincere thanks to the many people, too numerous to mention individually, whose assistance, co-operation and patience in dealing with my questions on the subject of the acoustics evidence has been invaluable. Finally, a special thanks to the FOIA staff at the National Archives, for all their assistance.

Endnotes

[1] "Report of the Select Committee on Assassinations, U.S. House Representatives, 95th Congress, Second Session", (U.S. Government Printing Office, Washington: 1979), p. 1 (hereafter in the format 'HR 1')

[2] HR 1, 41

[3] HR 1, 65, 91

[4] HR 7

[5] HR 7, 481-2

[6] "Report of the Committee on Ballistic Acoustics", (National Academy Press, Washington, DC: 1982), p. 3 (hereafter in the format 'RR 3'). The Report is on file in the National Archives as RIF 186-10001-10002. The RIF (Record Identification Form) reference can be used to locate the document in question in the National Archives and Records Administration (NARA) in College Park, Maryland.

[7] RR ii, 4

[8] RR 2

[9] HR 481

[10] Report to Hon. Peter W. Rodino, Jr., Chairman, House of Representatives Judiciary Committee, March 28, 1988, p.5

[11] Id. at 4, 5

[12] Report of The President's Commission on the Assassination of President John F. Kennedy", (United States Government Printing Office, Washington, D.C: 1964), pp. 19, 21, 195 (hereafter in the format 'WR 19')

[13] Id. at 22, 374-5

[14] HR 1

[15] Id. at 1, 41

[16] Id. at 1, 65, 91

[17] RR, 2

[18] Ibid.

[19] Ibid.

[20] Hearings before the HSCA, Vol. 8, p. 41 (hereafter in the format 'HH8, 41'); FBI report 89-43-10553, p.2 (RIF 186-10006-10078), October 1, 1980

[21] "*The Kennedy Assassination Tapes - A Rebuttal to the Acoustical Evidence*", by James C. Bowles (1979), p.10 [hereafter referred to as 'Bowles manuscript'] - on file at NARA as RIF 124-10053-10354

[22] Bowles manuscript, 10; Background Report prepared for NARA's Advisory Committee on Preservation of Dictabelts, 2004, p.2

[23] NARA internal "For the Record" memo dated July 14, 2005, written by Ms. Brenda Bernier, Senior Photograph Conservator, NARA Document Conservation Laboratory

[24] Ibid; *Albany Democratic-Herald*, June 28, 2008; Bob Swenson e-mail to the author, 5 March 2007; Bill McWilliams e-mails to the author, January 18, 2008 and April 9, 2009; Memo from Mark Ormsby to Brenda Bernier, NARA Senior Photograph Conservator, July 13, 2005; Les Waffen (NARA) e-mail to the author, March 12, 2009

25. Warren Commission Exhibit 1974 (hereafter in format 'WCE 1974') in Volume 23 of Warren Commission Hearings, page 832 (hereafter in format 'WH23, 832')

26. The "A" indicates a recording device, the "2" denotes two machines working with a single control box, the "T" indicates TimeMaster equipment, while the "C" indicates a Communication recorder, according to e-mail from Bill McWilliams to the author, dated April 7, 2008.

27. Bob Swenson e-mails (including relevant technical documentation/specifications) to the author in January and March, 2007; e-mail correspondence with Bill McWilliams, April 7, 2008.

28. HH8, 41

29. Ibid; WH23, 832; Background Report for Advisory Committee of Preservation of Dictabelts, NARA, 2004, p.2

30. "The Dallas Police Radio: Assassination on Tape", by Gary Mack, *The Continuing Inquiry*, (hereafter 'TCI') August 22, 1977, pp. 1-4; "The Sounds of Conspiracy", Gallery magazine, July 1979, p. 65-9; letter to the author from Gary Mack, November 15, 1981; "*The Plot to Kill the President*", by G. Robert Blakey and Richard N. Billings (New York: Times Books, 1981, pp. 91-2; HSCA "Critics Conference" transcript (HSCA record JFK 014688, RIF 180-10117-10024), September 17, 1977, p. 211

31. HH2, 110, McCaghren testimony; HSCA staff interviews with Paul McCaghren by Jack Moriarty, March 10 and 11, 1978 (HSCA records JFK 007058 and 007059, RIFs 180-10074-10388 and 180-10074-10389, respectively)

32. HH2, 16-17; HR 66-7; HH2, 89 and HH5, 645, Barger testimony; BBN Report at HH8, 34 and 62; letter to the author from Dr. Barger, January 29, 1982

33. HH2, 27, 41; HH8, 6

34. According to HSCA and FBI documents, DPD 2-wheel motorcycles were fitted with Motorola Model T-31 BAT-1130A radios, and 3-wheel motorcycles were equipped with Motorola Model FMT 41 radios. See HSCA record 010096, Outside Contact Report with John Griesel, DPD Radio Dept, July 19, 1978 (RIF 180-10071-10467) and FBI record 89-43-10553, Oct. 1, 1980, p. 4 (RIF 186-10006-10078)

35. "*Hear No Evil: Social Constructivism & The Forensic Evidence In the Kennedy assassination*", by Donald B. Thomas, Mary Ferrell Foundation Press, 2010, (hereinafter "*Hear No Evil*") pp. 569-570

36. "*Hear No Evil*", 570

37. HR 70

38. HH8, 101

39. Id. at 70-9; HH2, 46; HR 68, 602

40. HH8, 45, 70

41. HH8, 80

42. HR 68, HH8, 7-9

43. HR 69, HH8, 80

44. HR 69

45. Ibid.

46. "*The Sounds of Conspiracy*", Gallery magazine, July 1979, p.65

47. Ibid.

48. HR 69-70; HH8, 80-1, 97

49. Unfortunately, but for obvious safety and other reasons, a DPD motorcycle with its engine running and microphone jammed in the 'transmit' mode, was not used to record the test shot sounds in Dealey Plaza.

50. HH8, 94

51. HR, 70

52. HR, 70-1

53. Ibid.

54. HH5, 649

55. HR, 72; HH8, 101, 105

56. HR, 72; HH8, 4, 114

57. HH8, 4-5

58. HH5, 557-570 (Weiss testimony); HH8, 48, 115-6

59. HR, 72-3

60. HR, 73

Six | Unsound Acoustics?

61. HR, 73
62. HH8, 28-9
63. Weiss testimony, HH5, 570
64. HR, 74
65. HR, 74-5
66. HR, 75
67. WH20, 489
68. HH5, 650; letter to the author from Dr. Barger, April 2, 1979
69. HH5, 625; HR, 75
70. HH5, 629; HH8, 102, 107; "*The Application of Computers To The Photographic Evidence*", by Richard E. Sprague in *Computers And Automation*, May 1970, pp. 51-2
71. HH8, 103, 107
72. HR, 76; McLain's testimony at HH5, 617-41
73. Ibid.
74. Ibid.
75. Ibid.
76. Ibid.
77. HR, 80; HH8, 49-50
78. HR, 80; HH5, 722-4; HH6, 30, 32
79. HR, 78
80. HH8, 103, 107-8; letter to the author from Dr. Barger, April 2, 1979
81. See HH8, 183-5 for Robert Blakey memo of March 22, 1979 regarding Mannlicher-Carcano test firing, indicating that the rifle could be fired twice in 1.6 seconds, and three shots with two 'hits' could be achieved in 8.31 seconds
82. Ramsey Report, 4
83. "*Hear No Evil*", 618, citing "*The JFK Assassination: The facts and the theories*"; by Carl Oglesby (Signet, New York, 1992), p. 250-1
84. "*Hear No Evil*", 619, citing Don Thomas' personal communication from Dr. Barger
85. RR, 36
86. Ibid.
87. RR 38, 40
88. Norman Ramsey letter to HSCA acoustics experts Barger, Weiss and Aschkenasy, January 26, 1981, enclosing pages from Steve Barber letter of October 6, 1980; Barber's own account of his remarkable discovery is available on-line at http://mcadams.posc.mu.edu/barber.htm
89. RR 41ff
90. RR 5
91. RR 2
92. "*The Acoustic evidence in the Kennedy assassination*", by Michael O'Dell, November 2003, p. 10 (posted at http://mcadams.posc.mu.edu/odell/); O'Dell e-mail to the author, Jan. 6, 2004; e-mail group posting from O'Dell, Nov. 23, 2010)
93. Richard E. Sprague letter to author, Sept. 19, 1978
94. Author's meeting with Sprague in London, 29 Oct. 1978
95. "JFK Panel Staff Knew Motorcycle Wasn't There", by Earl Golz, *Dallas Morning News*, January 8, 1979; letter to the author from Sprague, February 24, 1979
96. "JFK Panel Staff Knew Motorcycle Wasn't There", by Earl Golz, *Dallas Morning News*, January 8, 1979
97. McLain testimony at HH5, 617ff.
98. Sprague letters to Jeff Fogel, DOJ, copies of which are in the author's files
99. Dale K. Myers, "Epipolar Geometric Analysis of Amateur Films Related to Acoustics Evidence in the John F. Kennedy Assassination", Second revision, November 1, 2010 [hereafter in the format, 'Myers Epipolar, nnn', and available on-line at http://www.jfkfiles.com/jfk/html/acoustics.htm]. p. 19 footnote 64, citing Bowles manuscript, 30-32 and 'Cop denies JFK gunshot tape', *Detroit Free Press*, January 6, 1979
100. CBS interview transcript, referenced in Haverford College Dept .of Political Science Senior Thesis "*An Evaluation of the House Select Committee on Assassinations' Finding of Probable Conspiracy in the*

Assassination of President Kennedy and an Evaluation of the Utility of the Committee", by Shanin Specter, April 1980, p.22ff; *London Daily Mail*, January 6, 1979, p. 4; *Boston Globe*, January 6, 1979

[101.] CBS transcript, referenced above; HR, 77-8; HH8, 112

[102.] HH8, 106, 112

[103.] HR, 76-78

[104.] Ibid.

[105.] Ibid.

[106.] "Doubt cast on theory that pair shot at JFK", by Earl Golz, *Dallas Morning News*, April 14, 1982, p. 1A.

[107.] Ibid.

[108.] Endnotes CD from *"Reclaiming History"*, by Vincent Bugliosi (W.W. Norton & Company, Inc., New York, 2007), p. 185

[109.] "Doubt cast on theory that pair shot at JFK", by Earl Golz, *Dallas Morning News*, April 14, 1982, p. 1A

[110.] RR, 94

[111.] "Doubt cast on theory that pair shot at JFK", by Earl Golz, *Dallas Morning News*, April 14, 1982, p. 1A.

[112.] Ibid.

[113.] Ibid.

[114.] Ibid.

[115.] Interview recording, courtesy of Denis Morissette, in author's files. See also *"The officer with the mike stuck"* posting to internet newsgroup alt.conspiracy.jfk on May 16, 2001, and *"This Officer Claims That HE Recorded The Shots"* in alt.assassination.jfk newsgroup on December 3, 2002.

[116.] *"REPOST: Dallas PD radio"* by Greg Jaynes, August 26, 1996,in Internet newsgroup alt.conspiracy.jlk. moderated

[117.] *"Acoustics - A little deeper down the rabbit hole"* by Greg Jaynes, March 27, 1997, in Internet newsgroup alt.conspiracy.jfk.moderated

[118.] Author's telephone conversation with Ian Griggs, December 1, 2005

[119.] See pp. 153-218 of Endnotes CD from *"Reclaiming History"*, by Vincent Bugliosi

[120.] Bugliosi Endnotes CD, pp. 217-8

[121.] Id. at 184-190

[122.] Id. at 184-5

[123.] Id. at 185

[124.] Ibid.

[125.] Id. at 185-6

[126.] Id. at 186

[127.] Ibid.

[128.] Ibid.

[129.] Ibid.

[130.] Id. at 189-190

[131.] Id. at 190

[132.] Ibid.

[133.] Ibid.

[134.] Lawrence Exhibit 2 at WH20, 492 (or HSCA Exhibit F-679 at HH5, 621)

[135.] Author's copy of Channel 2 radio recordings (Kimbrough transcript entry #345. See endnote 225)

[136.] Bowles manuscript, 103-4

[137.] Id. at 172, 187 (note 75)

[138.] Id. at 103

[139.] Author's copy of Channel 2 radio recordings (Kimbrough transcript entries #514-530). Price confirmed his presence near the limousine at Parkland during an interview for the Six Floor Museum's "Oral History" series on September 24, 1994 (Transcript, p. 7).

[140.] Bowles manuscript, 103; Sixth Floor Museum Oral History interview with Price, September 24, 1994.

[141.] Bowles manuscript, 104

[142.] Bowles manuscript, 132

[143.] Sixth Floor Museum Oral History interview with Price, September 24, 1994.

[144.] https://ieeetv.ieee.org/player/html/viewer#truth-about-assassination-signal-processing-tells-story

Six | Unsound Acoustics?

145. Author's e-mail exchange with J.C. Bowles, October 3, 2010
146. Bugliosi Endnotes CD, p. 185
147. Id. at 186
148. Ibid.
149. Endnotes CD, p. 186
150. Id. at 186-7
151. Id. at 187
152. Bowles manuscript, 60
153. Author's on-line searches of NARA records, July 25, 2011
154. Greg Jaynes (1997) [http://mcadams.posc.mu.edu/jaynes/], and his Video – "The Dallas Police Recordings" (1998); Michael Russ (2003) [http://www.geocities.com/jfkinfo4/sync/sync.htm]; Paul Seaton (2004) [http://www.paulseaton.com/jfk/acoustics/houston/houston.htm]; and Myers Epipolar, esp. 50-51. See also previously referenced Richard E. Sprague correspondence and meetings with DOJ and the author between September 1978 and April 1980.
155. Bowles manuscript, 62-3
156. HSCA document JFK 013886, Interview of Gerald Henslee, August 12, 1978 (RIF 180-10108-10192), p. 3
157. Bowles manuscript, 103-4
158. Michael Russ (2003) [http://www.geocities.com/jfkinfo4/sync/sync.htm]; Paul Seaton (2004) [http://www.paulseaton.com/jfk/acoustics/houston/houston.htm]; Myers Epipolar, 51
159. "Hear No Evil", 678-9
160. For Thomas' analysis in detail, see "Hear No Evil", 676-685
161. According to Myers Epipolar (92, 112), McLain is visible in the Hughes film frames H-631 to 648 (Zapruder film frames 133 to 150, or 9.84 to 8.91 seconds before Z-313, the headshot). Myers Epipolar, 93, says McLain is visible in Dorman film frames 456 to 496. Myers then says (103) that Dorman frame 456 equates to Zapruder frame 365 (2.84 seconds after the headshot), and Dorman frame 496 equates to Zapruder frame 409 (5.25 seconds after the headshot); Couch film begins 15.5 seconds after "Cop in Dorman" sequence ends (Z-409 - 5.25 secs after Z-313 – plus 15.5 secs = Z-313 21 secs) – Myers Epipolar, 175, fn. 210; Bond 4 photo, showing Hargis returning to his motorcycle, occurs at Z-313 31.3 secs, according to "*Photographic Proof: H.B. McLain and Acoustics*" by Dale K. Myers, April 7, 2008, at http://jfkfiles.blogspot.com/ endnote 31. For further material relating to the timing of films and photographs, see "*Seventy-Six Seconds in Dealey Plaza*", (1978) by R.B. Cutler, pp. 79-83; author's related correspondence with Bob Cutler through 1978-9; "*Pictures of the Pain*", (1994) by Richard Trask, (hereafter "Trask"), p. 156, 208, 218; JFK Lancer Forum discussion threads "*Baker Timeline Resolved*" and "*Update: Marion Baker's Timeline*" in July 2007; Richard Van Noord's final "Baker Timeline" document, based on his JFK Lancer 'November In Dallas' conference presentation, Dallas, November 2007.
162. Myers Epipolar, 50, Exhibit 22
163. Myers Epipolar, 52, Exhibit 23
164. HSCA document JFK 002378, interview H.B McLain, October 29, 1978 (RIF 180-10107-10184), p. 1
165. HH5, 629
166. Bowles manuscript, 28
167. Bowles manuscript, 139-140. Note: a 'Google Earth' check by the author on June 15, 2011, of the point at which McLain caught up with the limousine indicated that it was approximately 500 yards – and not 600-800 feet - north of the entrance to the Stemmons Freeway
168. "*No More Silence*", by Larry A. Sneed, University of North Texas Press, 1998, p. 163 (hereafter in the format 'Sneed, n')
169. Greg Jaynes' study, "*The Scene of the Crime*", at http://mcadams.posc.mu.edu/jaynes/mclain.htm)
170. "*Acoustic Evidence Revisited: A Controversial Study*", by Greg Jaynes, published in "The Kennedy Assassination Chronicles", Vol. 3 No. 4, p.20 (Winter 1997 issue) available at http://www.maryferrell.org/mffweb/archive/viewer/showDoc.do?docId=4261&relPageId=19
171. HH5, 630
172. Sneed, 163
173. Mark A. Oakes' "*Eyewitness Video – Part 3*", 1998.

174. HR 76, refer also to McLain's HSCA testimony at HH5, 631-7
175. Mrs. Dorman was a secretary with Scott-Foresman & Co., a book publishing company with offices in the TSBD
176. Myers Epipolar, 90, 94, 103
177. HSCA document JFK 002381, interview of J.W. Courson, September 26, 1977, RIF 180-10107-10189
178. Ibid. If Courson was immediately in front of the first Press Bus, there were actually 12 cars between Courson and the President at that time – "*Presidential Motorcade Schematic Listing, November 22, 1963, Dallas, Texas*", by Todd Wayne Vaughan, (Private printing, Michigan, 1993), p. i, 24
179. Bowles manuscript, 126
180. Myers Epipolar, p. 179, citing pp. 21-25 of Vaughan/Courson interview, 1986
181. Sneed, 128-9. The 'officer on the right' of the limousine to whom Courson referred was B.J. Martin, according to Courson's Sept 27, 1977 HSCA interview – RIF 180-10107-10189
182. Todd W. Vaughan, "*Presidential Motorcade Schematic Listing, November 22, 1963, Dallas, Texas*", p. 24
183. Researcher Sean Murphy e-mail to the author, May 20, 2008
184. "*Photographic Proof: H.B. McLain and Acoustics*" by Dale Myers, April 7, 2008
185. HH5, 635; e-mail to the author from Todd Vaughan, June 2, 2009
186. Arch Kimbrough channel 1 transcript, entries #1769 and #1798
187. In his HSCA interview of August 8, 1978 (HSCA JFK doc #014362, RIF 180-10113-10272), Hargis said that when he returned to his motorcycle, it was "still on the stand with the radio on (and working) and the engine off", just as he had left it. Eyewitness Malcolm Summers is the only other person to suggest that Hargis fell to the ground, telling author Larry Sneed that Hargis "laid his motorcycle down or fell down on it" (Sneed, 103, 106)
188. Myers Epipolar, p.179
189. Aschkenasy testimony, HH5, 592
190. Bowles – incorporated into his Channel 1 transcript in Bowles manuscript, pp. 167-174; Barber – in attachments to author's correspondence from R.B. Cutler, January-March, 1980; Barger – at HH8, 63 and HH5, 678; Vaughan – "The Acoustical Evidence in the Assassination of President John F. Kennedy", December 14, 1980, Vol. 2. Manuscript submitted to Ramsey Panel in December 1980.
191. HH8, 11, 63, 108-9
192. HH5, 678
193. HH8, 112
194. "*Mr. Chairman: Evidence of Conspiracy*", by R.B. Cutler (private publication, Manchester, MA, 1979), p.90
195. Bowles manuscript, 103
196. Bowles manuscript, passim, but especially in Bowles' commentary on the Channel 1 recording on pp. 181-190
197. Bowles manuscript, 71
198. WH6, 296; also reproduced at HH5, 506
199. Hargis was first considered as a possible source of the open microphone by this author in correspondence with author/researcher R.B. Cutler in April and May 1979. Cutler made all information then known regarding Hargis available to the Justice Department in a number of written submissions during July/August 1980.
200. Letter to Cutler from Dr. James Barger dated February 2, 1979, in which Barger acknowledged that Hargis' known movements "agrees with my (untested) impressions of motorcycle movement subsequent to the shots".
201. Steve Barber and Todd Vaughan were also involved in the early discussions regarding Hargis as a possible source of the open microphone. Barber dismissed Hargis as a candidate, however, after his discovery that Hargis had used Channel 2 at 12:34. See http://mcadams.posc.mu.edu/barber.htm
202. "*The Plot to Kill the President*", by G. Robert Blakey and Richard N. Billings (New York: Times Books, 1981), p.89; HR, 606, note 160. Note also that Hargis did not testify at the Clay Shaw trial – Officer B.J. Martin said that Hargis was ill in the Methodist Hospital in Dallas at the time – see Martin's Shaw Trial testimony, 14 February, 1979, p. 47.
203. HH11, 536, note 262
204. JFK document #003300, RIF 180-10107-10243

Six | Unsound Acoustics?

205. JFK document #014362, RIF 180-10113-10272
206. JFK document #014224, RIF 180-10109-10354
207. HH5, 608
208. HH5, 637
209. In compliance with the wishes of the person concerned, his identity is not revealed here
210. Memo from Margo Jackson to Gary Cornwell, "*Identification of motorcycle policemen for Acoustics project*", July 18, 1978, JFK document 014296, RIF 180-10108-101118.
211. Memo from Margo Jackson to Chief Investigator Cliff Fenton, "*Questions For Motorcycle policemen*", July 25, 1978, JFK document 014296, RIF 180-10108-10121
212. Interview records with only five of the seven officers identified for contact by HSCA investigators can be found, and their questioning did not follow the lines set out by Ms. Jackson in her July 25 memo.
213. McIntire's photograph is reproduced in Richard Trask's excellent book, "*Pictures of the Pain: Photography and the assassination of President Kennedy*" (Yeoman Press, Danvers, Mass., 1994), p. 475
214. John Hovland e-mail to the author, March 12, 2008
215. "Acoustics As Easy As 1-2-3...4", by Gary Mack, *TCI* March 22, 1980, p. 5
216. Letter to Prof. Norman Ramsey from Gary Mack, October 5, 1981, reproduced in *TCI*, September 1981, pp. 2-3; Mack letter to Ramsey, November 12, 1981
217. Posting by Bill Miller in Education Forum thread, "New Proof of JFK Film Forgery", February 16, 2008, quoting author/researcher Josiah Thompson
218. Letter to Prof. Norman Ramsey from Gary Mack, October 5, 1981, in *TCI*, September 1981, pp. 2-3
219. HSCA interview of William Greer by J.P. Kelly and B. Lawson, 28 Feb 1978 (RIF 180-10099-10491); "The Stop-And-Go Motorcade", by Gary Mack, in *TCI*, April 22, 1980, p. 1; "*The Hoax of the Century: Decoding the Forgery of the Zapruder Film*", by Harrison E. Livingstone (The Conservatory Press, Trafford Books, 2004), pp. 326-7
220. WH4, 161 (Curry testimony)
221. Courson's personnel recollection (Officer 'F') in Bowles manuscript, 126
222. Decker Exhibit 5323, WH19, 458
223. G. Paul Chambers, "*Head Shot: The Science Behind the JFK Assassination*", Prometheus Books, New York, 2010, pp. 141-4
224. "*Hear No Evil*", 621, citing Richard L. Garwin, "*Examining the Kennedy Assassination Evidence*", pp. 203-224 in Trower, W.P (Ed), "*Discovering Alvarez: Selected works of Luis Alvarez, With Commentary by his Students and Colleagues*", Univ. Chicago Press, Chicago, Illinois, 1987
225. Letter from Arch Kimbrough to researcher Paul Hoch, November 5, 1970.
226. An electronic copy of the Kimbrough transcript, created by researcher Russ Shearer, is available on the Internet at http://www.billdrenas.com/articles/policeTranscript.html A copy of the original typed transcript is in the author's files.
227. WCE 1974, in WH23, 857
228. Kimbrough transcript entry #841.
229. The spectrograms were produced using 'Goldwave', Version 5.13
230. See WCE 2175, reproduced at WR, 197
231. WCE 1974, at WH23, 844
232. Id. at 849
233. Id. at 850
234. Larry Harris letter to the author, April 24, 1984, p. 2
235. "*Reasonable Doubt: An Investigation into the Assassination of John F. Kennedy*'", by Henry Hurt (Holt, Rinehart and Winston, New York, 1986), p. 168
236. Paul Hoch letter to Stephen Trott, Assistant Attorney General, Criminal Division, Dept. of Justice, September 16, 1986
237. HSCA Executive Session Business Meeting, August 3, 1978, transcript, p. 104 (RIF 180-10116-10331)
238. Id. at p. 106
239. HH8, 62, BBN Report; HH2, 89, Barger testimony regarding damage
240. Audio Accession Preservation List and accompanying Preliminary Accession Inventory of JFK Assassination Records kept by Mr. Robert Keuch, Criminal Division, DOJ, and transferred to NARA, March

1990
[241.] HH8, 62; HH2, 89.
[242.] Ibid.
[243.] Weiss and Aschkenasy Report at HH8, 5
[244.] RR, 67
[245.] Based on information regarding the markings on the original audio tapes used by the Ramsey Panel, contained in e-mail to the author from Michael O'Dell, August 1, 2002.
[246.] A November 12, 1981 letter to Dr. Barger from Professor Ramsey refers to the "next draft of our report", which had been sent to Dr. Barger "last week". (NAS Public Access File, item #25)
[247.] RR, 20
[248.] Letter from Professor Ramsey to Roger Cubbage of the Justice Department, Bruce Koenig of the FBI and Charles Rader, a member of the Ramsey Panel, dated November 30, 1981 (RIF 186-10006-10392)
249. Cubbage "Memorandum to Files", dated December 10, 1981 (also part of RIF 186-10006-10392)
[250.] Michael O'Dell e-mail to the author, August 1, 2002.
[251.] Ramsey Panel member Charles M. Rader e-mail to the author, November 19, 1999.
[252.] Ibid.
[253.] HSCA document JFK 003090, interview of Murray Jackson, October 20, 1977, p.3 (RIF 180-10103-10353)
[254.] HSCA document JFK 013886, interview of Gerald Henslee, August 12, 1978 (RIF 180-10108-10192)
[255.] Id. at p. 4
[256.] Ibid.
[257.] Internet eBay auction site, item # 2161906270, March 2003.
[258.] http://archiver.rootsweb.ancestry.com/th/read/LEDFORD/2007-07/1183644238
[259.] "HSCA Administrative Folder – Field Office Personnel circa 11/63" (RIF 124-10371-10126) available at the Mary Ferrell Foundation website at http://www.maryferrell.org/mffweb/archive/viewer/showDoc.do?docId=10059 ; author's e-mail correspondence with Craig L. Wheeler, Head of Reference Services, Humanities Reference Librarian, James G. Gee Library, Texas A&M University – Commerce, May 10, 2006
[260.] Author's telephone interview with retired FBI Supervisory Agent Richard Rogge, May 5, 2008.
[261.] Secret Service Document 324 in Warren Commission Document 87, p.339; Reproduced in *TCI*, March 1982, p.5
[262.] Paul Hoch correspondence with National Archives and Secret Service in the period November to December 1970.
[263.] HSCA document JFK 004804 - Outside Contact Report with Tom Ferrell by Margo Jackson, January 24, 1978 (RIF 180-10070-10252)
[264.] Ibid.
[265.] Paul Hoch letter to Prof. Norman Ramsey, September 23, 1981, p.2
[266.] Author's correspondence with National Archives and Secret Service in the period September to December 1982.
[267.] HSCA document JFK 013886, Interview of Gerald Henslee, August 12, 1978 (RIF 180-10108-10192), p.4
[268.] Sawyer Exhibit B, WH21, 398; WH6, 326, Henslee's Warren Commission testimony of April 8, 1964
[269.] HSCA document JFK 013886, Interview of Gerald Henslee, August 12, 1978 (RIF 180-10108-10192), p.4
[270.] Sawyer Exhibit B, 21 WH21, 398; WH6, 326; "*Whitewash II*", by Harold Weisberg (private publication, Hyattstown, Md. 1966), p.25
[271.] HH4, 575, JFK Exhibit F-567, testimony of DPD Captain Jack Revill; HH2, 108, McCaghren testimony; "*The Plot to Kill the President*", by G. Robert Blakey and Richard N. Billings (New York: Times Books, 1981), p.92-3
[272.] HH2, 108, 110 - Paul McCaghren testimony; see "Discovery of file may break open JFK investigation", by Earl Golz, *Dallas Morning News*, Saturday March 18, 1978. Reprinted in *TCI*, March 1978, p.16.
[273.] Sneed, 172
[274.] WCE 705 at WH17, 390-455
[275.] "NAS Panel Stuck on Channel 1, Report Delayed", by Gary Mack, *TCI*, March 1982, p.6

Six | Unsound Acoustics?

276. Letter from J. Edgar Hoover to J. Lee Rankin, April 7, 1964. Copy in author's files.
277. Curry testimony at WH4, 184.
278. FBI report 89-43-10553, p.3 (RIF 186-10006-10078); *TCI*, March 1982, pp.6, 7
279. "NAS Panel Stuck on Channel 1, Report Delayed", by Gary Mack, *TCI*, March 1982, p.7
280. Letter to the author from Jim Bowles, October 22, 1983
281. Although not 'best practice', the DPD occasionally took the recorder 'off line' to allow copies to be made to another machine, according to one retired radio division officer – e-mail to the author from Gary Mack, July 1, 2008.
282. "NAS Panel Stuck on Channel 1, Report Delayed", by Gary Mack, *TCI*, March 1982, p.6
283. FBI report 89-43-10553, p.3 (RIF 186-10006-10078).
284. Bowles manuscript, 16-17
285. Letter to the author from Gary Mack, November 15, 1981; *TCI*, March 1982, p.6; FBI report 89-43-10553, p.3 (RIF 186-10006-10078); author's correspondence with Jim Bowles in October 1983.
286. "The Dallas Police Radio: Progress Update", by Gary Mack, *TCI*, September 1977, p.6; "National Archives - Security Classification Problems Involving Warren Commission files and Other Records", Hearings before the House Subcommittee on Government Information, 1976, referenced in *"Coincidence or Conspiracy"*, by Bernard Fensterwald Jr and Michael Ewing (New York; Zebra Books, 1977), p.430
287. "NAS Panel Stuck on Channel 1, Report Delayed", by Gary Mack, *TCI*, March 1982, p.7; letter to the author from Jim Bowles, October 22, 1983; Recently-obtained information indicates that the tape was, in fact, sent to a sophisticated audio facility located at Tinker Air Force Base in Oklahoma City.
288. *"With Malice: Lee Harvey Oswald and the murder of Officer J.D. Tippit"*, by Dale K. Myers (Oak Cliff Press, Millford, Michigan, 1998), p. 20
289. Gary Mack e-mail to the author, October 5, 2007; author's telephone conversation with Gary Mack, March 26, 2008
290. Dale Myers e-mail to the author, November 6, 2007
291. Ibid. It has been verified that CBS did indeed obtain a copy of the radio recordings from the DPD in 1964 – see e-mail to the author from Gary Mack, September 9, 1999; "Dallas police challenge JFK 4-shot theory", *Boston Globe*, January 6, 1979; "Dallas Police Responsible For Crosstalk Theory", by Gary Mack, in *"Coverups!"* newsletter, June 1983, p. 1-2
292. *"With Malice - Lee Harvey Oswald and the Murder of Officer J.D. Tippit"*, by Dale Myers, p.369; *"Who Was Jack Ruby?"* by Seth Kantor (Everest House, NY, 1978), p.224 fn. 10; HH2, 109, McCaghren testimony
293. HH2, 109, McCaghren testimony; HR 67
294. HH2, 109
295. HH2, 109-110; *"The Plot to Kill the President"*, by G. Robert Blakey and Richard N. Billings (New York: Times Books, 1981), p.93
296. HH2, 110
297. Bonner and Hill had both previously worked for the *Dallas Times Herald*, and both had worked there at the same time during 1953-4; Hill's Warren Commission testimony at WH7, 44, Bonner book review in author's files.
298. HSCA document JFK 013886, Interview of Gerald Henslee, August 12, 1978 (RIF 180-10108-10192), p.4
299. *"Investigation of A Homicide"* by Judy Bonner (Anderson, SC; Droke House, 1969), p.311-2; "Acoustical Analysis Confirmed: FBI Backs Down", by Gary Mack, in *TCI*, April 22, 1981, p.2; letter from Arch Kimbrough to Paul Hoch, November 5, 1970; author's e-mail correspondence with Gary Mack and Don Thomas in December 2006.
300. Arch Kimbrough letter to Paul Hoch, November 5, 1970
301. "Acoustical Analysis Confirmed: FBI Backs Down", by Gary Mack, *TCI*, April 22, 1981, p.2
302. Ibid.; e-mail to author from Gary Mack, September 9, 1999
303. *"The Plot to Kill the President"*, by G. Robert Blakey and Richard N. Billings (New York: Times Books, 1981), p.92
304. HH2, 110, McCaghren testimony
305. HSCA document JFK 007058 - Staff Interview of Paul McCaghren, by Jack Moriarty, March 10, 1978 (RIF 180-10074-10388)

306. Ibid.
307. HSCA document JFK 007059 - Staff Interview of Paul McCaghren, by Jack Moriarty, March 11, 1978 (RIF 180-10074-10389)
308. HSCA document JFK 014405 – "Inventory of Paul McCarhren's (sic) file" dated March 11, 1978 (RIF 180-10115-10093)
309. Ibid – item number 38.
310. Bowles manuscript, 143-175
311. Ramsey Report, Table C-3, 75-80
312. HSCA documents JFK 007415 (RIF 180-10078-10223) for tape #1, and JFK 007414 (RIF 180-10078-10222) for tape #2
313. HSCA document JFK 007416 (RIF 180-10078-10224)
314. Author's letter to Ms. Jackson of June 30, 2008, and subsequent telephone calls on July 28, August 10 and August 11, 2008, have all remained unanswered.
315. HH8, 62, BBN Report #3947 - "Analysis of Recorded Sounds Relating to the Assassination of President John F. Kennedy", by James E. Barger, Scott P. Robinson, Edward C. Schmidt and Jared J. Wolf, dated January 1979.
316. HH2, 108-110
317. HSCA document JFK 014405 – "Inventory of Paul McCarhren's (sic) file" dated March 11, 1978 (RIF 180-10115-10093); Letter to the author from Gary Mack, dated March 15, 1983
318. HH8, 62, BBN Report
319. HR 66
320. HR 67 and footnote on that page.
321. HH5, 645, Barger testimony
322. HH8 34, BBN Report; see also Barger testimony at HH2, 89
323. HH8, 62, BBN Report
324. Ibid.
325. HH5, 637
326. HH5, 638
327. Ibid.
328. Ibid.
329. WH23, 838 and 842
330. RR, 20
331. Letter from Professor Ramsey to Roger Cubbage of the Justice Department, Bruce Koenig of the FBI and Charles Rader, a member of the Ramsey Panel, dated November 30, 1981 (RIF 186-10006-10392)
332. *TCI*, February 1983, p.4
333. Copy in author's files.
334. Professor Ramsey e-mail to the author, March 6, 2006.
335. HH2, 89
336. RR, 81-2
337. *"No Case To Answer"*, by Ian Griggs (JFK Lancer Productions & Publications, Southlake, Texas, 2005), p. 11
338. According to Chief Dispatcher Gerald Henslee, the dispatcher on duty was meant to record the start and end time on each belt, and then initial the belt. HSCA interview of Gerald Henslee, August 12, 1978 (RIF 180-10108-10192)
339. RR, 82
340. Paul Hoch's *"Echoes of Conspiracy"* newsletter, Vol. 4, Issue 2, p.1; letter to the author from Gary Mack, October 25, 1982.
341. Handwritten 'Post-It' note from Matt Fulgham to author, dated May 24, 1999, attached to batch of documents received from NARA
342. CD containing photographs and internal NARA report, "Condition Report for RG 60 JFK.01, Dallas Police Department Dictabelt #10 NWTD service order #05-483", dated July 14, 2005, provided to the author on May 5, 2008
343. Sneed, 176

Six | Unsound Acoustics?

344. Call Report dated June 12, 1995, released in 2004 among documents relating to transfer of material from DOJ to NARA
345. Jim Bowles e-mail to the author, June 16, 2008.
346. Ramsey Panel member Charles M. Rader e-mail to the author, November 19, 1999
347. RR, 67
348. Timing tests were carried out using Goldwave (version 5.13) software
349. Ibid.
350. HSCA document JFK 003090, interview of DPD Channel 1 dispatcher Murray Jackson, October 20, 1977, p. 3 (RIF 180-10103-10353); HSCA document JFK 013886, interview of DPD Chief Dispatcher Gerald Henslee, August 12, 1978, p. 4 (RIF 180-10108-10192)
351. HH4, 575, JFK Exhibit F-567, testimony of DPD Capt. Jack Revill; HH2, 108, 110, Paul McCaghren testimony; "*The Plot to Kill the President*", by G. Robert Blakey and Richard N. Billings (New York: Times Books, 1981) pp. 92-3; "Discovery of file may break open JFK investigation", by Earl Golz, *Dallas Morning News*, March 18, 1978
352. HH2, 109
353. Blakey and Billings, "The Plot to Kill the President", p. 93; HH2, 109-110
354. Warren Commission Exhibit 1974 at WH 23, 832; author's telephone interview of retired FBI Investigation Supervisor Richard Rogge
355. Paul McCaghren e-mail to the author, May 1, 2008; HSCA documents JFK 007417 (RIF 180-10078-10225) and JFK 007418 (REF 180-10078-10226)
356. Paul Hoch letter to the author, May 10, 1983, quoting Dr. Barger letter to Hoch on May 5, 1982; Hoch e-mail to the author, May 28, 2008
357. Letter from G. Robert Blakey to Robert L. Keuch, March 24, 1979 (RIF 186-10001-10217)
358. Professor Blakey e-mail to the author, June 16, 2008
359. Receipt from Robert Keuch to the HSCA, March 30, 1979, which was included in material handed over by Justice Department to NARA in March 1990 as part of NN3-60-90-1. The receipt refers to HSCA items JFK 004717 and 004718, the dictabelts received from Paul McCaghren.
360. Internal memorandum from Les Waffen, NARA Motion Picture, Sound and Video Branch, to his then boss, William T. Murphy. The memo was released in 2004 along with other documentation relating to the transfer of material from DOJ to NARA.
361. Preliminary Accession Inventory of JFK Assassination Records kept by Mr. Robert Keuch, Criminal Division, DOJ, and transferred to NARA, March 1990; Audio Accession Preservation List; Background Report prepared for the NARA Advisory Committee on Preservation, by Les Waffen and Charles Mayn, February 2004, p. 7. This report also shows (p. 6) that from 1990 to 1998 the belts were stored in 65oF, 35% Relative Humidity, and since 1998 they have been stored at 50oF, and 35% Relative Humidity; e-mail to the author from Donna Wessel, NARA (NWCS section), February 18, 1999
362. Todd Vaughan e-mail group posting, August 31, 2010
363. BBN Communications Director Joyce Kuzman e-mail to the author, September 13, 2007
364. WCE 1974, at 23 WH 832
365. HSCA document JFK 014405 – "Inventory of Paul McCarhren's (sic) file" dated March 11, 1978 (RIF 180-10115-10093)
366. RR, 20
367. Ibid.
368. Id. at 25
369. Id. at 36; Letter from Professor Ramsey to Roger Cubbage of the Justice Department, Bruce Koenig of the FBI and Charles Rader, a member of the Ramsey Panel, dated November 30, 1981 and Roger B. Cubbage "Memorandum to Files", dated December 10, 1981 (both in RIF 186-10006-10392);
370. WCE 1974 at WH23, 906-939
371. Audio Accession Preservation List and accompanying Preliminary Accession Inventory of JFK Assassination Records kept by Mr. Robert Keuch, Criminal Division, DOJ, and transferred to NARA, March 1990.
372. Roger B. Cubbage "Memorandum to Files", dated December 10, 1981 (part of RIF 186-10006-10392)
373. Bowles manuscript, 16

374. Preliminary Accession Inventory of JFK Assassination Records kept by Mr. Robert Keuch, Criminal Division, DOJ, and transferred to NARA, March 1990.
375. Background Report prepared for the NARA Advisory Committee on Preservation, by Les Waffen and Charles Mayn, February 2004, p. 3; e-mail from Les Waffen to D.B. Thomas, April 7, 2008
376. Ibid.; Richard Garwin e-mail to Ms. Anjii Cornett, The Cutting Corporation, June 11, 2004; e-mail to the author from Ms. Anjii Cornett, January 24, 2006.
377. See, for example, TV report by Bill Blakemore on World News Tonight, August 3, 2004; *"Tape of Kennedy's Killing Is Getting Digital Analysis"*, by Michael Janofsky, New York Times, August 3, 2004; *"Digital tape may solve JFK shots riddle"*, by Andrew Buncombe, Irish Independent, August 5, 2004, p. 30; *"The JFK Murder – Can new technology finally crack the case?"* by Jefferson Morley, Reader's Digest, May 2005, pp. 84-91 (pp. 62-9 in UK Edition)
378. "For the Record" memo dated July 14, 2005, written by Ms. Brenda Bernier, Senior Photograph Conservator, NARA Document Conservation Laboratory
379. Ibid.
380. Ibid.
381. Ibid.
382. *"Status of Dictabelt Scanning Project"*, interim report by Carl Haber to NARA, September 9, 2005.
383. Final Report by Carl Haber, NARA, January 21, 2007, pp.1-2
384. Id. pp.7-8; Les Waffen e-mail to the author, May 8, 2007
385. Les Waffen e-mail to the author, December 16, 2008
386. Les Waffen e-mail to the author, November 3, 2009
387. Dan Rooney e-mail to the author, October 26, 2010
388. HH8, 62
389. Todd Vaughan e-mails, Aug 31, 2010 and Oct 13, 2011
390. Dr. Barger e-mail to Don Thomas and M O'Dell, Feb 21, 2002
391. Michael O'Dell group e-mail, Aug 30, 2010
392. Ibid.; http://raytheon.mediaroom.com/index.php?s=43&item=1424
393. Michael O'Dell e-mail, November 24, 2010
394. Via e-mail to the author through Raytheon/BBN Communications Director, Ms. Joyce Kuzmin, October 5, 2011
395. Author's e-mail exchanges with Ms. Alison Trulock, Office of Art and Archives within the Office of the Clerk, U.S. House of Representatives, Dan Rooney of the Motion Picture, Sound and Video Branch, NARA and Ms. Mary Kay Schmidt, Special Access and FOIA Office, NARA, October 13-20, 2011

Seven
The Single Bullet Theory

Russell Kent

"The great enemy of the truth is very often not the lie – deliberate, contrived and dishonest, but the myth, persistent, persuasive and unrealistic. Belief in myths allows the comfort of opinion without the discomfort of thought."
– John F Kennedy

The single bullet theory is a myth with the very qualities described by President Kennedy. It is persistent – all the official investigations of his assassination have confirmed their belief in it. It is persuasive because it appears, superficially, to be a simple account of the apparent physical evidence – it must be believed to allow Lee Harvey Oswald alone to be capable of the murder. Ultimately, however, it is unrealistic because a thorough, honest look at the evidence does not support it.

Belief in this myth has allowed a comfortable official opinion that the establishment was not at risk from the assassination and was not responsible for it. This relaxed position has only been achieved by a mass avoidance of thought by a judiciary, government, military and media more concerned with protecting their careers than finding the truth.

What Is The Single Bullet Theory?
Briefly stated, the official conclusion by all US Government investigations into the assassination of John F Kennedy is that Lee Harvey Oswald shot three bullets at the President and that these three bullets alone account for all the injuries sustained during the shooting. Three people were wounded, James Tague superficially on the cheek, Texas Governor John Connally seriously in the chest, wrist and thigh and JFK fatally in the back, throat and head.

The investigations concluded that one bullet must have caused JFK's head wound and that one bullet missed injuring bystander James Tague. This left one bullet to account for all seven other wounds to JFK and to John Connally who was also riding in the President's limousine. Furthermore, the official position is as follows:

- The bullet that caused all these wounds, dropped out of the Connally's thigh intact in Parkland Memorial Hospital.

- The bullet was found and matched to a weapon found in the Texas School Book Depository.

- This weapon belonged to and was fired by Oswald.

Put simply, this account of the assassination may sound entirely possible. Almost all the conclusions in the above, however, are at the very least debatable. The following points regarding the SBT have been skilfully disputed over the years and are certainly not facts:

- That Oswald did any shooting on the day

- That there were only three bullets

- That only one bullet caused JFK's head wound

- That the third bullet alone accounted for all seven other wounds

- That this bullet remained intact

- That this bullet dropped out of Connally's thigh.

This list highlights the major problem with the SBT – that *everything* must fit. If one part of the theory cannot be upheld, then the whole theory is unsustainable. There is an even more extensive list of facts which must be true for the SBT to work at the end of this chapter.

Where investigations rely upon a theory, we reasonably expect them to publish all the relevant data and for the data to lead towards the conclusion that the investigations claim. But the reality in the Kennedy assassination is that much of the relevant data was unpublished or hidden among reams of irrelevant garbage and the data we do have frequently does not support the conclusions. Worse, the evidence regarding the SBT has, along with most other areas of the crime, been substituted, modified or lied about.

Oswald, unfortunately, did not survive to be tried as he was murdered on 24th November 1963 by Jack Ruby. Nevertheless, the US investigations have always acted as his prosecutors. In this case, we must be Oswald's jury and it

SEVEN | THE SINGLE BULLET THEORY

is the duty of the investigations to convince us of their conclusions. As jurors, we can only find Oswald guilty if we are convinced beyond a reasonable doubt of his guilt.

If any doubt that is raised affects our reasonable belief that the defendant is guilty then we cannot be satisfied beyond a reasonable doubt and Oswald must be declared not guilty.

Despite what the Warren Commission, the House Select Committee on Assassinations (HSCA) and authors such as Vincent Bugliosi may have you believe, there is very little in the SBT which can be proven to this degree of certainty. I have calculated that out of the Warren Commission Report's 888 pages there are only 35 pages regarding the SBT[1]. This is a scant 4% of the report and yet without it the prosecution case must fail, because without the SBT Oswald could not have been the sole shooter.

The chapter in Bugliosi's massive book, "Reclaiming History", that specifically deals with the SBT, of which he is a staunch supporter, is 62 pages long[2]. But this chapter also covers the Zapruder film[3] and when his Zapruder coverage is taken out of the reckoning, Bugliosi spends just 22 pages on the SBT. Therefore, given that the total number of pages in Bugliosi's book is 1,648, he devotes under 2% of the pages discussing the core of the case.

Either the Warren Commission and Bugliosi believe that the SBT is simple and easily supported or they think it is shaky and therefore, best not dwelt upon. My aim in this chapter is to convince you that it cannot be tolerated.

The Warren Commission

From the very beginning, the US government worked hard to contain the investigation into the killing of JFK and the wounding of Connally. It is well known that the Dallas Police Chief Curry, Head of the FBI Hoover and Deputy Attorney General Katzenbach were determined to limit the responsibility for the crime to one individual, Lee Harvey Oswald, who was himself murdered on 25th November 1963. On that day, Hoover wrote a memo containing, among other things, the following statement:

"The thing I am most concerned about and so is Mr Katzenbach, is having something issued so that we can convince the public that Oswald is the real assassin."[4]

On the same day, the infamous Katzenbach memo to Bill Moyers stated:

"The public must be satisfied that Oswald was the assassin: that he did not have confederates who are still at large: and that the evidence was such that he would have been convicted at trial."

Again, on the same day, President Lyndon Baines Johnson (LBJ) ordered the FBI and the Department of Justice to investigate the assassination of JFK and the murder of Oswald. LBJ and Hoover then decided that the FBI investigation should be confirmed by a panel of the good and great. According to Walt Brown[5], based on tape recordings released by the Lyndon Baines Johnson Library, "... *the Warren Commission's charge was to verify the FBI's findings in the assassination: a secondary function ... was to ambush proposed investigations by both the House and the Senate.*"

The five-volume FBI Report[6] was completed on 9th December 1963. This effectively skewed the entire process from the start as the Warren Commission had no choice but to substantiate the FBI's findings. To do otherwise would have involved an independent gathering of information for which it had no investigative resources. There's no doubt that some of the Warren Commission staff worked hard to uncover the truth, but they could only work with what they were fed, particularly by the FBI.

Additionally, if the Warren Commission *had* discovered anything contrary to the FBI, they risked embarrassing a powerful establishment, including Hoover and LBJ, the latter being the very person who had appointed them. Worse, the Warren Commission could not examine any evidence which suggested Oswald was innocent or other parties were guilty because the FBI didn't provide any.

The lack of evidence showing anything other than the official position is often used against those who doubt the Warren Commission. But the scarcity of contrary evidence is not the fault of researchers, as they can only use that which was collected at the time. The gathering of forensic data was rudimentary, often slap-dash and even negligent. There never was an authority involved that was not concerned with protecting their own reputation or perhaps concealing their own involvement in the crime itself. Literally every piece of evidence assembled at the time is questionable, before one approaches the evidence which was *not* collected.

The result is that researchers are stuck with compromised evidence gathered by a combination of clueless cops and suspect Secret Service agents. The FBI agents involved were a mixture of incorruptible and devious, all operating under the direction of a pre-determined outcome set by Hoover (possibly at LBJ's bequest). The outcome is that honest historians are left to search between the flawed data of dishonest investigations.

The Necessity of a Single Bullet Theory

The FBI Report concluded that Oswald killed Kennedy and nobody else was involved. Oswald, according to the FBI, had fired three shots, these were the only shots that had been fired and all of them hit occupants of the presidential limousine. The FBI Report said the following regarding the distribution of the shots:

SEVEN | THE SINGLE BULLET THEORY

- The first shot hit JFK in the back and did not perforate his body

- The second shot hit John Connally in the back causing all his wounds

- The third shot hit JFK in the head.

This scenario, whilst requiring world-class marksmanship and the superhuman working of a poor weapon, did not require any magic bullet. But there were two problems.

Firstly, the FBI Report contained no mention of the President's throat wound. The FBI based their description of the Kennedy's wounds on the conclusions that the autopsy pathologists had made when the body was in the Bethesda morgue. The lead pathologist, Dr Humes, had stated at that time that the wound in Kennedy's back had not penetrated beyond three or four centimeters and that the bullet had dropped out of this wound when the President had been given external cardiac massage at Parkland.

Prior to writing the official autopsy report, Humes discovered that what he had assumed was a tracheotomy incision was also, in fact, a bullet wound. Dr Perry at Parkland had described the bullet wound in Kennedy's throat as an entrance wound. Ignoring this, as he had been told all the shooting was from behind the President, Humes conjectured as follows: if the throat wound is an entrance wound, either the bullet is still in Kennedy's body or there must be a corresponding exit wound. As neither was true, Humes simply presumed that the throat wound must be the exit for the back wound. With scant other evidence, Humes then changed the autopsy conclusion to say that the back wound was an entrance wound caused by a bullet that perforated Kennedy's body and caused an exit wound in his throat.

When the Warren Commission received the official autopsy report, they were confronted with evidence of a bullet leaving Kennedy's throat. They asked themselves the question, "Where did this bullet go"? Since Connally was sitting immediately in front of the President, it seemed likely to them that it went on to cause Connally's wounds. It was all based on guesswork.

The second problem was that the FBI had ignored a timing issue later revealed to the Warren Commission by the Zapruder film.

When the Warren Commission studied the Zapruder film, they concluded that the President and John Connally received their non-fatal wounds in less time than it takes to reload a Mannlicher-Carcano rifle, the type of weapon allegedly found in the Texas School Book Depository and allegedly owned by Oswald.

This created an immense problem for the Warren Commission. Oswald could not have shot Kennedy in the back, reloaded and then shot Connally in the back. The film showed that there was not enough time. So, for Oswald to be the sole assassin, the Warren Commission was forced to conclude that the shot which

JFK | ECHOES FROM ELM STREET
A SEARCH FOR HISTORICAL ACCURACY ON THE
ASSASSINATION OF PRESIDENT JOHN F. KENNEDY

hit Kennedy in the back also hit Connally in the back. They had been painted into a corner.

Later, James Tague made the corner tighter still. He had received several small cheek wounds from flying debris after a bullet struck the kerb close to where he was standing watching the motorcade. So with one shot causing the President's head wounds and one shot missing and wounding James Tague, the Warren Commission were left with only one shot to account for the remaining seven wounds to JFK and Connally.

But it gets worse. An intact bullet apparently from Connally's stretcher in Parkland was matched to the rifle found in the Texas School Book Depository. This bullet became Commission Exhibit 399 (CE399) and it *had* to be the single bullet which caused all seven non-fatal wounds to JFK and Connally.

The Warren Commission concluded that the other two bullets (the one which hit JFK in the head and the one that hit the kerb near Tague) had fragmented. So any intact bullet found anywhere at the scene of the crime or Parkland Memorial Hospital *had* to be that bullet.

The Warren Commission had no choice. Regardless of the condition of this bullet and regardless of where it was found, once it was matched to Oswald's gun it had to be the bullet that caused all seven separate wounds to JFK and Connally.

Once the SBT was born, the Warren Commission acted with huge confirmation bias – they strongly favoured evidence which supported it and ignored evidence that did not.

Supported?

The Kennedy assassination is a complex case and in some areas, extraordinarily complex. But the principal idea, the idea on which the choice of lone assassin or conspiracy rests, is a straightforward matter. If it can be proven that one bullet caused the seven wounds to the President and Connally, then the assassination could have been done by one gunman. If it can be shown, however, that one bullet could not have caused all the wounds to the President and the Governor in the manner claimed, then there have to be four or more shots. Given the timing limitations, this would mean that there was a second shooter in Dealey Plaza and a conspiracy to murder the President.

If the SBT is the truth, the evidence should largely support it. The entrance and exit wounds on Kennedy and Connally should show the correct pathological features of entrance and exit wounds. The tracks through their bodies should be supported by descriptions in an autopsy report and operative record. The trajectories should align and support a shot from behind at the correct elevation. Any films, photographs and eye witness testimony should be in agreement. The medical documents should be supportive and reliable. Any recovered ballistic evidence should be consistent and make sense given the wounds suffered.

SEVEN | THE SINGLE BULLET THEORY

But few, if any, of the official claims for the SBT are supported by the evidence. On the contrary, there is a mass of evidence that refutes the theory. This includes:

- Ballistics evidence – the bullet itself, CE399[7], which was barely distorted and almost whole despite the Warren Commission claiming that it broke 10cm of Connally's fifth rib and shattered his radius (a thick, solid bone). CE399 also has a very dubious chain of possession. This alone might result in CE399 not being allowed as evidence in a court.

- Trajectory evidence – recently, Alaric Rosman has thoroughly debunked the possibility that JFK and Connally were aligned in such a way that a shot from the 6th floor of the TSBD could hit both of them. In part four of his "The Single Bullet In Flatland"[8], Rosman skillfully showed that the bullet that entered Connally's chest had to be on a left-to-right trajectory (that is, fired from behind Connally, but to his *left*). This clearly exculpates Oswald who was accused of shooting from behind and to the *right* of the limousine.

- Arlen Specter even disproved his own theory when trying to line up the locations of wounds on JFK and Connally in a reconstruction using wires in a garage[9]. The picture of the reconstruction shows Specter having to hold a straight wire well above the marked location of JFK's back wound (near Specter's little finger) in order to line up JFK's throat wound with Connally's back wound.

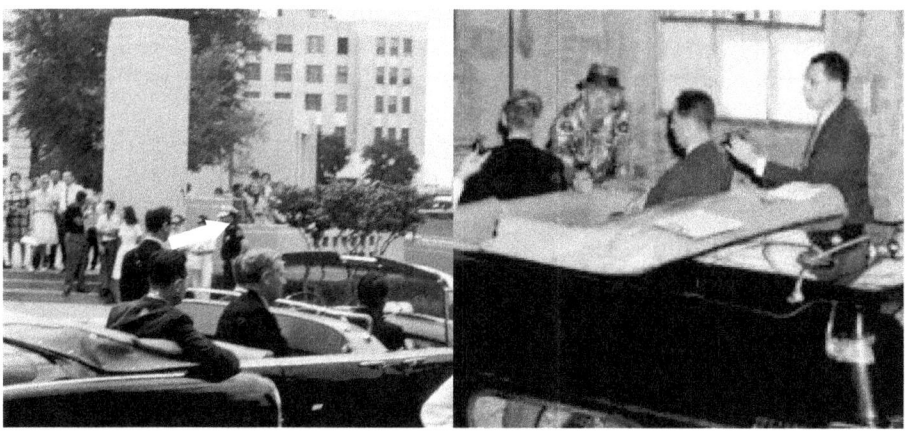

Specter Disproving His Own Theory

- Medical evidence – the bodies of JFK and John Connally.

- Eyewitness testimony, particularly that of John Connally himself[10]. Connally always insisted that he was hit after JFK was wounded in the throat.

- Photographic evidence – the Zapruder film, upon which the Warren Commission relied heavily, shows John Connally with his arm above his nipple line and unwounded, still holding his Stetson, after JFK has been hit[11].

Much of this stack of counter evidence is discussed below.

Bullet Fragments, Weights and Composition

Unfortunately for the investigating authorities and their supporters, the very piece of physical evidence, CE399, upon which the SBT and their conclusions rely, is suspect. While CE399 is not pristine (it is slightly flattened lengthways), it is fair to say that it is barely damaged. The Warren Commission and the HSCA used the results of two scientists to allege that:

- Any missing material from CE399 could be accounted for by the fragments of metal in Connally's body.

- The fragments recovered from Connally's body could be chemically matched to samples taken from CE399.

In my opinion, however, there is significant doubt over these allegations. CE399 may have lost only 2.4 grains[12] of its un-fired weight. The Warren Commission would have us believe that this very small loss of weight is accounted for by the lead found in Connally's wounds. However, the Commission's own scientist (at least, the only one they called on this matter), FBI ballistics expert Special Agent Robert Frazier testified that the difference between the weight of CE399 and the average for this type of bullet could be accounted for by normal manufacturing variation. Frazier testified that "there did not necessarily have to be any weight loss to the bullet"[13]. If that was true, then any metallic fragments found in Connally came from other bullets.

How Many Fragments?

Connally's body contained many bullet fragments when he was admitted to Parkland Memorial Hospital. During his three hours in surgery, only two were removed and they were taken only from his wrist. The rest remained in his body as it was thought that they posed no danger to the Governor's health and that it would be risky to attempt removing them.

Dr Gregory testified that he removed two fragments (but left other small fragments in the wound)[14]. This was good, clear testimony and so we should expect the exhibit purporting to be the fragments removed by Dr Gregory to show two pieces of metal. It does not. Warren Commission exhibit CE842 (see Figure 1 below) consists of three or four fragments. In other words, the evidence has changed.

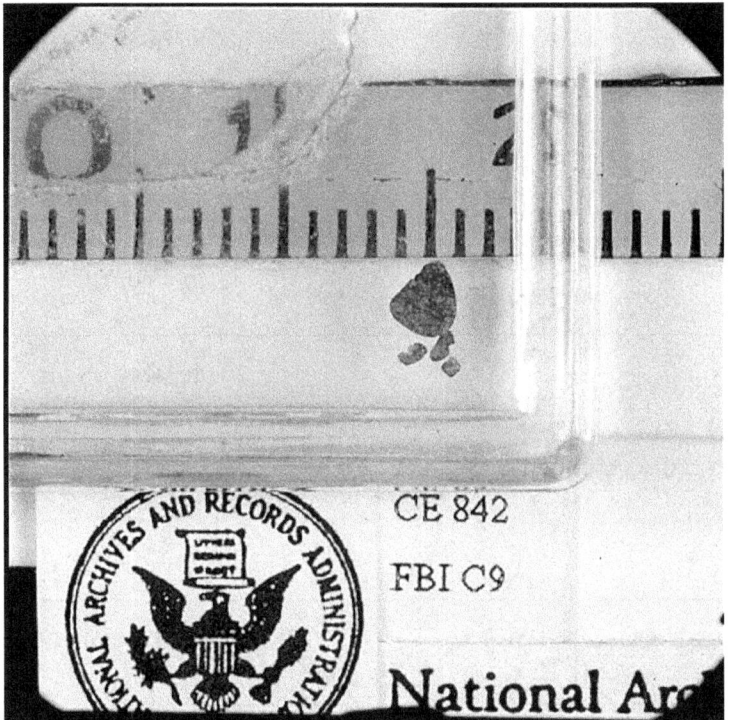

Figure 1: Part of CE842 (17H 841)

In fact, the confusion over the number of fragments removed from Connally's wrist is remarkable. Table 1, below, shows fifteen different references to the fragments removed by Dr Gregory from Connally's wrist[15]. The number of fragments ranges from one to five. Shouldn't a single exhibit be constant? How can the same exhibit consist of different numbers of fragments? Such inconsistency raises reasonable doubt over whether the fragments removed during surgery are the same as those shown in the exhibit.

JFK | ECHOES FROM ELM STREET
A SEARCH FOR HISTORICAL ACCURACY ON THE
ASSASSINATION OF PRESIDENT JOHN F. KENNEDY

Source & Date	Reference	No. fragments	Remarks
Dr Gregory's "Operative Record" (22 Nov 63)	WCR 533–534	More than 1	Several in wound: some removed
Original evidence envelope, PARKLAND (22 Nov 63)	17H 841 1HSCA 468 7HSCA 392	More than 1	Contains the description "Bullet fragments." Labelled "Q9"
WC photo of fragments in plastic box (Nov 64)	17H 841	3–4	One large fragment and 2–3 smaller ones
Dr Gregory's testimony (21 Apr 64)	4H 119–120	2	3 fragments in wound: 2 removed
Enhanced X-ray of wrist (22 Nov 63)	7HSCA 155	3–4	Before fragments removed
DPD's second list of evidence transferred to FBI, from DPD's report on the assassination (22 Nov 63) (CE 2003)	24H 260	More than 1	"Bullet fragments taken from body of Governor Connally." Mrs Audrey Bell, Operating room nurse, to Bob Nolan, D.P.S., to Capt. Fritz, to Crime Lab, to FBI.
FBI's list of evidence received from DPD, from DPD's report on the assassination (23 Nov 63) (CE 2003)	24H 262	1	Metal fragment

SEVEN | THE SINGLE BULLET THEORY

DPD's list of evidence transferred to FBI on 26 November 1963, from DPD's report on the assassination (CE 2003)	24H 252	1	"Bullet fragment taken from the body of Gov. John Connally".
FBI report by SA J. Doyle Williams (30 Nov 63)	7HSCA 155	1	"A small fragment of metal" was removed from Connally's arm.
Testimony of SA Robert A. Frazier (6 May 64)	5H 72	1	"A small fragment of metal."
V. P. Guinn's report to HSCA (Sep 78)	1HSCA 514	3	One larger (16.4 mg) and two smaller (1.3 mg combined)
V. P. Guinn's testimony to HSCA (8 Sep 78)	1HSCA 497	3	One larger and two smaller
Findings and Conclusions of the [HSCA] Firearms Panel, (Mar 79)	7HSCA 367	4	One weighed 0.3 grain: the others were too small to weigh.
HSCA photos of fragments in plastic box (15 Apr 78)	1HSCA 468 7HSCA 392	3-5	One large fragment and 2-4 smaller ones.
Caption to HSCA photo (15 Apr 78)	7HSCA 392	4	"Four lead-like fragments"

Table 1: References to Connally wrist fragments

There were other pieces of metal in Connally's body besides the fragments left behind in his wrist by Dr Gregory. Connally's left thigh contained at least one fragment. On 29th November 1963, Parkland Memorial Hospital sent Connally's X-rays to the FBI[16]. The dimensions of the thigh fragment, as shown on one of the X-rays, were 3.5mm by 1.3mm. Figure 2, below, is a drawing I made of the thigh fragment based on the dimensions given by Dr Reynolds from Parkland.

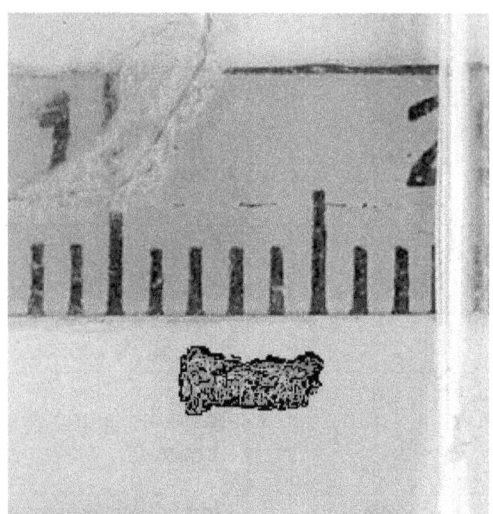

Figure 2: Drawing of thigh fragment

Figure 3, below, shows my drawing of the thigh fragment next to CE842 and the base of CE399 – all at the same scale. CE842's fragments don't appear to fit easily with any missing portion of CE399. I recognize that without an indication of the two fragments thickness and the depth of gouging to CE399 it is not possible to say this definitively. But when added to Dr Shires' testimony of another bullet fragment being visible on Connally's chest X-ray[17] and the fact that many fragments were left in his wrist I think it is reasonable to doubt that they all came from CE399.

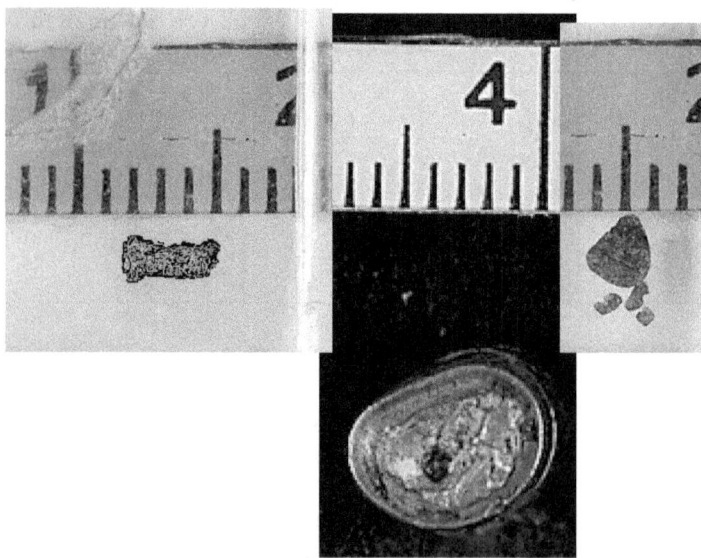

Figure 3: Comparison of Figure 2, CE399 and CE842 (same scale)

SEVEN | THE SINGLE BULLET THEORY

Bullet Composition

For the SBT to be true, the composition of any fragments recovered from Connally must match the composition of CE399.

Before looking at the way CE842 and CE399 were compared, I must digress into a discussion about the chain of possession. A chain of possession or chain of custody refers to a legal requirement that an exhibit is identified and retains its integrity from the place it was collected to a courtroom.

This is achieved by careful documentation. Each time the exhibit changes hands, the documentation should show the name or initials of the individual collecting the exhibit, each person or entity subsequently having custody of it, their employer or agency, the date the object was collected or transferred, any object number, any patient's or employee's name and a brief description of the object itself. Treated properly in this way, an exhibit might withstand legal challenges to its authenticity. Without a good chain of possession, the validity of an exhibit is weakened. It could even be declared inadmissible.

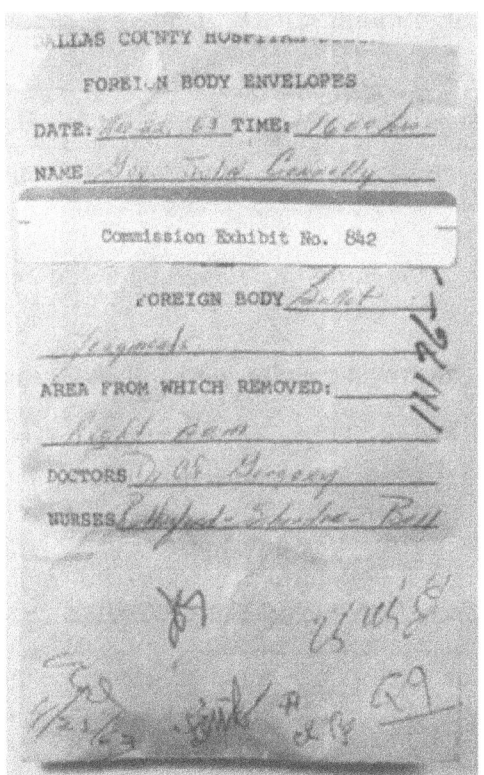

Figure 5: Part of CE842 (17H 841)

In a case involving the murder of the President, we would surely expect the chains of possession to be scrupulous. I doubt, however, that any of the evidence in this case would survive basic legal challenge. I do not intend to get into the provenance of CE399 as this is discussed extensively in the JFK literature, suffice to say that it is neither straightforward nor without legal problems. I will discuss the logic of its discovery later. For now, let's return to CE842, the alleged fragments from Connally's wrist wound. What does the chain of possession look like here?

Nurse Supervisor Audrey N Bell told the HSCA that she received the metal fragments from Connally's wrist and placed them in a one ounce medical jar[18]. She then prepared a foreign body envelope. This envelope together with the fragments from Connally's wrist and the jar they were in became Warren Commission exhibit CE842.

Nurse Bell gave the envelope containing the fragments to Texas Highway Patrol Trooper Bobby Nolan. In my opinion, Nolan then handed it to Dallas

Police Captain of Homicide and Robbery Bureau J W Fritz. Fritz gave most of the evidence (including the CE842) to FBI SA Vincent E Drain who took it to FBI SA Robert Frazier in Washington DC. All their initials are on the envelope.

The problem is that both the Parkland envelope (see above) and Dallas Police Department evidence list, (see below), call the evidence fragment<u>s</u> (plural):

> Bullet fragments taken from body of
> Governor Connally

Figure 6: Extract from CE2003 DPD evidence list (24H 260)

However, the FBI documents only ever refer to a fragment, (singular):

> Q9 Metal fragment from arm of Governor John Connally

Figure 7: Frazier's original (hand annotated) FBI evidence report November 23, 1963

> Q9 Metal fragment from arm of Governor John Connolly

Figure 8: FBI official evidence receipt from Hoover to Curry CE2003 November 23, 1963

I think it's fair to raise some doubt in the honest handling of the evidence here and suggest that either the FBI lost some of CE842 or the DPD didn't give them all of it.

To test whether the fragments allegedly from Connally's wrist (CE842) came from CE399, Dr Vincent Perry Guinn (Professor of Chemistry, University of California at Irvine) was asked by the HSCA to perform a neutron activation analysis (NAA). NAA is a highly accurate way to determine the concentrations of chemical elements in a sample of a specific material.

Of course, any testing of CE842 presumes that it is authentic evidence. I have already shown that it may not be. In fact, it is highly suspect. There are more fragments in evidence than the doctor said he removed. These extra fragments could have come from anywhere. If someone wanted to frame Oswald, the best place to take them from would be CE399. Any results showing that the compositions of CE842 and CE399 match must be considered with this in mind. If, however, they do not match then the fragments left in Connally did not come from the single bullet and must have come from one or more other bullets.

Guinn reported that the core of CE399 contained the metal antimony (in the lead core) at a concentration of 833 ppm (parts per million) and that the alleged Connally wrist fragments contained antimony at a concentration of 797 ppm[19]. He concluded that the miniscule difference in the concentration of

SEVEN | THE SINGLE BULLET THEORY

antimony between the two samples (36 ppm) was evidence that the alleged Connally wrist fragment came from CE399.

This is scientific nonsense and Guinn's own previous research shows it. It is not possible to use the levels of antimony to show that two fragments are from the same bullet of this type. Several years before the HSCA investigation, Guinn had performed NAA on several bullets of the same type as CE399. Table 2, below, shows the ppm of antimony that he found in three bullets[20]:

Fragment Number	Bullet 1	Bullet 2	Bullet 3
1	363	358	1062
2	395	869	1139
3	441	882	1156
4	667	983	1235

Table 2: Parts per million of antimony found in three WCC bullets by Dr Guinn

For the purposes of this chapter, it is not important to know what antimony is or the other metals for which Guinn tested. We only have to look at the way Guinn interpreted his results. Remember, according to Guinn, if a bullet has 833 ppm of antimony and a fragment has 797 ppm it's a match. That is, the fragment came from the bullet. But wait, *his own results* show:

- The levels of antimony within any one bullet vary widely.

- Any of the fragments from bullet 1 could be matched with bullet 1 *or* bullet 2.

- The first fragments of bullets 1 and 2 are *more closely matched* than CE842 and CE399. Had Guinn not known they came from separate bullets, using his HSCA nonsense science, he would have concluded that they came from the same bullet.

- *The alleged Connally wrist fragment (which contained 797 ppm of antimony) could have come from bullet 2 or any other similar bullet (and not CE399).*

Guinn should not have testified to the HSCA that CE842 came from CE399. That has never been proven. The HSCA should have checked – it's basic maths. If they had, they would have known that Guinn was wrong.

Two peer-reviewed scientific papers have proven the point. The first, by Drs Randlich and Grant, looked at the bullet evidence in the JFK assassination from both the metallurgical and statistical viewpoints. They found that "...the extant evidence is consistent with any number between two and five rounds fired in Dealey Plaza during the shooting."[21]

The second paper, by Doctors Spiegelman, Tobin et al, reported that Dr Guinn's statistical analysis was wrong. Their analysis showed that "evidence used to rule out a second assassin is fundamentally flawed" and their conclusion is that "the bullet fragments from the assassination that match could have come from three or more separate bullets"[22]. Any evidence of three or more bullets hitting the occupants of the car destroys the SBT.

These two scientific papers are crucial and support the proposition that Kennedy and Connally were hit by *separate* bullets.

JFK and the Evidence Against the SBT

The Warren Commission concluded that a bullet (CE399) caused a perforating wound when passing through JFK's neck entering "at the base of the back of his neck"[23] and exiting his throat.

There has been so much argument over the years about the wounds to JFK's back and throat and I will only give a brief summary here. For a more thorough discussion, see my other chapter in this book. Simply put, the wounds do not support the SBT. There is no real evidence that the wound in JFK's back was perforating (transitory). That is, there is nothing to prove that the wound in JFK's back and the one in his throat are connected.

The autopsy doctors, Drs James Humes, J Thornton Boswell and Pierre Finck did not dissect the path of the bullet[24]. They did not cut away the skin, muscle and organs of the neck to reveal a bullet track. They did try to probe the back wound with a finger and medical probe, but they could not define a path[25]. Dr Finck even testified that the wound did not penetrate deeply[26].

The base of the back of his neck entry was liable to fail a defence challenge in court for the following reasons:

- The autopsy (CE 387) more correctly describes JFK's wound as a back wound and not a neck wound.

- The JFK autopsy face sheet completed by Dr Boswell[27] and marked "verified" by the President's personal physician, Admiral Burkley, shows the wound to be in JFK's back.

- JFK's jacket and shirt[28] both show a hole in the back.

- The death certificate for JFK[29], prepared by the Admiral Burkley, also places

SEVEN | THE SINGLE BULLET THEORY

the hole at the level of the third thoracic (that is, the upper half of the back) vertebra and not at the level of the cervical (that is, the neck) vertebrae.

This physical evidence is backed up by the eyewitness statement of Secret Service Agent Glenn Bennett[30] and Secret Service Agent Clint Hill's testimony to the Warren Commission[31].

Furthermore, the evidence does not suggest that the back wound was an entry wound:

- No bullet was found in the wound

- No metallic fragments were found in the wound

- No abrasion collar was noted (entrance wounds often show a scorched border where the skin has been rapidly rubbed by the bullet as it penetrates)

- The slides made for microscopic examination of the back wound which might have shown evidence of a bullet entry have been lost. They are no longer available as proof.

The way that the back wound was treated created further problems in diagnosing its nature. Humes may have altered its appearance before anybody else got a good look at it because he probed it with his finger. This is significant because if it was an exit wound, by pushing his finger in, Humes may have pushed any tissue coming out of the wound back inside it. This may have changed the appearance of the wound from exit to entrance. In Humes' handwritten original autopsy report, the back wound is described as a "puncture" wound[32]. Even in the published autopsy report, Humes can only bring himself to call the back wound "presumably of entry."[33]

Turning now to the throat wound, there is no good evidence that it was an exit wound. During the autopsy, it was not carefully examined as the doctors assumed that the wound was caused by a tracheotomy. The official story is that only after the body was no longer available for examination did Humes discover that there had been a wound in the throat when JFK was admitted to Parkland. The throat wound may have been an entry wound - many of the Parkland doctors testified that it could have been either an entry or exit. The autopsy report prepared by Humes hedges and states that the throat wound was "presumably of exit."[34]

The Warren Commission's description of this wound as back to front through the neck would almost certainly not be upheld in court. According to the Warren Commission, this wound actually got smaller as it penetrated JFK from a 7 x 4mm "entrance" to a 3 – 5mm (almost half the size) "exit". This is contrary to medical experience – exit wounds are usually larger than entry wounds. But even if we ignore that and decide this wound did go through JFK, the Warren Commission puts the angle of the perforating path at around 17 degrees and slightly right to left[35]. This angle is 8 degrees shallower than the perforating wound to Connally's chest. What deflected the single bullet downwards? In fact, nothing could have. The men were hit by different bullets.

Recently, there has been a resurgence of the view that JFK's post-mortem X-rays show metallic particles in the neck. This is largely due to the Clark Panel Report which states, ". . . several small metallic particles are present in this region."[36] If this were true, then it might have been evidence of a bullet path through JFK's neck. However, as noted by Milicent Cranor[37] and more lately by Dr Gary Aguilar and Kathy Cunningham[38], these objects are artifacts –the film itself bore the marks before it was exposed. There were no bone or metal fragments in JFK's neck and none on the X-ray, so this is not evidence of a pathway through JFK's neck afterall.

Further evidence that no bullet could have penetrated JFK's neck in the way the Warren Commission would have us believe comes from a study by Dr David W Mantik[39]. By using a CAT scan of a body whose upper chest and neck dimensions were the same as those of JFK (see figure below), he found that the trajectory proposed by the Warren Commission would hit the cervical (neck) vertebrae. This shows that it would have been impossible for a bullet to have followed the official trajectory.

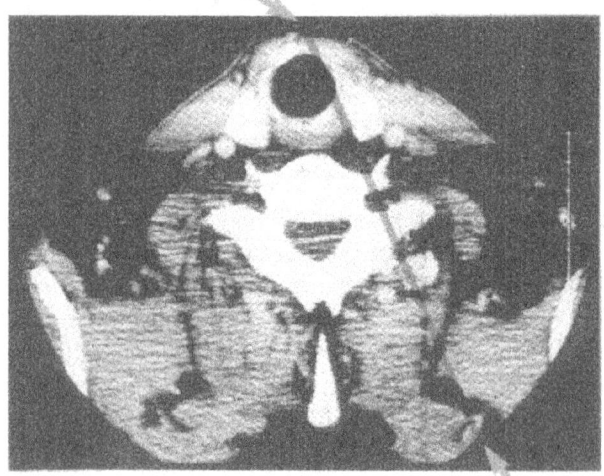

Location of Throat Wound

Location of Back Wound at Neck Level

Figure 9: CAT scan at the base of the neck showing official trajectory would have to damage spine (white area in the centre of the scan) (Mantik, 1998).

Seven | The Single Bullet Theory

This is where discussion about the viability of the SBT should end. There is no evidence that anything ever went through JFK's neck, but plenty of reasons that nothing ever could have done so in the way claimed. The last refuge of the SBT-believer, however, is to throw down the following challenge: if the back wound and throat wound are unconnected, then where are the bullets which caused these separate wounds?

It's a good question and I don't know the answer. The reason I don't know is because the collection of ballistic and medical evidence was, at best, negligent. The appearance and description of both wounds is in doubt. All the microscopic samples are missing. The ballistics evidence is compromised.

Legally speaking, for any reasonable person, the result of this is doubt. I can offer a guess at what the wounds may have been: The back wound may have been a short shot (a less powerful bullet manufactured with a low powder charge) which penetrated the President's back by only a few millimetres. The throat wound may not have been a bullet wound at all – perhaps it was caused by a piece of glass or projectile from another weapon. I have no evidence, but whose fault is that? The evidence is in such a mess that a whole range of things are possible. The truth cannot be stated with any degree of certainty.

So, I could stop here. Let's see though whether any other apparent evidence of Kennedy and Connally being hit by the same bullet is any more convincing.

Connally and the Evidence Against the SBT

Connally was treated for his gunshot wounds at Parkland Memorial Hospital by several doctors. He had three wounds:

- A perforating wound of the chest which broke a rib and damaged the pleural sac covering his right lung

- A perforating wound of the right wrist which broke his radius

- A penetrating wound of the left thigh.

Dr Robert Shaw led the surgical team that worked on Connally's chest wound. He gave testimony to the Warren Commission twice. Dr Charles Gregory led the surgical team that worked on Connally's wrist wound. Again, he gave testimony twice to the Warren Commission. Dr George Shires was head of the surgical team that worked on Connally's thigh wound and he gave testimony to the Warren Commission only once.

Between their two rounds of testimony in March and April 1964, Drs Shaw and Gregory were allowed to inspect some of the alleged physical evidence and watch the Zapruder film. This occurred during the "Strange Conferences" described in more detail later. The change in what Shaw and Gregory were willing to speculate on after seeing this alleged evidence is discussed in depth later.

Dr Robert Roeder Shaw

Dr Shaw was Professor of Thoracic Surgery at the University of Texas Medical School at the time of the assassination[40]. He had been a medical doctor since 1933. Crucially, Shaw had been in the US Army Medical Corp during the Second World War and had been stationed in England (1942) and France (1944). Shortly before joining the team at Parkland Memorial Hospital, Shaw had served with the MEDICO team in Afghanistan (1961– 63). By the time he treated Connally, Shaw had experience with over 1,000 gunshot wounds. I'd guess that was about 1,000 more than anybody in the Warren Commission.

He worked on Connally's chest wound. Shaw described the path of the bullet that caused this wound as entering Connally's back at the right armpit and leaving near his right nipple. The angle of perforation was about 25 degrees downward and only very slightly right to left[41].

Shaw was questioned twice by the Warren Commission[42]. Prior to his second appearance, he viewed the Zapruder film, CE399 and the Governor's clothes at the second "Strange Conference". His answers to questions in the first round are very different to the testimony he gave after viewing this physical evidence.

Shaw's testimony is important regarding:

- Whether the entrance wound in Connally's armpit was made by a tumbling bullet – the Warren Commission needed it to be tumbling to prove that it had gone through JFK first) – see later.

- The angle of trajectory through the chest, which needed to be about 25 degrees – and preferably slightly less – to match the rest of the Warren Commission Report.

Was the Bullet Tumbling?

Figure 10, opposite, shows the path of CE399 as believed by the Warren Commission and those authors that still trust its conclusions. It shows a relatively straight trajectory through JFK and Connally and that the bullet was tumbling after leaving JFK's throat.

SEVEN | THE SINGLE BULLET THEORY

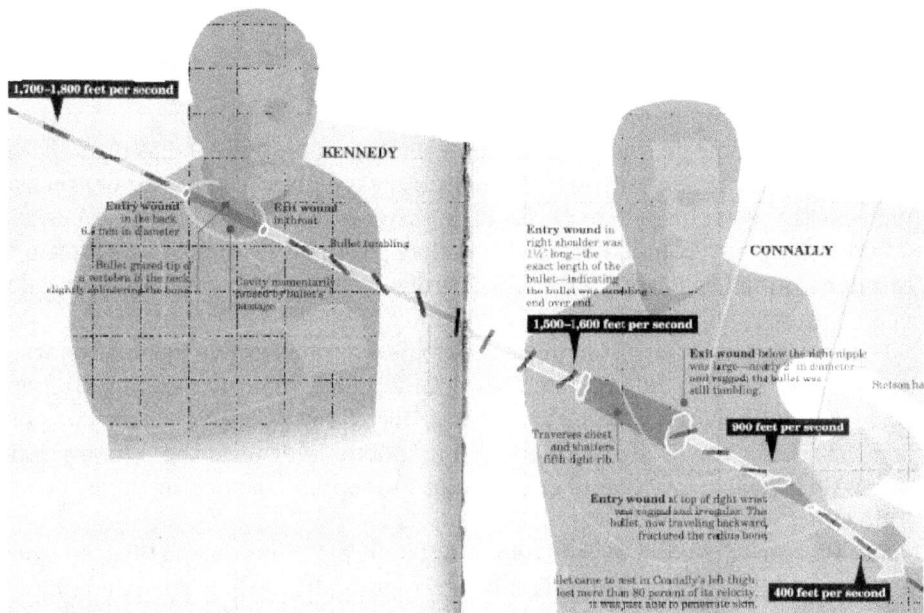

Figure 10: The smooth flight of CE399 according to Warren Commission supporters (from "Case Closed" Gerald Posner)

But if the bullet was tumbling when it hit Connally the resulting entrance wound in his back would have been expected by Shaw to contain mohair fibres and/or metallic fragments – and neither are mentioned in Shaw's detailed report. Dr Gregory testified that he asked Shaw *specifically* whether the chest wound contained foreign material or clothing. Gregory said, "Well, as I recall it, he said none was found and I would not have expected any to be found as I explained to you, if this was the initial impact of that missile."[43]

Furthermore, Shaw went off-the-record to state that the entry wound shown on the Gregory Diagram #1 was drawn too large[44]. To support the SBT, the Warren Commission needed a large entrance wound as that suggested a tumbling bullet. It's no surprise to me to find that the diagram bears a larger wound than the reality.

To summarise these two findings, the entrance wound was smaller than that which would have been caused by a tumbling bullet. Moreover, there was no debris in Connally's back wound. *The bullet was not tumbling* and this wound was *the first* caused by this bullet. It had not hit JFK or anything else before it hit Connally. Remember, if JFK and Connally were not hit by the same bullet, the SBT is not true and there was more than one shooter in Dealey Plaza.

This entire discussion, of course, assumes that the reader is naïve enough to forget that no bullet was ever proven to have perforated JFK's neck and if no bullet ever entered near the base of the back of President Kennedy's neck,

193

perforated his neck and exited his throat, there could never have been a bullet which hit both JFK and Connally.

The Angle Through Connally's Chest
To substantiate the SBT and match all the photographs of the Dallas motorcade, the angle of perforation through Connally's chest had to be about 17 degrees as this was the alleged angle of perforation through JFK's neck[45]. But the Warren Commission had a problem here. When they got Dr Shaw to measure the angle through Connally's chest[46] it was 25 degrees. They could not account for a dip of 8 degrees in mid-air and had to cover it up.

I believe they did this by having some crude diagrams drawn up and admitted into evidence during Dr Gregory's testimony (hence their names, the "Gregory Diagrams"). Then, using some slick semantics, they attempted to obscure the fact that no doctor produced them and no doctor ever used them in anything other than testimony. The doctors made numerous changes to them, but to little effect.

The Warren Commission used two sets of body diagrams during the testimony of Shaw and Gregory - Gregory Exhibit 1 (containing five diagrams) and CE 679 & 680. I have criticized these diagrams several times over the years. Simply calling them the "Gregory Diagrams" unjustly adds to their bona fides as they were not drawn by Gregory or any other doctor. Connally was actually present during the doctors testimony and removed his clothing to show the wounds. So why not just photograph them for the record?

The angle of perforation through Connally's chest was misrepresented in the following way. During Shaw's first round of testimony, he pointed out that the nipples were drawn too high and repositioned one of them about four inches (relatively) lower[47]. I believe that Specter was hoping that Shaw would not notice the "high nipple line" and that using the nipple to orientate the chest wound, Gregory would move the exit higher. This would give a shallower trajectory through Connally's chest from 25 degrees nearer to 17 degrees and aid the SBT. Compare the angle of perforation in Figure 11, below, with Figure 12 shown later.

SEVEN | THE SINGLE BULLET THEORY

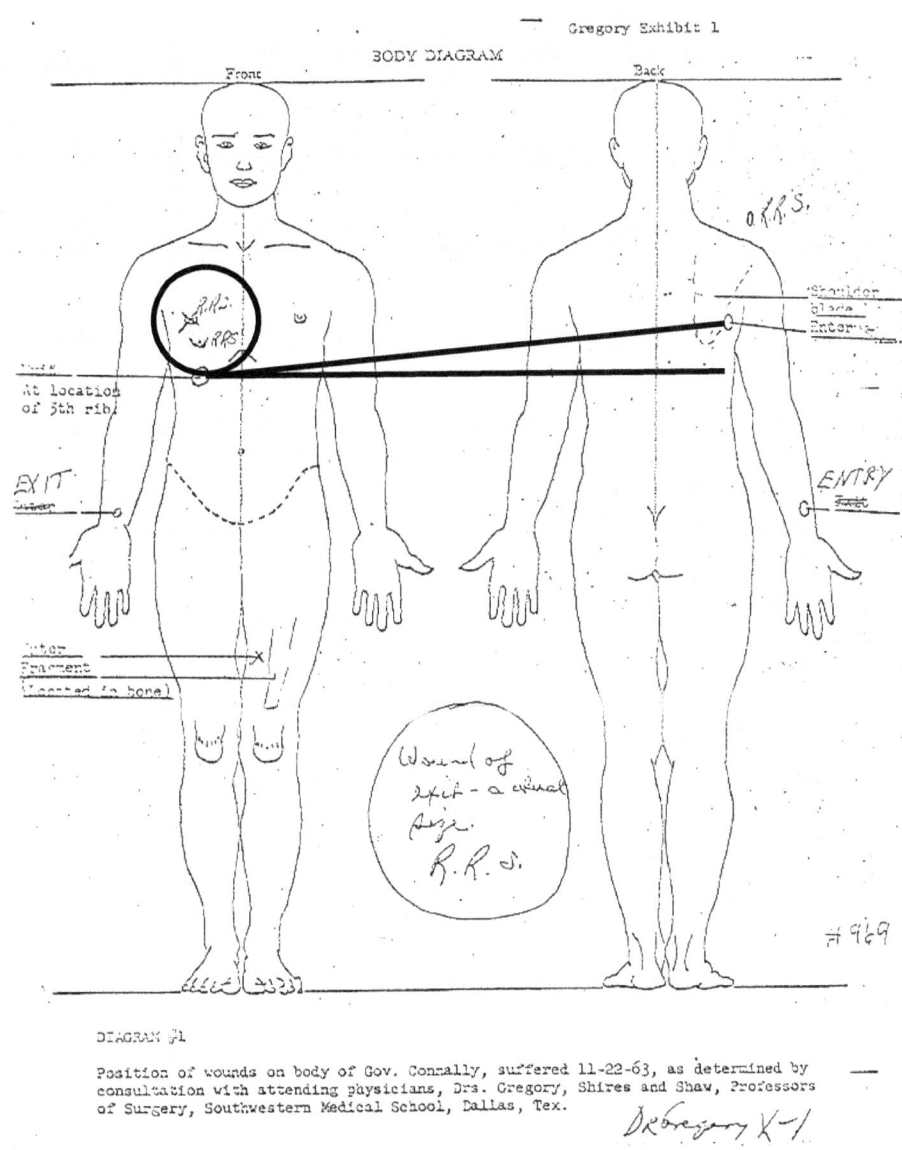

Figure 11: Gregory Exhibit 1 (G#1) – Nipple line drawn too high

Shaw's second testimony to the Warren Commission in April 1964 was taken by Cooper, Dulles and McCloy as well as Specter. It was taken after the second "Strange Conference" (see later) when he was allowed to view the Zapruder film and CE399. During the April testimony, Specter introduced a "new" set of diagrams:

"...the diagrams used now are new diagrams which will have to be remarked in accordance with your *recollection*."[48].

But these were *not* new diagrams. They were the *same* diagrams – Gregory Diagram 1 (see figure 11) and Gregory Diagram 2 – as shown to Shaw a month earlier, but now renumbered as CE679 and CE680. Furthermore, they still bore the errors pointed out in Shaw's and Gregory's March testimony.

Had CE679 and CE680 really been a new set of diagrams, they should have shown the wounds as testified to by the doctors in March 1964. I cannot think of an innocent reason to explain why the diagrams needed remarking. Underhand dealing with exhibits in this manner is damaging to the credibility of the Warren Commission.

This time, Shaw did not mention the "high nipple line", but simply moved up the position of the wound on the diagram. He did this on both CE670 and CE680[49]. The angle through the chest is radically different – much shallower.

In my opinion, this is highly indicative of coaching. We know that Shaw went off-the-record several times during his testimony (see later). The phrase "...new diagrams which will have to be remarked in accordance with your recollection" suggests to me that the original markings were not acceptable to Specter (that is, they didn't support the SBT) and that the required markings were discussed prior to the second round of testimony.

SEVEN | THE SINGLE BULLET THEORY

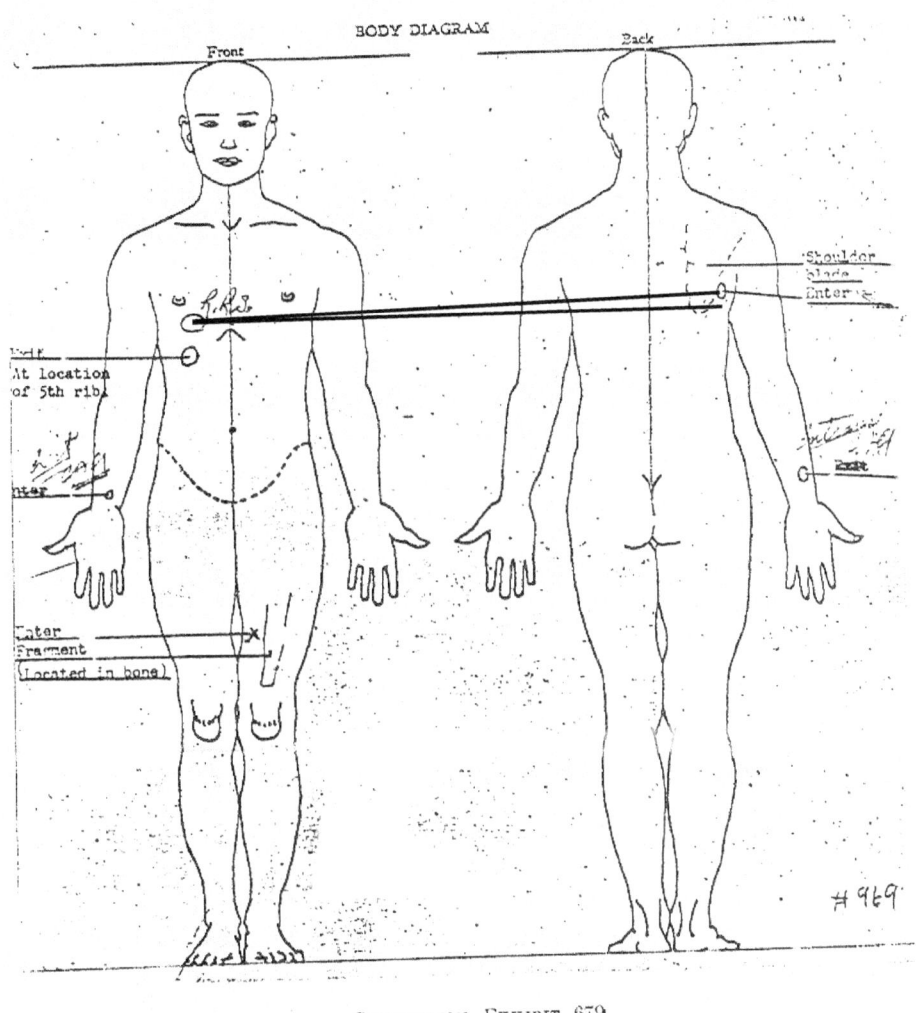

Figure 12: CE679

In his first round of testimony in March 1964, Shaw was willing to consider the SBT, but in April, after seeing the Zapruder film and CE399, he would not be held to that and discussed the possibility of several bullets[50]. Shaw also doubted that any single bullet could have been CE399[51] but the Warren Commission Report states:

"In their testimony, the three doctors . . . expressed independently their opinion that a single bullet had passed through his chest: tumbled through the wrist ... punctured his left thigh ... and had fallen out of the thigh wound."[52] This statement is untrue and provably so.

Dr Charles Francis Gregory
In November 1963, Dr Gregory was Professor of Orthopaedic Surgery at the University of Texas Medical School[53]. He had been a doctor since 1944 and had seen active service with the US Navy in the Second World War. By 1963, Gregory had treated over 500 gunshot wounds. Again, I'd put money on that being about 500 more than anybody in the Warren Commission.

Gregory worked on Connally's wrist wound and was assisted in surgery by Drs William Osborne and John Parker[54]. Gregory described the entrance wound on the upper (or dorsal) surface as 2cm round and ragged. He said it was about 5 cm above wrist joint. The exit wound on the underside, (volar), he described as 1cm round and smooth cut, about 1.5cm above the wrist joint[55]. Both were approximately in the midline of the wrist.

Gregory gave evidence to the Warren Commission twice, first in March 1964 (6H 95) and then a month later, in April 1964 (4H 117). The difference between the two occasions is before the second occasion Gregory was allowed to view the Zapruder film, CE399 and the Governor's clothes. This was at the second "Strange Conference". As with Shaw, Gregory's testimony was markedly different after viewing the physical evidence.

Dr Gregory's testimony is important regarding:

- Whether the wrist wound was made by a deformed bullet.

- The trajectory of the penetrating wound of the wrist.

Was the Bullet Broken or Intact After the Wrist Wound?
Gregory testified in April 1964 that he did not believe that one bullet would have had enough energy to fracture the radius and then go on to penetrate the thigh[56]. He thought it more credible for jagged, sharp fragments like CE 567 or CE 569 (allegedly found in the President's limousine see Figure 13 below) to have resulted from Connally's wrist injury[57].

It is difficult to over-emphasize the importance of this testimony and the fact that it is contrary to the Warren Commission Report. A *professor of surgery* after operating on a wound said that it was probably not CE399 that damaged it. He would have expected a mangled piece of metal to have exited the wound and not an intact bullet like CE399.

SEVEN | THE SINGLE BULLET THEORY

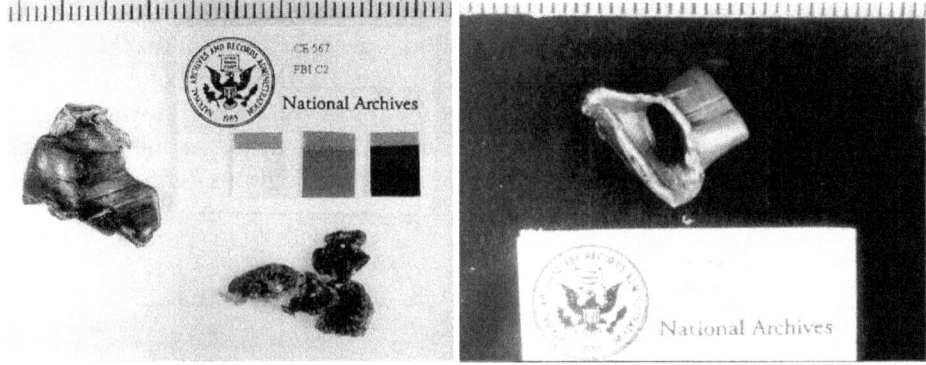

Figure 13: CE567 and CE569
[By the way, these exhibits are wrongly identified by Specter in Gregory's testimony as CE568 and CE570.]

There is more bad news for the SBT. Larry Sturdivan, a physical scientist for the US military gave testimony to the HSCA. He was considered to be an expert in the field of wound ballistics. He testified that a round like CE399 will deform if it hits bone at 1400 f/s (feet per second) nose on or 1000 f/s sideways[58]. If we look at Sturdivan's own numbers, it appears that a shot from a Mannlicher-Carcano from the 6th floor of the TSBD which first penetrated JFK's neck and Connally's chest would have hit Connally's wrist at about 1500 f/s[59]. Since this is faster than the speed at which a round like CE399 would deform when hitting bone, it should have emerged deformed. Remember, CE399 is almost intact.

To summarise, either the round which damaged Connally's wrist was moving too slowly to have caused the damage or was moving too quickly to have remained un-deformed. If CE399 did not damage Connally's wrist, then logically Connally's wrist was hit by another bullet.

What Was the Trajectory of the Wrist Wound?
For the SBT to work, the Warren Commission had to have Connally's penetrating wrist wound going from an under wrist (volar) entry to an upper wrist (dorsal) exit. Connally was sitting in the limousine, with his arm on the right-side of the car, holding his Stetson hat in front of his chest. The only natural way to do this is with the underside of the wrist pointing towards the chest. Any bullet coming out of the chest and then going through the wrist had to enter on the underside. Unfortunately for the Warren Commission, it didn't.

Gregory stated that Connally's wrist wound went from the upper (dorsal) surface to the under (volar) surface for five reasons[60]. Dr Gregory, remember, had treated hundreds of gunshot wounds. His testimony alone is seriously damaging to the SBT. It's just no use arguing that since the other evidence shows that all the shooting was done from the rear of the limousine, the trajectory had

JFK | ECHOES FROM ELM STREET
A SEARCH FOR HISTORICAL ACCURACY ON THE ASSASSINATION OF PRESIDENT JOHN F. KENNEDY

to be volar to dorsal. It simply wasn't - the best orthopaedic surgeon in the area saw the wound, worked on it and gave solid reasons why it couldn't be.

How did Specter deal with this? During Gregory's first round of testimony in March 1963, he introduced the Gregory Diagrams. When he showed Gregory the first diagram, the wrist wound was incorrectly marked as volar to dorsal. Gregory pointed out the error and marked the diagrams with the correct entrance and exit, see Figure 14, below.

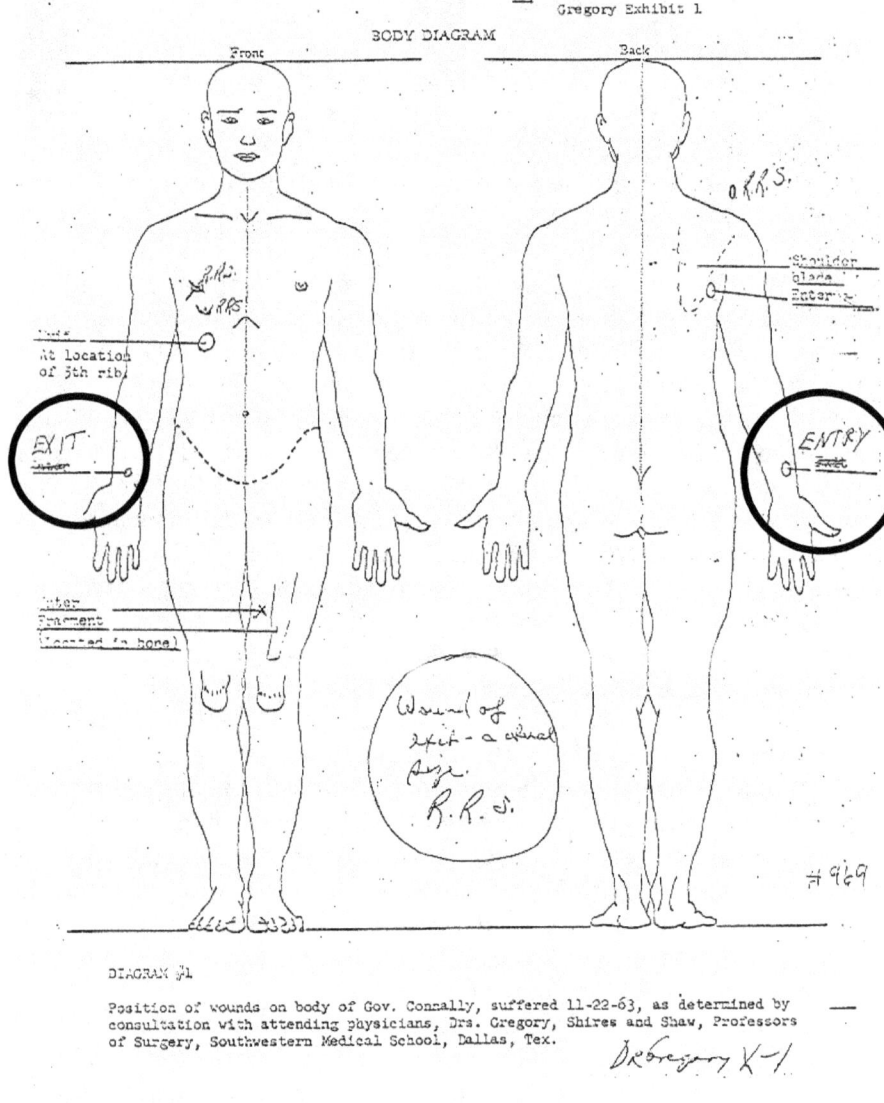

Figure 14: Gregory Diagram 1 (G#1) – Wrist wounds reversed

SEVEN | THE SINGLE BULLET THEORY

But Specter needed the wound to be the other way to substantiate the SBT. So during Gregory's second round of testimony in April 1963, he reintroduced G#1(then designated CE679, see Figure 15 below), with the entrance and exit wounds still incorrectly marked. Gregory was asked for a second time "whether these documents accurately depict the place and the identity of the entry and exit wounds [in the wrist]". He stated unequivocally: "They do not ... it is my opinion that the entrance and exit terms have been reversed."[61] Gregory wouldn't play ball and once again pointed out the wound reversal and re-marked the diagram accordingly.

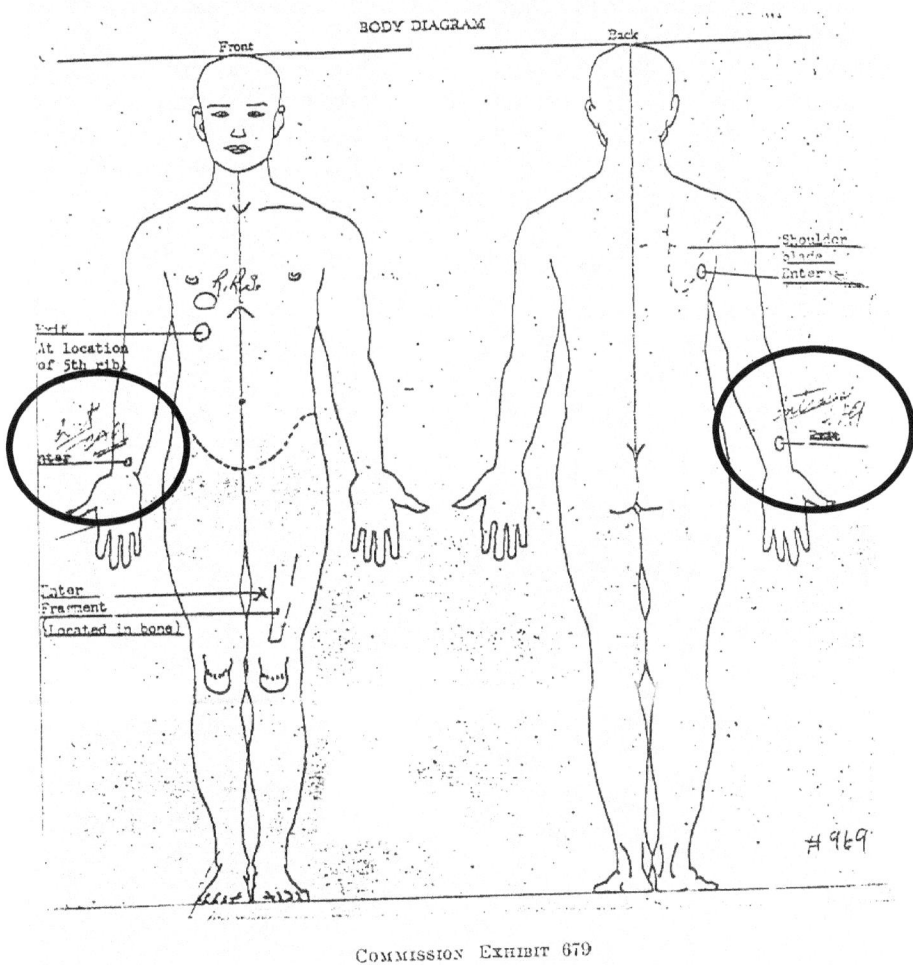

Figure 15: CE679 – Wrist wounds reversed again

JFK | Echoes from Elm Street
A Search for Historical Accuracy on the Assassination of President John F. Kennedy

Dr George T Shires

Dr Shires was Professor of Surgery at the University of Texas Medical School[62]. He became a medical doctor in 1948 after premed research for the US Navy at Bethesda Naval Hospital and service on the USS Haven (1945) as an associate surgeon. By 1963, he had treated many gunshot wounds. But if he had only treated one gunshot wound, he would have had more experience than anyone on the Warren Commission.

Shire's testimony is important regarding whether a bullet penetrated Connally's thigh and subsequently fell out. The Warren Report said of CE399 that it had "... *punctured his left thigh ... and had fallen out of the thigh wound.*" The evidence simply does not show this. Rather, it shows that no whole bullet ever penetrated Connally's thigh.

Shires described the thigh wound as a tangential hit. He said, "... The skin wound was either a tangential wound or ... a large fragment had penetrated or stopped in the skin and had subsequently fallen out."[63] If Shires meant a bullet, why did he say "large fragment"? If it was tangential, G#5 – in Figure 16, below – is wrong as it does not show a tangential hit.

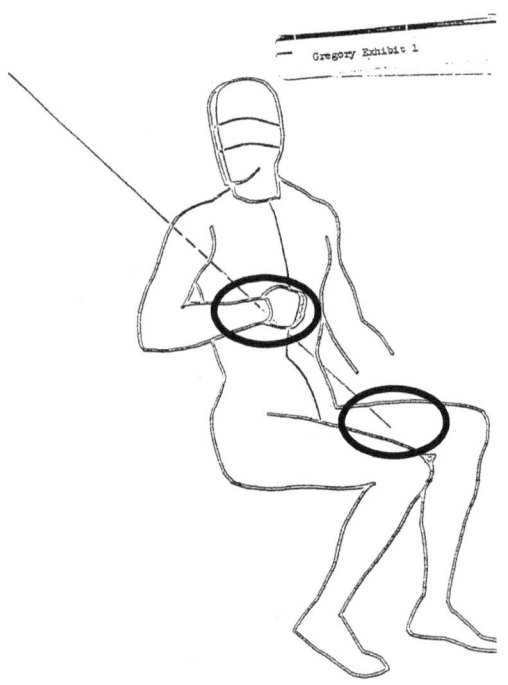

Figure 16: Gregory Diagram 5 (G#5) – Wrist and thigh wounds misrepresented and caption misleading

SEVEN | THE SINGLE BULLET THEORY

Gregory's amendments to G#1 and CE679 were damaging to the SBT. By publishing G#5, which ignores Gregory's previous corrections, the Warren Commission behaved as if Gregory had accepted their trajectory. Furthermore, if we add in a similar drawing of JFK so that a bullet going through his neck fits with the trajectory shown in G#5, the sheer audacity of the diagram becomes obvious:

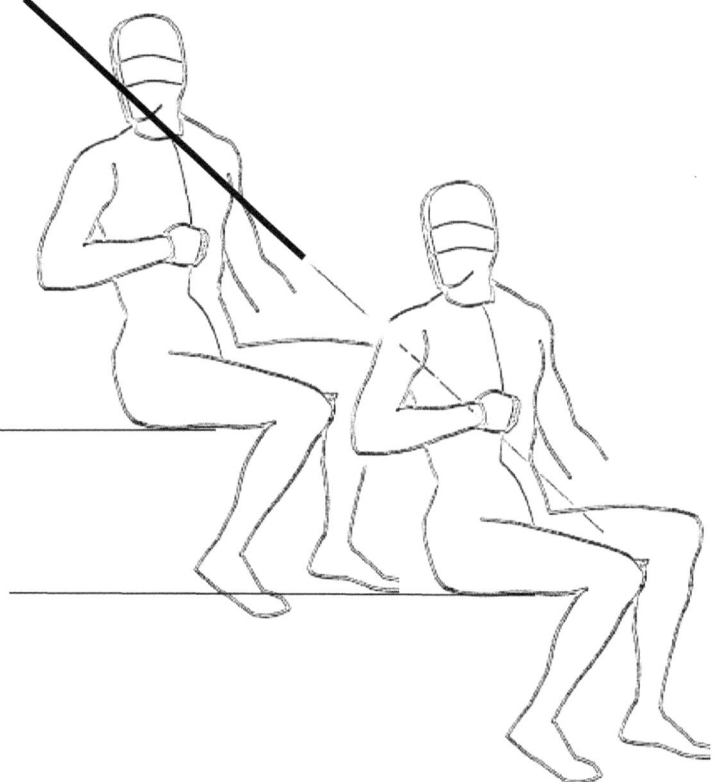

Figure 17: G#5 – The position of JFK for the SBT to work

For the trajectory through Connally to work, JFK would have had to either be sitting in the limousine at least 18 inches above Connally or to have stood up just at the moment the shot occurred. Of course, there's no evidence that he did and G#5 is another part of a mockery of an investigation.

Dr Perry told Weisberg that Shires called him in to give an opinion of the thigh wound (Dr Perry was an expert on arterial injury). Perry told Weisberg:

- The hole in Connally's thigh was too small for a bullet to have caused it.

- The fragment next to the femur could not have been deposited by a whole bullet that then backed out[64].

Specter avoided this and never questioned any Parkland doctor about it. As mentioned earlier when discussing the alleged fragments of CE399, the FBI was sent more evidence about the wound to Connally's thigh. The X-ray of Connally's left thigh sent by Dr Jack Reynolds and showing a small fragment was a problem for the Warren Commission[65]. It was difficult to explain how a whole bullet could have caused the thigh wound, deposited a fragment of this shape and then dropped out of the wound. For the SBT to work, the Warren Commission had to ignore this medical data. The bullet had to have been in Connally's thigh and then drop out at Parkland for it to have been found there.

Analysis of the Doctors Questions
In "Treachery In Dallas", Walt Brown records how he re-read all of the Warren Commission hearings and analysed the questions asked of the witnesses[66]. He divided the questions into eight categories. I will concentrate on just five of Brown's categories (all the other categories of questions I have summed into the "Others" column):

1. Preliminary – introductory questions regarding the witness's identity, qualifications and background.

2. Relevant – questions that had a direct bearing on the assassination of JFK (in this case regarding the wounding of Connally). For example, "Which to you appeared to be the point of entrance?"

3. Clarifications – questions calling for previous answers to be explained.

4. Hearsay – questions calling for the witness to say what he had heard. For example, "What did Mrs Kennedy say, according to Mrs Connally?"

5. Nonsense – gibberish or questions calling for an answer outrageously removed from the point of the investigation. For example, Senator Cooper's question, *"In the answers to the hypothetical questions that were addressed to you, based upon the only actual knowledge which you could base that answer, was the fact that you had performed the operation on the wound caused in the chest, on the wound in the chest?"* This is either claptrap or was misprinted. Neither is acceptable.

Table 4, opposite, shows the results of such an analysis of the questions asked of Connally's surgeons:

SEVEN | THE SINGLE BULLET THEORY

Doctor	Prelim	Relevant	Clarif	Hearsay	Nonsense	Others	Total
Shaw	12	13	60	58	0	150	293
Gregory	11	8	40	16	2	117	193
Shires	9	19	17	21	0	52	118

Table 4: Analysis of questions

Of Shaw's and Gregory's questions, only about 4% were relevant. Of Shire's questions, 16% were relevant, but he was asked far fewer questions. The average number of questions asked to the doctors was 225. This represents a tiny 0.2% of the total questions asked to all witnesses. Compare this to the 3,972 questions asked of Crafard, a nobody who sometimes slept in Ruby's Carousel Club. Craford's questions accounted for 3.6% of the total questions asked (second only to the Warren Commission questions champion, Ruth Paine, who was asked 5,236 questions) and did nothing to help clarify what actually happened on 22nd November 1963. How could it? Craford's questions were put to a vagrant about the man who shot the man who allegedly shot the President.

The Warren Commission's whole case rests on the medical evidence and specifically on the validity of the SBT. Wouldn't you at the very least expect questions to the doctors that treated Connally (a key to the SBT) to have vastly outweighed those to a bum with no information of value?

In fact, the top nine (by number of questions asked by the Warren Commission) were all character witnesses for Lee Harvey Oswald. Their total number of questions was 22,530 and represented over 20% of all the questions asked (109,930).

Here's another demonstration that I urge you to try.

- Get several long tape measures and layout 357 inches. Each inch represents a cubic foot of material gathered by the Warren Commission and originally locked away until 2039.

- Now mark four inches on one tape. This represents the four cubic feet of information published by the Warren Commission in its 26 volumes.

- Finally, hold a sheet of paper sideways against the tape. The thickness of this sheet of paper, on this scale, represents the *total* of all medical testimony and exhibits published.

Even in this miniscule amount of information, only a tiny percentage comprises relevant questions. With so little medical evidence to support the SBT and it being so difficult to find, you have to wonder whether the other hundreds of cubic feet are there to hide it.

Off-the-record
Dr Shaw went off-the-record with Arlen Specter several times at crucial points in his testimony in March and April 1964:

- When discussing the entrance/exit wounds on John Connally's wrist[67]
- When discussing the degree of injury in the wrist[68]
- When discussing the relatively intact nature of CE399[69].

Off-the-record discussion with counsel of this type compromises the testimony given by a witness. It is harmful to the Warren Commission's case that many of these off-the-record discussions relate to the roots of the SBT. It also does not help the credibility of the Warren Commission when Counsel lies to a witness. Specter tells Shaw that the Warren Commission has ascertained that CE399 came from Connally's stretcher[70], which is simply untrue. The Warren Commission came nowhere near to proving this. Unfortunately for us, Specter was not under oath.

Logic of CE399's Discovery
Specter went to great lengths to show that CE399 was found on Connally's stretcher without proving it. Remember, it had to be there, however, for the SBT to work. It couldn't have been still in Connally's thigh wound as it would have been seen during surgery. The fact that CE399 *had* to be on Connally's stretcher got me thinking how did it get there? The more I thought about this, the more unlikely it seemed. There are five situations that CE399 would have needed to avoid to have turned up under the mattress on Connally's stretcher:

1. It would have needed to remain in Connally's trousers when he was removed from the limousine and not rolled out when he was lifted onto a gurney.

2. It would have needed to hide when Connally was stripped in Trauma Room 2 (where it also had to evade being bundled up with his clothes).

3. It would have needed to dodge being noticed on the gurney's sheets during examination.

SEVEN | THE SINGLE BULLET THEORY

4. It would have needed to escape being wrapped in the sheets when they were removed from the stretcher.

5. It would have needed to avoid simply sitting on top of the stretcher and somehow to have managed to wriggle under the mattress.

At the Dealey Plaza UK Seminar 2005 in Canterbury, England, I demonstrated that this was farcical. I secreted a bullet inside my left trouser leg so that it was lying next to my thigh and sat down. When I was subsequently lifted from a sitting position onto a covered table, the bullet that I had in my trousers simply fell to the floor. Try it yourself with a coin.

Even when I stretched credibility by replacing the bullet and pretending that it had miraculously remained in my trousers, when they were removed, the bullet fell onto the sheets for all to see. I tried to recreate all five of the above scenarios and the bullet was always obvious.

It is highly illogical for CE399 to have ended up on the mattress, let alone under the mattress. If it's not logical for it to have got there without help, it must have got there with help – in short, it must have been planted.

The "Strange Conferences"

Two conferences were held in the VFW (Veterans of Foreign Wars) Building, 200 Maryland Ave, Washington DC, the first on the 14th April 1964 and the second on 22nd April 1963. I call these "strange conferences" for four reasons:
- The subject studied
- The participants
- The results
- The suppression of the records of the conferences – published here, in full, but not published by the Warren Commission.

The First "Strange Conference"

According to the memo produced by Assistant Counsel Melvin Aron Eisenberg, a group met "to determine which frames in the Zapruder film portray the instants at which the first and second bullets struck." This statement is very important. At this stage, most of the participants still believed that all three shots hit either JFK or JC. The conference was called to find out when the first and second bullets struck – not missed – as it was obvious to all that the third struck when JFK's head was hit.

The significance of this conference is that all but one person agreed that Connally was hit twice. Three bullets, three hits. Once Tague entered the equation, the Warren Commission were forced to conclude that only two bullets hit the occupants of the limo and were therefore led into the SBT. When they didn't have to force a conclusion, they looked – slightly – more openly for evidence.

Drs Boswell, Finck and Humes (JFK's autopsy surgeons) were there. The FBI was represented by Gauthier, Malley, Shaneyfelt and two unidentified others. John J Howlett (from the Dallas office) and Thomas J Kelley (later Assistant Director) appeared on behalf of the Secret Service. Edgewood Arsenal sent along Dr F W Light Chief of the Wound Assessment Branch, U.S. Army Chemical Research and Development Laboratories, Biophysics Division and Dr A G Olivier (Vet) Chief of the Wound Ballistics Branch. The Warren Commission was represented by Eisenberg, Redlich and Specter.

Some of these attendees had already been to a meeting on January 27th 1964 to study the Zapruder film. Eisenberg, Redlich and Specter for the Warren Commission met with FBI photographic expert Lyndal Shaneyfelt, FBI visual aids expert Leo Gauthier and Secret Service Inspector Thomas Kelley[71]. Obviously, no conclusions had been reached otherwise there would have been little need for the "strange conferences".

Eisenberg produced a three-page memo (not in the Warren Commission Report or any one of the 26 volumes), later obtained by Weisberg, which speaks for itself (see Appendix 1).

This memo is hugely destructive to the SBT for the following reasons:

- It explains that, "...the bullet recovered from Governor Connally's stretcher does not appear to have penetrated a wrist." This observation probably came from the Edgewood Arsenal doctors and is completely supportive of Dr Gregory.

- It suggests that the facts better match a different theory, "...if he [Connally] was hit by this (the first) bullet, he was probably also hit by the second bullet"

Of the fifteen people there, including five doctors (three of whom were experts in wounds) and two FBI photographic experts, only Specter, the architect of the SBT, dissented from the three bullets, three hits conclusion. The man either had guts or he knew that some powerful people were on his side.

The Second "Strange Conference"

The second "strange conference" was convened, according to the memo produced by Eisenberg also, "to determine which frames in the Zapruder film portray the instants at which the first and second bullets struck."

Again, the Warren Commission needed to find out when the first and second bullets struck the occupants of the limousine (not missed). In other words, most of them still believed that the wounds suffered by JFK and Connally were caused by three bullets, not two. This time, they invited people in a better position to answer.

SEVEN | THE SINGLE BULLET THEORY

Present were Mr and Mrs Connally along with Drs Gregory and Shaw who, whilst not in Dealey Plaza at the time of the assassination, at least got a first-hand look at Connally's wounds. The FBI sent along Gauthier, Shaneyfelt and one other unidentified agent. Belin, Eisenberg, McCloy, Rankin, Redlich and Specter represented the Warren Commission. From Edgewood Arsenal there was Drs Dolce, Light and Olivier.

This time, Eisenberg produced a two-page memo (not in the Warren Commission Report or any one of the 26 volumes), later obtained by Weisberg, which again speaks for itself (see Appendix 2).

Once more, the conference and the memo are hugely troublesome for the SBT, especially the final paragraph:

"...very strongly of the opinion that Connally had been hit by two different bullets, principally on the ground that the bullet recovered from Connally's stretcher could not have broken his radius without having suffered more distortion."

Of the sixteen people there, including five doctors, *all* of whom were experts in wounds, Specter alone dissented from the three bullets, three hits conclusion – and yet it was Specter that was allowed *the same day*, to take the testimony of Shaw, Gregory, Mr Connally and Mrs Connally.

That, to me, is appalling. It seems that the entire afternoon of testimony given to Specter was squarely aimed at bolstering the SBT. Had the Warren Commission been the slightest bit interested in the truth, why did they allow the one dissenting person to skew the questioning in this way? Why didn't the lawyers Belin, Rankin or Redlich, who were at both the conference and the taking of testimony, pipe up?

The Wounds Ballistics Experts
Melvin Eisenberg, to his credit, had called in some independent experts to look at the wound ballistics evidence. All these experts came from the US Army research departments at the Edgewood Arsenal in Maryland. Three were present at the "strange conferences" and three testified to the Warren Commission, *but not the same three*. Dr Olivier testified first and supported Specter, but could only produce badly damaged bullets in his tests some of which are shown in Figure 18, overleaf.

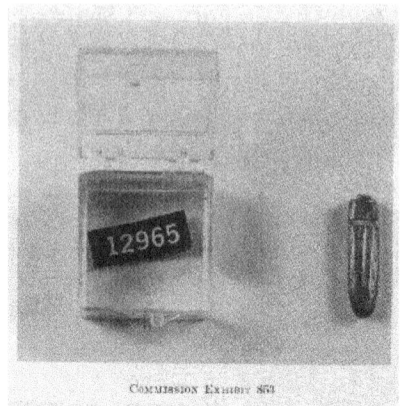 

Figure 18: CE853 (test bullet fired through goat rib) and CE856 (test bullet fired through human radius)

Dr Light testified next, but said, "...I am not quite as sure in my mind as I believe he [Olivier] is that the bullet that struck the Governor was almost certainly one which had hit something else first. I believe it could have produced that wound [in Connally's chest] even though it hadn't hit the President or any other person or object first."

Dr Dolce (Consultant to the U.S. Army Chemical Research and Development Laboratories Biophysics Division at Edgewood Arsenal) would naturally have been the third witness, but he was not called to testify. I am left wondering whether he was omitted as he appeared unwilling to support the SBT. Instead, Dr Dzieman (Chief of the Biophysics Division U.S. Army Chemical Research and Development Laboratories at Edgewood Arsenal), essentially Light's boss, testified. He supported the SBT but was not involved in the "strange conferences" and, therefore, *never shown the films, photographs or CE399*. We know from Connally's doctors (Gregory and Shaw) that seeing the physical evidence causes a change in scientific opinion about the SBT.

Conclusions

For the SBT to work and Oswald to be guilty alone, we firstly have to persuade ourselves that a bullet perforated JFK's neck. The evidence does not support this, so there's no real need to go any further. For the sake of argument, however, let's continue and see whether the other evidence is any more reliable or true.

A bullet allegedly shot by an assassin from the right of the limousine on a right-to-left trajectory either:

- Left JFK's throat and changed in mid-flight to a left-to-right trajectory to hit Connally's armpit and go straight through his chest or

SEVEN | THE SINGLE BULLET THEORY

- Was deflected within Connally's chest by 23.5 degrees so that it came out below his right nipple[72].

The first is impossible and the second highly unlikely according to Dr Shaw[73]. The investigations believed that a bullet went straight through Connally's chest. Since it is not possible for the SBT to result in a wound straight through Connally's chest it cannot be true.

Next, we have to imagine Connally with the upper side of his wrist pressed to his nipple while holding his Stetson lifting his left leg two feet diagonally to his right ready to catch a bullet emerging from the underside of his wrist. Few people short of highly-trained gymnasts or circus contortions can do this. Connally was neither and there's absolutely no evidence that he performed this bizarre movement on November 22nd 1963.

The descriptions of all five Connally's wounds have been manipulated to support the SBT. For the theory to work:

- The bullet must have been tumbling when it hit Connally. However, Dr Shaw found that the wound in the back of Connally's right armpit does not support a tumbling bullet.

- The angle through the chest had to be 17 degrees downwards. I have shown that the Commission allowed virtually any angle through the chest from the extremely shallow CE679, to the steeper CE680 and onto the ridiculous G#5 showing about 45 degrees. They never did prove 17 degrees.

- The entry wound on Connally's wrist had to be on the underside (volar). Dr Gregory proved a bullet entered on the upperside (dorsal).

- The exit wound on Connally's wrist had to be on the upperside (dorsal). Dr Gregory proved a bullet left on the underside (volar).

- Connally's thigh must have been penetrated by a whole bullet. However, both Drs Shires and Perry said that the thigh wound was caused by a tangential strike and a whole bullet did not penetrate. They were there and closely examined the wound.

The fragments of metal in evidence, allegedly from CE399, don't appear to fit easily with the missing portion of CE399. Without an indication of thickness of the fragments it is impossible to say for sure whether there is more metal in them than can be accounted for by the missing weight of CE399. However, we know that some of that metal was removed for analysis and it is entirely possible that CE399 was fully intact before samples were removed.

JFK | ECHOES FROM ELM STREET
A Search for Historical Accuracy on the Assassination of President John F. Kennedy

Logically and demonstrably, CE399 *could not have been* under the mattress on Connally's stretcher. The bullet was not found in Connally's leg, so for the Warren Commission to be correct that it was found under the mattress on Connally's gurney, it had to have been in his trousers on arrival at Parkland. The problem is that simply lifting a person onto a gurney causes a bullet loose in the trousers to roll out onto the floor.

Except for Specter, the attendees at two "strange conferences" (including doctors, the top wounds experts, the Secret Service, the FBI photographic experts, Warren Commission councilors and even Connally himself) concluded that Connally was hit at least twice by separate bullets. With the injury to James Tague, that is evidence for at least four shots and evidence of a conspiracy in the assassination. The "strange conferences" were never mentioned in testimony and the memoranda they generated were not part of the Warren Commission Report or any of the 26 volumes of supporting hearings and exhibits.

JFK was wounded in the back and separately in the throat. Neither wound was proven to be the result of any bullet let alone one fired by Oswald. Governor John Connally was wounded by more than one bullet. The injury to his chest was probably caused by a bullet shot from behind the limousine. The injury to his wrist was almost certainly caused by a bullet fired from in front of the limousine. It is more difficult to explain the thigh wound, but it was not caused by a whole bullet and, therefore, it was not caused by CE399.

It seems that despite its apparent certainty, some senior members of the Warren Commission itself could not be persuaded that the SBT was the truth. The minutes of the 27 January 1964 Warren Commission Executive Session record the following statement from the Chief Counsel J. Lee Rankin:

> "It seems quite apparent now, since we have a picture of where the bullet entered in the back, that the bullet entered below the shoulder blade, to the right of the backbone, which is below the place where the picture shows the bullet came out the neckband of the shirt, in front. So that how it could turn and..."

As Harold Weisberg noted, Rankin trails off because he realizes that he has just talked his way out of the SBT.

The SBT cannot be proved beyond a reasonable doubt using the alleged evidence. The surviving members of the Warren Commission and its supporters know that the single bullet theory should be replaced by a multiple bullet theory and conspiracy in the assassination of JFK.

Truth or Dare?
We must dare the US Government to rid us of reasonable doubt and prove that the following are true because if any – *any* – are not, then the SBT also cannot be true:

Seven | The Single Bullet Theory

- In the 0.75 seconds that he was behind the Stemmons Freeway sign (when the Warren Commission alleges JFK was first shot), JFK nodded forward about 20 degrees and then straightened up again

- At the same time, Connally rose up in his seat, twisted his wrist into an impossible position and lifted his left leg. Then he sat down again as if nothing had happened

- JFK's jacket *and* shirt were bunched up by *exactly the same* amount of 2 or 3 inches

- The FBI statements concerning the autopsy findings regarding JFK's back wound are mistaken

- The JFK's autopsy face sheet is inaccurate

- JFK's Navy death certificate is wrong

- The Parkland doctors could not identify an entry wound in JFK's throat

- A bullet could enter and exit JFK's neck where the WC say it did without going through his spine

- JFK and Connally were aligned to be wounded by one bullet

- That Governor Connally and Mrs Connally's memories of the assassination sequence are mistaken

- Connally's back wound was caused by a tumbling bullet

- Connally's wrist wound was volar to dorsal

- A bullet that caused the amount of damage noted to Connally's wrist could remain almost pristine

- Connally's thigh wound was caused by a whole bullet which remained in the wound

- A whole bullet can back out of a wound

- A whole bullet lodged in Connally or on his stretcher was missed by all the Parkland medical personnel

- The alleged single bullet could get out of Connally's trousers and hide underneath a mattress

- The alleged single bullet could swap stretchers

- The bullet found is CE399

- The alleged single bullet could be clean of all human tissue and unmarked (at *microscopic* level)

- The weight missing from the bullet could be accounted for by the fragments in the bodies of JFK and Connally

- The composition of the fragments removed from Connally matched CE399.

SEVEN | THE SINGLE BULLET THEORY

Appendix 1

April 22, 1964

MEMORANDUM FOR THE RECORD

FROM: Melvin A. Eisenberg

Subject: Conference of April 14, 1964, to determine which frames in the Zapruder movies show the impact of the first and second bullets

On April 14, 1964, a conference was held to determine which frames in the Zapruder film portray the instants at which the first and second bullets struck.

Present were:
Commander James J. Humes, Director of Laboratories of the Naval Medical School, Bethesda, Maryland:

Commander J. Thorton Boswell, Chief Pathologist, Naval Medical School, Bethesda:

Lt. Col. Pierre A. Finck, Chief of Wound Ballistics Pathology Branch, Armed Forces Institute of Pathology:

Dr F.W. Light, Jr. Deputy Chief of the Biophysics Division at Edgewood Arsenal, Maryland and Chief of the Wound Assessment Branch of the Biophysics Division:

Dr Oliver, Chief of the Wound Ballistics Branch of the Biophysics Division at Edgewood Arsenal:

Messers Malley, Gauthier, Shaneyfelt and two other unidentified agents of the FBI:

Messers Kelley and Howlett of the Secret Service:

Messers Redlich, Specter and Eisenberg of the Commission staff.

A screening was held of the Zapruder film and of slides prepared by LIFE from the film. Each slide corresponded with a separate frame of film, beginning with frame 171. The consensus of the meeting was as follows:

(a) The President had been definitely hit by frames 224-225, when he emerges from behind a sign with his hands clutching his throat.

(b) The reaction shown in frames 224-225 may have started at an earlier point - possibly as early as frame 199 (when there appears to be some jerkiness in his movement) or, with a higher degree of possibility, at frames 204-206 (where his right elbow appears to be raised to an artificially high position).

(c) If the reaction did not begin at 199 or 204-206, it probably began during the range of frames during which the President is hidden from Zapruder's camera by a sign, namely, frames 215-24.

cc: Mr Rankin   Mr Belin
        Mr Willens   Mr Specter
        Mr Redlich   Mr Eisenberg
        Mr Ball

Page Two:

(d) The President may have been struck by the first bullet as much as two seconds before any visible reaction began. In all likelihood, however, the maximum delay between impact and reaction would be under one second and it is possible that the reaction was instantaneous. Putting this in terms of frames, the President may have been struck as much as 36 frames before any visible reaction is seen. If the visible reaction begins at 199, the President may have been struck as early as 163: if the visible reaction begins at 204-206, he may have been struck as early as 168-170: if the visible reaction begins while the President is behind the sign, he may have been struck as early as 179-188.

(e) The velocity of the first bullet would have been little diminished by its passage through the President. Therefore, if Governor Connally was in the path of the bullet it would have struck him and (probably) caused the wounds he sustained in his chest cavity.

Strong indications that this occurred are provided by the facts that

SEVEN | THE SINGLE BULLET THEORY

(1) the bullet recovered from Governor Connally's stretcher does not appear to have penetrated a wrist

(2) if the first bullet did not hit Governor Connally, it should have ripped up the car, but apparently did not. Since the bullet recovered from the Governor's stretcher does not appear to have penetrated a wrist, if he was hit by this (the first) bullet, he was probably also hit by the second bullet.

(f) If Governor Connally was hit by the first and second bullets, it is impossible to say definitively at what point, or by what point, he had been hit by the second bullet.

(g) Governor Connally seems to straighten up at frames 224-226 and may be reacting to a wound at this point. (If so, it would be a wound from the first bullet).

(h) Governor Connally seems to begin showing an expression of anguish around 242. If he was hit with two bullets, this expression may have resulted from his second wound.

(i) After Governor Connally straightened up at frames 224-26, he starts to turn to the right. As a result of this turn, at no time after frame 236 was Governor Connally in a position such that a bullet fired from the probable

Page 3:

site of the assassin would have caused the wound in his chest cavity which Governor Connally sustained--that is, after frame 236, the Governor presented a side view to the assassin rather than a back view.*

(j) It is not possible to say whether prior to 236 Governor Connally was ever in a position such that one bullet could have caused the five wounds he sustained.

(k) As in the case of the President, Governor Connally could have conceivably been hit two seconds before he begins to react, but the maximum likely time interval between hit and reaction is one second and the reaction may have been instantaneous. The likelihood of an instantaneous reaction is particularly great in regard to the wrist wound, since pain is usually felt more quickly in a limb than in the torso.

*/ Mr Specter disagrees with this and feels the Governor was in position to receive the chest wound up to 242.

SEVEN | THE SINGLE BULLET THEORY

Appendix 2

April 22, 1964

MEMORANDUM FOR THE RECORD

FROM: Melvin A. Eisenberg

SUBJECT: Conference of April 21, 1964, to determine which frames in the Zapruder movie show The impact of the first and second bullets

On Tuesday, April 21, 1964, a conference was held to determine which frames in the Zapruder film portray the instants at which the first and second bullets struck.

Present were:

Dr F. W. Light Jr., Deputy Chief of the Biophysics Division and Chief of the Wound Assessment Branch of the Biophysics Division of the Edgewood Arsenal, Maryland:

Dr Olivier, Chief the Wound Ballistics Branch of the Biophysics Division at Edgewood Arsenal, Maryland:

Dr Joseph Dolce, Consultant to the Biophysics Division at Edgewood Arsenal:

Dr Charles F. Gregory and Dr Robert Shaw of Parkland Hospital, Dallas, Texas:

Messers Gauthier, Shaneyfelt and one other unidentified agent of the FBI:

Messers Redlich, Specter, Belin and Eisenberg.

Later in the proceedings, Governor and Mrs Connally, Mr Rankin and Mr McCloy joined the conference.

A screening was held of the Zapruder film and of slides prepared by LIFE from the film. Each slide corresponded with a separate frame of film, beginning with frame 171. The consensus of the meeting was as follows:

a) The President had been definitely hit by frames 224-25 when he emerges from behind a sign with his hands clutching at his throat.

b) After Governor Connally straightened up at frames 224-26 he starts to turn to the right. As a result of this turn, at no time after frame 236 was Governor Connally in a position such that a bullet fired from the presumed site of the assassin would have entered the wound in his chest cavity which Governor Connally sustained - - that is, after frame 236 the Governor presented a side view to the assassin rather than a back view. 1/

1/ Mr Specter disagrees.

c) In many frames up to 250, the Governor's wrist is held in a position which exposed him to the type of wrist wound he actually received.

d) After viewing the films and slides, the Governor was of the opinion that he had been hit by frame 231.

e) The Governor stated that after being hit, he looked to the right, looked to his left and then turned to his right. He felt the President might have been hit by frame 190. He heard only two shots and felt sure that the shots he heard were the first and third shots. Ho is positive that he was hit after the first shot, i.e. by the second shot and by that shot only.

In a discussion after the conference, Drs Light and Dolce expressed themselves as being very strongly of the opinion that Connally had been hit by two different bullets, principally on the ground that the bullet recovered from Connally's stretcher could not have broken his radius without having suffered more distortion. Dr Olivier withheld a conclusion until he has had the opportunity to make tests on animal tissue and bone with the actual rifle.

Endnotes

[1] Pages 79 – 117 plus 580 – 585 = 43. But 7 pages are figures with no bearing on the SBT and 1 page is a description of a rifle. 43 – 8 = 35 pages.
[2] "The Most Famous Home Movie Ever, the "Magic Bullet," and the Single-Bullet Theory" Vincent Bugliosi *"Reclaiming History"* (W.W. Norton, 2007) p450 – 512.
[3] The infamous "home movie" filmed by Abraham Zapruder which captured JFK's assassination
[4] 3 HSCA 471-473
[5] Walt Brown, *"The Warren Omission"* (Delmax: New Castle, Delaware, 1996)
[6] FBI Report – "Investigation of Assassination of President John F. Kennedy November 22, 1963" also Warren Commission Document CD1
[7] There are good pictures of CE 399 in several of the assassination books including Harold Weisberg *"Post Mortem"* (self published, 1975) p602
[8] Alaric Rosman *"The Single Bullet in Flatland"*, The Dealey Plaza Echo Vol. 12 No.2 July 2008
[9] See photograph on page 125 in Robert Groden *"The Killing of a President"* (1993)

10. John Connally interview Sept 28th 1964, *"Reasonable Doubt"* video (CS Films Inc, 1988)
11. Frame 232 of the Zapruder film shows Connally gripping his Stetson hat well after JFK is obviously wounded in the throat. The Warren Commission's single-bullet theory would have us believe that Connally had sustained all his injuries at this point. This is impossible:
Firstly, Connally shows no sign of distress at this point.
Secondly, Connally would not be able to hold his hat with a shattered radius, a severed tendon leading to the thumb and a damaged radial nerve (4H 124)
12. 1 grain = 0.065 grams. 2.4 grains = 0.15 grams.
13. 3H 430
14. 4H 123
15. Kenneth A Rahn *"Neutron Activation Analysis and the John F. Kennedy Assassination"* 2001
16. 7 HSCA 159-162 & 319-321
17. 6H 111
18. HSCA Record Number 180-10090-10264 Agency File Number 000915
19. V. P. Guinn and M. A. Purcell, "A very rapid instrumental neutron activation analysis method for the forensic comparison of bullet-lead specimens," *Journal of Radio analytical Chemistry*, 39, pages 85–91 (1977)
20. 1 HSCA 549
21. Erik Randich Ph.D., Patrick M Grant Ph.D. (2006) "Proper Assessment of the JFK Assassination Bullet Lead Evidence from Metallurgical and Statistical Perspectives", Journal of Forensic Sciences 51 (4), 717–728
22. Cliff Spiegelman, William A. Tobin, William D. James, Simon J. Sheather, Stuart Wexler, D. Max Roundhill, "Chemical and forensic analysis of JFK assassination bullet lots: Is a second shooter possible?", The Annals of Applied Statistics. Volume 1, Number 2 (2007), 287-301.
23. Warren Commission Report page 3
24. Testimony of Dr Finck during the Clay Shaw trial
25. Testimony of Dr Humes, 2H 361
26. Testimony of Dr Finck during the Clay Shaw trial
27. CE397 (17E 45)
28. See photograph on page 78 of Robert Groden's *"The Killing of a President"* (1993)
29. See photograph on page 79 of Robert Groden's *"The Killing of a President"* (1993)
30. 23 Nov 1963 Field Report of Secret Service Agent Glenn Bennett
31. Testimony of Clint Hill, 2H 144
32. Dr Humes' original, hand-written autopsy report is reproduced in Harold Weisberg *"Post Mortem"* (self published, 1975)
33. Autopsy Report, Kennedy, John F., CE 387
34. Ibid
35. Ibid
36. Clark Panel Report p13 (http://www.history-matters.com/archive/jfk/arrb/master_med_set/md59/html/Image12.htm)
37. Milicent Cranor "Trajectory of a Lie: Part 2 Neck and Torso X-Rays: Selectivity in Reporting" (http://www.history-matters.com/essays/jfkmed/NeckAndTorsoXrays/NeckAndTorsoXrays.htm)
38. Dr Gary Aguilar and Kathy Cunningham "How Five Investigations into JFK's Medical-Autopsy Evidence Got it Wrong Part 3: The Clark Panel" (http://www.history-matters.com/essays/jfkmed/How5Investigations/How5InvestigationsGotItWrong_3.htm#_edn192)
39. James H Fetzer *"Assassination Science"* (Catfeet Press, 1998) p153 – 158 and Stewart Galanor *"Cover-up"* (Kestral Books, 1998) Document 45
40. Testimony of Dr Robert Shaw, 4H 102
41. 4H 137
42. First in March 1964 (6H 83), then a month later in April 1964 (4H 101)
43. 6H 103
44. 6H 87
45. Autopsy Report, Kennedy, John F., CE 387

46. 4H 137
47. 6H 86
48. 4H 104
49. 4H 105
50. 4H 109
51. 4H 113-114
52. Warren Commission Report p95
53. 6H 96
54. 6H 97
55. 6H 97-98
56. 4H 127
57. 4H 128
58. 1 HSCA p396 - Sturdivan gives the figures for a Winchester Cartridge Company (CE399-type) round to deform when hitting bone. He tells Matthews (of the HSCA) that it will deform at 1400 feet/second nose on and 1000 feet/second sideways on. I notice that higher figures now appear in Sturdivan's book "The JFK Myths" Larry M Sturdivan (Paragon House, 2005) p118. It seems that CE399-type rounds got stronger in the years between the HSCA investigation and Sturdivan's book.
59. "Breakability: CE-399 and the Diminishing Velocity Theory" John Hunt (http://www.history-matters.com/essays/jfkmed/Breakability/Breakability.htm l
60. 4H 118-120
61. 4H 126
62. Testimony of Dr Shires, 6H 104
63. 6H 106
64. Harold Weisberg *"Post Mortem"* (self published, 1975)
65. Ibid
66. Walt Brown *"Treachery In Dallas"* (Carroll & Graf 1995)
67. 6H 89
68. 6H 92
69. 4H 114
70. 4H 112
71. 5H 141
72. Alaric Rosman *"The Single Bullet in Flatland"*, The Dealey Plaza Echo Vol. 12 No.2 July 2008
73. 6H 86

Eight
JFK at Risk

Larry Hancock

President Kennedy was at risk in 1963, that in itself is nothing new as threats to American Presidents occur on an ongoing basis. The Secret Service's Protective Research Service existed to receive and investigate reports of such threats; it was fairly standard procedure for individuals making such threats to go on a watch list and be re-investigated for a number of years. That process was followed for some of the reported 1963 threats, for others it was not. We will see that as one of the first indications that the system of Presidential protection, while appearing quite strong in the form of the White House detail of Secret Service agents that routinely surrounded the President, was fundamentally inadequate. Its protocols and resources were not prepared to deal with a new type of emerging threat – threats which involved groups rather than individuals and threats from trained, skilled and organized attackers, not just from mentally unbalanced "lone nuts". The Secret Service procedures had been developed on a history of Presidential attacks by such "lone nuts", that history changed in 1963.

The first concrete signs that a change was in place occurred during President Kennedy's address to the recently returned Cuban Brigade, back from prisons in Cuba and received in an honour ceremony at the Orange Bowl in Miami, Florida. The President's decision to attend the ceremony was a relatively last minute one, with some of his advisors reminding him that there was widespread animosity in the exile community, based on the perception that he had abandoned them at the Bay of Pigs. Still, Robert Kennedy had been a moving force in negotiating their release and the decision was made for Presidential participation. As it turned out, although little was made of it at the time, two incidents seem now to have confirmed the concerns for his safety. First, police found a dynamite bomb near the stadium, along the President's motorcade route and second, they received reports of a sniper within the Orange Bowl itself – a Cuban male, age 25 using the name Chino and carrying a scope equipped rifle in a duffel

JFK | ECHOES FROM ELM STREET
A SEARCH FOR HISTORICAL ACCURACY ON THE ASSASSINATION OF PRESIDENT JOHN F. KENNEDY

bag. They were unable to apprehend "Chino" but the description was quite complete, with his age, height, weight etc.[1]

This early threat, one involving a bomb (in today's terms an IED) on the motorcade route and a sniper, prepared to strike from a considerable distance, should have provided a warning that the nature of the threat to President Kennedy had changed – there is no evidence that it did. And in fact there is no indication that the Secret Service was even aware of the Orange Bowl incidents – which were reported in Miami papers and in Miami Police reports. The Secret Service itself did not have a general intelligence function or a threat analysis section. While this may seem somewhat unreal given the current state of the world, in 1963 its Presidential protection activities largely consisted of controlling access to the President, providing a personal security shield during his travels and personal security for his wife and family.

That lack of a true intelligence function became all too clear in Dallas, when statements and testimony from the Secret Service lead agents (following the assassination) revealed that they had been given no particular warnings about Dallas being a high risk stop. Over the previous twelve months Vice President Johnson and his wife had been surrounded and heavily jostled during a visit to downtown Dallas and UN Ambassador Stevenson had been physically attacked during a trip to Dallas. Both Stevenson and Senator Fulbright had each personally warned JFK to avoid Dallas. There had been numerous warnings from Texas Congressmen, local Dallas community leaders such as Stanley Marcus and top Dallas law enforcement officers; Chief of Police Curry had stated that citizens were encouraged to perform "citizen's arrests" in support of police efforts to quell protests and demonstrations. Indeed a special city ordinance (Ordinance No. 10046) had been passed by the Dallas City Council and Mayor, effectively "deputizing" the general citizenry. Yet the Secret Service agents claimed that they had received no warnings or direction in regard to special concerns about security in Dallas. They only noted that the headquarters threat files for Dallas had been checked twice and found to contain no entries at all.

As 1963 progressed, two consistent patterns of threats to the President emerged. Both threats involved groups of military or paramilitary individuals, with deep political agendas and generally a personal hatred of the President. In both instances the threats came from multiple locations around the country and clearly indicated that a network of such individuals existed, with the ability to act at multiple locations. That capability was totally lost on the Protective Services group, which continued to compartmentalize each reported threat report strictly by city of origin and Secret Service procedures which required that the lead agent for any Presidential trip review only the threat index for the particular city being visited.

In April of 1963, the FBI investigated a report that an ultra right wing California group was recruiting and training rifle teams to assassinated

Eight | JFK at Risk

targeted public officials, starting with the President and Cabinet. George Harding had supported the politics of the group but felt he had to go to the FBI when he was recruited to join an eight man assassination team. He "claimed that the leaders in the group were Dr. Wesley Swift, James Shoup and others.... The second in command was a Colonel William Gale...who was supposed to have been the youngest intelligence officer under MCARTHUR (sic)." Members of the group were associated with the Christian Identity movement, the Christian Defense League and the National States Rights party. The FBI picked up further reports in regard to the organization, including a related incident in April in which a Los Angeles physician was reported approaching individuals to form a group of young man to get rid of Kennedy and the Cabinet; the individual was known to be a friend of William Gale and a member of the National States Rights party.[2]

In August, both the FBI and Secret Service generated another report related to the group, when a close associate of Gale was overhead discussing the possibility of assassinating the President and was arrested later in the month for the possession of illegal firearms.

The Secret Service and FBI generated another report in August 1963 by the arrest of Gale's associate George King, Jr. King was overheard discussing the possibility of assassinating the president and was later arrested that month for the sale of illegal firearms.[3]

The reach of radicals such as Swift and Gale reached far beyond California, other FBI informant reports reveal the creation and training of sniper teams in Florida and in November of 1963, a Miami Police informant participated in a covert tape recording session of one of these ultra right figures, Joseph Milteer. Among other things, Milteer discussed the idea of killing President Kennedy by placing a sniper in a tall building on one of the President's motorcade routes. The plan would also involve a "patsy" who could be framed for the killing. In later remarks Milteer described the "patriots" killing the President and blaming it on the Communists. The FBI informant participating in the taping of Milteer was also a well trusted Miami police source, who had already assisted them in tracking a number of ultra right plots, including bombings in Miami. He had reported on secret meetings held in conjunction with a conservative political convention in New Orleans earlier that summer; members of a covert inner circle had discussed plans to form attack teams to target national political figures, Jewish judges and major financial figures.

The Milteer tape recordings serve to illustrate the fundamental weaknesses in the Presidential protective services effort. The incident generated reports to both the FBI and the Secret Service. While the FBI did question certain individuals mentioned by Milteer, the Miami Secret Service office merely passed the report on to Washington D.C., as Milteer had mentioned the possibility of the attack being made in D.C. Copies of FBI memoranda confirm that their was a Secret Service follow up out of at least one other field office but FOIA requests (as of 2010) to the Secret Service have resulted in the response that the Secret Service denies ever having held a file on Joseph Milteer.[4]

Finally, the week prior to the assassination, the FBI's San Antonio office reported a threat directly related to the upcoming Presidential trip to Dallas. The message contained the warning that "...a militant group of the National States Rights Party plans to assassinate the President and other high level officials."[5]

It may well have been this warning that produced an FBI Airtel which was reportedly transmitted to selected offices on November 17. This warning related a threat to assassinate President Kennedy in Dallas Texas on November 22. Information regarding the warning was related by a former FBI security file clerk working in the New Orleans field office at the time. The Airtel referred to "a militant revolutionary group and directed the offices to contact racial and hate group informants in investigating the threat. After the assassination Director Hoover would deny that any such warning had been transmitted however a related document suggests that FBI employees were briefed on withholding any comment on the matter and instructed to sign letters confirming the briefing – the briefing officers were "told not to place the letters in the office files on express instructions of the Deputy Associate Director."[6]

If all these threats and investigations had been reported to the Secret Service and evaluated together, it seems obvious (in retrospect) that protective services would have had to consider the possibility of the President being "stalked" by members of an armed paramilitary group, capable of staging relatively sophisticated sniper attacks at different locations. This would have called for a level of security totally beyond that of the "close in" shielding of the President that we see right up to the time of his murder. Clearly that was not done and the basics of the Presidential security protocols as of November, 1963 considered no such threat as had been described by Joseph Milteer in Miami.

Yet while President Kennedy was certainly at some level of risk from the ultra right radicals, there are also a number of other instances in which people talked about threats to JFK. These incidents occurred prior to his murder in Dallas, in some cases they were reported following the assassination. However, in virtually no instance were they neither investigated in any depth nor were they linked to each other for any sort of analysis or orchestrated criminal investigation. These "leaks" appear to provide us a clear direction to the individuals who were actually involved in the President's murder. Unfortunately, they also demonstrate that the FBI lacked the same sort of analysis capability as the Secret Service. In the Secret Service's case, this seems to have obviated any changes in security protocols for the President; in the case of the FBI, it underscores their inability to effectively investigate a conspiracy, a crime more complex than the act of a lone individual.

EIGHT | JFK AT RISK

One of the most revealing "leaks" prior to the assassination occurred in Miami, Florida, at the Parrot Jungle restaurant. On November 1, 1963, Lillian Spengler was working at the restaurant and being "chatted up" by a patron, one Jorge Soto Martinez. Martinez was apparently trying to impress Lillian, talking about being a crack marksman. During the conversation he described being as good a shot as his friend Lee Oswald. Lee, who spoke Russian and was currently in either Texas or Mexico, was an American Marxist, spoke Russian and either of them was good enough to shoot President Kennedy right between the eyes. Mrs Spengler was put off by Martinez's remarks and discussed them with some of her co-workers at the restaurant at the time. When she reported the conversation to the FBI, after the assassination, her co-workers corroborated her remarks.

Strangely, the FBI demonstrated little curiosity, the investigating agent suggested that they could simply bring Martinez in and Spengler could personally confront him with the story – understandably she was frightened at that prospect and declined. At that point the FBI Agent told her simply to "just drop it and not to mention it" any further. Interestingly, a private investigation of Martinez (a Cuban exile, fairly recently arrived in Miami) demonstrated that he was connected to some very interested individuals, people very heavily involved in anti-Castro activities.[7]

Also on November 1, a trip by President Kennedy to Chicago, Illinois, was cancelled at literally the last minute. All the advance work had been done, the motorcade was prepared and the President was on the verge of flying to the mid-west. The incident appeared to offer evidence of a known, significant threat to the President, and was investigated at some length by the House Select Committee on Assassinations. Sadly, their investigation was stonewalled by a variety of Chicago Secret Service office personnel as well as by Chicago FBI staff.

"I remember that case. Some people were picked up. And I'm telling you it wasn't ours. The whole Soldier Field matter was a Secret Service affair....you'll get no more out of me. I've said as much as I'm going to say on the subject. Get the rest from the Secret Service." FBI agent Thomas Coll.

However, when queried, not a single Secret Service officer assigned to the Chicago office would acknowledge any incident related to a Soldier Field event (a Presidential appearance at an Army-Navy football game) or a cancelled Presidential motorcade. When shown documents on the event one agent would only comment, "Isn't that the one that was cancelled at the last minute?" And the secretary, whose initials showed that she had typed them, denied ever having seen any of the related documents.[8]

Why would an FBI agent so adamantly refuse to discuss a cancelled Presidential trip, what would cause an entire Secret Service office to claim a loss of memory related to such an incident? At first researchers thought it might have to do with a reported threat from one Thomas Vallee; protective service files disclosed that he had indeed been investigated prior to the Chicago trip. Apparently he had made hostile remarks about the President during breakfast at a bowling alley a few days before the planned trip. The individual did report it and a visit (a pretext call to his land lady) to Vallee's apartment revealed that he did own a rifle and ammunition. The Secret Service advised the Chicago Police who put a watch on Vallee and actually picked him up for a minor traffic violation (or perhaps simply to take him into custody) very early on the morning of the President's planned visit.[9]

Was there more to Chicago than that? The answer is yes and the only reason we know it is that one of the local Secret Service agents, Abraham Bolden, provided considerable detail to the House Select Committee on Assassinations. Bolden admitted that he was not a first hand participant and that what he head heard came from office talk and from monitoring of the Secret Service radio frequencies the day prior to the President's visit. Bolden's information was explosive and there is little doubt that he suffered from trying to bring it forth following the assassination. For that story, readers are referred to his own story, told in The Echo From Dealey Plaza.[10]

What Bolden had to relate about the threat in Chicago was straight forward. The evening of October 30th, before the scheduled November 1st Presidential visit, the Chicago Secret Service office received a teletype from the FBI, which in itself was unusual. Even more unusual was that it described a potential threat to the President. Apparently the Bureau was monitoring four individuals that were in the process of travelling to Chicago, perhaps they were already there. For reasons unknown to us, the Bureau felt those individuals constituted a significant threat to the President. The warning gave some identification of the individuals and direction as to where they might be staying. And the Secret Service did locate them. Unfortunately the attempt to pick them up went awry, resulting in the capture of only two men. Bolden himself observed the two men being brought into the office, one he described as short and stocky, with a "swarthy" complexion, about five foot nine and with a crew cut – he was referred to as "Gonzalez". The two were interrogated and handed over the Chicago Police the day of the President's scheduled visit, what happened to them is not recorded but it is clear two individuals remained at large and represented an outstanding threat.

While we do have extensive documents (including follow-up annual PRS interviews over several years) relating to the Vallee report and investigation, nothing at all remains on the much more significant incident related by former Secret Service Agent Bolden. He related that it was known in the office that all documents, photos and notes pertaining to the incident were placed in a special, sensitive central office case file and hand carried back to Headquarters the evening of November 1, 1963 (via a commercial flight to Washington).

EIGHT | JFK AT RISK

What became of them is unknown however the Assassinations Records Review Board did discover that as late as 1995 the Secret Service destroyed several boxes of files relating to the President's travel in the fall of 1963.[11]

Unfortunately we simply don't know the details of the threat in Chicago, one apparently taken very seriously by both the FBI and Secret Service – so seriously that employees of both agencies later refused to discuss it with Congressional investigators. What we do know is that the President continued to be at risk during his final trip prior to Dallas. On December 11, the agent in charge of JFK's Miami trip prepared a summary report of the trip, ostensibly detailing all the threats, incidents, warnings and security measures for the Miami visit. The report only hints at certain threats (we do know that the Secret Service had actively worked with both the local JM/WAVE CIA station and certain Cuban exiles over concerns about exile anger with the President) and gives no details. However from other recently released documents we have indications of two very specific threats:

An interview with Richard Jamison states that "the threat of November 18 was posed by a mobile, unidentified rifleman with a high-powered rifle and scope."[12]

An interview with Lubert F. defreeze states that "there was an active threat against the President which the Secret Service was aware of in November 1963, in the period immediately prior to JFK's trip to Miami, made by a group of people.[13]

Once again we see the same indicators that seem to have become constant during 1963, the President was the target of an "active threat", a threat not from individuals but from individuals who are members of organized groups, from individuals equipped with high powered rifles, rifles with scopes, capable of attacking JFK from a distance. There is even some sign that in Chicago and in Miami, a response was made to the threats. In Chicago, with individuals still at large a visit and motorcade were cancelled. In Miami, travel by car (not a motorcade, simply transit travel) was replaced with transport by helicopter. But no special security precautions were implemented on the Texas trip. Was that because there had been specific threats reported in Chicago and in Miami but none in Dallas? Perhaps, if so it again illustrates the weakness over the over all protective system.

Apparently there was no discrete threat reported in Dallas, even though the entire community including the City Council, Mayor and Chief of Police had taken special action against perceived violent protests or demonstrations. But we do have two different incidents reported in Dallas, unfortunately not prior to the assassination. However, each was reported to the FBI afterwards. And each may tell us a great deal about the actual plot that killed President Kennedy.

On November 19, 1963 Woburn Aircraft was in the final stages of transferring the ownership of a series of DC-3 aircraft. Woburn had contracted with Ray January, at Red Bird airport, to perform repairs and inspections necessary

JFK | ECHOES FROM ELM STREET
A SEARCH FOR HISTORICAL ACCURACY ON THE ASSASSINATION OF PRESIDENT JOHN F. KENNEDY

to finalize transfer of the last of several aircraft which had been sold. Two individuals had arrived the previous day, to perform check outs and to take ownership; one was an Air Force Colonel, the other a Cuban exile pilot. The Cuban, obviously very familiar with DC-3 aircraft, told January that he previously flown similar aircraft as an officer in the Cuban Air Force.

While working with each other over several days January and the Cuban became quite friendly. By Thursday the 21st, they were routinely eating meals together and chatting during their lengthy work days. And during their lunch beak on the 21st, the Cuban paused, looked at January and simply said "they are going to kill your President". There was no doubt in January's mind that the man was not joking; he was deadly serious. Of course January asked him why he would say such a thing and the man gave him a very direct reply. The Cuban pilot had himself been involved with the Bay of Pigs and, along with others, had been told their friends had died solely because JFK had refused to provide the air cover that had been promised them. The word was that RFK had talked his brother out of sending the planes. And because of that both John and Robert were going to die. January remained convinced that the man was serious but it was something that he simply could not credit, he told his friend that and the reply was again simple, "You will see."

Early on the afternoon of November 22, the aircraft, the Cuban and the Colonel departed Love Field. January saw the Cuban briefly before, just as the first radio reports were coming in that something had happened on the Presidential motorcade. The Cuban, appearing rather sad, simply said, "It's all going to happen like I told you."

Research has confirmed all the basic elements of January's story, the sale of the DC-3, January's involvement with the airplane. The facts suggest the aircraft was sold to a CIA proprietary company and was intended to be used in a new anti-Castro initiative.

These "leaks", from Miami, from Chicago and in Dallas, suggest both the motive and the type of individuals actually involved in the murder of the President. They also suggest that Lee Oswald was known to these individuals and was introduced as a patsy in their plan. Support for that view comes in the form of one final pre-assassination incident in Dallas.

A couple of days before the President's visit, Ralph Leon Yates had been driving near the Burkley street extension on the R.L. Thornton expressway (the entrance closest to Lee Oswald's apartment). He noticed a man hitchhiking and had stopped to give him a ride. The young man was carrying a package some four feet long – he told Yates it contained curtain rods. During the ride, the young man was talkative, bringing up the President's upcoming visit – and showing Yates a picture of man with a rifle and asking if he thought the President could be killed with the gun shown in the photo. He went on to bring up the idea of whether or not someone might shoot JFK, perhaps from the top of a

EIGHT | JFK AT RISK

building or a window high off the ground. He also mentioned the Carousel Club (Jack Ruby's club) asking if Yates himself had ever been there. Finally the man mentioned that he was going to Houston Street and Yates obligingly turned off the Expressway and dropped the man at the intersection of Elm and Houston (the intersection being the location of the Texas School Book Depository).[14]

The whole exchange had seemed strange to Yates, strange enough that he mentioned it to a fellow employee, Dempsey Jones. Jones later gave a sworn statement verifying that Yates had discussed the whole thing with him prior to the assassination. We know about Yates story and Jones' corroboration because Yates (accompanied by his Uncle) went to the FBI with the story on November 27, apparently still disturbed because he felt the young man had closely resembled Lee Oswald (who, for the record, was working in the TSBD at the time of the incident).[15]

Yates story was detailed, Yates's himself was married with five children and told the FBI he most adamantly did not want any publicity over the information he was providing. Given the fact that it was corroborated by another individual, the FBI next administered a polygraph to Yates. His wife would later relate that she was told the polygraph verified that he was being truthful – but that of course his story simply could not be true. Based on that he was apparently encouraged to seek medical treatment and was told he should at once report to a psychiatric hospital. After several years of medication and shock treatments, he died of heart failure in 1975. His wife is of the opinion that the treatments were simply to make him forget the encounter but states that he stood by it until his death.[16]

The Yates story is significant for a number of reasons, implying that in the days before the assassination Lee Oswald was actively being set up as a patsy, an individual planning the shooting of the President. Interestingly, it also associates Oswald with the Carousel Club and very possibly Jack Ruby. One can only speculate what might have happened if Yates had gone to the Dallas Police with the incident the evening of the assassination or even the day following. Another interesting point is that the incident which contains some details which are not a match for the "official" story of Oswald and the assassination. It would have the rifle being taken into the Book Depository a day or more before the attack. It would introduce a totally different paper sack than the one attributed to Oswald.

Yet the Yates incident is certainly not the only report of Oswald being impersonated and "set up" prior to November 22. Several other incidents occurred when he should have been at work and in one a rifle was placed at a gun shop to have a scope mounted, when the "weapon of record" supposedly had already been purchased with a mounted scope. In fact it seems that the final work up to the assassination contained certain twists and turns, everything was not conducted to a perfect master plan. There were iterations, as there were "leaks".

JFK | ECHOES FROM ELM STREET
A SEARCH FOR HISTORICAL ACCURACY ON THE
ASSASSINATION OF PRESIDENT JOHN F. KENNEDY

In retrospect, that there was an active threat to the President seems perfectly clear. The nature of the attack, from trained, proficient riflemen, was repeatedly suggested. There is no sign that any action was taken to alter security protocols in response to the reported threats. Beyond that there is reason to suspect that certain groups and perhaps even individuals were under suspicion. But documents and records detailing that suspicion seem to have disappeared. Secret Service and FBI agents refuse to discuss key incidents. Witnesses describing certain leaks were either simply rejected or neutralized, especially if those leaks mentioned Lee Oswald and suggested that he might have been set up or framed as the assassin.

The conspiracy was far from perfect; it revealed itself in a number of ways. And it seems that those who did not deal with it before the fact certainly did not wish to deal with that afterwards.

Endnotes
[1] "The Kennedy's Greet the Cubans; Dynamite found at Stadium", *Someone Would Have Talked*, Larry Hancock, 2010, Exhibit 4-13 and Sons and Brothers, Richard Mahoney, Arcade Publishing, 1999, p. 407.
[2] WCD 39 and WCD 1107, also *"A League of their Own: A look inside the Christian Defense League"*, David Boylan, 1999
[3] FBI field report, CO2-26104 #6419, also *"A League of their Own, A look inside the Christian Defense League*, David Boylan, 1999
[4] Miami Police Intelligence report, Intelligence Division memo from Detective Sgt. Sapp to State Attorney Richard Gerstain, April 10, 1963 also RIF 124-10268-1000; agency file numbers 80-27-39, 40, 41 and 42.
[5] Warren Commission volume 17 H 566; report located by Vincent Palamara)
[6] *Someone Would Have Talked*, Larry Hancock, 2010, p. 202
[7] Dan Christianson, *Miami Magazine*, September 1976 and *Conspiracy*, Anthony Summers, p. 447
[8] Secret Service Agent James Griffiths to HSCA interviewer Harold Rose, January 23, 1978
[9] HSCA interview of Special Agent Edward Tucker pertaining to an interview with threat suspect Thomas Vallee, January 1, 1978 also *Someone Would Have Talked*, Larry Hancock, 2010, pp. 196-198
[10] *The Echo from Dealey Plaza*, Abraham Bolden, Harmony Books, New York, 2008
[11] HSCA interview with Abraham Bolden, 1978, RIF 180-10070-10273
[12] HSCA document 180-10074-10394
[13] HSCA document 180-10074-10394
[14] FBI report of November 27, 1963, Interview with Ralph Yates and Mr. J.O. Smith; exhibit 13-3 in *Someone Would Have Talked*, Larry Hancock, 2010
[15] Jones interview conducted by SA Arthur Carter, Dallas Office file DL 44-1639
[16] 2006 interview with Dorothy Yates, James Douglas, *JFK and the Unspeakable*, 2008, pp. 353-355

Nine
J.D Tippit: A Troubled Police Officer

Stuart Galloway

J.D. Tippit – a name forever associated with the brutal assassination of the 35th President of the United States, John Fitzgerald Kennedy.

Tippit was a Police Officer employed by the Dallas Police Department, who was also cut down by a murderer's bullets on that fateful day in November 1963. Was the event associated with the assassination of the President or was it simply a sheer coincidence that a second murder of a public official took place that day? History would have us believe that the two crimes were carried out by one individual but the evidence would seem otherwise. Some even believe that Tippit was a member of the team who was involved in formulating the assassination strategy against Kennedy. Conspiracy theories abound but what is certain that on the day of his death, J.D. Tippit was acting very mysteriously.

On the 22nd November 1963 just after the President of the United States had been assassinated by an unknown gunman or group of gunmen in Dealey Plaza, two miles away in Oak Cliff, a suburb of that city, another tragedy was about to take place. Tippit was driving his patrol car slowly down a quiet street when he stopped to talk to a pedestrian walking along the pavement. After a short conversation the pedestrian pulled a gun and shot the officer, fatally wounding him, before making off at a brisk pace to the horror of several bystanders.

The Early Years
J.D. was the eldest of five children born to Edgar Lee Tippit and Lizzie Mae Tippit (née Rush) on 18 September 1924 in Annona, Red River County, Texas.

JFK | ECHOES FROM ELM STREET
A SEARCH FOR HISTORICAL ACCURACY ON THE
ASSASSINATION OF PRESIDENT JOHN F. KENNEDY

Edgar Lee was born on 26th January 1902 and died on 24th February 2006, aged 104. Lizzie May was born in 1905 and died in 1990.

JD was growing up in Red River County just at the time that the Great Depression was to strike. His father was a reasonably successful cotton farmer. In 1929 Texas was optimistic about the future; after all the state population had increased by over 1 million people during the previous decade, climbing to nearly 6 million in total. The population of Red River County also peaked in the late 20's at about 35,000 but started to fall away soon afterwards. (The 2010 population was given as about 13,000).

Cotton was the most important industry in the area; in fact, by tracing the evidence of cotton, it is estimated that production began in Texas in the early 1800s. During the nineteenth century and up to World War I, the traditional "Cotton Belt" was made up primarily of the states of North Carolina, South Carolina, Georgia, Alabama, Mississippi, Arkansas, Louisiana, Tennessee, Oklahoma and Texas. Cotton can be grown with less water than any other crop so suited the dry and arid climate of that part of Texas.

The Great Depression struck on "Black Tuesday" – 29th October 1929, when the industrial average plunged on Wall Street. Unemployment soared, famine struck, and even drought exacerbated the situation. But the Tippit's survived as cotton farmers throughout this period moving eventually to a place called Baker Lane in 1939. Like many other youngsters in that part of Texas, J.D. automatically became a farmer on completion of his education. However, in 1944 at the age of 20, he decided that he wanted to help the war effort and joined the US Army. After several months of training he joined the 17th Airborne Division and became a paratrooper. In early 1945 the Division fought in Operation Varsity – the airborne assault on the Rhine. J.D. was awarded the Bronze Star for his actions during combat. He remained on active duty until 20th June 1946.

After the Second World War ended, J.D. returned to his father's farm and settled down to family life again, getting married on 26th December 1946 to Marie Frances Gasway, in Clarksville, Texas. The couple were to have three children over the coming ten years. J.D. worked for a while in the installation department of an American chain of department stores and even tried his hand at rearing cattle. After moving to Dallas he worked for a short time as a carpenter's helper and at a steel company doing odd jobs.[1] Tippit attended a Veterans Administration vocational training school at Bogata, Texas, from January 1950 until June 1952. However, he was to find his vocation with the Dallas Police Department and was made a patrolman on 28th July 1952.

The origins of formalized policing in the Dallas region can be traced to the formation of "Vigilance Committees" that were created to protect early settlers from skirmishes with the native population during the 1840s, and through the incorporation of Dallas as a town in 1856. Later in the nineteenth century, the

NINE | J.D TIPPIT: A TROUBLED POLICE OFFICER

city adopted a formal charter, and the Dallas Police Department came under the control of the Texas governor, who appointed the police chief through the police commissioner. The Dallas Police Department instituted formal uniforms and mounted patrols during the 1880s. Similar to other newly formalized police agencies during this period, the department was understaffed and overworked. By the turn of the twentieth century, Dallas had grown from a frontier outpost into a city of 45,000 inhabitants, and the Dallas Police Department had expanded to serve the increasing needs of a growing population. The department numbered forty-seven sworn officers by 1903, and it instituted its first motorized patrol units and had created a substation in the city's newly incorporated Oak Cliff section by the end of the decade.

The creation of the Texas Department of Public Safety in 1932 led to a much greater exchange of information amongst the various police agencies within Texas as well as the expanded use of fingerprint files and ballistics tests in the investigation of criminal suspects. By the end of the 1950's the DPD employed 966 sworn officers, who patrolled a city with a population of nearly 700,000.[2]

2. J.D.'s Working Life
J.D. became part of a rapidly developing police force utilizing modern systems of crime detection and prevention. He was very proud of his uniform, wearing badge number 848, and was diligent in the service that he provided to his community. He was cited for bravery in 1956 for his role in disarming a fugitive. On the night of 28th April 1956, he and his partner, Daniel Smith, responded to a call relating to "a demented person." It turned out that a man was threatening to kill his 25 year old wife and to then commit suicide. After an altercation with the husband, J.D. was struck in the stomach and knee with an ice pick. He was rushed to Parkland Hospital and received emergency treatment. Four months later he required knee surgery which left him with a permanent, slight, disability.[3]

In 1963 his salary in the police force was $5,880[4] - about $43,000 (£27,000) in today's money, but inflation was quite low, averaging out at about 1.0% per annum.

However, J.D. was looking to enhance his income so that he could better provide for his wife and children. He therefore took on part time work at several other places in Dallas. One of these was Austin's Barbecue at 2321 West Illinois Street in the Oak Cliff section of Dallas. Austin's Barbecue reigned as the destination of choice for thousands of Oak Cliff diners. Just about everyone eat there. The diner pulled in more customers than all the local eating places, not just because of its tangy-sauced barbecue but also because of its lunches, dinner plates, and breakfasts.

J.D. worked at Austin's every Friday or Saturday night from 10.00pm until 2.00am. He was employed to act as a deterrent to potential trouble-making teenagers who tended to hang out there late on weekend evenings. Because so many neighbourhood citizens gathered at Austin's to discuss what was going on in the area, the restaurant functioned, according to one local historian, as the unofficial Oak Cliff City Hall.[5]

J.D. also worked in the same capacity at the Stevens Theatre on 2007 Fort Worth Avenue, Oak Cliff, keeping order among the youthful moviegoers. Occasionally he also worked at football games on Saturday afternoons in the Cotton Bowl Stadium.[6] This stadium was originally known as the Fair Park Stadium. Originally constructed in 1930 and after expansion in the late 1940's the facility held over 75,000 people. Policing the area during some of the bigger American football matches must have been an enormous task because of the immense crowds that attended the games.

Many friends and acquaintances testified to the fact that Tippit was an upright member of the community and was a churchgoer who spent much of his spare time with his wife and children. However, was there a dark side to Tippit's life?

J.D. could be tied in very closely to Jack Ruby who, besides running strip clubs, was also heavily involved with narcotics and gun-running businesses, operations that considerably enhanced the income of certain Dallas police officers. Mack Pate, who owned a garage in the area and knew a large number of police officers, stated that Tippit was often referred to as a "dirty cop" by some of his fellow officers. A friend of Tippit's mother also reported that J.D. was "bad".[7] It would also seem that for some time he had been having an affair with a married waitress who worked at Austin's Barbecue. Some researchers have intimated that a jealous husband may have been involved with the murder of Tippit but this would seem unlikely bearing in mind that the shooting occurred in broad daylight and was carried out in a manner much more akin to a "mob" killing or execution. However, it would seem that J.D. had a very busy social schedule and was involved with a number of women.

Darrell Wayne Garner was a pimp and an alcoholic, a car thief and a gun runner, with thirty arrests to his credit in Dallas over a seven year period. However, in July 1967 Garner told Jim Garrison that he had known Officer Tippit, as a part-time gun runner.[8] (Jim Garrison was the District Attorney of New Orleans who began an investigation into the assassination of President Kennedy in late 1966, leading to the arrest and subsequent acquittal of Clay Shaw as being involved in the crime).

From the foregoing it can be deduced that J.D. may well have been deeply involved with certain criminal elements in the Dallas area.

3. The Day of Tippit's Murder

The sun rose at Love Field, Dallas, on 22nd November 1963 at 7.05am – it was drizzling, with overcast skies and the temperatures in the mid 50's. When John and Jackie Kennedy arrived later in Air Force 1 at Love field at

NINE | J.D TIPPIT: A TROUBLED POLICE OFFICER

11.40am, there was still rain on the tarmac but there was by now a clear blue sky with warm sunshine and temperatures heading towards the lower 70's.

J.D.'s shift started at precisely 7.00am and was to have continued until 3.00pm. He worked out of the Southwest Substation of the Dallas Police Department. His patrol district was number 78, situated about 6 miles from the Substation. J.D. was probably on the road soon after breakfast, before sunrise, leaving his house, 238 Glencairn, at about 6.15am in order to get to work on time.

The shift started normally enough. Lieutenant William Fulghum was in charge that morning and Sergeant Hugh Davis took the roll call requiring the patrolmen to formally acknowledge their names – along with J.D. on the early shift Truman Boyd, Rufus High, and Roy Walker were also signing on. All hands were reminded that they were to be especially vigilant because all suburban squads were short of men that day, and if trouble developed they would be moved from area to area, and Fulghum wanted an immediate response.[9]

By 8.00am J.D. had left the Oak Cliff Substation and was on his way south towards his assigned district located about five miles from downtown Dallas. At just before 10.00am he was called to investigate a disturbance at 2800 E.Illinois. Not much is known about this call except that Tippit was ordered there on a "Signal 4" which meant "Out on Investigation". At the time it was the location of the Aluminium Screen Manufacturing Company – today it houses a company by the name of Roberts Air Conditioning. Tippit was cleared back into service at 10.17am. So far the day seemed to have proceeded in a fairly normal pattern.

A few minutes later, at about 10.25am, J.D. stopped at the Rebel Drive-In on East Ledbetter to have a coffee break with his friend, Patrolman Bill Anglin. The latter later said in an interview with Dale Myers "I'd consider him to be one of the best officers I'd ever been around. He never looked anyone in the eye, nevertheless, he was able to give the impression that he was concentrating on you." The two officers were very close friends.

This could not have been a particularly long meeting between the two police officers, because at 10.40am J.D. stopped briefly at the home of Edith Davidson and by 10.45am was cleared back into service. At about 11.30am he arrived home to have lunch with his wife and his youngest son. He bolted down a sandwich with some fried potatoes and a glass of milk whilst watching the arrival of the President in Air Force 1 at Love Field on television.[10]

At 11.51am J.D. climbed back into his car, radioed that he was back in service from lunch, and started driving back towards his patrol district. However, did he ever actually reach that area? He seems to have gone to the North Oak Cliff area, several miles from where he was supposed to be. At 12:17pm Tippit checked out on an investigation near Bonnie View and Kiest. He radios the dispatcher and says "be out of the car for a minute, 4100 block of Bonnie View."

JFK | ECHOES FROM ELM STREET
A SEARCH FOR HISTORICAL ACCURACY ON THE
ASSASSINATION OF PRESIDENT JOHN F. KENNEDY

At 12.45pm the dispatcher on Channel 1 puts out a description of the suspect wanted in connection with the shooting of the President.

Dispatcher: *"Attention all squads, attention all squads. The suspect in the shooting at Elm and Houston is reported to be an unknown white male, approximately thirty, slender build, height five feet ten inches, weight one hundred sixty-five pounds, reported to be armed with what is thought to be a 30 calibre rifle. Attention all squads. The suspect from Elm and Houston is reported to be an unknown white male about thirty, slender build, five feet ten inches tall, one hundred sixty-five pounds, armed with what is thought to be a 30-30 rifle. No further description at this time, or information. 12:45."*

The dispatcher then points out that it is a signal 19 (shooting) involving the President. Several patrolmen report in and the dispatcher then orders Tippit and Patrolman RC Nelson into the central Oak Cliff area. Tippit responds "I'm about Kiest and Bonnie View". Nelson apparently reported that he was going north on Marsalis. More on this exchange later.

It would seem that Tippit falsified his position to the dispatcher because at about this time he was spotted at least 2 miles away, arriving in his patrol car at the GLOCO service station situated at 1502 North Zang Boulevard in the North Oak Cliff area. He reportedly sat in his car for about 10 minutes watching traffic crossing over the Houston Street Viaduct. This was less than a mile away from where the President had been shot in Dealey Plaza only 15 minutes previously.

Photographer Al Volkland and his wife both knew Tippit and stated that they saw him sitting in his car and actually waved to him. Three employees of the GLOCO station, Tom Mullins, Emmet Hollingshead, and JB "Shorty" Lewis also knew him and confirmed Volkland's story, and remembered that he sat in his car, stationary, for some time. Tippit was then seen by several witnesses to leave the service station in his patrol car at a high rate of speed, cross Zang Boulevard, drive a block east on Addison Street, and turn south onto Lancaster, only ten blocks from Jefferson Boulevard.[11] At 12.54pm the following radio transmission took place on Channel 1:

Dispatcher	78
78 (Tippit)	78
	You are in the Oak Cliff are, are you not?
	Lancaster and Eighth
Dispatcher	*You will be at large for any emergency that comes in.*
78	*10-4*

J.D. was next seen 8 minutes later (about 1.02pm) at the Top Ten Record Store on Jefferson Boulevard but this should have only been a 3 minute drive from his reported position of Lancaster and Eighth. Had he been following the slow-moving bus that Lee Harvey Oswald had alighted from in a traffic jam some 15

NINE | J.D TIPPIT: A TROUBLED POLICE OFFICER

minutes earlier? Author John Armstrong thinks that this may well have been the case. Had he parked at the GLOCO service station to actually meet and pick up Oswald but traffic density had thwarted his plans?

At 1.03pm the dispatcher called Tippit on Channel 1 and asked his location but received no reply. J.D. had actually parked his car on the west side of the record store at the corner of Bishop and Jefferson and rushed into the store, asking the store clerk Louis Cortinas for permission to make a telephone call. Both Cortinas and the owner of the store, J.W. Stark, had seen Tippit dial a number but apparently no connection was made because Tippit rushed out of the store again, extremely agitated, without saying a word, and sped north for one block, turning east on Sunset Avenue towards Zang running parallel with Tenth Street.

Tippit may have called in again soon afterwards but this time the dispatcher failed to reply so we will never know what it was that Tippit wished to report.[12]

A minute or so later and less than half-mile away, Tippit drove up behind a car heading west along Tenth Street very close to where he would subsequently be murdered. The route that he must have taken means that he must have cut back on himself. The car was driven by James Andrews who was a salesman for the American National Life Insurance Company. Suddenly Tippit overtook the car and pulled to the right in front of Andrews, blocking any further movement forward. J.D. then rushed to the driver's side of the car and searched the space between the front and the back seats. Apparently not finding what he was looking for he left without a word, jumped back into his patrol car, and drove away quickly, reversing his direction and heading back east again.

It is fairly obvious from Tippit's movements that he was desperately searching for somebody but what had triggered off this sudden panic and why was he not working in the area to which he had been assigned? The district in which he was cruising just before his death was actually assigned to Officer William D. Mentzel.[13] A number of murder witnesses and others who knew Tippit reported that he would leave his area a lot and drive around to other assigned areas. In fact some thought that this area of Oak Cliff was in fact Tippit's assigned area and that he lived close to where he was murdered.

And so, unbeknown to J.D., the last few moments of his life were fast approaching.

Warren Commission document 630

The statements of witnesses to the murder vary significantly as can happen when people are confronted with a sudden, unexpected, short-lived, occurrence. Their positions in relation to the scene of the crime were also significantly different. Their statements will be dealt with in the next section of

JFK | ECHOES FROM ELM STREET
A SEARCH FOR HISTORICAL ACCURACY ON THE ASSASSINATION OF PRESIDENT JOHN F. KENNEDY

this chapter. However, most witnesses agree that J.D. was driving fairly slowly, east, down Tenth Street when he **may** (my emphasis – see 4C below) have spotted a man walking along the pavement in front of him. He pulled his patrol car in towards the kerb just next to the man and stopped, about 50yds. east of the intersection of Tenth and Patton. (See photo taken at the scene) The man walked over to the passenger's window of the car and seemed to acknowledge the policeman although nobody was close enough to hear any conversation. Some witnesses said that the passenger window was closed although J.D. may have been trying to open it. J.D. then opened his car door and climbed out quite nonchalantly stepping towards the front of the car, leaving the driver's door partially open. One witness (Benavides) reported that J.D. was in the act of drawing his gun at this point. As he drew level with the front of the car the man pulled out a gun and fired three quick shots across the bonnet of the car fatally wounding the officer. The man then went back around the squad car, back up towards the front, and shot him again, in the head – like a *de grâce* or a gangland killing. J.D. was probably dead before he hit the ground.

4. Some Discrepancies

A. Why did the dispatcher direct Tippit to the quiet residential area of Oak Cliff when all the other officers had been told to proceed to Dealey Plaza under a Signal 19 (shooting) where the assassination of the President had taken place? This order was not in the first radio transcript produced by the DPD and then suddenly appeared in a later transcript. This has caused many researchers to speculate that the dispatcher's words were later dubbed into the tape by Tippit's police colleagues in order to account for his presence there. There is a break in the 60Hz background interference that runs through the tapes at the point of the insertion. As can be seen from the transcript at 12.45pm, Nelson was also ordered into Oak Cliff, but when his movements were later checked he apparently moved directly to Dealey Plaza, oblivious of any such instruction.[14]

B. The Warren Commission would have us believe that when Tippit was cruising slowly east down Tenth he was actually searching for the suspected assassin of the President based on the description put out by the dispatcher at 12.45pm – only a quarter of an hour after the assassination. This poses two questions. How did the DPD arrive at the description so quickly – after all there were quite a few people who had not returned to the Book Depository after the shooting of the President?

Secondly – If J.D. had suspected that the assassin was walking down the pavement in front of him, would he not have stopped short of the suspect, radioed in to headquarters, got out of his car, drawn his pistol, and challenged the man from a distance or perhaps even waited for back-up? What he

NINE | J.D TIPPIT: A TROUBLED POLICE OFFICER

would not have done is to have allowed the suspect to get the "jump" on him. C. Helen Markham was one of the principle witnesses to the murder of Officer Tippit. (Her deposition to the Warren Commission is considered in some detail in the section on Witness Statements in this chapter). Alaric Rosman (researcher and member of Dealey Plaza UK) points out in his detailed article on Helen Markham's affidavit ("Document 106") given to the Dallas Police only 90 minutes after the murder, that there is no evidence that Tippit stopped anybody. Her typed and signed affidavit states:

"At approximately 1.06("pm" added in pen), November 22nd 1963—I was standing on the corner of E. 10th and Patton Street waiting for traffic to go by when I saw a squad car stop in front of 404 E. 10th about 50 feet from where I was standing. I saw a young white man walk up to the squad car opposite the driver's side, lean over and put his arms on the door of the car for a few seconds, then straighten up and step back from the car two or three feet. At this point the officer got out of the squad car and started around in front of the car and just as he got even with the left front wheel this young white man shot the officer and the officer fell to the pavement. I screamed and the man ran west on E. 10th across Patton Street and went out of sight."

So Helen Markham clearly states that Tippit had already stopped his patrol car outside 404 E.10th when the young white man walked up to the front passenger window of the car. In other words Tippit's murderer initiated the encounter. This makes nonsense of the Warren Commission findings that Tippit had stopped the man as a possible suspect in the assassination of the President.

D. The timings are all important here and whilst we can never be sure of exactly when the various incidents occurred in the build up to Tippit's murder, we can be reasonably sure of events based on the timed transmissions of the Dallas Police Department on Channel 1 and 2 and the more reliable witness statements. Again the Warren Commission would have us believe that the movements of Lee Harvey Oswald, after he had supposedly assassinated the President, gave him time to reach the Tippit murder site at Tenth and Patton by 1.15pm – when they say the event occurred.

The Warren Commission Report surmises that Oswald arrived back at his lodgings having travelled by bus and taxi from Dealey Plaza, a strange method of transport for an assassin escaping the scene of his crime, at 1.00pm. He picked up a pistol and immediately left, walking the 9/10th of a mile to the site of the Tippit murder in about 15 minutes – perfectly feasible at a fast walking pace. Bear in mind that nobody had reported anybody running in that area at the time. However, it will be shown from the witness statements that it would have been impossible for Oswald to have reached Tenth and Patton in the time that

JFK | ECHOES FROM ELM STREET
A SEARCH FOR HISTORICAL ACCURACY ON THE
ASSASSINATION OF PRESIDENT JOHN F. KENNEDY

would have been available to him, bearing in mind the time that the murder was actually committed and the testimony of Oswald's housekeeper.

E. In Dale Myers book on Tippit entitled "With Malice" he opens Chapter 1 with the words "Lee Harvey Oswald murdered Officer J.D.Tippit." Well, I believe that after due consideration of the evidence that the witnesses provided that day, and later when some were deposed by the Warren Commission, such a definitive statement is illogical. This along with the fact that the subsequent, very limited, investigation by the police, and the associated cover-ups that were perpetrated, makes it just as plain to me that one can say with some certainty that "Lee Harvey Oswald did not murder Officer J.D.Tippit."

Let us now proceed to the evidence collected from, and the statements made by, the witnesses themselves.

5. Witness Statements

The Warren Commission was set up by Lyndon Johnson under Executive Order No.11130 on 29th November 1963. It was clear from the outset that their instruction was to establish that a lone nut (Lee Harvey Oswald) had been killed by a lone nut (Jack Ruby). This was an unimpeachable panel of personnel who were ordered to rubber stamp an FBI report that pinned the blame for the murder of President Kennedy and Office J.D.Tippit entirely on Lee Harvey Oswald. This the Commission did by selective interviewing, deposing only those who were likely to support that conclusion and suppressing any contrary evidence collected during the hearings in the final report.

There were many witnesses or persons attending the site of the murder that day. These included private citizens, police officers, ambulance attendants, and others. However, the Warren Commission chose to depose only the following people: William Scoggins, Helen Markham, Barbara Davis, Virginia Davis, Ted Callaway, Sam Guinyard, Domingo Benavides, William Smith, and Warren Reynolds. As we shall see, the evidence from these people was changed and distorted when necessary so as to ensure Oswald was found guilty, and other witnesses who were likely to disagree with these findings were simply not formally questioned or their evidence ignored. The evidence of some of these witnesses will be considered in the following section.

A. *William Scoggins*

Scoggins was a cabdriver who had dropped a fare at about 1.00pm at 321 North Ewing. In his deposition to the Warren Commission he stated that he was parked on the east side of Patton facing north, a few feet from the corner of Tenth Street, just round the corner from where J.D. had stopped. He reported that he had earlier bought a Coke and watched the reports of the assassination on TV at the Gentlemen's Club (125 Patton) before coming out to his cab to

NINE | J.D TIPPIT: A TROUBLED POLICE OFFICER

eat his lunch. Scoggins stated that he did not see the shooting itself because of shrubbery in the way. An extract of his submission to the WC is given below.
 (David Belin was an Assistant Council to the Commission and was a close friend of Gerald Ford who in turn was appointed by President Johnson to the Commission. Allen Dulles was also appointed by Johnson as one of the seven commissioners, even though he had been forced to resign by President Kennedy after the debacle of the Bay of Pigs.)

BELIN. When you saw the officer fall, when was the next place that you saw the man, or did you see him at the same time you saw the officer fall, the other man?

SCOGGINS. No, I saw him coming kind of toward me around that cutoff through there, and he never did look at me. He looked back over his left shoulder like that, as he went by. It seemed like I could see his face, his features and everything plain, you see.

BELIN. Was he walking or running or trotting?
SCOGGINS. Kind of loping, trotting.
BELIN. Kind of loping or trotting?
SCOGGINS. Not in too big a hurry. It didn't seem like at first.
BELIN. At first not too big a hurry?
SCOGGINS. Yes.
BELIN. Did he change that at all?
SCOGGINS. Never did change his pace as long as I saw him. I don't know where he went after he passed the cab and got down a little piece, because then I was busy trying to get my dispatcher, and I never did look and never did get to see him.
BELIN. Did he have anything in his hand?
SCOGGINS. He had a pistol in his left hand.
BELIN. Did the pistol appear to be - did he appear to be doing anything with the pistol or not?
SCOGGINS. Yes. He had it, holding it, in his left hand in a manner that the barrel was up like this, and the stock was down here, curved back in here.
BELIN. Did it look like the gun had been flipped open at all or not?
SCOGGINS. I wouldn't say.
BELIN. You don't know?
SCOGGINS. No; I don't.
DULLES. You said he had it in his left hand?
SCOGGINS. Yes, sir.
BELIN. Did you see where his right hand was?
SCOGGINS. He was kind of running, kind of like this, in this manner.
BELIN. Did you hear the man say anything?
SCOGGINS. I heard him mutter something like, "poor damn cop," or "poor dumb cop." He said that over twice, and the last, I don't know whether the middle word

was "damn" or "dumb," but anyway, he muttered that twice.
BELIN. Did you hear him say any other word or phrase?
SCOGGINS. No.

Not exactly a positive identification of the fleeing assailant! Scoggins admitted that he ducked down behind his cab as the assailant came by and yet he was one of the principal witnesses said by the WC to prove beyond any reasonable doubt that Oswald was the culprit. He picked out Oswald in a farcical Dallas police line-up – only four people with Oswald shouting that he should not be put in line with three other teenagers. Scoggins again identified Oswald as the assailant on the Saturday but had to admit that he had seen pictures of Oswald in the newspaper. After the line-up he was then shown several pictures of men by an FBI agent - Scoggins narrowed these down to two. He told the agent that one of these two was Oswald but was then told by the agent that the one he had not selected was actually Oswald. Scoggins was actually one of the two principal witnesses for the Warren Commission report.

B. Helen Markham

Mrs Markham was the chief witness for the Warren Commission even though her credibility overall was extremely dubious. However, she gave the most important testimony in the whole affair. This was based on the evidence that she gave to Detective Graves only 90 minutes after Tippit's death. She was in emotional shock being still really frightened and certainly in no frame of mind to fabricated or consciously exaggerate.[15]

She told the Commission that at the time of Tippit's murder she was standing on the northwest corner of Tenth and Patton waiting for traffic to pass. She had left her house at the same time as she did every day to catch the 1.15pm bus to go to work. An extract of part of her submission to the Commission is given below. (Joseph Ball was a trial lawyer and appointed as a senior counsel to the Warren Commission.)

BAL. You left your home to go to work at some time, didn't you, that day?
MARKHAM. At one.
BALL. One o'clock?
MARKHAM. I believe it was a little after one.
BALL. Where did you intend to catch the bus?
MARKHAM. On Patton and Jefferson.
BALL. Patton and Jefferson is about a block south of Patton and 10th Street, isn't it?
MARKHAM. I think so.
BALL. Well, where is your home from Patton and Jefferson?
MARKHAM. I had came – I come one block, I had come one block from my home.

NINE | J.D TIPPIT: A TROUBLED POLICE OFFICER

BALL. You were walking, were you?
MARKHAM. I came from 9th to the corner of 10th Street.
BALL. And you were walking toward Jefferson?
MARKHAM. Yes, sir.
BALL. Tenth Street runs the same direction as Jefferson, doesn't it?
MARKHAM. Yes, sir.
BALL. It runs in a generally east and west direction?
MARKHAM. Yes, sir.
BALL. And Patton runs north and south?
MARKHAM. Yes, sir; up and down this way.
BALL. So you were walking south toward Jefferson?
MARKHAM. Yes, sir.
BALL. You think it was a little after 1?
MARKHAM. I wouldn't be afraid to bet it wasn't 6 or 7 minutes after 1.
BALL. You know what time you usually get your bus, don't you?
MARKHAM. 1:15.
BALL. So it was before 1:15?
MARKHAM. Yes, it was.

From the above exchange between Helen Markham and Joseph Ball, one can assume that Markham was probably on the corner of Tenth and Patton by about 1.06pm., much earlier than the Warren Commission would have us believe, so her evidence completely destroys their case.

Alaric Rosman (a member of Dealey Plaza UK), pointed out in his article on the subject of the Tippit murder that it was a brilliant piece of cross examination by Bell. If he hadn't been so quick thinking the Commission would have been in real trouble. He was terrified, as were the commissioners attending the hearing, that Markham would repeat what she had said in her affidavit (which is probably the most important document in the whole affair), that Tippit was killed just after 1.06pm. He switched her away from her comments on exact timings just to record the fact that she was in time for the bus at 1.15pm!

On page 165 of the Warren Commission Report it is stated: "According to Chief Curry, Tippit was free to patrol the central Oak Cliff area. Tippit must (why must? – my comment) have heard the description of the suspect wanted for the President's shooting; it was broadcast over channel 1 at 12.45pm, again at 12.48pm, and again at 12.55pm ...."
"At approximately 1:15pm, Tippit, who was cruising east on 10th Street, passed the intersection of 10th and Patton, about eight blocks from where he had reported at 12:54pm. About 100 feet past the intersection Tippit stopped a man walking east along the south side of Patton."

So the Commission would now have us believe that the murder probably didn't take place until getting on for 1.20pm. If they would also have us believe that Tippit was simply cruising around in the hope of finding the President's assassin, why did it take him 20 minutes to drive eight blocks?

DALLAS POLICE OFFICER J.D. TIPPIT MURDER SCENE

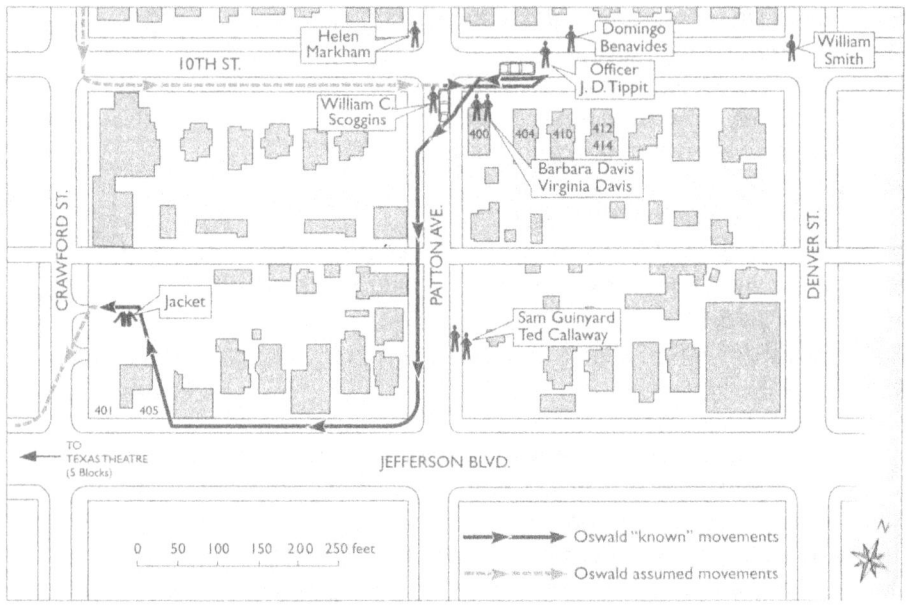

Acknowledgement: Diagram from "The Encyclopedia of The JFK Assassination" by Michael Benson – Figure 1

Although in this diagram it shows "Oswald's movements", it is far from certain that Oswald would have taken this route to the Texas Theatre where he was arrested or was ever at the scene of the crime. The solid black line is the known route taken by Tippit's killer after the murder. However, the broken grey line from where the jacket was dropped at a Texaco service station showing the route to the Texas Theatre is unlikely to have been taken by the killer. He was more likely to have gone straight ahead at this point and into the back door of the Abundant Life Temple which stands on Tenth and Crawford.

Markham's subsequent testimony indicated that the meeting between Tippit and his killer was very relaxed right up to the time that the shots rang out. Even after the murder, the killer does not seem to have rushed away from the scene with undue haste. Would this have been the case if Tippit had thought the man to be a suspect in the assassination of the President?

NINE | J.D TIPPIT: A TROUBLED POLICE OFFICER

BALL. Where was the police car when you first saw it?
MARKHAM. He was driving real slow, almost up to this man, well, say this man, and he kept, this man kept walking, you know, and the police car going real slow now, real slow, and they just kept coming into the curb, and finally they got way up there a little ways up, well, it stopped.
BALL. The police car stopped?
MARKHAM. Yes, sir.
BALL. What about the man? Was he still walking?
MARKHAM. The man stopped.
BALL. Then what did you see the man do?
MARKHAM. I saw the man come over to the car very slow, leaned and put his arms just like this, he leaned over in this window and looked in this window.
BALL. He put his arms on the window ledge?
MARKHAM. The window was down.
BALL. It was?
MARKHAM. Yes, sir.
BALL. Put his arms on the window ledge?
MARKHAM. On the ledge of the window.
BALL. And the policeman was sitting where?
MARKHAM. On the driver's side.
BALL. He was sitting behind the wheel?
MARKHAM. Yes, sir.
BALL. Was he alone in the car?
MARKHAM. Yes.
BALL. Then what happened?
MARKHAM. Well, I didn't think nothing about it; you know, the police are nice and friendly, and I thought friendly conversation. Well, I looked, and there were cars coming, so I had to wait. Well, in a few minutes this man made –
BALL. What did you see the policeman do?
MARKHAM. See the policeman? Well, this man, like I told you, put his arms up, leaned over, he just a minute, and he drew back and he stepped back about two steps. Mr. Tippit –
BALL. The policeman?
MARKHAM. The policeman calmly opened the car door, very slowly, wasn't angry or nothing, he calmly crawled out of this car, and I still just thought a friendly conversation, maybe disturbance in the house, I did not know; well, just as the policeman got –
BALL. Which way did he walk?
MARKHAM. Towards the front of the car. And just as he had gotten even with the wheel on the driver's side –
BALL. You mean the left front wheel?
MARKHAM. Yes; this man shot the policeman.

JFK | ECHOES FROM ELM STREET
A SEARCH FOR HISTORICAL ACCURACY ON THE ASSASSINATION OF PRESIDENT JOHN F. KENNEDY

Poor Mrs Markham was very muddled on the day of the murder – in fact hysterical. A police officer at the site of the murder admitted that she just kept screaming and shouting and he had to slap her just to bring her back to some kind of sanity. Whilst all agreed that Tippit had died instantly, she stated that it was 20 minutes before the ambulance arrived and that she was trying to talk to the dying officer during that time, before anybody else turned up. In fact a fairly large crowd had gathered at the scene within minutes of the shooting. Her depiction of the killer did not match that of Oswald although the authorities tried desperately to get her to change her statement.

The police wanted her to identify Tippit's killer as Oswald as soon as possible so carted her off to the police station where she was in such a state that ammonia had to be administered to her in order to bring her to a suitable state to even attend a line-up. Again the line-up was a complete farce – with Oswald protesting his innocence and sporting a black eye that he had suffered during his arrest in the Texas Theatre only three hours before.

The following is a further extract of Mrs Markham's evidence to the Warren Commission describing what happened during the line-up she attended on the day of the murder.

BALL. Now when you went into the room you looked these people over, these four men?
MARKHAM. Yes, sir.
BALL. Did you recognize anyone in the line-up?
MARKHAM. No, sir.
BALL. You did not? Did you see anybody – I have asked you that question before did you recognize anybody from their face?
MARKHAM. From their face, no.
BALL. Did you identify anybody in these four people?
MARKHAM. I didn't know nobody.
BALL. I know you didn't know anybody, but did anybody in that lineup look like anybody you had seen before?
MARKHAM. No. I had never seen none of them, none of these men.
BALL. No one of the four?
MARKHAM. No one of them.
BALL. No one of all four?
MARKHAM. No, sir.
BALL. Was there a number two man in there?
MARKHAM. Number two is the one I picked.
BALL. Well, I thought you just told me that you hadn't –
MARKHAM. I thought you wanted me to describe their clothing.
BALL. No. I wanted to know if that day when you were in there if you saw anyone in there –

NINE | J.D TIPPIT: A TROUBLED POLICE OFFICER

MARKHAM. Number two.
BALL. What did you say when you saw number two?
MARKHAM. Well, let me tell you. I said the second man, and they kept asking me which one, which one. I said, number two. When I said number two, I just got weak.
BALL. What about number two, what did you mean when you said number two?
MARKHAM. Number two was the man I saw shoot the policeman.
BALL. You recognized him from his appearance?
MARKHAM. I asked – I looked at him. When I saw this man I wasn't sure, but I had cold chills just run all over me.
BALL. When you saw him?
MARKHAM. When I saw the man. But I wasn't sure, so, you see, I told them I wanted to be sure, and looked, at his face is what I was looking at, mostly is what I looked at, on account of his eyes, the way he looked at me. So I asked them if they would turn him sideways. They did, and then they turned him back around, and I said the second, and they said, which one, and I said number two. So when I said that, well, I just kind of fell over. Everybody in there, you know, was beginning to talk, and I don't know, just –

The foregoing is just one example of many showing how the Warren Commission staff quite outrageously led witnesses to state what needed to be recorded in order to nail Oswald as the murderer of both President Kennedy and Officer Tippit. Mrs. Markham's evidence would never have stood up in a court of law. Any defence lawyer would have had a field day with her. Joseph Ball later said that she, his own witness, was full of mistakes and utterly unreliable. Later in a debate in December 1964, he described her as an "utter screwball"! Yet she was the Warren Commission's star witness! Ball was still trying to undermine the credibility of Markham's statement regarding her 1.06pm assertion as to the time of her arrival at the scene.

Returning now to the movements of Lee Harvey Oswald after the assassination of President Kennedy. Based on the testimony of Earlene Roberts, Oswald's housekeeper at his lodgings in North Beckley Street, he arrived back at almost exactly 1.00pm. She knew this because the news had just started on the television. He was in a hurry but was in the house for two or three minutes, time enough to pick up a jacket and a pistol. He then stood at the bus stop just outside for a couple of minutes before moving off at a fast walking pace. This would now put the time at no earlier than 1.04pm. We know from Mrs. Markham's evidence that Tippit was shot at no later than 1.10pm, giving Oswald no more than 4 minutes to walk nearly a mile. (She had seen him crossing the intersection as she arrived at the scene approximately 2 minutes before the shooting.) This alone makes it impossible for Oswald to have been the murderer of Officer Tippit. In addition, Deputy Sheriff

Roger Craig who was in Dealey Plaza at the time of President Kennedy's assassination, stated that a police radio message had been received when he and others were in the School Book Depository, advising that a Dallas policeman had been shot in the Oak Cliff area. The time on his watch was 1.06pm.

C. Domingo Benavides

Benavides was an auto mechanic who had stopped to help a man whose car had stalled in the middle of Patton street between Jefferson and Tenth. He had driven off to get a carburettor part but was returning in his 1958 Chevrolet pick-up truck to the scene of the breakdown in order to check a part number. He was travelling west on Tenth Street. He first spotted Tippit's car as he drove past the junction of Tenth and Denver Street, about 100yds. away from where the car had stopped. Benavides stopped his truck about 10 yards from Tippit's car on the other side of the street.

BELIN. *How fast were you going when you watched the policeman getting out of his car?*
BENAVIDES. *Oh, I imagine not maybe 25 miles an hour. I never did pay much attention to it.*
BELIN. *You say you stopped the car right away? Your vehicle, I mean?*
BENAVIDES. *Yes, sir. I just didn't exactly stop because I just pulled it into the curb.*
BELIN. *Then you say you heard a shot and you then ducked?*
BENAVIDES. *Yes. No; I heard the shot before I pulled in.*
BELIN. *Oh, I see. You heard the shot and pulled in and then what?*
BENAVIDES. *Then I ducked down.*
BELIN. *Then what happened?*
BENAVIDES. *Then I heard the other two shots and I looked up and the Policeman was in, he seemed like he kind of stumbled and fell.*
BELIN. *Did you see the Policeman as he fell?*
BENAVIDES. *Yes, sir.*
BELIN. *What else did you see?*
BENAVIDES. *Then I seen the man turn and walk back to the sidewalk and go on the sidewalk and he walked maybe 5 foot and then kind of stalled. He didn't exactly stop. And he threw one shell and must have took five or six more steps and threw the other shell up, and then he kind of stepped up to a pretty good trot going around the corner.*
BELIN. *You saw the man going around the corner headed in what direction on what street?*
BENAVIDES. *On Patton Street. He was going south.*

NINE | J.D TIPPIT: A TROUBLED POLICE OFFICER

Why would a killer throw away shells like that fired from his gun at the scene of a crime knowing that this would easily facilitate the subsequent identification of the weapon? Were these shells being planted as a decoy?

BELIN. Now, the first time that you saw him, what was his position
BENAVIDES. He was standing, the first time I saw him. The man that shot him?
BELIN. Yes.
BENAVIDES. He was standing like I say, on the centre in front of the windshield, right directly on the right front fender of the car.
BELIN. He was not moving when you saw him?
BENAVIDES. No; he wasn't moving then.
BELIN. All right, after you saw him turn around the corner, what did you do?
BENAVIDES. After that, I set there for just a few minutes to kind of, I thought he went in back of the house or something. At the time, I thought maybe he might have lived in there and I didn't want to get out and rush right up. He might start shooting again. That is when I got out of the truck and walked over to the Policeman, and he was lying there and he had, looked like a big clot of blood coming out of his head, and his eyes were sunk back in his head, and just kind of made me feel real funny. I guess I was really scared.
BELIN. Did the Policeman say anything?
BENAVIDES. The Policeman, I believe was dead when he hit the ground, because he didn't put his hand out or nothing.
BELIN. Where was the Policeman as he fell, as you saw him?
BENAVIDES. I saw him as he was falling. The door was about half way open, and he was right in front of the door, and just about in front of the fender. I would say he was between the door and the front headlight, about middleway when he started to fall.
BELIN. Did you notice where the gun of the policeman was?
BENAVIDES. The gun was in his hand and he was partially lying on his gun in his right hand. He was partially lying on his gun and on his hand, too.
BELIN. Then what did you do?
BENAVIDES. Then I don't know if I opened the car door back further than what it was or not, but anyway, I went in and pulled the radio and I mashed the button and told them that an officer had been shot, and I didn't get an answer, so I said it again, and this guy asked me whereabouts all of a sudden, and I said, on 10th Street. I couldn't remember where it was at the time. So I looked up and I seen this number and I said 410 East 10th Street.

It wasn't Benavides who actually got through successfully to the Dallas Police dispatcher on the radio in Tippit's car. He did attempt to do so. It was in fact another witness by the name of Temple Ford Bowley who had had more experience in using radios, who managed to make the necessary contact.[16]

So Benavides sat in his truck *for just a few minutes* before getting out and going over to Tippit's lifeless body. It is known from police tape records that the radio message from J.D.'s car was received from a citizen at 1.15pm, so allowing for the fact that Benavides had sat in his truck for say 2 minutes, that it would have taken some time for Ted Callaway to reach the scene of the crime from near Jefferson, and that it would have taken time to get the radio working and handed over to Callaway, this still puts the murder at no later than 1.11pm.

Benavides had a clear view of the killer as he threw away the empty shells, unloading them from his pistol one at a time. This is important because the pistol taken from Lee Harvey Oswald at the Texas Theatre had an extractor that ejected all shells simultaneously.[17] In fact the police at the scene stated that the weapon used to kill Tippit was an automatic so could not have been the weapon found on Oswald. Benavides picked up two shells and put them in an empty packet and handed them to Officer J.M.Poe who was told to maintain the chain of evidence. (More on this later)

Benavides absolutely refused to identify the man he had seen at Tenth and Patton as Oswald. As a result, the police did not call him to an official identification parade because this would have helped to exonerate Oswald. He never budged that in his assertion that Oswald was not the killer until he felt that his life was threatened, his brother having been murdered – after which he went along with an Oswald identification, but one which would not have had any validity in a court of law.[18]

D. Warren Allen Reynolds

Reynolds was employed at the Johnny Reynolds Motor Company, a used car dealership on East Jefferson Boulevard, one block away from the scene of the murder. He saw the assailant fleeing the crime scene. At first Reynolds refused to identify the man as Oswald but after he recovered from having been shot in the head by an unknown assailant with a .22 rifle, he expressed concern to the FBI that the attempt on his life may have been associated with his statement concerning Oswald. When he was deposed by the Warren Commission in July 1964 he therefore decided that it was Oswald that he had seen fleeing the scene of the crime.

The following is an extract of the submission made by Reynolds on 22nd July 1964 after he had recovered from his head wound. (Wesley Liebler was an Assistant Council appointed to the Warren Commission).

LIEBELER. You were in no way, if I understand it correctly then, properly identified as anyone who had told the authorities that this man that was going down the street was the same man as Lee Harvey Oswald, is that correct?
REYNOLDS. Well, yes and no. When it happened, and after I seen – and you probably know what I did – after I saw the man on the corner of

NINE | J.D TIPPIT: A TROUBLED POLICE OFFICER

Patton and Jefferson, I followed him up the street behind the service station and lost him. I went back there and looked up and down the alley and didn't see him, and looked through the cars and still didn't see him. Then the police got there, and they took my name. While they were taking my name, some television camera got me, and I was on television, I am sure nationwide. Then some man that I worked with wanted to be big time, I guess, so he called some radio station and told them what I had done, and they recorded that and ran it over and over and over again over the radio station. And other than that, no.
LIEBELER. Well, what was it that they said you had done? All you had done was try to follow this man and he got away from you?
REYNOLDS. And he got away.
LIEBELER. Then you went back and you looked around for him around the car lot in the area and you weren't able to find him?
REYNOLDS. I looked through the parking lot for him after. See, when he went behind the service station, I was right across the street, and when he ducked behind, I ran across the street and asked this man which way he went and they told me the man had gone to the back. And I ran back there and looked up and down the alley right then and didn't see him, and I looked under the cars, and I assumed that he was still hiding there.
LIEBELER. In the parking lot?
REYNOLDS. Even to this day I assume that he was.
LIEBELER. Where was this parking lot located now?
REYNOLDS. It would be at the back of the Texaco station that is on the corner of Crawford and Jefferson where they found his coat.
LIEBELER. They found his coat in the parking lot?
REYNOLDS. They found his coat there.
LIEBELER. So that he had apparently gone through the parking lot?
REYNOLDS. Oh, yes.
LIEBELER. And gone down the alley or something back to Jefferson Street?
REYNOLDS. Yes. When the police got there, and they were all there, I was trying to assure them that he was still there close. This was all a bunch of confusion. They didn't know what was going on. And they got word that he was down at a library which was about 3 blocks down the street on the opposite side of the street.
LIEBELER. Down Jefferson?
REYNOLDS. Down Jefferson. And every one of them left to go there. So when they left, well, I did too, and I didn't know this man had shot a policeman. I wouldn't probably be near as brave if I had known that. The next time, I guarantee, I won't be as brave.

So Reynolds did not know that the man he saw walking down Patton Avenue had shot a police officer? Would he have bothered

253

JFK | ECHOES FROM ELM STREET
A SEARCH FOR HISTORICAL ACCURACY ON THE
ASSASSINATION OF PRESIDENT JOHN F. KENNEDY

to take in the man's features sufficiently to later make a positive identification, if the man was just another pedestrian passing him by? Note also that Reynolds saw the killer go through to the back of the Texaco station on the corner of Crawford and Jefferson. It was only the fact that the police searching the area got word that somebody suspicious was down at a library three blocks away down Jefferson that they departed. As stated earlier in this chapter, why would the killer have doubled back down Jefferson? It is far more likely that, as Reynolds said, the killer was still in the parking lot when the police left and that he later moved into the Abundant Life Temple on the corner of Tenth and Crawford.

E. *Ted Callaway & Sam Guinyard*
Callaway worked at a used-car lot called Harris Brothers Auto Sales situated at 501 East Jefferson Boulevard, close to Patton Avenue. At about 1.00pm he and his assistant, B.D. Searcy, were standing on the front porch of the car-lot when Callaway heard five pistol shots that sounded like they came from the back of the car lot, toward Tenth. He ran out onto the street and observed a man in a white shirt as he was crossing from the east to the west side of Patton. Callaway said the man was wearing dark trousers and a white jacket. He yelled at the man "Hey man, what the hell is going on!" The man slowed his pace, shrugged his shoulders, made an unintelligible reply, and continued south on Patton. Before reaching the intersection of Patton and Jefferson, he turned right, cut through the corner of a front yard and ran west on Jefferson.[19] Searcy went back to his office and did not follow the man as Callaway suggested, fearing that he might be shot. Callaway and another fellow worker Sam Guinyard, hurried up Patton towards the scene of the shooting. Guinyard also saw the man emptying shells from his pistol.

Callaway seemed to take some sort of charge at the scene because he took the radio microphone from Benavides who seemed to be having some trouble in contacting the police dispatcher. By this time five or six people and a couple of cars were already at the scene. It may be that Benavides had actually got through to the police because at virtually the same time the dispatcher (Cliff Hulse) radios a Code 3 on Channel 1 (Emergency Assignment – use Red Lights and Siren). The ambulance signalled a Code 5 (En Route) and actually arrived at the scene within minutes. Callaway in his statement to the Warren Commission:

Radio Transmission at 1.15pm. – Channel 1

Citizen: Hello, police operator?
Dispatcher: Go ahead. Go ahead, citizen using the police radio.
Citizen: There's been a shooting out here.

NINE | J.D TIPPIT: A TROUBLED POLICE OFFICER

Dispatcher: Where's it at?
Dispatcher: The citizen using the police radio . . .   Citizen Tenth Street.
Dispatcher: What location on Tenth Street?
Citizen between Marsalis and Beckley. It's a police officer. Somebody shot him. What – what's . . . 404 Tenth Street.
Dispatcher: Can you hear me?   (*Man and woman's voices in background*)
Dispatcher: 78.   (Tippit)
Citizen: It's in a police car, number 10.
Dispatcher: 78.
Dispatcher (?): 78.
Citizen: Got that?   - Hello, police operator. Did you get that?
Dispatcher: Attention. Signal 19 (Shooting), police officer, 510 E. Jefferson.
Citizen: Thank you.
35 (Ptm. J.M. Lewis): 35.
259 (unknown): 259.
Dispatcher: The citizen using the police radio: Remain off the radio now.

At 1.17pm.the dispatcher on Channel 2 (Gerald Henslee) puts out a general broadcast about the shooting to all squads. Several officers respond to say that they elsewhere to do with the Kennedy assassination but car 19 (Sergeant CB Owens) radios "almost a code 6" (Arrived – at the scene)

Callaway then helped others load Tippit's lifeless body into the ambulance and noticed the patrolman's pistol on the front seat of the car. It was originally under Tippit's body but had been placed in the car by Bowley (see below). Callaway then ran towards Scoggins cab, where the latter had just reported in to his controller, and suggested that they chase the assailant. Rather dubiously Scoggins agreed, and he drove Callaway west on Tenth, south on Crawford, and west on Jefferson. They returned quite soon having been unable to trace the culprit.

BALL. And you say you identified a man. How did you do that?
CALLAWAY. Well
BALL. Tell us what happened.
CALLAWAY. We first went into the room. There was Jim Leavelle, the detective, Sam Guinyard, and then this busdriver and myself. We waited down there for probably 20 or 30 minutes. And Jim told us, "When I show you these guys, be sure, take your time, see if you can make a positive identification."
BALL. Had you known him before?
CALLAWAY. No. And he said, "We want to be sure, we want to try to wrap him up real tight on killing this officer. We think he is the same one that shot the President. But if we can wrap him up tight on killing this officer, we have got him." So they brought four men in.

JFK | ECHOES FROM ELM STREET
A SEARCH FOR HISTORICAL ACCURACY ON THE ASSASSINATION OF PRESIDENT JOHN F. KENNEDY

I stepped to the back of the room, so I could kind of see him from the same distance which I had seen him before. And when he came out, I knew him.
BALL. You mean he looked like the same man?
CALLAWAY. Yes.
BALL. About what distance was he away from you--the closest that he ever was to you?
CALLAWAY. About 56 feet.
BALL. You measured that, did you?
CALLAWAY. Yes, sir.
BALL. Last Saturday morning?
CALLAWAY. Yes, sir.
BALL. Measured it with a tape measure?
CALLAWAY. Yes, sir.
BALL. Did he have the same clothes on in the lineup – did the man have the same clothes?
CALLAWAY. He had the same trousers and shirt, but he didn't have his jacket on. He had ditched his jacket.

So although Callaway identifies Oswald as the man he saw leaving the scene of the crime, as previously stated, Oswald would have been fairly obviously the odd man out amongst only four by the way he was acting during the line-ups and the bruise on his face. There was also a significant amount of pressure being applied by Detective Jim Leavelle during the line-up. Another point to note is that if Callaway had seen nothing on the television, or had not heard any reports on the radio, about the crime, how did he know that Oswald had "ditched his jacket"?

F. Temple Ford Bowley
Bowley, who was not deposed by the Warren Commission, was driving up Denver Street and had just turned west on Tenth Street when he came upon the murder scene. He reported that he looked at his watch and it indicated 1.10pm. That would mean that the officer was already down only four or five minutes after Oswald had apparently left his rooming house, on foot, 9/10ths of a mile away! Quite impossible if Oswald had committed the murder. Bowley would have been very aware of the actual time because he was to pick up his wife and daughter at a certain time to go to a family event. Bowley had placed Tippit's gun on the front seat of the patrol car before Callaway grabbed it and set out with Scoggins on their futile bid to find the fleeing gunman.

Barbara & Virginia Davis
Barbara lived at 400 East Tenth and her sister-in-law, Virginia, lived around the side of the apartment house in the same building. They were in bed resting

NINE | J.D TIPPIT: A TROUBLED POLICE OFFICER

at the time of the murder. Barbara reported that she heard two gunshots close together. When she opened her door she saw Markham and a man walking across her lawn, apparently emptying shells from a gun. Virginia was standing behind her. They went back into the house and Barbara phoned the police saying that a police officer had been shot. She went outside but only viewed Tippit's body from a distance. She later found one shell in the grass and Virginia found another one later on. One wonders exactly what sort of examination of the area the police undertook after the murder if these ladies actually found two of the shells! Surely it must have been declared a crime scene with access strictly limited while a search by detectives was conducted?

Both ladies, together, attended a line-up later that day and were asked to identify the man that they had seen. Barbara picked number 2 from the left (Oswald, who had not changed his position – there were still only four persons in the line-up). Virginia was then asked the same question and she also chose number 2. However, due to the sloppy way in which the viewing was conducted she may well have just heard her sister-in-law's selection when she made her choice.

Virginia Davis also let slip the remark that she thought Tippit lived at the house outside of which he was shot. Presumably this was because Tippit was a frequent visitor to that house.

Later in her deposition, Barbara failed to identify either the jacket or shirt that supposedly belonged to Oswald.

BALL. I have a jacket, I would like to show you, which is Commission Exhibit No. 162. Does this look anything like the jacket that the man had on that was going across your lawn?
DAVIS. No, sir.
BALL. How is it different?
DAVIS. Well, it was dark and to me it looked like it was maybe a wool fabric, it looked sort of rough. Like more of a sporting jacket.
BALL. I show you a shirt which is Commission Exhibit No. 150. Was that--does that shirt look anything like something he had on, that the man had on who went across your lawn?
DAVIS. I thought that the shirt he had on was lighter than that.
BALL. I have no further questions. Where was Mrs. Markham when you first saw her?

G. Mrs Acquilla Clemons

Mrs Clemons was never deposed by the Commission – in fact a great deal of pressure was applied to make sure that she spoke to no one on the subject of what she had seen. She told several independent investigators that she saw two men shoot Tippit. The killer then waved to the other man, and they ran away in different directions. On 23rd March 1966, Mark Lane (a lawyer and investigator), interviewed Mrs Clemons at her home in Dallas. During the interview she described the gunman as 'kind of short guy' and 'kind of heavy' and said that the other man was tall and thin and wore light khaki trousers and a white shirt.[20] Neither description seems to match that of Oswald.

One investigator asked her "Has anyone talked to you and told you not to talk to anyone?"
She responded: "Yes they have"
Investigator: "Is that the Dallas police?"
Mrs Clemons: "Some of them"

In the interview with Mark Lane Mrs Clemons said that a man who wore a gun and looked like a policeman came round to her house only two days after the day of the killing. He told her that it would be best if she didn't say anything because otherwise she might be hurt! Again pressure was being applied to a witness because her testimony would not have matched what the authorities wanted to hear.[21]

H. Frank & Mary Wright / Mr & Mrs Donald Higgins

All four were witnesses to the murder. The Wrights lived at 501 East Tenth and the Higgins' at 417 East Tenth. Mary Wright probably made the first call to the Dallas Police, who then summoned an ambulance from the Dudley Hughes Funeral Home. Mrs Higgins may also have made a similar call. Evidence of these calls to the civilian operators should have been kept but the details were lost or destroyed. It is quite likely that these calls were made as early as 1.06pm so needless to say none of these witnesses were interviewed by the F.B.I. or summoned by the Warren Commission. Their evidence would not have matched the official story line.

Frank Wright actually saw Tippit fall to the ground at the moment he was shot. He stated that the killer was of medium height and wore a long coat. He said that he saw the killer get into a grey car, probably a Chrysler Plymouth of about 1950 vintage, and drive off at speed. He stuck to this version of events rigidly when questioned by investigators.

I. Mrs Higgins

In a book entitled "The Girl on the Stairs" by Barry Ernest, the author tells the tale of a young lady, Victoria Adams, who worked in the Texas School Book Depository at the time of the Kennedy Assassination. She stood on the fourth floor of the building at the very instant that the assassin's shots rang out. She testified to hearing three shots coming from the right of the building, from the Grassy Knoll. She was absolutely certain that she did not hear or see anyone coming down from upstairs so why did she not see Lee Harvey Oswald rushing

NINE | J.D TIPPIT: A TROUBLED POLICE OFFICER

down to the second floor from the sixth floor, the sixth floor being the place from where he had supposedly shot the President? Victoria Adams was apparently hounded by the authorities and her deposition to the Warren Commission later discredited. However, she remained adamant for the rest of her life as to what happened in the School Book Depository that day.

While Barry Ernest was researching the book he visited the site of the Tippit murder and met a witness that no agent of the government had talked to, a Mrs Higgins who lived nearby. She had heard the shots and ran out of her front door to see Tippit lying in the street. When asked what time it was she said it was 1.06pm. Ernest asked her how she recalled that specific time. She said because she was watching TV and the announcer had said it. So she automatically checked her clock and found that it tallied. She also said she got a look at the man running from the scene with a handgun. When Ernest asked her what he looked like she replied it was definitely not Oswald. So again the evidence points to the fact that Oswald could not have murdered Tippit.

6. The Revolver and the Shells
Sergeant Gerald Hill at the scene of the murder went on air and described the weapon used to shoot Tippit as an automatic – the markings on the first cartridge found early in the investigation clearly indicated this. Empty cartridges are automatically ejected from such a gun. The gun taken from Oswald at the Texas Theatre was a revolver but this was never marked as evidence which was at least very sloppy policing, and at worst corrupt, in that a substitute weapon may have been later planted. Oswald purportedly purchased the weapon only a short time before but the weapon had already been re-chambered and the build up of carbon deposit in the barrel indicated that it had already been used on a significant number of occasions. When had Oswald had the opportunity to use the gun to this extent?

As mentioned earlier, Benavides handed two shells to Officer J.M.Poe. He initialled them so that they could be identified later. Two more shells were subsequently found, one by Captain George Doughty close to a bedroom window and one by Virginia Davis close to her front door. These again were identified to maintain the chain of evidence. However, when shown the shells during his deposition to the Warren Commission, Poe was unable to find his initials and was inaccurate in his attempted identification.

BALL: Now, I have here a package which has been marked "Q"--FBI lab. Q-74 to Q-77. Would you look those over and see if there is any identification on there by you to indicate that those were the hulls given to you by Benavides?
POE: I want to say these two are mine, but I couldn't swear to it.
BALL: Did you make a mark?

POE: I can't swear to it; no, sir.
BALL: But there is a mark on two of these?
POE: There is a mark. I believe I put on them, but I couldn't swear to it. I couldn't make them out any more.
BALL: Now, the ones you said you made a mark on are you think it is 'these two? Q-77 and Q-75?
POE: Yes, sir; those two there.
BALL: Both marked Western Special? They both are marked Western Special. How long did you stay there?

So here Officer Poe is just guessing as to which shells were handed to him by Benavides. The other police office involved in identifying the shells, Sergeant Barnes, also incorrectly identified one shell, picking out Q-75 instead of Q-77.[22]

Four bullets were found in Tippit's body during the autopsy; three were copper coated and manufactured by Winchester Western Company and the fourth was a lead bullet made by the Remington-Peters company. Bullets were not sold in mixed lots so how could these have all come from Oswald's gun?

The Dallas Homicide Unit initially sent only one bullet to the F.B.I labs, at the same time informing the Bureau that this was the only bullet found in Tippit's body. The F.B.I. declared that the bullet did not match Oswald's revolver. Dr. Rose, who performed the autopsy on Tippit, stated that there were four bullet wounds in Tippit's body, but when questioned by the F.B.I. Capt. Will Fritz of the Homicide Bureau could not recall receiving any other bullets. Records did not, apparently, show that they were held by the Police Department. However, on 13th March 1964, nearly four months after the murder, the other bullets were located by the Police and turned over to the F.B.I. The firearms expert at the F.B.I. again stated that because of distortion it was impossible to establish from which gun these bullets had been fired. A second opinion was sort from an independent police expert and he stated that on one of the bullets there were sufficient characteristics to conclude that the projectile was fired from the same weapon as the test projectiles. However, was it Oswald's gun that had been used in the tests?

All in all the firearms evidence against Oswald as the slayer of Tippit was very tenuous indeed.

7. The Jacket & Shirt

A light grey zipper jacket said to belong to Oswald was found under the rear of a car in the parking lot on 400 East Jefferson (see Figure 1) and was said to have been discarded by him in his flight from the scene of the shooting. This would seem to be yet more planted "evidence" to incriminate Oswald.

It has been shown in a previous section that Barbara Davis failed to identify Oswald's jacket and shirt as the clothes worn by the fleeing assailant

NINE | J.D TIPPIT: A TROUBLED POLICE OFFICER

The shirt Oswald wore at the time of his arrest

Domingo Benavides was shown a jacket by Commission Attorney David Belin, who said, "I am handing you a jacket which had been marked as Commission's Exhibit 163, and ask you to state whether this bears any similarity to the jacket you saw this man with the gun wearing?" Benavides responded: "I would say this looks just like it..." The problem was that Commission's Exhibit 163 was Oswald's dark blue jacket. The grey jacket was Commission's Exhibit 162.[23] So Benavides seems to be simply saying what he assumed the Commission wanted him to say. Rather disingenuous?

Further evidence from Helen Markham
BALL. *Did you recognize him from his clothing?*
MARKHAM. *He had on a light short jacket, dark trousers. I looked at his clothing, but I looked at his face, too.*
BALL. *Did he have the same clothing on that the man had that you saw shoot the officer?*
MARKHAM. *He had, these dark trousers on.*
BALL. *Did he have a jacket or a shirt? The man that you saw shoot Officer Tippit and run away, did you notice if he had a jacket on?*
MARKHAM. *He had a jacket on when he done it.*
BALL. *What kind of a jacket, what general colour of jacket?*
MARKHAM. *It was a short jacket open in the front, kind of a greyish tan.*
BALL. *Did you tell the police that?*
MARKHAM. *Yes, I did.*
BALL. *Did any man in the lineup have a jacket on?*
MARKHAM. *I can't remember that.*
BALL. *Did this number two man that you mentioned to the police have any jacket on when he was in the lineup?*
MARKHAM. *No, sir.*
BALL. *What did he have on?*
MARKHAM. *He had on a light shirt and dark trousers.*
BALL. *Did you recognize the man from his clothing or from his face?*
MARKHAM. *Mostly from his face.*
Were you sure it was the same man you had seen before?
MARKHAM. *I am sure.*
BALL. *Now, what time of day was it that you saw this man in the lineup?*
MARKHAM. *I would say it was four, a little after.*

JFK | ECHOES FROM ELM STREET
A SEARCH FOR HISTORICAL ACCURACY ON THE ASSASSINATION OF PRESIDENT JOHN F. KENNEDY

BALL. That was four in the afternoon?
MARKHAM. I was so upset I couldn't even tell you the time. In fact, I wasn't interested in the time.
BALL. Yes.
DULLES. Could I ask just one question?
BALL. Yes.
DULLES. You referred to his eyes; they were rather striking. Can you give any impression of how his eyes looked to you? I realize that is a very vague question.
MARKHAM. Yes. He looked wild. They were glassy looking, because I could see –
DULLES. He had no glasses on?
MARKHAM. No. When we looked at each other, he just stared, just like that. I just don't know. I just seen him – I would know the man anywhere, I know I would.
DULLES. Thank you.
BALL. I have here an exhibit, Commission Exhibit 162, a jacket. Did you ever see this before?
MARKHAM. No; I did not.
BALL. Does it look like, anything like, the jacket the man had on?
MARKHAM. It is short, open down the front. But that jacket it is a darker jacket than that, I know it was.
BALL. You don't think it was as light a jacket as that?
MARKHAM. No, it was darker than that, I know it was. At that moment I was so excited –
BALL. I show you a shirt here, which is Exhibit 150. Did you ever see a shirt the colour of this?
MARKHAM. The shirt that this man had, it was a lighter looking shirt than that.
BALL. The man who shot Tippit?
MARKHAM. Yes, sir; I think it was lighter.

It is quite staggering how, as soon as the "evidence" that the Commission wanted to hear was likely to be contradicted by a witness, the counsel started to apply surreptitious pressure to that witness, or simply shifted to another subject altogether. In this case Helen Markham refused point-blank to identify either the jacket or the shirt that Lee Harvey Oswald was wearing at the time of his arrest, as the clothes that she had seen on the fleeing gunman. Even Joseph Ball didn't have the nerve to suggest that Oswald changed his clothes in the Texas Theatre!

The jacket bore a laundry tag and the authorities did their best to trace a laundry/dry cleaners in the area who could have cleaned the item, but to no avail. The search was undertaken in Dallas, Fort Worth, and New Orleans, all places where Oswald had lived. Oswald's wife, Marina, stated that she thought that the jacket had belonged to her husband but by now pressure would have been applied to her to "toe the party line" if she wanted to remain in the USA.

NINE | J.D TIPPIT: A TROUBLED POLICE OFFICER

Marina also stated that she hand-washed her husband's jackets. The jacket was medium size whereas all Oswald's other clothes were small size. It had been made in California and sold only there or in Philadelphia, both places not visited by Oswald as a civilian.

Officer H.W.Summers gave a description of the suspect killer to the dispatcher while still at the scene of the crime. An "eyeball" witness had told Summers that the man was about 27, nearly 6 foot tall, 165 pounds, and black wavy hair wearing a light gray jacket, dark trousers, and a white shirt. Again this does not sound like Oswald and certainly does not describe the clothing that he was wearing when arrested.

So the evidence of ownership by Oswald of either item seems fairly flimsy but the Commission, nevertheless, concluded that the items belonged to him.

8. Official Views of the Murder

The Captain of Police (Patrol Division), **Cecil E Talbert**, had made up his mind by 28th November 1963 as to who was responsible for the murder of both Tippit and the President. In a letter of that date to Jesse Curry (Chief of Police) recommending that Tippit be awarded the Police Cross posthumously for losing his life in the performance of his duty, Talbert writes: "The murderer of Officer Tippit was arrested a short time later in the Texas Theatre, 231 West Jefferson. He was subsequently proven to be the same man that assassinated the President and wounded Governor Connally."[24]

The Dallas Police Department might have operated a very efficient service in relation to crime busting, but to be able to make that statement less than a week after the murders had taken place was somewhat disingenuous. The investigation into both deaths had been closed down and poor old Oswald, who never had a chance to plead his case, was dead. The Dallas Police were overwhelmed that day – a President slain on their patch and a Patrolman cut down in his line of duty, or possibly for some other reason, but where was the evidence that Oswald was guilty?

David Belin, Assistant Counsel to the Warren Commission and one of the chief defenders of the Warren Report, asserts that "the Rosetta Stone to the solution of President Kennedy's murder is the murder of Officer J. D. Tippit. . . . Once it is admitted that Oswald killed Patrolman J. D. Tippit, there can be no doubt that the overall evidence shows that Lee Harvey Oswald was the assassin of John F. Kennedy." But this is an entirely illogical statement. The proof that Oswald assassinated President Kennedy could only possibly be established by investigating every aspect of that murder in its own right. The proof cannot possibly be found by examining the facts of a separate murder committed at a totally different time and place.

Chief Jesse Curry and his men have often been criticised as being very amateurish and failing in their duties in not having undertaken a much fuller investigation into both murders. However, in the early afternoon of the murders the Dallas Police had swung into action at both murder scenes. In Dealey Plaza a list of all cars in the parking lots had been taken and drivers were being individually interviewed. The names of all the people in the Texas Theatre had been recorded and statements were being taken. However, both these lists subsequently, under very mysterious circumstances, disappeared.[25]

It was later on the same day that pressure was applied from the very top echelons of the government, namely Lyndon Baines Johnson himself, to bring about a sudden closure to any further investigation of the Tippit and Kennedy murders. Johnson had his reasons, but that is an entirely different story. Suffice to say that it suited him to state that "they had their man."

Earl Warren was pressurised, much against his wishes, by Johnson, to head up the Commission that has been much referred to in this chapter, to investigate the Assassination of the President and thus by default the murder of Officer Tippit. Clearly, from the start, the Commission was a tool established to declare a political truth rather than to determine the facts in the matter. The Commission was told unequivocally what the results of their findings must be. Lee Harvey Oswald was a "lone nut" who committed both murders.

At 7.54pm on Friday 18th September 1964 at the end of the Warren Commission and just before publication of the final Report, Johnson called Senator Richard Russell, one of the seven members of the Commission, at his home in Winder, Georgia, to ask about what the Report contained[26]. Russell was fed up and admitted that he had been fighting over that "damned report". He just could not accept what has now become the cornerstone of the Commission's findings, the Single Bullet Theory. Acceptance of this was the only way that Oswald could be considered the lone killer, so a unanimous decision from the Commission members was demanded.

LBJ: Well, what difference does it make which bullet got Connally?
RUSSELL: Well, it don't make much difference. But they said that....the commission believes that the same bullet that hit Kennedy hit Connally. Well I don't believe it.
LBJ: **I don't either** (my emphasis).

Eventually Russell did sign after John McCloy brokered a deal to use compromise language saying that there was "very persuasive evidence from the experts to indicate that the same bullet which pierced the President's throat also caused Connally's wounds." So here we have the top man really admitting that it was impossible for Oswald to have committed the assassination of the President, at least on his own, which therefore blows apart Belin's "Rosetta

NINE | J.D TIPPIT: A TROUBLED POLICE OFFICER

Stone" because we now no longer have a "solution to the President's murder" so by default no solution to the murder of Officer J.D.Tippit.

9. Possible Suspects for the Murder of J.D.Tippit

It is virtually certain that the man arrested in the Texas Theatre on the afternoon of 22nd November 1963 did not murder either the President or J.D.Tippit. Significant evidence exists that Oswald was a Central Intelligence Agency operative of some sort who had been set up as a "patsy" to take the rap for both murders. He was probably tied up with Operation Mongoose, a secret programme of propaganda and sabotage developed by the C.I.A during the Kennedy administration to wrest power from the communists in Cuba. This included developing plans to assassinate Castro. It must be remembered that, at the time, the spread of communism was seen as a horrific threat to the U.S.A and the western world in general. Some believe that it might have been Tippit who was supposed to meet Oswald and take him to a local airport (Redbird) so that he could be flown out of the country, possibly to Cuba, or maybe simply murdered to silence him. Jack Ruby was to successfully complete that task two days later.

It is certain that Oswald lookalikes were used on many occasions during 1963 in places like New Orleans and Mexico City to propagate the idea that Oswald was a communist sympathiser working for the pro-Castro forces. So there may well have been an Oswald lookalike in the vicinity of Dealey Plaza and Oak Cliff that fateful day, whose job it was to furnish the finishing touches in the framing of Lee Harvey Oswald for the two murders. Different researchers have come up with different names as to who this person might have been.

Roscoe White – He joined the Dallas Police in September 1963 and was a "rooky" at the time of the Assassination. He had served in the Marine Corps with Lee Harvey Oswald. The two were stationed together in Marine Air Wing 1 at Japan's Atsugi Air Base, home of the highly secret CIA operation U2 Flights over the Soviet Union. Roscoe's wife claimed that she overheard her husband and Jack Ruby plotting the assassination of the President just prior to the event. White had already left the police force at the time that he died of severe burns in September 1971. He was caught up in an industrial fire. In his diary Roscoe White claimed that he shot both the President and Officer Tippit. His son discovered the diary some time after his father's death and made the details known in 1990.

It is thought that Roscoe White asked Tippit to drive Oswald to Redbird Airport but Tippit was very concerned suspecting that the request may have been tied up with the Kennedy Assassination. White then shot Tippit to keep him quiet. At 1.00pm on the day of the murders just as Lee Harvey Oswald had returned to his apartment at 1026 North Beckley Avenue, his housekeeper, Earlene Roberts, reported that she had seen a police car drive up to the house and sound its horn. She suspected that this was some sort of signal to Oswald and the driver may have been Tippit.[27]

William Seymour – William Torbitt (a pseudonym for David Copeland) is the author of a manuscript entitled "Nomenclature of an Assassination Cabal". In that document he claims that the Kennedy Assassination was planned by a fascist cabal, whose members included J Edgar Hoover, Lyndon Johnson, Werner von Braun, and others, who planned to lay the blame on right wing conservatives. Torbitt argues that a Swiss Corporation named Permindex (a CIA front) engineered the Assassination along with the Defense Industrial Security Command. William Seymour, an Oswald impersonator for many months prior to the Assassination, was seen leaving the School Book Depository fifteen minutes after the Kennedy Assassination. He was later to murder J.D.Tippit so that Oswald could be blamed for both crimes.

Lee Oswald – Perhaps the most controversial idea, but one which is brilliantly researched and developed by John Armstrong in his book "Harvey and Lee", relates to the fact that there were two Oswalds groomed from childhood by the C.I.A. *One was a Russian speaking youth, possibly the child of Hungarian parents who preferred to be called "Harvey." The other was a taller but similar looking boy with a Southern U.S. accent, who preferred to be called "Lee." Both youths became entangled at an early age in an American intelligence operation designed to give a U.S. identity to a Russian-speaking child. It was "Harvey" who defected to Russia, and later returned to the USA with a Russian wife, who was shot dead by Jack Ruby. It was "Lee" who framed "Harvey" for the assassination of JFK and the murder of Officer Tippit. Both were brought together in 1963 and became entangled in the plans to murder JFK and then helped to provide what must be considered one of the most skilful cover-ups in the annals of crime.*

Endnotes

[1] Warren Commission Exhibit (WCE)-2985 - *The Warren Commission: The Presidents Commission on the Assassination of President Kennedd:* (Washington, DC. US Government Printing Office, 1964). Volume XXVI - pages 483-492

[2] Stowers 1983: http://what-when-how.com/police-science/dallas-police-department/

[3] Dale Myers: *With Malice: Lee Harvey Oswald and the Murder of Officer J. D. Tippit:* -(Oak Cliff Press, Nov 1998) - p.33

[4] Wikipedia: http://en.wikipedia.org/wiki/Main_Page

[5] Oak Cliff Advocate – Internet based Magazine http://oakcliff.advocatemag.com/

[6] WCE 2985

[7] Harrison Livingstone: *The Radical Right and the Murder of JFK:* (Trafford Publishing, 2006) - Footnote 2, Chapter 7

[8] Joan Mellen: *A Farewell to Justice:* (Potomac Books Inc, 2005) - p.259

[9] Jim Bishop :*The Day Kennedy was Shot*:(Gramercy Books/Random House, New York,1968) - p.49

[10] Dale Myers: *With Malice*- p.39

[11] John Armstrong: *Harvey & Lee, How the CIA Framed Oswald:* (Quasar, ltd, Arlington Texas, 2003) - p.829

NINE | J.D TIPPIT: A TROUBLED POLICE OFFICER

12. Anthony Summers: *The Kennedy Conspiracy:* (Sphere,2002) - p.67
13. John Simkin - *The Education Forum:* http://educationforum.ipbhost.com/index.php?showforum=126
14. Matthew Smith: *JFK- The Second Plot*: (Mainstream Publishing, 1992) - p.96
15. Alaric Rosman: *Dealey Plaza Echo, Volume Eight, No 1. March 2004* - p.50 http://www.maryferrell.org/mffweb/archive/viewer/showDoc.do
16. John Armstrong: *Harvey & Lee* - p.853
17. John Armstrong: *Harvey & Lee* - p.855
18. Matthew Smith: *JFK The Second Plot* - p.89
19. John Armstrong: *Harvey and Lee* - p.852
20. Mark Lane: *Rush to Judgment: A Critique of the Warren Commission's Inquiry into the Murders of President John F. Kennedy, Officer J. D.Tippit and Lee Harvey Oswald* : (The Bodley Head Ltd, London 1968) - p.194
21. Mark Lane: *Rush to Judgement* - p.280
22. Mark Lane: *Rush to Judgement* - p.198
23. Jim Marrs: *Crossfire: The Plot That Killed Kennedy:* (Carroll and Graf Publishers. Inc. New York) - p.346
24. Dale Myers: *With Malice:* - p.482
25. Larry Hancock: *Presentation to DPUK Seminar* (April 2011)
26. Michael Beschloss: *Taking Charge: The Johnson White House Tapes:* (Simon & Schuster, 1998) - p.559
27. Matthew Smith: *The Kennedys: The Conspiracy to Destroy a Dynasty:* (Mainstream Publishing, 2005) - p.102

Please note: Website addresses correct at time of writing.

JFK | Echoes From Elm Street
A Search for Historical Accuracy on the
Assassination of President John F. Kennedy

Ten
A Man of Unusual Training: The Oswald Enigma

Alaric Rosman

Introduction

It is significant that a deep, questioning interest in Oswald as a person is very rare amongst JFK researchers. To substantiate, I draw attention to the fact that of the 328 articles I have checked, published in the last 40 journals (1998/2011) of the Dealey Plaza Echo (the thrice yearly research journal of the British JFK research group), only 7 (excluding two articles I have written) have anything to do with Oswald, and these are all limited in scope to some particular incident in his life. None is concerned with Oswald's identify or character. And my experience of other journals confirms this. We can say then that until recently probably only about 2% of Assassination research has been devoted to the alleged assassin.

Why is this?

I think the reason is that irrespective of viewpoint – lone assassin or conspiracy – there is the natural assumption that the key to the Assassination lies in what actually happened at Dealey Plaza – the medical, ballistic and eye-witness evidence, etc. – and, secondly, to a considerably lesser degree, in what happened on East Tenth Street where Patrolman Tippit was gunned down. It follows then that Oswald's biography is seemingly irrelevant to the Dealey Plaza/ East Tenth Street evidential base.

To appreciate this point fully and to see things in perspective, it might be a good idea to list, without comment, the 16 assertions that constitute the mainstream belief in Oswald's guilt:

(1) A 6.5 millimetre Mannlicher Carcano rifle allegedly owned by Oswald was found on the 6th floor of the Texas School Book Depository.
(2) Three empty 6.5 millimetre shells were discovered nearby.
(3) Oswald's palm print was found on the gun.

JFK | ECHOES FROM ELM STREET
A Search for Historical Accuracy on the Assassination of President John F. Kennedy

(4) Oswald worked at the book depository.
(5) A witness saw a man resembling Oswald aiming a rifle to fire from the 6th floor window.
(6) It is alleged that medical and ballistic evidence confirm that all the wounds sustained by both Kennedy and Connally were caused by two shots fired from Oswald's rifle.
(7) Oswald disappeared from the book depository immediately after the Assassination.
(8) Oswald was identified as the killer of Dallas police officer J.D.Tippit 45 minutes after the assassination. The mainstream belief is that Tippit, spotting Oswald walking along a sidewalk, thought that he resembled the description of the assassin, and tried to question him. Oswald, fearing arrest, shot Tippit dead.
(9) Four ejected, .38 caliber shells were found in the vicinity of the dead Tippit.
(10) Witnesses claim to have seen Oswald, while leaving the scene of the crime, emptying shells from a pistol.
(11) Ballistics confirmed that the thrown away shells could have been fired from Oswald's .38 Special Smith and Wesson.
(12) The pistol was in Oswald's possession at the time of his arrest.
(13) The Dallas police, acting on a tip off, arrested Oswald in a movie theatre. He resisted arrest.
(14) After shooting Patrolman Tippit, Oswald, fearing pursuit and identification, was seen dumping his jacket in an area between where Tippit was killed and the movie theatre where he was arrested.
(15) Oswald's psychopathic character was confirmed by his wife who claimed that her husband told her that he was responsible for the Assassination attempt, in April '63, on retired General Edwin Walker, an extreme right-wing activist.
(16) A 6.5 millimetre bullet fired from Oswald's rifle was found at Parkland Hospital after it had seemingly fallen from Governor Connally's thigh.

It is obvious that were these assertions all true – if they fully represented the reality of the assassination – then Oswald's guilt would be established beyond doubt, and his character, biography, and motivation would be a matter of curiosity only.

On the other hand, if doubt can be cast on many of the above assertions (as most certainly it can: too much evidence coming in too quickly, being just one point) then Oswald's guilt becomes a matter of doubt – the case for a frame-up could be argued – but again his character, etc. would be irrelevant, at least in establishing the frame-up.

It is easy to see then, given the nature of the evidence against him, why initially Oswald's character was of secondary concern. However, later there was an exception. Over the 2/3 months before the Commission settled to collecting evidence, many people were beginning to find the case against Oswald far from convincing, and the Commission in response sought to make the lone assassin

Ten | A Man of Unusual Training: The Oswald Enigma

case more credible by depicting Oswald as a man of pathological discontent, nitroglycerin in his stability, worm eaten with a sense of failure, who sought compensation in delusions of superiority. Such a character, mainstream belief asserted, had nothing to lose by killing Kennedy. However, over many years, this depiction ran into difficulties. Slowly there was accumulated a considerable amount pointing to the reverse.

Oswald – it was realised – was obviously intelligent: he was, for example, able to talk on equal terms to George De Morenschildt, a worldly, much experienced, aristocratic, geologist. And moreover, he had a warm human side, well illustrated by his devotion to his 21-month-old daughter June. Moreover, he had always expressed great admiration for President Kennedy[1].

Sixteen years later, Marina, testifying to the House and Select Committee on Assassinations, took part in the following exchange:

Marina Porter, Testimony 2, afternoon session].

Chairman STOKES -..........We will proceed as far as we can this afternoon. Mrs. Porter, throughout your testimony here today you have indicated that Lee Harvey Oswald always spoke of liking President Kennedy; is that correct?
Mrs. PORTER - That is true, sir.
Chairman STOKES - You never heard him speak of him in a hostile manner?
Mrs. PORTER - No.
Chairman STOKES - Then is it consistent, in your opinion, then, that a man who spoke of President Kennedy as he did also was accused of having killed the President?
Mrs. PORTER - That is very hard for me to comprehend.
Chairman STOKES - Now, have you on occasions indicated that you thought perhaps he was not shooting at President Kennedy but was trying to hit someone else?
Mrs. PORTER - It was my aloud speculation which doesn't have any foundation for it because it was very hard for me to even think about a person who could like someone can do such a thing to him. The reason I mentioned Mr. Connally, I mentioned his name only because Lee was corresponding at one time in his life with Governor Connally.
Chairman STOKES - Can you tell us a little bit more about that? What had he in effect said about Governor Connally?

Marina and De Morenschildt were expressing their opinions about 13 years after the Assassination, and of course what they say contradicts the view that the Warren Commission was trying to perpetuate. They raised serious questions about Oswald's motivation – and therefore his character.

To those, however, who at the time seriously questioned the Dealey Plaza evidential base, and who centered all their doubts on what happened at Dealey Plaza, interest in Oswald's character was confined to his patsy role, and the Assassination, in consequence, was seen as a political conspiracy, in which the character of Oswald was lost against a political background that was large, turbulent and conspiratorial. However behind these considerations lay (and still lie) a further assumption. It was that we know a lot about Oswald – therefore, superficially, not much to enquire into –and that although his involvement in the Assassination is a matter of heated contention, his life and character are not.

On the surface there are three seemingly strong reasons for this view:

(1) Oswald lived to be only 24. Hardly long enough for the development of a duplicitously complicated life.
(2) As I shall demonstrate in this chapter, Oswald lived his life in a goldfish bowl. He was always under some firm of surveillance, to such an extent that, in principle, there could be nothing about Oswald that was not known about.
(3) As I shall show, the Commission devoted more time enquiring about Oswald's character and past life than the circumstances of the Assassination. The Commission interviewed 71 people who knew Oswald at various stages of his life, and the accumulative testimonies of all these witnesses amounted to just under a million words.

We should therefore know nearly everything about Oswald. There may be disagreement as to whether he killed Kennedy, but there should be plenty of agreement over his life and character.

Disconcertingly, this is far from the case. It is my contention that nothing in the official version of Oswald's life makes sense; the Warren material doesn't stack up.

I would like to be able to cover all the major aspects of Oswald's life, but obviously this could not be done within the space of a single chapter. I therefore have to limit myself considerably.

I am not going to deal with the issue of "two Oswalds", nor with the mysteries of Oswald in Russia, nor with the conflicts over "Oswald in Mexico", not because I question the importance of these topics – on the contrary, I consider them to be immensely important – but because they have been dealt with very fully elsewhere.

This chapter, will, instead, concentrate on four topics which I have researched because in addition to being key issues (at least, to the way I see the Assassination), they are, in addition, comparatively neglected areas.

(a) The Enigma of Oswald's Character
(b) The Enigma of Oswald's Height. Do the measurements refer to two people?
(c) The Enigma of Oswald's Politics and Defection to the Soviet Union.

Ten | A Man of Unusual Training: The Oswald Enigma

(d) The Enigma Oswald's arrest.
(e) The Enigma of His Subsequent interrogation at Dallas Police Headquarters.
(f) The Enigma of Oswald and the Russian Language

Points (a)-(e) are however are all leading to the greatest enigma of them all: ***why is it that nobody knows how Oswald not only learnt to speak Russian, but how he learnt to speak the language with remarkable fluency and with a marked Polish (?) accent.*** This last section is the most important part of this chapter.

The enigma is, then, how was it possible for there to be so many doubts about someone always under constant surveillance? Oswald comes across as a rabbit always in someone's headlights. But more: it is my argument that the existence of so many enigmas where everything should be straightforward makes the whole issue of Oswald's identity part of the evidentiary base of the Assassination, for the question, who was Oswald? points to a vast fabrication of evidence at a very high level.

Where This Chapter Is Heading
All the arguments I shall put forward in covering these four points will be used to defend the three assertions listed below. These assertions lead to the conclusion of this chapter.
Conclusion Number One: That there is plenty of evidence, even from official sources, to suggest that Lee Harvey Oswald was seriously connected with American intelligence.
Conclusion Number Two: That Oswald's ability to speak Russian fluently (with a marked Polish accent) cannot be accommodated within his official life story, and is, in consequence, an Exocet missile aimed at the fuel tanks of his official biography.
Conclusion Number Three: That the official biography of Oswald simply does not make sense in any of its parts, and is just a mass of confusions and contradiction.**These three conclusions in combination suggests that Oswald's official biography, full of loose ends and contradictions is in a large part a fabrication.**

The conclusion of this chapter is, then, that the propagation of such a fabricated biography – its creation and massive dissemination – could only have been carried out by (at least) the very senior echelons of the CIA, reaching, I should imagine, as high as James Jesus Angleton, CIA Chief of Counterintelligence, from which it would follow that the CIA was heavily implicated in the Assassination.

A Backdrop To My Arguments
Before going any further, I would like to create a backdrop – a sort of context –

to all the facts and arguments that I am going to use, and for this purpose I shall make central to my background the fifty-one year old man who, although just a member of the House of Representatives at the time (but re-elected eleven times), was eleven years later to be the country's unelected Vice President and who one year later was to be its unelected President. I am of course referring to one of the Warren Commissioners, Congressman Gerald Ford.

The Gerald Ford Background

On Friday 13th February, 1964 (the 39th day of the Warren Commission Hearings), at about 1150 am, Dr. Peter Paul Gregory gave his testimony to the Commission in the presence of two of the seven Commissioners: the Commission's Chairman, Chief Justice Earl Warren, and Republican Congressman Gerald Ford (of Michigan), at the time the Chairman of the Republican Conference.

Dr. Peter Gregory had been called upon by the Commission because of his extensive dealings with Lee Harvey Oswald on Oswald's return from the Soviet Union.

Dr Gregory was a consulting petroleum engineer and part-time Russian instructor at the Fort Worth Public Library. He was Siberian by birth, and avoided the Revolution by moving to Japan, where at the American school in Tokyo he learnt English. He came to the USA in 1923, and studied at the University of California at Berkeley, and became a leading member of the Texan White Russian Community (Fort Worth) amongst whom Oswald and his Russian wife lived. Dr Peter Gregory was Marina Oswald's initial translator during her Warren Commission interrogations.

As the clock approached 1 pm, in the very final moments of Dr. Gregory's cross-examination (by Mr. Wesley J. Liebeler, a former Wall Street lawyer.), Mr. Ford interjected a few questions of his own, and in response to Mr. Gregory's replies, gave utterance to one of the most startling assertions ever heard by the Commission.

Here is the revelatory exchange:
Representative FORD – Did Oswald tell you when he first visited you that he had learned to speak Russian, where?
Mr. GREGORY – In the Soviet Union.
Representative FORD – He never gave you any indication he had learned or studied prior to going to the Soviet Union?
Mr. GREGORY – No, sir.
The dialogue continued:
Mr. GREGORY – .... Now, I thought that Lee Oswald spoke with a Polish accent that is why I asked him if he was of Polish descent.
Mr. GREGORY –............. it would be rather unusual, rather unusual for a person who lived in the Soviet Union for 17 months that he would speak so well that a

Ten | A Man of Unusual Training: The Oswald Enigma

native Russian would not be sure whether he was born in that country or not.
Representative FORD – That would be a very unusual kind of a person?
Mr. GREGORY – It would be, yes.
Representative FORD – Or a person who had unusual training? (WC 2, 346)[2]
Mr. GREGORY – Right, or unusual ability or training, yes, that is right. "

Ford's description of Oswald as a person of "unusual training" was a knee-jerk response to his surprise at Oswald's mastery of Russian. If Oswald was trained, then clearly by whom? Where? When?

The implication of Ford's surprised comment – that Oswald must have had an intelligence background – would have been as welcome to Mr. Liebeler and Earl Warren as a runny egg in a salmonella outbreak, and it's no wonder that immediately the words had dropped from his lips – with the shattering effect of broken glass – Liebeler and Warren, saved by the 1 pm clock face, adjourned for lunch. And until I wrote this chapter nothing more was ever heard of Oswald as a person of "unusual training".

As we shall see, if Oswald was indeed a person of "unusual training", then this is something that could not be accommodated within the biography supplied by the FBI to them on December 9th

Why did Ford blurt out such a remark? The answer very likely lies in a major problem that had confronted the Commission 52 days earlier, and whose puzzling and worrying details were possibly swilling around in the bilges of Mr. Ford's mind.

The idea of Oswald as a person of "unusual training" chimed unwelcomely with the idea of Oswald as a FBI informer, a possibility that had confronted the Commission immediately it came into being.

Quite possibly, when he unwarily described Oswald as a "person of unusual training" Ford had at the back of his mind this "informer" possibility. The story behind Oswald as a possible FBI informer is as follows:[4]

Late in January (1964) the Commission held its first formal staff meeting, at which they all agreed that "Truth was to be their only client". Little did the staff members realise that such a good intention was to fall at the very first hurdle.

And the first hurdle came a few days later (21st of January) in the form of a nasty shock – analogous to a cow-patch in a dining area. The Commission was suddenly confronted with the "news" that Oswald had very possibly been an FBI informer. The Commission's source for the "news" came from two Texas attorneys: Waggoner Carr, the Attorney General of Texas, and Henry Wade, the Dallas District Attorney.

The implications, if the allegation was true, were potentially enormous. If Oswald had been an FBI informer, then what was there about him that had prompted his selection? One answer could be that his FBI involvement was a development of previous intelligence/informer work under the Office of Naval Intelligence when in the Marines, and since Oswald had served at Atsugi in Japan, where the CIA had an operational base, he might have a CIA history.

And this led to the chief problem the Commission had in this connection: if Oswald had been involved in intelligence work, then how deep had his involvement been? Because if it had been deep, then possibly his whole biography was an intelligence fabrication?

To be specific: the FBI, as we have said, had supplied the Commission on December 9th with a massive Summary Report on the Assassination, the very largest part of it about Oswald, but was the FBI summary about the real Oswald, or was it an intelligence fabrication?

So serious were these implications, that within a matter of hours the Commissioners held an emergency meeting ("most tense and hushed", Epstein put it) the outcome of which was an agreement that the Commission's Chairman (Warren), and it's Executive Director (Rankin) should jointly instruct the two senior public attorneys to fly to Washington to discuss matters.

Although neither attorney knew the precise source of the information, they did have in their possession what was claimed to be Oswald's FBI informant number (179), his salary ($200 a month), and alleged period of employment (from September 1962 up to date of his arrest).

On January 27th the four men (Warren, Rankin, Carr and Wade) secretly met to discuss what was to be done. They had five reasons for believing Oswald to be an FBI informer.

(1) It was believed that Oswald's address book contained the telephone number and car registration number of James Hosty who was in the Dallas FBI. On December 21st The Commission had received what purported to be a list of the names in Oswald's address book, but Agent Hosty's name was omitted.
(2) A government voucher for $200 was found in Oswald's personal possessions.
(3) A Western Union employee had claimed that Oswald was periodically telegraphed small sums of money.
(4) Wade at one time had been himself an FBI agent, and knew the habit of setting-up postal boxes as "covers" for each time an agent moved. It was significant that Oswald did the same thing.
(5) Three days after the issue raised its head, the Commission received investigative reports from the Secret Service: they had traced the rumours to a journalist who seemed reliable and who claimed as his source the Chief of the Criminal Division in the Dallas Sheriff's Office.

Despite these five factors, the emergency meeting came to the un-heroic (but prudent) conclusion that since the matter could not be established either way, the Commission, faced with such uncertainty, should turn to what was certain, which was its duty to uphold the faith of the American people

TEN | A MAN OF UNUSUAL TRAINING: THE OSWALD ENIGMA

in their institutions. It would therefore, the Commissioners concluded, be very inappropriate to speculate on anything that could damage the FBI's reputation. The conclusion was to put the matter to Hoover and accept his word as final.

On January 28th Rankin saw Edgar Hoover, Director of the FBI and Hoover – surprise! surprise! – flatly denied that Oswald had ever worked for his organisation, and, nine days later, supplied affidavits from FBI agents to support his assertion.

The Commission dropped the matter immediately, and made no further enquiries. Hoover's assurance was considered sufficient.

And there we have it: within a few days of their first meeting, the Commissioners, deep within their hearts, must have realised that beneath the evidentiary base of the Assassination lay dark waters through which it was not prudent to wade.

Life In A Goldfish Bowl
According to the FBI version of Oswald's life, he lived his old life in a goldfish bowl. Oswald lived for $8,803^3$ days, of which 2,205 days were spent in childhood, 3,662 at school (a total of 5,867 days of unremitting surveillance). Then, after school, 351 days in paid employment (under the eyes of his three different bosses and fellow workers), followed by 300 days in Marine training, leading to 416 days stationed with the Marines in Japan, and 263 days at the El Toro Marine base in California (979^4 days of close supervision by officers and NCOs, not to mention constant shoulder rubbing with barrack mates) Then a complete change: Oswald's defection to Russia: 82 days in Moscow, followed by 876 days of factory work in Minsk (in which he lived in very close contact with the family of one of the factory managers).

We have also to take into account that for the last 397 days of his stay in Minsk Oswald was heavily closeted by his marriage to Marina.

This gives a total of 958 days in Russia, during which his apartment was bugged by the KGB who were in addition receiving regular reports from all his friends, workmates and supervisors.

Then another change in life – and another goldfish bowl
On the 13th June, 1962, Oswald returned (with Marina) to America. Fate was allowing him only 529 days to live, and during those days everybody in the "White" Russian Fort Worth community was keeping a critical (and gossipy) eye on both Oswald and his wife. In addition, several leading community members made a point of watching Oswald intently, one of them in particular, a Mr. George De Mohrenschildt, a geologist with alleged CIA connections, became, for the last 14 months of Oswald's life, his close friend and mentor.

JFK | ECHOES FROM ELM STREET
A SEARCH FOR HISTORICAL ACCURACY ON THE ASSASSINATION OF PRESIDENT JOHN F. KENNEDY

And of course in these 529 days there were the 176 days that Oswald was employed by Jaggars-Chiles-Stovall Co, the 70 days that he worked at the Reily Coffee Co, the 84 days he worked for the Leslie Welding Company, and the 37 days that he moved book cartons for the Texas School Book Depository.

These figures mean that for 367 days, Oswald was under a double "whammy" of supervision: at work, he was under the supervision of employers and workmates, and on his return home there were "supervisory" visits from various members of the "White "Russian community.

Add up, this means that of the 8,803 days of his life, Oswald spent at least 8,768 days under close supervision (i.e. 99.6%) of his life.

In short, Oswald – if the official version is correct – had no individual, private life. He was never alone.

Then there is further important factor (one we have already referred to): the sheer amount of biographical information on Oswald available to the Warren Commission through witness depositions and affidavits. As we shall see later, this amounts to a million words of biographical information, alas, a lot of it contradictory.

To make it clear just how great in quantity this material was, it is necessary to put matters in a wide, number-crunching perspective.

And to facilitate this perspective, we can start by recalling the actual purpose of the Commission, which following Executive Order 11130[5] of President Johnson, was "to ascertain, evaluate, and report upon the facts relating to the assassination of the late President John F. Kennedy and the subsequent violent death of the man charged with the assassination".[6]

The way the Commission sought after the "facts relating to the Assassination" was to take testimonies from the 21 doctors and the 4 nurses who gave medical attention, either at Parkland Hospital in Dallas, or at the Bethesda Naval Hospital in Maryland. I have calculated that their testimonies totalled 190, 950 words. Then, of course, the Commission brought in 6 ballistics and firearm experts. Their testimonies, I have estimated, totalled 104,692 words. The Commission then went to the 7 Secret Service agents who were involved in the fatal motorcade. Their testimonies and reports provided the Commission with 20,024 words of evidence. Other Secret Agents, FBI men and senior Dallas police officers – a total of 9 men in all – contributed, through depositions and affidavits an estimated total of 152,375 words. Then there were the occupants of Kennedy's car. All 5 gave evidence totalling a calculated 74,712 words. Finally, there were the 26 people who at some point on the route witnessed the assassination. Through their testimonies, affidavits and FBI statements I estimated a word total of 123,822. Adding these 6 totals we get 666,575 words. This figure gives a good representation of the time and effort the Commission spent on investigating the actual Assassination.

But Oswald, as well as being charged with the assassination of the President,

Ten | A Man of Unusual Training: The Oswald Enigma

was also charged, in his attempt to escape the assassination scene, with the shooting dead of Patrolman J.D. Tippit. The Commission, in relation to this charge, deposed (and took affidavits from) a combined total of 11 people, giving an estimated word count of 54,469 words. This leads to a final, investigative total (for the murders of both Kennedy and Tippit) of 721,044 words.

An impressive total, admittedly, but it is dwarfed by another total which is even more impressive, but only by size, because it is profoundly depressing in its implications.

The Commission quickly enlarged the directions of President Johnson's Executive Order, claiming that the investigation of the assassination required the "interviewing and taking the testimony of various persons who, among other things, came in contact with a man named Lee Harvey Oswald". (WCT Kerry Thornley, XI, 82). With this intention, the Commission spent far more time questioning Oswald's family, friends and associates than it did investigating the actual circumstances of the assassination.

The Commission acquired vast amounts of information about Oswald, especially his early life. The Commission's depositions of Oswald's immediate family (mother, brother and half brother) ran to 205, 500 words, of which Oswald's full brother Robert provided 62%. His more remote family (uncle, aunt and two cousins) supplied the Commission with depositions totalling 70,862 words. (Incredibly, the Commission spent nearly as much time on these distant relations as it did on the occupants of the presidential car, and vastly more time than it did on the 7 Secret Service agents in the motorcade.)

This assertion can be confirmed by totalling all the words supplied by the 72 people who either through testimonies or affidavits gave the Commissioners information about Lee Harvey Oswald. The word total of their efforts comes to 996,949.[7]

But, in terms of understanding what happened at Dealey Plaza, enquiring about Oswald's background was an utterly fatuous exercise since none of his family, friends or associates had anything to do with the assassination: their only connection with the assassination was through their relationship with Oswald, and this relationship only had value if Oswald was the sole assassin, since if he had been part of a conspiracy a lot of the motivation might not have come from within his own character, but from his fellow conspirators.

A few instances show how absurd the Commission's bias was.

(1)The Commission allowed Oswald's full brother, Robert to testify to an extent of 127,000 words. Utterly amazing! Robert Oswald had nothing to do with the assassination – nobody could ever claim otherwise – and he witnessed nothing since he was in Fort Worth at the time. Robert left home to join the Marines when Lee was just 12, and the two brothers did not live together until 10/11 years later when Lee had returned from Russia. From the time when Oswald joined the Marines (24/10/56), up to his death (24/11/63), a period of 2,587 days, his brother only saw him for three periods totalling 68 days.

The 5 other leading relatives had equally nothing to do with the assassination, and equally were not at the assassination scene at the time. Moreover, these 5 other leading relatives had even less contact with Oswald than had Robert, yet the Commission spent 45% more time talking to these 7 family members than it did to the 25 medical staff who could give expert, first-hand testimony on the President's wounds.

(2) Many of the 72 people who supplied the Commission with their experience of Oswald had very limited contact with him. There was for example a Mr. Blalock, who occasionally observed Oswald in New Orleans. There was also Anne Boudreaux who knew Oswald for a bit in his youth; and then there was Mr. and Mrs. Evans who, when Oswald was a child, were close friends of his mother. There was also Mary Bledsoe who claimed to have seen Oswald on a bus shortly after the Assassination..Of her 16,293 word deposition,5023 were spent on describing Oswald's 5-day rental stay with her. Judging by the number of words (32,210 against 20,024), the Commission was prepared to give these 5 people 61% more time than the 7 Secret Service Agents who were at the head of the motorcade at the time of the assassination.

One fact stands out very clearly – I've mentioned it before – none of this biographical information would have been of any use unless Oswald was the sole assassin, which is unless the motivation for the assassination came entirely from within his supposedly twisted mind.

The Commission's strong biographical bias is grounded in its attempt to substantiate their psychopathic estimate of Oswald.

Also the Commission was trying to do something else. By devoting so much time to Oswald – it was Oswald this, Oswald that, Oswald something else – by making him the dominant factor in their enquiries, the Commissioners were trying to hammer into the public mind his name as the sole assassin.

(a) The Enigma of Oswald's Character.
In the opinion of KGB officers, Oswald was highly strung, anxiety ridden, a neurotic, schizoid personality, with hands too trembling to squeeze a rifle trigger, and eyes always on the verge of tears.

"As the three of us reflected on the assassination, we simply could not picture Oswald as being capable of making-rapid fire, precise shots at a moving target. We all remembered teary eyes, trembling hands and overall nervousness."[8]

According to the Dallas police, Oswald was unnervingly calm – nearly pathologically so – resolute, difficult to intimidate, and highly articulate.

Everybody who dealt with the arrested Oswald – the officers who made the actual arrest at the cinema[9], and the officers who escorted him along the

Ten | A Man of Unusual Training: The Oswald Enigma

corridors[10], and the detective in charge of his interrogation[11] – all testified to Oswald's calmness, articulacy, and intelligence.

However, according to Daniel Powers, who knew Oswald more or less continuously for about a year (they had been to radar school at the same time, had met at El Toro, and were on board the troopship USS Bexar together),Oswald was a "meek mild individual" – "Ozzie the Rabbit" – with "a large homosexual tendency". [WCT Daniel Powers 8H, 270].

Powers' testimony is confirmed by the recollections of Thomas Bagshaw, a career Marine, who described Oswald as a "very thin, almost frail, shy and quiet", who avoided group activity and womanising and, in consequence, was known as "Mrs. Oswald", and much bullied. (Epstein[12], "Legend", p 68)

Peter Gregory – we have just mentioned him – in his testimony (to which we have just referred) saw Oswald as "a peculiar person" "that carried some sort of a chip on his shoulder". (WCT Peter Gregory, 2H, 343)

On the other hand, Zack Stout, a fellow Marine who for a total of ten months worked, bunked and took leaves with Oswald in Atsugi, the Philippines, Corregidor and Subic Bay, found Oswald "intelligent", "honest and likeable", and well informed on politics and history, "absolutely truthful, the sort of guy I'd trust completely". (Epstein, "Legend", ps 69, 77).

Even as a teenager, there were severely contradictory opinions on him. When he was 14 an experienced social worker, noting that Oswald was "emotionally starved" nonetheless found him "affectionate" and "appealing" [WCT Evelyn Siegal, 8H,227,Exhibit 1], whereas Julian Evans, who along with his wife Myrtle, had known the young Oswald and his mother, on and off for 6/7 years described Oswald as "arrogant", "insolent", and "demanding", frequently shouting (with a "foghorn" voice) at his mother. In his testimony to the Commission, Mr. Evans reported on a very cruel streak in Oswald's character:

"Lee and the boys were down there fishing, but Lee didn't talk to the other kids or anything. He just seemed to want to be alone, and he just fished by himself, and the odd part of his behavior that we all thought was very strange was the way he would just let the fish die on the bank after he would catch them. Now, the other small boys would catch them and, and if there was enough for eating and everything, they would throw the others back, but not Lee. He would pull them in and just throw them down on the river – I mean on the bank by the pond and just let them lay there, and when he got through he just walked off and left them there. Something like that is hard to understand. He didn't catch them for eating, and he didn't want to throw them back in. He just left them on the bank and walked off after he got tired of fishing. We couldn't understand that at all. It showed how totally inconsiderate he was of everything. It was a good example of how he acted, and his general attitude." (WCT Julian Evans, 8H, 70)

However, it would appear that by the time Oswald arrived in Japan (some 6 years after the period Mr. Evans was referring to) his character seems to have changed: a fellow Marine recalled to journalist Edward Jay Epstein that he found Oswald "a good egg" who was prepared to lend him money, and the sort of friend that could be "counted on" [Epstein, p 70].

A similar, positive opinion is given by George De Morenschildt, whom I shall be frequently referring to in this chapter. Writing about Oswald 13 years after the Assassination, De Morenschildt who, with his wife, strongly befriended Oswald on his return from Russia, wrote of him:

"Only someone who had never met Lee could have called him insignificant. "There is something outstanding about this man," I told myself. One could detect immediately a very sincere and forward man. Although he was average-looking, with no outstanding features and of medium size, he showed in his conversation all the elements of concentration, thought and toughness. This man had the courage of his convictions and did not hesitate to discuss them. "["I'm A Patsy! I'm Patsy!" a memoir, 1976, by George De Morenschildt]

(b)The Enigma of Oswald's Height
Two Oswalds?
It would be agreed that the one certain, unarguable fact about somebody would be their height, where officially recorded. One would also suppose that any variations in measurements would be random. However, in the case of Oswald this would be wrong on both counts. There were variations in Oswald's officially recorded height, but these variations were not random. Measurements of Oswald's height can be divided into two groups: his Marine height (i.e. his height before his 'defection' to the Soviet Union), and his height on his return. The facts are these: the 10 volumes of the Warren Commission Exhibits contain 27 documentary readings for Oswald's height, plus one guess (from a 5-year memory) given by a Marine friend in deposition to the Commission.

Eight of these 27 documentary readings were recorded while Oswald was in the Marines, of which 5 were unarguably fully official, that is taken by some Marine officer. Three (of these 5 official measurements) gave Oswald's height as 71".

The remaining 3 (of the 8 Marine measurements) were self submissions, and in each case Oswald put his height as 71".

On his return from the Soviet Union, 19 documentary recordings were made of Oswald's height.

6 (of these 19 documentary readings) were taken either by a Marine officer, or by an FBI agent. 5 (of these 6 readings) gave Oswald's height as 69"; 1 (of these 6 readings) gave Oswald's height as 69.5".

That leaves 13 readings which were either submitted by Oswald himself, or were possibly based upon previous recordings; all but 2 (of these 13 readings) put Oswald's height as 69".

Ten | A Man of Unusual Training: The Oswald Enigma

Very significant are two opposing facts:

On September 3rd, 1959, at Santa Ana, California, Oswald underwent a full medical examination prior to his release (8 days later) from active service in the Marines (and transfer to the inactive reserves). His height was ruler-measured and recorded as 71". [WC XIX, 584; WC XXIII, 744]

On the day of his murder (24th September, 1963), two doctors at Parkland hospital recorded Oswald's height as 69". (WC XXVI, 521; WCE 3002).

It is interesting to note that Rimma Shirakova[13], Oswald's Intourist guide, described him (when he arrived at the Hotel Berlin in Moscow) as being of "medium"* height (i.e. not tall). The arithmetic average for the height of the Russian adult male (aged 20 and above) is now 69",[14] and may well have been less when Oswald was in Moscow.

Note that no scaled measurement of Oswald's height after he left the Soviet Union gave a reading of 71."

Given this fact, it is difficult to believe that if the 'Russian' Oswald had been 71" tall – well above the average height for the Russians – that Rimma Shirakova would have remembered him as "medium" height. Of the 28 figures, only 2 are deviant. The remaining 26 figures support (but very far from establish) the possibility of two Oswalds:

(1) An Oswald in the Marines 71" in height, and who, applying for a passport, put his height as 71" because that was his actual height. It is alleged that he 'defected' to the Soviet Union.

(2) A smaller man, 69" in height, who arrived from the Soviet Union, falsely claiming to be the Marine Lee Oswald, This imposter consistently put his height as 69" on all applications (because that was his actual height), etc., with the exception of a passport application because (presumably) he didn't want to draw suspicious attention to himself. On his passport application he gave the September '59 height of the Marine Oswald he was impersonating since this was the height recorded for 'Lee Oswald' by the passport authorities.[15]

(c) The Enigma of Oswald's politics and his Defection to the Soviet Union
Oswald's official biography portrays him as a fervent Marxist.
All Oswald's biography seems – on the surface – to shout "I am a Communist". At the age of 17, Oswald worked as a messenger for a dental laboratory, and in the course of his duties he struck a friendship with a young fellow messenger, Palmer McBride; the basis of their friendship was a shared love of classical music.

To McBride's surprise (and annoyance), Oswald spoke incessantly of the virtues of communism, claiming that capitalism was based on the exploitation of the working class, and that America, through its capitalist system, was being forced along a path of exploitive imperialism, thereby destabilising the world.

JFK | ECHOES FROM ELM STREET
A SEARCH FOR HISTORICAL ACCURACY ON THE
ASSASSINATION OF PRESIDENT JOHN F. KENNEDY

In view of all this cruelty and exploitation, President Eisenhower, a symbol of working class oppression, deserved to be shot.

This red-blooded declaration of hostility rocked McBride.

OSWALD was very anti-Eisenhower, and stated that President EISENHOWER was exploiting the working people. He then made a statement to the effect that he would like to kill President EISENHOWER because he was exploiting the working class. This statement was not made in jest, and OSWALD was in a serious frame of mind when this statement was made."

And it wasn't just teenage Palmer McBride who was receiving this political ear-bashing.

Another teenager was equally pummeled. He was William Eugene Wulf, the head of a local amateur astronomical association, and a friend of Palmer McBride. Wolf's testimony to the Commission shows the sort of ear-bashing he had to endure.

Mr. WULF – I made that statement to McBride after my second meeting with Oswald when we got into a discussion—I being a history major and always been interested in history, some way or another we got around to communism. I think Oswald brought it up, because he was reading some of my books in my library, and he started expounding the Communist doctrine and saying that he was highly interested in communism, that communism was the only way of life for the worker, et cetera, and then came out with the statement that he was looking for a Communist cell in town to join but he couldn't find any. He was a little dismayed at this, and he said that he couldn't find any that would show any interest in him as a Communist, and subsequently, after this conversation, my father came in and we were kind of arguing back and forth about the situation, and my father came in the room, heard what we were arguing on communism, and that this boy was loud-mouthed, boisterous, and my father asked him to leave the house and politely put him out of the house, and that is the last I have seen or spoken with Oswald.
Mr. LIEBELER – Now you indicated that your argument was rather loud and boisterous?
Mr. WULF – Yes.
Mr. LIEBELER – Did Oswald generally impress you as a loud or boisterous person?
Mr. WULF – Well, he impressed me as a boy who could get violent over communism, who, if you did not agree with his belief, he would argue with you violently over it. This, as you know, was the period right before he moved, I believe, to Dallas. I did hear that he had moved to Dallas. I got that from McBride. And he struck me as a very boisterous boy and very determined in his way about communism.
Mr. LIEBELER – Did he strike you as boisterous in any other respect or strong headed about other things?

Ten | A Man of Unusual Training: The Oswald Enigma

Mr. WULF – Generally a strong headed boy that knew his own mind, thought he knew his own mind, and would do his own will. He wanted his way, in other words.

Oswald comes across as a compulsive yapper on communism. He even barked Marxism when he was invited to a meeting of Wulf's astronomical society.

Now fast forward nearly a year, – it is early 1957 – and Oswald, roughly a third the way through his 19th Year is in the Marines. He has successfully completed his basic training, and has been sent for combat training to the Marine Infantry Training Regiment at Camp Pendleton, California.

A young recruit, Allen R. Felde shared a tent with Oswald, and he underwent the same intellectual coshing – exactly the same ideas – as McBride and Wulf.

He was frequently told by Oswald that American capitalism was the threat to world peace, and had to be opposed. Only a strong communist party could accomplish this.

Now fast-forward about a couple of years, and we've jumped from California to the Far East (principally Japan), where Oswald served for about 14/15 months, and, by December '58 back again to California with Marine Aircraft Squadron 9. Within a year Oswald will be "defecting" to the Soviet Union, but in the meantime he made friends with a young Marine called Kerry Thornley, who suffered the same ideological buffeting as McBride, Wulf and Felde. It wasn't only Thornley who received Oswald's machine-gun fire of Marxist dogma; many other Marines were similarly subjected. Not only that, but Oswald made a point of being strongly pro-Russian, reading Russian newspapers and books.

Thornley told the Commission:

Mr. THORNLEY. It became obvious to me after a while, in talking to him, that definitely he thought that communism was the best–that the Marxist morality was the most rational morality to follow that he knew of. And that communism was the best system in the world.
I still certainly wouldn't – wouldn't have predicted, for example, his defection to the Soviet Union, because once again he seemed idle in his admiration for communism. He didn't seem to be an activist.
Mr. JENNER. Would you explain what you mean by idle in his admiration of the communistic system?
Mr. THORNLEY. Well, it seemed to be theoretical. It seemed strictly a dispassionate appraisal–I did know at the time that he was learning the Russian language. I knew he was subscribing to Pravda or a Russian newspaper of some kind from Moscow. All of this I took as a sign of his interest in the subject, and not as a sign of any active commitment to the Communist ends.
Mr. JENNER. You felt there was no devotion there. That it was somewhat of an intellectual interest, a curiosity. But I don't want to put words in your mouth, so tell me.

Mr. THORNLEY. *I wouldn't put it quite that weakly. While I didn't feel there was any rabid devotion there, I wouldn't call it a complete idle curiosity either. I would call it a definite interest.*
Mr. JENNER. *A definite interest.*
Mr. THORNLEY. *But not a fanatical devotion.*
Mr. JENNER. *You said you knew at that time that he was studying Russian. How did you become aware of that?*
Mr. THORNLEY. *Probably by hearsay once again. I do remember one time hearing the comment made by one man in the outfit that there was some other man in the outfit who was taking a Russian newspaper and who was a Communist and when I said, "Well, who is that?" he said, "Oswald," and I said, "Oh, well." That is probably where I learned it.*
Mr. JENNER. *How did you learn that he was a subscriber to Pravda and the other Russian publications you have mentioned?*
Mr. THORNLEY. *Well, I don't think – it was either Pravda or some other similar paper.*

However, as we shall see, in a few pages following, Oswald, despite his defection to the Soviet Union, also on his return keenly supported extreme right wing views.

Oswald's Defection to the Soviet Union

The Enigma of Oswald's Dependency Discharge
Referring to the concluding part of Oswald's period in Japan, Epstein in his The Secret World of Lee Harvey Oswald" (Arrow Books, 1978) writes:
"Unknown to his fellow Marines, Oswald was making careful plans and preparations to defect to the Soviet Union – at least, that is what he told reporters when he arrived in Moscow one year later." [P 83]
To this end, within 8 months of his return from Japan, and his subsequent posting to Santa Ana, California (Marine Air Control Squadron 9), Oswald requested a dependency discharge because of an alleged injury sustained by his mother.
(A glass jar she was stretching for had fallen on her nose, but did not break it). Eleven days later the dependency discharge was granted, and three weeks after notification of approval, Oswald was officially discharged from active duty in the Marine Corps. (September 11th, 1959)
Oswald's discharge from the Marines was very mysterious. He enlisted in the Marines on the 24th of October 1956 on a six year basis (three years on active service, and three years in the reserves). [Folsom[16] Exhibit 1, p 92]
His discharge would therefore have been on that date three years later. However his disciplinary record was poor. On the 11th of April, 1958 Oswald was sentenced to 20 days in a Marine prison for the illegal possession of a firearm, and 57 days

Ten | A Man of Unusual Training: The Oswald Enigma

after completing this sentence, he was sentenced on the (27th June) to a further 28 days for pouring a drink over a Sergeant. That means a total of 48 days, and, in accordance, with Marine custom, this should have postponed his discharge to 7th December, 1959.

However, he was not fully a private citizen: he had been discharged only from active duty; officially Oswald was still in the Marines, although only in an inactive capacity. This meant that he was (ultimately) still under Marine jurisdiction, one consequence of which was that (in theory) he could not go abroad without Marine approval; certainly the Marine authorities had to be informed of any travel intentions.

And yet Oswald was given permission to go abroad, and, moreover, he did so within 9 days of his discharge, spending only two days with his allegedly dependent mother.

He went – of all places – to the Soviet Union, and he did so as a private citizen, to become what he always ostensibly wanted to be – a communist in a communist country. Why the Marine authorities, following normal procedure, would have allowed a skilled radar operator, trained in the latest equipment (as Oswald was) to depart to an enemy country is totally inexplicable, all the more so as Oswald's discharge – mysteriously approved in eleven days – was based on a deception: Oswald, following his discharge stayed with his mother, as we have said, for only a couple of days.

The Facts Behind a Mystery

With the notable exception of John Armstrong's "Harvey and Lee" (2003), and with the possible exception of Robert Groden's (1995) " In Search of Lee Harvey Oswald", all other accounts of Oswald's Dependency Discharge are disingenuously brief, as if anything detailed would raise awkward questions. I have in mind:

(1) The coverage in the Warren Report (1964),
(2) "LEGEND: The Secret World of Lee Harvey Oswald" (1978) by Edward Jay Epstein,
(3) The HSCA Report (1979),
(4) "Oswald's Game" (1983) by Jean Davison,
(5) "Oswald's Tale" (1995) by Norman Mailer,
(6) Diane Holloway's "The Mind of Oswald" (2000), and
(7) Vincent Bugliosi's "Reclaiming History" (2007).

Behind a façade of routine normality described by these five books, and two Government reports, lies yet another Oswald enigma, a series of confusions, contradictions and obfuscations which point to an intelligence connection. Let's start the ball rolling by quoting the Government Reports on the subject. It's a good idea to quote from the Reports so as refresh our memories on a neglected area.

First, the 1964 Warren Report. This contains 63,303 words of biographical material, divided into two sections: Chapter V11 (Lee Harvey Oswald: Background and Possible Motives) [24.365 words], and a larger coverage (38,938 words) in Appendix Xlll

From Chapter Vll:

At his own request, Oswald was transferred from active duty to the Marine Corps Reserve under honorable conditions in September of 1959, 3 months prior to his regularly scheduled separation date (137) ostensibly to care for his mother who had been injured in an accident at her work [P 386]

From the Appendix:

On August 17, he [Oswald] submitted a request for a dependency discharge, on the ground that his mother needed his support. The request was accompanied by an affidavit of Mrs. Oswald and corroborating affidavits from an attorney, a doctor, and two friends, attesting that she had been injured at work in December 1958, and was unable to support herself. Oswald had previously made a voluntary allotment of part of his salary to his mother, under which arrangement she received $40 in August, and had submitted an application for a "Q" allotment (dependency allowance) in her behalf of $91.30; one payment of the "Q" allotment, for the month of August, was made in September. On August 28, the Wing Hardship or Dependency Discharge Board recommended that Oswald's request for a discharge be approved; approval followed shortly. On September 4, he was transferred from MACS-9 to the H. & H. Squadron, and on September 11, he was released from active duty and transferred to the Marine Corps Reserve, in which he was expected to serve until December 8, 1962. He was assigned to the Marine Air Reserve Training Command at the Naval Air Station in Glenview, Ill. [Ps 688/9]

From the HSCA Report:
[The quickest way to access the Report is through the website http://jfkassassination.net/russ/m_j_russ/hsc.htm. or through a Google search "JFK alphabetical list of Witnesses", and choose "House Select Committee" (4th item down)].

Finally, with one exception, the circumstances surrounding Oswald's rapid discharge from the military do not appear to have been unusual. Oswald was obligated to serve on active duty until December 7, 1959, but on August 17 he applied for a hardship discharge to support his mother. About 2 weeks later the application was approved. (193) 31

It appeared that Oswald's hardship discharge application was processed so expeditiously because it was accompanied by all of the necessary documentation. In response to a committee inquiry, the Department of Defense stated that "... to

Ten | A Man of Unusual Training: The Oswald Enigma

a large extent, the time involved in processing hardship discharge applications depended on how well the individual member had prepared the documentation needed for (221) consideration of his or her case."(195)

A review of Oswald's case indicates that his initial hardship discharge application was accompanied by all of the requisite documentation. Oswald had met the, preliminary requirements of having made a voluntary contribution to the hardship dependent (his mother) and of applying for a dependent's quarter's allotment 32 to alleviate the hardship. (196) Even though all of the supporting affidavits for the quarters allotment had not been submitted at the time that the hardship discharge application was filed, the endorsements on the application indicated that the reviewing officers were aware that both the requisite voluntary contribution and the application for a quarters allotment had been made. (197) Moreover, that application was accompanied by two letters and two affidavits attesting to Marguerite Oswald's inability to support herself. (198)

Documents provided to the committee by the American Red Cross indicate that Oswald had sought its assistance and therefore was probably well advised on the requisite documentation to support his claim. (199) Indeed, Red Cross officials interviewed Marguerite Oswald and concluded that she "could not be considered employable from an emotional standpoint."(200) The Fort Worth Red Cross office indicated a quarters allotment was necessary for Marguerite Oswald, rather than a hardship discharge for Lee, and assisted her in the preparation of the necessary application documents.(201) Nevertheless, Oswald informed the Red Cross office in El Toro, Calif., where he was then stationed, that he desired to apply for a hardship discharge. (202)

The unusual aspect of Oswald's discharge application was that, technically, his requisite application for a quarters allowance for his mother should have been disallowed because Marguerite's dependency affidavit stated that Oswald had not contributed any money to her during the preceding year. (203) Even so, the first officer to review Oswald's application noted in his endorsement, dated August 19, 1959, that "[a] genuine hardship exists in this case, and in my opinion approval of the 'Q' [quarters] allotment will not sufficiently alleviate this situation."(204) This quotation suggests the possibility that applications for quarter's allotments and hardship discharges are considered independently of one another. In addition, six other officers endorsed Oswald's application. (205) The committee was able to contact three of the seven endorsing officers (one had died); two had no memory of the event, (206) and one could not recall any details. (207) The committee considered their absence of memory to be indicative of the Oswald, case having been handled in a routine manner.

Based on this evidence, the committee was not able to discern any unusual discrepancies or features in Oswald's military record.

However, by studying the timetable behind Oswald's discharge and the evidence given to the Commission by Robert Oswald, it becomes obvious how false the Government reports are and how they contradict their own evidence published in the Warren Hearings and Exhibits.

Timetable of Oswald's Dependence Discharge

December 1958
December 5th Marguerite suffers an unwitnessed accident. She is working for the King Candy Company who has rented a sales area in the Fair Ridglea Departmental Store, Fort Worth She is reaching for a box of candy jars, when of the jars falls on top of her, landing on her nose. Presumably there is plenty of bleeding. She is offered immediate first aid. No bones broken.

December 6th Marguerite complains of a headache and discomfort in the neck. Very possibly due to nasal obstruction.

December 11th
The Fair Ridglea store legally files the accident with the Industrial Accident Board of Texas. The King Candy Company gives Marguerite's monthly income as $175, and her probable period of disability as one week. [Armstrong[17], Harvey and Lee p 209]

January 1/7 1959. From the first week Marguerite's insurance company starts compensation payments of $28 weekly [Armstrong p 224].

January 9th
Marguerite sees a Dr Goldberg. He doesn't believe that she is suffering from anything more than a bruised nose, but to make sure he forwards her to two other doctors, the last of whom (a Dr Harris) is an ear, nose and throat specialist. Dr Harris applies poultice treatment to Marguerite's nose, and draws pus from the right side. Clearly there has been damage to her nose. [Armstrong, "Harvey and Lee", document 59-03].

This comes from a statement (contained in the same document) that Dr. Goldberg made to the FBI of his own accord the day after the Assassination. In addition to supplying medical details, he also told the FBI two startling pieces of information:

Firstly, that Marguerite told him that her son, Lee, was going to defect to Russia, and,

Secondly, that Lee had beaten her on several occasions. This statement might reflect the fertility of Dr Goldberg's imagination, but all the same it has a ring of truth. John Pic in his Warren Commission testimony related an incident when, according to his wife, Lee, over a row about what television channel to watch, pulled a penknife on Marguerite and struck her. According to John Pic, Lee

TEN | A MAN OF UNUSUAL TRAINING: THE OSWALD ENIGMA

bullied his mother and was very much in control. [WCT John Pic, XI, 38/41], and there is the confirmatory remark of Julian Evans (quoted at the start of this article), who along with his wife, Myrtle, knew Lee very well. Julian Evans told the Commission about Lee, when a teenager, bullying and shouting at his mother. [WCT John Pic XI, 69/70]

February 1959
February 6th From the first week of this month, Marguerite's insurance company starts compensation payments of $29weekly (i.e. $116 Monthly). Given that her budgeted expenses (to be discussed later) amounted to $230 (if genuine), her financial distress was obvious. (Folsom Exhibit 1, ps 89, 90, 94)

February 20th
We have a documentary coverage for what follows [Armstrong, "Harvey and Lee,document 59-04]. Marguerite receives treatment under the direction of Dr.Lester Hamilton (a doctor of osteopathy) at the Hamilton-Everett Clinic (Fort Worth, Texas). The treatment consists mostly of penicillin injections, various types of osteopathic manipulation, and physiotherapy over the temple and face. Beginning February 20th she attended the clinic for this type of treatment on fourteen occasions over a period of 4 weeks from her first visit.

March 1959
On March 23rd, and roughly for every other day until April 11th, Marguerite has her sinuses drained at the clinic, with pus found in the washings. Clearly, her suffering has been genuine, not from the direct effects of the candy-jar fall, but from its secondary effects: the bruising of the nose – still apparent 5 months after the accident – had caused an infection deep within her nasal cavity, [Armstrong, "Harvey and Lee,document 59-04] a misfortune which would explain Marguerite's wide variety of symptoms: tenderness of the neck, heavy feeling in the head, and her jaw not opening properly.

April 1959
Robert Oswald visits his mother at her place of work. He can see that she has been injured, but he believes that she has largely recovered. From his testimony to the Commission:
Mr. JENNER. You say for three to four months prior to September 11, you had not seen your mother, that for several months prior to that you had not talked with her.
I take it from that that you were not aware of her well being, whether she was in good health, poor health, or otherwise?
Mr. OSWALD. During the approximate date of three or four months prior to Lee's release from the service, I was aware that she did have an accident at her place

of employment there in Fort Worth, at which time, if memory serves me correct, something fell on her, on her face, and injured her nose.

I was aware from conversations with her at that time that she was consulting or going to various doctors. And she told me at that time

Mr. JENNER. Excuse me. Having reached that point – is that how you first discovered that your mother had suffered an accident? You say she told you.

Mr. OSWALD. Yes, sir; that is correct.

Mr. JENNER. And I take it, then, that you had not talked with her for several months prior to September 11 nor seen her before sometime, or later than sometime in April of 1959, that this telephone conversation must have taken place several months prior to September 11. Am I correct about that?

Mr. OSWALD. It was not a telephone conversation, sir.

Mr. JENNER. You saw her?

Mr. OSWALD. Yes.

Mr. JENNER. In the month of April '59?

Mr. OSWALD. Approximately that date.

Mr. JENNER. And did you visit her, or did she visit you?

Mr. OSWALD. I saw her at her place of employment.

Mr. JENNER. And how did that come about?

Mr. OSWALD. I do not remember, sir.

Mr. JENNER. Would it refresh your recollection if I recited some possibilities–that she called you and asked you to come to see her, that you desired to inquire of her, see if she was all right, or was it that you just happened to be in the downtown Fort Worth area, and you stopped by to see her, knowing where she was employed?

Mr. OSWALD. I believe the latter would possibly be more accurate.

Mr. JENNER. Is that your best recollection at the moment?

Mr. OSWALD. Yes, sir. She was not employed at that time at the downtown area of Fort Worth, but rather at a suburb store, Cox's Department Store.

Mr. JENNER. This is a shoe store?

Mr. OSWALD. No, sir, this is just a large department store, from wearing apparel to toys, a full line store.

Mr. JENNER. How did you become aware she was employed there?

Mr. OSWALD. I do not remember, sir.

Mr. JENNER. How long–did you know then how long she had been employed at Cox's Department Store?

Mr. OSWALD. No, sir, I did not.

Mr. JENNER. How did you become aware of the fact she was so employed?

Mr. OSWALD. I do not remember, sir.

Mr. JENNER. You have no recollection?

Mr. OSWALD. No, sir, I do not.

Mr. DULLES. About how long was this after the accident, or was it after the accident?

Ten | A Man of Unusual Training: The Oswald Enigma

Mr. OSWALD. My recollection of that, sir-this was shortly after the accident. She was still employed there, even though I understand from our conversation that day that she had been off for a while I don't know how long a period-and that she was still employed there. Because this is where I did see her, at her counter in this department store.
Mr. JENNER. On this occasion, when you stopped by to see her, she related to you an accident she had suffered–that was the first news you had of it?
Mr. OSWALD. That is correct. Yes, sir.
Mr. JENNER. You had not known she was ill or what her state of well being was prior to that time?
Mr. OSWALD. None that I remember, sir.
Mr. JENNER. Where is the Cox's Department Store located with respect to your place of business? I am seeking now distance, and the convenience of getting there.
Mr. OSWALD. From my place of business at that time in Fort Worth this was approximately four or five miles west. I might further state, sir, it was approximately two miles from my home.

Although Marguerite had recovered and was at work, she was at the same time continuing to claim that she was unwell – something that was out of character. This was confirmed by Robert Oswald in his testimony:
Mr. JENNER. All right. Now, if we can return to the events of April 1959, did your mother appear to you to have been injured?
Mr. OSWALD. Yes, sir; she did.
Mr. JENNER. What evidence was there of her injury?
Mr. OSWALD. There appeared to be a little swelling in the upper part of the nose.
Mr. JENNER. Any scratch or other skin break?
Mr. OSWALD. No, sir; none that I recall.
Mr. JENNER. Did you form an opinion at that time as to whether her injury was major or minor?
Mr. OSWALD. I asked her about it, or she volunteered the information of how the accident occurred, and that she had been seeing doctors, and so forth And I did recall her stating to me that she had been to either two or three doctors, and none of them had said anything was wrong with her, and then she was insisting that there was definitely something wrong, and she was continuing to see other doctors.
Mr. JENNER. Had that sort of thing occurred prior thereto, in which your mother felt that she was ill and she went to physicians, and the physicians indicated otherwise?
Mr. OSWALD. Not to my knowledge, said at any time in connection with this injury?
Mr. OSWALD. Not to my knowledge, sir.
Mr. DULLES. Did she have to give up her work for a period of time, or did she continue working?
Mr. OSWALD. I believe she did miss a short period of time when the accident occurred.

JFK | Echoes From Elm Street
A Search for Historical Accuracy on the
Assassination of President John F. Kennedy

Mr. DULLES. Thank you.
Mr. JENNER. But she was at work on the day you visited her?
Mr. OSWALD. Yes, sir, that is correct.

May 1959
May 19th Marguerite's insurance company suspended payments, as according to their doctor she was physically capable of working. Remember: according to her son, Robert in his Warren Commission testimony, she was at work by April latest. Sometime in June (?)

Marguerite writes to Lee, stationed with the Marines in California, saying that she had been injured, is very short of money – has had to sell most of her furniture – she claims that she needs his help at home.

July 1959
July 6th In response to her letter, Oswald visits the American Red Cross at the US Marine base at El Toro, California and tells them of her extreme distress, and then, in an undated letter writes to his mother as follows:

> Dear Mother
> Received (sic) your letter and was very unhappy to hear of your troubles, I contacted the Red Cross on the base here, and told them about it. They will send someone out to the house to see you, when they do please tell them everything they want to know, as I am trying to secure an Early (hardship) discharge, in order to help you such a discharge is only rarely given, but If (sic) they know you are unable to support yourself than (sic) they will release me from the U.S.M.C. and I will be able to come home and help you. The Red Cross cannot give you funds of any kind they can (sic) only give you me and only If (sic) you make to/right imprestion (sic) on them only aif they know you cannot and are not reciving (sic) help from any other kin, and only if they know you are in dire need now! Please tell them I will be able to secure (sic) a good job, as this is important, also send me the names of some actual business's/that I may write them and get an acceptance letter. This last point is not required but It would help my case for a hardship discharge if and when I bring it before my commanding office. Just inform them I have been your only source of income.
> Lee – (Commission Exhibit 201)

July 10th A Red Cross worker visits Marguerite. Marguerite is described as unstable, neurotic and in need of company. The Red Cross worker must have realised that Marguerite's accommodation was totally unsuitable for two people. Marguerite told the Commission:

Ten | A Man of Unusual Training: The Oswald Enigma

I was ashamed when he arrived home. I was in a one bedroom and bath and a small kitchen. (WCT Marguerite Oswald, 1H, 202)

If the Red Cross were really serious about Lee's coming home to look after his mother, they would surely have helped Marguerite find more spacious accommodation? But they didn't.

14th July
Marguerite's case comes before the Texas Industrial Accident Board.

July 17th
Liberty Insurance Company agrees to Marguerite having a medical examination, but Marguerite finds out that the doctor is a psychiatrist,[John Armstrong, p241] and she doesn't turn up. Although it is now obvious that Marguerite has recovered from the damage caused by her accident, she is still claiming to be unwell, and the Red Cross feels that her symptoms are heavily psychosomatic.

July 21st
Mr. Lester L. Hamilton of the Hamilton-Everett Clinic, whose osteopathic treatment of Marguerite in March has been described, supports Lee's dependency with the following letter:

To whom it may concern
Mrs. Marguerite Oswald came to us Feb. 20 1959 with traumatic arthritis of tempero–mandibular and cervical joints and also right maxillary sinusitis and 5th cranial nerve neuritis. She was last treated by us on May 26th, 1959, and was not well of her ailments at that time. [Folsom Exhibit P 1, P 90]

There are four important points to make about this letter.
(1) Although the letter was dated 21 July, the osteopath had not seen Marguerite since May 26th, a period of 56 days, and was therefore not aware of her present condition, let alone able to provide a prognosis.
The reason why he hadn't seen her since May is explained in the Armstrong document we have from the clinic (Point 5): her sinusitis had completely cleared.
(2) No reference is made to Marguerite's accident, although possibly an echo of it can be found in the description of her arthritis as "traumatic".
(3) The phrase "not well of her ailments" suggests that Marguerite's symptoms would not necessarily cause her to be unwell, and that therefore her condition is possibly psychosomatic.
(4) The letter makes no reference to Marguerite being physically dependent and therefore unable to work. In short, as a letter of support, Dr. Hamilton's contribution is useless, and it is significant that Marguerite could not produce anything more impressive. The obvious reason is that there was nothing really wrong with her.

22nd July
Oswald, possibly to add credibility to his dependency claim, put into effect two allotments from his service pay. One was what was called a D allotment, and it was money deducted from a serviceman's pay by the government and forwarded by them to whomever was nominated. Oswald nominated his mother, and made to her just one payment of $40.

The other type of allotment was known as a Q allotment. Nominations had to be government-recognised dependents, and part of the money was contributed by the government. Under this classification, Oswald nominated one monthly payment of $91.30, making a total one-off contribution of $131.30. According to his mother's budget (Folsom Exhibit 1, p 89), this sum would only have covered (just for one month) about half her average monthly expenditure.

July 27th
Marguerite Oswald submits an affidavit in which she outlines her accident and subsequent incapacity. She claims that her minimum regular outgoings are $230.75 [Folsom Exhibit 1 ps 89/90]

July 28th
Two lady friends sign affidavits claiming that Marguerite needs her son's help. They both claim that Marguerite has no income and can't work.

August 1959.
August 14th The Industrial Board reports their findings:

The Liberty Insurance Company to pay Mrs. Oswald $29.19 for 32 weeks (i.e. 224 days) as from Saturday 06/12/58. To 18/07/59, that is $931.84 (29.19 x 32). But they had already paid her $28 a week from Friday 02/01/59 to Friday 29/05/59, i.e. $4 a day for 147 days, which amounts to $588, meaning that the Insurance company had to pay up a further $343.84 (${931.84-588}). [Armstrong, Harvey & Lee, p 241]

August 17th
Lee submits a formal request to the Commanding General of the 3rd. Aircraft Wing, MCAS, El Toro, Santa Ana, California asking for a Dependency Discharge, in support of which he furnishes the affidavits from Marguerite's two lady friends, and the letter from Dr. Hamilton. He states "I want to be with my mother and provide support for her, as she is unable to provide support for herself."(Folsom Exhibit 1 ps 84/85)

This is complete nonsense as Lee deserts his mother two days after arriving home from his discharge, then spends a couple of day seeing his brother Robert, and, on leaving Robert, begins his route to Moscow, exactly 6 days after his

TEN | A MAN OF UNUSUAL TRAINING: THE OSWALD ENIGMA

discharge. He doesn't see his mother, whom he is so keen to support, for 1033 days. (15.09.59/14.07.62)

A few days later: A reply comes from Oswald's Commanding Officer at MACS-9, Santa Ana, California. The CO forwards Oswald's request with a positive recommendation, asserting that in Oswald's case there was "a genuine hardship"

August 28th
The senior member of Oswald's squadron Dependency Discharge Board, in a letter to the Commanding General of Oswald's Aircraft Wing, states that neither of Oswald's brothers are able to offer help because they are both married with children and are financially fully committed (Folsom Exhibit 1, p 79). [This is totally dishonest as neither brother was approached. It was obvious from his testimony that Oswald's half brother, John Pic knew nothing of Lee's early discharge, and his full brother Robert, in his testimony, denied that he had ever been approached on the matter. Indeed, one can go further: it is obvious that Marguerite and the Marine authorities deliberately excluded Oswald's brothers from the machinations of his discharge.]

This Marine document contains the following paragraph:

The home situation of private First Class Oswald has been aggravated subsequent to his enlistment date through the incapacitation of his mother as a result of an industrial accident. The mother is no longer gainfully employed due to her physical condition and has no source of income. The presence of her son, Private First Class OSWALD, is required for physical and financial assistance.

Two points:
(a) Marguerite had not been badly or permanently incapacitated. That was a lie. Even her medical letter of support never made this claim.
(b) Marguerite may not at the time have been gainfully employed, but it was not "due to her physical condition", she had been at work some time before April, and whether or not she continued her employment is not known.

The purpose of the letter is to seek the Commanding General's authorisation for Oswald's premature discharge on hardship grounds. [Folsom Exhibit 1, p 79]

August 31st
General Hayes, Commanding General of the 3rd.Marine Aircraft Wing, replies to the communication, and gives his necessary authorisation for Oswald's discharge. [Folsom Exhibit1, p 78]

September 1959
September 4th Marguerite writes to the Marine Headquarters [Folsom Exhibit 1, p 94], at the Department of the Navy, and tells them of her circumstances. She received, so she claims, $543 from the Workers Disability Compensation and this was her sole source of income from January to May ('59). She then claims that from May through to September her only source of income was the sale of her furniture and a litter from her dog, a total of $255. The implication is that from January to September the total of money sustaining her was $798. We have seen that towards the end of July Marguerite gave her budget as $230,75 a month, which over a 9 month period would amount to $2,076.75, meaning that by September (the time of her letter) she was (presumably) $1,276.75 in debt [$(2,076.75 - 798)].

However, John Armstrong researches (see our entry under 17th August), show that up to the August of that year Marguerite's had received $931.84 from her personal insurance, (Liberty Insurance) meaning that her actual loss would have been $344.91[$(1,276,75 - 931.84)]. Clearly she was misleading the Marine authorities.

In the same letter, Marguerite writes:

I have not worked since December 5th, 1958, which was the date of my accident.

This, was a total fabrication. After leaving work at Ridglea, Marguerite got work at Cox's department store.

September 11th
Oswald is released from the Marines and arrives at Marguerite's house at Fort Worth on the 14th, leaving 3 days later for New Orleans, after spending a day with his brother Robert and his wife; 3 days after that (on the 20th) he is on the SS "Marion Lykes " for an 18 day voyage bound for Le Havre, France. By 16 October he arrives in Moscow, registers at the Hotel Berlin, and meets meeting his in tourist guide Rima Shirakova.

On July 10th, 1963, Oswald, just over a week before he leaves the Reilly Coffee Company, and 12 days before the denial of his requests for an official review of his "undesirable discharge" ("undesirable" because of his attempt to renounce his American citizenship while in Moscow), Oswald seeks to re-enlist in the Marines. In Folsom Exhibit 1, p 42, Oswald is referred to as "the petitioner", and the document states:

*Petitioner requests recommendation for reenlistment, review of case and appropriate action. He [Oswald] submitted a brief which essentially **states that his discharge was improperly issued**........* (My emphasis)

Overall Comment on the Discharge Evidence
The extract from Robert Oswald's Warren Testimony throws a hand-grenade

TEN | A MAN OF UNUSUAL TRAINING: THE OSWALD ENIGMA

into the official version, and the fact that I haven't seen it quoted anywhere, suggests an ignorance that is wilful rather than accidental.

Robert Oswald is saying four things, all of which makes nonsense of the official version:

(1) Although his mother originally had been genuinely injured – her nose was still slightly swollen 4 months after the accident –she had made a fairly quick recovery, and by the time Robert was seeing her, she was exaggerating her condition, and for some reason, unguessed at by him, and uncharacteristic of her, she went unsuccessfully from doctor to doctor trying to get her condition recognised as serious.

(2) Although her injury necessitated some time off work, the damage to her finances was never so serious that she had to contact Robert.

[It emerged from his mother's Warren Testimony that when she suddenly became homeless (from a job dismissal), she had no hesitation in seeking help from Robert. Presumably therefore she would have done so if destitute through loss of work (income) following her accident].

(3) By April 1959 (at the latest) she was back at work, and therefore receiving regular money. I write "at the latest" because this bit of dialogue between Mr. Jenner and Robert Oswald suggests that she was at work before April:

Mr. JENNER. Would it refresh your recollection if I recited some possibilities–that she called you and asked you to come to see her, that you desired to inquire of her, see if she was all right, or was it that you just happened to be in the downtown Fort Worth area, and you stopped by to see her, knowing where she was employed?
Mr. OSWALD. I believe the latter would possibly be more accurate.
Mr. JENNER. Is that your best recollection at the moment?
Mr. OSWALD. Yes, sir. She was not employed at that time at the downtown area of Fort Worth, but rather at a suburb store, Cox's Department Store.

What is being said here is that Robert Oswald, finding himself In the vicinity of Cox's Department Store, and remembering that his mother was working there, decided to drop in and give her a call. Clearly then he must have known before that April day that his mother was working at Cox's. In December, she had been working at the Fair Ridglea Department Store (where she had the accident), so apparently sometime between December and April she had changed her place of employment.

(4) In talking to his mother at her counter in the department store, he never got the impression that there was anything seriously wrong with her, either physically or psychologically.

(5) The "Dependency Discharge" was a total scam in which the Marine authorities and Marguerite played a knowing part. One possible explanation is that although Marguerite's accident was genuine; when somehow she learned

in January that her son was going as a "defector" to the Soviet Union, she decided that in addition to benefitting from the insurance, she could also assist her son get an early discharge. All this was ignored by the maritime authorities because (presumably) an early discharge suited those they were working for. Having persuaded Oswald to risk the defector venture, the intelligence authorities were wary in case something may cause him to change his mind, say, for example, he might have found a new girl friend, with the possibility of an engagement. If that were to happen, the "defection" plan would most likely have collapsed.

No doubt it all came back to the old adage of striking while the iron is hot.

To my mind, the full facts of Oswald's premature discharge, ostensibly on dependency grounds, indicate clearly – as obvious as white chalk on redbrick – that his defection was an Intelligence operation.[18]

Moreover, quite apart from a possible intelligence connection, the incident, dealing with what should have been a not-infrequent routine procedure, is interesting because it encapsulated all the confusions and contradictions that accompanied everything about Oswald. Knowing what the reader knows now, it might be a good idea for the Report section to be re-read. Its dishonesty will become apparent – the discharge was a scam.

On September 20th – one month short of his 20th birthday – Oswald left America, headed towards the Soviet Union, which he reached in 28 days (16th October), in a highly planned trip travelling by way of Le Havre, England and Helsinki.

Immediately, Oswald told his Intourist guide of his desire to become a Soviet citizen, the situation was totally farcical. Oswald, having only just planted his feet on Russian ground, declared the greatness of the country and enthusiastically expressed his desire to be a Soviet (Communist) but was told on October 21 that his application had been refused. Oswald then inflicted a minor but bloody wound to his left wrist in his hotel room bathtub, after which the Soviets put him under psychiatric observation at a hospital.[19] The wrist cutting has often been treated as hysterical. However it served its purpose: it not only prevented Oswald from being sent home immediately, but got him a job at a radio factory (admittedly far away in Minsk, and gave the opportunity of an indefinite stay in the country whose politics and people he professed to love.

On October 31st, Oswald went to the United States embassy in Moscow, dramatically expressing a desire to renounce his U.S. citizenship and confronted the American Head Consul (Richard Snyder[20]) with a request for his immediate renunciation. the news that he wishes to renounce his US citizenship Oswald told the interviewing officer at the U.S. embassy, Richard Snyder,

"..He stated that he had recently been discharged from the Marine Corps. He also volunteered the information that he had offered to the Soviet authorities any information which he had acquired as an enlisted radar operator in the Marines" [WCH 5, 266.]

TEN | A MAN OF UNUSUAL TRAINING: THE OSWALD ENIGMA

[Such statements led to Oswald's hardship/honourable military discharge being changed to "undesirable."]

The Associated Press story of the defection of a U.S. Marine to the Soviet Union was reported on the front ps of some newspapers in 1959.

At this point I am going to do a lot of skipping – Oswald's lack of faith in the Soviet Union, his decision to return to America, and his vigorous defence of Castro's Cuba, etc, his radio confrontation with Carlos Bringuier – not because these things are unimportant (far from it, they are very important), but because they have been covered exhaustively, and instead I want direct attention to a very important (and comparatively little discussed) aspect of Oswald's politics.

Was Oswald A Right Winger Posing As a Communist?
Oswald's official biography portrays him, as I have already discussed, as a fervent Marxist, but – and here everything turns upside down – history professor Dr. Michael Kurtz provides evidence from his personal encounters with Oswald that Oswald was in fact right wing – far more General Walker than Lenin.

At the time of the Assassination, Professor Kurtz was a student at the Louisiana State University (now University of New Orleans). The university was politically one of the most important in the southern states: about five years before Professor Kurtz attended as a student, the university had become one of the first to become racially integrated. One of the greatest opponents of this progressive move was W. Guy Banister, a private detective and CIA operative who was an ex-FBI agent.

W. Guy Banister, in his attempt to prevent desegregation, had made several regular visits to the university organising opposition to the intended integration.

Who was Guy Banister? He was one of the FBI agents involved in the gunning down of John Dillinger His FBI career climaxed with his appointment as Special (FBI) Agent-in -Charge of Chicago city. In WW2 he worked for the Office of Naval Intelligence. Since then he had, on and off, worked for the New Orleans police department, He had a history of anti-communist activity, and was currently running a private detective agency, (Guy Banister Associates) thought to be in large part, a front for FBI and CIA anti-communist activity. Politically Guy was on the extreme right, belonging (amongst other groups) to the John Birch Society and the MINUTEMEN.

One day in May 1963, Michael Kurtz (as a student) attended an informal political meeting in one of the university's empty classrooms. The principal speaker was to be Guy Banister, who was accompanied by a fellow student of Kurtz's (George Higginbottom), and another young man whom Kurtz didn't know at the time.

Higginbottom introduced Banister, who then introduced the young man who had accompanied him. This young man was introduced to the meeting as "Lee Harvey Oswald".

Bannister's talk was extremely right wing, indistinguishable from the politics of General Walker. He asserted that Kennedy's administration was riddled with Communists, and in consequence, treasonably soft on Cuba.

Banister warned about the evils of racial integration, and (the climax of his speech) fiercely advocated the necessity of invading Cuba.

Oswald remained silent during the entire visit.

But on a second visit it was Oswald who did the speaking. Oswald – astonishingly for a communist – argued passionately against desegregation[21].

Two or three months later, Professor Kurtz saw Banister and Oswald sitting together enjoying a friendly coffee.

From the perspective of these three assertions, it follows that the Oswald of tradition – the "YouTube" Oswald, what is going to be the Oswald of 2013 – is a fiction.

For a start, was Professor Kurtz correct? I certainly don't believe that Oswald was a Marxist. To my mind, Oswald's association with the extreme right winger Banister correctly represents his politics. Five considerations support my assertion:

(1) On his return from the Soviet Union, Oswald never sought out fellow Marxists. All the people he was caught up with were extreme right wingers, with law enforcement/intelligence connections. Communism is a collectivist philosophy. Communists do not believe in the efficacy of private action, which is why they meet frequently on a collaborative basis, usually working through trade unions. On this basis alone – his lack of Communist friends and collaborators – Oswald could not have been a Communist.

On the contrary, the people he associated with were the very reverse of what a Communist would look for.

Two outstanding examples:

(a) George De Mohrenschildt –"Uncle George" to Jacqueline Kennedy. Oswald was very closely with this alleged Nazi collaborator. De Mohrenschildt persuaded Oswald and is wife to move to Dallas, and once there he helped Oswald to get employment.

De Mohrenschildt was a contact of H.L. Hunt, the Dallas billionaire, and was very strongly believed to be a CIA operative. Hardly good company for a Marxist!

(b) Guy Banister. We have already mentioned him. The last person any Marxist would associate with

(2) It was through Guy Banister that Oswald turned many Marxists over to the FBI.

This apparent treachery took place through the infamous Fair Play for Cuba Committee. This organisation, set up by Banister and Oswald, produced leaflets arguing for tolerance towards Cuba and the cessation of all aggressive threats. Those sympathetic were asked to fill in a leaflet – they were publicly handed

TEN | A MAN OF UNUSUAL TRAINING: THE OSWALD ENIGMA

out by Oswald – and to return it to the Fair Play for Cuba Committee, address given on the leaflet. Unfortunately – that is for those Marxists who fell for the ploy – the address on the leaflets was the 544 Camp Street address of Banister's office.

The exercise served two purposes: firstly, it enabled Oswald to pose publicly as a Marxist and thereby to develop his role as a Communist.

Secondly, it handed to the FBI (through Banister's strong FBI connections) the names of a large number of "subversives".

It is difficult to reconcile any of this with Oswald's commitment to Communism. Why would he be reporting his comrades to the FBI?

(3) For a supposedly committed Communist, Oswald never helped the working class in any of their struggles. He never attended picket lines

Indeed, Oswald, outside his work at the Book Depository, never came anywhere near the working class (let alone join a trade union), but, on the contrary, spent all his time, when not working, with the right-wing white Russians and with people like De Mohrenschildt and Banister.

(4) There is no logical (let alone a necessary) connection between being a Marxist and defecting to the Soviet Union.

Oswald, in defecting, was seeking a private solution to the public question, as he saw it, of class oppression, whereas a true Marxist would have no other option but to work within the parameters of public solutions.

Had Oswald ever bounced ideas off any of his fellow communists, they would, all of them, have told him the same story.

They would have said: "Don't waste your time learning Russian and defecting. You could achieve nothing in Russia. Only the Russian working class can save themselves. The best way you can help the Russian working class is by communising the American working class."

Anyway, his fellow American Communists would remind him, the Soviet workers would probably always see him as a foreigner, and resent his criticisms – not because they would be unfair or wrong – but because they come from a foreigner.

The advice they would have given Oswald would – surely? – have been to leave the Marines, get a job (say, in the car industry),and work through the trade union movement for better conditions and pay, whilst at the same time trying to 'drip' a Marxist consciousness into the workforce.

(5) There is also another important factor. If Oswald's defection (for life) was entirely his own private decision, he would have made exhaustive private enquiries from journalists and business people who had been there. Obviously so: Russia was going to be his new home, and the fact that he liked its political set-up would be no assurance that everything else would be to his liking. He would surely have been anxious about food, climate, working life, communications, housing transport, consumer goods.etc.

Seen from this point of view, Minsk, as Richard Synder indirectly told the Commission, was not a place that anybody would voluntarily choose to live.

Yet – astonishingly – not an enquiry from Oswald: nobody has ever come forward to say that Oswald asked them about life in the Soviet Union; similarly, in the same way that nobody has ever come forward to say they taught Oswald Russian.

For these reasons, I just don't believe the official defection line. It seems to me that Oswald's defection was an intelligence operation, viewed by him as a hush-hush posting.

The backyard photos show Oswald, keen to demonstrate his Communist allegiances, by holding two Communist journals, the Daily Worker and the Militant. However nobody with any acquaintance with Communism would pose in this way. Certainly not Oswald, if he was a Communist. The Daily Worker in those days was a Stalinist paper, whereas the Militant supported Trotsky. Nobody could support both parties at once – they fought together like two cats tied by their tails – any more than anybody could be at one and the same time both a Roman Catholic and a Protestant.

The pictures do not establish Oswald's Marxism. Politically, they are simply nonsense.

(6) Nobody who was as politically aware as Oswald was suppose to be would have mistaken the Soviet Union for a Marxist paradise worthy of defection

(7) If the Marines had thought that Oswald was a real Communist they would have discharged him automatically. Being thought to be a Communist in America, let alone, actually being one, was an act of suicide in Oswald's day. Just read the Internet Wikipedia article on the history of the American Communist Party. About 30% of its active membership were FBI informers. Read also the Wikipedia article on McCarthyism.[22]

No one in Oswald's very straitened circumstances – on minimum wage employment and married with one child and another on the way – could have afforded to let anyone think he was a Communist.

(d) The Enigma of Oswald's Arrest

I shall now show that there are serious enigmatic factors surrounding Oswald's arrest.

At 1:38 pm., sixty-eight minutes after the assassination, and twelve minutes before Oswald's, arrest, Lyndon Johnson told Robert Kennedy, in his (Kennedy's) role as Attorney General, that it was a matter of national urgency that there should be a strong hand at the helm of state, and that, in consequence, he (Johnson) should be made president as soon as possible. The assassination, Johnson argued "might be part of a world-wide plot". (William Manchester, Death of a President, p269)

Ten | A Man of Unusual Training: The Oswald Enigma

Johnson had no need to take the oath of office immediately on Kennedy's death He had automatically become President the moment Kennedy was pronounced dead. And there was certainly no need for him to do so in Kennedy's personal aircraft with Jacqueline Kennedy by his side, her clothes heavily stained with the blood of her slain husband.

It was a ruthless, dramatic gesture designed to underline that power now lay in his hands. And Johnson had to exercise that power swiftly and with unyielding resolution if he was to initiate immediately what was probably the biggest cover-up in history.

He had to convince everybody that the nation could be facing a worldwide conspiracy which it could not surmount unless there was a strong arm – his – at the tiller.

And, in the light of this fear, full security measures were taken:
(1) Air Force One, where Lyndon Johnson (now President Johnson) had taken occupation, was ringed by the Secret Service.
(2) The rooftop of the terminal building at Love Field was scanned for snipers. This two measures confirm that President Johnson was portraying the assassination as a *coup d'état*.[23]

Fear of conspiracy, started by Johnson in his new role as President, had spread so far that:

"At the Pentagon, Defence Secretary Robert McNamara called the Chairman of the Joint Chiefs of Staff, General Maxwell Taylor, and suggested that they place all troops on alert because they did not know whether a foreign power had been involved in the shooting."[24]

On p.296 of his memoirs, published 28 years after the assassination, Dean Rusk, the then Secretary of State described the fear that seemed to be gripping everybody:
"My greatest concern during that long return flight home and in the assassination aftermath was whether or not Kennedy's murder had international ramifications. Was it a conspiracy involving the Cubans or the Russians? We just didn't know."

(1) Under Section 1111 of TITLE 18 of the US code murder was a federal crime in 1963, but only if it was committed in a place or on a property owned (or controlled) by the federal government. Clearly Elm Street did not come under this description, and therefore the shooting of Kennedy was not a federal offence.
(2) However Sections 372 and 871 of TITLE 18 are interpreted to mean that

conspiring to kill the president is a federal offence, so that a presidential assassination, were it to involve a conspiracy, would, even in 1963, in its initial investigative stages, at least, come under federal jurisdiction.

This conspiracy fear meant that the autopsy could arguably be put under federal authority.
However the battle for Kennedy's body at Parkland Hospital lasted for nearly half-an-hour. Dr. Earl Rose, the Dallas Medical Examiner, tried physically to block the attempt of the Kennedy aides (Ken O'Donnell and Larry O'Brien), and the Secret Service agents (including Kellerman) attached to them, to take the body from Parkland Hospital. Dr. Earl Rose pointed out very fiercely that it was Dallas law that no homicide could leave the county without an immediate autopsy. The argument of the Kennedy men was that the fact that the body was that of the president changed things, but a Dallas judge, Theron Ward, joined forces with Dr. Rose, and asserted that legally Kennedy's body was just one more homicide case.
But the Dallas authorities were, in principle, wrong.

Bugliosi[25] attributes this decision (a military hospital for reasons of national security) to Admiral Burkley ("Four Days in November", p 219, and footnote 711), but given the magnetism and strength of Johnson's personality, and the fact that he had so dramatically made himself president (and was therefore so obviously in charge), it can be assumed – safely, I think – that Admiral Burkley was following Johnson's instructions.
But as a reason, National Security was a nonsense. The coup d'état danger (which Johnson knew never existed; see the next Point)) was over hours ago. (See points 18 & 19) Oswald, as we shall see, had been declared a lone assassin within 90 minutes of the Assassination. Adequate security, for the limited period of an autopsy, could have been applied at any private hospital, or the appropriate forensic team could have been flown to Bethesda.
There was no rational reason for choosing the forensically inadequate military doctors other than, being military men; they could/would act under orders.

THE LONE ASSASSIN CARD NOW APPEARS AS SUDDENLY AS A RABBIT FROM A CONJUROR'S HAT.
Despite his talk of a *coup d'état*, President Johnson dropped the subject the moment Kennedy's body was aboard Air Force One.[26]
2.14 pm Kennedy' body, in its very heavy casket, is taken aboard Air Force One. Thanks in basis to Johnson's Conspiracy Card.
At 2.20 pm Will Fritz, Head of Homicide and Robbery at Dallas police HQ, takes over the interrogation of Lee Harvey Oswald. This would ONLY have been

Ten | A Man of Unusual Training: The Oswald Enigma

possible if the Assassination had been placed under the jurisdiction of Dallas law, and this would only have been possible if Lee Harvey Oswald was held to be the LONE Assassin.[27]

The Warren Commission Report makes the matter very plain:

"................once it became reasonably clear that the killing [of Kennedy] was the act of a single person, the State of Texas had exclusive jurisdiction" [Warren Report, p 454. My emphasis].

NOTE! The corollary of this is that Will Fritz could not have had exclusive jurisdiction over Oswald's interrogation unless it had become reasonably clear by the early afternoon (actually, 2.20pm) that Oswald was the sole assassin.

In other words, the belief that Oswald was the lone assassin was not the conclusion of Will Fritz's interrogation, but its pre-condition. [Bear in mind that had Oswald's interrogation been conducted in Washington – i.e. under FBI jurisdiction – this would have strongly fuelled rumours of a conspiracy].

Between 1.30 and 2 pm the death of the President Kennedy was treated as a likely *coup d'état*, possibly with foreign involvement.

After 2pm, it is agreed to be the act of a lone assassin. How did this change come about?

The Report raises three questions:
(1) When did it become "reasonably clear"? (2) What is meant by "reasonably clear"? (3) Who made the decision?*

[*No, I'm not going to answer these questions. That's up to the reader. His/her opinion is probably as good as mine. However, in what follows I will indicate what is at stake.]

These questions are raised very starkly by the recollections of Rufus Youngblood (Head of the Vice Presidential Detail at the time of the Assassination) in his 1978 book "20 Years in the Secret Service".

From Rufus W Youngblood's book:

Commenting on the situation on the way to Air Force One at Love Field Airport, Rufus Youngblood wrote:

"One of the motorcycle officers ahead of us had begun to sound his siren, and I quickly told Curry to have him stop. Unlike the trip into Dallas from Love Field, we had no desire to attract attention. I felt that if we could get through the next few minutes, then conspiracy or no conspiracy, we would have Lyndon Johnson in a secure situation." (p 121)

Aboard Air Force One, Rufus Youngblood continued:

"The interior of the plane was stiflingly hot. But it was secure. I had one final thought of security – a sniper* atop one of the airport buildings could conceivably get a shot at LBJ through the plane's window. (p 121) [* He seems to be thinking of a coup d'état]

"I looked at my watch. It was slightly past 1:40 ...." (p 121)
"As of the time we boarded the plane (about 1415), we had not heard the name of Lee Harvey Oswald. The possibility that the death of John Kennedy was part of a far-reaching conspiracy that had not yet run its course was very real indeed and was in the thoughts of everyone – and especially in the thoughts of the Secret Service." [p 123 Emphasis mine]

This means that the 'conspiracy' fear was running "its course" up to the point of Oswald's arrest (until we "heard the name of Lee Harvey Oswald").

So what was there about Lee Harvey Oswald (about his name) that automatically made it (in the words of the Report) "reasonably clear" that he was acting entirely on his own, and, in consequence, put a stop to the "course run" by the fear of a far-reaching conspiracy?

As I have said in an earlier part of this chapter – and it needs repeating – one thing is certain: everybody who dealt with the arrested Oswald – the officers who made the actual arrest at the cinema, the officers who escorted him along the corridors, and the detective in charge of his interrogation – all testified to Oswald's calmness, articulacy, and intelligence. And Dale Myers (With Malice[28], 1998) has described Oswald as "a master of self control" [p 208].

These qualities separated Oswald from all previous assassins, with the arguable exception of John Wilkes Booth, and would have made him appear an ideal conspirator.

What this means is that whatever reason there was for believing that Oswald, from the moment of his arrest, to be the sole assassin, it was very much despite his personality, not because of it. By the very character of Oswald, and because the assassination involved multiple high – powered rifle shots (i.e. the shots could have come from more than one rifle) – by these facts alone –a red light should have been given to conspiracy, and therefore to Federal jurisdiction.

And yet, immediately on his arrest, the red light was switched off. Federal jurisdiction was jettisoned, and replaced by local (State) jurisdiction, and Will Fritz took over Oswald's interrogation?

Here is what Jesse Curry, the Dallas Chief of Police told the Commission on his second appearance (22 April, '64):"

Now, subsequent to that, we felt this, that this was a murder that had been committed in the county, city and county of Dallas, and that we had prior, I mean we had jurisdiction over this. The FBI actually had no jurisdiction over it; the Secret Service actually had no jurisdiction over it. But in an effort to cooperate with these agencies we went all out to do whatever they wanted us to do that we could do to let them observe what was taking place, but actually we knew that this was a case that happened in Dallas, Tex., and would have to be tried in Dallas, Tex., and it was our responsibility to gather the evidence and present the evidence." (WCT Jesse Curry, 4H, 195)

TEN | A MAN OF UNUSUAL TRAINING: THE OSWALD ENIGMA

Bugliosi, justifiably the star defender of lone-assassin orthodoxy, agrees with this. He writes: "Personally, Curry doesn't give a hoot what the FBI wants. This is a Dallas case under Dallas jurisdiction and the responsibility is his."(Four Days in November, p 260)

But, as the Report makes clear (p 454), the county of Dallas would never have had this jurisdiction had it not PREVIOUSLY been decided that Oswald, as I have argued. was the sole assassin.

Who made the decision – and why? It certainly wasn't Hoover.

"The only Bureau communications which could have been construed as an instruction to interview security informants [teletypes timed at 2140 and 2300 hrs, 22nd November '63] were rescinded by an instruction issued the following day at 1120 hrs." This teletype instruction informed FBI agents that Lee Harvey Oswald has been DEVELOPED [!] as the principal suspect in the assassination of President Kennedy.[29]

"The truth is that nobody, outside a very small, heavily closeted circle knew why, from the moment he was taken into custody, Oswald was treated as the sole assassin (with the binning of all conspiracy talk), but the speed and certainty of the polar change – an international conspiracy mutating into the anger of a single malcontent – suggests the pre-planning, directing force of a personality strong in itself and strong from its power of office – maybe Lyndon Johnson.

(e) The Enigma of Oswald's Interrogation
As we shall see, the official version makes no sense.

Oswald's Interrogation
Oswald was in police custody from 2.02 pm on Friday, 22nd November until he was murdered on Sunday, 24th November at 11.21 am. That is just under 46 hours. His periods of interrogation, directed by Will Fritz, were given by the Report as follows:
Friday, intermittent interrogation, for a period of more than 7 hours;
Saturday: for 3 hours
Sunday: Just under two hours.

This gives a total of about 12 hours, which means that one quarter of Oswald's time at the police station was allegedly spent under the guided interrogation of Will Fritz.

Main Points:
1) The Poor Quality of the Interrogation.
What did these 12 hours produce? The answer is absolutely nothing. Reading Bugliosi's "factional"[30] account of Will Fritz' interrogation one is impressed

not by Fritz' perspicacity, but by the slow, repetitive plodding nature of his questioning. Bugliosi cannot offer one incriminating item of information that Will Fritz teased from Oswald.

From Will Fritz's statements to the Commission, he seems to have missed every salient point.

The following is a good example, where many could be chosen:

Will Fritz, in his Warren testimony (4H, 226) told Mr. Ball that, as regards the backyard photos, Oswald had claimed that his face in those photos was a superimposition, and that therefore the photos were fakes.

Oswald, according to Will Fritz in his written submission, immediately after Oswald's death (WR 601, CE 203:24H, 269) continued this assertion by claiming that his superimposed face was from a recent police-station picture snapped by one of the (seemingly) hundreds of press photographers.

This claim (attested by the WCT (7H, 231) of James Bookout was an absurdity. Oswald's left eye had been cut and bruised during a struggle at his arrest, and it showed so clearly that the TV coverage of his police station appearances has a reporter loudly commenting on his injured face.

How Oswald looked at Dallas Police HQ and in one of his backyard photos

However Oswald's face in the backyard photo shows no such cut or bruising, and corresponds to an obviously younger Oswald. Yet, incredibly, Will Fritz – I'm going from the Bugliosi version – was not astute enough to have noticed this, nor, bafflingly, were any of the FBI or Secret Service officers attending the interrogation.

Here is another example of Will Fritz's incompetence.

Oswald contradicted himself on a mightily important point. On what floor was he when the President was shot? Oswald must surely have remembered that. But according to the Commission records, he didn't. He claimed (if the Commission records are to be believed) to have been at two places at once – and Will Fritz was too incompetent to notice.

On Friday afternoon, about two hours after his arrest, Oswald was asked by Will Fritz (in the presence of Special Agents), where he was in the building when the President was shot. He replied that he was having his lunch on the on the first floor, and implied that he went up to the 2nd floor for a Coke.

Two days later, on the Sunday morning of his final interrogation, in the presence of four Dallas detectives, plus the note-taking presence of a Secret Service Postal Inspector, and the Head of the Dallas office of the Secret Service, Oswald was again asked by Will Fritz where he was at the time of the shooting, and this time instead of talking about going deliberately up a floor for a Coke (on the second floor), he spoke of going down to check on the commotion following the shooting, and, on his way down , he noticed a Coke machine, and, on an impulse, had a Coke.

Ten | A Man of Unusual Training: The Oswald Enigma

Therefore, on this Sunday morning interrogation, Oswald claims, at the time of the shooting, to be not on the first floor (as he asserted on the Friday), but to have been on the third floor or above, and to have moved *downwards* to the 2nd floor.

This major contradiction – the very type of contradiction that interrogations are intended to reveal – and yet (if the Commission records are true), it went completely unnoticed by Will Fritz, thereby putting a question-mark over all his interrogation sessions.[31]

Police Chief Jesse Curry summed the utter failure to get a confession by saying that all that emerged from the 12 hours of interrogation was that Oswald knew "nothing about anything". (4H,154)

Appendix XI of the Report deals exclusively with Oswald's interrogation. It provides" the most important recollections" of what happened in those 12 hours, and was prepared for the Commission by Oswald's 4 senior interrogators.

The recollections (written within a day or two of Oswald's death) are those very principally of Will Fritz, and to a lesser extent of FBI agent James Hosty, Special (FBI) Agent James Bookout, Secret Service Inspector Thomas Kelley, and Postal Inspector H.D Holmes.

A total of only 57 questions are contained in these memoranda.

However there is a very serious query here. We know from the Commission how many questions can be covered in a 12 hour period.

On the 22nd April (1964), the Commission, given the normal breaks, sat for 12 hours, and in that period deposed of 3 people: Police Chief Jesse Curry, Will Fritz, and J.C. Day of the Identification Bureau. Their questions covered 129 pages from the Hearings, but I chose 20 of these pages at random and counted 345 questions, suggesting that the Commission in 12 hours covered something like 2,200 questions.

Therefore if Oswald, as the Report asserts, was interrogated for 12 hours, we would expect him to have answered at least about 2,000 questions. The interrogators, as we shall see, were not handicapped by the delays of note-taking.

But the Report acknowledges, on my counting, only 57 topics,and these topics, at the most, covered no more than about 190 questions, (9% of the estimated total), which implies that we do not have Oswald's answers to about 91% of what he was asked.

This means that we cannot take any notice of the answers that we do have, firstly, because we cannot put any trust in those who suppress information on such a massive scale, and, secondly, because anything that Oswald allegedly said in his 9% of recorded answers could have been moderated (if not contradicted) by what he said in the 91% that was deliberately unrecorded.

The record of questions that we do have indicates that every significant avenue was unexplored. For example:

There were three possible conspiracy dimensions

On Friday at 7.55 pm – just 5 hours after being in police custody – Oswald made his first and only volunteered comment on his arrest. He said: "They've taken me in because of the fact that I lived in the Soviet Union. I'm just a patsy." Oswald was prevented from continuing this revelation because he was cut short by a reporter shouting at him "Did you shoot the President?"

Yet not one question from either Will Fritz, or from any of the FBI/Secret Service Agents attending the interrogations, or, for that matter, from any of the Commission lawyers, touched on this claim.

If this is correct, then Will Fritz' incompetence is on a cosmic scale and also that of the FBI, the Secret Service, and the whole Commission. No Commission lawyer ever referred, even tangentially, to Oswald's "patsy" claim, and yet this claim is one of the very few unarguable truths of the Assassination.

But there were, on the surface of things, excellent reasons for believing in a conspiratorial dimension. All of which Will Fritz ignored:

Mafia connection

Nobody knew better than Will Fritz the depths to which the Mafia was embedded in the politics and commerce of Dallas. He had, after all, spent 32 years in the city fighting organized crime.

(a) Will Fritz would have quickly learnt that Oswald spent some of his childhood and formative years in a Mafia infested area of New Orleans. One particular address was 126 Exchange Alley, a well-known Mafia gambling territory.

Moreover, the school Oswald went to (Beauregard High school) had a reputation for producing a nearly endless supply of Mafia gunmen and 'helpers'. Oswald could easily have acquired Mafia connections, as indeed could his mother and her relatives.

In fact, there is plenty of evidence to suggest that this is what happened.

As recently as three months before the Assassination, when Oswald was arrested in New Orleans over the Fair Play for Cuba fracas, he was bailed out by an alleged Marcello associate, and, for the one night that he did spend behind bars, he was visited by his uncle, another alleged Marcello associate.

In addition, the Mafia, given their own vantage point, had every reason to both .hate and fear Kennedy. Their motivation in this respect was beyond argument.

(b) On 7th September '63 – a mere 71 days before the Assassination – President Castro, who believed that, at the instigation of President Kennedy, the US government had organized 24 assassination attempts on him, gave an interview to Daniel Harker, of the Associated Press. In the course of the interview, Castro remarked

"*If American leaders persist in their terrorist attacks upon the lives of the Cuban leaders, they themselves would not be safe.*" [32]

TEN | A MAN OF UNUSUAL TRAINING: THE OSWALD ENIGMA

Direct Communist Threat
Bill Alexander, the Assistant Dallas District Attorney, and a great friend of Will Fritz, described Oswald as "a card-carrying member of the Communist party with overseas connections", and on this basis his immediate thoughts were of a conspiracy. Bugliosi supplies evidence that these immediate thoughts became firmly rooted, and were, in part, privately held by the Attorney Generals for Dallas and Texas.[33]

Bill Alexander attended some (if not all) of Will Fritz's Friday 12 hours interrogation of Oswald.

It is impossible to believe that Bill Alexander did not discuss these communist conspiracy fears with his old friend, Will Fritz.

No tape recording or note-taking (4H, 232,209)
A tape recorder could – surely? – have been easily obtained.

If, as we shall see later, two armoured cars, from within Dallas City, were made available within 75 minutes, early on a November Sunday morning (24th November), then surely on a Friday afternoon Dallas Police HQ could acquire a tape recorder?

If the Dallas Police were not up to the job, then what about the FBI, and if the FBI couldn't lay their hands on a tape-recorder, couldn't the Secret Service?

And what about President Johnson?

He took so much interest in the case that the day after the Assassination he made a commiserating 'phone call to Mrs. Tippit which very cleverly carried the oblique implication that Oswald was Kennedy's assassin. Couldn't the White House provide a tape-recorder?[34]

Equally, stenographers were available. This is a key point. Alan Belmont, Hoover's deputy, had agreed, amongst other provisions, to supply Will Fritz with four stenographers[35] – so why weren't they used?

It is simply beyond belief that it did not occur to any of the attending FBI officers or to any of the Secret Service agents – let alone to Will Fritz – that for this, the Crime of the Century, notes had to be taken at the actual time, and not from memory days afterwards. But none were taken, as Will Fritz himself told the Commission [4WCH, 209], and as was reflected in his (at times) very vague testimony.

He was not certain when he left off (and re-joined) an interrogation nor could he remember who was present at any particular interrogation, and, in any of his absences, what questions were asked. Even when he was asking the questions, he was not always certain of the order in which he asked them. Also he was sometimes confused between Mrs Paine and Mrs Oswald. [See 4WCH, 211-213; 217/218]

Why wasn't the interrogation, like the autopsy, carried out in Washington by, say, Alan Belmont, Hoover's assistant, and third in command at FBI

Headquarters? Instead of having to liaise between Curry and Hoover, and having to send down stenographers, why didn't Belmont have Oswald sitting in front of him at FBI headquarters?

The question is sharpened by two facts:

Firstly, that several rifle shots were fired at the President, indicating the obvious possibility that there was more than one shooter – therefore a conspiracy – and secondly, that the alleged assassin within the first day of his arrest, had publicly declared himself to be "just a patsy" who was innocent of any wrong doing. This public declaration – recorded on TV – despite its enigmatic qualities, is one of the few certain facts about the Assassination. It is therefore worthwhile investigating.

Oswald's famous "I'm a patsy" declaration.

Such a declaration is to my mind an important part of the Oswald Enigma", but before I justify my assessment, I would like to put forward the mainstream view. Strangely, the best exponent is not Bugliosi – he inexplicably dismisses Oswald's declaration without comment – but David Von Pein in his website "JFK Archives", which contains a blog directly on this topic[36]. The following quotation comes from Mr. Von Pein's blog:

OSWALD'S "I'M JUST A PATSY" LIE

When Lee Harvey Oswald's "I'm just a patsy" statement (which was uttered by Oswald at approx. 7:55 PM on 11/22/63, per reporter Seth Kantor's notes) isn't broken up into smaller sections (which it usually is, so that people don't get to hear Oswald's incredibly silly lie about being "taken in" because of his once having lived in Russia), it becomes fairly clear that the Patsy statement is nothing more than a whitewash/lie being spoken by Lee Harvey in an obvious attempt to divert suspicion away from the man (Oswald) who really did kill two people in Dallas on November 22, 1963.

My reply is that Oswald's statement – that the Dallas Police have taken him into custody because of his visit to the Soviet Union – was, if taken literally, so idiotically absurd that it obviously couldn't have been what he intended to say. It must be understood that Oswald, in circumstances, of the greatest stress – he had forty-five minutes earlier been arraigned for the murder of a police officer – had just emerged, at the time of his declaration, from the jail's lift, following his third line-up and was headed towards Will Fritz's office for further interrogation.

In the process he was being rushed along a hallway crammed with probably over a hundred journalists, with dozens of camera bulbs flashing and dozens of microphones thrust into his face. Oswald only had seconds to speak. His patsy declaration was over in 14 seconds.

TEN | A MAN OF UNUSUAL TRAINING: THE OSWALD ENIGMA

The Soviet reference can be understood by considering what Oswald was implying by calling himself a "patsy". The word "patsy" meant the same in 1963 as it does today. We know what the world meant in those days because the word appears eight times in the Commission's Hearings [1WCH, 491/2/6/7; 8WCHH, 353; 9WCHH, 56/9 11WCHH, 330], and each time it carries the same meaning: it refers to a framing, but not by the police, but by the criminals.

This interpretation puts Oswald's Soviet reference into a rational perspective. He is claiming that he has been framed as a Communist lone assassin. As I have suggested, his Soviet "defection" was very likely an intelligence operation – an important part of the creation of his Communist "legend" – and it was possibly because of this convenient Communist background that he was chosen by the conspirators as a patsy. Oswald's "patsy" declaration, interpreted this way, carries the following implications:

(a) That there was a conspiracy to kill the President;
(b) That Oswald knew some of the conspirators (otherwise how could they have framed him?);
(c) That through his involvement with them they had been able to frame him (and therefore his involvement must have been more than tangential);
(d) That Oswald was led to believe that he was working undercover for the US government. This follows from his declaration in the same video clip that he had done nothing wrong and nothing of which he could be ashamed. Clearly the only way he could have associated innocently with conspirators (which is what he was implying) is if were working under cover for some form of law enforcement.
(e) Such a crucial intelligence assignment – 'under-covering' an assassination plot against the president – was unlikely (if true) to have been his first assignment. The obvious implication is that Oswald, on the strength of his "patsy" claim, was in fact asserting (if the claim was true) a long-standing intelligence background

But, as I shall show, this "patsy" declaration carries, a further and more revealing implication.

(f) It is that the conspiracy was possibly two layered. The operatives on the ground, and a direction from above. This implication will now be justified. Its justification lies in the mysterious timing of Oswald's "I'm a patsy" declaration which has not, so far as I know, been pointed out. The following timetable will make this point obvious:

7.04 p.m:
Will Fritz tells Curry that he is getting ready to file on Oswald for shooting Tippit. Curry takes it for granted that Oswald shot the President, and was acting entirely on his own. Will Fritz indicates that he, too, thinks the same.

JFK | Echoes From Elm Street
A Search for Historical Accuracy on the
Assassination of President John F. Kennedy

7.10 p.m:
Will Fritz informs Oswald that he will be charging him with Tippit's murder.

7.28 p.m:
Asked by a reporter whether he had shot the President. Oswald replies "I didn't shoot anybody, Sir"

8:30 p.m:
During interrogation, Will Fritz accuses Oswald of killing the President. Oswald replies by firmly denying the charge.

8:55 p.m:
Oswald is tested for gunpowder on his hands and cheeks, and he tells the officers doing the testing that he knows nothing about the shootings. The use of the plural indicates that Oswald is aware that the police department is considering arraigning him for the deaths of both Tippit AND Kennedy.

11.20 p.m:
Five senior law officers meet in the Dallas police HQ Homicide and Robbery office. They are Chief Curry, head of police, Will Fritz, head of Homicide and Robbery, District Attorney Wade, and Alexander his assistant, and Judge Johnston. They decide to proceed with filing against Oswald for the assassination of President Kennedy, and complete the paperwork by 11:26 p.m.

11:50 p.m:
Chief Curry tells s large collection of third –floor reporters that they are about to charge Oswald officially with Kennedy's murder.

12:10 a.m:
Oswald is taken to meet the press. He looks baffled.

"I really don't know what this situation is about. Nobody has told me anything except that I am accused of....ah...of...ah murdering a policeman*

[*Oswald up to this moment has only been arraigned for the murder of Patrolman Tippit]
A journalist challenges him: "Did you kill the president?"

"No I have not been charged with that. In fact nobody has said that to me yet. The first thing I heard about it was when the newspaper reporters in the hall....."...
His voice drowned by the pandemonium background noise. The TV coverage shows Oswald shattered his voice uncertain.

TEN | A MAN OF UNUSUAL TRAINING: THE OSWALD ENIGMA

"You have been charged," a reporter tells him.

Oswald on hearing this rocks on his feet. A look of astonishment crosses his face. This dismay is clearly picked up by the TV camera, and must have been obvious to everybody present. And one of those present in the room was the British disc-jockey John Peel (1934/2004), who at the time of the assassination was only 6 months older than Oswald.

John Peel had been in the United States since 1960, mostly as a travelling insurance salesman for a Texas-based company, and at the time of the Assassination he was in Dallas.

Hearing that the man arrested for the Assassination was at Dallas Police Headquarters, for a televised press parade, John Peel seized the opportunity of a lifetime. Taking advantage of the lax security, he gained entry pretending to be a reporter for the British Liverpool Echo (he was born near Liverpool).

The TV footage confirms that he was pushed very near to Oswald by the crowd in the Assembly-room, which was swelling by the second*. [* So enormous was this crowd that Will Fritz became separated from his prisoner, and had great difficulty in squeezing himself into the Assembly Room]

In his (uncompleted) autobiography John Peel described Oswald as "convincingly bewildered", and remarked that "Oswald didn't seem to have a clue as to what was going on", and was either a damn good actor or he was innocent.[37]

However all this presents a serious problem. Granted that Oswald obviously was shattered by the news that he was to be charged with Kennedy's assassination, the question is why he was so surprised, given that just four hours previously, as we have shown in the timetable, a reporter had directly asked him whether he had shot the President?

Moreover, as I have argued Oswald's 7.55 pm "I'm a patsy" remark was obviously referring to the assassination of the President. It is, therefore, obvious that Oswald had correctly guessed the under currents of his fate hours before he was paraded as the assassin.

And yet Oswald was rocked by the news. Why was he shocked by something he had every reason to anticipate?

The only answer I can give is that although Oswald knew that Dallas law enforcement was keen to arraign him for the assassination of the President, and that therefore a charge had already been formulated, he was convinced that it would be blocked.

In other words, following his patsy claim, Oswald possibly saw the conspiracy as being two layered. It was the lower layer – the ordinary 'workmen' of the Assassination, as it were – who had framed him, but there was, so he may have felt, a higher layer – maybe a "Mr. Big"– who Oswald was convinced would overrule his framing.

Of course to be that confident, Oswald must have had dealings with "Mr. Big" Clearly, if this was so, then no man in Oswald's position could be expected to live for long.

Of course all this is very speculative, with no room for dogmatism. But for all that three questions still remain:

(a) At what was Oswald so surprised?
(b) Why didn't Oswald's interrogators question him on his patsy claim?
(c) Why didn't the Commission question his interrogators as to what they thought he meant?

Of course he may have been asked these questions. Remember; as I have argued, Oswald was virtually interrogated in secret, and so may well in reality have been grilled on this topic. It is just the answers – too many people seriously incriminated – were not for our knowledge.

As we shall see, according to the US constitution, this "patsy" defence on its own should have placed Oswald under federal jurisdiction. Instead – if the official records are correct – not only did the Dallas Police totally ignore what Oswald said, despite their alleged 12 hours of interrogation, but also – utterly astonishing this – none of the of the Commission lawyers ever raised the issue of Oswald's "patsy" claim with any of his interrogators

(f) The Enigma of Oswald and the Russian Language

In this, the most important part of my chapter, I shall make a case against the view, held alike by orthodox believers and many conspiracists, that Lee Harvey Oswald learnt to speak Russian while in the Marines.

I also argue against the view that Oswald was taught Russian while in the Soviet Union. I put forward evidence that Oswald was an easy Russian speaker before he went to the Soviet Union.

My purpose is to open the possibility that the enigmatic person called Lee Harvey Oswald was a natural Russian speaker. I am aware, of course, that the idea of Oswald as a natural Russian speaker is an argument basic to John Armstrong's 2003 " Harvey and Lee" (and the numerous Harvey and Lee website articles he has produced), but, to my mind, John Armstrong doesn't argue this linguistic aspect of his case very convincingly.

What follows, therefore, is a much more detailed defence of Armstrong's assertion than he himself supplies.

IF one accepts the mainstream, official view of the Assassination, then there is an unsolvable mystery about Oswald and the Russian language.

As an introduction to this mystery, I provide 8 quotations (seven from the 1964 Warren Commission Hearings, and one from the 1978/9 House Select Committee on Assassinations) which by their sharp clarity put the issue in excellent focus.

Ten | A Man of Unusual Training: The Oswald Enigma

From the Warren Commission Testimony of George De Morenschildt.
NOTE! George De Morenschildt, in addition to being a geologist was also an educated foreign nobleman with very high social and commercial connections.

He was "Uncle George" to Jacqueline Kennedy, and he was linked to H.L. Hunt, the Dallas oil billionaire.

De Morenschildt had considerable influence over Oswald – it was possibly he that encouraged Lee and Marina to leave Fort Worth and join the Russian community in Dallas – and the involvement between such polar opposites in the externalities of life has convinced many people that the two contrasting men were brought together by an Intelligence connection.

First Quotation
Mr. De Mohrenschildt. Well, he spoke fluent Russian, but with a foreign accent, and made mistakes, grammatical mistakes, but had remarkable fluency in Russian.
Mr. JENNER. It was remarkable?
Mr. De Mohrenschildt. Remarkable–for a fellow of his background and education, it is remarkable how fast he learned it. But he loved the language. He loved to speak it. He preferred to speak Russian than English any time. He always would switch from English to Russian."
Mr. JENNER. Oswald was pretty proud, was he, of his ability to speak Russian
Mr. De Mohrenschildt. He was proud of it, yes; because it is quite an achievement for a man with a poor scholastic background to have learned the language. It is surprising to me. It was an extraordinary surprise for my wife and myself that he was able to learn to speak it so well for such a short time as he was supposed to have stayed in Russia. As I understand it, he stayed there some 2 years, I gather.
Mr. JENNER. That is all.
Mr. De Mohrenschildt. And it is amazing.
Mr. JENNER. In speaking of that, as I recall, you noted he had a conversational command of the language.
Mr. De Mohrenschildt. Yes.
Mr. JENNER. But that he did not speak a refined Russian.
Mr. De Mohrenschildt. No, no; not a refined Russian.
Mr. JENNER. He had trouble with his grammar?
Mr. De Mohrenschildt. Yes, yes.
WCT *George De Morenschildt* [WC 9 226, 259]

More from De Morenschildt:

Second Quotation
"Incidentally I never saw him [Oswald] interested in anything else except

Russian books and magazines. He said he didn't want to forget the language – but it amazed me that he read such difficult writers like Gorki, Dostoevsky, Gogol, Tolstoy and Turgenieff – in Russian. As everyone knows Russian is a complex language and he was supposed to have stayed in the Soviet Union only a little over two years.

He must have had some previous training and that point had never been brought up by the Warren Committee - and it is still puzzling to me. In my opinion Lee was a very bright person but not a genius. He never mastered the English language yet he learned such a difficult language! I taught Russian at all levels in a large University and I never saw such a proficiency in the best senior students who constantly listened to Russian taped and spoke to Russian friends. As a matter of fact American-born instructors' never mastered Russian spoken language as well as Lee did".
[George De Morenschildt, "I Am a Patsy! I Am A Patsy!" 1976]

But De Morenschildt was not the only person to comment on Oswald's preference for speaking Russian rather than English. His 20-year-old daughter, Mrs Donald Gibson supported him:

Third Quotation
Mr. JENNER. When Oswald came to your house that evening, did he speak English
or Russian?
Mrs. GIBSON. He spoke English to us and Russian to Marina.
Mr. JENNER. When he arrived, did he speak with his child?
Mrs. GIBSON. Oh, yes.
Mr. JENNER. In what language did he speak with the child?
Mrs. GIBSON. Russian.
Mr. JENNER. That was not merely small talk? All of his conversation with his child was in Russian?
Mrs. GIBSON. Some was small talk. You could tell that he was just playing around, and when he really talked to her, it was in Russian. Of course once in a while he'd lapse into English.
Mr. JENNER. When Oswald came to your house that evening, did he speak English or Russian?

Fourth Quotation
Another witness who confirmed that Oswald preferred to speak Russian than English was Ruth Paine, Oswald' landlady, who was learning the language. She told the Commission:

Mr. JENNER. I think you said to me this morning, and please correct me if my

Ten | A Man of Unusual Training: The Oswald Enigma

recollection is not good, that he always spoke to you in Russian.
Mrs. PAINE. With, perhaps, a couple of rare exceptions, yes, he spoke to me in Russian. When I tried to teach him to drive I tried to explain to him, proceeded to explain to him in English.
Mr. JENNER. Excuse me; you tried to teach him to do what?
Mrs. PAINE. To drive. This is later.
Mr. JENNER. Drive, yes.
Mrs. PAINE. But he would answer me in Russian, which is a way of getting the person to go back to Russian. But I couldn't explain driving in Russian, so I did it in English.
(2WC, 458)

Fifth Quotation
From the Warren Commission testimony of Marguerite Oswald:
Mrs. OSWALD ......And, of course, Marina and Lee spoke Russian all the time, even in front of me. And you asked about this time it was a very happy time. They would sit at the table. They were playing a game, and I said to Lee, "What is it you are doing?' Because they were always talking in Russian. Mother, we are playing a game which is similar to American tic-tac-toe. [WC1, 134]

Sixth Quotation
From an FBI Report, dated 7th December, 1963:
"She [Marina Oswald] said that Oswald's Russian, though good, bore a definite accent. She thought that he had probably come from one of the Russian speaking Baltic countries." [WC 22, 745 (CE 1401, page 6/25)]

Seventh Quotation
From the testimony of Paul Gregory:[38]
Mr. GREGORY: She said she met him at a dance, I guess in Minsk, and she didn't know who he was, and she danced with him or something, and thought he was, because of his accent, thought he was from the Baltic States, and later somebody called her aside and said, 'I guess you don't know who he is' and so forth, and I guess they more or less left him alone." [WCH x, 146]
Mr. LIEBELER. What about Oswald's proficiency in Russian?
Mr. GREGORY. He spoke a very ungrammatical Russian with a very strong accent.
Mr. LIEBELER. What kind of accent?
Mr. GREGORY. Well, I can't tell you, because I am not that much of a judge. You would have to ask an expert about that. It was this poorly spoken Russian, but he was completely fluent. He understood more than I did and he could express any idea, I believe, that he wanted to in Russian. But it was heavily pronounced and he made all kinds of grammatical errors, and Marina would correct him, and he

would get peered at her for doing this. She would say you are supposed to say like this, and he would wave his hand and say, "Don't bother me." [WC H 9, 149]

Eighth Quotation
From Marina Oswald:
Marina's HSCA testimony, Vol 2 of the HSCA Report. Marina testified throughout the day on 13.09.78.

Mr. McDONALD. Can you recall what you talked about at this first meeting?
Mrs. PORTER. Just typical young people everyday talk, routine talk, about the weather. I do not really recall what it was about. Mr. McDONALD. Do you recall how long this initial meeting lasted?
Mrs. PORTER. About 2 or 3 hours.
Mr. McDONALD. In other words, you continued to talk with Lee Oswald for 2 to 3 hours?
Mrs. PORTER. No, I didn't. When he asked to dance, we just talked very little.
Mr. McDONALD. Did he tell you he was an American?
Mrs. PORTER. No, not at that – not during the dancing, no.
Mr. McDONALD. At this time you were speaking in Russian together?
Mrs. PORTER. Yes. He spoke with accent so I assumed he was maybe from another state, which is customary in Russia. People from other states do speak with accents because they do not speak Russian. They speak different languages.
Mr. McDONALD. So when you say another state, you mean another Russian state?
Mrs. PORTER. Yes, like Estonia, Lithuania, something like that.
Mr. McDONALD. Did you suspect at all that he was an American?
Mrs. PORTER. No, not at all.
Mr. DEVINE - Mrs. Porter, taking you clear back to the time that you originally met Lee, this was in Russia, you said you did not know he was from America or from the United States until someone later told you; is that accurate?
Mrs. PORTER - Yes. During the few dances with him he spoke with accent, but I did not know he was from America. Mr. DEVINE - But his Russian was sufficiently fluent that you did not necessarily think he was necessarily a foreigner to the Soviet Union?
Mrs. PORTER - He spoke with accent but lots of people in Russia do speak with accent. They don't speak Russian very well, they have different nationalities than Russians.
Mr. DEVINE - But his Russian was pretty good at that time?
Mrs. PORTER - It was pretty good, yes..

[Note! Three natural Russian speakers (De Morenschildt, Dr. Peter Gregory

TEN | A MAN OF UNUSUAL TRAINING: THE OSWALD ENIGMA

and Marina Oswald), and one fluent graduate student (Paul Gregory) all say that Oswald spoke Russian with a marked accent which none of them was able to identify. One of the reasons why Marina didn't spot Oswald as an American was not because he spoke Russian – she would have had no difficulty in believing that an American could learn the language – but she did not expect an American to speak the language with a regional accent, especially one she couldn't identify. Bear in mind that Oswald's accent could not have come from his stay in Minsk because Marina, when they met, had been in Minsk for about 18 months, and she would have identified his accent immediately, indeed, would probably not have commented on it.

Oswald's regional accent is analogous to (say) a German speaking English with an accent found only in some remote corner of south-west England. Puzzling. Intriguing. It needs some explaining. However, in 50 years, no explanation has come forward. It is difficult to believe that the CIA, for example, would have taught Oswald to speak Russian in a dialect which would attract (suspicious?) attention.]

How Did Oswald Learn Russian?

Four Quotations

First Quotation
From the Commission testimony of Marguerite Oswald:
Mrs OSWALD: And Lee spoke and wrote Russian fluently when he went to Russia. So Lee learns Russian in the Marines.
Mr. RANKIN. Did he ever talk about reenlisting into the Marines after he returned?
[Note Mr. Rankin doesn't answer Marguerite's question. He quickly changes the subject]

Second Quotation
From the Warren Commission Testimony of John Pic (Oswald's half-brother):
Mr. JENNER. Did you have any discussion with him on that subject – where he had learned Russian?
Mr. PIC. Well, sir, I knew he had been in Russia over 2 years, so evidently he had learned Russian while there.
Mr. JENNER. There was no occasion because of that, it never occurred to you to ask him about how and when he had learned?
Mr. PIC. I wasn't going to pry into his affairs, sir.
Mr. JENNER. You didn't?
Mr. PIC. No, sir; I didn't. (1H, 521)
[Most likely it was Oswald's repeated evasiveness on the topic that gave John Pic the "prying" feeling.]

JFK | ECHOES FROM ELM STREET
A SEARCH FOR HISTORICAL ACCURACY ON THE
ASSASSINATION OF PRESIDENT JOHN F. KENNEDY

Third Quotation
From the Commission testimony of Oswald's brother, Robert:
Mr. (Robert) OSWALD. No, sir; I had not. There is also one of his first letters from the hotel in Russia that he pointed out to me that I didn't even know that he could write or speak Russian. He was being rather sarcastic in his first letters, and he pointed this out. I would answer it that I was not aware that he could speak or could write any foreign language when he was in the Marine Corps and after he got out of it.
Representative FORD. You had no prior knowledge that he was studying Russian or had become articulate in Russian?
Mr. OSWALD. No, sir; I did not.
Representative FORD. In your experiences with Lee during your lifetime, did he ever show a skill at language, for languages?
Mr. OSWALD. No, sir; I know of no time nor can I recall of any time that he studied any foreign language or in my presence that he even read a book in a foreign language or attempted to teach himself any type of foreign language.
[1WCH,318/319]

I start my argument by imaginatively reconstructing a very important and revealing meeting that actually took place[39], and which, to my mind, supplies an important clue to the Assassination.

So here is my reconstruction of this important meeting.

This is a meeting the world doesn't want to know about.

It is the summer of '59.

The scene is a cafeteria in Santa Anna, California.

If you believe, as I do, that the character of the alleged assassin can tell us as much about the Assassination as the medical and ballistic evidence, then this meeting is of supreme importance.

So, let's get back to it.

Sitting in the cafeteria is an extremely attractive and very ambitious Pan American World Airways stewardess.

Her ambitions are not, however, about the airline business: she is determinedly planning for a State Department career, and considers, given the cold war, that fluency in Russian to be the surest way of starting work in the State Department.

To this end she is planning to sit a State Department Russian language examination, and has been studying the language with extreme intensity for over a year under the guidance of a Berlitz tutor.

At the moment she is anxious because she is expecting to meet a very young marine (19/20).

There is all the anxiety of a first-time meeting.

No, its not romance.

TEN | A MAN OF UNUSUAL TRAINING: THE OSWALD ENIGMA

She wants to test her conversational Russian, and she is told that this young marine speaks Russian.

Then, to her relief, she spots a very young man – boy, really – anxiously entering the cafeteria. He seems only 17.

He looks nothing like a Marine. Too boyish. Too frail.

His eyes are rotating like a radar turret. He has spotted her. He couldn't miss her. She is so attractive She would be spotted at once even in a crowded room.

He moves directly towards her. He is very slim (about 130 lb), pale, with hazel/blue eyes; his height is medium (5" 8'), and his hair a medium brown.

His personality radiates an in-built tension. His face – boyish though it is – manifests a resolute character.

"Miss Rosaleen Quinn?"

"Yes". She replies. He looks relieved.

"I'm Lee Oswald – Henry's friend."

She beckons him to sit down. They each order a cup of coffee.

Here goes, she thinks. I must speak. I must use my Russian. No English small talk. Practising my Russian – that's what meeting is about. This is California, and I'm all the way from New York, partly for this meeting.

Summoning all her courage – she is frightened that her Russian will come out all wrong – she ventures in Russian an introductory remark.

He smiles sympathetically. He has obviously understood her. And answers her fluently in the language.

Her confidence floods back.

Thereafter they talk earnestly – for two hours – in Russian, comparing their ideas about life in the Soviet Union.

And a few days later they have another meeting. He takes her to see the film South Pacific. Then afterwards they go to a bar and talk for another two hours in Russian.

What do they make of each other? He likes her, wants to see more of her.

Her attitude is different. As a Russian speaker he is just what she needs. Although she had been studying Russian with a Berlitz tutor for more than a year, she found that this young marine had a far more confident command of the language than she did and could string entire sentences together without much hesitation.

Looking back, she could see that this schoolboy-Marine had three good points: He had genuine affection for the Russian language. He was intellectually curious, and perfectly happy to admit to what he didn't know, and one part of him – the intellectual part of him – seemed guileless.

But there was something off-putting about him. He was very guarded about himself – very unusual for anybody so young – and you can't make close friends with someone you can't get to know. Indeed, the youngster was so guarded about himself that he could not (would not) explain how he learnt Russian. She

JFK | ECHOES FROM ELM STREET
A SEARCH FOR HISTORICAL ACCURACY ON THE
ASSASSINATION OF PRESIDENT JOHN F. KENNEDY

felt if she met him a hundred times she would know no more about him than she did at their first meeting. He was really something of an oddball.

All this has been my imaginative reconstruction of the meeting based on the work of Epstein; the Warren Testimony of John Donovan; Rosaleen Quinn's statement to the FBI, and the affidavits of Oswald's Marine associates (in volume 8 of the Hearings).

Oh, just one thing: the young Marine she had met, whoever he was, he was not, in my opinion, Lee Oswald, that is, he was not Robert Oswald's kid brother Lee. He was obviously somebody else. Before I continue, I would like to emphasise a point.

The evidence for the belief that Robert Oswald's kid brother Lee was not the Russian-speaking man shot by Jack Ruby does NOT solely depend on the doppelgänger evidence of John Armstrong's "Harvey and Lee" (great though Armstrong's work is), but is contained in Commission Exhibit 2015 and in the abundantly supportive evidence contained in the Commission's Hearings. It should have been obvious decades ago that the man interrogated (allegedly for 12 hours) by the Dallas Police Department was not the Lee Oswald born in Alvar Street, New Orleans in October 39, but an immigrant of Baltic origin, using the Alvar Street identity, and therefore claiming to be Robert Oswald's kid brother.

What follows in this chapter will support this idea. I present my case in fourteen logical steps.

Step ONE
12 Important Points about Rosaleen Quinn
(1) Rosaleen Quinn was the '"extremely attractive" young aunt of acting Lance Corporal Henry Roussel.
(2) She lived in an apartment in New York
(3) Prior to the summer of '59, she had been a Pan American Airline stewardess for 7 years.
(4) At the time she met "Oswald", she was on a leave of absence from the airline.
(5) She was keen to have a career in the US State Department (hopefully at the Moscow Embassy), and to this end she had, for over a year, been doing a Berlitz course in Russian in preparation for her State Department examinations.
(6) She planned to spend a week in California, at a boarding house near where her nephew was stationed (Santa Ana). In her nephew's radar unit were two people who could advance her prospects:
(7) The first was a fellow marine called Lee Harvey Oswald. Her nephew had discovered that Oswald spoke Russian, and could therefore strengthen his aunt's conversational Russian.

The second was the radar unit's immediate commanding officer, First Lieutenant John E. Donovan, who as a Bachelor of Science Foreign Services

TEN | A MAN OF UNUSUAL TRAINING: THE OSWALD ENIGMA

graduate would have successfully covered a lot of the academic work facing Rosalen Quinn.
(8) The meeting took place in the summer of '59.
(9) On the 13th December, '64 Rosaleen Quinn was interviewed by Roger H. Lee of the FBI.[40]
(10) She told the FBI agent that the purpose of the meeting was "to practise speaking the language".
(11) Rosaleen Quinn was never interviewed by the Commission. Henry Roussel did supply a affidavit.(25/05/64; 8WCH, 320).
(12) Nor was she interviewed by any researcher until, in the late '70s, Epstein interviewed her for his forthcoming book "Legend" (1978), in which he devoted only half a page to her. Nonetheless what Epstein said was of decisive importance. Since Epstein, no researcher has contacted her .Nonetheless,. two years after Epstein's "Legend", while the Rosaleen Quinn affair still had a certain freshness, Anthony Summers ("The Kennedy Conspiracy", 1980) saw that the Rosaleen Quinn incident opened a "Pandora's box of nagging questions", but (strangely) he didn't pursue his insight. Since Summers, the incident has been dropped until 23 years later it was resurrected (but with no new research) by John Armstrong ("Harvey & Lee" 2003).

Step TWO
Some thoughts about the meeting
(1) FBI records say Henry Roussel joined the Marines in July '57.[41]
(2) Oswald's reputation as a Russian speaker must have been very widespread, for Henry Roussel knew of Oswald's accomplishment, despite the fact that there is evidence that he was a close friend.[42]
And, of course, this was the case. Erwin Donald Lewis, who as a marine served with Oswald at Santa Ana, told the Commission in an affidavit that it was "a matter of common knowledge among squadron members that Oswald could read, write and speak Russian". (8WCH, 323) Also another marine (James Anthony Botelho) told the Commission (again through an affidavit) that "It was common knowledge that Oswald had taught himself Russian." (8WCH, 315). Also John Donovan told the Commission (8WCHH, 292) that when he arrived at Santa Anna he quickly learnt that Oswald could read and speak Russian.
(4) However, Henry Roussel would not have arranged a 'linguistic' meeting between Oswald and his aunt had he not been certain that Oswald did in fact speak Russian to a high standard.
(5) To this end, he would surely have interrogated Oswald as to his actual ability, as opposed to his self-professed ability.
(6) Would Rosaleen Quinn have made the journey from her New York apartment to Santa Ana unless she was convinced that her nephew had correctly assessed Oswald's spoken Russian?

But it wasn't only Rosaleen Quinn who had a lot at stake; Oswald was obviously putting his reputation on the line. Of the 11 marines who served with Oswald who were asked to submit affidavits, 4 claimed that Oswald considered himself intelligent, and wanted to impress others of his intelligence.

(7) There are 3 probable reasons why Rosaleen Quinn would have agreed to the meeting:

(a) She probably felt she was due for a holiday, and a sunny week in California, where her nephew was stationed, seemed a good idea. (b) Her nephew's immediate commanding officer had a degree in foreign affairs, and his graduate studies would be a preparation for her State Department syllabus, and, decisively, (c), a Russian-speaking marine (Oswald) could give her invaluable practise in conversational Russian. In this respect, she probably had the same experience as Ruth Paine, that it was difficult to find anyone in America who spoke modern Russian[43] [WCH2,440].

(8) Similarly, there are three reasons why Oswald would have agreed to the meeting. (a) He was told that Miss Quinn was very attractive. (b) It would confirm to his mates his ability to speak Russian, and (c) it would give him an opportunity to speak the language. Dr Peter Paul Gregory told the Commission that Oswald lived in fear of losing his fluency in Russian. (WCH 2,342)

Step THREE

IF ROSALEEN QUINN IS TRUE, THEN LEE HARVEY OSWALD WAS <u>FLUENT IN RUSSIAN BEFORE THE AGE OF 20.</u>

This fact cannot be accommodated within Oswald's accepted biography.

Rosaleen Quinn was (and still is) a circular saw hitting a nail. Had she been asked to appear before the Commission, she would have jarred it to its foundations.

What she told John Donovan and Epstein – that Oswald was a fluent Russian speaker – collided with the Report.

In Oswald''s life, as told in the Report (twice), and as recounted by Bugliosi ("Reclaiming History"), Oswald was in August '59 struggling to learn the language, entirely self-taught.

The Report says that so great was the struggle that: "when Oswald reached the Soviet Union in October of the same year he could barely speak the language." [Report page 257]

This is a lie – not a mistake.

John Donovan[44], Oswald's immediate officer commanding. twice told the Commission in his May 5th('64) deposition (8WCH, 294/7) that Rosaleen Quinn told him that Oswald could speak Russian (meaning that he was fluent in the language before his defection).

[* Some information about John Donovan:

TEN | A MAN OF UNUSUAL TRAINING: THE OSWALD ENIGMA

(1) "Oswald" served on a radar crew, John Donovan, as a first lieutenant, was the officer in command of that crew.
(2) At the time he gave evidence to the Commission (5th May,'64), John Donovan was aged 29/30, and was teaching at a a high school, Ascension Academy, Alexandria.
(3) Before serving in the Marines he had a completed, in 1956, aged 21, a Bachelor of Science course (including) philosophy and theology) in foreign studies (BSFS) at the School of Foreign Service, Georgetown University.
(4) He joined the Marines on graduation, aged 21, and served for 39 months.
(5) After serving in Japan – Donovan never encountered Oswald there – he was posted as operations and training officer to Marine Air Control Squadron 9 at the helicopter and radar base at Santa Anna, arriving on the 1st.March, 1959.
(6) He was the senior first lieutenant on a radar cree of 3 officers (including himself) and 7 enlisted men.
(7) Amogst the enlisted men was "Oswald" – he'd been at Santa Anns since December 22nd,'58, and was to remain there until his transfer to H & H squadron on 4th September '59 (286 days).
(8) Donovan worked very closely with Oswald: every day, five days a week they were on the same radar shift.
(9) Also they had one big interest in common: international affairs."Oswald" was (or pretended to be) a marxist, and was fond of discoursing on the imperialism and capitalism, whilst Donovan had studied the 'science' of forein affairs.
(10) Of Oswald's 286 days of radar work at Santa Ana, Donovan was his close-contact supervisor for 248 of them (i.e. 87%).]

Step FOUR
Rosaleen Quinn has been totally ignored – her name not even mentioned – by the following biographers of Oswald, or writers concentrating on him:
(1) Priscilla Johnson McMillan,"Marina & Lee" (1978) 467 pages. Only passing references to Oswald's Russian. No mention of Rosaleen Quinn.
(2) Jean Davison, "Oswald's Game"(1983), 297 pages She virtually ignores the fact that Oswald spoke Russian. No mention of Rosaleen Quinn.
(3) Robert J. Groden, "The Search for Lee Harvey Oswald" (1995). No mention of Rosaleen Quinn.
 253 large pages. Assumes that Oswald was taught Russian by Naval ((or some other) intelligence No details.) No mention of Rosaleen Quinn.
(4) Norman Mailer,"Oswald's Tale" (1996), 791 pages. No account of how Oswald learnt Russian; nor are there any insights into how well Oswald spoke Russian. He fights shy of the topic. No mention of Rosaleen Quinn.
(5) FBI Agent James Hosty, "Assignment: Oswald", 1996. 328 pages. Hosty admits that Oswald could write in Russian (page 106), and since Marina could not speak English, the reader is left to conclude that Oswald must have been

fluent in the language. However, Hosty avoids any direct reference to Oswald's fluency or how he learnt the language.

(6) Diane Holloway, Ph.D, "The Mind of Oswald" (2000).Dr. Holloway believes that Oswald learnt Russian in a "matter of weeks", p 9. Need one say more! Surely, how Oswald learnt Russian would reflect his psychology. Yet Dr. Holloway marginalises the topic. No mention of Rosaleen Quinn.

(7) Vincent Bugliosi, "History Reclaimed: The Assassination of John F. Kennedy" (2007), 1518 pages. Oswald taught himself Russian in the Marines. A mere paragraph. (p 556). [See below] Marginalises the Quinn issue by:
(a) not mentioning her name (nor Roussel's) and (b) by grossly misrepresenting the episode. (p565). [See below]

Of Bugliosi's 1518 pages, 252 deal with Oswald's biography, and 16 (the chapter on his motivation for the assassination) focus on Oswald's psychology. This is a total of 278 pages (18/19)% of the book.

As I shall argue later, Bugliosi is of decisive importance in the two-Oswald question, not by what he says, nor by what he doesn't say, but by what he can't say [See below].

(8) Jack R Swike, "The Missing Chapter: Lee Harvey Oswald in the Far East", 2008, 268 pages. Mr Swike says (page 226) that Oswald did not start to learn Russian until after he arrived at Santa Ana, as he can find no evidence of any interest in the language whilst in the Far East. This is in contradiction to the Report (Report CD Section 111), which states that Oswald started to learn Russian whilst at Atsugi.

(9) Professor John Newman, "Oswald and the CIA", 2008, 664 pages. An excellent account of how the CIA worked and their possible relationship with Oswald, and the labyrinth of files they kept on him. Nonetheless the book is disappointing in that has nothing of significance to say about how Oswald and the Russian language, about how good his Russian was, and, above all, how he learnt the language, etc.

The total is just under 3,00 pages written on Lee Harvey Oswald. The total amount written in all these books on how Oswald learnt Russian would amount to no more than 50/60 words, or less than a quarter of a page.

Step FIVE

The Federal Services Institute (FSI) used to have a CIA backed website called "Languages of the World".[45]
This website states:

"Food for thought: Duration of language instruction in U.S. colleges and universities:
Compare the figures on the duration of instruction compiled by the U.S. Government agencies to the average number of class hours per year in a

Ten | A Man of Unusual Training: The Oswald Enigma

college language course. A typical college year is 9 months, or 36 weeks. A typical language course is 3-5 hours a week, or 108-180 hours per year plus preparation outside of class. It's no wonder that students who start a foreign language from scratch in college, rarely achieve higher levels of proficiency. Unless they have done significant language work in high school, they will need to supplement their college program with intensive summer schools and study abroad in order to achieve a high level of proficiency.

The inevitable conclusion is that one must begin the study of a foreign language as early as possible and pursue it for many years in order to achieve higher levels of proficiency."

The FSI is the Federal Governments primary institution for training officers and support personnel for the US foreign affairs community.

Their intensive one-year Russian course (designed for people in the 30/ 40 age group, who have already acquired proficiency in another foreign language) requires 25 hours a week of directed study, and 15 hours a week of self-directed study for 44 weeks a year.

That is (25 15) x 44 = 40 x 44 = 1760 hours. This would have been the type of course that Rosaleen Quinn undertook.

Clearly what the FSI had in mind was stable, mature people who had control over their lives.

But the poorly educated, teenage Oswald (18 changes of address, 13 changes of school and plenty of truanting) had to teach himself – no one to help him with difficult points of grammar, etc.,– so it would be reasonable to increase this figure by at least 50% – ie 2640 hours.

But the official view (strongly supported by Bugliosi) is that Oswald was heavily dyslexic (i.e. "word blind").This would have caused him considerable problems (verging on the impossible) in handling the Cyrillic alphabet. It would be reasonable to add at least another 50% to his 2640 hours, giving a minimum total of 3,960 hours.

Step SIX
Oswald enlisted in the Marines on 24th October, 1956 (5 days short of his 17th birthday), and started on his intensive training programme two days later (26th October). Oswald's training programme lasted 234 days, terminating on the 17th June, 1957.

During his 234 days of intensive training, Oswald was pushed to the limits – square bashing, weapons training, physical fitness, aircraft identification, and radar (theory and operation), for example.

And on the last two items he had to face a battery of examinations he would have had no time for anything other than Marine life.

However, from the 17th June, when his training was completed, Oswald (in theory) had a less intensive life, and, if he was going to teach himself Russian, his studies could have started then. In August he demonstrated to Rosaleen Quinn a strong command of Russian. The maximum time Oswald would have had to attain this command of the language would be from 17thJune, 1957 to 31st. August, 1959 (less 47 hard, exhausting, humiliating days (27.06.58/13.08.58) he spent in a military prison in Japan)– i.e. 758 days

Step SEVEN
A minimum of 3960 hours of study over a maximum of 758 days equates to an average of at least 5 hours and 13 minutes a day.

This is obviously an impossible achievement, and is not something that could pass unnoticed. The withdrawal from social life would have been widely commented upon. No such comments have been recorded.

Step EIGHT
The independent researches of Swike[46] and Epstein point to Oswald being full of distractions at Atsugi:
(1) Drinking to excess (Swike p 218;Epstein,p70);
(2) establishing communist contacts (Swike pages 17, 42/44, 213, 230; Epstein, p71);
(3) visiting areas outside the Atsugi Naval Air Station (Swike p 106; Epstein p71;79);
(4) visiting bars in the Chinatown section of Yokohama (Swike p 211;Epstein p70);
(5) engaging in substantial black-market activities (Swike p 42). The first four of these activities had been indicated by Epstein 30 years earlier. The fifth (the black-market activities) had not been noted by Epstein, and is new.

However, Epstein had noted two distractions which Swike did not research: firstly, that Oswald had a love affair with a Japanese bar hostess (Epstein, page 71). and, secondly (possibly in consequence) that he was studying the Japanese language.

This makes a total of at least 7 major distractions. How, amongst all these distractions, did Oswald find time for 5 hours study daily? There is no answer.

Step NINE
Epstein wrote: "Oswald would have had to have begun his training in Russian while he was still in Japan. None of his barrack-room mates, however, remember Oswald's using a linguaphone or records to learn Russian, which suggests that he had some private means." (ps 85/86).Oswald received private tuition. This is Epstein's solution. However it is open to several objections:
(a) Oswald, on his marine pay (<$85 monthly) could not have afforded private tuition.

TEN | A MAN OF UNUSUAL TRAINING: THE OSWALD ENIGMA

(b) Private tuition requires a control over one's time. Lessons cannot be given at a moment's notice; arrangements have to be made in advance. Oswald, living a controlled life, had no knowledge as to where and when he would be sent to next. Hence there could be no long-term planning of lessons. For example, the sudden posting of his unit to the Philippines in October '57. (Epstein 72/73)

(c) Whoever gave Oswald this private tuition would be putting into the task as many hours as Oswald himself. He (they) would– surely? – be well known to all Oswald's friends and associates. Yet no such person (or persons) has ever been identified.

(d) If such a person (or persons) existed, then he (or they) would certainly make their presence known: a book, possibly: "How I/We Taught Oswald Russian"

No such book has ever appeared. Why not? The author(s) would have had a unique opportunity to assess Oswald's character and intellectual prowess, and to commercialise their unique closeness to a Presidential assassin.

(e) If Edward Jay Epstein really believed in this private tuition theory, he would surely have investigated the matter?

Epstein was a highly competent and experienced investigative journalist. He searched out and interviewed Oswald's marine colleagues. Why would he have stopped with the person(s) who were so regularly closeted with Oswald in such a demanding and shared pursuit?

Twenty-seven years later John Armstrong conducted his own enquiries:"....... I gathered FBI, Warren Commission and HSCA interviews of Marines who had known and served with Oswald in Japan. I wanted to see if any of the marines who knew Oswald in Japan saw him with a Russian book, Russian records, or Russian reading materials. Not surprisingly no one remembered seeing Oswald study the Russian language in Japan, where he was stationed until November 1958."*(Website excerpt (page 7/21) from John Armstrong's "Harvey and Lee: How the CIA Framed Oswald" (2003). See www.jfkresearch.com/jfk.101htm).

Step ELEVEN

In view of this, Swike has had to admit (p 226), in contradiction to the Report, that Oswald didn't start to study Russian until he reached Santa Anna: Oswald left Japan on 2nd November, 1958, and was speaking fluently in Russian to Rosaleen Quinn by the end of August (latest), 1959. A maximum of 302 days, meaning that for Oswald to attain this fluency would require a minimum of (3960/302) hours a day – i.e. 13 hours – an impossibility.

[*As an officer serving at HQ Marine Air Group 11, Swike was not actually stationed with Oswald's part of the Air Group (Marine Air Squadron 1, MAC 1), nor was his service contemporaneous with Oswald's tour of duty: Swike left Japan a few months before Oswald arrived (in 1957).

It is worth noting that in addition to his intelligence work while a serving officer, Swike, on leaving the military, also worked for the counter-intelligence arm of the US government – hence his access (by correspondence) to James Angleton, the then CIA Counter Intelligence Director.

"Because [writes Swike, p 7] I served as an Intelligence Officer with MAG- 11, and was in charge of security and top secret materials, I took a personal interest in Oswald's military activities in the Far East after the Kennedy Assassination. I began my research in 1978 and will now make my findings public."(p 7) [THE MISSING CHAPTER: LEE HARVEY ODEALD IN THE MIDDLE EAST, self-published].

Disappointingly, Swike's book is more about the military, and political context in which Oswald (as an ordinary marine) worked, than about Oswald himself.

Moreover, having worked in counter-intelligence, Swike is over-reliant on official sources, seemingly confining himself to what officialdom can (is prepared?) to offer.

On the other hand, these official sources do provide him with some interesting documents, which are well worth studying. Swike is not concerned with arguing for the official view on Oswald's guilt; he simply assumes it. Nonetheless his orthodoxy is sufficiently flexible to allow for Oswald not to have acted on his own (p 230)].

Step TWELVE
Oswald and the Russian language
Consider the following facts:
(1) Oswald's Russian was ungrammatical, and he spoke with a marked accent (possibly Polish) [WCH 9, 149; 2WCH,347]. His marked accent – equivalent to (say) a Glaswegian speaking English – suggests that he was neither taught Russian by the CIA, nor did he learn the language whilst in Minsk.
(2) Not even one person has ever come forward to say that Oswald, whilst teaching himself Russian, asked him/her for help.
(3) Oswald never told anybody how he learnt Russian, not even his brother (1WCH, 319) and avoided any questions on the topic (Epstein p87; 11WCH, 456).
(4) Every comment made on Oswald's Russian refers to his conversational fluency. Whatever Oswald wanted to say he could put it quickly into Russian.
(5) Whatever was said to him in Russian, his understanding was immediate (9WCH, 149).
(6) He could translate from Russian into English accurately and with immediate ease. (2WCH, 338)
(7) There has never been any agreement (because no serious discussion) as to how any of this was possible.

Step THIRTEEN
A quick canter through these twelve steps leads to three conclusions:

Ten | A Man of Unusual Training: The Oswald Enigma

(A) Oswald spoke Russian fluently – for two double-hour sessions with Rosaleen Quinn – before he was 20, and 46 days before he defected.
(B) No biographer of Oswald wants to admit this.
However, Oswald could not possibly have taught himself (the Commission's view) because:
He was (1) a poorly educated truant, (2) a teenager, (3) heavily dyslexic, with (4) an unstable background (effectively no father, 13 changes of school).
Dyslexic, and working entirely on his own, Oswald did not have the 3960 hours of time minimally required.
(C) Nobody in Japan (where Oswald must have laid the foundation of his studies) knew of Oswald studying Russian, nor was he ever withdrawn from normal duties. No one in the past 50 years has admitted to giving him help in his Russian studies.
To add further support to this part of my chapter, I supply, firstly, a critique of Bugliosi in his treatment of the Rosaleen Quinn evidence, and, secondly, an account of how the Warren Commission were confronted with the evidence of Oswald's ability to speak Russian, all of which they ignored.

A Critique of Bugliosi

The Report had nothing to say on how Oswald learnt Russian from scratch. It acknowledged the suspicion that Oswald was officially (but secretly) taught Russian, but unequivocally denied such a claim, and with equal emphasis asserted that Oswald taught himself Russian, entirely on his own initiative, and without assistance of any sort [Report page 656]. Oswald, the Report asserted, could barely speak the language when he defected (as would be expected from a solo effort). [Report page 257]

However, there are four very severe problems with this approach, problems that Bugliosi should have been able to solve, but, as we shall see, failed to do so.

Here are the four problems:

(1) As we've been pointing out, nobody knows anybody who, whilst Oswald was in the Far East, saw (or knew) he was studying Russian, nor does he seem to have had the time.

(2) Other than a two-way Russian/English dictionary (which Oswald gave Dr. Peter Paul Gregory as a keepsake), no Russian self-instruction material associated with Oswald was (or has) ever been found, and the FBI – strangely – conducted no search.

(3) The Commission accepted, in its Exhibit 2015, that Rosaleen Quinn met Oswald to "PRACTISE SPEAKING THE LANGUAGE".

However this completely contradicts the Commission' assertion (through its Report) that Oswald could "barely speak the language"

(4) Oswald was depicted in the Report (it was echoed by Bugliosi) as having had only a very mediocre education, and, in consequence, deficient

in intellectual training, and, in addition, an unstable, nitroglycerin character, and in consequence undisciplined, and doomed to failure. Such a person could never have mastered on their own, a difficult foreign language.

Bugliosi's "Reclaiming History" was published 43 years after the Report, and one would have thought that in this lengthy interval, research would have established how Oswald, living in a goldfish bowl, studied Russian from zero.

After all, whereas ordinary researchers in contacting official America find themselves swimming in treacle, Bugliosi, writing the supposedly definitive official version, was, by comparison, paddling in calm, clear and shallow waters. He had ready, easy and friendly to the FBI, CIA, Dallas Police, army and Marine records – indeed, to all America's information and intelligence agencies.

Disappointingly (and surprisingly) he comes up with nothing.

This is what Bugliosi says. It's pitifully disappointing:

"It was clear to all his mates [at Santa Ana] that Oswald was now concentrating on learning Russian – he would sit in his room for hours on end poring over Russian newspapers bought in Los Angeles and a Russian English dictionary. (Source Note 351; page 359)

Source Note 351 (Bugliosi's only source of information) reads as follows:
From the Affidavit of Mack Osborne

"I, Mack Osborne, 2816 43rd Street, Lubbock, Texas, being first duly sworn, depose and say:

That while I was in the United States Marine Corps, I served in Marine Air Control Squadron 9 in Santa Ann, California, with Lee Harvey Oswald. Prior to his discharge, I shared a room with him.

Oswald was at that time studying Russian. He spent a great deal of his free time reading papers printed in Russian–which I believe he bought in Los Angeles–with the aid of a Russian-English dictionary. I believe he also had some books written in Russian, although I do not remember their names. (53 words)

Executed May 18th, 1964"

These 53 word were (and still are) the sole source of knowledge available on how Oswald learned to speak Russian with a (regional) accent.

Bugliosi's Errors of Commission

If it is believed that the false identity "Lee Oswald" was 'manufactured' and disseminated by the CIA, as part of a cover-up, then by logic it must be accepted that the power behind the Assassination was the intelligence arm of the US government.

And it is because the implications of Rosaleen Quinn's evidence supports (if not leads to) this conclusion. that Bugliosi doesn't mention Epstein's interview. He daren't. If he did, then a 1510 page book would go down the toilet.

The total dishonesty of Bugliosi's treatment of the Rosaleen Quinn/Epstein interview is exhibited in what he writes:

TEN | A MAN OF UNUSUAL TRAINING: THE OSWALD ENIGMA

"…..two dates in Santa Ana that had been arranged by a squad mate who thought that Oswald would like to meet his attractive aunt, an airline stewardess who was studying Russian preparing for a US Department of State foreign language test,(390) ….. "(p 565)
This is, of course, totally dishonest: involving a sin of commission and one of omission. [Epstein, Legend, p.87; WC affidavit of Henry J. Roussel 8 WCH, 321]

Bugliosi states authoritatively that the meeting was arranged for Oswald's benefit, largely because Rosaleen Quinn was "attractive". But this goes against the evidence.
As I have said, the "squad mate" (the Marine Henry J. Roussel, jnr) was not a close friend of Oswald, from which it follows that any meeting would have been arranged not for Oswald's benefit, but for the advantage of his aunt.
It is difficult to see why Rosaleen Quinn would have agreed to a meeting unless it was to her advantage, and if she was "attractive", she would have had no need to involve herself with a marine unknown not only to herself, but probably, in any deep sense, to her nephew also.
Rosaleen Quinn told the FBI that the purpose of the meeting was to have an "opportunity to practise speaking the language" (CE 2015) – not, as Bugliosi implies, to provide Oswald with "attractive" company.

Bugliosi's Major Error of Omission
Bugliosi's treatment is a disgrace because he doesn't mention Epstein's interview with Rosaleen Quinn, despite the fact that he quotes from Epstein 8 times. Rosaleen Quinn's assertion that Oswald was fluent in Russian blew the traditional view of Oswald out of the water.

The Warren Commission's Confrontations with Oswald's Ability to speak Russian
Here is a time-sheet showing how, as the Hearings progressed, the Commission were increasingly confronted by the mystery of Oswald's ability to speak Russian fluently.
  5th February (1,59): Marina Oswald told the Commission that when she and Oswald met they chatted endlessly about everything under the sun. Such a width of conversation would only be possible if Oswald was very fluent in the language (1WCH, 92). Hence the Commission, right at the outset, was confronted by Oswald's competence in Russian.
  (b) On the 10th February, Oswald's mother told the Commission that Lee's love of Russian more or less obliged her to apply for admission to Dr Peter Paul Gregory's Fort Worth Russian class,
  (c) 20th February (1,264): Robert Oswald told the Commission that he had no idea how or when his brother Lee learnt Russian, and in answer to a question

from Representative Gerald Ford, he said that Lee, while at school, had never shown any interest in languages. (1,319)

(d) 13th March (2,295).Dr Peter Paul Gregory told the Commission that in June 63, he had made Oswald an official translator/interpreter for the County of Dallas.

Dr Gregory was a consulting petroleum engineer and part-time Russian instructor at the Fort Worth Public Library.

He was Siberian by birth, and avoided the Revolution by moving to Japan, where at the American school in Tokyo he learnt English.

He came to the USA in 1923, and studied at the University of California at Berkeley.

He was a leading member of the Russian-speaking Dallas community.

Following the assassination, Dr Peter Gregory was Marina Oswald's initial translator during her interrogation by the Secret Service.

He told the Commission three things:

(A) That he did not think that Oswald's fluency in the language could be accounted for by his stay in Russia[47].

(B) That Oswald spoke Russian with a heavy accent, which Dr Gregory penciled in as polish.

(C) That Oswald's ability to read Russian was as fluent as his ability to speak the language. (WCH2, 338)

On the 18th March, Mrs. Ruth Paine (landlady to the Oswalds) told the Commission three important things. Firstly, that that Oswald was so fond of the Russian language that he spoke to his 6 year-old daughter only in Russian. (WCH2, 446)

Secondly, that Oswald preferred speaking Russian rather than English. And, thirdly (by implication) that despite her years of tutor-directed study, she was not up to Oswald's standard. (WCH2, 458)

(e) 25th March(WCH 8,379,415). Mrs. Anna Meller, and Mrs. Frank (Valetina) Ray, both Russian ladies married to Dallas Americans, echoed what Peter Paul Gregory had told the Commission nearly a fortnight before: like him, they did not believe that Oswald's Russian fluency could be accounted for by his 3 years in the Soviet Union. (WCH8,382,421)

Mrs. Valetina Ray told the Commission that Oswald spoke Russian to baby June. (WCH8, 422)

Also questioned on this date (WCH9,27) was Mrs. Thomas (Natalie) Ray. She was strongly convinced that Oswald's Russian was too strong to be explained by his Russian sojourn (WCH9, 31).

(f) 31st March (WCH9, 141): Paul Roderick Gregory, the son of Peter Paul Gregory, and like his father, a prominent member of the Fort Worth Dallas community, who (again, like his father) knew Oswald well, testified that he was studying Russian at Oklahoma university. He told the Commission (WCH9,

TEN | A MAN OF UNUSUAL TRAINING: THE OSWALD ENIGMA

149) that Oswald's Russian was often ungrammatical, "poorly spoken"(i.e. with a strong accent), but very fluent

(g) On the 22nd April, De Mohrenschildt supported Paul Gregory's assessment of Oswald's Russian ("foreign accent, made mistakes, especially grammatical ones "), but, like Paul Gregory, he emphasized Oswald's" remarkable fluency" He also remarked (in agreement with Mrs. Paine) on Oswald's preference for Russian over English.(WCH9,226)

(h) On the 5th of May (WCH8, 289), John E. Donovan, who was in charge of Oswald's radar unit, and his immediate commanding officer, told the Commission, firstly, that when he took up his position on Oswald's radar unit, he quickly learned that Oswald had a reputation among the radar crew of being fluent in Russian (WCH8, 292), and, secondly, he twice told the Commission that Rosaleen Quinn told him that Oswald could speak Russian (WCH8, 293,297). Since the Rosaline Quinn meeting took place well before Oswald's 20th birthday and therefore well before his defection to the Soviet Union, it follows that Donovan was indirectly telling the Commission that Oswald's Russian fluency could not be attributed to his stay in that country.

(i) On the 13th May the Commission was informed by Lt.Col Folsom that while in the Marines (in Santa Ana, California) Oswald had undergone a Russian-proficiency test.

Lt.Col A.G.Folsom, when he testified to the Commission, was in his fourth year as the Head of the Records Branch, Personnel Department, Headquarters, US Marine Corps, Washington, DC. He gave the Commission (through its lawyer, Mr. John Ely) details of all Oswald's Marine tests, etc. Included in this list was something totally unexpected: results for a Russian proficiency test in which Oswald' s scores approached 50%. Three very peculiar features:

(1) Lt. Col Folsom never explained (and Mr. Ely never enquired) why, seemingly out of the blue, Oswald, a mere private who had been busted from Private First Class, was given a Russian language test.

(2) Lt. Colonel Folsom never vouchsafed (because Mr. Ely never prompted) how Oswald learnt the Russian he was tested on.

(3) Bewilderment at the incuriosity of Mr. Ely doubles when one knows that he was assigned to help Warren staffers Albert E. Jenner and Wesley Liebeler in their research into Oswald's life! Incredible though it may seem Mr. Ely was Oswald's "Boswell"!

(j) On the 28th May (WCH11,123), Mrs. Donald Gibson, a 20/21 year old Russian wife of an American (and De Mohrenschildt's daughter) supported Mrs. Valetina Ray's statement that Oswald even spoke Russian to his baby. When Oswald spoke English, she described this to the Commission as "lapsing into English".

(k) On the 25th July (WCH11,442), Priscilla Mary Post Johnson, a journalist who had known Oswald as a defector and who, 14 years later, was to be the authoress of "Lee and Marina ", told the Commission that Oswald was tight lipped about how he learnt Russian, something she could never understand (WCH11,456).

Conclusion

The conclusion seems obvious: firstly, Oswald was an instrument of US intelligence, and, secondly, as John Armstrong has always argued, there must have been two "Oswalds": the one born in Alvar Street, New Orleans in 1939, and another "Oswald" who was a fluent Russian speaker. These two "dots" seem well established, even though one may not agree (as I don't) with the way John Armstrong links them.

In order to present these two people as one individual, and for the Russian speaking Oswald to pass himself off successfully as the New Orleans Marine, a massive amount of fabrication must have been involved.

This extensive fabrication –sustained by the creation of so many false documents and the destruction of so much genuine evidence – probably explains why Lee Harvey Oswald of orthodox belief comes across as such a mysterious person. The answer to the Oswald enigma is possibly that Oswald never existed as an actual person. He was, in large part, a CIA creation.

Endnotes

All the Warren Commission material used in this chapter can be accessed straightforwardly on the internet. Witness depositions can be found at jfkassassination.net/russ/wit.htm, and the full range of Commission Exhibits can be found at history-matters.com/archive/contents.htm

[1] De Moreschildt, who possibly knew Oswald better than anybody else, wrote in his memoir of Oswald ("I Am A Patsy! I am A Patsy!", 1976 that Lee actually admired President Kennedy in his own reserved way. One day we (De Morenschildt and his wife) discussed with Lee, Kennedy's efforts to bring peace to the world and to end the cold war. "Great, great!" Exclaimed Lee. "If he succeeds, he will be the greatest president in the history of this country." "Talking to Lee was a balm for his raw nerves, a sincere conversation calmed him down and it wasn't bad for me either. Fortunately I remember well so much of what he said. I remember distinctly that one of those evenings together we talked of John F. Kennedy. Lee liked him and certainly did not include him among those despicable politicians he mentioned before. I showed him President's picture of the cover of Time Magazine and Lee said -"How handsome he looks, what open and sincere features he has and how different he looks from the other ratty politicians. I don't remember exactly the words but Lee spoke most kindly of the gradual improvement of the racial relations in the United States, attributing this improvement to the President. Like most young people he was attracted by the Kennedy's personality but he also knew that JFK's father was a rascal who made money off whisky and being bullish on the stock-market which is betting against this country's economy".

[2] WC stands for the Warren Commission set of 26 volumes; the first of the two figures is the volume number; the last figure is the page number.

[3] All the facts I'm going to mention can be found in pages 30/35 of the 1966 Bantam (paperback) edition of Edgar Jay Epstein's book "Inquest", his controversial enquiry into the Warren Commission. Epstein was one of the first journalists to look at the Warren Commission wih a critical eye. Note! The opinions expressed and the linkage of facts come not from Epstein, but from me.

[4] The information I use comes from the Lee Harvey Oswald Timeline on http://mcadams.posc.mu.edu/parnell/chrono.htm. My calculations are done using a Hewlett Packard 19b calculator which

Ten | A Man of Unusual Training: The Oswald Enigma

has a day-count facility.
5. Released November 30, 1963. Dated November 29, 1963
6. Notice that the Executive Order refers to Oswald not as the assassin, but objectively as merely the man "charged" with the President's murder, therefore nominally giving the Commission an Investigative function. However, as my number crunching shows, this objectivity was merely a veneer.
7. 45% of this total comes from the 47 people who knew Oswald from schooldays, from early employment days, and from his period in the Marines; 38% comes from his wife, Marina, and the 7 members of his immediate family, and 17% comes from the 16 members of the Fort Worth Russian community who supplied their assessments of Oswald.
8. "Passport to Assassination", by KGB Colonel Oleg Maximovich Nechiporenko, Carol Publishing Group 1993, p 106].
9. 7H, 61 WCT of Detective Gerald Hill, one of the arresting officers.
10. http://www.city-data.com/forum/history/198980-news-lawmen-lee-harvey-oswalds-side.htmli David Flhick, Dallas Morning News 22 Nov. 2
11. WC 5, 240, WC testimony of Will Fritz.
12. The book referred to is "Legend: The Secret World of Lee Harvey Oswald", Arrow Books Ltd, 1978.
13. [Norman Mailer, "Oswald's Tale: An American Mystery", Random House 1995. UK editionm, Little Brown & Company", 1995. See p 43.UK edition. Rimma Shirakova said this 34 years later to either Mailer or one of his researchers.
14. http://forums.interbasket.net/showthread.php?9287-Average-Male-Height-By-Country-Updated-(official-data)Scientific-research.
15. The facts in this survey were suggested by an analysis from Michael Eddowes which he included (as Chapter 7) in his book "November 22: "How They Killed Kennedy", published by Neville Spearman (Jersey Ltd) in 1976. Eddowes used his analysis to support his theory that the Oswald who returned from Russia was a Russian imposter. One of his leading arguments was Oswald's fluency in Russian on his return from the Soviet Union.]
16. Commander Folsom was in charge of Marine personnel records. He was in charge of all Oswald's marine records.
17. John Armstrong, "Harvey and Lee: How the CIA Framed Oswald", Quasar Ltd., Arlington, Texas, 2003.
18. This chapter will include plenty of evidence that Oswald was working for US intelligence. Two websites which give good arguments for Oswald's intelligence connection are:
"Harvey Oswald---a U.S. Intelligence Agent: The Evidence"
(http://www.acorn.net/jfkplace/09/fp.back_issues/07th_Issue/copa_lho.html), and "JFK Assassination: The Oswald-CIA Connection"
(http://www.trutv.com/conspiracy/assassinations/jfk-oswald-cia/marines-defection-marriage.html) Also a very easy-to-follow discussion can be found in the article on Lee Harvey Oswald in "Who's Who in the Kennedy Assassination" by Michael Benson, Carol Publishing Group, 1993.
19. The wrist cutting has often been treated as hysterical. However it served its purpose: it not only prevented Oswald from being sent home immediately, but got him a job at a radio factory
(admittedly far away in Minsk, and gave the opportunity of an indefinite stay in the country whose politics and people he professed to love.
20. Richard Snyder was a CIA agent (joined June 1949) who worked under State Department cover. His previous posting was in Tokyo [Epstein, op.cit,. page 94.
21. Thirty-five years later (1998),Researcher David Reitzes heard from Professor Kurtz (in an interview) that George Higginbottom, Kurtz's fellow student back in '63, had told Professor Kurtz that Banister made a second visit to the university. [http:/http://www.whokilledjfk.net/dave_reitzes.htm]
22. Here is an extract: In the federal government, President Harry Truman's Executive Order 9835
initiated a program of loyalty reviews for federal employees in 1947. It called for dismissal if there were "reasonable grounds...for belief that the person involved is disloyal to the Government of the United States.Truman, a Democrat, was probably reacting in part to the Republican sweep in the 1946 Congressional election and felt a need to counter growing criticism from conservatives and anti-communists. When President Dwight Eisenhower took office in 1953, he strengthened and
extended Truman's loyalty review program, while decreasing the avenues of appeal available to

JFK | ECHOES FROM ELM STREET
A SEARCH FOR HISTORICAL ACCURACY ON THE
ASSASSINATION OF PRESIDENT JOHN F. KENNEDY

dismissed employees. Hiram Bingham, Chairman of the Civil Service Commission Loyalty Review Board, referred to the new rules he was obliged to enforce as "just not the American way of doing things." The following year, J. Robert Oppenheimer, scientific director of the Manhattan Project that built the first atomic bomb, then working as a consultant to the Atomic Energy Commission, was stripped of his security clearance after a four-week hearing. Oppenheimer had received a top-secret clearance in 1947, but was denied clearance in the harsher climate of 1954.

Similar loyalty reviews were established in many state and local government offices and some private industries across the nation. In 1958 it was estimated that roughly one out of every five employees in the United States was required to pass some sort of loyalty review.] Once a person lost a job due to an unfavorable loyalty review, it could be very difficult to find other employment. "A man is ruined everywhere and forever," in the words of the chairman of President Truman's Loyalty Review Board. "No responsible employer would be likely to take a chance in giving him a job."

[23.] See Rufus Youngblood, the Secret Service agent assigned to Johnson, in his 1973 book "Twenty Years in the Secret Service", p 121.

[24.] This is a quotation from Steven M. Gillon, "The Kennedy Assassination, 24 hours After"(2009), Footnote 27, Chapter 6, quoting a Newsweek (22.11.'93) article by Evan Thomas; also an interview published in Washington Mutual news agency, given by George Ball (the then Under Secretary of State on April 10th 1964.

[25.] Vincent Bugliosi is the leading defender of the Warren Commission orthodoxy. His 1 510-page book, "The Reclaiming History: The Assassination of President John F. Kennedy", complete with Source Notes and Endnotes on a CD) was published in 2007 by W.W. Norton & Company, New York. In the same year the publishers brought a paperback abridgement called "Four Days in November".

[26.] Neither William Manchester nor Steven Gillon make any mention of President Johnson contacting the National Command Centre, the White House Situation Room, or any of the joint Chiefs of Staff, etc.]

[27.] JFK researcher Russ Burr* some time in 1995/7 interviewed Jim Leavelle, the Dallas homicide officer who was in charge of the Tippit case. Leavelle told him that Oswald, immediately on his arrival at Dallas police HQ (2:15 p.m), "was suspected of having a possible hand in the President's murder". [*http://www.jfklancer.com/pdf/DidOTalk.pdf]

[28.] While allegedly trying to escape justice, Oswald is alleged to have shot dead a patrolman (J.D. Tippit). Dale K. Myers' 1998 book ("With Malice: Lee Harvey Oswald and the murder of Officer J.D. Tippit", Oak Cliff Press) strongly defends these charges.

[29.] Church Committee: Book V - The Investigation of the p 27. endnote 14] Assassination of President John F. Kennedy: Performance of the Intelligence Agencies pages 38, 39 ,40. The upper-case and the exclamation mark are mine.

[30.] Bugliosi, especially in his coverage of Oswald's interrogation, somewhat fictionalises his data. He has, admittedly done a great service to JFK research by thoroughly examining all the Commission testimonies and documents in search of interrogational material. However, for all his hard work, Bugliosi comes up with a meagre 190 questions, which he imaginatively recasts in the form of a dramatic script, complete with descriptions of imagined body language. Unfortunately, Oswald's interrogation is not dealt with as a complete topic in itself, but is fragmented throughout the book as the presentation is unremittingly chronological. This fragmentation by reducing the impact of what was happening (or not happening) hides the feebleness of Will Fritz's interrogation.

[31.] Bugliosi ps 130 and 263. Commission records: CE 832(17H, 786): CE 2064 (24H, 491), 7H, 302/6]

[32.] "Crime of the Century", by Professor Michael Kirtz (1982): the Cuban Connection (xiii-xiv). Professor Kurtz outlines how he thinks elements in the CIA and the Mafia possibly linked up to assassinate Kennedy.

[33.] Bugliosi, Reclaiming History, p 177]

[34.] Dale Myers, op.cit., p 27.and endnote 14

[35.] Dale Myers, op. Cit., reproduces, on page 579, the FBI Report detailing contact between Dallas FBI Special Agent in Charge, Gordon Shanklin, and FBI Assistant Director, Alan Belmont. The memorandum was dated 22/11/63, and timed at 8.18 pm (CST)] The FBI memorandum stated:

"In view of the fact a number of leads are developing in Dallas and it is necessary to conduct numerous interviews at once, I told Shanklin we would send an additional 20 agents, four stenographers and ten

Ten | A Man of Unusual Training: The Oswald Enigma

cars. The administrative division is handling this tonight."

[36] http://jfk-archives.blogspot.com/2011/03/oswalds-patsy-lie.html.

[37] "Margrave of the Marshes" by John Peel and Sheila Ravenscroft, Corgi Books, 2006, p 253.

[38] Paul Gregory was Dr.Peter Gregory's son, and, at the time of his testimony, he was a first-year graduate student, studying Russian Language and Literature at Oklahoma university.

[39] My reconstruction is based on what the investigative journalist Edward Jay Epstein claimed Rosaleen Quinn told him in a personal interview. The account is found on page 87 of the 1978 Arrow paperback edition of Epstein's "Legend: The Secret World of Lee Harvey Oswald". Also I have taken information from two more sources:the Warren Commission Testimony of John Donovan (WCH 8,
293,297) who knew both Oswald and Rosaleen Quinn, and CE 2015 (volume 24), which describes the FBI interview with Rosaleen Quinn.

[40] FBI File Reference: NY 105-38431; the FBI document appears in the Warren Commission exhibits as CE 2015.

[41] FBI 105-82555 Oswald HQ File Section 38, p 44]

[42] FBI 105-82555. Oswald HQ File Section 53, p 248]

[43] According to FBI Agent James Hosty, in his 1996 book "Assignment Oswald", of the 300 Secret Service agents at the time of the Assassination, only one could read Russian (page 106), and for him Russian was a second language (page 90).]

[44] Some information about John Donovan: "Oswald" served on a radar crew, John Donovan, as a first lieutenant, was the officer in command of that crew. At the time he gave evidence to the Commission (5th May,'64), John Donovan was aged 29/30, and was teaching at a a high school, Ascension Academy, Alexandria. Before serving in the Marines he had a completed, in 1956, aged 21, a Bachelor of Science course (including) philosophy and theology) in foreign studies (BSFS) at the School of Foreign Service, Georgetown University. He joined the Marines on graduation, aged 21, and served for 39 months.
After serving in Japan – Donovan never encountered Oswald there – he was posted as operations and training officer to Marine Air Control Squadron 9 at the helicopter and radar base at Santa Anna, arriving on the 1st March, 1959. He was the senior first lieutenant on a radar crew of 3 officers (including himself) and 7 enlisted men. Amongst the enlisted men was "Oswald" – he'd been at Santa Anns since December 22nd, 1958, and was to remain there until his transfer to H & H squadron on 4th. September 1959 (286 days). Donovan worked very closely with Oswald: every day, five days a week they were on the same radar shift. Also they had one big interest in common: international affairs."Oswald" was (or pretended to be) a Marxist, and was fond of discoursing on the imperialism and capitalism, whilst Donovan had studied the 'science' of forein affairs. Of Oswald's 286 days of radar work at Santa Ana, Donovan was his close-contact supervisor for 248 of them (ie 87%).]

[45] The website was closed down, but the information it contained is now reproduced in the website "About the Languages of the World" [http://www.aboutworldlanguages.com/LanguageDifficulty.

[46] As an officer serving at HQ Marine Air Group 11, Swike was not actually stationed with Oswald's part of the Air Group (Marine Air Squadron 1, MAC 1), nor was his service contemporaneous with Oswald's tour of duty: Swike left Japan a few months before Oswald arrived (in 1957). It is worth noting that in addition to his intelligence work while a serving officer, Swike, on leaving the military, also worked for the counter-intelligence.

[47] Residence in a country does not ensure fluency in its language. Two very relevant examples:
Marina Oswald, could not speak English at the time of the Hearings, some 20 months after her arrival in America. Mrs. Natalie Ray (a Russian with an American husband; see later) on being questioned by the Commission, had difficulty speaking English despite 20 years' American residence].

JFK | Echoes From Elm Street
A Search for Historical Accuracy on the Assassination of President John F. Kennedy

Eleven
The Autopsy of John F. Kennedy

Russell Kent

> *"There are risks and costs to a program of action, but they are far less than the long-range risks and costs of comfortable inaction."*
> – John F. Kennedy

Military autopsy number A63-272 was performed on the evening of Friday 22nd November 1963 in the morgue of the Bethesda Naval Hospital in Washington D.C. on the body of President John Fitzgerald Kennedy. The autopsy pathologists (or prosectors) were led by US Navy Commander James Joseph Humes MD. His assistant was US Navy Commander J Thornton Boswell MD. US Army Lieutenant Colonel Pierre Antoine Finck MD was called as a consultant. They may have been some of the most senior autopsy pathologists available, but they were far from the best.

Both Dr Humes and Dr Boswell were anatomic pathologists not specifically experienced in forensic pathology. In other words, neither was qualified to perform a medicolegal autopsy which is required in the case of a homicide. Humes told the Warren Commission where his experience lay:

"My type of practice, which fortunately has been in peacetime endeavour to a great extent, has been more extensive in the field of natural disease than violence. However, on several occasions in various places where I have been employed, I have had to deal with violent death, accidents, suicides, and so forth. Also I have had training at the Armed Forces Institute of Pathology, I have completed a course in forensic pathology there as part of my training in the overall field of pathology."[1]

Humes's training in forensic pathology was a one-week course completed ten years before the President's autopsy (he remembered it because it snowed)[2]. Not only was Humes inexperienced with medicolegal autopsies, he was at that time a senior administrator rather than an active pathologist. As he explained to the Warren Commission:

"My current title is Director of Laboratories of the Naval Medical School at Naval Medical Center at Bethesda. I am charged with the responsibility of the overall supervision of all of the laboratory operations in the Naval Medical Center..."[3]

Dr James Joseph Humes

Boswell was Chief of Pathology at the National Naval Medical School. He too was at that time a senior administrator rather than an active pathologist. He had time between desk duties to do unauthorised work for Suburban Hospital.[4]

Dr J Thornton Boswell

Dr Finck was a qualified forensic pathologist. He was Chief of the Wound Ballistic Pathology Branch and the Director of the Armed Forces Institute of Pathology. There were, however, two reasons why Finck was not the best man for the job of consultant forensic pathologist to the President's autopsy. Firstly he was no longer in practice: He too was a senior administrator and had not performed an autopsy on a gunshot victim for five years. Secondly, he was a US Army doctor in a US Navy morgue full of officers that out-ranked him and intimidated him. As Finck himself stated, "Oh, yes, there were admirals, and when you are a lieutenant colonel in the U.S. Army you just follow orders..."[5]

Dr Pierre Antoine Finck

Critically, Finck was not present for the beginning of the President's autopsy. Humes testified that the President's body arrived at 19:35 and that autopsy began at 20:00, but that some X-rays and other examinations had been made previous to that time[6]. Sometime between 19:35 and 20:00, Humes requested Finck to join the team at Bethesda[7]. Finck reported that he arrived at Bethesda at 20:30[8]. But it may not have been until 21:15 that he actually *entered* the morgue to begin assisting Humes and Boswell[9]. Humes told the Assassination Records Review Board (ARRB): "Pierre had a terrible time, incidentally, getting into the place because the Marines were not about to let this Army guy come in that night"[10].

Over the years, the autopsy doctors have been questioned several times about their actions that night. Humes always took a superior tone – he often appeared to be quite angry. Boswell was the "me too" doctor during both the Warren Commission and HSCA investigations – he simply agreed with what Humes said. Finck, however, was left to flounder.

The Unenviable Position of Finck
I believe that Finck was in an unenviable position when he finally gained access to the Bethesda morgue. As a forensic pathologist he knew that a specific procedure is required to gather, record and interpret evidence. That procedure would begin by examining the surface of the body[11] and then proceed in a methodical way with specific dissections, weighing of organs and so on.

However, when he arrived, JFK's brain had been removed and his chest had been eviscerated[12]. Even the nature of JFK's back wound had been compromised by Humes who had stuck his finger into it (possibly enlarging it and pushing its margin inwards)[13]. Put simply, it was no longer possible for Finck to apply his specialist training to this autopsy.

Finck and the Warren Commission
Finck's Warren Commission testimony was taken by Assistant Counsel Arlen Specter immediately after that of Humes and Boswell on March 16th 1964. He brought with him a teaching aid to show "coning" as a result of a bullet going through the skull[14]. Using this and Commission Exhibit 388 (the Rydberg drawing of JFK's head wound), Finck characterised the wound in the back of JFK's head as an entrance wound. There are several reasons to believe that this was not the whole truth:
- This wound was not seen by anyone (including all the Parkland doctors) before JFK arrived at Bethesda.
- Despite specifically requiring an autopsy photograph, there is no photograph clearly showing this wound.
- During testimony to the House Select Committee on Assassinations (HSCA), Humes identified the wound in Kennedy's scalp in two different locations: Once in the "hairline"[15] and once 10cm higher in the "cowlick"[16].
- Sometimes the wound was described by an autopsy doctor as being a complete hole in the occipital bone. In other testimony, however, they described how the hole could not be seen until skull fragments were delivered to the autopsy room – in other words there were only parts of a hole visible.

If Finck really believed that there was an entrance wound in the back of Kennedy's head, he would have looked specifically for additional evidence such as friction burning of the skin on the edges of the wound. But, when Finck was asked whether any other characteristics (apart from the "coning") would show this wound to be an entrance, he answered "No".[17]

In the Supplementary Autopsy Report, however, Humes describes "coagulation necrosis of the tissues at the wound margins"[18] which *is* characteristic of an entrance wound. Humes though is the only one of the pathologists who signed this supplement, he didn't mention taking such samples in the main autopsy report and the microscope slides noted are no longer in evidence. It's obvious that Finck never saw these slides – he would have mentioned them. I doubt whether they ever actually existed as there would be every reason in the world to keep them (they would support the US government case) and none to hide or dispose of them.

Eleven | The Autopsy of John F. Kennedy

When asked by Specter whether the President was shot from the front, rear or side, Finck answered that he had been shot from the rear and that the exit wound measured "approximately 13 centimetres"[19]. However, this was not a direct observation by the forensic pathologist. Prior to his arrival, Humes and Boswell had enlarged the wound so that JFK's brain could be removed. So Finck never saw the head wound in its original state.

The Warren Commission decided that two bullets, fired from the same weapon, hit two people riding in the President's limousine. The first, they concluded went straight through Kennedy's neck and then hit Texas Governor John Connally who was seated in front of the President. According to the Warren Commission, this bullet caused all the wounds to Connally including breaking bones in his chest and wrist. They concluded that this bullet (CE399) remained intact. The second bullet hit Kennedy in the head where it disintegrated into scores of particles and, allegedly, two large pieces. So, amazingly, the Warren Commissions conclusion was that two identical bullets behaved in totally different ways during the assassination. Despite their assertion that both hit bone, they concluded that one remained practically undamaged and the other split into many fragments. I am particularly sceptical to find that there was off record discussion with Finck regarding this very conclusion.[20]

Finck and the Clay Shaw Trial

Finck is the only one of the pathologists who was ever exposed to a proper legal cross-examination. During the Garrison trial of Clay Shaw, the defence called Finck as a witness. He was cross-examined for the prosecution by Alvin Oser on February 24th 1969. Finck struggled in several areas, the most infamous of which follow.

When he was asked who was in charge of the autopsy, Finck testified as follows:

OSER: You were a co-author of the report though, weren't you, Doctor?
FINCK: Wait. I was called as a consultant to look at these wounds; that doesn't mean I am running the show.
OSER: Was Dr. Humes running the show?
FINCK: Well, I heard Dr. Humes stating that – he said, "Who is in charge here?" and I heard an Army General, I don't remember his name, stating, "I am." You must understand that in those circumstances, there were law enforcement officers, military people with various ranks, and you have to co-ordinate the operation according to directions.
OSER: But you were one of the three qualified pathologists standing at that autopsy table, were you not, Doctor?
FINCK: Yes, I am.
OSER: Was this Army General a qualified pathologist?

FINCK: No.
OSER: Was he a doctor?
FINCK: No, not to my knowledge.
OSER: Can you give me his name, Colonel?
FINCK: No, I can't. I don't remember.

Only one person should have been in charge of the JFK autopsy – Finck himself. He was the only qualified forensic pathologist. However, as the autopsy took place in a naval hospital and it had begun before Finck arrived; Humes had already taken the role of chief pathologist. If a medically-unqualified army general was directing the autopsy, at the very least it would have undermined the autopsy report and opened it to challenge in court. The autopsy report on the body of the deceased person is, in legal terms, the "best evidence"[21] – it is a first-hand verification of the wounds suffered by the deceased. Where would any court case regarding the President's assassination be without the best evidence actually being proof? What a mess.

When he was asked why he did not dissect the organs of the neck, Finck gave the following answers:

OSER: Why did you not trace the track of the wound?
FINCK: As I recall I didn't remove these organs from the neck.
OSER: I didn't hear you.
FINCK: I examined the wounds but I didn't remove the organs of the neck.
OSER: You said you didn't do this; I am asking you why didn't do this as a pathologist?
FINCK: From what I recall I looked at the trachea, there was a tracheotomy wound the best I can remember, but I didn't dissect or remove these organs.
OSER: Your Honor, I would ask Your Honor to direct the witness to answer my question.
OSER: I will ask you the question one more time: Why did you not dissect the track of the bullet wound that you have described today and you saw at the time of the autopsy at the time you examined the body? Why? I ask you to answer that question.
FINCK: As I recall I was told not to, but I don't remember by whom.
OSER: You were told not to but you don't remember by whom?
FINCK: Right.
OSER: Could it have been one of the Admirals or one of the Generals in the room?
FINCK: I don't recall.

As you will see later, dissection of the organs of the neck is absolutely necessary and is a routine part of any autopsy. Where injury to the neck is suspected, dissection of the neck organs is mandatory.

Eleven | The Autopsy of John F. Kennedy

Finck and the House Select Committee on Assassinations (HSCA)
Finck's testimony to the HSCA lasted almost two hours on the afternoon of March 11th 1978. The most remarkable feature of this testimony is the number of times he responds to valid questions with "I don't remember" or "I don't know" or similar phrases.

It strains credibility that, after several years of absence from the morgue, a forensic pathologist would walk into an autopsy, see the President's lifeless body with its brain, heart and lungs removed and not have it indelibly printed upon his memory. Most people can remember in some detail where they were and what they were doing when they received news of the President's death. I simply don't believe that Finck would forget much about that day.

Finck's responses suggested that the 15 years which had passed since he participated in the most important and highest profile autopsy of his career had practically wiped his memory. His attitude seemed to suggest that it was wholly unreasonable to expect him to remember such details as "Was there injury to the cerebellar hemispheres?" to which Finck replied, "I don't remember."[22]

I think that this remarkable memory loss was entirely deliberate. Finck was on the ropes because it was he who should have made sure that the autopsy ran according to the medicolegal methods mandated by the military and by law. The major problem for Finck was that, before he arrived, Humes and Boswell had removed the very organs where they claimed "missile" damage - the brain and lungs. The body was no longer in a position where a forensic pathologist could have made honest and accurate assessments of the wounds. Finck simply had to forget. His only alternative was to accept that the autopsy of the most important man on the planet was totally botched and that he had signed an unscrupulous autopsy report.

Finck and the Assassination Records Review Board (ARRB)
Finck's next sworn testimony was to the ARRB on May 24th 1996. He was questioned by T. Jeremy Gunn, Head of Research and Analysis and General Counsel. By this time, Finck's apparent memory loss was so profound that during his testimony he even forgot things he had remembered seconds previously:

GUNN: So that I'm clear here, the two parts of the body of President Kennedy that were actually struck by the bullets were not weighed during the course of the autopsy, is that correct?
FINCK: Oh, you don't weigh the organs of the neck. Even if you remove them, you don't weigh them.[23]

Incredibly, this is followed almost immediately by:

GUNN: Could you tell me what, in just a very brief way, the thyroid is ...
FINCK: Well, the thyroid is a gland in the front of the throat. Removed with the organs of the neck, it would be weighed separately.
GUNN: So it would have been possible to weigh an organ of the neck and that would have been a standard ...
FINCK: Oh.[24]

Yes, oh dear. Together with Doug Horne, Gunn had sourced a copy of the 1960 tri-service US Military Autopsy Manual (much more of this later) and questioned Finck about it:

GUNN: At the time that you completed the autopsy of President Kennedy, did you believe that the standards as set forth in the autopsy manual had been satisfied for the autopsy of President Kennedy?
FINCK: You mean at the time the autopsy was completed?
GUNN: Yes.
FINCK: I didn't – I did not ask myself the question.[25]

And yet, just a few minutes earlier, Finck had been shown a memo that he prepared where he had apparently questioned whether the autopsy was complete:

GUNN: Did you write those documents?
FINCK: I wrote those documents, but I don't recognize a sentence handwritten, this is not my handwriting on page 23, the lines crossed out and someone wrote by hand. I don't recognize my handwriting here.
GUNN: Let me read those lines to you that are handwritten. "One officer who outranked me told me that my request was only of academic interest. The same officer did not agree to state in the autopsy report that the autopsy was incomplete, as I had suggested to indicate." Do you now recall whether those are your words, even though that is not your handwriting?
FINCK: That could be my words. I don't recognize my handwriting. I don't know what happened.[26]

It is possible that the handwritten entry over the redacted portion was not the original wording. Finck, however, has stated elsewhere that he considered the autopsy to be incomplete. In his interview with Dennis L Breo for the Journal of the American Medical Association, just five years earlier, Finck stated: "At the time, it may not have seemed as 'complete' to me as some other autopsies I have done, but for the purposes of history, yes it was complete."[27] Finck was the master of answering a question in the negative *and* the positive.

ELEVEN | THE AUTOPSY OF JOHN F. KENNEDY

The US Military Autopsy Manual

Critiques of the autopsy report on the remains of JFK can be found in many books on the case and even amongst those who accept the Warren Report's conclusions. Arch Warren supporter Vincent Bugliosi describes the autopsy report as "admittedly, less-than-perfect". The autopsy report is thoroughly deficient and displays the very characteristic that JFK had warned about, "comfortable inaction". In the remainder of this chapter, I hope to reveal how poor the autopsy was and offer my thoughts on why certain procedures were omitted.

I have used the "US Military Autopsy Manual"[28] to compare what should have been done with what actually was done during JFK's autopsy. This is the manual used by the US Army, US Navy and US Air Force. It was first prepared by the US Armed Forces Institute of Pathology over fifty years ago. In the forward, its purpose is defined as follows: ". . . a guiding directive toward uniformity in the selected techniques and objectives of an autopsy". Although my copy is dated 1981, many of the techniques and references within it predate JFK's autopsy. A check of a section of the 1960 manual reproduced in Dr Charles Wilber's book, "Medicolegal Investigation of the President John F. Kennedy Murder", confirms this[29].

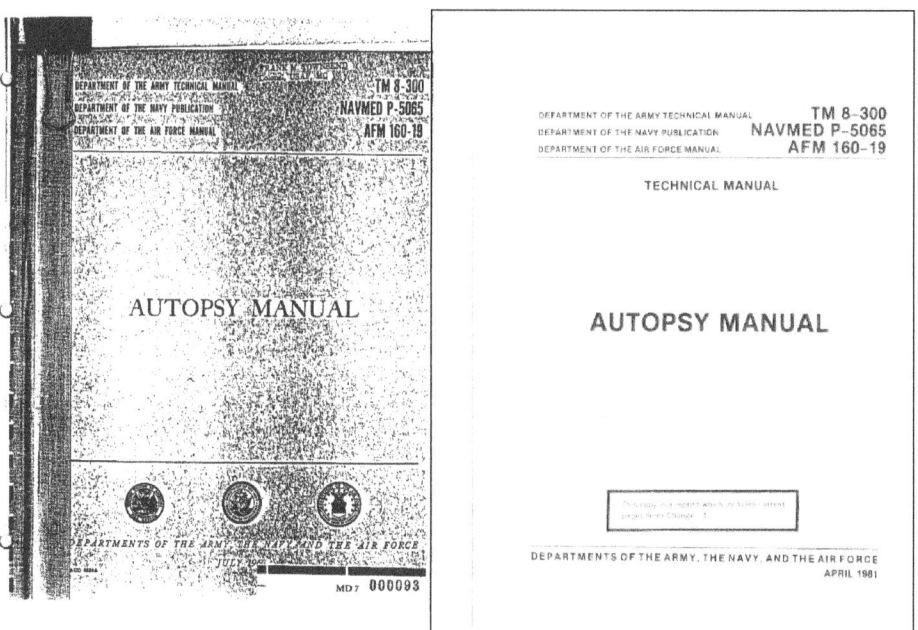

Front Page 1960 Manual　　　　　Front Page 1981 Manual
ARRB MD7　　　　　　　　　　　Author's Copy

Drs Humes, Boswell and Finck, would have performed every autopsy they ever did based on this manual (although Humes claimed, remarkably, that he had never seen it before[30]). Doing things "by the book" is the military way and I suggest that they would have known this book's contents thoroughly.

In the case of a homicide, the US law in 1963 required a full medicolegal autopsy (it still does of course). A report of the autopsy is required so that all medical aspects of the case can be discussed in court and any trial can be as fair as possible to those accused of the crime. Since JFK was murdered, his remains too should have been subject to a full medicolegal autopsy. Chapter 6 in The US Military Autopsy Manual consists of ten *extra* pages on the specific subject of a medicolegal autopsy. It defines such a specialised autopsy as follows:

"The medicolegal autopsy has the special purpose of securing information needed for the administration of justice. This requires a pathologist to direct attention to areas not normally examined during the routine autopsy of a person dying within a hospital."[31]

A typical definition is that a medicolegal autopsy (sometimes called a forensic autopsy) is a series of tests and examinations performed on a body to determine the presence of injury or to identify any disease that may have caused or contributed to the death. This internal and external examination must be carried out by a forensic pathologist who has been specially trained to recognise patterns of injury, collect evidence and investigate the circumstances surrounding the death. During a medicolegal autopsy, the body and the internal organs must be thoroughly examined.

The US Military Autopsy Manual goes further still requiring, where possible, the pathologist to "... be called to the scene of an incident in any case involving violent death or death under suspicious circumstances"[32]. For JFK this was not possible as his body was removed from Dallas (where he was shot and subsequently died) and flown back to Bethesda Naval Hospital in Washington D.C. for his autopsy [see my chapter on the medical evidence elsewhere in this book]. The manual continues, "In the event the pathologist cannot visit the scene of the incident, a written preliminary report from the investigating authorities concerning the circumstances surrounding the death should accompany the body to the morgue."[33] Nothing like this occurred for JFK. The pathologists instead made references to newspaper reports[34].

The section in the US Military Autopsy Manual covering the required extent of a medicolegal autopsy states the following:

"A medicolegal autopsy should never be a partial autopsy, and should always include the examination of the brain, neck organs, thorax, abdomen and pelvis."[35]

Incredibly, given this crystal clear obligation in the manual, the President's autopsy appeared to be wanting in *all* these areas. I will be looking at the

ELEVEN | THE AUTOPSY OF JOHN F. KENNEDY

examinations (or lack of them) of the President's brain, neck organs and so on later in this chapter. Let me begin with the first condition that the autopsy should never be partial.

Naturally, in a medicolegal autopsy, examination, measurement and description of injuries are the most important aspects. This does not mean, however, that the usual autopsy procedures are omitted. As the US Military Autopsy Manual stresses:

"Whatever type of autopsy is performed, the examination should not be restricted to only those areas which are the seat of obvious alteration, but should include all organs of the body, for the normality of certain viscera is often as significant as the disease of others, and organs that appear normally macroscopically are frequently abnormal microscopically."[36]

The manual continues that the exception to this is, "... where the authority to conduct the autopsy derives from the consent of the next-of-kin and such consent has limited the extent of the autopsy."[37] This is one of the reasons used for years by the pathologists to excuse the very limited autopsy performed on JFK. And yet, it was never the truth.

Finck, at least, would have known that claiming family restriction was wrong on three counts: Firstly, it was based on hearsay. None of the pathologists ever heard directly from any of the Kennedy family regarding restriction.[38] Secondly, family wishes always take second place to the needs of justice in a medicolegal autopsy (and the US Military Autopsy Manual says so[39]).

Finally, there is a document specifically permitting a full autopsy and this would be the strongest evidence in court. While completing his book "Post Mortem" in 1969, Harold Weisberg finally received a full copy of the Warren Commission file CD362a. Within the file he discovered a poor photocopy of JFK's "Authorization for Post-Mortem Examination"[40]. It was signed by the President's brother, Robert Kennedy (then the Attorney General – the chief law enforcement officer of the United States government). It states "You are hereby authorized to perform a complete post-mortem examination on the remains of John F. Kennedy." This authorisation was the legal basis for the autopsy of JFK and it specifically permits a complete post-mortem examination.

There can be no doubt that any excuses used over the years for a restricted autopsy are false. And yet, over thirty years after the event, the autopsy doctors *still* tried to convince the ARRB otherwise.

Missing Test for Pneumothorax

JFK's autopsy report[41] begins with a clinical summary and a general description of the body. Then there is a section entitled "Missile Wounds" later elaborated upon by the "Summary" section. I have separated out the discussion of wounds for special attention later in this chapter.

Next, under the title "Incisions", Humes notes that the scalp wounds were extended across the top of the skull to enable "examination of the cranial content" and the usual Y-shaped incision used to expose the thoracic and abdominal cavities. A one-paragraph description of the thoracic (chest) cavity follows:

"*The bony cage is unremarkable. The thoracic organs are in their normal positions and relationships and there is no increase in free pleural fluid. The above described area of contusion in the apical portion of the right pleural cavity is noted.*"

This is an insufficient description and Humes specifically deviates from a US Military Autopsy Manual requirement. Humes noted in the general description that, "Situated on the anterior chest wall in the nipple line are bilateral 2cm long recent transverse surgical incisions into the subcutaneous tissue." This means that just to the side of each nipple, Humes noticed a 2cm cut through the skin, which he recognised as being recently made by a surgeon. He would have known that these recent incisions were done in the emergency room to relieve a possible pneumothorax (collapsed lung). A pneumothorax is caused when the pleural membranes, which form a closed sac around the lungs, is punctured. The resulting air in the chest causes the respiratory system, which relies on pressure differences, to fail. Humes knew very well what these wounds represented:

"These wounds were bilateral, they were situated on the anterior chest wall in the nipple line, and each were 2cm. long in the transverse axis. The one on the right was situated 11 cm. above the nipple the one on the left was situated 11 cm. on the nipple, and the one on the right was 8cm. above the nipple. Their intention was to incise through the President's chest to place tubes into his chest."[42]

Given that a pneumothorax had been suspected, he should have followed the US Military Autopsy Manual which requires a specific test for it[43]. Humes continued to explain in his Warren Commission testimony why he did not:

"We examined those wounds very carefully, and found that they, however, did not enter the chest cavity. They only went through the skin. I presume that as they were performing that procedure it was obvious that the President had died, and they didn't pursue this."[44]

If Humes believed that a pneumothorax was even suspected in the Dallas trauma room, post-mortem testing for pneumothorax would have been mandatory, as the manual requires.

It has always bothered me that the Parkland doctors specifically noted inserting chest tubes, but that Humes apparently found otherwise. They cannot both be right. The Parkland doctors were quite matter-of-fact about how they inserted chest tubes and attached them to sealed underwater drainage (this helps re-inflate a collapsed lung). Insertion of a chest tube is invasive and

Eleven | The Autopsy of John F. Kennedy

uncomfortable for a conscious patient. It involves cutting through the skin followed by blunt dissection of the intercostal muscle (between the ribs) and parietal pleura. The surgeon then pushes a finger into the wound to loosen any adhesions before inserting a chest drain tube (see diagram below).

The Dallas doctors certainly knew what they were doing, two were assistant professors and one was a chief resident. They would have performed this routine procedure many times before. It is inconceivable to me that surgeons would have got this procedure wrong once let alone twice *and* on the President.

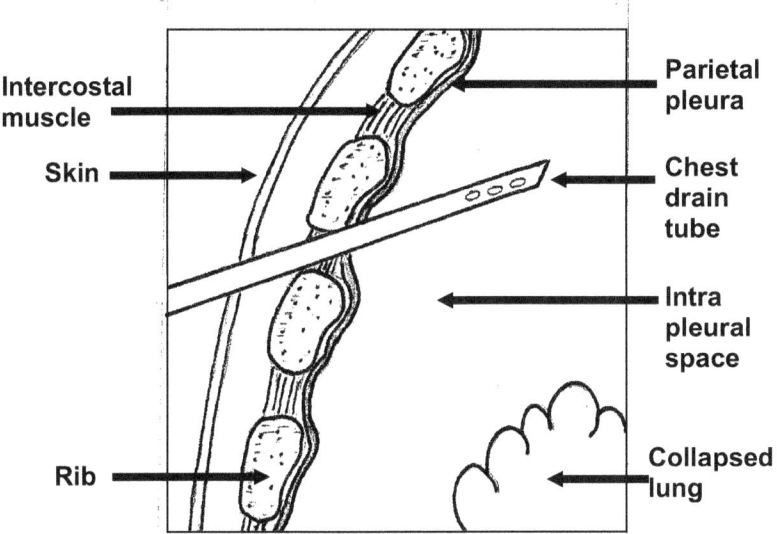

Technique of Intercostal Tube Drainage of Chest[45]

Dr Ronald Jones (Chief Resident of Surgery) inserted the left chest tube and gave the following testimony to the Warren Commission on 24th March 1964:

"Dr. JONES – Well, as Dr. Perry started the tracheotomy, I started the cut down in the left arm to insert a large polyethylene catheter, to give an I.V. so that we could give I.V. solutions as well as blood, and at the same time another doctor or two were doing some cutdowns in the lower extremities around the ankle. We made the cutdown in the left arm in the cephalic vein very rapidly and I.V. fluids were started immediately and as I was doing this, Dr. Perry was performing the tracheotomy, and it was about this time that Dr. Baxter came in and went ahead to assist Dr. Perry with the tracheotomy, and as they made a deeper incision in the neck to isolate the trachea, they thought they saw some gush of air and the possibility of a pneumothorax on one side or the other was entertained, and since I was to the left of the President, I went ahead and put in the anterior chest tube in the second intercostal space.
Mr. SPECTER – Was that tube fully inserted, Doctor?

Dr. JONES – I felt that the tube was fully inserted, and this was immediately connected to underwater drainage.
Mr. SPECTER – What do you mean by "connected to underwater drainage", Dr. Jones?
Dr. JONES – The tube is connected to a bottle whereby it aerates in the chest from a pneumothorax and as the patient breathes, the air is forced out under the water and produces somewhat of a suction so that the lung will re-expand and will not stay collapsed and this will give adequate aeration to the body..."[46]
Dr Charles Baxter (Assistant Professor of Surgery) and Dr Paul Peters (Assistant Professor of Urology) inserted the right chest tube and gave the following testimony to the Warren Commission on 24th March 1964:
Dr. PETERS – Dr. Perry and Dr. Baxter were doing the tracheotomy and a set of tracheotomy tubes was obtained and the appropriate size was determined and I gave it to Baxter, who helped Perry put it into the wound, and Perry noted also that there appeared to be a bubbling sensation in the chest and recommended that chest tubes be put in. Dr. Ron Jones put a chest tube in on the left side and Dr. Baxter and I put it in on the right side I made the incision in the President's chest, and I noted that there was no bleeding from the wound.
Mr. SPECTER – Did you put that chest tube all the way in on the right side?
Dr. PETERS – That's our presumption – yes."[47]

Note that Specter asks both doctors if they were sure the chest tubes were fully inserted. He asks because he knows it is significant, but he leaves the matter there as he dare not pursue it further. I believe that Specter worked with Humes for weeks before his testimony on 16th March 1964 to get the best story together to explain why Humes had not tested for a pneumothorax.

To sum up on the pneumothorax:
- The Dallas doctors had good reason to suspect the chest had been penetrated[48].
- Three experienced doctors inserted chest tubes on both sides and connected them to underwater drainage. They would not have done this had the tubes not been fully inserted.
- Having connected the back wound and throat wound (see later), Humes could not allow for a bullet to penetrate the pleural sac – the trajectory would be too low. So, he avoided all mention of the mandatory test for a pneumothorax and lied in his testimony to the Warren Commission.
- Specter coached Humes to testify as he did because he too could not allow a chest wound. The single-bullet theory demands that no missile penetrated the pleural sac.

ELEVEN | THE AUTOPSY OF JOHN F. KENNEDY

What's missing from The Autopsy Report?
The US Military Autopsy Manual suggests the following headings and contents for a medicolegal autopsy:

Section	Description from page 73 Section 140
Summary of the Circumstances	How the death occurred based upon law enforcement investigation.
External Description	"... clothing, general appearance, description of rigor mortis and liver mortis, temperature and identifying features."
Evidence of Injury	"In this section the tracks of stab wounds or gunshot wounds should be described in their entirety."
Evidence of Medical and/or Surgical Treatment	"Identify any evidence of therapy as contrasted to injuries."
Internal Examination	"Organs systems are described as in the routine autopsy."
Summary	"... only those things that are factual and no speculative ideas should be given."

Humes, who wrote the autopsy report, could have verified what his report should contain by checking the US Military Autopsy Manual before putting pen to paper. Having never before performed a medicolegal autopsy and knowing that the manual contained a specific section regarding such autopsies; wouldn't you expect Humes to have checked? Either he did not, which is at least negligent, or he did but ignored the manual because JFK's autopsy report contains the following sections and contents:

Section	Description
Clinical Summary	• How the death occurred based largely upon newspaper reports • Summary of treatment in emergency room (Parkland).

General Description of Body	• General description • Brief wound description • Brief description surgical treatment • No description of clothing, temperature and identifying features.
Missile Wounds	See later
Incisions	Mentions some cutting to extend the scalp wounds (so that the brain can be examined) and the usual Y-shaped cut to expose the thorax and abdomen.
Thoracic Cavity	See earlier discussion regarding testing for pneumothorax.
Lungs	• Missing description of the trachea and bronchi specifically mentioned in the US Military Autopsy Manual.[1] • Missing description of larynx, pharynx, hypopharynx, tongue, thyroid and parathyroid mentioned in the US Military Autopsy Manual.[2]
Heart	This section contains the most thorough notes in the whole autopsy (except for the "Missile Wounds").
Abdominal Cavity	Missing description of the adrenal glands – the lack of these in JFK would have been obvious and should have been noted. The US Military Autopsy Manual is quite specific about this "Weigh the organs if the size is abnormal"[3]
Skeletal System	No dissection of the skeleton is noted. If Humes suspected that the back wound was an entry wound for a missile, he should have dissected and checked all bones in that region (ribs and vertebrae).
Photography	Photographs were taken but not developed. They were immediately handed over to the Secret Service. If they were not for use by the autopsy doctors, you have to wonder what was the point (see below) in taking them.

Eleven | The Autopsy of John F. Kennedy

Roentgenograms	Humes wrote, "Roentgenograms are made of the entire body..."[4], **but that is untrue (see below).**
Summary	Contrary to the US Military Autopsy Manual, the summary contains the following speculation: • "two perforating gunshot wounds inflicted by high velocity projectiles " • "fired from a point behind and somewhat above " • "exit through the anterior surface of the neck" • "this missile struck no bony structures "[5]

Dr Charles Wilber listed 27 observations required by the US Military Autopsy Manual which are missing from the JFK autopsy report[54].

Photographs & X-rays

Using the US Military Autopsy Manual it is possible to see exactly what is missing from JFK's written autopsy report[55]. Firstly and most obviously missing are photographs and X-rays. Whatever the reason given for the photographs not being attached, it is a serious dereliction and the autopsy report is incomplete without them. The manual states: "Copies of photographs, X-rays and toxicology reports should be attached as part of the completed report."[56] The pathologists should have had access to the photographs which they had taken so that they could be referred to within the text of the autopsy report. I have mentioned elsewhere the requirement for at least three colour photographs of each item of interest (wide-angled, mid-range and close up), but the manual goes further:

"Each photograph must have the autopsy number and a scale within the field of view. A photograph of the face should be made for identification purposes. Photographs should be made with the clothes on and off, and before the wounds are cleaned and after the wounds have been cleaned."[57]

None of JFK's autopsy photographs have the requisite three views, none have a visible autopsy number and none show the wounds before and after cleaning. Hardly any even contain a scale.

The X-rays do not support the conclusions in the autopsy report and are not consistent with the photographs. If there were X-rays taken of the extremities (where bullet fragments might have lain), they are no longer in evidence[58] - X-rays of the lower arms, wrists, hands, lower legs, ankles and feet are missing. From this I conclude either that none were taken (most likely) or that they have been destroyed as they contained evidence of bullet fragments which would not support the official story (quite possible).

Organs of the Neck

Most astoundingly, given that Humes described a bullet wound through JFK's neck in the autopsy report, the organs in that area were *specifically* not dissected. These organs include the trachea, bronchi, larynx, pharynx, hypopharynx, tongue, thyroid and parathyroid. All three pathologists would know that they were neglecting their duty to the President and to justice by not dissecting this area. To begin with, how can the nature of the wound (angle of perforation, track through the body and so on) be determined without it? Importantly, the US Military Autopsy Manual clearly requires it[59].

In fact, in Chapter 6 "Objectives of The Medicolegal Autopsy", the US Military Autopsy Manual outlines a specific technique for anterior neck dissection[60]. This is important particularly for examining the tongue because fresh, self-inflicted, bite marks may be evidence that a seizure preceded death. Some researchers believe that the President was in some way paralysed before he was shot in the head – this test may have provided some evidence one way or the other.

The manual also suggests that this technique gives a good view of the upper air passage so that it can be checked for possible foreign bodies such as might be suspected from a throat wound. Furthermore, where damage to the cervical spine (neck bones) is a possibility, the manual also includes a specific technique for dissecting this area[61].

It is clear to me that this dissection was not done for fear of revealing that the President was shot from behind (causing the back wound) and from in front (causing the throat wound). This would, of course, show that there had been a conspiracy to assassinate the President. I do not believe that the back wound was perforating – I think it was a shallow hole. Nor do I believe that the missile that caused the throat wound ever left JFK's body. There is simply no evidence to show otherwise.

Heart, Lungs and Brain

Kennedy's heart, lungs and brain were removed before the forensic pathologist, Finck, arrived. I don't believe that the significance of this can be overstated. The very organs which were alleged to have been wounded by bullets were dissected from the President's body by the anatomical pathologists before the expert arrived. I can imagine Finck's dismay, once he had fought his way past the US Marines guarding the morgue, to be confronted with the President's empty head and chest and the puzzled looks of Humes and Boswell.

The heart, lungs and brain are the only three organs specifically described in the autopsy report. Where are the required descriptions of the neck organs, intestines, spleen, lymph nodes, pancreas, liver, kidneys and so on? If these organs were examined during the autopsy, why are they not in the report? Could it be that there was evidence of bullet wounds to these organs or even poisoning? An incomplete autopsy performed by out-of-practice doctors produced nothing but questions. And yet this would have been the proof relied upon in court to convict the murdered President's assassin(s).

The Missing Notes and Drafts
When conducting an autopsy, it is routine for pathologists to make many notes concerning the dimensions, weights and appearances of body tissues. The notes also indicate the taking of samples, X-rays and photographs which will be used later to illustrate specific autopsy findings.

It would be rational to expect the President's autopsy report to contain facts based on the written measurements taken and noted by the pathologists as they worked on 22nd November 1963, but it does not. Of the autopsy report's 88 facts, only 24 are contained in what remains of the notes that the autopsy doctors took[62].

An astounding 64 facts appear to have come from nowhere as they are not backed up by contemporaneous notes. 15 of the 64 facts relate to numbers and figures which it is unlikely Humes could have memorised until the report was written[63]. Where are the missing notes? Oh, Humes burnt them! This is worrying for three reasons:

- It is worrying firstly because the autopsy notes would have been required in court. Oswald's defence would have demanded disclosure of the notes as source materials for the autopsy report. As they could not have been produced, this would have been a serious blow to the credibility of the autopsy report. It is highly suspicious that they were destroyed by Humes at all, but it is particularly suspicious that they appear to have been destroyed shortly after he heard of Oswald's death[64] when he knew there would be no trial.

- It is worrying secondly because the notes themselves may have contained data which contradicted the official record. The notes could have contained different details of the sizes and locations of wounds and the results of "probing" the back wound. Now we may never know.

- Finally, not only were notes destroyed, but the first draft of the autopsy report *itself* was also destroyed[65] (which may well have contained different conclusions prior to Oswald's death). This was not mentioned by Humes in his Warren Commission testimony where he referred to the first draft as "certain preliminary draft notes"[66]. I cannot believe that Arlen Specter was unaware of the significance of this. I believe that by coaching the autopsy doctors over a period of weeks prior to their testimony to the Warren commission, Specter was responsible for keeping such information out of the record.

The "Head Wounds"

The autopsy report makes a wretched job of describing the head wounds. Before beginning to look in detail at the description, it may help you to visualise the measurements described if you have a small template to hand. This is easy to do. Please find a piece of A4 or US letter paper. A piece of A4 paper is about 21cm by 30cm (US letter paper is slightly wider and shorter). If you fold this paper into half and half again, you should have a rectangle of roughly 10cm by 15 cm. The skull diagram below should help you to locate the bones of the skull and better understand Humes' description.

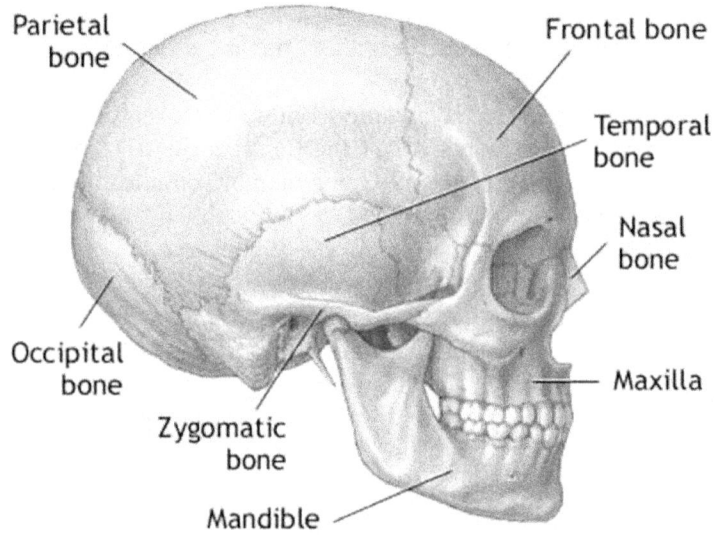

Skull Diagram

Now, let's look at the autopsy report, written by Humes:

"There is a large irregular defect of the scalp and skull on the right involving chiefly the parietal bone but extending somewhat into the temporal and occipital regions. In this region there is an actual absence of scalp and bone producing a defect which measures approximately 13 cm. in greatest diameter."

The important point here is that if the hole had a measurement of 13cm at *any* point and it extended into both the temporal and occipital regions, it was huge. What Humes was saying in the autopsy report was that a large part of the right side of JFK's head was missing. The defect ran from his right temple to the middle of the back of his head. This is a massive defect. Just hold the piece of paper on your head and you will get an idea of its size. It is vital to

Eleven | The Autopsy of John F. Kennedy

note that the autopsy report describes this area as having an "actual absence of scalp and bone . . . " So you must imagine about a quarter of JFK's head gone with whatever was left of his brain exposed. The autopsy report continues to describe the wound in JFK's head:

"From the irregular margins of the above scalp defect tears extend in stellate fashion into the more or less intact scalp as follows:
a. From the right inferior temporo-parietal margin anterior to the right ear to a point slightly above the tragus.
b. From the anterior parietal margin anteriorly on the forehead to approximately 4 cm. above the right orbital ridge.
c. From the left margin of the main defect across the midline antero-laterally for a distance of approximately 8 cm.
d. From the same starting point as c. 10 cm. postero-laterally."

What this means is that there were four tears in JFK's scalp which ran from the edges of the large hole in a more-or-less star pattern. The first went from the right and back edge of the large hole forward almost to the middle of JFK's ear (the tragus is the triangular part of the external ear that sits over the ear canal). The second went from the front edge of the large hole forwards into JFK's forehead and ended 4cm above his right eyebrow. The third began at the left edge of the large hole and ran 8cm diagonally forward and left. The fourth tear began at the same place as the third and ran 10cm diagonally backwards and left. The diagram below may help to better understand these tears. The large hole is an approximation because a true representation *cannot* be drawn from the descriptions in the autopsy report.

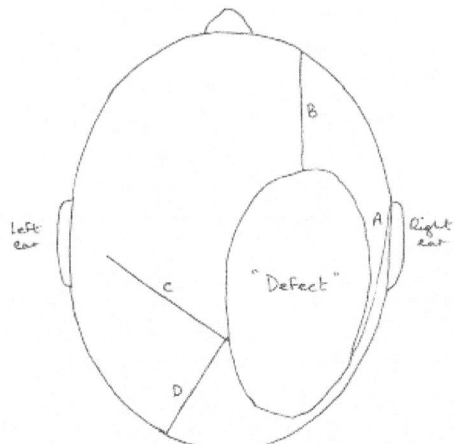

Author's Diagram – Scalp Tears in Top of JFK's Head

Note that the *"actual absence of scalp and bone . . ."* a horrifying quarter of the President's head actually gone is now described as a *"scalp defect"*. Doesn't sound so bad does it? Next, Humes goes on to describe a much smaller hole in the back of JFK's head which he later characterised as a bullet entrance wound:

"Situated in the posterior scalp approximately 2.5 cm. laterally to the right and slightly above the external occipital protuberance is a lacerated wound measuring 15 x 6 mm."

What this means is that there was a small oval hole in the back of JFK's scalp. Humes clearly wants us to believe that this is a bullet entrance wound as he mentions it as such in the summary section. However, he could not prove it, so he too described it as a *"lacerated wound"*. Firstly, use of the word "lacerated" " (meaning cut or wounded in a jagged manner) seems to be an odd way to describe a bullet entrance wound which would normally be described as "punctuate" and "smooth edged". Secondly, the *"lacerated wound"* apparently showed no signs of being a bullet entrance wound since there is no description of any such signs in his autopsy report. For example, there is no mention of a circumferential margin of abrasion or an "abrasion collar", which is one of the effects of the rapid scraping created by a bullet going into a body.

The strangest thing about this paragraph though is that is appears to exonerate the alleged assassin. Oswald allegedly shot JFK with bullets measuring 6.5mm in diameter, but this wound is smaller. Whatever the length of the wound, a bullet with 6.5mm diameter should cause a wound of at least 6.5mm diameter not 6mm.

"In the underlying bone is a corresponding wound through the skull which exhibits beveling of the margins of the bone when viewed from the inner aspect of the skull."

The bevelling on the inner aspect of the skull could have been caused by a missile. The critical point here is whether the *". . . corresponding wound through the skull . . ."* was a complete hole in the occipital bone or a part of an alleged hole. If it was only a part of an alleged hole, the bevelling could have been caused by the edge of the wound being bumped in some way post-mortem. The autopsy report is silent on this, but over the years, the pathologists have been questioned. Reading from his own memo[67], Finck gave the following testimony to the ARRB:

FINCK: Right occipital, lacerated occipital corresponds to the wound. "The skull shows a portion of a crater, the beveling of which is obvious on the internal aspect of the bone. On that basis I told the prosectors and Admiral Galloway that this occipital wound is a wound of entrance." This is unquestionable.
GUNN: And so just so I am clear, I understand that you have identified as being beveled but I want to know whether the wound is a circular wound

Eleven | The Autopsy of John F. Kennedy

in the sense that the shell, the skull all around the wound is intact, or is part of the adjacent skull blown away from the portion of the entrance wound? FINCK: It was a perforation of the occipital bone.[68]

According to Finck, there was a complete hole in the occipital bone. However, Humes and Boswell's testimony to the HSCA gave another story. Boswell told the HSCA that, "there was a hole here, only half of which was present in the bone that was intact, and this small piece then fit right on there and the beveling on those was on the interior surface."[69] So, according to the Navy pathologists, the only bevelling present was on bones bought into the morgue after midnight[70]. In court, the chain of possession of the "late arriving fragments" would have been closely examined. If the chain had been found to be anything other than complete, then the evidence of an entry into JFK's skull would have been even further in doubt.

It is highly suspicious that there are two accounts of this "wound of entrance" – this, after all, is one of the "proofs" that the shooting was from above and behind. If this "proof" is nothing of the sort, then what is the truth?

"Clearly visible in the above described large skull defect and exuding from it is lacerated brain tissue which on close inspection proves to represent the major portion of the right cerebral hemisphere. At this point it is noted that the falx cerebri is extensively lacerated with disruption of the superior saggital sinus."

What this means is that the pathologists could see a mass of cut and torn brain tissue, which appeared to be most of the right of the brain, oozing out of the large hole in the top and side of JFK's skull. A tough membrane that separates the two cerebral hemispheres (the falx cerebri) was cut though many times. The chamber bordered by the falx cerebri (the superior saggital sinus, which is a drainage channel for venous blood) was damaged.

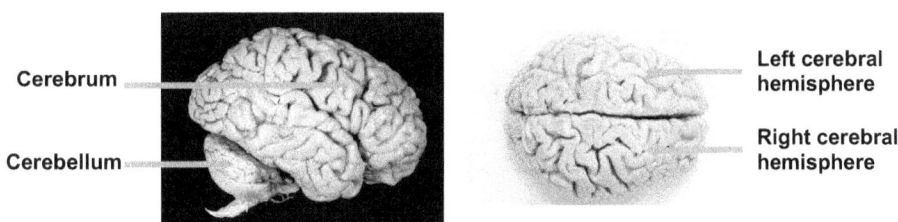

Human Brain – Right Side View and Top View

The falx cerebri is the shape of a sickle and lies in the long gap, which separates the two cerebral hemispheres.

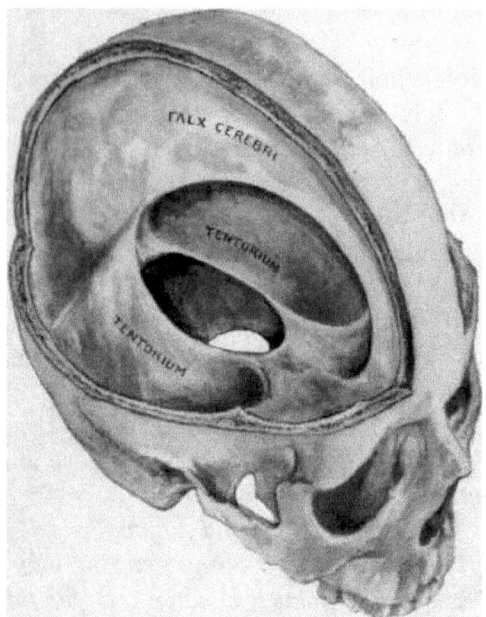

Diagram Showing the Tough, Fibrous Falx Cerebri (Brain Removed)

The autopsy report asserts that this tough membrane at the centre of the brain was substantially ripped, torn or cut. If this membrane was so badly damaged, there must have been significant damage to the left cerebral hemisphere of JFK's brain. As you can see from the diagram below, if the falx cerebri is cut or torn, whatever caused it must have continued into the left cerebral hemisphere (line a to b).

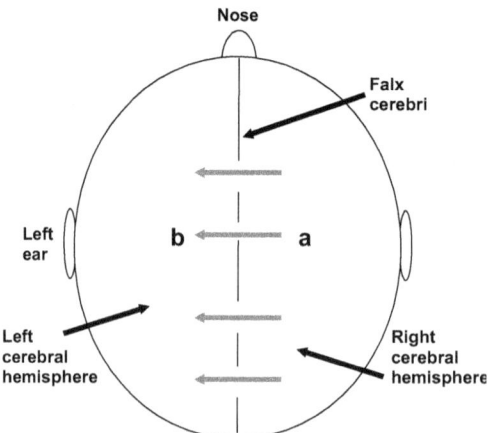

Diagram Showing Top of JFK's Head with Cuts to Falx Cerebri

Eleven | The Autopsy of John F. Kennedy

But a supplementary report (written by Humes within days of the main autopsy) that gave a detailed account of an examination of Kennedy's brain reveals no such damage: *"When viewed from the vertex the left cerebral hemisphere is intact."*

This observation adds some weight to Doug Horne's conclusion that there were two brain examinations and that the descriptions published in the supplementary report may not have been of JFK's brain[71].

The main autopsy report continues:

"Upon reflecting the scalp multiple complete fracture lines are seen to radiate from both the large defect at the vertex and the smaller wound at the occiput. These vary greatly in length and direction, the longest measuring approximately 19 cm. These result in the production of numerous fragments which vary in size from a few millimeters to 10cm in greatest diameter."

This means that when the doctors pulled back JFK's scalp to look at the skull underneath, they could see cracks which went completely through the skull bone. These ran in all directions from both the large hole in the top of the skull and the small hole in the back of the skull. The longest crack was 19cm. The cracks resulted in many bits of skull bone some small and some large.

Note that the *"actual absence of scalp and bone . . ."* is now described as a *"the large defect at the vertex"*. The wound has changed *within* the autopsy report! The large wound is described as being in the uppermost surface of the head (vertex) whereas, only a few paragraphs previously it was mainly in the *"parietal bone but extending somewhat into the temporal and occipital regions"*. If you look at a skull diagram, then by definition, this original description means the wound was side and rear and not uppermost.

Furthermore, in this paragraph, we have two other strange things. Firstly, if the right and rear of JFK's head is gone (*"actual absence of scalp and bone . . . "*), then a crack of 19cm must either be in the left of the skull or at the front of the skull. But Humes doesn't tell us which it was. Secondly, the 10cm fragment that he mentions must also be in the left or front. The X-rays also show large cracks, but they do not show the right rear of JFK's skull to be missing.

"The complexity of these fractures and the fragments thus produced tax satisfactory verbal description and are better appreciated in photographs and roentgenograms which are prepared."

What Humes means is that he cannot describe the mosaic of cracks and bits of skull bone in JFK's skull. He says that photographs and X-rays will give the best picture and that these were taken.

Humes was working largely from memory here as, remarkably, the photographs were not available to him when he wrote the autopsy report. They were taken away by the Secret Service before they were even developed. The whole point of taking photographs is to aid the preparation of the autopsy report and its interpretation. Incredibly, those from JFK's autopsy were not seen again for several years.

JFK | ECHOES FROM ELM STREET
A SEARCH FOR HISTORICAL ACCURACY ON THE
ASSASSINATION OF PRESIDENT JOHN F. KENNEDY

The authenticity of the photographs and X-ray photographs in evidence is in doubt. Firstly, they do not support the conclusions reached in the autopsy of even the observations of the autopsy doctors. Secondly the fact that they were not made available to the autopsy doctors for writing the autopsy report is suspicious. Thirdly, it is possible that they are not even the ones taken by the official medical photographer and radiologist on the night of the autopsy. While they were hidden away, there was enough time to modify the images. One thing is certain, the photographs and X-ray photographs do not help our appreciation of the President's wounds whatsoever.

"Received as separate specimens from Dallas, Texas are three fragments of skull bone which in aggregate roughly approximate the dimensions of the large defect described above. At one angle of the largest of these fragments is a portion of the perimeter of a roughly circular wound presumably of exit which exhibits beveling of the outer aspect of the bone and is estimated to measure approximately 2.5 to 3.0 cm. in diameter."

This means that at sometime during the autopsy, Humes received three bits of skull bone. When he put them together, they roughly filled the large hole where there was "*actual absence of scalp and bone . . "* the corner of one piece of bone there was part of the edge of a hole which he thought might be an exit as there was shelving on the outside surface of the bone.

So the autopsy evidence that the "large defect" was an exit wound was also based on bone fragments that arrived after midnight. The X-ray taken of these fragments is not helpful in identifying which surface the bevelling was on (the circled area is where the pathologists found apparent bevelling):

Photograph of an X-ray of Three Skull Fragments[72]

Eleven | The Autopsy of John F. Kennedy

But is this the inner or the outer surface? If the fragments showed bevelling, wouldn't the edges of the bone still making up JFK's skull also show it (that is, the other edges of this hole)? As the chain of possession is incomplete, it is suspicious to me that bevelling was only noted on fragments of skull which did not arrive with the body. Humes can only use the weasel-word "presumably" when describing the alleged exit wound.

The Back Wound
The autopsy report[73] describes the back wound in the most uncertain way. The reader should not be intimidated by the medical terms used in this extract from the autopsy report as I analyse it in standard English afterwards:

"The second wound presumably of entry is that described above in the upper right posterior thorax. Beneath the skin there is ecchymosis of subcutaneous tissue and musculature. The missile path through the fascia and musculature cannot be easily probed. The wound presumably of exit was that described by Dr Malcolm Perry of Dallas in the low anterior cervical region. When observed by Dr Perry the wound measured "a few millimeters in diameter", however it was extended as a tracheostomy incision and thus its character is distorted at the time of autopsy. However there is considerable ecchymosis of the strap muscles of the right side of the neck and of the fascia about the trachea adjacent to the line of the tracheostomy wound. The third point of reference in connecting these two wounds is in the apex (supra-clavicular portion) of the right pleural cavity. In this region there is contusion of the parietal pleura and of the extreme apical portion of the right upper lobe of the lung. In both instances the diameter of contusion and ecchymosis at the point of maximal involvement measures 5 cm. Both the visceral and parietal pleura are intact overlying these areas of trauma."

Let's take that paragraph out of medical-speak and dissect it along the way:

"The second wound presumably of entry is that described above in the upper right posterior thorax." The best that Humes can write is that the wound in the rear was "presumably of entry". The word "presumably" almost never occurs in an autopsy report. The report should include only objective observations drawn from proper scientific processes.

The "upper right posterior thorax" is a large area, could he not have noted that the wound was X cm to the right of a certain vertebra and Y cm from the top of the head? That would be the standard autopsy procedure.

JFK | ECHOES FROM ELM STREET
A SEARCH FOR HISTORICAL ACCURACY ON THE
ASSASSINATION OF PRESIDENT JOHN F. KENNEDY

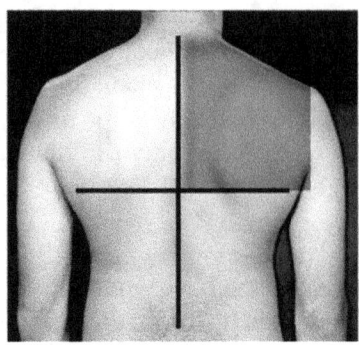

Upper Right Posterior Thorax (shaded area)

Earlier in the autopsy report, Humes did make a half-hearted attempt to locate the wounds. He wrote: "This wound is measured to be 14 cm. from the tip of the right acromion process and 14 cm. below the tip of the right mastoid process."

The right mastoid process is the bump of bone you can feel immediately behind your right ear. The tip of the right acromion process is the bump of bone you can feel at the very right of your shoulder. The problem here is two fold: Firstly, it's difficult to imagine any doctor locating a back wound starting from the ear and the tip of the shoulder when there are nearer, fixed anatomical references. Secondly, both of these points can be moved (simply by raising the shoulders and flexing the neck). A measurement from either of these points is unprofessional. Why didn't Humes position the wound in relation to a fixed anatomical point, like say a vertebra? This is exactly what was done on JFK's death certificate signed by Dr Burkely, JFK's personal physician. On the death certificate, the back wound is marked as being at the level of the third thoracic vertebra where it corresponds closely with the holes in JFK's jacket and shirt.

"The missile path through the fascia and musculature cannot be easily probed."

What does that really mean? Humes should never have been allowed by his fellow pathologists, his superiors or an honest investigation to get away with not explaining this properly. Did he mean that he couldn't probe it? Surely, it was very easy to actually take a finger or a rod and poke it in the wound. In fact, the Sibert & O'Neill Report describes Humes doing so.

Referring to the back wound, the FBI field report notes: "*This opening was probed by Humes with the finger, at which time it was determined that the trajectory of the missile entering at this point had entered at a downward position of 45 to 60 degrees. Further probing determined that the distance traveled by this missile was a short distance inasmuch as the end of the opening could be felt with the finger.*"[74]

Perhaps Humes meant that he could probe it, but it didn't go very deeply into the body. This is the more likely explanation as, in his testimony to the

Eleven | The Autopsy of John F. Kennedy

ARRB, Finck remembered the back wound being probed and describes it as "*unsuccessful*"[75]. A fourth pathologist present at the autopsy of JFK, Dr Robert F Karnei, also remembered the back wound being probed[76]. Autopsy technician James Jenkins too had good recollection of probing[77].

So what Humes meant by "*cannot be easily probed*" was that the back wound was shallow and did not pierce through the body. He never showed during the autopsy or subsequently that the hole in the back connected with the hole in JFK's neck. This is corroborated by the next statement and the re-use of that strange word, for an autopsy, "presumably".

"The wound presumably of exit was that described by Dr Malcolm Perry of Dallas in the low anterior cervical region." Note that this suggests that Perry himself reported an exit wound. In fact, Perry had described the throat wound as an entrance.

"When observed by Dr Perry the wound measured "a few millimeters in diameter", however it was extended as a tracheostomy incision and thus its character is distorted at the time of autopsy."

If anything, the small size of the wound ("a few millimeters in diameter") should make an autopsy doctor think "entrance" and not "exit".

"However there is considerable ecchymosis of the strap muscles of the right side of the neck and of the fascia about the trachea adjacent to the line of the tracheostomy wound."

So, there was more bruising. Humes claims that when he examined the throat wound, he had thought it was only a tracheotomy incision. So, presumably, Humes felt that the bruising he noted was consistent with a tracheotomy and not indicative of a bullet wound.

"The third point of reference in connecting these two wounds is in the apex (supra-clavicular portion) of the right pleural cavity. In this region there is contusion of the parietal pleura and of the extreme apical portion of the right upper lobe of the lung."

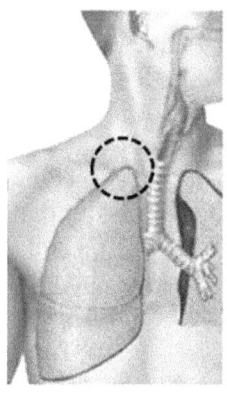

(Supra-Clavicular) Apex of Right Pleural Cavity

373

In layman's terms, this would be a bruise at the top of the right lung and its lining. Such a bruise though is not necessarily indicative of a bullet path. Even if it were, it cannot show the direction of wounding. Fourteen years before JFK's murder, Dr W C Sealy wrote a paper showing that lung contusions could be caused by non-penetrating injuries. He wrote:

"In an army hospital receiving patients with combat injuries from the army air forces all gradations of injury from contusion to rupture of the lung from non-penetrating injuries were seen. The agents responsible for the changes in the lung were blast from high explosive shells, blows from blunt objects and *non-penetrating wounds caused by high velocity missiles.*"[78]

According to Sealy's paper, the contusions noted by Humes could also have been caused by a non-penetrating wound, which is, according to Sibert & O'Neill's FBI Report, how the wound to JFK's back was described during the autopsy. In any event, the photograph that Humes allegedly asked to be taken of this contusion is missing from the collection at the National Archives[79]. How convenient.

"In both instances the diameter of contusion and ecchymosis at the point of maximal involvement measures 5 cm. Both the visceral and parietal pleura are intact overlying these areas of trauma."

What this means is that the bruise on the lung was up to 5cm in size. Also, the lining of the chest above the bruise did not have any holes in it. It is worth comparing Humes's description of what he *presumed* to be a perforating wound of JFK's neck with part of the autopsy report on somebody that definitely was shot through the neck almost 100 years before.

John Wilkes Booth assassinated President Abraham Lincoln, fled from the scene, but was cornered and killed on 26 April 1865[80]. His autopsy took place aboard the *Montauk* at 2pm on 27 April 1865. Surgeon General Joseph K. Barnes and Dr Joseph Janvier Woodward performed the autopsy and both men wrote autopsy reports. The following is an extract from Dr Woodward's report, note the precise detail and cross-referring to a specimen:

"The missile perforated the base of the right lamina of the 4th lumbar vertebra, fracturing it longitudinally and separating it by a fissure from the spinous process, at the same time fracturing the 5th vertebra through its pedicle and involving that transverse process. The projectile then transversed the spinal canal almost horizontally but with a slight inclination downward and backward, perforating the cord which was found much torn and discolored with blood (see Specimen 4087 Sect. I AMM). The ball then shattered the bases of the left 4th and 5th laminae, driving bony fragments among the muscles and made its exit at the left side of the neck, nearly opposite the point of entrance. It avoided the 2nd and 3rd cervical nerves."[81]

Note the discussion of passage of a projectile. Look too at this description of the course of a missile from Dr Rose's autopsy Report on J D Tippit, the Dallas

Eleven | The Autopsy of John F. Kennedy

policeman which Lee Harvey Oswald was also accused of murdering on November 22, 1963:

"The courses of the missiles are followed. The wound described as No. 2 is found to go between the second and third rib. The missile is found to penetrate the anterior edge of the right upper lobe. The bullet is found to go into the pericardial sac, there is extensive hemorrhage in the pericardial sac, approximately 4 ounces. Passes through the superior vena cava. It exits into the mediastinum, strikes the fourth thoracic vertebra to the left of the midline, courses in the substance of the vertebra and is recovered slightly to the left of the vertebra approximately 16 inches from the top of the head, having pursued a course very slightly upward, to the left and backwards."[82]

Compare this with the Humes' autopsy report on JFK where there is no discussion of the course of the missile until the summary section, where he wrote that a missile: "*traversed the soft tissues of the supra-scapular and the supra-clavicular portions of the base of the right side of the neck*" but this was never shown by dissection as it was in the autopsies of Booth and Tippet and is only a guess.

Note too, there's no hedging in the Booth and Tippet autopsy reports, no use of "presumably", only straight-forward description of direct observations. The type of unambiguous and straightforward language used in both the Booth and Tippet autopsy reports is typical autopsy language. The noncommittal and sometimes disingenuous language used in the Kennedy autopsy is unusual to the point of being unknown.

Until recently, it was believed that, remarkably, Humes didn't find out that the throat wound had been caused during the shooting until some time after JFK's body had left the Bethesda autopsy room on Saturday 24th November 1963.

Without the body in front of him to dissect, this means that the linking of the two wounds was, at best, a hunch based on the relative positions of the injuries. Therefore, Humes had to use the weasel words, "*As far as can be ascertained this missile struck no bony structures in its path through the body*". The truth is that it could not be ascertained at all because Humes did not dissect the path and, moreover, it is impossible for a missile to have followed the path claimed by Humes without it hitting bone.

In fact, the situation is even worse than this. Recent evidence appears to show that Humes called Perry during the autopsy and was told that there was a wound to the throat prior to the tracheotomy[83]. Dr Perry's own Warren Commission testimony on this matter supports this possibility, although it also seems to me to show signs of being coached by Specter[84]. But if there was contact between Humes and Perry during the autopsy, Humes cannot claim ignorance for not dissecting the path of the wound. The likelihood is that Humes was told not to do it, as Finck testified in the trail of Clay Shaw.

The reason he was told not to dissect the wound was because, in my opinion,

Kennedy's throat wound was caused by a shot from the front which, if proved, would have totally contradicted the Warren Report's conclusion that Kennedy was shot only from behind by Oswald. It is possible that what hit Kennedy was not a bullet but a piece of glass from the car's windscreen. There are photographs showing a hole in the windscreen and evidence that this was covered up. But whether it was a bullet or a piece of glass, the point is that it could only have come from the front, which means at least two shooters and conspiracy.

Classic Mistakes in a Forensic Autopsy
In 1956, Dr Alan R. Moritz published what has become a landmark paper on forensic pathology, "Classical Mistakes in Forensic Pathology"[85]. Moritz would have been well known to Humes, Boswell and Finck. He was famous for having established the first department of legal medicine in the US at Harvard University where he was the George Burgess McGrath Professor of Legal Medicine (1937-1949). Additionally, during the time that Humes, Boswell and Finck were senior pathologists, Moritz was the President of the American Association of Pathologists and Bacteriologists (1959). Moritz's 1956 "Classical Mistakes" paper would also be familiar to Humes, Boswell and Finck. They could hardly argue otherwise because its conclusions are reproduced in the US Military Autopsy Manual[86]. Moritz's paper lists the following thirteen mistakes:
1. Not being aware of the objective of the medicolegal autopsy.
2. Performing an incomplete autopsy.
3. Permitting the body to be embalmed before performing a medicolegal autopsy.
4. Regarding a mutilated or decomposed body as unsuitable for autopsy.
5. Mistakes resulting from non-recognition or misinterpretation of post-mortem changes.
6. Failure to make an adequate examination and description of external abnormalities.
7. Confusing the objective with the subjective sections of an autopsy protocol (report).
8. Not examining the body at the scene of the crime.
9. Substituting intuition for scientifically defensible interpretation.
10. Not making adequate photographs of the evidence.
11. Not exercising good judgment in the taking or handling of specimens for toxicological examination.
12. Permitting the value of the protocol (report) to be jeopardised by minor errors.
13. Talking too soon, too much or to the wrong people.

How many of these "classic" mistakes would you expect to have been made

Eleven | The Autopsy of John F. Kennedy

at the President's autopsy? I expect the most common answer would be "none", but after reading this chapter, you will be aware that Humes, Boswell and Finck made almost all of these errors during the autopsy of the 35th president.

Not being aware of the objective of the medicolegal autopsy
The purpose of a medicolegal autopsy is to secure the data needed for the administration of justice. Over the years, Humes wrongly described his objective as to "ascertain the cause of death"[87].

Performing an incomplete autopsy
Humes, Boswell and Finck did not dissect the organs of the neck. X-rays were not made of JFK's lower arms and legs. The only organs described in the autopsy report are those removed prior to the arrival of the forensic pathologist - the brain, heart and lungs.

Permitting the body to be embalmed before performing a medicolegal autopsy
Since a medicolegal autopsy was never performed, strictly speaking the body was embalmed before such an autopsy could take place.

Regarding a mutilated or decomposed body as unsuitable for autopsy
I cannot accuse the pathologists of this, although Lifton and others might well describe JFK's body as "mutilated" prior to the official autopsy. Lifton has written, somewhat persuasively, that he believes JFK's body was surgically altered prior to the official autopsy to hide wounding from the front[88].

Mistakes resulting from non-recognition or misinterpretation of post-mortem changes
Again, I cannot specifically accuse the pathologists of this, but Lifton definitely would as he believes the President's body was altered post-mortem, but before the autopsy.

Failure to make an adequate examination and description of external abnormalities
Humes' use of the word "presumably" to describe putative entrance and exit wounds is simply unacceptable and suggests strongly that there was inadequate examination. Also surrendering description of the skull "fractures and the fragments" to an extremely poor set of photographs and X-rays is a failure.

Confusing the objective with the subjective sections of an autopsy protocol (report)
Humes was desperate to find the bullet which he believed entered the

President's back: "It was bothering me very greatly, like nothing you can imagine . . ."[89]. But instead of dissecting the neck, which would have been the unbiased approach, he left it. When writing the autopsy report, he then allowed a prejudiced opinion (that the only shooting was from behind the President) to colour his descriptions.

Not examining the body at the scene of the crime
The crime scene was unusual in that it was moving to begin with. When the President was ambushed, the natural reaction of the Secret Service was to get him away from danger. And JFK did not die until he was in the Parkland trauma room. The point of examining the body at the scene of the crime is to reduce any weaknesses in the chain of possession. This would have been minimised had the President been autopsied in Dallas.

Substituting intuition for scientifically defensible interpretation
Use of "intuition" is a very good way to describe the conclusion that a bullet went through JFK's neck.

Not making adequate photographs of the evidence
The existing photographs are all poor. They do not identify the subject, are badly lit, frequently out of focus and few bear a scale. There are several photographs of the same thing where the camera appears to have moved fractionally, but not zoomed from wide angle to close up. Specific views of wounds appear never to have been taken. Furthermore, some photographs of wounds that the pathologists particularly remember being taken are now missing.

Not exercising good judgment in the taking or handling of specimens for toxicological examination
There is no mention of any toxicological specimens taken, no remarks about any tests made and no citation for any results of such examination.

Permitting the value of the protocol (report) to be jeopardised by minor errors
This entire chapter is devoted to the errors made at the autopsy and in the report. Other authors have devoted complete books. There can be no doubt that the protocol is spectacularly poor.

Talking too soon, too much or to the wrong people.
Humes obviously spoke with the wrong people to get information about how the President died (which he then used in the "Clinical Summary" section of the autopsy report). Furthermore, I believe he was wrong to spend so much time with Specter – together they conspired to enter dishonest testimony into the record.

ELEVEN | THE AUTOPSY OF JOHN F. KENNEDY

If you needed to choose an autopsy to best illustrate Moritz's "classical mistakes" you would select Kennedy's.

Conclusion

In any homicide, the victim's body represents much of the reality of the crime. A poisoned woman will often preserve traces of the poison in her body fluids. A stabbed man will be wounded according to the length and width of the knife. Ordinarily, these elements of the truth are fixed at the time of the murder. An honest investigation seeks to reveal the truth and to preserve it for later use in court.

I believe that those that conspired to kill the President understood this well. They knew that the autopsy had to be managed for the conspiracy to work. The reality of the assassination, captured in JFK's body (that he was shot from at least two different directions), could not be revealed.

The legal process concerning the President's body had to be steered towards covering the conspiracy while appearing to be absolutely genuine.

JFK, like all Presidents, was the Commander-in-Chief of the US military forces. Forgetting for a moment that his autopsy should have taken place in Dallas, an autopsy at a military hospital could be argued, without much vigour, to be perfectly reasonable. Where many have not questioned the choice of a military autopsy, they have largely overlooked the fact that in a military hospital the information available to any investigation could be controlled through career promotions and threats of courts martial.

I believe that the obvious choice of The Armed Forces Institute of Pathology at Walter Reid Hospital had to be avoided as there would be too many qualified doctors there to enable full control. As the deceased President was a US Navy veteran, Bethesda Hospital could be made to appear to be just as reasonable a choice for the autopsy location.

The most senior but least experienced pathologists had to be chosen for the job. Their seniority would appear to be appropriate, but their medicolegal inexperience and lack of recent practice would be a bonus. It could almost be guaranteed that they would make irrevocable mistakes. They could also be more easily influenced by their superiors. As this might look negligent, a qualified consultant had to be involved. He must be from a different hospital so that he can be made to arrive after the relevant parts of the body had been removed and so that he cannot apply his expertise. This was achieved by ordering Humes to call for help only after JFK's body was in the morgue and then by ordering him to start the autopsy immediately – specifically to remove the brain, heart and lungs.

The extent of the autopsy had to be controlled. A full autopsy report could not be allowed, yet it had to be characterised as the best possible given the circumstances. To achieve this, a hierarchy of excuses was suggested: I believe the pathologists were told to begin by claiming that the aim was "just to find ballistics evidence" (plan A). If that unravelled, they were given a plan B which was to claim that the autopsy was "just to find the cause of death". If that came apart, plan C was to use the "the family wishes argument". I believe they were ordered never to accept that the autopsy was anything but complete by arguing that it was complete given their constraints (A to C).

The evidence collected during the autopsy (including the photographs and X-rays) had to be kept out of the official record. Then it could be subjected to whatever alterations and redactions necessary for the official conclusion and to blame a lone assassin.

The initial investigation by the Warren Commission could not be allowed to call any witnesses to the autopsy apart from the pathologists. Earl Warren himself should be used to justify keeping the autopsy photographs and X-rays out of the public record. The documentation provided to the Warren Commission must be different to that provided to the FBI. It must be degraded, altered, substituted or manufactured for the purpose of concealing the conspiracy which killed the President of the United States.

Endnotes

1. 2H 348
2. Testimony of Humes to ARRB p42
3. 2H 348
4. Assassination Records Review Board testimony p17
5. Transcript of testimony of Dr Pierre A Finck during the trial of Clay Shaw in New Orleans, La. February 24-25 1969, p52
6. 2H 349
7. Transcript of testimony of Dr Pierre A Finck during the trial of Clay Shaw in New Orleans, La. February 24-25 1969
8. ARRB Medical Document 28 p4, Finck Memo to Brigadier General Blumberg
9. JAMA, May 27, 1992, Vol 267 No.20 p2798
10. Testimony of Humes to ARRB p40
11. US Military Autopsy Manual p64 Section 125c
12. ARRB Medical Document 28 p4, Finck Memo to Brigadier General Blumberg
13. ARRB Medical Document 44 – Sibert and O'Neill Report on the Autopsy (11/26/63)– "Gemberling Version"
14. CE400
15. HSCA Appendix to Hearings 7 p246 on September 11 1977
16. ARRB Medical Document 21 p 323, HSCA sworn testimony 7 September 1978
17. 2H 379
18. Warren Commission Report Appendix IX CE 391
19. 2H 380
20. 2H 384
21. David S Lifton, *Best Evidence*, (New York, Carroll & Graf, 1991) Chapter 6
22. ARRB Medical Document 30 Transcript of Finck testimony to HSCA p24 (p91 of stenographic transcript)
23. Transcript of Finck's testimony to ARRB p53
24. Transcript of Finck's testimony to ARRB p54
25. Transcript of Finck's testimony to ARRB p41
26. Transcript of Finck's testimony to ARRB p27

ELEVEN | THE AUTOPSY OF JOHN F. KENNEDY

27. JAMA, October 7, 1992, Vol 268 No.13
28. US Military Autopsy Manual, 1981 (Department of the Army Technical Manual TM 8-300, Department of the Navy Publication NAVMED P-5065, Department of the Air Force Manual AFM 160-19). Hereafter "US Military Autopsy Manual"
29. Charles G Wilber, *Medicolegal Investigation of the President John F. Kennedy Murder*, (Charles C. Thomas, 1978)
30. Testimony of Humes to ARRB p41
31. US Military Autopsy Manual p64 Section 124
32. US Military Autopsy Manual p64 Section 125a
33. US Military Autopsy Manual p64 Section 125b
34. Warren Commission Report Appendix IX CE 387
35. US Military Autopsy Manual p65 Section 128
36. US Military Autopsy Manual p1 Section 3
37. Ibid
38. James Folliard, *Blaming The Victims: Kennedy Family Control Over The Bethesda Autopsy*, The Fourth Decade Vol 2 No.4
39. US Military Autopsy Manual p65 Section 128
40. Harold Weisberg, *Post Mortem* p507
41. Warren Commission Report Appendix IX CE 387
42. 2H 363
43. US Military Autopsy Manual p6 Section 14a
44. 2H 363
45. Burkitt & Quick, *Essential Surgery*, 3rd Edition (Elsevier Science Limited, 2002) p331 – illustration by P J Deakin
46. 6H 54
47. 6H 70
48. 3H 370
49. US Military Autopsy Manual p17 Section 24
50. US Military Autopsy Manual p19 Section 26
51. US Military Autopsy Manual p25 Section 35
52. Warren Commission Report Appendix IX CE 387
53. Ibid
54. Charles G Wilber, *Medicolegal Investigation of the President John F. Kennedy Murder*, (Charles C. Thomas, 1978)
55. Ibid
56. US Military Autopsy Manual p74 Section 140
57. US Military Autopsy Manual p66 Section 131
58. Clark Panel Report p3 1968 (ARRB Medical Document 59)
59. US Military Autopsy Manual p17 Section 24 and p19 Section 26
60. US Military Autopsy Manual p72 Section 139a
61. US Military Autopsy Manual p72 Section 139b
62. 17H 29 CE397
63. Harold Weisberg, *Post Mortem* p255 - 256
64. 2H 374
65. Humes testimony to Jeremy Gunn ARRB quoted in Douglas P Horne, *Inside the Assassination Records Review Board*, Vol 1 p95
66. 2H 373
67. ARRB Medical Document 28, Finck Memo to Brigadier General Blumberg
68. Transcript of Finck's testimony to ARRB p99 - 100
69. HSCA Appendix to Hearings 7 p246
70. David S Lifton, *Best Evidence*, (New York, Carroll & Graf, 1991) p534
71. Douglas P Horne, *Inside the Assassination Records Review Board*, Vol 3 p777
72. A computer scan of the photograph of the X-ray made by John Hunt at NARA, John Hunt, "*A Demonstrable*

Impossiblity: The HSCA Forensic Pathology Panel's Misrepresentation of the Kennedy Assassination Medical Evidence", www.history-matters.com

73. Warren Commission Report Appendix IX CE 387
74. ARRB Medical Document 44, Sibert and O'Neill Report on the Autopsy (11/26/63)–"Gemberling Version"
75. Douglas P Horne, *Inside the Assassination Records Review Board*, Vol 1 p122
76. Ibid p127
77. ARRB Medical Document 65, Copy of HSCA Interview 29/08/77
78. W. C. Sealy, "Contusions of the Lung from No penetrating Injuries to the Thorax", Archives of Surgery, 1949: 59(4): 882-887
79. Douglas P Horne, *Inside the Assassination Records Review Board*, Vol 2 p337
80. James L Swanson, *Manhunt* (New York, HarperCollins, 2006)
81. http://rogerjnorton.com/Lincoln83.html
82. http://www.acorn.net/jfkplace/03/JDT/jdtaut.txt
83. Harrison Livingstone, *High Treason 2*, (New York, Carroll & Graf, 1992) p121
84. 6H 16
85. Dr Alan R. Moritz, "*Classical Mistakes in Forensic Pathology*" American Journal of Clinical Pathology, 1956 (also Am J Forensic Med Pathol. 1981 Dec; 2(4): 299-308)
86. US Military Autopsy Manual p74 Section 142
87. ARRB Medical Document 21 p 324, HSCA sworn testimony 7 September 1978
88. David S Lifton, *Best Evidence*, (New York, Carroll & Graf, 1991)
89. JAMA, May 27, 1992, Vol 267 No.20

Endnotes Table pp. 353-355

1. US Military Autopsy Manual p17 Section 24
2. US Military Autopsy Manual p19 Section 26
3. US Military Autopsy Manual p25 Section 35
4. Warren Commission Report Appendix IX CE 387
5. Ibid

Twelve
Jack Ruby
Tony Austin

> *"The great enemy of the truth is very often not the lie – deliberate, contrived and dishonest, but the myth, persistent, persuasive and unrealistic. Belief in myths allows the comfort of opinion without the discomfort of thought."*
> – John F. Kennedy, Yale University, June 1962

On the 24th day of November 1963, in the basement of Dallas Police Department headquarters, groups of journalists, radio reporters and television crews were gathered in anticipation of the arrival of one man. The public was still reeling from the shock of the murder of President Kennedy only two days earlier but the police had the prime suspect for the crime, an ex-marine by the name of Lee Harvey Oswald, safely in their custody. The Dallas Police were required to transfer Oswald to the county jail that morning and at 11:20am Oswald arrived down in the basement and emerged into the bright lights of the TV crews handcuffed and flanked by two police officers. There were more than seventy members of the police department present and dozens of people from the world's media there to cover the event.

Suddenly a heavy set man in a dark suit lunged forward from the onlookers and shot Oswald at point blank range before the police officers were able to force him to the ground and disarm him. Oswald was seriously wounded and soon he was being bundled into an ambulance and hurriedly transferred to Parkland Hospital. However, attempts to save his life proved futile and within two hours Oswald was pronounced dead.

The man who shot Oswald was quickly identified as Jack Ruby, the owner of a Dallas nightclub called the Carousel Club. But who was Jack Ruby? How did he get into the basement of police headquarters and manage to shoot dead a man being guarded by over 70 members of the Dallas Police Department? Why did he do it? Was he acting alone or was he acting on the orders of others? Was he somehow involved in the killing of President Kennedy? Was he trying to silence Oswald?

These questions have been repeatedly asked over the years and different individuals and investigatory bodies have reviewed the matter and come to

JFK | ECHOES FROM ELM STREET
A SEARCH FOR HISTORICAL ACCURACY ON THE
ASSASSINATION OF PRESIDENT JOHN F. KENNEDY

different conclusions. The Warren Commission was first official body to look in detail at these questions about Jack Ruby.

The Warren Commission
The Warren Report came out in 1964 and included a biography of Jack Ruby in the appendix section. Some of the details provided in this biography are as follows:

Jack Ruby was born in 1911 and he was the fifth of his parents' eight children. His parents were Jewish immigrants from Poland. His father was a carpenter and he was known for his excessive drinking and violent behaviour, sometimes against his wife. His mother was said to have "domestic shortcomings" that were accompanied by symptoms of mental disease. In 1927 she was said to be suffering from psychoneurosis with marked anxiety state. In 1937 she was committed to Elgin State Hospital for a few months and she was committed again in 1938. Jack Ruby grew up in a series of poor Jewish neighbourhoods in Chicago. His parents' problems made life hard for him, particularly in 1921 when they separated. In 1922, at the age of 11, he was referred to the Institute for Juvenile Research by the Jewish Social Services Bureau because of "truancy and incorrigible behaviour at home". Jack was described as being "quick tempered" and disobedient. He was placed in a foster home for the next 4 or 5 years.

The Commission was uncertain about the education Ruby received as a child but they noted that he had an apathetic attitude towards school and they doubted that he ever went to high school. As a young man in Chicago he tried to make money selling "novelty items and knickknacks" associated with popular sports. Buried in the 26 volumes of evidence and testimony of the Warren Commission is exhibit 1288 which shows that Barney Ross told the FBI that in 1926 (when Ruby would have been 15 years old) he and Jack Ruby were members of a group of about 12 young boys that ran errands for the infamous Chicago Gangster Al Capone. However, this information was not included in biography of Ruby in the main Warren Report, where all the findings of the Warren Commission are summed up in one volume. In contrast, the Warren Report biography states that some of Ruby's friends eventually became criminals but they did not believe that Ruby had been involved with Chicago's criminal element on the basis of statements made by family, friends and acquaintances of Ruby.

Some people spoke of Ruby as being mild mannered, quiet and even tempered in his youth but others reported that he had the reputation of being a good street brawler.

In 1933, at the age of 22, Ruby moved to San Francisco where he lived for 4 years. He had a number of different low paid jobs during this time. He appears to have lived quietly and kept out of trouble during this period of his life. In 1937 he returned to Chicago and remained there for the next 6 years. During

TWELVE | JACK RUBY

this time, Ruby's friend Leon Cooke arranged for him to work for the Scrap Iron and Junk Handlers Union. In December 1939 Cooke was shot dead by John Martin, the president of the union. Martin was acquitted on the grounds of self-defence. Ruby was upset by the event and left the union. The Warren Commission considered the possibility that Chicago's criminal element was involved in these events but said that they found nothing to support this idea. After this event, Ruby earned money selling various items. At one stage he was selling "Remember Pearl Harbor" plaques. His friends reported that Ruby had no interest in political affairs during this period. He was more interested in sports and he liked to associate with boxers. Ruby was sometimes involved in fights at this time, usually with persons making derogatory comments about his ethnic background or being overtly pro-Nazi or anti-Semitic in his presence. The Warren Commission stated that he was familiar with some Chicago criminals but again stated that there was no evidence that he ever participated in organised criminal activity.

In May 1943, Ruby was called up into the armed services and he served at various airbases in America. It was reported that on one occasion a sergeant called him a "Jew bastard" and he responded by beating him with his fists. Ruby attained the rank of private first class and he was honourably discharged in February 1946. Following his discharge, Jack Ruby went to work for a small company in Chicago owned by his brother Earl Ruby. He was in charge of sales for the company that made and sold items such as small cedar chests.

Jack Ruby went to Dallas in early 1947 to help his sister Eva Grant manage the nightclub she owned called the Singapore. In October 1949 agents of the Bureau of Narcotics interrogated Jack and his brother about their association with Paul Roland Jones. Mr Jones had recently been convicted of attempting to bribe Steve Guthrie the newly elected sheriff of Dallas. He represented a group of Chicago criminals that wanted to move in and manage illegal activities in Dallas. Ruby and his brother admitted knowing Jones but denied any awareness of his connection with narcotics.

The Warren Commission accepted Ruby's denial and rejected suggestions by Steve Gutherie that Ruby was to be a front man for the proposed criminal activities.

According to the Warren Commission, except for a brief period of time when he managed the Evray Theatre motion picture house, the operation of nightclubs and dancehalls was his primary source of income and his basic interest in life during the 16 years he spent in Dallas prior to his shooting of Oswald.

During this time Ruby developed a reputation for violence. He acted as an unofficial bouncer at the Carousel Club and the Warren Report mentioned that "on about 15 occasions since 1950, he beat with his fists, pistol whipped, or blackjacked patrons that became unruly." Ruby could be equally violent towards his own employees if he got into a heated argument with them. He was reported once to have hit one of his employees over the head with a blackjack and he also knocked a guitarist to the ground and kicked him in the groin. On another occasion he beat another musician with brass knuckles. Ruby punched entertainer Joe Peterson in the mouth and knocked a tooth out and he reportedly gave handyman Frank Ferraro a severe beating. Even the women were not immune to violent tendencies, in March 1963, during an argument about wages, Ruby threatened to throw a cigarette girl down the steps of the Carousel. There were other reports of Ruby physically assaulting women. Jack Ruby could be warm and generous to his friends but he was not really the sort of guy you would want to get on the wrong side of!

The Warren Commission reported that Ruby was arrested eight times by the Dallas Police Department. These arrests were for disturbing the peace, allegedly carrying a concealed weapon and violating a peace bond, allegedly violating State liquor laws by selling liquor after hours, allegedly permitting dancing after hours (twice), simple assault and allegedly ignoring traffic summonses. However, there were only three occasions when he received some form of penalty following these arrests.

Possible ties between Ruby and the organised crime were considered in the Warren Report. The Warren Report noted that two individuals had reported that Ruby's consent was necessary before gambling or narcotics operations could be launched in Dallas. However, the individuals were not named and described as being "of questionable reliability". The Warren Report went on to say: "The Commission believes that the evidence does not establish a significant link between Ruby and organised crime."

Ruby the criminal

The Warren Report gave the impression that Jack Ruby's personal involvement in crime during his time in Dallas had been minimal and trivial. However, independent researchers have found evidence that contradicts this point of view. For example, David Scheim, in his book "Contract on America" presents evidence for Ruby being heavily involved in gambling, narcotics and prostitution. The Warren Report is 888 pages long and there are 26 volumes of reports, evidence and testimony that, in theory, support the report. Surprisingly, most of the evidence for Ruby being heavily involved in gambling, narcotics and prostitution comes from these 26 volumes. The next three sections contain information that comes only from this source.

Involvement in gambling

In December 1963 William Abadie told FBI agents that he was hired by Jack Ruby's foreman as a slot machine and juke box mechanic for a period of about seven weeks. He also reported seeing Jack Ruby engaging in illegal bookmaking during that time. Commission Exhibit 1750 is a copy of the relevant FBI report

Twelve | Jack Ruby

but, strangely, it misses off the first page where important details can be found. However, on page 2 of the report, there is the following comment: "...He stated that working in his warehouse, however, it was obvious that to operate the gambling in the manner that he did, he must have racketeering connections with other individuals in the City of Dallas, as well as Fort Worth Texas. He also said that this opinion applied also to police connection with the two cities and this had to be obvious in order to operate. While he was making book for Ruby's establishment, he did observe police officers in and out of the gambling establishment on occasion..."

The FBI interviewed Jack Hardee in prison in December 1963. During that interview, Hardee stated that when he attempted to set up a numbers game in Dallas a year earlier he was told that he would need to have clearance from Jack Ruby. A Secret Service report, dated the 30th of November 1963, concerned statements made by Harry Hall. The report mentioned that this man had provided useful and accurate information to the authorities previously and they regarded him as being a reliable witness. Hall told the Secret Service that in the 1950s he was involved in a scheme to defraud rich Texans through high stake bets. He also said that Jack Ruby was involved in this activity and he spoke of Ruby having good connections in gambling circles in a number of cities he had visited with him. Harry Hall also said that when he made money through the scheme Ruby would be given a 40% cut as he was regarded as having influence with the police and he would not have to worry about being arrested for gambling because of this.

Involvement in narcotics

Jack Ruby was the subject of a CIA memorandum to the Warren Commission dated the 24th of February 1964. In one section it states that he was the subject of a narcotics investigation in 1947 along with his brother Hyman and Paul Roland Jones. Ruby avoided prosecution over this matter but Jones was convicted of flying 60 pounds of opium over the Mexican border. Eileen Curry acted as an informant for the FBI in the 1950s. One FBI report reveals that she told them that in January 1956 she had moved to Dallas with her boyfriend, James Breen, after they had jumped bond on narcotics charges. Breen told her at that time that he had made connections with a large narcotic set up operating between Texas, Mexico and the East. The report includes the sentence: "In some fashion James got the okay to operate through Jack Ruby of Dallas."

Another FBI document records an interview of Eileen Curry in June 1964 in which she confirms her previous account but also states that in early 1956 she saw James Breen drive off with Jack Ruby. Breen told her later that he had accompanied Ruby to an unknown location where he had been shown moving pictures of various border guards plus narcotics agents and contacts on the Mexican side. Breen had been impressed by what he regarded as an extremely efficient narcotics trafficking operation. Eileen Curry had seen Jack Ruby several times at her apartment and at Ruby's club and she easily recognised him as Oswald's killer from news photos.

Involvement in prostitution
Former Dallas County Sheriff Steve Guthrie told the FBI in December 1963 what he knew about Jack Ruby. Paragraph seven is as follows: "Guthrie advised he has never heard a good thing about Jack Ruby to the best of his knowledge. He believes Ruby has operated some prostitution activities and other vices in his club since Ruby has been in Dallas."

Jack Hardee has already been mentioned regarding his comments about Jack Ruby being involved in illegal gambling activities. In the same FBI report he mentions other activities that Ruby was engaged in. At one point it states: "Hardee stated that he knows of his own personal knowledge that Ruby hustled the strippers and other girls that worked in his club. Ruby made dates for them accepting the money for dates in advance, and kept half, giving the other half to the girls."

The FBI interviewed the Dallas restaurant operator Carl Maynard in November 1963 and noted certain information that he had obtained from Diana (last name unknown). She was one of his employees who previously worked as a waitress for Jack Ruby. The report states: "Ruby had strict rules that strippers and waitresses should not leave the Carousel with dates, but Diana said that all girls employed did fill $100 a night dates after work, particularly after convention nights. She did not say that Ruby received a cut as a pimp, but Maynard's impression of Ruby is that he would do anything for money and undoubtedly got a percentage of prostitution dates. Dallas disc jockey Kenneth Dowe testified to the Warren Commission in July 1964 and told them about Jack Ruby. At one point he said "he was known around the station for procuring women for different people who came to town."

Ruby's relationship with the Dallas Police
The Warren Commission acknowledged that Jack Ruby was on friendly terms with many members of the Dallas Police Department and quoted Chief Curry who said that he knew 25 to 50 of the 1,175 men in the DPD. However, statements by witnesses who knew Ruby such as hotel manager Joseph Cavagnaro, musician Johnny Cola and Dallas bartender Edward McBee suggest this was a gross underestimation. Ruby employee William O'Donnell stated that: "Ruby is on speaking terms with about 700 out of the 1200 men on the police force." The Warren Commission mentioned Ruby serving free coffee and soft drinks to Dallas Police Department members at his Carousel Club. However, O'Donnell said that police officers were admitted to the Carousel without charge and given a free round of drinks. Police officers such as Theodore Fleming and Hugh

Smith confirmed that Ruby would give free alcoholic drinks and even bottles of liquor at times to DPD members. If Ruby was on friendly terms with so many men who worked for the Dallas Police department it might well explain how he managed to avoid being arrested for his gambling, narcotics and prostitution activities. It might also help to explain the ease with which he got into Dallas Police Department to stalk Oswald and later kill him.

Other Ruby associations
In 1964 staff within the Warren Commission were aware of some possible associations between Jack Ruby and CIA-Mafia activities connected to Cuba. Burt Griffin and Leon Hubert were running the Warren Commission enquires into Ruby and they wrote a memo in March of 1964 which stated: "The most promising links between Jack Ruby and the assassination are established through underworld figures and anti-Castro Cubans and extreme right-wing Americans."

A month later they wrote another memo: "We believe the possibility exists, based on evidence already available, that Ruby was involved in illegal dealings with Cuban elements who might have been in contact with Oswald."

The Warren Commissions 26 volumes of evidence and testimony did include investigations by the FBI into the possibility that Jack ruby was involved in illegal gunrunning between the USA and Cuba. It has been suggested that the investigations were superficial and the FBI did not pursue the leads to their logical conclusions.

Warren Commission exhibit 3063 shows that the FBI interviewed Blaney Mack Johnson (also known as confidential informant AT T-2) in 1964. In the early 1950s he was a pilot working in Miami and he told them that Jack Ruby was involved in the illegal smuggling of weapons to the pro-Castro forces in Cuba at that time under the name of Jack Rubenstein. The FBI report tries to undermine Johnson's statement by including statements made by Leslie Lewis, Joe Marrs and Clifton T. Bowes, three men who could have corroborated his claims. Their statements contradict Johnson's assertions, although Johnson says in his statement that he believes that these individuals had lied in their own interest.

In Warren Commission exhibit 3065 the FBI interviews Mary Thompson and she describes travelling to Islamorada in Florida in 1958 with her daughter and son-in-law Dolores and Richard Rhoads to visit her brother and sister-in-law, James and Mary Lou Woodard. She met two people known to the Woodards called Jack and Isabel and ended up spending a night at their home. Jack told her he grew up in Chicago and he ran a bar in Dallas. Mary Lou told her that Jack had a trunk full of guns and inferred that he was going to supply them to the Cubans. Mary Thompson claimed that Jack was in fact Jack Ruby. Dolores Rhoads spoke to the FBI and confirmed Mary's story and said that she thought jack was part of a syndicate. James Woodard told the FBI that he had participated in the Bay of Pigs invasion and that he had furnished ammunition and dynamite to both Castro and Cuban exile forces. There is no record of him being asked if the "Jack" he was with was in fact Jack Ruby.

The FBI report includes statements from relatives of the Woodards saying that they were liars or that they readily made things up. This approach was used to dismiss all the information they had provided. The Warren Commission was dismissive of the idea that Jack Ruby was involved in gunning to Cuba. However, support for this idea comes from an interview of James E. Beaird by Earl Golz that appeared in the Dallas Morning News (18th of August, 1978). In the article Beaird identifies himself as a poker-playing friend of Jack Ruby who associated with him in the Houston suburb of Kemah on Galveston Bay in 1957. Beaird claims Ruby stored guns and ammunition in a two-storey house near the waterfront. Beaird reported seeing Ruby and his associates load "many boxes of new guns, including automatic rifles and handguns" on pickup trucks, transporting them to what looked like a 50-foot surplus military boat." Beaird stated that Ruby would take the boat across the Gulf of Mexico to Castro's rebels in Cuba.

There is further support for the idea of Jack Ruby being a gunrunner and that comes from his links to a man called Thomas Eli Davis the third. Going back to Warren Commission staff members Burt Griffin and Leon Hubert, it can be noted that in a memorandum dated the 19th of March 1964 they said, in part: "Ruby has acknowledged independently that, prior to the time that Castro fell into disfavour in the United States, he had been interested in selling jeeps to Cuba. Ruby states that he contacted a man in Beaumont Texas, whose name he recalled was Davis. The FBI has been unable to identify anyone engaged in the sale of arms to Cuba who might be identical with the person named Davis."

The FBI never made progress on this matter and the Warren Commission ignored this memo. However, in his book "Who was Jack Ruby" (on page 15) the veteran newsman Seth Kantor writes that Ruby's first lawyer, Tom Howard of Texas, asked Ruby if there were any names of people of people the prosecution could produce who could be damaging to his defence. Ruby came up with Thomas Davis immediately, he told Tom Howard that he had been involved with Davis, who was a gunrunner entangled in anti-Castro efforts. Ruby even told Howard that he intended to go into the gunrunning business in partnership with Davis sometime in the future.

Kantor writes that Davis was a professional deep-sea diver who operated a boat on the Gulf of Mexico. He had become involved in training anti-Castro units at a hidden encampment in Florida and at another site in South America according to knowledgeable sources in Texas. At the time of the assassination of Kennedy, Davis was in Jail in Algiers, charged with gun running to men planning to assassinate French Premier Charles de Gaulle. Evidence shows that Davis was freed from jail through the efforts of QJ/WIN, the code name given by the CIA

TWELVE | JACK RUBY

to a foreign agent with a network of Mafia contacts. He specialised in recruiting and directing other criminals to handle CIA assignments. QJ/WIN worked on African and European projects. If the Warren Commission had established an association between Thomas Eli Davis III and Jack Ruby it might have established links between Ruby and elements in CIA and the Mafia that were involved in gunrunning to Cuba. However, that was one can of worms that the Warren Commission made no attempt to open.

The next large scale official investigation of the assassination of President Kennedy came in the 1970s when the House Select Committee on Assassinations was formed to re-examine the crime.

The House Select Committee on Assassinations

Still on the subject of Jack Ruby and illegal dealings with Cuba, the HSCA looked into the question of Jack Ruby associating with Robert Ray McKeown in 1959. McKeown lived in the Houston area of Texas and he had been arrested by federal agents a year earlier for conspiring to smuggle guns to Castro. He received a 2-year suspended sentence and five-year probation. The FBI made the Warren Commission aware that there had been a close association between McKeown and Fidel Castro and Carlos Prio Socarras (the President of Cuba from 1948 until 1952 when a military coup brought Batista to power). The HSCA reported that the Warren Commission had not interviewed Robert McKeown and that it could be argued that it had failed to investigate the matter adequately.

When interviewed by the FBI on the 24th of January 1964, McKeown spoke of his first contact with Jack Ruby on the phone: "...a person called him, identified himself as Jack Rubenstein from Dallas Tex, affirmed McKeown's connections with Castro and solicited McKeown's assistance in obtaining the release of three people detained in Cuba. Rubenstein offered $5,000 per person, stating that someone in Los Vegas could provide the money. McKeown said he would accept the offer on the condition that he first received some money. Rubenstein replied by saying that he would think about it and call again. About 3 weeks after the call a man visited the J and M and offered him $25,000 for a letter of introduction to Castro. The visitor, who could not introduce himself, stated that he had access to a large number of jeeps in Shreveport, La, which he wished to sell to sell to Cuba. McKeown said that he would provide a letter upon a $500 cash down payment. McKeown said that the man "never returned nor did he ever see him again."

According to the HSCA: "McKeown told the FBI his visitor strongly resembled Jack Ruby; McKeown stated, however, "He is not certain that the above-described telephone caller from Dallas or the man who personally appeared at the J and M Drive-In was identical with the Jack Ruby who killed Lee Harvey Oswald."

It is of note that large sums of money were being discussed. You would not expect a man like Jack Ruby to have come up with $25,000 by himself; however, he could have obtained this sort of money if he was acting on behalf of the Mafia or the CIA, both of whom were active in supplying arms and military supplies to Castro at this time.

The HSCA was aware of statements made by Jack Ruby suggesting he had been in contact with Robert McKeown and also statements had been made by his sister, Eva Grant, that Ruby had spoken to her about using someone in Houston to sell jeeps to people in Cuba. The HSCA remained sceptical about statements made by McKeown due to differences in the comments made by Ruby and also inconsistencies between various statements made by McKeown made at different times.

However, it had to admit that something could have been going on between these two individuals. The HSCA report states: "The most that can be said is that Ruby probably made some kind of contact with someone, possibly McKeown, in Texas regarding something related to Cuba. The statement alone is consistent with the inference that Ruby's trips to Cuba were not merely for vacation. If McKeown's allegations are in fact true, which again the committee was unable to determine, this would lead more credence to the committee's theory regarding Ruby's trips."

The report continues: "If Ruby did in fact take at least three trips to Cuba and on at least one of these trips was acting as a courier, there is a strong possibility that he was interested in pursuing other interests, such as selling jeeps or guns to Cuba or obtaining the release of prisoners. This possibility is supported not only by McKeown's statements, but also Ruby's. Ruby admitted he had contacted someone regarding the sale of jeeps to Castro. Ruby also reportedly told Wally Weston, "They're going to find out about Cuba, they're going to find out about the guns."

Ruby and the Mafia

The HSCA probed more deeply into the question of Mafia involvement in the assassination of John Kennedy than the Warren Commission had done earlier.

The findings of the HSCA included the following: "The committee believes, on the basis of the evidence available to it, that the national syndicate of organised crime, as a group, was not involved in the assassination of President Kennedy, but that the available evidence does not preclude the possibility that individual members may have been involved."

The HSCA believed in the possibility that some members of organised crime could have been involved in the assassination because they believed that Ruby had shot Oswald with the help of others and they had found that Ruby "had a significant number of associations and direct and indirect contacts with underworld figures, a number who were connected to the most powerful La Cosa Nostra leaders.

Additionally, Ruby had numerous associations with the Dallas criminal element."

Twelve | Jack Ruby

The HSCA established that David Yaras and Lenny Patrick were acquainted with Ruby in the 1930's and 1940's. They also established that Yaras and Patrick were notorious gunmen closely associated with an organised crime leader in Chicago called Sam Giancana. They were believed to be responsible for numerous syndicate executions. The HSCA stated that Ruby had probably talked to Patrick during the summer of 1963.

The Committee noted that one of Ruby's closest friends was Lewis McWillie and stated that: " McWillie moved from Dallas to Cuba in 1958 and worked in gambling casinos in Havana until 1960. In 1978, Mc Willie was employed in Las Vegas, and law enforcement files indicate he had business and personal ties to major organized crime figures, including Meyer Lansky and Santos Trafficante."

Both Ruby and McWillie claimed that Ruby visited Cuba in late summer or early fall of 1959 at the invitation of McWillie. They described it as a single social visit lasting for about a week. However, the HSCA found clear evidence for Ruby moving backwards and forwards between America and Cuba in August and September 1959 so that he had to have made at least three trips to Cuba. The committee reached the judgement that Ruby most likely was serving as a courier for gambling interests when he travelled to Miami from Havana for 1 day, before flying to New Orleans.

The HSCA also deemed it likely that Ruby at least met various organised crime figures in Cuba, possibly including some who had been detained by the Cuban government. The committee quoted declassified CIA document from the 28th of November 1963: "On 26 November 1963, a British Journalist named John Wilson…gave information to the American Embassy in London… In prison in Cuba, Wilson says he met an American gangster/gambler named Santos who could not return to the U.S.A. … While Santos was in prison, Wilson says, Santos was visited frequently by an American gangster type named Ruby…"

The HSCA arranged for an extensive computer analysis of the telephone toll records of Jack Ruby for the month prior to the President's assassination and this revealed that "he either placed calls to or received calls from a number of individuals who may be fairly characterized as having been affiliated, directly or indirectly, with organized crime."

In 1963, Jack Ruby had to deal with the AGVA, an entertainer's union, regarding a dispute between himself and other nightclub operators over the use of amateur performers in the clubs. Individuals that spoke to Ruby over the phone usually said that he was discussing AGVA union business with them. The HSCA thought it would be possible that other matters had been discussed on the phone. The committee was not satisfied with the explanations of three individuals concerned. Ruby phoned Irwin Weiner, a Chicago bondsman well known as a front man for organised crime, on October 26, 1963. "Weiner suggested that Ruby was seeking a bond necessary to obtain an injunction in his labor troubles, yet the committee could find no credible indication that Ruby contemplated seeking court relief, nor any other explanation for his having to go to Chicago for such a bond.

Robert "Barney" Baker was a lieutenant of James R Hoffa and associate of several convicted organised crime executioners. He told the FBI that he received just one call from Ruby on November 7 during which he curtly dismissed Ruby's plea for assistance. The committee established that Baker received a second lengthy call from Ruby only one day later. The committee found it hard to believe that Baker, who denied the conversation ever took place, could have forgotten it. The committee were concerned about a call that Ruby made on the 30th of October to the New Orleans Trailer Park Office of Nofio J. Pecora who they described as a long time Marcello lieutenant. Pecora claimed he would have answered the phone but not spoken with Ruby or passed on a message.

The HSCA noted that James Henry Dolan, a Dallas AGVA representative was reportedly an acquaintance of Mafia bosses Carlos Marcello and Santos Trafficante and the FBI had identified him as being an associate of Nofio Pecora. While Dolan worked with Ruby on labour matters they were also allegedly associated with some criminal activities that involved the Dallas Adolphus Hotel. The committee noted further that reported links between AVGA and organised crime figures had been the subject of Federal and State investigations for years leading up to their report. The committee's difficulties in separating Ruby's AGVA contacts from his organised crime connections was, in large degree, based on the dual roles that many of his associates played.

The HSCA established that Jack Ruby was a friend and business associate of Joseph Civello who has been described as being a deputy in Dallas for the New Orleans Mafia boss Carlos Marcello. In 1964 Civello told the FBI that he had been a casual acquaintance of Ruby for about ten years and he had seen Ruby about four or five times during that period. The committee also established that Ruby was on friendly terms with Joseph Campisi who owned the Egyptian Lounge in Dallas. His roommate, George Senator, testified that Campisi was one of Ruby's closest friends. This can clearly be seen to be true because Ruby dined with him at the Egyptian Lounge the night before Kennedy was assassinated and Campisi and his wife were two of the first people to visit Jack Ruby in prison after he killed Oswald. Campisi told the HSCA that he knew Carlos Marcello and his brothers very well and he even spoke of going with them on fishing trips to Grand Isle where he would cook spaghetti for Carlos and his brothers on several occasions. Campisi would also send the Marcello brothers 260 pounds of homemade sausages every Christmas.

Warren Commission defender Vincent Bugliosi writes that neither Civello nor Campisi were actively involved in Mafia activities in Dallas at the time of the assassination. He acknowledges that Civello was a Mafia figure and head of the small Mafia group present in Dallas at that time. He even mentions that when

TWELVE | JACK RUBY

the police uncovered a large gathering of Mafia bosses from all over America in Apalachin, New York, in 1957 that Civello was amongst the 59 high ranking Mafia men that were detained. However, he quotes a FBI report in which it was concluded that in 1962 there was "no evidence of illegal activities by Joseph Francis Civello."

Bugliosi quotes former Dallas district attorney Bill Alexander as saying: "we had no organised crime in Dallas. Our local criminals were too tough for them..." which makes you wonder what kind of violent, murderous place was Dallas back in those days if the local criminals were too tough for the Mafia, were the bank robbers mugged on their way to their getaway cars?

Alexander is also quoted as saying: "I would be the one to have known because I screened all the cases that came through the district attorney's office. Carlos Marcello had no influence here, and as far as two of our locals, Joe Civello and Joe Campisi, they never did anything here." In 1957 a US Senate Committee stated that Dallas had its own Mafia boss, Joseph Civello and in November of that year Civello represented Dallas at the meeting of national organised crime bosses at Apalachin. According to another Senate document; Civello's arrest by the police at Apalachin led to him being sentenced to five years for conspiracy to obstruct justice in 1960. However, ten months later he was successful in his appeal against this sentence. In 1967 Dallas was included in a federal report as one of 25 centres of Mafia activity in the USA.

It seems strange that there should be an active Mafia group in Dallas in 1957 and again in 1967 but no Mafia activity in 1962 and 1963. Did the activity of the Dallas Mafia really diminish to nothing by 1963, only to re-emerge in the years that followed?

Vincent Bugliosi does not mention that Bill Alexander and Jack Ruby were well acquainted, Ruby even went to see him about some 'bad checks' the day before the assassination of Kennedy. On one occasion, Jack Ruby was testifying in Court and he claimed that Bill Alexander had said to him "Jack, I have been your friend for 13 years" and also he spoke about giving Alexander a courtesy pass to his nightclub (Moment of Madness by Elmer Gertz, p187). It should be noted that, in fact, a permanent pass for the Carousel Club in the name of Bill Alexander was found amongst Ruby's possessions in his car following his arrest.

Could it be that the relationship between Alexander and Ruby had been rather too friendly? And, if so, would this have made Alexander inclined to play down Ruby's association with organised crime? After all, nobody would worry about their District Attorney being on friendly terms with a humble nightclub owner but most people would worry about their District Attorney being friendly with a nightclub owner who was involved in gambling, narcotics, prostitution and associating with a local and very active Mafia boss.

However, having said this, it is also possible that Alexander was telling the truth and he had not seen any information suggesting that Campisi and Civello were active in organised crime activities when, in fact, the opposite was the case. The reason for this could have been that there was a significant amount of corruption within Dallas law enforcement circles.

With this in mind it is interesting to note that in volume 9 of the House Select Committee on Assassinations you can find a biographical summary for Joseph Campisi. In paragraph 913 of this summary there is mention of a 1970 FBI report that contains an assertion by an informant that Joe Campisi was close with both State Judges and members of the Dallas County District Attorney's office. According to the informant, he also had contacts within the Dallas Police Department. The possibility of Mafia activity being hidden by corruption should be considered but is there any real evidence that either Civello or Campisi were activity involved in organised crime activities in 1963? Let us consider the evidence in the FBI files that suggests that this was the case: On the 30th of October 1961 Lieutenant Jack Revill from the intelligence Unit of the Dallas Police Department told FBI Special Agent Carl X. Underhill that, for a period of at least 10 years, information had been received that Joe and Sam Campisi were running illegal gambling and prostitution activities from the Egyptian Lounge. He went on to say that they had been unable to substantiate any of the allegations. (According to this report there had been 10 years of smoke without any fire!)

On the 31st of January 1963 FBI Special Agents Barret and Ivan D. Lee reported that they had observed known Dallas gamblers Jesse Ray McPherson, Gerald Francis Burch and John Benton Turns in contact with Joe Campisi in the Egyptian Lounge, the Dallas restaurant owned by Campisi. On the 7th of August 1963 Lieutenant Jack Revill from the Intelligence Unit of the Dallas Police Department advised Special Agent Charles T. Brown that numerous known bookmakers and dice hustlers were frequenting the Egyptian Lounge on a daily basis. The year after the assassination, on the 17th of December 1964, Lieutenant Revill told Special Agent Barrett that Campisi was associating with gamblers Frank J. Tortiello and Riley B. Bawcum but he went on to say that there was no information to suggest that the Campisi brothers were involved in illegal activities at that time or the recent past. However, Revill went on to say that Joe Campisi had been severely reprimanded by his brother Sam to cease any bookmaking activity as it would jeopardise their legitimate business activities. This, of course, suggests that Joe Campisi had been involved in bookmaking up until this reprimand by his brother, almost certainly, sometime in 1964. If Joe Campisi had stopped bookmaking activities prior to 1964 it is unlikely that his brother would have given him a severe reprimand about this criminal activity more than a year after Joe Campisi had completely stopped his involvement in that type of activity. Therefore, it seems very likely that the bookmakers and dice hustlers noted to be going into the Egyptian Lounge on a daily basis in

Twelve | Jack Ruby

August 1963 were there to engage in illegal gambling run by Joe Campisi.

If nothing else, it would appear that Campisi was involved in illegal gambling at the time of the assassination. What about Joe Civello the friend of both Campisi and Ruby? The Chief Counsel and Staff Director of the House Select Committee on Assassinations, Robert Blakey, wrote in his book "The Plot to Kill the President" that the HSCA were interested in Joe Campisi and Joe Civello. On page 313 Blakey states that in 1963 Captain W.P. Gannaway was the commander of the Special Service Bureau and he told the HSCA "emphatically" that the national syndicate's Dallas representative at that time was Civello and that Campisi belonged to his organisation. There was no suggestion made that these men were "inactive" with regards to organised crime at this time.

Did the Mafia have "a hold" over Jack Ruby in November 1963?
In 1963 Jack Ruby was a man with big financial problems. Anthony Summers looks at his problems in his book "The Kennedy Conspiracy (page 345). In March 1963 the Internal Revenue Service was after him for nearly $21,000 and by the mid-summer of that year the figure was nearer to $40,000 (a debt of this size would be amount to nearly $300,000 in today's money). In early October 1963, Ruby was engaged in difficult negotiations with the IRS. However, in November, he started to act as if his luck was going to change. According to Summers, on the 15th of November Ruby began to use a safe and discussed plans to embed it in concrete in his office. On the 19th of November he told his tax lawyer that he now had a "connection" who could supply him with money to settle his tax debts. Ruby also signed a form giving his lawyer power of attorney to control his financial dealings with the government. Ruby's bank records show that he only had $246 in his bank at that time.

Jack Ruby was acting in a way that suggested that he expected to receive a large amount of money to pay off his debts. There is no record of him approaching any legal institution to get a loan and it is unlikely that any legitimate institution would have agreed to give him money. So where was Ruby expecting to receive his huge rescue package from? There is evidence that Ruby was involved in crime and that he had contacts with numerous people associated with the Mafia. We know that he knew Dallas Mafia boss Joseph Civello and we know that he was friends with Joseph Campisi who was on very friendly terms with the powerful New Orleans Mafia boss Carlos Marcello. It is not unreasonable to suggest that Ruby could have used his contacts to arrange for a large loan from Carlos Marcello's organisation. If this had happened, then it would have come 'at a price'. That price might have been an agreement that if at any time Ruby was called upon to do a "special job" for the Mafia then he would do it and his debt would be cancelled. If Ruby refused, he and his family would suffer the consequences. Could it be that on the 24th of November 1963 Jack Ruby called upon to do a special job?

We could speculate that there was a conspiracy to assassinate President Kennedy and that in the original plot Lee Harvey Oswald was supposed to have been shot dead by angry Dallas 'cops' when he was resisting arrest in the Texas Theatre. However, something went badly wrong and Oswald was captured alive. The HSCA concluded that it could not preclude the possibility that certain individuals from organised crime might have been involved in the assassination of Kennedy. If that was the case, then did certain people in the Mafia get nervous that Oswald would talk and say too much? Had things gone so badly wrong that it was time for a damage limitation strategy to be used?

Jack Ruby had engaged in activities such as gambling, prostitution and narcotics and he had associated with Mafia people but he had always managed to avoid prosecution for anything other than trivial crime. He was on friendly terms with dozens of men who worked for the Dallas Police Department so if anybody could find a way of getting into their headquarters it would be Ruby. The Mafia could have had a strong financial hold over Jack Ruby.

Let us speculate for a moment and say what if, following Oswald's capture, Carlos Marcello had contacted his friend Joe Campisi and told him that he wanted to have Oswald killed and he would like him to suggest a suitable local man to do the job. Marcello might then add that the killer would have to be somebody who had no criminal records that could link him to organised crime. He might also say that it would be better if he was familiar with the Mafia and it ways. It would have to be a man that was in debt to the Mafia in some way and, of course, he would have to have a violent streak in his character and be tough enough to kill somebody in cold blood. It would also be an advantage if he had friends in the Dallas Police Department who could help him to gain access to their headquarters when he wanted to carry out the murder. Faced with those requirements, who would Joseph Campisi have suggested? With that question in mind let us look more closely at how Jack Ruby came to murder Lee Harvey Oswald.

Ruby's murder of Oswald
The rest of this chapter will be devoted to a review of the controversial issue of how Jack Ruby entered the basement of the Dallas Police Department headquarters so that he was able shot Lee Harvey Oswald when the police brought him out. The Warren Commission stated: "Although the evidence on Ruby's means of entry is not conclusive, the weight of evidence indicates that he walked down the ramp leading from Main Street to the basement of the police department." The Warren Commission accepted the conclusion of a Dallas Police Department investigative team that stated that Jack Ruby had walked down the ramp at the time a police car driven by Lieutenant Pierce was coming out and going on to Main Street. The Commission also stated: "There is no evidence to support the rumor that Ruby may have been assisted by any

Twelve | Jack Ruby

members of the Dallas Police Department in the killing of Oswald."

However, the House Select Committee on Assassinations reached different conclusions and stated in its report: "The evidence available indicates that Jack Ruby did not come down the Main Street Ramp when Lieutenant Pierce exited." It also stated: "The alley route was the most likely alternative..." The HSCA went on to conclude: "...it is unlikely that Ruby entered the basement without some form of assistance. This might have been in the form of knowledge of the Oswald transfer plans, direct help in entering the basement, or direct help in both entering and shooting Oswald." What follows is a systematic review of the key events in an attempt to determine which official body was correct in its assessment. We shall start with a brief review of the events between the death of President Kennedy and the death of Lee Harvey Oswald.

President Kennedy was shot in Dealey Plaza on Friday the 22nd of November at 12:30pm and the Secret Service took him immediately to Parkland Hospital where he was pronounced dead at 1pm. Jack Ruby said that he was at the offices of the Dallas Morning News at the time of the assassination where he had gone to place an advertisement for his club. The Warren Commission was of the opinion that Ruby was there from about 11am until about 1:30pm. Gladys Craddock told the FBI that she saw Ruby at about 11am in the lobby of the Dallas Morning News. She recalled that he had called out to her: "Hi, the President is going to be here today!" Don Campbell told the FBI that he found Jack Ruby in the advertising offices when he arrived there at 12 noon and he was still there when he left at 12:25pm.

Georgia Mayor informed the FBI that she saw Jack Ruby at about 12:30pm. She said that Hal Coley had told her that Kennedy had just been shot and then she went to cash a 'check' before going upstairs and encountering Ruby at a desk. Hal Coley was in Dealey Plaza at 12:30pm so Georgia Mayor must have seen Ruby some minutes after this time. John Newnam testified to the Warren Commission that he saw Ruby when he came into the offices at 12:40pm and he left around 1:30pm. None of the witnesses can place Ruby at the offices of the Dallas Morning News between 12:25pm and 12:40pm, around the time of the assassination, so it is possible that Ruby slipped out and went to Dealey Plaza for a short time before returning back to the offices by 12:40pm. There are a number of witnesses who claim to have seen Ruby in Dealer Plaza at the time of the assassination. However, Jack Ruby maintained that he remained in the offices of the Dallas Morning News.

After the assassination, friends and relatives of Ruby would claim that he "loved Kennedy" so it was strange that he would not bother to walk a few blocks to see his beloved President. If Ruby was correct in saying that he stayed at the offices of the Dallas Morning News that morning and that he never went to Dealey Plaza it means that he spent two and a half hours there rather than going to watch President Kennedy go by. Bugliosi quotes William Howard, a man who knew Ruby well, as saying "He liked to be in the middle of things no matter what it was." If this is the case, why did he spend more than 2 hours loitering around in the offices of the Dallas Morning News when he could have gone to watch the President's motorcade go by?

It turns out that Ruby might have spent even longer at the newspaper offices that morning. Jerry Colley was an employee in the advertising department of the Dallas Morning News at that time. He was interviewed by Len Osanic on 'Black Ops Radio' on the 3rd of November 2011 about his recollections of that day. He recalled going to the cafeteria in the Dallas Morning News building at 8am and finding Jack Ruby already there. He clearly remembered Ruby chatting with him and another employee in the cafeteria. Ruby was still there at 9am when Colley left the building for a couple of hours. Jerry Colley went back to the offices at 11am and was there for half an hour before he went out again. He noted that Ruby was there over that time and this fits in with statements made by other witnesses that day.

If Colley is correct, then Jack Ruby spent at least 3 and a half hours at the offices of the Dallas Morning News that morning and he did not find the time to walk a few blocks to go and watch the President of the United States drive past in his motorcade. The question is did he specifically want to make sure that people remembered him as being in the offices of the Dallas Morning News around the time of the assassination?

At about 1:30pm, Jack Ruby was seen at Parkland Hospital (where President Kennedy had been taken) by a journalist called Seth Kantor who knew him well. However, Ruby denied being at the hospital and the Warren Commission chose to accept Ruby's word on the matter. Support for Kantor's claim came from Wilma Tice who claimed to have seen Ruby at the hospital and Roy Stamps, a former radio newsman, who claimed some years later that he saw Ruby in the hospital that day. In 1979 the House Selected Committee on Assassinations concluded that Seth Kantor was not mistaken and that Ruby was at Parklands Hospital at about 1:30pm. After this, Ruby went back to the Carousel Club and gave orders for the club to be closed for the weekend. He then made numerous phone calls to people he knew and told them how upset he was about the death of the President. Later that day, in the early evening, Ruby was seen on the third floor of Dallas Police Department headquarters by police and media personnel. One reporter witnessed him trying to enter Captain Fritz's office where Oswald was at the time. Two police officers stopped him "You can't go in there, Jack" he was told. Like many of the police officers in Dallas, they knew Ruby by name.

Ruby left and was later seen attending an evening service at his local synagogue being held in memory of the dead President. He arrived near the end of the service and the rabbi, who talked to him, noticed that he said nothing at all about the assassination.

Later, Ruby was seen again in police headquarters at the midnight press conference. He was posing as a newspaper reporter and even corrected District Attorney Henry Wade when he said that Oswald was a member of the Free Cuba Committee (an anti-Castro group) calling out to him that it was the Fair Play for Cuba Committee (a pro-Castro group) that he really meant to say. After the conference, Ruby went around to a local radio station and spent some time talking with people there. Later he spent at least an hour with an off duty police officer by the name of Harry Olsen and his girlfriend who was one of Ruby's nightclub girls. They talked about the assassination and Ruby cursed Oswald and said that he should be cut to ribbons. Ruby then went on to the Times-Herald offices and expressed his feelings about the assassination to the few people still around at that time.

At 4:30am Ruby woke up his roommate, contacted an employee, and made both of them go out with him to take photographs of a political poster aimed against the Chief Justice of the United States. Only then did Jack Ruby go home and go to bed.

On Saturday the 23rd of November, in the early afternoon, Ruby made two phone calls to local newsmen asking when Oswald would be moved to the county jail. There had been some early discussion amongst the police about transferring Oswald at 4pm and Ruby was seen at police headquarters at 4pm that day. Nothing happened at that time, but some time later, Police Chief Curry told reporters that they should come back next day at 10am. Jack Ruby was still around at this time.

At 10:44pm a call was made from Jack Ruby's sister's apartment to the Bull Pen, a restaurant owned by Ralph Paul, the friend and financial backer of Ruby. Paul would later claim he had left the restaurant by this time and that he never spoke to Ruby. However, a waitress called Wanda Yvonne Helmick testified to the Warren Commission that she remembered Ralph Paul being called to take a call from 'Jack'. She also said: "...he had been talking quite a while and he said something. He either said, "Are you crazy, a gun?" or something like that, or he said something about a gun."

At 11pm Ruby was at his club and making phone calls again. He phoned Galveston to try to speak to his friend Breck Wall a few times and he also phoned Ralph Paul again. At midnight, Jack Ruby was seen at the Pago club with the owner Bob Norton and left about half an hour later. He telephoned his sister from his apartment at about 12:45am and later he would claim that he went to bed between 1 and 1:30am.

Researchers have looked at Jack Ruby's activities between the 21st of November and the 24th of November and found that he probably slept for less than 14 hours over that three-day period. He seemed to be very emotional and numerous witness statements show that he was obsessed with the events of the assassination. Ruby was seen in close proximity to Oswald on the Friday and Saturday of that weekend. He was also making efforts to find out when Oswald would be transferred to the County Jail. He would have known that Oswald was supposed to be transferred at 10am on the Sunday morning. According to the Warren Commission, on the Sunday Morning, Ruby stayed at his apartment until after 10am and then drove over to the Western Union office near to Dallas Police Department headquarters with no plans to go into that building at that time.

Given this background, the question is: why didn't Ruby try to be at Dallas Police Department headquarters before 10am to watch the transfer? This was the man who 'loved President Kennedy' and who 'liked to be in the middle of things no matter what it was', so why was he not at the headquarters bright and early? There is some evidence that Ruby had his revolver with him when he attended the midnight press conference. Another question is: why did Ruby not try and shoot Oswald earlier when he was near him in Dallas Police Department headquarters? If we were to assume that Ruby was acting under orders when he killed Oswald, then the answer to both these questions probably relates to the fact that Ruby would have known that shooting Oswald in the police headquarters after stalking him, to use a modern expression, would have had two consequences. Firstly, he would have been arrested by the police almost immediately and, secondly, he would almost certainly have received the death sentence for premeditated murder. However, if Ruby could appear to have arrived down in the basement area by chance within seconds of Oswald appearing and then appear to be overcome by overwhelming emotion when Oswald was brought out, then it would be possible for him to plead for murder without malice. If this plan worked, he would received a 5-year jail sentence and avoid a death sentence.

In order for this plan to work, Ruby would have needed some help. He would also have needed a good excuse for attending somewhere very close to Dallas Police Department headquarters and some way of showing he was at that place within minutes of Oswald's transfer. The day before Oswald's transfer, a way of solving this problem appeared to Ruby in the form of his employee, Karen Carlin.

Karen Carlin
Karen Carlin, also known as 'Little Lynn', worked as a stripper for Jack Ruby at the time of the assassination. Contacts between Ruby and Carlin between the death of Kennedy and the death of Oswald were highly significant. Nancy Powell, also known as Tammi True, testified to the Warren Commission that she drove Karen Carlin and her husband Bruce to Dallas the night before Oswald's murder and drove them back home again later that evening. She said that she took Karen to the Carousel Club where she expected to be working that night but they found that the club was closed. Nancy testified that Karen phoned Ruby because she wanted either $20 or $25 and she wanted to pick the money

Twelve | Jack Ruby

up from his apartment. Ruby told her that he would send her the money next day.

Karen and Bruce Carlin gave a slightly different account. They both told the Warren Commission that they phoned Ruby twice at his home and said that she needed $5 as she did not have enough money to get home. Karen Carlin said that during the first phone call Ruby said he would come around to meet her at the club but 30 or 40 minutes later he had not arrived so she had to phone him again. Karen stated that Ruby said he could not come around because he was busy and Bruce Carlin testified that Ruby did not want them to come to his home because he had people there "and company" and he also said that he could hear people talking as he spoke to Jack Ruby. He arranged for Huey Reeves at Nichol's garage next to the Carousel to give her the $5 and he made her sign a receipt for the amount that was stamped with the time and date. The time was recorded as 10:35pm.

Karen Carlin was asked about the amount she requested from Ruby and she said: "Just enough money to get home on and I happened to mention I would need money for rent tomorrow, and he said to call him." She then confirmed he wanted her to call him the next day.

Karen Carlin was asked by the Warren Commission if her landlord had been pressing her for the rent and she said "no". When her landlord was interviewed by the FBI, he said that there was never any argument if the rent was late by a few days and that he had not presented Karen Carlin with a demand for payment. These observations raise a number of questions. Firstly, why did Karen Carlin tell Ruby she needed $5 to get back home when she was getting a lift back home from Nancy Powell? Nancy Powell made no mention of Karen giving her money for fuel, in fact she was under the impression that Karen had no money on her and she had not received any money from anyone that evening. Secondly, why did Ruby say that Karen and Bruce could not come around to his apartment because he had company when he would later claim that he was alone in his apartment at that time? Thirdly, if the landlord was not pressing Karen Carlin for rent that Saturday, why did she not tell Ruby that she could wait until she saw him on Monday or Tuesday evening (when the club reopened) and she would collect her wages from him at that time? Fourthly, if Ruby was made aware that Karen Carlin would need money for rent the next day why did he not lend her $30 that evening to cover all her needs instead of lending her $5 immediately and asking her to call him the next day about the rest of the money?

It is of note that we know, from the testimony of Karen and Bruce Carlin, that Ruby specifically asked Karen to phone him the next day. This was also more than 30 minutes after their first contact so Ruby had had time to think about what he was doing. Karen claimed he did not mention a time, but her phone call did give Ruby an excuse for going down to the Western Union office very near to Dallas Police Department headquarters only minutes before Oswald's transfer. Ruby would be able to get a receipt with a date and time stamp on it from the Western Union office to back his claim that he was on an errand at the Western Union and it was only by chance that he encountered Oswald shortly afterwards.

Secret Service agent Roger C. Warner interviewed Karen Carlin on the day that Oswald was murdered and recorded that "she was reluctant to make any statement." She explained that she suspected an assassination conspiracy and that "she would be killed if she gave any information to the authorities." He noted that she twisted in her chair, stammered in her speech and seemed on the point of hysteria."

When Karen and Bruce Carlin testified before the Warren Commission they brought a lawyer with them, something that not many witnesses did. Why did she suspect a conspiracy? Why was she so anxious about talking to the authorities? Here we could ask a speculative question: if Ruby had asked Karen Carlin to phone him at a specific time on the Sunday but "on her life" never to tell anybody about this, would this explain her high level of fear and anxiety?

Signs of premeditation
On Sunday the 24th of November 1963 at about 2:15am an anonymous male caller twice phoned the Dallas County Sheriff's office and warned that Oswald would be killed. The Dallas FBI office received a similar call at 2:30am. At about 3am lieutenant Billy R. Grammer was in the communication room at Dallas Police Department headquarters when he received an anonymous call but this time the man described the transfer plans for Oswald, including the use of a decoy vehicle and he said "You're going to have to make some other plans or we are going to kill Oswald right there in the basement." The man appeared to know Grammer but his accent was not that of a local Dallas citizen, however, it did sound familiar to Grammer. At the time of the phone call he could not place it. However, later that day, after Ruby shot Oswald, Billy Grammer realized that the voice on the phone was that of Jack Ruby. He knew Ruby and had only spoken to him a week earlier. Grammer was still convinced that he had spoken to Jack Ruby when he was interviewed for a British television programme 25 years later.

At the time of the assassination Jack Ruby was sharing an apartment with a friend by the name of George Senator. The House Select Committee on Assassinations noted some inconsistencies by Senator in his statements made to different agencies regarding the weekend of Oswald's murder. These were not deemed significant and the committee was willing to accept his explanation that he had been very stressed at the time and they regarded Senator as being a benign character with no involvement or prior knowledge regarding the death of Oswald. However, there is evidence to show that Senator knew that Ruby planned to shoot Oswald in the 24 hours prior to the event.

Twelve | Jack Ruby

Senator gave a statement to the FBI on the day that Oswald was killed. He stated that he went to the Eatwell Restaurant at about 11:30am on that day. He overheard a waitress say that Oswald had been shot and a short time later he learnt that it was Jack Ruby who shot him. Soon after this he telephoned Attorney Jim Martin who was a friend of his. Martin was not at home so he drove to his house and found him there when he arrived. Martin was then able to go with Senator down to Dallas Police Department headquarters.

The statement that Senator gave to the Warren Commission a few months later was slightly different. He stated that he was in the Eatwell Restaurant drinking coffee when he heard a girl say that Oswald had been shot. He phoned his friend Jim Martin but was told by Martin's daughter that his friend was out and that he would be back in half an hour. About five minutes later he heard that it was Ruby that had shot Oswald and then he decided to drive straight over to Jim Marin's house. Senator was asked why he phoned an Attorney who could have been useful to Ruby at a time when all he knew was that Oswald had been shot and it would be a few minutes before he heard that Ruby had done the shooting. Senator claimed he only had a few friends and it was only a matter of chance that he chose to phone a friend that just happened to be an Attorney. Another suspicious event involved Senator's friend William Downey. The FBI interviewed Downey about what happened on the day that Oswald was shot and according to their report: "Downey heard a radio announcement that Oswald had been shot by Jack Ruby, and, knowing that Senator and Ruby lived together, Downey attempted to reach Senator at the residence of Jim Martin, where Senator mentioned he had been staying." The problem is that Senator had not been staying with Martin he had been staying at Jack Ruby's apartment for a year. Senator did go to stay with Jim Martin after the killing of Oswald but he twice told the Warren Commission that fear had overwhelmed him and it was this fear that made him ask Martin if he could stay with him for the night. Downey's statement shows that Senator was planning to stay with Jim Martin before Oswald was shot.

Downey told the FBI that Senator had phoned him on the morning that Oswald was killed and offered to come around to make breakfast for him and his wife, an offer that Downey declined. Senator could have let slip that he would be staying with Jim Martin at that time, before Oswald's murder. Strangely, when Senator was asked by the Warren Commission about the phone call to Downey he denied that this event had happened. It would have been a strange story for Downey to make up, so was Senator trying to cover himself should Downey reveal more about their phone conversation?

These two events taken together suggest that Jack Ruby's roommate knew that Ruby planned to kill Oswald before the event. Did Ruby tell him about his plans on the Saturday evening, the day before he shot Oswald, and ask for his help? Senator told the Warren Commission that on the Saturday evening he got

JFK | ECHOES FROM ELM STREET
A SEARCH FOR HISTORICAL ACCURACY ON THE
ASSASSINATION OF PRESIDENT JOHN F. KENNEDY

back to Ruby's flat at 7:30pm and stayed there until about 8:30pm but Ruby was not there. He then met up with his friends Bill Downey and Mike Barclay in the Burgundy Room of the Adolphus Hotel, with whom he stayed until he went back to Ruby's apartment at about 10:30pm. He saw Ruby briefly, back at the apartment before Ruby went out.

The problem with this account is that Downey and Barclay both, separately, told the FBI that they met up with Senator on the Sunday night and not the Saturday night. Senator was with Barclay at the Eatwell Café to start with and then later Barclay and Senator went to Dee's Lounge and met up with Downey.

This account by the two men is supported by the FBI statement of Chris Elson who owned and operated the Burgundy Room at that time. In his statement, Elson said that the Burgundy Room was closed on the 23rd and 24th of November and he specifically stated that none of his employees saw George Senator from the 22nd to the 28th of November 1963. If George Senator had not gone out to the Adolphus Hotel on the Saturday night it is possible he could have stayed in with Jack Ruby that evening. Jack Ruby told his lawyers he was at home by himself at this time, however, if you remember from the last section, this was the time that Bruce Carlin spoke to Ruby on the phone and told Bruce that he did not want Bruce and Karen to come over as 'he had people there and company' and Bruce testified he could hear people talking in the background. Was Jack Ruby having a meeting with his sponsors the evening before he shot Oswald and was George Senator in on that meeting?

The morning of Oswald's murder
John Smith was in a TV truck outside Dallas Police Department headquarters on the morning that Oswald was shot. He told the FBI that between 8am and 10am a man came to the truck and enquired about Oswald's transfer on two occasions. He told the FBI that he saw "mug shots" of Jack Ruby on television later that day and he was positive the man he saw was Ruby.

Dallas Police Officer Jack Revill testified before the Warren Commission and told them that a preacher by the name of Ray Rushing had informed him about a short conversation he had with a man in an elevator at Dallas Police Department headquarters at about 9:30am on that Sunday morning. He recognized him as being Jack Ruby when he saw pictures of him in the TV and newspaper reports later that day and on subsequent days.

WBAP cameraman Ira Walker testified to the Warren Commission that a man came up to his TV truck at just after 10:30am and enquired about Oswald's transfer. He saw a mug shot of Ruby on a TV monitor in the truck a few hours later. He immediately recognized him as being the man who came up to the TV truck. Ira Walker was able to see Ruby "in the flesh" at his trial and he was still convinced that he was the person he had seen that morning. Warren Richey was working on top of the truck that Ira Walker was inside. He also told the

TWELVE | JACK RUBY

Warren Commission about seeing a man near the truck that he later concluded was Ruby when he saw his "mug shot" on TV.

From this information it appears that Ruby was in and around Dallas Police Department headquarters between 8am and 10:30am that morning and he was taking a keen interest in what time Oswald would be brought down. However, the Warren Commission dismissed the testimonies of Smith, Walker and Richey. It was noted that none of them had ever seen Ruby before, none of them looked at him for very long, and that their descriptions of him as being shabby and wearing a grayish over coat did match with how Ruby appeared when he was arrested (of course Ruby could have been wearing on a shabby coat that he later discarded.)

The Warren Commission took more notice of the claims made by Jack Ruby's roommate George Senator. He claimed that on that Sunday morning Ruby was in his apartment until about 10:30am. However, Elnora Pitts had been doing cleaning Sunday for Ruby on Sunday mornings and she telephoned the apartment between 8:30am and 9:00am to check if it was alright for her to come around that morning. The man who spoke to her claimed to be Ruby but she testified that it did not sound like him, he did not seem to recognize her and he did not seem to know anything about the cleaning arrangements Ruby had with her. In theory, it could have been Senator that spoke and Ruby could have already left.

Telephone company records show a call at 10:19am from Karen Carlin's residence to Jack Ruby's apartment. She would later claim that she spoke to Ruby to ask him for a loan of $25 but, again, it could have been Senator answering the phone at that time. We know that Karen Carlin was very scared after Oswald was shot; it is interesting to note that Senator was also in fear. Attorney Jim Martin told the FBI that Senator was practically "overwhelmed with fear" and his fear was "one of the primary reasons he left the Dallas area." We saw earlier that there is evidence that Senator knew Ruby would shoot Oswald in advance of the event and he claimed to be out with friends the night before at the Burgundy Room of the Adolphus Hotel. All the evidence, however, shows this was not the case and he could have stayed at home with Ruby. George Senator might have been used by Ruby to make it look as though he left home late that morning when, in fact, he left quite early. This would certainly explain his various claims that do not stand up to examination and his high level of anxiety.

Before Jack Ruby went to trial, he worked out the timeline for his activities that weekend with his legal team and he claimed that he left home at about 10:45am. The entry reads: "Then left the apartment and spoke to a neighbor for a minute (Curtiss?), about some fences that I promised him then left to go to Western Union to send some money to Lynn. 10:45am".

FBI agent C Ray Hall testified to the Warren Commission that Ruby told him the neighbour was the father in law of police officer Buddy Munster and from this information they determined that the neighbour was in fact Mr J Doyle Stokes and not "Curtiss" as Ruby had guessed. Doyle Stokes was interviewed by the FBI on two occasions and both times he asserted that he saw Ruby on the Saturday morning and not the Sunday morning of that weekend. He even gave reasons why he was certain that he saw him on Saturday morning. Given this information it appears that Ruby could have left early and arranged for Senator to answer the phone on his behalf that morning.

The scene of the crime

On the morning of Sunday the 24th of November 1963 Lee Harvey Oswald was taken down into the basement of Dallas Police Department headquarters so that he could be transferred to the county jail. At that time, most of the basement area consisted of the garage space where police vehicles were parked. On the east side of the basement there were some elevators and stairs to higher levels. Running along the west side of the garage space there were two ramps in direct line with each other. The Main Street ramp ran in an approximately north to south line from the Main Street entrance at ground level down to a level stretch along the middle of the basement. To the south of this level stretch in the basement the Commerce Street ramp ran upwards to the Commerce Street exit at ground level, again running in a roughly north to south line. In the minutes leading up to the shooting of Oswald the Commerce Street ramp was blocked by an armoured truck parked at the top of the ramp. This was going to be used as a decoy vehicle when Oswald was driven away to the county jail.

At about 11:20 am, Oswald was escorted out of an elevator and taken around the jail office and through a door into an open area visible to most of the garage area. From here he was led to the level area at the foot of the Main Street ramp. It was here that Jack Ruby pushed his way forward out of the crowd of reporters and TV personnel and fired a fatal shot into the abdomen of Oswald.

Events down in the basement

We shall start by looking at statements made by key witnesses that were down in the basement of Police Headquarters at the time of Oswald's murder. The HSCA noted that several police officers stationed in the basement had stated that during the period encompassing Lieutenant Pierce's departure and the Oswald shooting, they may have glanced toward the Main Street ramp at various times without consistently focusing on the area. None of them had stated that they had seen Ruby or any other individual come down the ramp.

It should be said, however, that the bright lights of the TV crews in the area in front of the Main Street ramp would have made it hard for the officers to see clearly up the ramp. Also, they might have been looking in the wrong direction at the time Ruby came down the ramp if this is what happened. Terrance McGarry, a United Press International reporter, told the FBI that he was at the bottom of the Main Street ramp, in the middle, and nobody came down the ramp during the 5 minutes preceding the shooting.

Detective W.J. "Blackie" Harrison was stationed in the centre of the Main Street ramp at the lower end in the basement. His comments appear to confirm the statement by McGarry according to a HSCA summary of events. The Committee reports that "...he saw Lieutenant Pierce's car go up the ramp and stop at the ramp entrance for a very short time. He did not see Ruby come down the ramp. His response was deemed truthful when the Dallas Police Department administered a polygraph test to him."

This information is based on a letter from Lieutenant Wallace to Chief Curry in which he reports that on the 1st of December 1963 Harrison had informed him that he was looking towards the Main Street ramp at the time the police car was turning left onto Main Street and he did not see anybody coming down the ramp at that time. However, the HSCA failed to report that Detective Harrison made no mention of this when he was interviewed by the FBI five days later. He did say that he saw Ruby go past him on his left side as he was watching Oswald being brought out.

A polygraph (lie detector) examination was given to Detective Harrison on the 16th of December 1963 and during the pre-test interview he stated that he was not sure that he saw the police squad car actually make a left turn on Main Street. During the polygraph test, Harrison was asked: "Did you see Jack Ruby come down the Main Street ramp just before the shooting?" to which he replied truthfully "No". However, there were no questions as to what extent he was looking up the ramp before the shooting of Oswald.

The HSCA also failed to mention that Detective Harrison was interviewed by the Warren Commission three months later and he stated that he only watched Lieutenant Pierce's car until it cleared the group of people at the bottom of the ramp and that he did not look up the ramp after that. Harrison was keen to tell the Warren Commission that Ruby might have come down the ramp even though he did not witness this himself.

Harrison's evidence suggests that Ruby came past him on the left side, just before the shooting, moving as if he had come down the Main Street ramp but Harrison did not see if he had actually came all the way down the ramp. One witness was certain he did see Ruby coming down the Main Street ramp and that was WBAP-TV director Jimmy Turner. He told the Warren Commission that he saw Lieutenant Pierce's car going up the Main Street ramp and that about the same time he glanced towards the ramp and saw Ruby coming down it. Turner did not know Ruby but he was certain that the individual he saw was the same man that shot Oswald. Turner stated that he saw Ruby from approximately two-thirds of the way down the ramp.

At this point we shall digress for a while and consider how Ruby could have got into position to shoot Oswald without coming down the full length of the Main Street ramp. The HSCA considered the possibility that Ruby may not have come all the way down the ramp, but may have come from the garage area, crossed the railing dividing the parking area from the ramp at some point and then continued down the ramp incline. They expressed a view that the Warren Commission never properly explored this idea. The HSCA wrote on the matter as follows: "Last is the alley theory. The alley in question is situated between the Western Union office and the Dallas Police Department (DPD) headquarters, running from Main Street to Commerce Street.

In the middle of the alley is a door leading to the first floor of the municipal building... Once inside the door of the alley and in the first floor corridor of the municipal building, a person would normally be able to reach the DPD basement parking lot by either elevator or fire escape stairway. The stairway has doors at the first floor and the basement. If Ruby had left Western Union and started to walk down Main Street toward Patrolman Vaughn's position [at the top of the Main Street ramp] he would have passed the alley and had access to the building.

Although Commission counsels Hubert and Griffin indicated an awareness of the alley in questioning the witnesses, the Warren Commission Report does not mention this possible route. Further, the special DPD investigation unit did not consider it at all."

The HSCA also said: "The possibility that Ruby entered via the alley, went down the stairs and through the basement door is logistically attractive. Through his knowledge of Dallas Police Headquarters, Ruby may have been aware of the alley, the stairs and the door, and this mode of entry would have been much less conspicuous than the others. It would have enabled Ruby to get into position without having to pass many persons, since the route went through a fairly empty parking lot in the basement. Further, most, if not all, people were probably focusing on the area nearest to the jail office and the ramps, awaiting Oswald's appearance. This path would also have taken Ruby across the garage area through a railing at a point near the bottom of the Main Street ramp. With respect to timing, Ruby could have entered the basement via this route in the four minutes that elapsed between his visit to Western Union and the shooting. On June 26, 1964, an FBI agent walked through the route (including going through the railing near the bottom of the ramp) in response to a request from the Warren Commission; he found it required 189 steps and 2 minutes and 25 seconds."

The HSCA went on further to look at the doors Ruby would have had to go through and whether or not they would have been locked had he chosen this alternative route:

"Although there were at least three doors along this route, it is possible they were not or could not be secured. The Warren Commission noted that there

TWELVE | JACK RUBY

were doubts about whether the door at the bottom of the fire escape was secured. John O. Servance, the head porter for these buildings in 1963, said that even when the bottom of the door of the fire escape is locked in such a way as to prevent egress from the basement, a person could still open it from within the stairwell. This was corroborated by two other maintenance employees, Edward Pierce and Louis McKinzie."

The HSCA reviewed the statements from several people on this matter and concluded: "...this information raises the possibility that the alley door was left open, albeit inadvertently, and that if Ruby had gone through this door, he would have been able to continue to the basement without locked barricades. Additionally, security at the relevant point in the basement was not airtight. Patrolman Alvin R. Brock had been assigned to watch the door leading from the fire escape to the nearby elevator doors, but he was reassigned by Sergeants Putnam and Dean at 10:45 am."

Basically, the HSCA did not believe that Ruby walked down the Main Street ramp when a police car driven by Lieutenant Pierce exited and it stated: "The alley route was the most likely alternative because of the factors of time and distance, the lack of security in the garage area and along the entire route, and the testimony concerning the security at the doors along the route. This possibility was not considered or investigated by the FBI or the Dallas Police Department and was virtually ignored by the Warren Commission."

If we now return to the witness Jimmy Turner we can see that the fact that he first saw Jack Ruby on the lower part of the Main Street ramp does not necessarily mean that Ruby had walked all the way down the ramp. Indeed, when Turner was interviewed by the Warren Commission he was asked to mark on a plan of the basement the position that he first saw Ruby. The mark he made shows a position on the lower part of the ramp that could be accessed from the garage part by climbing over a simple railing.

The upper two thirds of the Main Street ramp had a wall on either side and could not be accessed directly from the garage area. Therefore, the important question to ask is did anyone in the basement see Ruby higher up the ramp coming down in the minute before the shooting?

The only other witness to a man coming down the ramp was a police reservist by the name of William. J. Newman. He was stationed guarding a door on the far south side of the basement area. Newman claimed that about 1 minute before the shooting, just after a shout of "here he comes" he saw an individual coming down the ramp.

The HSCA was rather dismissive of Newman's claim, mainly because he could not identify the individual as Ruby; all that he could say was that he was a white male. The commission noted that in 1978 Newman had declared that he was only sure that it wasn't Santa Claus!

The statements by Newman are entirely understandable if you consider that he was approximately 140 feet from where he could see the man on the ramp. He was also looking beyond the large crowd gathered in the central area waiting to see Oswald with bright spotlights on this area but not on the ramp in the background. The description of 'a white male' is about the best you could expect under these circumstances.

The HSCA was critical of Newman because he stated that the man had come down the far (jail office) side of the ramp. This contradicted the Warren Commission view that Ruby had come down the near side of the ramp. Again, the statement of Newman is understandable given that he was looking at the ramp at an acute angle and from about 140 feet away. At such a position it would be difficult to tell exactly where the man was positioned on the ramp when he first saw him and exactly where he was moving down on the ramp. William Newman was asked by the Warren Commission to mark on a plan of the basement exactly where he thought he saw the man when he first spotted him. Newman used a small cross to mark a point on the ramp. The cross was two thirds of the way over to the far (jail office) side and slightly above the part of the ramp that can be accessed directly from the garage. However, he was being interviewed four months after the event. There was also all the problems involved in trying to be accurate in judging the position of something about 140 feet away.

The important points to remember with regard to William Newman are, firstly, that he could not identify the man he saw on the ramp and secondly, he was too far away to accurately judge exactly where the man was on the ramp at the moment he first noticed him.

Another important question to ask is: did anyone see a man climbing over the railing between the garage and the Main Street ramp before the shooting? If Ruby was in the garage part of the basement and he wanted to make it look like he had just walked down the ramp he would probably pause by the railing and look down at the crowd gathered below and wait until he thought nobody was looking in his direction and then climb over the railing. However, he might not have been aware of being observed by someone in the far south part of the basement. It turns out there could have been such a witness.

Here we go back to police reservist William Newman who was standing by a door on the south side of the basement. According to a memo sent to Lieutenant Revill dated the 6th of December 1963 Newman stated that he saw someone going over "the railing at the ramp leading into the parking area of the basement..." He could not remember whether this was before or after the shooting. The memo also stated "he saw the person was wearing a suit, and he saw only his back, and could not identify him."

When Newman testified before the Warren Commission in March 1964 he said that his observations of a man coming down the ramp and of a man climbing over the railing related to "two different instances". However, he still could not recollect exactly when he saw the man climbing over the railing onto the Main Street ramp. This does make you wonder why he was so confident that he really was observing "two different instances" as the Warren Commission phrased it.

Did Newman see Ruby climbing over the railing having used the 'alley route' to get into the basement? It is still possible but there is no clear evidence from William Newman's statements to prove that this is what he actually saw.

Some extra notes about basement security
Sergeant Patrick Dean had been in charge of security in the basement that morning.

Richard Blakey, who was the Chief Counsel and Staff Director of the House Select Committee on Assassinations, made some interesting observations about Dean in his book "The plot to kill the President". He writes that Dean was a good friend of Jack Ruby and that this friendship endured even after he acted as a principle witness in his prosecution. He also says that a background check on Dean revealed that he had been on good terms with prominent organized crime figures, in particular Dallas Mafia boss Joseph Civello. The relationship between Jack Ruby and Civello has already been discussed.

Blakey notes that a police investigation in 1964 led to Dean being given a polygraph test. He failed the test when he was asked questions concerning how Ruby got into the basement.

Burt Griffin from the Warren Commission found out that Dean had lied when he claimed that Ruby would have needed a key to the door into the basement if he entered via the side alley. Three members of the building's maintenance staff said that this was not the case. Griffin became annoyed by Dean's deceptions and wrote a memo that stated:
- Dean was derelict in securing all the doors to the basement.
- Griffin had reason to believe Ruby did not come down the ramp
- He suspected Dean was now part of a cover-up and was advising Ruby to say he came down the Main Street ramp even though he knew he didn't.

The newspaper reporter, Seth Kantor, wrote in his book "Who was Jack Ruby?" (on page 3) that Dean was furious with Griffin and complained about him to Dallas D.A. Henry Wade who then phoned Griffin's superiors in Washington. Rankin's deputy, Howard P. Willens told Kantor that "The situation was critical and tense…My own judgment was that Burt Griffin was a very competent and aggressive investigator, and was right in pursuing it aggressively." However, Rankin conceded to pressure from Henry Wade and other Texas officials and he ordered Griffin to return to Washington where he had to stay through April and May that year and was not allowed to attend the meeting of Jack Ruby with The Warren Commission on the 7th of June 1964. Willens felt that the punishment and sanctions had been applied to Burt Griffin inappropriately.

The result of all this was that the actions of Patrick Dean were not pursued further and the Warren Commission promoted the "Ruby came down the ramp without any assistance" viewpoint.

The only other key witness to events in the basement before the shooting is Jack Ruby himself. We will look at his statements later in this chapter. If we look at the information provided by key witnesses excluding Ruby we can see that Ruby used the lower part of the Main Street ramp before the shooting. However, he could have used one of two possible routes to arrive there, either a route which involved him walking down the full length of the ramp or the 'alley route'. There is no conclusive proof available from the key witnesses to establish beyond any doubt which route Ruby took.

Events at the top of the Main Street ramp

At the time of Oswald's murder the Main Street ramp was guarded by Patrolman Roy E. Vaughan. Most of the time he was standing in middle of the ramp at the top making sure that only persons with the correct identification could go past him. About a minute before the shooting a police car came up the ramp and Roy Vaughan had to move out of position to allow the car to exit the building. Jack Ruby left the nearby Western Union office less than three minutes prior to this event.

If Ruby did enter the basement of Dallas Police Department (DPD) headquarters via the Main Street ramp then logically there are only two periods of time during which he could have done this. Firstly, when there was no car in the process of exiting the building via the ramp and secondly, when there was a car in the process of exiting via the ramp. We shall examine these two periods of time separately.

(1) When no car was exiting via the Main Street ramp

Patrolman Vaughn was interviewed twice by the FBI in the month following the murder of Oswald. He told them that he only allowed the members of the police department that he knew and other individuals whom he had checked their identification access to the basement.

The interview dated the 2nd of December 1963 states: "Vaughn advised he is positive Jack Ruby did not enter the Main Street entrance to the ramp of the Dallas Police Department between 9:30am and 12:45pm, November 24 1963. He said he does know Jack Ruby by sight as he met him on official business in 1959…"

At about 11am that morning Vaughn was joined by a former police officer by the name of Napoleon Daniels. He stood on the east side of the entrance to the

Twelve | Jack Ruby

ramp and remained there until after the shooting. He spoke with Vaughn from time to time as he stood there. His presence that morning was confirmed by Roy Vaughn in his formal FBI statements.

On the 29th of November 1963 Daniels signed an Affidavit. In this he stated that nobody went down the Main Street ramp at the time that a police squad car was exiting and Roy Vaughn was out of position. He went on to say that he saw a man go down the ramp shortly after this when Vaughn was back in position on the ramp. Daniels indicated that the man passed between Vaughan and the east side of the ramp and continued down the ramp. He stated that Vaughn did see him but he did not challenge him or show any signs of recognising him.

This sounds as if Daniels could have witnessed Ruby going down the Main Street ramp. However, the authorities soon became aware of many problems with the Affidavit made by Daniels and later statements he made to the authorities.

Firstly, the description of the man given in the Affidavit, made only 5 days after the event, does not fit with how Ruby would have appeared that day. Daniels stated that the man was "...a white male, approximately 50 years of age, 5'10", weighing about 155 – 160 pounds, wearing a dark (blue or brown) single breasted suit, white shirt and dark colored tie, this man was not wearing a hat, he had light colored hair thinning on top, round face, kind of small head, fair complexion....." The famous photograph of Jack Ruby shooting Oswald shows a man wearing a hat with dark coloured hair visible below the brim of his hat.

When interviewed by the FBI on the 4th of December 1963, Daniels described the man he saw as now being a little shorter at 5'8-9" and "he also seemed to recall that he was partly bold" in the interview. He also stated that he could not recall whether or not the individual was wearing a hat (if he had a hat on how could he tell he was partly bald?).

Secondly, the timing of events given by Daniels was completely wrong. When the Dallas Police Department studied tapes of TV recordings made in the basement that morning they calculated that the time between the police car driven by Lieutenant Pierce leaving the basement and the shooting of Oswald was 56 seconds. If we allow 6 seconds for the car to drive up the ramp and turn on to Main Street then the interval between Roy Vaughn getting back into position and the shooting of Oswald would be about 50 seconds. However, in his Affidavit, Daniels states that Vaughan got back into position and then "several minutes later" the unknown man appeared and walked down the ramp. He went on to say that he heard the shot being fired in the basement 2 minutes after that.

Daniels was later informed by the Dallas Police about the 56 second time interval between the squad car leaving the basement and the shooting but when he was interviewed by the Warren Commission a few months later he still said that he thought there was 3 or 4 minutes interval between the car exiting the ramp and the shooting. When questioned by Mr. Hubert from the Warren Commission as to when he saw a man go down the ramp, Daniels said "...I am not sure it was before or after the car came out. I am not sure I have run that in my mind a thousand times, but I can't place one before the other."

The following exchange occurred shortly after this when Mr. Hubert asked him about the time he saw a man walk down the ramp:

Mr. Hubert: "Do you know how long that was before the shot was fired?"
Mr. Daniels: "3 or 4 minutes, I guess."
Mr. Hubert: "But what you say is confusing you is as to whether or not that was after the Rio Pierce car came out?"
Mr. Daniels: "I'm not sure – I can't place one before the other – if I had to guess at it I would say it was before."
Mr. Hubert: "In other words you now think you saw the man go down past Vaughn before the Rio Pierce car came?"
Mr. Daniels: "Right."

At this point Mr. Hubert made Napoleon Daniels look through all the previous statements that he made to the authorities. Daniels then said: "Well I said I think I have changed my mind now – I believe it was after the car was gone out when I saw him."

It was obvious to the Warren Commission that there were inconsistencies in Daniels's various statements and even within the same statement as we have just seen. In addition, the timing of events he described did not correspond with the timing of events worked out by the police. The Commission expressed the view that Daniels's story "merits little credence."

It should also be noted that Mr. Daniels's version of events does not fit with Jack Ruby's claims. Ruby made clear statements that he had gained access at the time the police car was exiting and Vaughn was out of position. If Ruby had arrived even just a few seconds after the car pulled out onto Main Street he would not have been able to tell the police about Lieutenant Pierce driving out of the building.

We can also note that it contradicts Patrolman Roy Vaughn's version of events. If Vaughn had let Ruby walk right past him less than 50 seconds before the shooting without challenging him in any way, then it would suggest some form of collusion between the two men. However, Vaughn consistently stated that he only allowed people with proper authorisation go down into the basement. He also stated that he never saw Jack Ruby that morning.

Vaughn underwent a polygraph test and he was assessed as being truthful in all his replies when questioned about his time guarding the ramp. In contrast, Daniels was subjected to the same test and was assessed as being untruthful in all but one of his responses. This is probably another reason why the Warren

Commission was keen to reject his testimony completely.

The day after the shooting Vaughn was aware that Ruby had claimed he entered via the Main Street ramp. He telephoned Daniels and asked him if he saw anybody go down the ramp when the police car came out of the building. Daniel said that he did not and Vaughn left the matter at that. Both men told the FBI about this episode and described it the same way. If Vaughn had deliberately let a man go down into the basement unchallenged at a time when there was no police car exiting it is very likely that he would have asked Daniels something about this matter when he spoke to him on the phone. However, the only thing on his mind was what happened when Lieutenant Pierce's car came out of the building.

There were two other witnesses who could have seen Jack Ruby go down the ramp during the time that Patrolman Vaughn was in position guarding the entrance. They were taxi driver Harry Tasker and Sergeant Flusche who were in separate vehicles across the road from the entrance of the Main Street ramp at that time. We will consider their statements more in the next section but the main thing to note is that they were in a good position to see Ruby go down the ramp and neither of them reported seeing him do so.

It should be noted that Napoleon Daniels never positively identified the man he saw going down the ramp as being Jack Ruby. When he testified before the Warren Commission he said very early on "Well actually, I don't feel I really know anything, but I saw a guy go down into the basement, but I don't think it was Ruby."

When Daniels underwent his polygraph test there was only one question that he was assessed as replying with a truthful answer. The question was: "Do you think the person you stated you saw enter the basement at that time was Jack Ruby?" to which he replied "No."

It is highly unlikely that Jack Ruby could have walked straight past Patrolman Roy Vaughn as he guarded the top of the Main Street ramp without being stopped for identification. The evidence that he did this is very weak and easily challenged whilst the evidence that Ruby did not go down the ramp when Vaughn was standing in position is very strong. It can be stated with a high degree of certainty that this was not how Ruby entered DPD headquarters.

(2) When a police car driven by Lt Sam Pierce was exiting via the Main Street Ramp

This was the time that Jack Ruby told the police that he slipped down the ramp and into the basement of DPD headquarters.

Patrolman Roy Vaughn had to move out of position until the police car had turned left onto Main Street. Defenders of the Warren Commission often overstate how busy and distracted Roy Vaughn was at this time. For example, Vincent Bugliosi tells us that Vaughn was surprised by the car coming up the

JFK | Echoes from Elm Street
A Search for Historical Accuracy on the
Assassination of President John F. Kennedy

ramp because it was normally used as an entrance to the basement and not an exit. However, in Vaughn's Warren Commission testimony you find:

Mr. Hubert: "What did you do when the car came up?"
Mr. Vaughn: "The first thing I noticed the car – still standing inside the ramp – and I heard someone at the bottom of the ramp holler, "Watch the car," and when I looked down you could just get a view of the front end of the car coming up the ramp. It had its red light, which were in the grill. As it come on up the ramp, I stepped to my right, and it come up the ramp."

So Vaughn was given plenty of warning that a car was on its way. Roy Vaughn never mentioned being surprised by the car exiting and neither did any of the other witnesses that saw the event.

Bugliosi went on to say that Vaughn had to clear people away from the area in front of the Main Street entrance. However, Vaughn did not describe having to do this and neither did any of the other witnesses who saw the car come out from the top of the ramp. The driver of the police car, Lieutenant Pierce, told the Warren Commission that people were on both sides of the car when he pulled across the sidewalk. He was then asked how far they were from the entrance to which he replied "Well, probably 6 or 7 feet." He does not mention Patrolman Vaughn having to move them back.

Sergeant James Putnam was Pierce's front seat passenger. In his statement to the Warren Commission he describes people on the sidewalk as being further back, as the following exchange demonstrates:

Mr. Hubert: Can you go as far as to say, turning again to you right side, that there was nobody on your right-hand side at all?"
Sergeant Putnam: "I can say that there was no one in the immediate vicinity within, I would say – well, it was apparent that – 15 feet away from me I saw a group of people standing, and to the right."
Mr. Hubert: "On the ..."
Sergeant Putnam: "To the left and to the right I saw no one in the immediate vicinity of us."

Again there is no mention of Vaughn clearing people from the sides of the ramp entrance. Sergeant Maxey was in the back of the car and, according to his Warren Commission testimony; he was looking straight ahead when the car exited the building. He did not comment as to how far back people might have been on the sidewalk. Once again there was no mention of Vaughn clearing people from in front of the ramp. Taxi driver Harry Tasker was in his taxicab parked across the road and a little to the east of the Main Street ramp entrance. He was watching the entrance from about 90 feet away. He was questioned by the Warren Commission as to how close people were standing to the Main Street entrance to which he replied "7 or 8 feet".

Yet again, he makes no mention of Patrolman Vaughn having to clear people away from the sides of the entrance.

So, what exactly did he do that morning? Patrolman Roy Vaughn gave a very precise account of his actions in his testimony to the Warren Commission:

Mr. Vaughn: "...I stepped to my right in order to get out of the car's way, and I stepped out on the sidewalk somewhere between the sidewalk and the curb, I believe it was right around the curb, and I glanced – it would be toward the eastbound traffic, which would be traffic towards Pearl Street to see that traffic was clear, and then motioned them on and turned around and walked back."
Mr. Hubert: "You did not pass the curb?"
Mr. Vaughn: "No, sir; not that I recall – I don't believe I did at all."
And later:
Mr. Hubert: "Was your back then towards the ramp entrance?"
Mr. Vaughn: "No, sir; my back was not toward the ramp, I was standing to the right of the ramp where I still had a view of the ramp itself, the entrance to the ramp. My back would have been toward Pearl Street – it would be towards the east."
Mr. Hubert: "Did you ever turn your head or body toward your right, that is, toward Pearl Street?"
Mr. Vaughn: "No, sir; not that I recall. All I done on that, Mr. Hubert, like I say, I walked out – I glanced west towards the eastbound traffic going west [he means coming from the west] and due to the fact that there were cars parked along here on Main Street, I glance to the west and seen there was an opening in the eastbound traffic which would be coming from the west, and I just motioned them on."
Mr. Hubert: "You did not go out in the middle of the street to halt traffic?"
Mr. Vaughn: "No, sir; I did not."

So it appears that Vaughn did not have to move away any pedestrians near the ramp. When he got to the curb edge all he had to do was to briefly turn his head to the west, notice there were no cars coming, and then look back and wave on the police car before moving back to the ramp. At no time was the police car between Vaughn and the left edge of the ramp entrance (where Ruby claimed he entered) and Vaughn probably had his head turned towards the west for only a couple of seconds at most. The account by Vaughn is well supported by the testimonies of the three police officers in the car.

Vaughn was certain that Ruby could not have got past him at the time that the car driven by Lieutenant Pierce came out. He underwent a polygraph test regarding this matter and he was assessed as being truthful for all the answers he supplied.

There were other witnesses who could have seen Jack Ruby enter the Main Street ramp when a car exited. The nearest one was Napoleon Daniels the former member of the Dallas Police Department who was standing on the east side of the entrance to the Main Street ramp. As mentioned earlier, the Warren Commission rejected Daniels's testimony mainly due to inconsistencies between his various formal statements. However, there was one thing that Daniels was completely consistent about and that was his assertion that he saw nobody go down the ramp when Patrolman Vaughn moved out of position to allow the police car to exit the building. He even told the FBI on the 4th of December 1963 that he was making a particular effort to look out for anyone that might try to slip down the ramp when Roy Vaughn was out of position. When Daniels was asked if he thought it was possible that someone could have gone passed him without him knowing he replied that he did not think this was possible.

Next we should consider the testimonies of the three police officers that were in the squad car that came up the ramp. If Jack Ruby had been standing still near to the entrance as they came out, particularly if he had been close to the wall of the building, then the three men could easily have failed to spot him there. However, Ruby claimed that he never stopped walking. He walked west along Main Street and as he reached the entrance he saw Patrolman Vaughn out of position. Without slowing or stopping, he simply changed direction and headed down the ramp.

If this account by Jack Ruby was correct then the chances that one of the three police officers would have spotting Ruby heading for the ramp would have been increased dramatically.

The human eye, optic nerve and visual cortex have developed over millions of years of evolution. One feature of this visual system is that each one of us is very sensitive to movement in the peripheral part of our field of vision. If out of "the corner of our eye" something is moving we are aware of it immediately and we instinctively turn towards it to see exactly what it is that is moving.

If we get back to the Main Street entrance, the fact that Ruby was in constant motion means it is highly likely that one of the three police officers would have noticed a man walking towards the ramp and turned their head to look at the source of movement. However, the three men were questioned by the Warren Commission and none of them saw Ruby, or anybody else, walking outside the Main Street entrance that morning.

Taxicab driver Harry Tasker was sat in his taxicab that morning. He was parked across the road and to the east of the Main Street entrance. He testified that he was about 90 feet away and he was waiting for a newspaper reporter who had hired his services that morning. He was expecting him to come out from the Main Street entrance so he was watching the entrance carefully as he sat waiting.

Twelve | Jack Ruby

Tasker testified that he did not see anybody walking along Main Street from the direction of the Western Union office in the minutes leading up to the shooting of Oswald. Surprisingly, he was never specifically asked if he saw a man walk into the Main Street entrance at the time Patrolman Vaughn was out on the sidewalk.

The next witness was Sergeant Don Flusche of the Dallas Police Department. It should be noted that his statement was not available to the Warren Commission but it was available to the HSCA. His statement is in fact one of the main reasons that the HSCA came to a different conclusion to the Warren Commission as to how Ruby gained access to the basement. Jack Moriarty interviewed Sergeant Flusche in 1978 and the following is a direct quote of Moriarty's report as recorded by the HSCA:

"The sergeant had his cruiser parked to the curb with the right front door opened on to the side walk area. He was listening to the Police Department radio (he was on duty) Although assigned to the Northeast District at the time, he was also working as the Watch Commander and had driven to Main Street to see if he could see Lee Harvey Oswald as he was moved to the Sheriff's Office.

He stood there long enough to see (Lt.) Rio Sam Pierce drive up the ramp and Vaughn step towards the street. He was still there when the obvious commotion told him that something was amiss in the basement. The street was void of pedestrians in the downtown section on this Sunday morning and he knows beyond any doubt in his mind, that Jack Ruby, whom he had know for many years, did not walk down Main Street anywhere near the ramp. Asked why he hasn't mentioned this before, he advised he did as soon as he found out what had happened. He immediately notified his superior, Lt. Knox. He didn't hear any more about it until yesterday [i.e. 15 years later!] talking with Vaughn who asked him to mention it to me."

This is clear, strong evidence from an on duty police officer that had known Jack Ruby for years. It is evidence that Ruby did not use the Main Street entrance to gain access to the basement when a police car was exiting or at any other time.

So we can say at this point there is the evidence of five on duty police officers, an ex-member of the Dallas Police Department and a working Taxicab driver to show that Ruby did not go down the Main Street ramp when Lieutenant Pierce drove his car out from the basement. There is only the evidence of one man to shows that he did go down the ramp and that is the evidence of Jack Ruby. In the next section we shall consider what he had to say on his own movements that morning.

Claims made by Jack Ruby

In his book "Reclaiming History" Vincent Bugliosi reviews the murder of Oswald and states in a matter-of-fact way that Ruby got into the basement of Police Headquarters by going down the Main Street ramp when a police car driven by Lieutenant Pierce was coming out via the ramp. The only evidence that Bugliosi presents to support his position is the various comments made by Jack Ruby following his arrest. Twice Bugliosi quotes Jack Ruby as saying to police officers that he came down the Main Street ramp when Sam Pierce was exiting the building in a police car. He also quotes Ruby as saying "I just walked to the bottom of the ramp when he walked in" when asked how long he was in the basement before Oswald came out.

You can see the logic that Mr. Bugliosi has used to reach his conclusion. A last minute decision was made to send Lieutenant Pierce and two other officers out of the building via the Main Street ramp. If Ruby reported that Sam Pierce was driving a squad car out via the ramp within minutes of his arrest then he must have been at the Main Street entrance and seen this for himself. Ruby stated that the police officer guarding the ramp moved out of position and came out onto the sidewalk when the police car came up the ramp. This means he must have been at the Main Street entrance to witness Patrolman Vaughn come out onto the sidewalk.

Ruby said that it was at this time that he went down the ramp and logically this would be the time when the ramp was less well guarded. If Ruby walked down the ramp he would have arrived at the bottom only about thirty seconds before Oswald came out. His claim that he was only in the basement for a few seconds before he shot Oswald is consistent with him coming down the ramp at the time that Lieutenant Pierce's car was exiting.

With evidence like this why should we need to consider the matter further? The answer is that we need to consider the matter further because this "logic" is hopelessly flawed.

An FBI agent determined that it would have taken Jack Ruby 2 minutes and 25 seconds to walk from the Western Union office to the spot where he shot Oswald if he had gone via the "alley route" and used stairs and doors on the east side of the building. The Warren Commission took the view that there was a time interval of four minutes between Ruby leaving the Western Union office and the shooting of Oswald. This means that if Ruby had used the "alley route" he would have arrived down in the basement with plenty of time to see a police car go up the Main Street ramp. He could have seen Lieutenant Pierce getting into the car or driving his car around to the bottom of the ramp or else he could have overheard police officers talking about Sam Pierce taking a squad car out of the building. The fact that Ruby came up with the name of Sam Pierce as the driver of the police car exiting the building does NOT prove that he must have seen him at the Main Street entrance. He could have gathered that information from inside the basement a short time before the event.

Patrolman Roy Vaughn was standing just inside the Main Street entrance at the top of the ramp and in this position he could have been seen by anybody at the bottom of the ramp. Anyone looking up at him would be able to see that Vaughn would have to move out of the way of any exiting cars. In fact, if Ruby used the "alley route" to get into the basement and then climbed over the railing onto the Main Street ramp just after the police car had driven up it, he could have looked up the ramp and seen Patrolman Vaughn moving out of position out on to the sidewalk. Again, the fact that Ruby knew patrolman Vaughn moved away from the ramp and onto the sidewalk does NOT prove that Ruby must have been at the Main Street entrance.

In theory, there was an increased chance of someone slipping down the ramp unnoticed when Patrolman Vaughn was out of position. However, Ruby's repeated claim that he went down to the basement at this time is contradicted by the witness statements of five police officers, an ex-police officer and a taxicab driver. So there are reasons to believe that Ruby was simply lying on this point!

Ruby did say that he was in the basement for only a matter of seconds before he shot Oswald. However, if he had been in the basement before the police car came out he would have known full well that the police car went up the ramp less than a minute before the shooting. He would know that anybody who walked all the way down the ramp at this time would arrive within seconds of Oswald being brought out so he could have told the police about being in the basement for a matter of seconds to keep his story plausible. What is interesting to note is that one police officer (Sergeant P.T. Dean) reported Ruby as saying that he was in the basement for about 3 minutes before Oswald was brought out. For a moment, did Ruby slip up and give his real feelings as to how long he thought he had been in the basement?

We can now see that the evidence for Jack Ruby using the Main Street entrance to gain access to the basement that is based purely on the statements made by Ruby is actually worthless. At this point it is worth seeing just how well Ruby's statements about his entry into the basement stand up to close scrutiny.

Key statements by Jack Ruby
Ruby told the FBI that as he approached the Main Street entrance he saw the police officer guarding the entrance go up to the police car driven by Sam Pierce and bend down to look inside the vehicle. When testifying to the Warren Commission he said the officer was talking with Sam Pierce. However, we looked at Vaughn's testimony to the Warren Commission earlier in this article and we saw how he described exactly what he did when the car came out. In his testimony there is no mention of him going over to the car or trying to talk with Pierce in any way.

If you look at the statements made by the three officers in the car you find that they support Vaughn's version of events. Sergeant Putnam gives the Warren Commission the most detailed account as the following exchange shows:

> Mr. Hubert: "Where was Vaughn now when you first saw him?"
> Sergeant Putnam: "In front of our automobile about the middle of the sidewalk."
> Mr. Hubert: "What did he do?"
> Sergeant Putnam: "He stepped to the right and about to the curb, or just off the curb, glanced to his right and looked back and waved us on."
> Mr. Hubert: "You went into Main Street and turned left?"
> Sergeant Putnam: "Right."
> ...a little later...
> Mr. Hubert: "And he stepped off the curb just about 2 feet?"
> Sergeant Putnam: "Well, I would say in one step, 2 feet."
> Mr. Hubert: "Didn't go into the middle of the street?"
> Sergeant Putnam: "No, sir."
> Mr. Hubert: "And he waved you on?"
> Sergeant Putnam: "He immediately turned back and glanced like this [indicating], and turned back, and was walking back to his position on the sidewalk."
> Mr. Hubert: "Would you say from the time you all reached the Main Street exit point to the time that Vaughn started to walk back to his position, it only took a matter of 3 or 4 seconds?"
> Sergeant Putnam: "We didn't even stop the car. It would be very few seconds."
> Mr. Hubert: "No stop at all?"
> Sergeant Putnam: "Just a – to prevent from hitting a pedestrian walking on the sidewalk. Now, there wasn't one walking, but to take a quick glance like you would do approaching a sidewalk, the car was slowed, and immediately – at this time everything happened at once. He slowed the car, Vaughn walked and glanced and waved us on. He accelerated and we went on to Main Street."

There you have it, no attempt by Vaughn to look into the car. No attempt to talk with the driver. No stopping of the car by the driver and no time for Jack Ruby to slip down the ramp unnoticed.

Lieutenant Pierce was asked by the Warren Commission what happened when he got to the top of the ramp where Patrolman Vaughn was stationed. Pierce replied: "Well, actually, nothing happened outside the fact that he had to move out of the way to let us out." He makes no mention of Vaughn coming over to his car and trying to talk with him or "acknowledge" him as Bugliosi phrases it in his book.

Sergeant Maxey was in the back seat. In his testimony to the Warren Commission he mentions that when the car got to the top of the ramp there was a momentary hesitation. Again he does not report the car stopping and Vaughn trying to talk to the driver.

An FBI report dated the 4th of December 1963 reports that an ex-member of the Dallas Police Department, Napoleon Daniels, told the FBI "While he was standing there, a black unmarked squad car carrying three officers drove up the

Twelve | Jack Ruby

Main Street ramp. He does not recall this car stopping or anyone in it talking to Vaughn ..."

So when Ruby talks about Vaughn going over to the police car that came out and talking to the driver, he is describing an event that never happened. There is the testimony of four police officers and a former member of the Dallas Police Department to confirm that this is the case.

Another claim made by Ruby was that he was half way down the ramp when he heard a voice calling out "Hey you!" and he just put his head down and carried on down the ramp. This is a nice little embellishment, the wily night club owner slips down the ramp and just hurries on down faster when he hears someone behind him trying to get him to stop.

As the nearest pedestrians to the ramp entrance were between 6 and 15 feet away (according to witness statements) the only people likely to have shouted out "Hey you" and to have been heard by Ruby would be Patrolman Vaughn or Napoleon Daniels. In fact neither of these men reported that they cried out "Hey you!" to Ruby or anybody else in any of their official statements. If Daniels shouted "Hey you!" down the ramp then Vaughn would have followed his gaze down the ramp and immediately ran down the tunnel after Ruby. If Vaughn has shouted "Hey you!" he would have done so as he ran down the tunnel after Ruby. How can we be sure of this? If we look at the testimony of Harry Tasker to the Warren Commission we find that he describes what he saw of Vaughn's actions that morning:

Mr. Tasker: "...he had a little difficulty now and then. Somebody would try to slip by him and he would hail them and bring them back out."
Mr. Hubert: "Did that happen once or more than once?"
Mr. Tasker: "It happened a few times – I've forgotten just how many."
Mr. Hubert: "Did he grab them?"
Mr. Tasker: "Oh, yes; he just went and got them and brought them back out. He didn't mistreat them or anything like that."

Vaughn was dragging back anyone who tried to slip past him that morning, so it is hardly likely that Vaughn would have treated Jack Ruby any differently. Once again, when Ruby describes hearing someone shouting "Hey you!" as he gets half way down the ramp, he is describing something that the evidence suggests did not happen.

It is of note that, in order to get down into the basement via the ramp, Ruby would have had to walk right past Napoleon Daniels. This black ex-police officer was standing on the east side of the ramp entrance away from nearby pedestrians. Ruby could hardly have failed to notice him there and yet, in a statement to FBI agent C. Ray Hall, the report reads: "As he entered the ramp, he does not recall seeing any person standing around the entrance, and he does not know a former police officer named Daniels."

Patrolman Roy Vaughn was a large man, at 6 feet 4 inches he was one of the tallest officers in the Dallas Police Department. In theory, Vaughn came out from the top of the Main Street ramp and walked right in front of Jack Ruby and within a few feet of him. In those circumstances it is unlikely that he would have failed to notice that this man was rather tall. You would expect Ruby to refer to him as 'the tall officer' when talking about him but Ruby never refers to his size or height in any of his conversations recorded by the authorities.

Lastly, there is the question about the number of police officers in the car that came up the ramp just before the shooting. Roy Vaughn correctly referred to three officers and named them all in his statements but then he could have spoken with his colleagues later before he made his official statements. Napoleon Daniels did not know who was in the car but in his early FBI statements he said that he saw three officers. When he testified to the Warren Commission a few months later he thought he had seen four men. It can be said that he always thought there were at least three officers in the car. Which brings us on to Ruby, who in theory would have had a similar view of the police car to that of Daniels. When Ruby gave a statement to FBI agent C. Ray Hall on the 21st of December 1963 the following comment was made: "Ruby did not recall seeing anyone else in the police car with Lieut. Pierce in either the front or back seat of the police car."

Looking in detail at the statements made by Ruby following his arrest does not help to provide evidence to support his claim that he entered the basement of Police Headquarters by going down the Main Street ramp. On the contrary, the evidence suggests that Ruby was nowhere near the Main Street entrance in the last few minutes before Oswald was shot.

A question of timing

Jack Ruby claimed that he gained entry to the basement of Dallas Police Headquarters via the Main Street ramp. One way to assess the validity of this claim is to analyse the time sequence of events in the minutes leading up to the shooting and see if this method of entry fits in easily with the known timing of events or whether inconsistencies are brought to light.

Exactly when did Ruby leave the Western Union office?

Shortly before he shot Oswald, Jack Ruby visited the Western Union office near to Dallas Police Department headquarters and wired some money to an employee. Mr. Doyle E Lane, who dealt with the transaction, testified to the Warren Commission. When asked about the accuracy of the clocks at his branch of the Western Union he explained that the clocks were extremely accurate because every morning at 11 am the clocks would be precisely set against a national standard, the US Naval Observatory at Washington D.C.

Twelve | Jack Ruby

There are four Warren Commission exhibits that are photocopies of the paperwork filled in by Doyle Lane that morning. Exhibits 2420 and 2421 are the front and back views of what is described as: "the face of the Western Union receipt" and exhibit 2421 has the time stamped on it as 11:16am. Exhibit 5118 is the "copy of an application by Jack Ruby for a money order" and exhibit 5117 is the "copy of a money order receipt given to Jack Ruby" and both these exhibits show the time stamped on them as 11:17 am.

Exhibit 2421 was obviously stamped before exhibits 5117 and 5118 and when the last two exhibits were stamped the time had probably just changed to the next minute.

Doyle Lane informed the Warren Commission that stamping the last two documents and passing the receipt over to Ruby would be the last thing done before Ruby left the building. We can see that Jack Ruby must have left within seconds of 11:17 am.

Exactly when was Oswald shot?

The Warren Commission established that the shooting occurred very close to 11:21 am. The Commission stated: "This time has been established by observing the time on a clock appearing in motion pictures of Oswald in the basement jail office, and by records giving the time of Oswald's departure from the city jail and the time at which the ambulance was summoned for Oswald."

Exactly how long would it take to walk from the inside of the Western Union office to the Main Street entrance? The special Dallas Police Department investigation unit calculated this time on the 29th of November 1963. Lieutenants Revill and McCaghren found that it took 1 minute and 13 seconds to walk this distance.

What was the length of time between the car driven by Lt Sam Pierce arriving at the Main Street entrance and Oswald been shot?

Lieutenants Revill and McCaghren found it took 22 seconds to walk down the ramp to the spot where Oswald was shot. Given that a car can move much faster than a man we could guess that it would take the car about 6 seconds. As stated earlier, the Dallas Police looked at video tape of TV footage made down in the basement and worked out that there was a 56 second interval between the police car leaving the basement and Oswald being shot. If we subtract 6 seconds to allow for the time the car took to get up the ramp this leaves us with 50 seconds. This means that there were about 50 seconds between the time Ruby claimed he slipped past Patrolman Vaughn to go down the ramp and the moment Oswald was shot dead.

What does all this add up to?

Ruby left the Western Union office at almost exactly 11:17 and he shot Oswald at almost exactly 11:21. This means there are four minutes of time to be accounted for. Walking from the Western Union office to the Main Street entrance would take 1 minute and 13 seconds, if we then add 50 seconds for the time interval between Ruby starting down the ramp and the shooting of Oswald we arrive at a figure of 2 minutes and 3 seconds. If this is subtracted from the 4 minutes of available time we end up with 1 minute and 57 seconds of time unaccounted for.

The Warren Commission accepted that there was a four minute interval between Ruby leaving the Western Union office and Oswald being shot and offered some simple explanations for the approximately two minutes of unaccounted time. It then quickly moved on to other matters. Their explanations effectively "swept the matter under the carpet". The problem is that the explanations are complete nonsense. The exact wording in the report is "Ruby could have consumed time in loitering along the way, at the top of the ramp, or inside the basement." Let us consider them in reverse order:

Loitering inside the basement
We know that the police calculated that the car driven by Lieutenant Pierce arrived at the top of the ramp about 50 seconds before the shooting. Lieutenants Revill and McCaghren found it took 22 seconds to walk down the ramp to where Oswald was shot. So that would leave Ruby with 28 seconds in the basement, a little longer if he hurried. However, this time is fixed by the time of the police car exiting the building. Ruby could not loiter for longer because of the fixed time when an exiting car made access possible.

Loitering at the top of the ramp
Jack Ruby made it clear in his statements following his arrest that he did not stop when he reached the Main Street entrance. He claimed that he saw the officer who was guarding it move out of position and he simply changed his direction and headed straight down the ramp. The idea of loitering at the top of the ramp contradicts Ruby's own claims.

Loitering along the way
Let us consider the background here. The Warren Commission looked at Ruby's activities over the weekend in detail and it was obvious that he was in a state of emotional turmoil. He appeared to be totally obsessed with the events of the assassination and he went into the DPD headquarters to watch Oswald being moved around the building and to watch him appear at a midnight press conference. Ruby appeared to be fascinated and obsessed with Lee Harvey Oswald.

Detective D.R. Archer was with Ruby after his arrest and, in a report to Chief Curry, he mentions that Ruby explained to Sergeant Dean how he got into the basement of Police Headquarters. At one point Ruby states that, after leaving

Twelve | Jack Ruby

the Western Union, "I walked up that way, thinking I might get a chance to see Oswald..."

Jack Ruby left Western Union at 11:17am and he started walking towards the Main Street entrance believing he might have a chance to see Oswald, the man he had been obsessed with for the previous two days. He also still had to sort out one of his dogs that he had left behind in his car in a nearby parking lot. Can we really believe that under such circumstances Ruby would loiter along the way? If anything we would expect him to hurry to the entrance as he would be anxious not to miss anything. The idea that for a short walk, which would normally take 1 minute and 13 seconds, took him 3 minutes and 10 seconds to complete is really unbelievable. It is much easier to believe that Ruby used a different means of entry and one that did not depend on him arriving at the ramp at the exact moment that a car was exiting.

Why would Ruby lie?
If Jack Ruby had used the 'alley route' and entered DPD headquarters via some doors and stairs at the east side of the building, then why did he not just say so? He could have said that he knew about this route into the building and when he entered this way he found that the doors were unlocked and there was nobody guarding them.

However, the evidence does suggest he was lying and the most likely explanation would be that he had something to hide. If Ruby had entered the east side of the building it could have been that somebody working for the Dallas Police Department helped him to enter the building or simply "turned a blind eye" when they saw him coming into the basement.

Ruby would not want this information to come to light. Assistance from someone inside the Dallas Police Department would suggest that Ruby had some pre-arranged help. He wanted his arrival in the basement to be regarded as a chance event and his shooting of Oswald to be regarded as a sudden, unplanned, impulsive action.

When Ruby saw a police car going up the Main Street ramp, within a minute of Oswald coming out, he probably thought it would be useful to claim that he came down the ramp as the car exited. He may have thought that it would divert attention away from the 'alley route' and make it less likely that his assistance from somebody on the inside would ever come to light.

It appears that the plan worked for about 15 years as his entry into the basement via the 'alley route' was never given serious consideration until the late 1970s when the HSCA reviewed the matter.

Peripheral issues: The black sweater question
Some defenders of the Warren Commission like to make out that the shooting of Oswald by Ruby was just a matter of chance. Ruby was obsessed with the

events of the assassination of Kennedy and Lee Harvey Oswald in particular, even attending a midnight press conference when Oswald was brought out to face the press. However, in spite of this obsession, he made no plans to attend this transfer but arrived at the Western Union near to Dallas Police Department just before the transfer by pure chance (he had to wire some money to Karen Carlin) He walked from Western Union office and arrived at the top of the ramp at the moment that Roy Vaughan was out of position, by chance. He then arrived at the bottom of the ramp within a minute of Oswald being brought out, again by chance.

If these were not enough chance events to believe happened, Warren Commission defenders point to another chance event involving Oswald's black sweater. An example of this is in Gerald Posner's book 'Case Closed' where he states that when the police had finished interviewing Oswald in Captain Fritz's office, before taking him down to the basement, Oswald asked if he could change his clothes. Posner then claims that Captain Fritz sent for some sweaters and Oswald tried on the beige one, and then changed his mind and switched to a black sweater. Posner then goes on the state that if Oswald had not decided at the last moment to get a sweater, he would have left the jail almost five minutes earlier, whilst Ruby was still in the Western Union office.

However, in the section of the Warren Commission "Chapter 5, Detention and Death of Oswald" on page 215 we find the sequence of events described. Captain Fritz and others finish interviewing Oswald at about 11:15 am. Captain Fritz instructs police personnel to move cars in preparation for the transfer, this includes Lieutenant Pierce. After they leave to do this, Oswald is given his sweater and then he is handcuffed to Detective Leavelle after which Oswald is taken down to the basement. From this we can see that Lieutenant Pierce has already left to get the police car when the sweater incident occurs. This means that the car driven by Pierce would have arrived at the top of the ramp at 11:20am irrespective of whether Oswald spent zero time over the matter of his sweater or 10 minutes over the matter of his sweater. The only thing that would change would be that the longer the time Oswald spent over putting on a sweater, the longer the time between the car driven by Lieutenant Pierce coming out at the top of the ramp and Oswald arriving in the basement at the place where he was shot. In fact, we know that the time interval between Lieutenant Pierce coming out at the top of the ramp and Oswald being shot was only about 50 seconds.

This suggests that the time involved in the sweater incident could not have been very long, why would that be? To answer that question we need to look at the testimony of Detective L.C. Graves before the Warren Commission. He was the only person present when Oswald put on his sweater to give much detail on the matter when he was interviewed. In his testimony he states that "We asked him if he would like to put something on" and not "He asked if he could change his clothes" as Posner writes in his book. Graves goes on to say "we got these clothes off the rack and started to give him the light colored jacket or

Twelve | Jack Ruby

shirt…" and Oswald said "if it's all the same to you…I'd rather wear the black sweater"…."so we let him put it on". So Oswald did not actually try on a beige sweater before putting on the black one as Posner suggests.

Posner says that Captain Fritz sent for some sweaters, implying that somebody had to go and fetch them from another part of the building. However, when Detective Graves was asked about where Oswald's clothes were he tells the Warren Commission that they were at the back of Captain Fritz's office. So it appears that Oswald was offered some sweaters and shirts from the back of Fritz's office, he then chose the black one and put it on and he was then ready to be taken down to the basement. This whole event probably only took between 30 and 60 seconds.

So what would have happened if Oswald said he did not want to put the sweater on?

If Ruby had walked along to the top of the ramp, as he claimed, he would still arrived there as the car driven by Lieutenant Pierce was exiting (having spent nearly 2 minutes loitering along the way, as we saw earlier) and gone down the ramp. Without spending time putting on a sweater, Oswald would have arrived down in the basement earlier and he would have been placed in a car when Ruby was still walking down the ramp. It is unlikely that Ruby would have been able to get a clear shot at Oswald had this occurred.

However, the evidence suggests that Ruby did not go down the ramp, so what would have happened if Oswald had said he did not want his sweater under these circumstances?

Ruby left the Western Union office at 11:17am. At walking pace, the police determined it would take him 2 minutes and 25 seconds to get to the site of Oswald's murder in the basement from the Western Union office. This means that Ruby could be in place to kill Oswald at 11:19am and 25seconds. Of course, Oswald would have come out earlier had he not put his sweater on but the earliest he could have been brought out would have been the time that Lieutenant Pierce was starting to drive up the ramp. Captain Fritz would have wanted to allow some time for Pierce to drive his car into position and Fritz asked his men check that everything was ready for Oswald to come out before he was brought out from the jail area. The men in the basement would not have given the all clear if they could see that Lieutenant Pierce was still driving his car in the basement. They would have waited until they saw his car going up the ramp before giving Captain Fritz the all clear.

We know from TV pictures taken that morning that Lieutenant Pierce's car cleared the area at the bottom of the ramp 56 seconds before Ruby shot Oswald. This means that the earliest time Oswald could have been shot if he did not put his sweater on would have been 11:20am and 4 seconds. This would have given Ruby 39 seconds to ready himself for when Oswald was brought out. Ruby would still have been able to shoot Oswald, the only thing that might have changed is that if Lieutenant Pierce's car was only just starting up the ramp when Oswald was shot then Ruby could not have claimed he came down the ramp when the car was exiting at the top of the ramp. He would have had to say he came in via the side entrance through doors that were not secured and not guarded. The blame for Ruby getting into the basement would have gone to the police officers in charge of basement security. History would have only been slightly different, Patrick Dean would have been blamed for incompetence leading to Ruby getting into the basement and not Roy Vaughan.

Peripheral issues: The Sheba question
One argument used by those who support the Warren Commission version of how Jack Ruby got into the basement has to with a certain dog. At the time of the assassination, Ruby kept Dachshund dogs at the Carousel Club and his favourite was a bitch named Sheba. He would take Sheba back to his apartment every night and leave his other dogs behind at the club.

The Warren Commission stated that: "Ruby was extremely fond of dogs" as shown by statements from William G Serur and George Senator in which they spoke about Ruby's having extreme fondness for his dogs and Sheba in particular. Ruby would refer to his dogs as 'his family' and Sheba as 'his wife'. The official story is that, on the day that Oswald was shot, Ruby drove down to a car park near to the Western Union with Sheba in his car. He left her in the car with the doors unlocked and went off to go to the Western Union office. The argument is that if Ruby intended to shoot Oswald that morning he would never have brought Sheba with him. He was so fond of Sheba that he would have left her back at the Carousel Club with the other dogs where his trusty bartender, Andrew Armstrong, could take care of her.

The problem with this argument is that there is no proof that the dog recovered from the car was Sheba and, in fact, there are good reasons to believe that the dog was not Sheba.

Firstly, after his arrest, Ruby showed very little awareness or concern about the dog in his car. The first formal statement Ruby made was to FBI agent Mr. C Hall within hours of the shooting. Ruby gave details of how he drove to the car park near to the Western Union but he made no mention of Sheba at all.

Oswald was killed at 11:21am and the police went to Ruby's car at about 1pm (according to two car park attendants). Ruby must have told the police about the dog in his car between these two times. Records show that he was with a jailer and detectives Clardy, McMillon and Archer during this time. You would expect that Ruby's attempts to get somebody to go and fetch his dog from the car would have been quite memorable. Given his deep affection for Sheba, you would expect Ruby to become very vocal and animated about her being struck in the car in a quiet car park on a Sunday afternoon. However, the statements and testimonies of the detectives do not show this happening.

Twelve | Jack Ruby

Detective Archer never commented about the matter of the dog in the car. Detective McMillon was asked by the Warren Commission how the subject of the dog came up and he gave a vague reply: "I don't remember that, but maybe Jack asked us to take care of his dog or something like that. I don't know. I made no note of it after they impounded the car..." and when Detective Clardy was asked if Ruby had said anything about his car having a dog in it he replied: "Sir, I recall that he said there was some money in the car. I don't recall him saying in my presence, about the dog being in it. I do recall he talked later about some dogs that he thought so much of."

It appears that Ruby's comments about there being money left in his car were memorable but comments he made about the dog in his car were totally unmemorable, not at all what you would expect given Jack Ruby's well documented affection for Sheba.

A visitor's pass was given to Eva Grant to see her brother, Jack Ruby at 5:55pm on the day of his arrest. Six days later his friend Joe Campisi and his wife visited him for 10 minutes. Sometime after this, Ruby's barman, Andrew Armstrong visited Ruby in jail. Armstrong testified to the Warren Commission that when he first visited Ruby in jail he asked Ruby where Sheba was and Ruby told him that she had been left in his car. According to Armstrong, Ruby went on to ask him to find out if the dog pound had Sheba and if they would release her.

So here we have a situation where a man is totally besotted by Sheba, his dog, and more than six days after his arrest he is not sure where the dog is and has made no arrangements for her to be cared for. He could have asked his sister to sort out his dog on the first day or he could have asked Campisi for his help six days later. Ruby knew dozens of people in the Dallas Police Department and could easily have used his contacts to, at the very least, find out where Sheba was and check that she was alright yet it appears Ruby made no such effort. It looks like Ruby's wife had grounds for a divorce!

George Senator told the FBI that Ruby left his apartment on the morning of Oswald's murder and took Sheba with him. Ruby would later tell Andrew Armstrong that he had left Sheba in his car that day. However, after Ruby left his car, somebody could have gone to his car and swapped Sheba for another Dachshund. This sounds a rather strange and far-fetched idea until you look at some of the details of the event.

Larry Crafard worked for Ruby and often used his car keys to move objects in or out of the car for him. In his testimony before the Warren Commission he stated that Ruby only ever used one large set of keys that included keys to his apartment, his nightclub and his car. However, after his arrest, a set of key were removed from Ruby and given to Detective McMillon. He was ordered to take the keys to the car park so that Ruby's car could be impounded. However, when he got there the car had already been taken away. Earlier, Detective Swain had arrived at Ruby's car and found the doors to be unlocked. In the glove compartment he found as single key to the boot (or 'trunk' as they call it in America). Ruby did not use a single key to the boot normally. In the boot (trunk) Swain found a bunch of keys that included the ignition key for the car. This means that there were keys for the car separate to the bunch of keys taken from Ruby's person after his arrest. Ruby's use of keys had inexplicably changed on the day he shot Oswald. Two sets of keys relating to one car does raise the possibility that two individuals had been accessing Ruby's car on that day before the police came along.

Sheba eventually went back into the care of Ruby's bartender Andrew Armstrong. The dog removed from Ruby's car went to the city dog pound so if there had been a clear record of somebody taking Sheba from the dog pound into the custody of Armstrong then the idea that she had been swapped for another dog would be highly unlikely.

Armstrong told the Warren Commission that one of Ruby's employees by the name of Joy Dale picked Sheba up from the pound and took her back to the Carousel so that he could take over her care. However, some time later, Joy Dale told researcher Gary Mack that she had no memory of doing this and she thought that Andrew Armstrong must have fetched her. Some years later, Armstrong told the HSCA that he remembered collecting Sheba himself and that somebody must have given him a lift because he did not have a car at that time. He said that he could not remember who gave him the lift or if he collected Sheba from the Carousel Club or the police station.

There appears to be confusion over this issue and no clear statement from anybody that Sheba was taken from the dog pound and passed on to Andrew Armstrong.

You might want to ask the question: why would Ruby want to switch Sheba for another dog? This is a difficult question to answer as it involves trying to get into the mind of Jack Ruby. We can only speculate that he might have wanted to get Sheba into the care of a friend before he went to DPD headquarters. He might have worried that things could have gone wrong when he shot Oswald and that he might have been shot and seriously wounded or even killed in the confusion. If this happened he could not tell them about Sheba in the car and she might then be left in the car for many hours.

Ruby might have just not liked the idea of Sheba going into a dog pound. We can never know the reason; all we can do is look at the evidence and see what it shows us.

To sum up, a dog was recovered from Jack Ruby's car after he was arrested. Both Ruby and George Senator would later claim that this dog was Sheba; however, the behaviour of Ruby in his contacts with the police and his visitors strongly suggests that this dog was not Sheba. Swapping Sheba for another dog suggests deliberate deception and pre-planning. We know that Jack Ruby knew some magicians and illusionists and that he liked to have magic acts

Twelve | Jack Ruby

performing at his club, perhaps he was doing his own little trick that afternoon with a couple of small dachshunds.

Summary of how Jack Ruby entered the basement

Careful examination of witnesses statements from individuals who were down in the basement show that Ruby used the lower part of the Main Street ramp just before he shot Oswald. However, he could have come all the way down the ramp or he could have used the 'alley route' and walked across the garage area. There is no decisive proof to show exactly which route he chose.

Witness statements from individuals around the Main Street entrance are more helpful. They provide good solid evidence that Ruby did not use this entrance to gain entry to the basement.

Looking closely at the comments made by Jack Ruby following his arrest we find there is nothing in his words that prove that he must have used the Main Street entrance and walked down the ramp. Jack Ruby failed to observe certain things around the Main Street entrance that he might reasonably have been expected to see. He also spoke of events taking place around the entrance that all the evidence from other witnesses suggests never occurred. A detailed examination of the timing of events relating to Jack Ruby's movements that morning do not support his claim that he walked up to the Main Street entrance and then went down the ramp without stopping.

When all this information is brought together it is clear that the House Select Committee on Assassinations was correct in its assessment as to how Ruby gained access to the basement of DPD headquarters before he shot Oswald. Ruby did not use the Main Street entrance and walk down the ramp as described by the Warren Commission. Ruby almost certainly used the 'alley route' and went through doors and down stairs in the east part of the building. Ruby went to considerable efforts to try and persuade his captors that he did not use this route. However, it is highly likely that he did use this route and he was probably helped by someone who worked for the Dallas Police Department. The investigations of Burt Griffiths of the Warren Commission suggests that help could have come from Sergeant Patrick Dean, however, pressure from Dallas officials led to Griffiths being removed from Dallas and the matter being dropped from the Warren Commission investigations.

Chapter Summary

- Jack Ruby came from a broken home and he lived his formative years in the poor and rough districts of Chicago.
- As an adult, Ruby moved around and did various jobs before he settled in Dallas where he spent 16 years running dancehalls and nightclubs.
- FBI documents suggest that Jack Ruby was involved in criminal activities such as gambling, prostitution and narcotics. His narcotics

- activities would have brought him into contact with criminal gangs that were involved in the import and distribution of narcotics in Texas.
- There is evidence that Ruby was involved in gun running and other illegal activities between the USA and Cuba. It is possible that Ruby associated with people in the CIA and the Mafia because of his involvement in such activities.
- Jack Ruby was on friendly terms with many of the men who worked for the Dallas Police Department.
- There is evidence that Jack Ruby had planned to kill Lee Harvey Oswald in advance and that he accessed the basement of the Dallas Police Department headquarters with inside help.
- Jack Ruby may have been looking to somebody within organized crime to solve his dire financial problems. That person may have manipulated Ruby into killing Oswald.
- The murder of Lee Harvey Oswald was a pre-planned event designed to silence him forever.

Final thoughts
Earlier in this chapter we noted that Jack Ruby was in the offices of the Dallas Morning News on the day that President Kennedy was shot but there was nobody that could confirm he was there at the exact time of the assassination. It just so happened that Jack Ruby telephoned a friend on that morning but he was unaware that the man that he had become friends with was in fact an informant for the criminal intelligence division of the Internal Revenue Service. There is a declassified FBI document dated 4/6/77 number 62-109060-6799 in which the information that this IRS informant had on the matter is revealed as follows: "The informant stated that on the morning of the assassination, Ruby contacted him and asked if he would 'like to watch the fireworks.' He was with Jack Ruby and standing at the corner of the Postal Annex Building facing the Texas School Book Depository Building at the time of the shooting. Immediately after the shooting, Ruby left and headed toward the area of the Dallas Morning News Building."

It appears that this informant never appeared before the Warren Commission or the House Select Committee on Assassinations. If he had done so his testimony might have been quite explosive. How did Ruby know of the "fireworks" that were about to go off in Dealey Plaza? Was he given a minor role in the event? If so, who gave him the role? What was his role? And how much did he understand about what was going on? When it comes to Jack Ruby, like most aspects of the Kennedy Assassination, there are always more questions to ask and there is always so much more to find out.

Twelve | Jack Ruby

References

Black Op Radio:
Web site: http:///www.blackopradio.com/
Interview with Jerry Colley (access date 10.11.2011)

Bugliosi, Vincent: Reclaiming History, The Assassination of President John F. Kennedy. (W.W. Norton & Company Inc New York. 2007) pp1101 – 1102

Coup D'Etat in America: nodule 28, Jack Ruby and the contact out on Oswald (2012) web site: http://www.scribd.com/doc/120973657/COUP-D-ETAT-IN-AMERICA-VOLUME-EIGHT (access date 01.05.2012) section on the Campisis.

Douglass, James W: JFK and the Unspeakable, Why he died and why it matters: (Orbis Books New York. 2009) p368

R. Ecker (2004) web site: Jack Ruby's Dog or Goodbye Little Sheba available at http://hobrad.angelfire.com/rubysdog.html (access date 01.05.2007) refers to a personal communication between Gary Mac and Ron Ecker about Joy Dale.

House Select Committee on Assassinations: (Washington, DC.US Government Printing Office, 1979) hereafter referred to as the HSCA

The House Select Committee on Assassinations: appendix Volume 9 p595-809
Ruby's entry to the basement: HSCA Report p156-157

Kantor, Seth: Who was Jack Ruby? (Everest House New York 1978) p3 and p15

Marrs, Jim: Crossfire, The plot that killed Kennedy: (Great Britain. Pocket Books 1993) p366

Posner, Gerald: Case Closed, Lee Harvey Oswald and the assassination of JFK: (Great Britain. Warner Books 2003) p394-395

Schweim, David E.: Contract on America:
(Shapolsky Publishers Inc, New York 1988) pp 87-93 and pp109-113

The Warren Commission: Hearings before the Presidents Commission on the Assassination of President Kennedy: (Washington, DC.US Government Printing Office, 1964) hereafter referred to as WCH:

JFK | ECHOES FROM ELM STREET
A SEARCH FOR HISTORICAL ACCURACY ON THE
ASSASSINATION OF PRESIDENT JOHN F. KENNEDY

Ruby the criminal:
WCH Volume 13 p359   WCH Volume 13 p372-273
WCH Volume 23 p362   WCH Volume16 p466-473
WCH Volume 23 p369   WCH Volume 23 p370
WCH Volume 22 p360   WCH Volume 13 p372-373
WCH Volume 26 p262   WCH Volume 15 p432

Other Ruby associations:
WCH Volume 16 p634 and p644

Ruby at the offices of the Dallas Morning Post:
WCH Volume 25 p281-282   WCH Volume 15 p563
WCH Volume 25 p189   WCH Volume 20 p651

Karen Carlin:
WCH Volume 15 p404-430   WCH Volume 13 p205-221
WCH Volume 13 p201-205

Signs of premeditation:
WCH Volume 21 p431   WCH Volume 15 p245
WCH Volume 16 p 551 WCH Volume 14 p259
WCH Volume 14 p234   WCH Volume 26 p550

Events down in the basement:
WCH Volume 24 p465   WCH Volume 14 p105
WCH Volume 20 p83   WCH Volume 14 p107
WCH Volume 12 p250-255 WCH Volume 13 p135-136
WCH Volume 12 p331-334 WCH Volume 20 p647

Events at the top of the Main Street Ramp:
WCH Volume 21 p684   WCH Volume 14 p82
WCH Volume 19 p421   WCH Volume 12 p231
WCH Volume 14 p180   WCH Volume 14 p83
WCH Volume 12 p361   WCH Volume 12 p340
WCH Volume 12 p346   WCH Volume 12 p287
WCH Volume 15 p681 and 683

The statements of Jack Ruby:
WCH Volume 14 p51

The claims made by Jack Ruby:
WCH Volume 12 p345   WCH Volume 12 p339

WCH Volume 12 p287   WCH Volume 19 p421
WCH Volume 15 p681   WCH Volume 20 p43

A question of timing:
WCH Volume 14 p50

Comments about loitering:
WCH Volume 24 p51

The black sweater question:
WCH Volume 13 p5

The Sheba question:
WCH Volume 25 p484   WCH Volume 14 p185 and p319
WCH Volume 20 p37-46   WCH Volume 19 p22
WCH Volume13 p51   WCH Volume 12 p413
WCH Volume 12 p395   WCH Volume 25 p184
WCH Volume 13 p355   WCH Volume 13 p500 and 501
WCH Volume 13 p84   WCH Volume 13 p272-273
WCH Volume 13 p51

The Warren Commission Report: The President's Committee on the assassination of President Kennedy (Washington, DC:US Government Printing Office, 1964) hereafter referred to as WCR:

Ruby's entry to the basement:
WCR Chapter 5 p222

Ruby's 'loitering':
WCR Chapter 5 p221

Dismissing Napoleon Daniel's evidence:
WCR Chapter 5 p231

JFK | ECHOES FROM ELM STREET
A SEARCH FOR HISTORICAL ACCURACY ON THE
ASSASSINATION OF PRESIDENT JOHN F. KENNEDY

Thirteen
The Authenticity of the Zapruder Film

Chris Scally

> *"Reason does not always appeal to unreasonable men."*
> – John F. Kennedy
> University of Washington Centenary Speech
> November 16, 1961

Introduction

It was raining in Dallas on that fateful November morning when Abraham Zapruder left his home at 3909 Marquette Street[1], and began the seven-mile journey to the offices of 'Jennifer Juniors', his dress manufacturing business located on the 4th and 5th floors of the Dal-Tex building at 501 Elm Street, directly across Houston Street from the Texas School Book Depository (TSBD). On the previous day Zapruder, a great admirer of the President, had talked about bringing his new 8mm movie camera to work so that he could film the motorcade as it passed almost directly below his 4th floor office, but clearly the rain had deterred him from doing so.[2]

The rain eased off as the morning progressed, and by 10 am Zapruder's receptionist Marilyn Sitzman and his secretary Lillian Rogers had persuaded him to return home and collect his camera.[3] But did their persuasiveness ultimately result in the production of "the greatest home movie ever made", or "the hoax of the century"?

There has always been discussion, debate and even controversy regarding the authenticity of the Zapruder film, but rather than diminish over time, the question is still very much to the fore. A 'show-of-hands' straw poll, conducted at the Dealey Plaza UK (DPUK) annual conference in Canterbury, England in April 2012 revealed an almost equal number of people who (a) believed the Zapruder film has been 'doctored' or deliberately altered in some way; (b) fully believed that the film is authentic; and (c) were still undecided one way or the other.

Zapruder film alteration claims are predicated on five main areas of contention – the alleged removal of frames showing the President's limousine as it made the turn from Houston Street onto Elm Street; the further removal of frames said to show the limousine coming to a halt on Elm Street during the shooting itself; the existence of another version of the Zapruder film, which allegedly shows the deleted events; the alleged manipulation or alteration of the film in order to hide the exact nature of the President's head injuries; and the mysterious appearance of two different versions of the Zapruder film (both of which were believed by those who saw them to be the "original" film) at the National Photographic Interpretation Center (NPIC) in Washington, D.C. on the nights of Saturday and Sunday, November 23 and 24, 1963. Central to all of these issues is the question of when and where any substitution of Zapruder's camera-original film could have taken place.

It therefore seemed logical that the first requirement in any evaluation of the authenticity of the film was the establishment of whether or not there were any gaps or inconsistencies in the whereabouts of the film – and the three first-day copies created on the afternoon of the assassination – in the days immediately following the assassination. A chance discussion in April 2010 with fellow DPUK member Mark de Valk[4] prompted the author to attempt the task of creating the most detailed possible chronology of the film, incorporating *all* the available material, with the result that in November 2010, the author's updated Zapruder film timeline was presented at the *JFK Lancer* conference in Dallas, and appears in tabular form at the end of this chapter.[5]

When the author first began researching the chronology of the Zapruder film, a well-known researcher and author warned: "Anyone who embarks upon a study like this has endless decisions to make about whose account to believe, and whose account not to believe". Compiling the chronology certainly proved the truth of that warning, but every such decision was based on what was considered to be the weight of the available evidence. Some of those decisions may ultimately turn out to be wrong, but they were always made in good faith, since the author began this task as an "alteration agnostic", with no idea of where the search would ultimately lead. However, as research into the chronology progressed, it became apparent that the timeline, or chronology of the film, simply did not allow for changes on the scale alleged by a number of very well-known researchers and authors. That conflict of views was not, in itself, a cause for concern, since such differences of opinion are at the heart of all research. However, in the back of the author's mind at all times was the nagging doubt that, because the camera-original film and the three first-day copies which exist today are not in the same physical layout and condition as they were on the afternoon of the assassination, there just *might* still be a possibility that somehow they might not be the ones created in Dallas that day – and furthermore, there appeared to be no way in which it could be proven one way or the other.

Thirteen | The Authenticity of the Zapruder Film

However, in February 2011, the author began to research the origin and history of three black-and-white 16mm copies of the film, which had apparently been made very shortly after the assassination. These three copies of the film were not even known about until late 1999, when they turned up among material handed over to the Sixth Floor Museum in Dallas by *Life* magazine and the Zapruder family.[6] Nobody had apparently looked at – or even shown any interest in – these three films since 2000 when they were examined on behalf of the Sixth Floor Museum by retired Kodak scientist Roland J. Zavada, but the author quickly realised that they might turn out to be crucial evidence in the search for clarity – if not certainty – about the authenticity of the camera-original Zapruder film. As a result, the question of their provenance became vitally important.

This chapter attempts to document the story of these three copies of the film, and what the author believes is their pivotal role in determining whether or not there might have been any opportunity for the original film to have been clandestinely altered, or replaced with a forgery. But first, it is perhaps appropriate to briefly review what is known about Zapruder's camera and the current status of his historic film.

The Camera
In May 1963, 58-year old Abraham Zapruder – a keen amateur photographer – purchased a top-of-the range Bell & Howell Zoomatic Director Series 8mm home movie camera from Peacock Jewellery Company on Elm Street in Dallas.[7] The camera, which had a price tag of just over $200, was a Model 414 PD (the "P" indicated "Power Zoom", while the "D" indicated "Dual Electric-Eye"[8]), and had the serial number AS 13486 stamped on a metal plate in the compartment where the film is loaded. Weighing 3.5 pounds (or 1.5 kilos), Zapruder's camera was a "transition" model, and was equipped with a Varamat 9-27mm F/1.8 lens with manual zoom capability, which could be operated by a lever attached to the lens or by the zoom control buttons.[9] The camera had exposure speeds of 'Run' (16 frames per second), 'Slow Motion' (48 frames per second) and 'Animation' (single frame).[10]

When fully wound, the camera ran for approximately 73 seconds, exposing about 15 feet of film. It was spool-loaded with double-8mm film (which is actually 16mm wide film, consisting of two rows of 8mm wide exposures alongside each other in opposite 'heads-to-tails' orientation, representing the two passes required to completely expose the double-8mm in-camera film), with 25 feet of usable film on each 8mm row and approximately 4 feet of 'leader' at each end, making a total of 33 feet of film per side. When one side of the film was exposed, the user manually reversed the roll of film in the camera, and then continued filming, thereby exposing the second half. Under normal conditions, when the film was developed it was slit down the middle, the two

JFK | ECHOES FROM ELM STREET
A SEARCH FOR HISTORICAL ACCURACY ON THE ASSASSINATION OF PRESIDENT JOHN F. KENNEDY

sides were spliced together, and the developed film was returned to the user as a single roll of 8mm film, each frame being 0.192 x 0.144 inches in size – giving a total of approximately 4,166 frames on a 50-foot roll of film.[11]

On the day of the assassination, Zapruder's camera was loaded with a roll of 1961-manufactured Kodachrome II safety film, which was Kodak's 'outdoor' film,[12] and as some film had already been exposed on Side A of the roll, Zapruder used up the remaining available footage on Side A by filming his secretary, Lillian Rogers.[13]

Zapruder then turned the film spool over to Side B, and to bring the footage indicator on his camera to the correct starting position for Side B, he exposed about 60 frames of what appears to be the arm of an office chair.[14] Zapruder then went down to Dealey Plaza where, before filming the motorcade on Side B, he exposed 117 frames (or approximately 6.5 seconds worth of film) of Marilyn Sitzman standing by a bench at the top of the grassy knoll. Seated on the bench was fellow Zapruder employee Beatrice Hester, with her husband Charles sitting on the steps to her left.[15]

The Film today

The camera-original Zapruder film and the two Secret Service first-day copies are today stored under tight security at the National Archives and Records Administration (NARA). All three films have now been slit to 8mm format, and have been spliced and damaged to varying degrees.

On Monday November 25, 1963, Zapruder sold all rights to his film to *Life* magazine, who kept the film for over 11 years until their owners, Time Inc., returned the camera-original film to Zapruder's family on April 9, 1975. Three years later, the family handed the film over to the National Archives. We do not know how or where the film was stored, or how it was handled or otherwise cared for, during the three-year period it was in the possession of the family, nor indeed during the entire period when it was in the custody of *Life*.[16]

After the film was given to NARA in June 1978, it was initially stored in the National Archives building in Washington at between 70 and 74 degrees Fahrenheit (F), and 40 to 55% Relative Humidity (RH). In 1987, it was moved to the NARA Annex in Alexandria, Virginia, where it was stored at 35 degrees F, and 35% RH. In 1994, the original film (officially identified as "200 ZAP 1; 1 ORSK {P} 8 mm") was moved to its current location at NARA in Maryland, where it is "wound on a large slotless core 7 inch x 0.25 inch plastic audiotape reel in an unsealed aluminized plastic bag in a NARA standard flame-retardant, inert polypropylene vented plastic container" at 25 degrees F and 30% RH.[17] Whenever the film is taken out of 'cold storage', it is first kept for 24 hours in a temperature of 50 degrees before the container in which it is stored can be opened.[18] In 1996, film shrinkage was measured at 0.5%, and the film was described as scratched, containing splices, and having broken sprocket holes.[19]

Thirteen | The Authenticity of the Zapruder Film

In addition, there are reports that the film is showing some signs of mould.[20]

In its present state, the camera-original film consists of the last 14 frames of the original 117-frame sequence of Marilyn Sitzman and the Hesters in Dealey Plaza, followed by 480 frames of motorcade footage. The motorcade footage begins with 132 frames showing the lead motorcycles, followed by the 'assassination' sequence. At 25 inches into the exposed film there is a broken sprocket hole and a splice where frames 155 and 156 are missing. A second splice occurs at 32.5 inches, where frames 207 and 212 are spliced, and frames 208 through 211 are missing. The exposed footage amounts to fractionally less than 6 feet 2 inches in length, and runs for approximately 26.5 seconds at 18.3 frames per second.[21]

The perforated identifier '0183' is missing from the film, as is Side A (the home movies and the Lillian Rogers office scene) in its entirety. The current whereabouts of the original Side A footage is unknown.[22]

Turning to the two Secret Service copies of the film (both of which are identified at NARA as "87.010; 1 MPPSK {P} 8 mm"), neither one shows splices following frames 154 or 207, nor are there any other frames missing from the assassination sequence on either copy (apart from the five burned-through frames in copy #1, mentioned below).[23]

The original perforated identification is missing from Secret Service copy #1, and the film contains "3 completely burned-through frames, 2 partially burned-through frames, and many ripped sprocket holes" in the assassination sequence. The Side A 'home movie' footage is described as being approximately 32' 7" in length, while the Side B footage is approximately 7' 6" long, consisting of the pre-assassination footage of Marilyn Sitzman and the Hesters in Dealey Plaza, which Zapruder filmed prior to the arrival of the motorcade, and the entire assassination sequence itself.[24]

According to Roland Zavada,[25] Secret Service copy #2 has "been cut and reassembled, apparently to provide 'looping' to facilitate examinations of selected scenes."[26] The original perforated identification number '0186', punched onto this copy of the film by Kodak in Dallas on the afternoon of the assassination, appears at the beginning of the motorcade side of the film, making this the *only* print of the film made on November 22, 1963 to still contain its original identification number.[27]

The third first-day copy of the film, the so-called "*Life*/LMH" copy, is now housed in the Sixth Floor Museum in Dallas.[28] Like the original and the two Secret Service copies, it is in slit 8mm format. The original perforated identification is also missing from this copy of the film, and the film has been spliced and rearranged such that Side B – the assassination footage side of the film – appears first. All the pre-assassination footage on Side B is missing, as are all the frames prior to approximately frame 214 of the assassination footage (when the President is hidden behind the Stemmons Freeway sign). In total, only 3' 6" of Side B remains. All of the Side A footage (the 'home movies' and the Lillian Rogers office footage) is present on this copy of the film.[29]

It is interesting to note that, while it is now missing from the original film, the perforated identification number '0183' given to the camera-original film on November 22, 1963 is photographically copied onto all three of the first-day copies, further verifying their authenticity.[30]

Provenance of the Extant Film
According to the Zavada Report, NARA records "provide reasonable assurances of the traceability of copies identified as Secret Service copies 1 and 2, which we, in general, accepted as first generation copies..."[31] However, this conflicts with NARA's Accession Report dated 12 May 1975 and their Inventory dated 13 December 1996, which state that these are "duplicate copies made for the Secret Service by *Time-Life, Inc.* 59 feet. Copy 1 has a written note in the can on blue paper stating 'original Secret Service copy of Zapruder film'."[32] This discrepancy was effectively resolved on April 19, 1999, when NARA's Motion Picture, Sound and Video Branch chief Les Waffen said that this was a "mistake" on the part of NARA, and admitted that there was no documentation to support the conclusion that the two Secret Service copies were made by *Life*. He further acknowledged that he had no idea how that misidentification got into the record.[33]

In order to 'prove' the provenance of the original film, Roland Zavada suggested that a sample be removed from the film in order to conduct a spectrometry test. This test, which would cause the destruction of a single frame from the non-motorcade sequence, would determine whether the extant film was of Kodachrome II type (which it should be), or some type of indoor film, as might be the case if the film had been 'recreated' in a film laboratory. The Assassination Records Review Board (ARRB), set up in 1994 to oversee the implementation of the JFK Assassination Records Collection Act of 1992, and to whom Zavada suggested the test, were clearly opposed to the idea, and the test was never carried out.[34]

A second test suggested by Zavada, which would permit him to verify that Zapruder's film was taken with the camera in evidence, to the possible exclusion of any other Bell & Howell model 414PD camera, was also rejected by NARA with the endorsement of the ARRB. As Zavada reported, "we were encouraged to obtain and test a comparable camera rather than use Zapruder's camera held by NARA".[35] While the reluctance of NARA to risk any unnecessary or unjustifiable damage to such historic artifacts is fully understandable, allowing such tests – and presumably proving the authenticity of the artifacts – is surely preferable to their integrity being regularly called into question?

However, the current state of the original film, and the three first-day copies, is such that we can no longer rely on their unquestioned integrity, with the

Thirteen | The Authenticity of the Zapruder Film

result that the three black-and-white copies, made on November 23 from the camera-original film before it was split or damaged, must now be regarded as the 'best evidence' of what Zapruder captured on film during those less than 30 seconds in Dealey Plaza.

The black-and-white copies

After the US Government took possession of the Zapruder film in 1998, the Zapruder family decided to turn over a large quantity of material to the Sixth Floor Museum in Dealey Plaza. The handover took place in January 2000, and the treasure trove of material included the third remaining first-day copy of the film (the *Life*/LMH copy), copyright ownership of the Zapruder film, and three 16mm black-and-white copies of the film, made from the original film before it was damaged. The three 16mm copies of the film consisted of two high-quality 16mm negative copies of the film, and a third copy which had been processed through a reversal process to yield what is commonly-referred to as a "Dirty Dupe".[36]

The Zapruder Film – a brief history

In order to determine the origin of these three 1999-discovered black-and-white 16mm copies of the film, it is necessary to look briefly at the chronology of the Zapruder film on the afternoon of the assassination.

Between 3 and 4 o'clock that afternoon, Zapruder had his camera-original double-8mm home movie developed by Kodak at their processing plant at 3131 Manor Way, near Love Field airport in Dallas.[37] An affidavit was obtained from Kodak Production Supervisor Phil Chamberlain confirming the work that had been done, and that "at the end of the processed film and carrier strip", the identification number 0183 had been punched by Kodak processing staff.[38] Zapruder subsequently took the film to the Jamieson Film Laboratory at 3825 Bryan Street to have three copies made, a task which was completed by around 7:30 pm.[39] He obtained an affidavit from Laboratory Manager Frank Sloan that only three copies were made [as Jamieson did not have the necessary film, they could only make the same number of copies as Zapruder had rolls of film from Kodak].[40] Once again highlighting the frailties of the human memory, however, Sloan told the ARRB in 1997 that he had no memory whatsoever of signing the affidavit for Zapruder that afternoon.[41] At approximately 8 pm, Zapruder and his business partner Erwin Schwartz returned to Kodak to have the three copies printed[42], a job which was finished at around 9 pm.[43] When the three 16mm duplicates were developed, the lab perforated identification number 0185, 0186 and 0187 to the end of the filmstrips.[44] After everything had been completed, Zapruder obtained affidavits from Kodak Production Foreman Tom Nulty that only three copies (bearing identification numbers 0185, 0186, and 0187) were processed.[45] The original film and one of the copies were left in unslit (16mm) format, while the other two copies were slit to 8mm format, as was the normal practice.

However, Doug Horne of the ARRB subsequently suggested to author Richard Russell that this "almost-too-good paper trail" was questionable, in that these affidavits were probably created on Monday, November 25, and backdated to the afternoon of the assassination. Horne believes that Zapruder "created the appropriate paper trail in the form of the backdated affidavits" in order to satisfy *Life* magazine that they were getting what they paid for, when he sold all rights to the film to them on November 25, 1963. Unfortunately, however, Horne offers no concrete evidence in support of his seemingly unfounded allegation.[46]

At approximately 9 pm, Schwartz and Zapruder left the Kodak plant and drove the 10-15 minute journey to Dallas police headquarters at 106 South Harwood Street to look for Dallas Secret Service Special-Agent-In-Charge (SAIC) Forrest V. Sorrels, to whom Zapruder had earlier promised to provide a copy of his film. They eventually found him and told him they had two copies of the film for him. Sorrels asked them to take the films to the Secret Service office at 505 North Ervay Street, less than half a mile away.[47]

Sorrels clearly alerted his office to the pending arrival of Zapruder, because agent Max Phillips was expecting them after they had driven the short distance to Ervay Street.[48] The films were handed over to Phillips, who noted the time as 9:25 pm on the box containing the copy of the film perforated with the identifier '0186'.[49] By a process of elimination, we now know that Zapruder gave one 8mm slit and one 16mm unslit copy of his film to Phillips, leaving Zapruder still in possession of the unslit original film and the remaining, slit format, first-day copy. Phillips told them that one of the two copies would be sent to Secret Service headquarters in Washington that night by Navy jet from Hensley Field Naval Air Station on Mountain Creek Lake in southwest Dallas.[50] Zapruder then "signed something", before he and Schwartz left.[51] One of these copies (not the one perforated with "0186") was shipped from Dallas to Secret Service Chief Rowley in Washington that night with a covering memo, dated at 9:55 pm from Agent Phillips.[52] The handwritten memo concludes, "Note: Disregard personal scenes shown on Mr. Zapruder's film. Mr. Zapruder is in custody of the "master" film. Two prints were given to SAIC Sorrels, this date. The third print is forwarded."[53]

This seemingly throw-away comment by Agent Phillips has led to some controversy over the years. It has been interpreted to mean that four (rather than the acknowledged three) copies were made of Zapruder's film at the Jamieson processing plant that afternoon, with Zapruder keeping the original and one copy, giving two more of the copies to Sorrels, with the fourth being forwarded by Phillips to Secret Service headquarters in Washington. This would leave one additional first-day copy of the film still unaccounted for today. The

Thirteen | The Authenticity of the Zapruder Film

author's interpretation is that Zapruder kept the original 'master' print of the film and one copy (eg. #0185), and that two copies (#0186 and #0187) were given to Sorrels indirectly through Phillips, with the third print (#0187) being forwarded to Washington. This would alleviate the need for a non-existent, unaccounted for fourth copy.

Fig. 1: Front and back of box containing Zapruder film copy 0186, given by Zapruder to Secret Service agent Max Phillips at 9:25 pm on the night of the assassination (Photo Credit: National Archives)

At some time between 9 and 9:40 pm, Sorrels and others took a short break, and returned to police headquarters around 10 pm.[54] Sorrels is alleged to have subsequently carried out a detailed frame-by-frame study of Zapruder's film in his office. According to Dallas Postal Inspector Harry D. Holmes, who claimed to have been present for this examination of the film, "...we thumbed (through) that thing for an hour or more... push(ing) it up one frame at a time."[55] Holmes' story is questionable however, as Agent Max Phillips was in possession of the only copy of the film held by the Secret Service in Dallas at that time, and he told the ARRB that he believed that he gave the film to Sorrels via his secretary – "I don't think I personally gave it to the SAIC. I might have given it to the secretary to make sure the agent-in-change had it".[56] Phillips reassuringly added, "I know I didn't handle that film like I would handle a ham sandwich! And it was well taken care of until it was given to Mr. Sorrels".[57] As Sorrels was at police headquarters, and Inspector Kelley – the only other person to whom Phillips said he would have given the film – did not arrive in Dallas until 10:30 pm, after which he joined Sorrels at DPD headquarters[58], then it is most likely that the person to whom the film was actually given was Ms. Lillian L. Rhyan, Sorrels' administrative assistant.[59] Presumably, Phillips could not have given the film to her until she arrived in the office on Saturday morning.

After handing over the two copies of the film to Phillips, Schwartz took Zapruder to his car, and they both apparently went home.[60] Schwartz said he was home by 10:30 to 11 pm.[61] However, although he never apparently repeated the story, Zapruder suggested to the Warren Commission that he personally delivered the copy of his film to Hensley Field Naval Air Station on behalf of the Secret Service.[62] Could he have done so within the available time constraints? According to a Google Maps search, the present-day distance from the Secret Service office on Ervay Street to the northwest corner of Mountain Creek Lake (where the Hensley Base was located in 1963) is 14 miles, or approximately 28 minutes driving time. If a further 32 minutes are added to cover the 20-mile journey back to Zapruder's home, the minimum elapsed time is approximately one hour, with no allowance for a few minutes to complete the handover over of his film to someone. Accordingly, if Zapruder left the Secret Service office immediately after Secret Service agent Max Phillips wrote his covering note at 9:55 pm, he could not realistically have been home before 11 pm.[63]

When Zapruder arrived home sometime "after 10 pm", his wife Lillian, daughter Myrna, and her husband Myron Hauser, were there. Zapruder got out his 8mm projector and showed the film to his wife and son-in-law, but his daughter could not bear to watch.[64]

Our attention is therefore drawn to the period from about 10:30 to 11 pm on Friday night – when Zapruder got home – until approximately 7:30 am on Saturday morning, when Zapruder must have left home, because we know he was in his office before 8 am. All we really know about the whereabouts of the original film and the one remaining copy during that 9-hour period is what we have heard from Zapruder's daughter Myrna, who confirmed that her father arrived home "after 10 pm", and that he had his film with him at that time.

At 8 am on the morning after the assassination, Zapruder was back in his office in the Dal-Tex building for a meeting with Richard Stolley of *Life* magazine. Stolley had spoken to Zapruder at home by telephone the previous night around 11 pm, and had arranged to meet Zapruder on the Saturday morning to discuss the purchase of rights to the film on behalf of *Life*. Between 10 and 10:30 am on Saturday morning a deal had been done, giving *Life* worldwide print rights to the film for $50,000. As part of the deal, Zapruder gave the original film to Stolley, but kept the remaining (and allegedly the best) copy for further bargaining power with other prospective buyers.

As soon as they agreed the deal, and Zapruder had handed over the film, Stolley left Zapruder's office and immediately sent the film by courier on a commercial flight from Dallas to *Life*'s printing plant in Chicago, where work was already under way to put together the November 29 issue of *Life*, which actually appeared on newsstands on Tuesday, November 26. Roy Rowan, the *Life* editor in Chicago who received the film, has confirmed that he received only one film from Stolley, and that it was the unslit 16mm original film. We also know that the film could not have been in Chicago before midday, at the

Thirteen | The Authenticity of the Zapruder Film

earliest, as the flight time from Dallas to Chicago was unlikely to be less than it is today, which is a minimum of 1.5 hours.[65]

Author and former ARRB staff member Doug Horne believes, for reasons which will be examined later in this chapter that the accepted chronology of the film is in error, and he openly declares that Richard Stolley of *Life* magazine's recollection that the original film went to *Life's* printing plant in Chicago on Saturday, November 23 "requires re-examination".[66]

To the best of his recollection, Stolley believes that the film was taken directly to Love Field airport by someone trustworthy, most likely a member of the *Time-Life* Dallas bureau staff. The film was almost certainly addressed to Roy Rowan at the address of the Donnelley Printing plant. From Love Field, the film was sent on a commercial flight to Midway airport in Chicago, where someone from the *Life* bureau in Chicago probably met the courier on arrival.[67]

Very shortly after the film arrived in Chicago, it was sent to a local photo laboratory, where two high-quality 16mm black-and-white copies and a 'dirty dupe' copy were made.[68] The evidence indicates that these are our 1999-discovered black-and-white copies of the film, as Roland Zavada has since confirmed that the absence of a 'septum line' on these films proves that they were made from the undamaged original film, and not from one of the first-day copies.[69] Markings on these black-and-white copies suggest they were used to create the photos in *Life*'s November 29 issue.[70]

One of the boxes containing the black-and-white copies received by the Sixth Floor Museum was marked "Allied Film Laboratory, 306 West Jackson Boulevard, Chicago 6, Illinois", and despite earlier claims that Allied did not exist prior to 1967, Roland Zavada has confirmed that such a lab did exist in 1963.[71]

Joe Cook, a Chicago freelance photographer and technical specialist who frequently worked on black-and-white film projects for *Life*, said he received a call at some unspecified time on Saturday, November 23, informing him that *Life* were flying a film to a local photo lab at 53 West Jackson, which Cook described as a "drop-off point" because it was the only place a helicopter could land at that time.[72] Cook and some of his work colleagues were invited by the lab to view the film, which Cook said "really wasn't that sharp, you know. It was a fuzzy film."[73]

Cook said he had no involvement in processing the Zapruder film, work which he said was done at the 53 West Jackson 'drop-off' site, although the author believes it may well have been done at the Allied Film Labs premises.[74] Cook said that among those who were present when he saw the film were a few of his colleagues, and some of the people who worked at 53 West Jackson.[75]

If Cook's recollection of the film as "fuzzy" is accurate, what if any inference can be drawn regarding what generation of the film he saw? Did he see the film before or after it was copied? Did he only see the 'dirty dupe' copy? In any event, Cook's account supports the view that the camera-original film may have been copied in Chicago on Saturday evening, November 23, 1963.

In December 2011, the assistance of the Chicago Public Library was sought in an effort to identify the names of any companies which operated out of the 53 West Jackson address in 1963-4. However, the CPL said they did not have a reverse lookup directory for the time in question, without which it was impossible to make any further progress.[76]

Will Emaus, a former employee at *Life*'s R.R. Donnelley Calumet Plant in Chicago, and one of the last people to work there prior to its closure in 1991, has stated that, at the time the President was murdered in Dallas, some 300,000 copies of the planned November 29 issue had already been printed. A 'kill order' for these copies was issued, and the new version of the November 29 issue was worked on "until roughly 3:30 am on the 24th, when it went to press. The presses then went down again after Oswald was shot, and after the Ruby/Oswald material was inserted, (they) went back to press (on) Sunday evening." Emaus has further indicated that two members of the *Life* print team who were working on the first revision of the November 29 issue have said that the black-and-white frames from the Zapruder film were available at the Donnelley plant at around 8 pm on Saturday evening, a further strong indication that the black-and-white copies were made – probably mid-afternoon or early evening – on November 23.[77]

Although *Life* have never revealed the identity of the person who damaged the original film, or when that damage was done, it is known that a junior technician accidentally broke the original film in at least two places, resulting in splices at what would later be numbered frames 155 and 207-212.[78] According to some sources, however, the damage was actually done in Chicago on the night of November 23, in the mayhem surrounding the production of the November 29 issue of *Life*.[79] Roland Zavada, however, believes the original film was probably slit to 8mm format for viewing in New York, and it was in the 8mm format that the damage occurred while making colour inter-negatives for a subsequent issue of *Life* magazine.[80] In any event, we know that the original film was sent to *Life* headquarters in New York on Sunday morning, November 24, so the copies must have been made before the film left Chicago.[81]

Irrespective of when the original film was slit, Zavada said of the three copies: "In March 2000, I was asked to examine film materials returned to the Zapruder family by *Time-Life* 1975 and subsequently donated to the Sixth Floor Museum in 1999. We now had the third Jamieson copy available for study together with two 16mm negative copies of the double 8mm original and a corresponding dirty dupe... By analyzing the perforated lab identification of the Jamieson copy compared to a print-through of the identification number on the Allied negative, we can conclude that Zapruder did not allow his valuable original to be slit... I believe the resulting double 8mm Allied Laboratory negative became the source of selected images... for the assassination sequence photos in *Life*, November 29, 1963."[82]

Zavada further reported that the "Dupe copy made by Allied in Chicago does not contain a septum line, which allows us to conclude that the negative is a direct copy of the Zapruder camera original". He further noted the existence of what he called "callout tabs" on one of the negative copies, which were used to identify selected images for printing in the November 29 issue of *Life*. Zavada added that the Sixth Floor Museum collection also contained a splice-free 'dirty dupe' in unslit double-8mm width format, which revealed that the film stock used to print the 'dirty dupe' was the same negative material used in creating the other two double-8mm negative rolls.[83]

Taking all the foregoing evidence into account, one can reasonably deduce that the 'dirty dupe' and the two high-quality black-and-white copies were probably made in Chicago sometime between 2 pm and 5 pm on Saturday, November 23, 1963.

Or were they?

Authenticity issues

There are many who have persistently questioned the authenticity of the extant Zapruder film and its three first-day copies. Since the first low-quality copies of the film came into the hands of researchers at the time of the Clay Shaw trial in New Orleans in 1968, numerous claims have been made regarding anomalies in individual frames of the film.[84] Many of these claims were as much the result of the study of low contrast, inferior quality copies of the film, and camera-specific peculiarities, as they were from "alterations" to the film,[85] and – through the availability of high-quality copies of both the film and individual frames – they have subsequently been shown to be in error. The digital age heralded an even more widespread problem – the production of digital enlargements of individual frames from the film, followed by the study of highly-pixelated images, which can lead to almost any conclusion the 'researcher' cares to make.

More recently-discovered or publicised claims about the authenticity of the film have been based on copies of the film which are as close to the original as third-generation; however, it must be remembered that these new copies of the film have been made in recent years from an original which is now acknowledged to be scratched, dirty, damaged, and showing indications of mould.[86] Furthermore, many of these more recent studies have been done after digital cleaning, sharpening, and high-definition enhancement, such that any number of artifacts and anomalies may have been introduced along the way. As a result, many of the claims are based on subjective personal interpretations, rather than objective scientific analyses, and are far beyond the scope of this chapter.[87]

It has long been this author's belief that, if the film had been altered or replaced after Monday, November 25, when it supposedly became freely available to executives in *Life*, the original unaltered film would have surfaced somewhere by now. In fairness, there have been claims that a small number of people have seen this 'other' film – however, even the nature of that other film is in some doubt, since some claim that it is a version of Zapruder's film which precedes the version we now know, while others believe that it is a completely different film. This 'other' film is said to contain two events that are not in the Zapruder film as we know it today – first, the film allegedly shows the President's limousine making the turn from Houston onto Elm Street, and shows the driver having some difficulty negotiating the sharp turn, in contrast to the obvious break in filming between the appearance of the lead motorcyclists and the arrival of the limousine on Elm Street, which we see in the film today. The second significant event that we do not see today, but which allegedly appears in the 'other' film, is a two to four-second 'stop' on Elm Street, just before frame 313, the headshot.

The Other Film
Up to a dozen people claim to have seen this 'other' film at various times. While the descriptions of the film they have seen have varied, the film has been most clearly and concisely described by researcher Rich DellaRosa, who said that he saw the film three times – once in 1974, again in 1976, and once in the 1990s. He added that while he saw the film on three separate occasions, he never had possession of it and was therefore unable to watch it in slow motion or frame-by-frame. The film, according to DellaRosa, was professionally shot in 16mm colour format, and was very sharp in terms of both the image and the colour quality.[88] DellaRosa added that it is important to understand that no two people who have seen the film have ever seen it in company with someone else. Those who had seen the 'other' film and with whom he had discussed it did not believe that they all saw the same film. According to DellaRosa, the film shows:[89]

- the limousine making the turn onto Elm from Houston Street, without any break in filming between the appearance of the lead motorcycles and the limousine itself;
- the limousine driver, Secret Service agent William Greer, having difficulty making the turn onto Elm, turning too wide, and almost hitting the curb on the north side of the street, nearest the TSBD;
- the limousine coming to a complete halt just prior to the President's fatal head injuries being inflicted. While the car was stopped, believed by DellaRosa to have been for "maybe three or four seconds", Greer turned around and looked directly at the President, during which time the President was hit twice in the head – once from the rear causing his head to move forward slightly; and once in the right temple, by a shot fired from the front.[90]

DellaRosa did not believe that the film he saw was "in any way" a version of the Zapruder film. In his opinion, the Zapruder film was "amateurish and

Thirteen | The Authenticity of the Zapruder Film

unrealistic" by comparison, making it look no more than an animated "cartoon". The 'other' film, however, seemed to have been professionally made, with great colour rendition and smooth panning.[91]

In DellaRosa's opinion, what we know as the Zapruder film replaced the 'other' film in order to (a) remove all evidence of multiple shooters; (b) remove evidence of shots from any direction but the rear if possible; and (c) remove evidence of Secret Service complicity. Finally, DellaRosa expressed the view that it was unlikely that the film would become generally available. He described it as "dangerous property" because it proves that Kennedy was murdered as a part of a well planned and executed conspiracy. DellaRosa claims to have known of about half-a-dozen people who have seen the film in the distant past, yet no two ever saw it in the same place at the same time.[92]

Another researcher who has seen the 'other' film, and described it in detail, is Greg Burnham. Burnham also believes that the film he saw is not an unedited version of the Zapruder film, adding that the film he saw "impeaches the authenticity of the Zapruder Film because it (the "other film") shows events that are absent from the extant Zapruder film."[93]

Burnham also claims to have seen the film on several occasions over a number of years, and his description of what he saw is similar to that of DellaRosa.[94]

According to Burnham's account, the limousine came into view on Houston Street and the entire, uninterrupted, turn onto Elm Street is visible. The limousine made an extremely wide turn, almost striking the curb on the northwest corner of Elm and Houston, and was moving very slowly.

There is, according to Burnham, absolutely no question as to whether or not the limousine came to a stop at the time of the shooting, stating that the limousine came to a complete halt, and "remained motionless for approximately 2 seconds". He said that the headshot "most obviously" came from the right front.

Burnham highlights a few differences between his recollections and those of DellaRosa. For example, Burnham does not recall a shot from behind that caused the President's head to move forward initially just before the fatal head shot from the front. "That doesn't mean it didn't happen. I just may not have registered that for whatever reason", he said. He also recalls that several Secret Service agents climbed out of the President's Secret Service follow-up car with what he believed to be automatic weapons drawn, apparently looking to return fire, although DellaRosa recalled no such incident. Burnham also says that there was a considerable time interval between the President's limousine speeding off and the follow-up car leaving the scene.

In Burnham's opinion, the quality of this 'other film' is extremely high, and that – unlike the Zapruder film – there is nothing "jittery" in it, and he believes it to undoubtedly be the work of a professional cameraman, who was in the "right place at the right time, but perhaps for all the wrong reasons."

Furthermore, he believes that there is "no way of knowing whether or not those who saw a 'non-Zapruder Film' each saw the same film or whether what they saw, even if edited, was from the same film." He does not find it strange or suspicious that some of the details cannot be recalled by those who saw the other film, since they were not analyzing the film at the time of viewing it. "They were focused on content not authenticity", he said.[95]

Finally, Burnham says that it has not been possible to determine if the film he and DellaRosa saw was the unaltered original Zapruder film (although they both tend to believe that it was not), or if it was a separate film taken that day from a similar location (they both tend to believe that it was), or if they even both saw the same film, although the similarities of their respective recollections are sufficient enough to accept that as highly probable. He said they both refer to what they saw as the "other film" rather than a copy of the unaltered "original" Zapruder film. He noted that the quality of the 'other film' was extremely high in comparison to that of the extant Zapruder film.[96]

French journalist William Reymond also claims to have seen the film, but unlike DellaRosa and Burnham, he refers to it as an "unaltered copy" of the Zapruder film. In an interview with researcher Jim Marrs in 2000, Reymond said that he had seen the film a number of times, and claims that the film shows the complete turn of the limousine from Houston onto Elm Street, and the driver - having swung too wide – struggling to negotiate the turn. He also claims that the limousine stopped for about two seconds on Elm Street, during which time the President was struck twice in the head.[97]

According to professional videographer David Healy, a strong believer in film alteration, the alteration of the film to remove what he called the "limo left turn problems" would require the removal of "probably 100-140 frames", and the deletion of "the limo stop (momentarily or extended)" would require the removal of "10-40 frames" (but other estimates range from 2 to 4 seconds, which is 36 to 72 frames). Healy also suggests that within this "limo stop" could have been "indications of additional weapon(s) being discharged in Dealey Plaza". Taken together, the removal of these 110 to 180 frames would excise between about 6 and 10 seconds from the film.[98]

According to Harrison Livingstone, "someone cut out hundreds of frames" at Zapruder frame 132, between the end of the footage of the lead motorcycles and the start of the actual assassination footage.[99] Elsewhere, he suggests that the removed film was "only a half block of the motorcade... no more than two feet of film – probably closer to 1.5 feet".[100] An excision of this magnitude would result in the removal of 125-167 frames.

The allegation that a number of frames were removed from the early part of the Zapruder film to hide the perceived difficulties of Secret Service driver William Greer in negotiating the turn from Houston onto Elm Street first came to light during testimony to the Warren Commission in 1964 by

Thirteen | The Authenticity of the Zapruder Film

TSBD building superintendent Roy Truly. Truly testified that Greer had such difficulty negotiating the turn from Houston onto Elm that he came within "an inch" of hitting the curb on the north side of Elm Street, and "he had to almost stop to pull over to the left. If he had maintained his speed, he would probably have hit this little section here".[101] In fairness, Greer told the House Select Committee on Assassinations (HSCA) in 1978 that, as he made the turn from Houston onto Elm, his speed had dropped to about three to five miles per hour. He explained this very slow speed by saying that he had no prior knowledge of the motorcade route, and was simply following the lead car up ahead of him.[102] However, by slowing to such a very low speed, it is possible that vehicles further back in the motorcade did, indeed, come to a momentary halt, an explanation that could equally be applied to the claim that the limousine also stopped at the time of the headshot.

Truly's claim is also allegedly supported by the fact that, until frame 132, the Zapruder film depicts the Dallas police motorcycle escorts as they turn from Houston onto Elm. Starting with frame 133, however, we see the President's limousine as it proceeds down Elm Street, thus implying that footage was deleted from the film at this point. To support their claim, those who support the alteration theory rely heavily on Zapruder's interview by the FBI on December 4, 1963, in which he reportedly said that he "first picked up the motorcade as it made the turn onto Elm Street from Houston Street. The motorcade then passed behind a street directional sign and from that point on until it disappeared from sight to his right, or the west, he was taking moving pictures of the President's car."[103] In his testimony before the Warren Commission, Zapruder said he "started shooting – when the motorcade started coming in, I believe I started and wanted to get it coming in from Houston Street".[104] Both of these quotes would seem to suggest, at first glance, that Zapruder began filming as the motorcade began the turn onto Elm Street, and that he continued filming until it passed under the Triple Underpass at the foot of Elm Street, nearly ten seconds after the shooting had ended. However, Zapruder's secretary, Marilyn Sitzman, told a different story when interviewed about this specific question. When asked if Zapruder ever stopped filming, she said, "Yes, I think so". She was then asked at what point Zapruder stopped, to which she replied, "Well, you see, he had vertigo, or whatever, so he asked me to hold on or steady him when he got up on the wall, (pedestal) over here (pointing to her right), he started filming when the motor cycles came around on to Houston, and he kept turning (i.e. panning) to his left, to follow them when they go to Elm, and started to turn he started to fall away from me." She was then asked, "So you started to grab him?" and she replied, "Yes and I think he stopped filming then! I think he started to film again, when the President's car came down Elm."[105]

The second allegation – that the motorcade stopped immediately before the President was fatally shot in the head – also has its origins in testimony given to the authorities immediately after the shooting. The allegation has also resulted in the specific actions of Secret Service driver William Greer coming under close scrutiny from those who believe that Greer, as the driver of the limousine, was solely and directly responsible for inexplicably stopping the car moments before the fatal headshot, thereby creating an 'easy target' for an assassin.

In 2000, widely-respected researcher Vincent Palamara published an analysis of the testimony of 59 witnesses who claimed to have seen the limousine either slow dramatically or come to a complete halt after the shooting began.[106] Australian researcher John P. Costella published a similar analysis in 2007.[107] However, Dallas researcher Duke Lane has concluded that, on closer examination, less than 25% of those witnesses cited by Palamara as offering a direct opinion actually said that the limousine came to a complete halt.[108] (Part of the problem is the interpretation and use of the word "stop". Even the Dallas police used the term "a rolling stop", meaning to slow down to a speed which would allow the occupants of one vehicle to talk to those in another nearby vehicle). This finding notwithstanding, one cannot deny that a number of eyewitnesses said the limousine stopped. However, given the evidence of the Zapruder film to the contrary, one must again ask if these witnesses actually saw the limousine itself come to a standstill, or if they are referring to one or more of the other vehicles behind the limousine, any of which would be forced almost to a halt if any the cars at the front of the cavalcade slowed down to speeds below the "crawl" at which they were already travelling.

For a film that is apparently so similar to the Zapruder film that those who claim to have seen it are in dispute as to whether it is an un-edited version of Zapruder's film or a completely different film, the 'other film' must have been filmed from a point very close to where Zapruder was standing in Dealey Plaza. However, it has not been possible to uncover any evidence (credible or otherwise) of a professional cameraman in Zapruder's immediate vicinity at the time of the assassination. It has been suggested that the film is, in fact, a composite that was created by unknown conspirators from a combination of an 'un-edited' version of the Zapruder film and a second film, shot possibly in advance of the arrival of the motorcade. However, it seems incomprehensible that an 8mm amateur movie, shot with a hand-held camera, could be merged with a professional, high quality, clear and sharp 16mm movie in such a way as to withstand critical study and not be detected for what it is.

However, whether or not one believes *any* of the Zapruder film alteration claims, be they based on old, grainy copies of the film, poor quality Internet cropped images, or high-quality logarithmic colour scans made from a third-generation copy of the film obtained from NARA, one is still left with the same question – can the source material be traced back to the camera-original film? As previously mentioned, even the integrity of the film which current resides in NARA can be questioned on the basis that it is not in the same unslit format

Thirteen | The Authenticity of the Zapruder Film

as was the original film on November 22, 1963. Furthermore, it has been damaged, frames are missing, and the chain-of-possession from 1963 until 1999 cannot be accurately, comprehensively and conclusively documented. Therefore, any research based on such evidence must be tainted with some degree of uncertainty.

Unfortunately, the documented history of the film has been ignored in creating at least one scenario in which the film was allegedly altered on the evening on the assassination.

According to authors Mike Pincher and Roy Schaeffer, the original film and at least one of the three Jamieson copies were flown from Love Field airport in Dallas to Andrews Air Force base in Washington at 4 pm CST on November 22, 1963. The flight arrived in Washington around 9:30 pm EST, and the films were taken directly to NPIC, where they arrived shortly after 10 pm. According to Pincher and Schaeffer's account, the original film was "at least partially edited", and the production of new copies was completed by approximately 3 am EST on November 24. The films were then returned to Dallas, arriving at Love Field at 6:45 am CST. From there, they were returned by the Secret Service to Zapruder's office by 7 am.[109]

This scenario is, of course, completely at odds with the known chronology of the film, and is not supported by a scintilla of credible, documented evidence. However, it is the sort of 'evidence' which, when presented in a supposedly scholarly work, gains credence and public acceptance.

Only one researcher has come even close to providing a scenario which could undermine the integrity of the black-and-white 16mm copies of the film given to the Sixth Floor Museum in 2000 by the Zapruder family.

The two NPIC Events
In an on-line article in May 2012, updating information first published in his 2009 book, "Inside the Assassination Records Review Board", Doug Horne presented an alternative to the generally accepted chronology of the film, in an effort to explain two completely unrelated appearances by the Zapruder film at NPIC on the nights of November 23 and November 24, 1963, which Horne believes are central to the 'recreation' of the Zapruder film before it ever reached *Life* magazine's offices in Chicago.[110] The circumstances surrounding these two events have led Horne and others to the inevitable speculation that a deliberate attempt was made to "compartmentalise" these two separate events, with sinister implications.[111]

According to Horne, the Zapruder film sent by *Life*'s Richard Stolley to Chicago on November 23 was "intercepted" by the Secret Service either on arrival at Chicago airport, or at the *Life* offices after the film was delivered there.[112] The film was then sent to Washington, a journey of approximately two hours, where it was taken to the NPIC facility located in Building 213 at the Navy Yard in Washington D.C.[113]

JFK | ECHOES FROM ELM STREET
A SEARCH FOR HISTORICAL ACCURACY ON THE ASSASSINATION OF PRESIDENT JOHN F. KENNEDY

Around midnight, two Secret Service agents arrived at the NPIC building, where duty officer for that weekend, Dino Brugioni, met them personally.[114] Brugioni, who served as Chief Information Officer at NPIC for nearly 25 years, was of the opinion that the two agents had not seen the film themselves, and had come to NPIC directly from the airport.[115]

The film the two agents brought had already been slit to 8mm format, and Brugioni told Doug Horne that he was "almost sure there were images between the sprocket holes", implying that what they had was the camera-original film. During a follow-up interview, Brugioni said definitively: "I'm sure it was."[116] The two Secret Service agents wanted 'briefing boards', made from selected frames from the film, to be produced. After prints had been made from the individual frames, the two Secret Service agents left NPIC at around 3 am on Sunday morning, bringing the film with them. Meanwhile, the production of the briefing boards ended at about 6 or 7 am, at which time NPIC Director Arthur Lundahl collected the briefing boards, along with briefing notes which Brugioni had prepared. Lundahl then went to the office of CIA Director John McCone, and briefed McCone using the boards and notes Brugioni had prepared. Lundahl returned to NPIC later on Sunday morning, November 24, and thanked everyone for their efforts the previous night, telling them that his briefing of McCone had gone well.[117]

While Horne claims that the film was "intercepted" in Chicago and brought to NPIC, there may be another, less sinister explanation. The Secret Service regularly used the CIA-run NPIC for specialist photographic work, which would explain why the request would have come to NPIC via the CIA Director; and the fact that a slit 8mm version of the film was delivered to NPIC by two Secret Service agents suggests that the film might equally have been the first-day copy sent by Dallas Secret Service agent Max Phillips to Washington on the night of the assassination.[118] The only reason for suspecting that the film came from any other source is Brugioni's belief that the film he saw had imagery between the sprocket holes – the implication being that it was the camera-original film, since there was no inter-sprocket imagery on any of the three first-day copies made by the Jamieson laboratory in Dallas. However, the documented chronology shows that the camera-original Zapruder film was in double-8 un-slit format, and was in the possession of *Life* at the time Brugioni claims to have received it at NPIC. In the absence of any tangible evidence to support Brugioni's personal belief, one may reasonably ask if it carries more evidentiary weight than the "logical" source of the film suggested above, namely, Secret Service headquarters in Washington. It is the author's personal view that Brugioni was simply mistaken.

Horne posits that, following an examination of the briefing boards produced the previous night by Brugioni's team, it was deemed necessary by the CIA and the Secret Service to 'recreate' a 16mm unslit version of the Zapruder film, as a result of which the film was then flown the relatively short distance to

Thirteen | The Authenticity of the Zapruder Film

the Eastman Kodak Hawkeye film processing facility in Rochester, New York, where the 'new' Zapruder film was created sometime on Sunday, November 24. According to Dino Brugioni, this state-of-the-art facility where "they could do anything", was operated by Kodak on behalf of the CIA.[119]

The second 'appearance' of the Zapruder film at NPIC on Sunday night is, perhaps, even more controversial and mysterious than the first.[120]

Homer McMahon was Head of the NPIC Colour Photo Lab at the time of the assassination. In 1997, McMahon told the ARRB that, at around 8 pm on the evening of Sunday November 24, a man representing himself as "Secret Service agent Bill Smith" arrived at NPIC with an un-slit double-8mm format copy of the film. Once again, the purpose of the visit was the preparation of briefing boards, although the intended recipient of this set of briefing boards is unknown.

In a series of interviews with the ARRB, McMahon consistently claimed that he had enlarged individual frames from the original film, and that it was a 16mm wide unslit double-8mm home movie film. During his first ARRB interview, McMahon stated he was "sure we had the original film", because "we had to flip it over to see the image on the other side in the correct orientation."[121] This film (which McMahon claims to have seen "at least 10 times that night") was apparently viewed on the existing 16mm projection equipment at NPIC.[122] McMahon confirmed this recollection of a 16mm unslit film with opposing image strips during his ARRB in-person interview which was tape recorded on July 14, 1997.[123]

However, the most significant revelation by McMahon regarding the events of that evening was the story he claims was told to him by the mystery Secret Service agent Bill Smith regarding the source of the film that Smith brought to NPIC that night.

According to McMahon, Smith said that he had collected the film from the unnamed amateur photographer (presumably Zapruder) who shot it; that he had flown to the main Kodak plant in Rochester, New York, where the film was processed and copied at the CIA's top-secret Hawkeye Facility, which was located in the Kodak plant; and that he had then flown directly to Reagan National airport in Washington with the film, so that three briefing boards could be produced at NPIC, just a short distance from the airport. Smith also told McMahon about the type of camera used, the make and exact type of film used, the story of how the film was processed, and the number of copies made from it.

Every single aspect of Bill Smith's story did actually take place, except that it happened in Dallas and not elsewhere, and the established chain of custody of the Zapruder film actually makes it impossible for McMahon's version of the story to be correct.

A review of the original film in the National Archives by Doug Horne failed to reveal any edge-printing or other indications that would indicate the film was processed in Rochester – indeed, all indications were that it was produced in Dallas,[124] a fact confirmed independently by Roland Zavada in his report for the ARRB.[125]

Furthermore, Horne subsequently checked a roster of all Secret Service agents attached to the White House Detail in 1963. There was no agent named Bill (or William) Smith on that list.[126] But was McMahon's story a complete fabrication, or is there another explanation? As an elderly (and now deceased) witness, could his ability to accurately recall details of events that occurred almost 34 years earlier be fully relied upon?[127]

It is this author's belief that McMahon did not set out to deliberately mislead the ARRB investigation. McMahon – because of the references to the Secret Service being the initial source of the film – may have simply erred by assuming that Bill Smith was a Secret Service agent, and then assumed the reference to Kodak was to the Kodak plant in Rochester (with which McMahon would have been familiar), rather than Kodak in Dallas. By then mixing facts and assumptions together, he finished up with the story he told to the ARRB. A simple explanation, perhaps – but the simple explanation is often the correct one.

In August 2010, researcher William Kelly and this author – working completely independently of each other – identified a man we both believe may have been the mysterious "Secret Service agent Bill Smith".[128]

This man, now retired, worked for NPIC at the time of the assassination. Whether or not Homer McMahon knew him is open to debate. The man was eventually traced to his home in Virginia, and in a subsequent telephone interview he revealed that he had worked in the print shop at NPIC for a number of years, including the time in question, but said he did not see or handle the Zapruder film at NPIC at any time. The man's identity is being withheld at the time of writing in order to protect his privacy, and in the hope that he may yet provide a more detailed and formal statement.

It would therefore appear realistic to suggest that the film which McMahon saw at NPIC on the night of Sunday, November 24, 1963, was almost certainly the one which the Dallas Secret Service loaned to the FBI, and which was sent to FBI headquarters in Washington on the Saturday evening.

Interestingly, neither McMahon nor his support team had attended the Brugioni-supervised creation of briefing boards at NPIC on the previous evening, and Brugioni and his team from the previous evening were not involved in the McMahon event, despite the fact that Brugioni was still the duty officer.[129]

The chronology espoused by Horne also purports to deal with the three 16mm black-and-white copies of the film discovered in 2000 and discussed earlier, by relying on Homer McMahon's claim that "Bill Smith" told him that copies of the film were made in Rochester.[130] Horne then goes on to suggest that "there is strong evidence" to suggest that these copies were produced as black-and-white copies, of which at least one was "rushed to Chicago Sunday night so that (*Life*) magazine could begin its layout for the revised November 29th issue."[131]

Thirteen | The Authenticity of the Zapruder Film

In the author's opinion, Doug Horne's alternative chronology – while feasible at first glance – simply does not stand up to close scrutiny.

The interception of the film in Chicago, whether it happened at the airport or at *Life*'s offices, is purely speculative, and does not appear to have any evidentiary basis. This author's interpretation of the versions of the film which were at NPIC, which does not require any correction, revision or re-evaluation of the accepted chronology, is that the copy of the film sent to Secret Service headquarters from Dallas on Friday night was the 8mm slit copy which appeared at NPIC on Saturday night, while the 16mm wide copy which was given to McMahon on Sunday night was the version loaned to the FBI by the Dallas Secret Service on Saturday morning, and flown that evening to FBI headquarters in Washington D.C.

The rationale for the creation of a 16mm unslit version of the film at Rochester, when the film had already been seen in 8mm slit format by Brugioni, is also unexplained. The reliance on the account of Homer McMahon, a man by his own admission was an unreliable witness, who was suffering from senile dementia and was a recovering drug addict and alcoholic, also detracts from the credibility of Horne's chronology.[132] Finally, the out-of-hand dismissal of all accounts regarding the events at the R.R. Donnelley printing plant in Chicago on Saturday night, saying they were "simply off by 24 hours", is hardly adequate or acceptable under the prevailing circumstances.[133]

Was the original film slit?
Central to Doug Horne's hypothesis is the question of whether or not the camera-original film was in slit or unslit format when it left Dallas.

Phil Chamberlain, Richard Blair, and Tom Nulty (senior staff in the Dallas Kodak plant on November 22, 1963) "all said it was slit", according to Horne.[134] In his 1970s typed recollection, Chamberlain does say he was "almost positive" that "we slit and spliced the films" after the copies were made,[135] although he acknowledges that the FBI were back at Kodak the following morning, where they examined the film at length on a Kodak Analyst Projector, which is used with unslit, 16mm wide film. Chamberlain simply dismisses the discrepancy by saying that it must have been another projector – although he was the one who first mentioned the use of the Analyst projector.[136]

However, the author cannot find where Blair or Nulty said specifically that the original film was slit – the claim that they *all* said it was slit is based entirely on a single paragraph in Zavada's report to the ARRB.[137] This was the product of a breakfast meeting between Chamberlain, Blair, Nulty and Zavada on Monday July 28, 1997 at which they developed a "sequence of events for the processing of the Zapruder films". However, if we look at the final Zavada report itself, we see that it described the outcome of the meeting as no more than the "*most* probable sequence" of events they could develop at the time (emphasis added).[138] Furthermore, we have already seen that, following his examination of the material turned over by the Zapruder family to the Sixth Floor Museum,

Zavada was convinced that the original film was not slit on the afternoon of the assassination.[139]

A second key area in Horne's theory revolves around the question of whether or not those involved in the events at NPIC could accurately identify what they saw as "original" or "duplicate" films.

Horne quotes Dino Brugioni as saying, "I'm almost sure there were images between the sprocket holes", implying that what they had was the camera-original film. During a follow-up interview, Brugioni said definitively: "I'm sure it was (the original)."[140] Brugioni had an 8-mm film, which he knew "was an original because we all put on white gloves", according to a May 5, 2009 taped interview with author Peter Janney.[141] Horne's response to those who would question how Brugioni knew it was the original film rather than a copy is: "This man's photographic credentials were impeccable. Are we to believe that a photo professional at the CIA's preeminent national photographic analysis center did not know the difference between an original film and a copy?"[142]

Homer McMahon's assistant, Ben Hunter said it was his "reasonably strong impression" that there were no inter-sprocket images on the film he and McMahon saw, and that the film was "not high resolution".[143] Interestingly, Phil Chamberlain said that the duplicates made at Jamieson on the afternoon of the assassination were "soft, or fuzzy" in comparison with the original, but still of good quality.[144]

Homer McMahon himself said he was "sure we had the original film" because it was on Kodachrome film stock and because it was a double-8 movie (i.e. in non-standard, unslit format). He was pretty sure the film was unslit because they had to "flip it over to see the image on the other side in the correct orientation".[145] When asked by Doug Horne what he was basing his opinion upon, McMahon said it was "a combination of everything you said" and "the quality of the film."[146]

If Horne's hypothesis is incorrect, as this author very strongly believes, every possible Zapruder film manipulation or alteration scenario is dependent on the camera-original film being altered between 10:30 pm on Friday night, when Zapruder arrived home, and around 7:30 am on Saturday morning, when Zapruder would have left home in order to be in his office by 8 am, when he met *Life*'s Stolley and handed over the film.

Is Abraham Zapruder's film authentic?

There is, in this author's opinion, solid evidence to refute the claims that frames have been removed from the Zapruder film, or that the entire film is a forgery.

Author Richard Trask has described in detail the non-motorcade footage shot by Zapruder.[147] Trask notes that the home movies on Side A of the film consist of five short scenes showing two of Zapruder's grandsons in the rear garden of his house.[148] As previously mentioned, this footage is now missing from the camera-original film.[149]

Trask further notes that the remainder of side A is made up of footage shot by

Thirteen | The Authenticity of the Zapruder Film

Zapruder in his office on the morning on the assassination. This footage shows Zapruder's secretary, Lillian Rogers, seated at her desk.[150]

As his source for these descriptions, Trask cites a VHS tape of Secret Service copy #1 of the film which he obtained from NARA. If his calculations are based on this version of the film, there are 90 additional frames to be added to the beginning of the "home movies", which are only contained in Secret Service copy #2.[151]

Using Trask's five grandchildren scenes, and adding his 36-second Lillian Rogers sequence, we get a total length for Side A of 22' 2", calculated as follows:

The height of each Zapruder frame is 0.144";[152]
Zapruder's camera was filming at 18.3 frames per second;[153]
Therefore,
- there would be 2.6352 inches of film exposed per second;
- it would take 4.5537 seconds to expose one foot of film;
- there would be 83.33 frames per foot of exposed film.

Scene (1): Boy in shorts -	7 seconds	=	1' 6.5"
Scene (2): Toddler walking -	13 seconds	=	2' 10.25"
Scene (3): Toddler walking -	16 seconds	=	3' 6"
Scene (4): Boy on grass -	7 seconds	=	1' 6.5"
Scene (5): Boy at Tree -	22 seconds	=	4' 10"
Rogers office scene -	36 seconds	=	7' 10.75"
Totals =	101 seconds		22' 2"

Examination of the Lillian Rogers scene, as shown on the Sixth Floor Museum website, indicates that it runs for approximately 44-45 seconds, and not the 36 seconds suggested by Trask. More recent study indicates that the complete Rogers scene is actually 46.428 seconds long. If an elapsed time of 45.5 seconds is used for the length of the scene, it equates to 10' 2.5" in length, which means a further 2' 4" should be added to the above, giving a total Side A "home movies" length of 24' 6".

If an additional 90 frames need to be added at the start of the "home movies", assuming Trask's calculations are based on Secret Service copy #1, it would add yet another 1' 1" (90 x 0.144") to the above calculations, giving a **total length of 25' 7"**.

Roland Zavada also produced a detailed Film Map of the non-motorcade footage as part of his examination of the *Life*/LMH copy of the film in December 1999.[154] If Zavada and Trask's calculations are compared, we get the following:

Zavada Scenes and lengths

Scene	Length	
Young boy in white shirt	1' 5"	equals Trask's scene (1)
Toddler (baby) at various zoom lengths	8' 4.5"	equals Trask's scenes (2) and (3)
Young boy by lawn chair	2' 0.5"	equals Trask's scene (4)
Boy by tree	6' 4.5"	equals Trask's scene (5)
Lillian Rogers office scene	9' 6"	equals Trask's Office scene

=======
27' 8.5" in total

It will be noted that the duration of the scenes differ by almost two feet in these two sets of results. Trask's calculations indicate that the "grandchildren" scenes total 65 seconds. Adding a further five seconds for the missing 90 frames at the beginning increases the total to 70 seconds. The pre-Rogers scenes in Zavada's evaluation come to 18' 2.5", which is 83 seconds worth of film, some thirteen seconds more than Trask estimated. Similarly, their calculations also differ in respect of the duration of the Rogers office scene. This problem is primarily caused by the different measuring techniques used – Trask's calculations were based on his measurement of time, while Zavada was measuring inches of film. If, for example, Trask's VHS tape was recorded at a speed which was only fractionally different from the official film speed of 18.3 frames per second, or his VHS player was operating at a slightly different speed to the recording device, these differences could be both explainable and acceptable.

In any event, these calculations clearly demonstrate that, based on all known measurements of the film, Side A of the original film was "full".

Therefore, if Side A of the original film was "full", it would have been impossible for another 6-9 seconds (or 109-165 frames, or 1' 4" to 2 feet) to have been excised or missing from Side B, the assassination footage side of the film, unless the film was slit, Side B was altered to remove frames, and the film was then seamlessly reconstructed in double-8mm format, all the while retaining the integrity of the Side A footage, which was of interest only to Zapruder and his family. Otherwise, all such alteration or manipulation of the assassination footage would have required corresponding additions or deletions in the Rogers office scene on Side A of the film. Examination of this scene (by simply viewing it on the Sixth Floor Museum website) reveals no evidence whatsoever of any such splices.[155]

The 16mm black & white copies

It will be recalled that the camera-original film was unslit when Zapruder gave it to Richard Stolley of *Life* on Saturday morning, November 23, 1963. Our film chronology showed that Stolley left Zapruder's office between 10 and 10:30 that morning and immediately had the film sent by commercial flight to Chicago, a journey of just over ninety minutes' duration.[156] It will also be recalled that the black-and-white frames for inclusion in the November 29 issue of *Life* were

Thirteen | The Authenticity of the Zapruder Film

reportedly available in Chicago at around 8 pm that evening. If one assumes that as little as three hours elapsed between the production of one or more black-and-white copies of the film and the final selection and subsequent printing of the individual frames, it would be reasonable to conclude that these copies of the film were probably made between 1 pm and 5 pm that afternoon.

We also know that three double-8mm format 16mm-wide black-and-white copies of the film, which were turned over to the Sixth Floor Museum by the Zapruder family in 2000, were made from the original film, before it was slit and before it was damaged in any way. The reader will recall that there is ample evidence to suggest that the film was damaged – after it had been slit to 8mm width – by a *Life* technician in Chicago on the evening of November 23, and the film had almost certainly been slit to 8mm width before being shown to *Life* executives in New York on Sunday morning, November 24.

As a result, these three 16mm black-and-white copies constitute the best available evidence of how the camera-original film looked within about 30 hours of the assassination, or perhaps more importantly, within no more than seven hours of its having first come into the possession of *Life* magazine's Richard Stolley. In light of the foregoing, therefore, the evidentiary value of these 16mm black-and-white copies simply cannot be underestimated.

In July 2011, the author had the very good fortune to be given access by The Sixth Floor Museum at Dealey Plaza to a DVD copy of one of those 16mm black-and-white films made directly from the unslit, camera-original Zapruder film, which provided a unique opportunity to examine the film from a perspective which had apparently never previously been attempted.

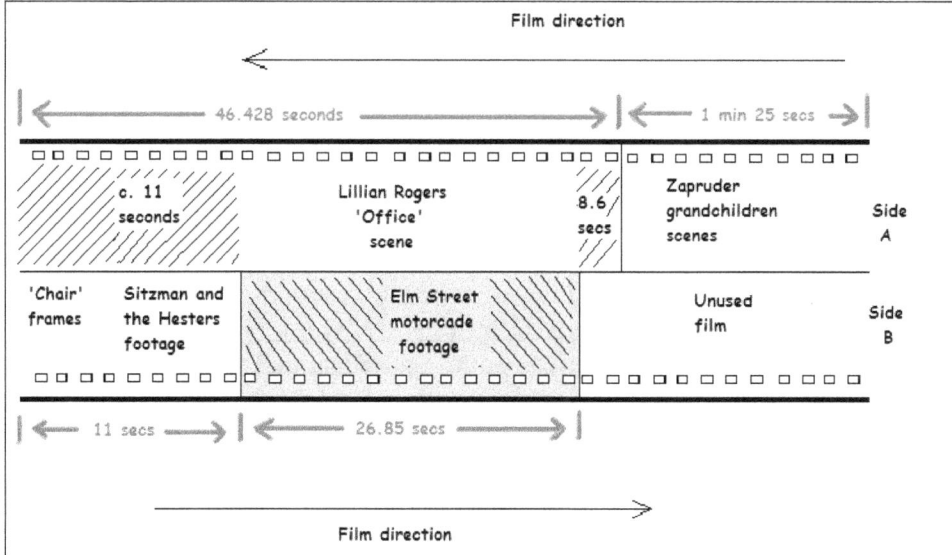

Fig. 2: Author's representation of Zapruder film, as it appears in 16mm format (Not to Scale)

467

JFK | ECHOES FROM ELM STREET
A SEARCH FOR HISTORICAL ACCURACY ON THE ASSASSINATION OF PRESIDENT JOHN F. KENNEDY

On viewing the film for the first time, one is immediately struck by the remarkable sharpness and clarity of the imagery, which is superior to anything currently in the public domain. It is also somewhat disconcerting at first to watch the assassination footage on Side B run in one direction, while the home movies and the Lillian Rogers office scenes on Side A are simultaneously running 'upside-down' and in the opposite direction on the screen.

The contents of both sides of the film are in agreement with what we have already discussed. A series of timing tests showed that an average of one minute and twenty-five seconds of Side A of the film (the non-assassination side) consists of footage of the Zapruder grandchildren, followed by an average of 46.428 seconds of the Lillian Rogers office scene.[157] The timing tests revealed that the overall average total duration of Side A was just over two minutes and eleven seconds.

At 18.3 frames per second, and a frame height of 0.144", this equates to 28' 10" of film, yet further evidence that Zapruder had fully exposed all the available film on Side A of the roll. Indeed, the film which Zapruder used was a 25-foot roll, so Zapruder obviously got the very most out of his roll of film. [The author has been able to confirm that it was neither impossible nor improbable to get almost 29 feet of film off a 25-foot roll, as Zapruder apparently did.[158]]

This figure of just less than 29 feet of film on Side A is not inconsistent with the similar, previously-discussed exercises carried out by Richard Trask and Roland Zavada on the two Secret Service first-day copies of the film. It will be recalled that they arrived at figures of between 26 and 28 feet on copies of the film that had been spliced and damaged in various ways over the years. They also used different measuring techniques – Trask's calculations, like those of this author, were based on the film's 'run time', while Zavada was actually able to measure the film with a tape-measure.

If Trask or the author were playing the film at even a fractionally different speed to that at which the film was originally recorded, it is possible that the obtained results could be in error by a small amount.

Also, because these timings were done with a manually-operated stopwatch, it is possible that small differences will occur. So, while there is not *exact* agreement between the measurements, the author believes that there is enough consistency between these three sets of figures to confidently state that Zapruder utilised every available frame of usable footage on Side A of his film.

Side B of the film begins with about eleven seconds of pre-motorcade footage, briefly showing a few blurred frames of what appears to be part

Thirteen | The Authenticity of the Zapruder Film

of a chair, followed by film of Zapruder's receptionist Marilyn Sitzman, her fellow employee Beatrice Hester, and Mrs. Hester's husband, Charles, taken in Dealey Plaza shortly before the motorcade arrived. The remainder of Side B consists of the motorcade footage, which amounted to between 26.8 and 27 seconds in the author's timing tests. The motorcade footage is undamaged – there are no splices.

While already noted, it must be emphasised again that all or any removal of frames from Side B of the film, without corresponding alterations being made to the Rogers footage on Side A, was impossible on an unslit copy of the film without major reconstruction being performed – something for which there is simply no documented or physical evidence, as we have already seen.

Accordingly, it is this author's firm belief that Sides A and B of the Zapruder film as it exists today are totally consistent with one another, and with the black-and-white copies obtained by the Sixth Floor Museum in 2000.

Therefore, on the basis of both the length of Side A and the consistency of the black-and-white copies and the original film, we can be confident that for *any* changes to have been made to the assassination sequence on Side B, the original film *must* have been slit before the alterations were made – otherwise, Side A would have to be altered as well, and there is not a shred of evidence to indicate that.

Viewing the film in its 16mm unslit format, however, also identified a single, simple test of the authenticity of the Zapruder film, which relies entirely on a study of the Lillian Rogers scene on Side A of the film rather than the motorcade footage on Side B, as has always previously been the case.

To validate the accuracy of the author's timing tests, six individual Zapruder 'assassination' frames on Side B of the film were matched with their corresponding frames in the Lillian Rogers office sequence on Side A of the 16mm copy of the film. (See Figure 3 below)

The timing tests showed that the Rogers scene on Side A begins 8.66 seconds before the motorcade footage ends on Side B, and continues for between 10.9 and 11.2 seconds beyond the start of the assassination footage on Side B. To view this in context, the reader is invited to look at the Lillian Rogers scene, which is shown in colour on the Sixth Floor Museum's website. The final frame of the motorcade footage on Side B corresponds with a point between 8 and 9 seconds into the Rogers office scene, where Ms. Rogers is seen standing, with her back to the camera, looking sharply to her left.

The shot to the President's head at Zapruder frame 313 equates to a point 18 seconds into the scene, where Ms. Rogers finishes replacing the dark vest/waistcoat which she had previously removed. Zapruder's break in filming at frames 132-133, when he briefly stopped filming the lead motorcycles before starting to film again as the presidential limousine began its journey down Elm Street, occurs at 27 seconds into the Rogers scene, as Ms. Rogers nods her head while on the telephone. The first motorcade frame corresponds with the point where Ms. Rogers puts down the telephone receiver, 35 seconds into the scene.

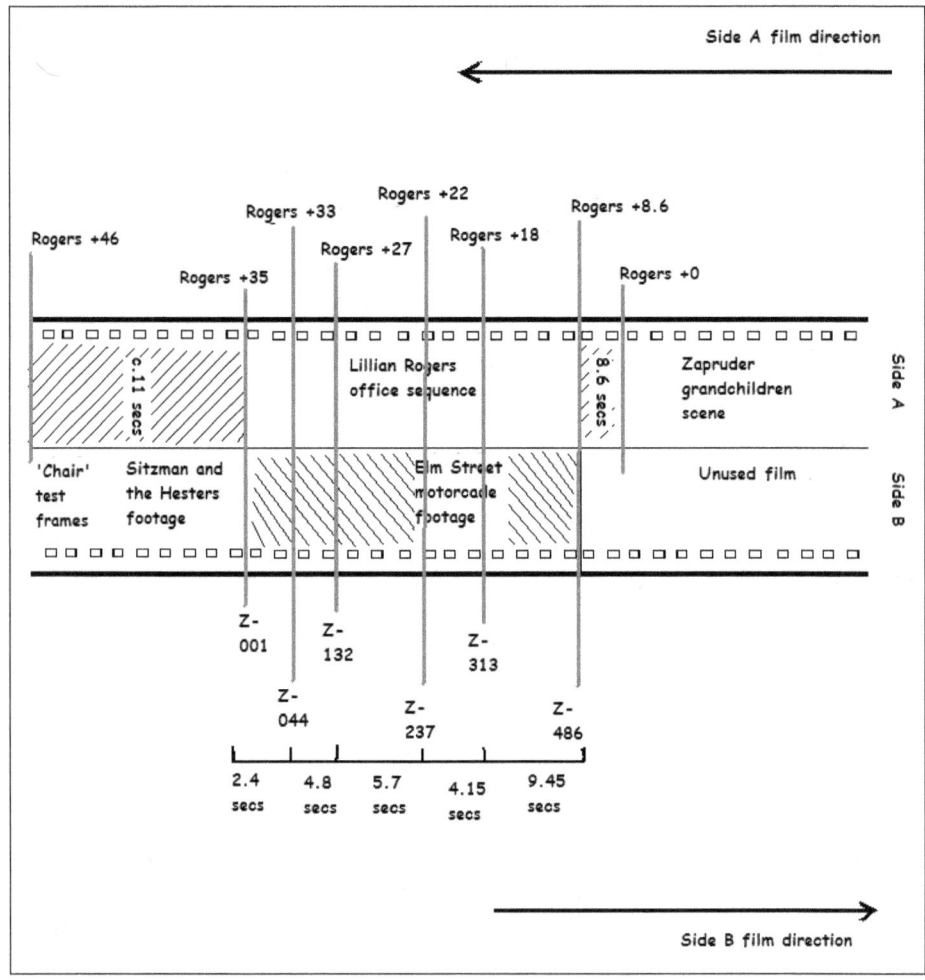

Fig. 3: Correlation between frames on Sides A and B of 16mm film

The calculated time difference between any two frames is equal on both sides of the film – for example, Zapruder frames 001 and 237 in the assassination sequence are 12.9 seconds apart. The corresponding Rogers frames are 13 seconds apart. Similarly, frames 001 and 486, the first and last frames in the assassination sequence, are a total of 26.85 seconds apart, according to the

Thirteen | The Authenticity of the Zapruder Film

timing tests. (The accuracy of this can be confirmed by taking 486 frames, at 18.3 frames per second, which was the actual running speed of Zapruder's camera, and it will yield a total of 26.55 seconds). The corresponding time interval, according to the author's timing tests, on Side A is from Rogers 8.6 to Rogers 35 – a total of 26.4 seconds, which is acceptably close to the 26.85 seconds obtained on Side B.

Another means of validating the accuracy of the tests, and the consistency between Sides A and B, was based on the total length of the Lillian Rogers scene on Side A (See Figure 2). This was measured repeatedly, and produced an average of 46.428 seconds. Turning to Side B, if one takes the 'pre-assassination' footage, which runs for an average of 10.9 seconds, adds the 26.85 seconds of assassination sequence, and also adds the 8.66 seconds additional Rogers footage after the assassination sequence ends, the total is 46.41 seconds – a very close match to the corresponding 46.428 seconds on Side A.

Examination of the 16mm black-and-white copies additionally allows a new perspective on the question of when any of the alleged alterations could have been made to the film. If the limousine's turn from Houston onto Elm Street was removed from the film and/or if frames showing the motorcade coming to a complete halt on Elm Street around the time of the headshot were excised from the film – as those who believe that the Zapruder assassination footage is a forgery so vehemently claim - the 16mm copies of the film allow us to narrow down the time-frame within which such alterations could have been made.

But can the films now in the possession of the Sixth Floor Museum in Dealey Plaza be incontrovertibly linked to the three films created in Chicago on November 23, 1963?

In his response to Chapter 14 of Doug Horne's 2010 book, Roland Zavada published a photograph from the 'dirty dupe' copy of the film. The photograph shows a series of 14 complete frames on both sides of the 16mm film, the first in the motorcade sequence being frame 040 of the Zapruder film.[159] Careful examination of the same series of frames in the 16mm black-and-white copy of the film to which the author had access in July, 2011 shows them to be corresponding exactly on sides A and B of the film.

A second photograph, which the author obtained from Zavada in May 2012, was taken from one of the negative 16mm copies of the film, which has been marked with 'callout tabs'. The photograph shows Zapruder frames 223 to 232, with frame 232 (and possibly 226) arrowed to indicate that they were selected for printing by *Life* magazine staff. Both of these frames, Z-226 and Z-232, were indeed published in the November 29, 1963 edition of *Life* magazine.[160] Examination of the same frames in the author's black-and-white copy of the film reveals that the corresponding Side A frames are exactly the same as those in Zavada's photograph.

Zapruder frames 237 and 238, along with their corresponding Side A

471

frames showing Lillian Rogers, were published by author Richard Trask in his excellent book on the Zapruder film.[161] As published, the photograph appears to contain what could possibly be the edge of a 'callout tab' at the bottom of the frame – and frames 237 and 244 were also published by *Life* on November 29, 1963. Once again, comparison of the frames published by Trask with the same frames in the author's black-and-white copy of the film show them to be identical.

A fourth and final photograph, also published in Zavada's response to Doug Horne, shows Zapruder frames 363 to 386, with a 'callout tab' pointing to frame 371, presumably for identification as a still photo to be printed for inclusion in the November 29, 1963 issue of *Life* magazine. Frame 371 was used in that issue, and it was not used again until the October 2, 1964 issue.[162] The film was damaged before the Warren Commission asked *Life* for colour enlargements of frames from the original film, and the record shows that these slides were received by the Commission in April 1964.[163] Therefore, the call-out tab must refer to the November 29, 1963 issue. It is almost superfluous at this stage to add that, as with each of the previously-discussed photographs, examination of the author's 16mm copy of the film reveals it to be totally consistent with the content of this photograph.

Therefore, if Zapruder's assassination footage had been altered at *any* time after the creation of the three black-and-white prints on the afternoon of November 23, some of the early footage on Side B (showing Marilyn Sitzman, and the Hesters) must have been added to fill the same amount of space, or some of the Rogers frames must have been deleted from Side A, to reduce the length of that side and retain consistency between the two sides. There is absolutely no evidence that either of these two eventualities took place.

In summary:
- Side A of Zapruder's roll of film (the non-assassination side) was full – Zapruder used every possible inch of it;
- The original film was in double-8, 16mm width unslit format when it was received in Chicago on November 23, 1963;
- Evidence suggests that the original film may well have been damaged that night;
- The film is believed to have been slit to 8mm format before being sent to *Life* headquarters in New York the following day;
- The 16mm black-and-white copies were made from the original film, before it was damaged, and before it was slit;
- With the exception of the known damage to the film at frames 156/7 and 207-212, the assassination footage on the 16mm copies is identical to the Zapruder film as we know it today;

Thirteen | The Authenticity of the Zapruder Film

- The 16mm copies are also consistent with copies of the film made in Chicago on Saturday afternoon, during the selection of frames for inclusion in the November 29, 1963 issue of *Life*;
- The evidence of the 16mm black-and-white copies of the film militates strongly against any alteration of the camera-original film.

The only alternative – which would require no manipulation of Side A – would be for the film to have been slit, the assassination footage on Side B altered, and the whole film reassembled to its original unslit format *before* the camera-original was given to Richard Stolley of *Life* on Saturday morning, November 23. If this had happened, claims that the film was altered in any way on either Saturday or Sunday in the Kodak plant in Rochester, or at NPIC, would also be rendered both unsustainable and irrelevant.

The only remaining opportunity for any such work to be done was between 10:30 pm on Friday night – the earliest time the film could have been delivered to the Hensley Naval Air Station in Dallas - and approximately 7:30 am on Saturday morning, when Abraham Zapruder left home in order to be in his office by 8 am, when he met Stolley.

Notwithstanding any possible logistical obstacles which will be discussed below, could the film have been altered, manipulated or re-created in the available time?

It has been claimed that it was technically possible in 1963 to alter the Zapruder film in a way that would withstand cursory examination at least. While 'special effects' technology undoubtedly existed in 1963, this author has not yet seen or heard of any convincing evidence which indicates that it was possible to create any realistic alteration or replacement of the double-8mm Zapruder film in the available time-frame. After the film reached Chicago, and especially after it reached *Life* headquarters in New York, there were too many copies of the film in circulation for any replacement or alterations to have even been considered. Furthermore, given what we know about the chain-of-possession of the original film and each of its three first-day copies during that period of time, would it have been possible to isolate the original film and the three first-day copies – either together or individually – for long enough to make the alterations or replacement anyway, without it being noticed by someone?

In his presentation at a Zapruder Film Symposium in Duluth, Minnesota in May 2003, researcher and photographer David Healy said: "If someone was to give me the Zapruder film, today, right out of the camera, and I had the time and the money, and I could guarantee it's not going to take much time, today; but if we used the optical printer of yesterday, with the proper people, I think it could be done in a couple of days".[164]

According to Healy, "it should have taken between two to three weeks of lab time, maximum" to make these changes using 1963 equipment, standards and techniques.¹⁶⁵ In fairness to Healy, he wrote as recently as February 8, 2011 that "I can't prove it's altered (as I've said all along)."¹⁶⁶

Researcher/author John Costella, who claims that the film was "substantially edited", believes that "as a motion picture" it had to be "in a fairly consistent form" by the time it was shown to the members of the Warren Commission at the end of January 1964, but that the fine details need not have been completed until the Warren Commission published individual black-and-white frames from the film in November 1964. Costella says that the film, "as a complete entity" didn't really need to exist until the time of the Shaw trial in 1968, and that further work to ensure that the inter-sprocket imagery was consistent throughout the film and slides could have been left until the 1990s.¹⁶⁷

Bruce Jamieson, at whose film lab in Dallas the three 'first-day copies' of Zapruder's film were made, described the theory that the film was processed, altered, and re-spooled on the afternoon of November 22 as "the biggest pile of <vulgarity deleted> I've heard in a long time." Referring to proponents of such alteration theories, Jamieson said they "obviously don't understand the technicalities" involved. According to Jamieson, "the time required to execute the Kodachrome process, not to mention the complex optical art and matte printing you suggest, won't fit within the known time scale involved". Finally, Jamieson dismissed "the comments, third party statements, innuendo, gossip, etc. about who processed what" as "rampant speculation and rumour." ¹⁶⁸

Author Vincent Bugliosi notes that it is "highly doubtful that even the most modern advances in film and photography technology" could do what has since been ascribed to those who allegedly altered the Zapruder film in the 1960s. He further notes that there is even disagreement among those who subscribe to these theories regarding the timeframe during which the film was supposedly altered.¹⁶⁹

Renowned Kodak film expert Dr. Roderick Ryan highlighted the fact that the Kodachrome II process was relatively complicated compared with that needed for Ektachrome film, taking nine different steps requiring special equipment, as opposed to only five steps for Ektachrome film processing.¹⁷⁰ In Dr. Ryan's view, alteration of the film would require it to be enlarged to 16mm or 35mm format (neither of which was available on Kodachrome II stock), edited, and then reduced back to 8mm format on Kodachrome II film stock. He also pointed out that the capability for the special effects film editing that is possible today was not commercially available in 1963.¹⁷¹

Roland Zavada told Harrison Livingstone that the alleged alterations could "never be achieved with an 8mm original", and said it is "blatantly unrealistic even if one began with a 35mm original".¹⁷² He said that he did "not believe that it is possible to start with 8mm and end up with 8mm."¹⁷³ He added that "Hollywood professional photography never tried to shoot and add optical effects with the result on the same film type as the original – the goal was

Thirteen | The Authenticity of the Zapruder Film

(always) a projectable print", a point he repeated in his presentation at the JFK Lancer conference in Dallas in November 2010.[174] In a May 2004 meeting with Livingstone, Zavada again explained the difficulty if not the impossibility of going from 8mm film through multiple processes to alter the film, and get back to an 8mm film on original Kodachrome stock without leaving detectable evidence of alteration. Zavada says such a process does not exist, to his knowledge or that of experts with whom he consulted. He said that even to simply cut out frames and put the film back without any trace would be impossible without some loss of quality.[175]

According to Zavada, the proposition that the film was altered over the weekend of the assassination, as proposed by Doug Horne in 2009, "just doesn't add up!" It would require five different processing machines to be set up, along with the necessary certified chemistry and personnel on a Sunday. In Zavada's opinion, even the most rudimentary 'quick-and-dirty' approach would require a minimum of 7.6 hours processing time alone, which he says is "just NOT attainable" (emphasis in original).[176]

Kodak's Dr. Roderick Ryan said that the only independent non-Kodak facilities which could process Kodachrome II film in 1963 were located in Chicago, Los Angeles, Kansas and New York. There was no such company in Dallas, and neither the FBI nor the CIA had the capability at that time. [The problem was not that the film could not be copied, but it could not be altered and then reprocessed back onto Kodachrome II film stock, which Zapruder's film was on.][177] The film was clearly not altered in Dallas, since Kodak were the only people in Dallas who were equipped to do so, unless a number of people in the Kodak plant there were prepared to lie about the entire processing of the film on the afternoon of the assassination. Indeed, there is documentary evidence to suggest that simply having copies of the film made on the weekend of the assassination was problematic, much less having it altered. Two memos dated November 23 from the FBI's Cartha DeLoach to John P. Mohr, administrative assistant to FBI Director J. Edgar Hoover, indicate that the FBI had been trying unsuccessfully to have a copy of the Zapruder film – which had earlier that day been loaned to them by the Secret Service – duplicated in Dallas.[178]

But let us assume for a moment that – as part of some grand conspiracy involving Zapruder and the Secret Service, for which there is absolutely no evidence – the original film was substituted for the Secret Service copy, and instead of being sent to Washington it was sent elsewhere instead for some nefarious purpose.

Getting to Kansas
Assuming also that any attempt at alteration would have used the nearest facility capable of doing so, further research revealed that Calvin Laboratories in Kansas City was the nearest one to Dallas, a flight time of 54 minutes away.[179]

JFK | ECHOES FROM ELM STREET
A SEARCH FOR HISTORICAL ACCURACY ON THE
ASSASSINATION OF PRESIDENT JOHN F. KENNEDY

Calvin Labs was located at 1105 East 15th Street, Kansas City, and the nearest airport to the Calvin plant in 1963 was the Fairfax Army airfield (which was closed in 1985), located approximately 8 miles (or a 15-minute drive) away.[180]

The Dallas Secret Service said that the 8mm slit format copy of the film given to them by Zapruder on the evening of the assassination was sent by Army jet from Hensley Field Naval Air Station in Dallas to Secret Service headquarters in Washington DC that same evening. It is universally accepted that Secret Service agent Max Phillips wrote a covering note to accompany the film to Washington, and that the note was time-stamped at 9:55 pm. If one assumes that the film was then sent immediately from the Secret Service office to the Hensley Field airbase, it could have been there at 10:20 pm. With the immediate availability of a jet to fly the film to Kansas, the film could have left Dallas by 10:30 on Friday evening, and could theoretically have been 'on the ground' in Kansas at 11:25 pm. If one then allows just over 15 minutes to get from the airport to Calvin Laboratories, the film could have been in the Calvin processing lab by 11:45 pm. If nothing more sophisticated than the most rudimentary 'quick-and-dirty' alterations - which Kodak's own expert Roland Zavada said would take at least 7.5 hours – were then carried out, it takes the timeline forward to 7:15 am on Saturday morning. Adding a further 15 minutes to get back to the airport, a 54-minute flight back to Dallas, and an additional 25-30 minutes to get back to Zapruder's office, the earliest possible time the film could have been available to Zapruder was 8:45 to 8:50 am on Saturday morning, three-quarters of an hour *after* he and Stolley met in Zapruder's office. In reality, therefore, it is almost certain that alteration of the film between Friday night and Saturday morning could not have been achieved in the available time.

One might reasonably ask why the possibility that the film was altered in Chicago after *Life* got the film early on the Saturday afternoon has not been addressed. The Colburn photo lab in Chicago was capable of processing Kodachrome II film, and while they undoubtedly did some work for *Life* in relation to assassination material, there is uncertainty as to whether or not they ever handled the Zapruder film. However, as the photos to be used in the November 29 issue of *Life* had already been selected and printed by 8pm on Saturday evening, there would actually have been *less* time available in Chicago for any alteration of the film than there would have been the previous night in Kansas. It simply could not have been done in the time available.

There is one further possibility that warrants consideration. It has previously been noted that the high-quality 16mm black-and-white copies of the film were made before the original film was damaged and before it was slit to 8mm format, both of which are believed to have happened on the Saturday night or Sunday morning after the assassination. But "what if" the original film was not damaged until some later date, and the original film was not slit to 8mm format that weekend either? If that were true, it would open up the possibility that

Thirteen | The Authenticity of the Zapruder Film

the original film could have been altered at any time before it was damaged or slit. Therefore, the only absolute certainty we have is that the black-and-white copies were made in Chicago on Saturday evening. Furthermore, by comparing the frames on Sides A and B in the photographs identifying the frames which were to be published by *Life* on November 29, 1963, and the corresponding frames in the 16mm copy obtained by the author in 2011, they can clearly be seen to be identical.

Therefore, it can be concluded that because the black-and-white copies created in Chicago on November 23 are identical to the high-quality 16mm black-and-white copies given to the Sixth Floor Museum in 2000, and they in turn are identical in content to the Zapruder film as we know it today, the content of the extant camera-original film in NARA is exactly the same (allowing for the known and acknowledged damage to specific frames) as it was on the evening of November 23, 1963.

Conclusion

This odyssey began as an attempt to produce the most detailed chronology possible of the history of the Zapruder film in the days immediately after the assassination. However, the discovery of the existence of the previously-unknown 16mm black-and-white copies of the film and the author's opportunity to study one of them in 2011, has not only validated the benefit of the chronology, but also converted the author from an 'alteration agnostic' to a true believer in the authenticity of the film.

For those who have studied the Zapruder film over many years, it is perhaps easy to forget that the film is, first and foremost, the graphic depiction of the cold-blooded murder of a fellow human being. That said, the film is also perhaps the most closely studied and analysed piece of home movie film ever made.

This chapter has clearly demonstrated that the established chronology would leave little or no time for any alteration of the film, irrespective of how technically possible it was. The experts say it was not possible anyway, due to the film being in 8mm format. The possibility of the existence of 'the other film' – as opposed to an altered version of Zapruder – begs the question of who the photographer was, how he took the film without being seen, why it has not been more widely circulated, even in the research community, and where it is now.

Turning to the alteration claims, many of them are based on the study of poor copies of the film and/or eyewitness accounts of a brief but very traumatic event. As such, they must be regarded with a considerable degree of scepticism, which is reinforced by more recently available high quality images from the film. Other claims of forgery and alteration, by their extraordinary nature, will require extraordinary and incontrovertible proof if they are even to be considered.

JFK | Echoes From Elm Street
A Search for Historical Accuracy on the Assassination of President John F. Kennedy

If – as those who believe that the Zapruder assassination footage is a forgery so vehemently claim – the limousine's turn from Houston onto Elm Street was removed from the film and / or if frames showing the motorcade coming to a complete halt on Elm Street around the time of the headshot were excised from the film, or if there was any other manipulation of the film, then we are left with just three possibilities:

- The original film must have been slit, the deletions made, and then the whole film reassembled in its original unslit format in order to retain the integrity of the non-motorcade Side A footage of Lillian Rogers, and this all took place prior to Zapruder giving the film to Richard Stolley of *Life* on the morning after the assassination. Furthermore, all or any such alterations to the film must have been made between 10:30 pm on the night of the assassination and about 7:30 am on the following morning – and the chronology simply does not allow enough time for this to have happened;

- Zapruder was not using a standard 25-foot roll of Kodachrome 8mm home movie film, and was using a much longer roll of film. This possibility flies directly in the face of everything we know about Zapruder's camera and its film, all the evidence the author has been able to gather, and what both the FBI and Zapruder himself said about it;

- The third and only remaining alternative is simple. As this chapter has shown, there is tangible, straightforward and non-scientific evidence in the form of the 16mm black-and-white copies of the film given to the Sixth Floor Museum in 2000 to show that frames have not been removed from the film. It is the author's contention that this chapter has shown that the key to the whole question of Zapruder film authenticity lies, *not* in the assassination footage on Side B of the film, but in the Lillian Rogers sequence on Side A of the film; and as previously demonstrated, there is not a single piece of evidence to indicate any manipulation of that side of the film. Indeed, the opposite is true – all the evidence points unmistakeably to the fact that the Rogers footage is completely intact.

Nobody is infallible, and nobody has an exclusive right to the truth. So, while the opinions expressed in this chapter are those of the author, based on the totality of the evidence available at the time of writing, there is no doubt that further research may find otherwise in the future. Such is the very essence

Thirteen | The Authenticity of the Zapruder Film

Date / Time	Event	Reference
Nov 22: 8 am	Zapruder arrives at his office	Trask, 29
10 am	Sitzman and Rogers persuade Zapruder to go home for his camera	Wrone, 9; Trask, 29-30
11:30 am	Zapruder returns with his camera	Wrone, 9; Trask, 30; Thompson 1998
12:25 pm	Zapruder films Sitzman and the Hesters in Dealey Plaza	Trask, 33-4; Horne, 1196
12:30 pm	Zapruder films shooting	
12:40 pm	DMN reporter Harry McCormick fortuitously meets Zapruder in Dealey Plaza, and discovers he has filmed shooting.	Trask, 94; McCormick recollections, 1964 (Belo Interactive CD 2003)
12:45 pm	Zapruder returns to his office, and tells Rogers to call authorities	Zapruder testimony, WH7, 571; Wrone, 17; Trask, 33
12:50 pm	Darwin Payne (DTH) tries unsuccessfully to purchase film rights; two DPD officers arrive, asking for film, but Zapruder refuses	Wrone, 17; Trask, 95, 97-8; Payne/SFM interview; Dealey Plaza Echo article, July 2010
1:40 pm	Erwin Schwartz contacts office, and tells secretary (Mildred) to put camera (still containing film) into office safe	Trask, 32, 98; Wrone, 18; Thompson, 1998; Schwartz/SFM interview
1:50 pm	Schwartz arrives at office, followed by Harry McCormick and Forrest Sorrels of Secret Service	Trask, 99; Schwartz / SFM interview
2 pm	Sorrels orders DPD officers Osborn and Jones to take himself, Zapruder, Schwartz, and McCormick to DMN offices	McCormick, Belo CD, 2003; Schwartz interview; Dealey Plaza Echo article, July 2010

	DMN unable to process film – Zapruder & party walk next-door to WFAA studios	Mack/SFM chronology; Trask, 101
2:10 pm	Zapruder agrees to do live TV interview	Trask, 101
2:10-2:20 pm	WFAA's Bert Shipp and Sorrels speak to Jack Harrison at Kodak about processing film	Wrone, 20; Trask, 106; Shipp and Harrison SFM interviews
2:21 pm	DPD Officer Osborn tells dispatcher that he and Officer J.B. Jones are on "special assignment" with Sorrels	WH17, 428, 480; WH23, 885
2:45 pm	Osborn & Jones drive Zapruder party to Kodak, arriving before 3 pm.	Trask, 106; Wrone, 21; Zavada Report, Study 1
3:15-3:30 pm	Sorrels returned to DPD HQ following arrest of Oswald	Bugliosi, 128; WH13, 57
4 pm	Original unslit film (perforated with processing identification #0183) shown at Kodak	Thompson 1998; Wrone, 23; Trask, 109; Horne, 1197; Zavada Study 1
4:30 pm	Osborn and Jones take Zapruder and Schwartz to their office, and McCormick to DMN office	Wrone, 24; Trask, 112; Schwartz interview
6 pm	Zapruder & Schwartz drive to Jamieson to get three copies of film made	Wrone, 24; Trask, 112; Schwartz interview
6:30-7:45 pm	Three copies produced	Wrone, 25; Trask, 114-5; Zavada Study 1
8-9 pm	Zapruder & Schwartz return to Kodak with original and three copies. Copies developed and perforated with nos. 0185, 0186 and 0187	Trask, 115-6; Wrone, 26; Zavada Study 1

Thirteen | The Authenticity of the Zapruder Film

9 pm	Zapruder & Schwartz leave Kodak, and drive to DPD HQ in search of Sorrels. Sorrels asks them to take 2 copies to agent Max Phillips at Secret Service office on Ervay Street	Horne, 1199; Trask, 119-120; Wrone, 26-7; Schwartz/SFM interview
9:55 pm	Phillips sends one copy to Secret Service Chief Rowley in Washington, and retains other copy (0186) for Sorrels	CD87, 66; Wrone, 28, 279-280; Thompson "Six Seconds...", 311-2
By 10:30 pm	Zapruder and Schwartz both reach their homes	Wrone, 31; Trask, 126-7; Schwartz & Reis SFM interviews
11 pm	Richard Stolley *(Life)* makes initial contact with Zapruder. Agree to meet next morning	Trask, 127; Stolley; Wrone, 32
Nov 23: 8 am	Stolley arrives in Zapruder's office	Wrone, 32; Trask, 127
Unknown time	Secret Service Insp. Kelley loans copy #0186 to FBI's James Bookhout, who gives it to SA Barrett, who later gives it to SAIC Shanklin	Trask, 120; Wrone, 30
Morning	Two FBI agents view 16mm copy of film at Kodak for nearly an hour	Trask, 120; Wrone, 26; Zavada Study 1
9 am	Zapruder shows 8mm copy of film to Stolley and others in his office. Zapruder sells print rights to *Life*	Wrone, 33; Trask, 128-9; Schwartz SFM interview; Horne 1200

JFK | ECHOES FROM ELM STREET
A SEARCH FOR HISTORICAL ACCURACY ON THE ASSASSINATION OF PRESIDENT JOHN F. KENNEDY

10:30 am	Stolley leaves Zapruder's office with original 16mm print of film (#0183), which is immediately couriered to Donnelly printing plant in Chicago, where *Life* magazine is being prepared. Zapruder retains the best of the 3 first day copies.	Stolley, "What happened next", Esquire, November 1973, 134-5; Thompson and Mack e-mails to author, May 2010; Wrone, 34; Richard Bartholomew/ Schwartz interview, 1994
	Three 16mm b/w copies of film made by Life in Chicago	Wrone, 27, 35; Horne, 1199; Trask, 119; Zavada 2010
5:20 pm	Dallas FBI office send 16mm film (#0186) on American Airlines flight 20 to Washington HQ	Wrone, 30; Trask, 122; Horne, 1346
10 pm	CIA Director McCone alerts NPIC Director Lundahl to expect film. Lundahl calls in Brugioni	Horne, 1231, 1236
12 pm	Brugioni meets two Secret Service agents with 8mm copy of film	Horne, 1231, Wrone, 28-9
Nov 24: 6-7 am	NPIC complete production of briefing boards and notes for Lundahl / McCone	Horne, 1230 ff
During day	Zapruder shows 8mm copy of film for Sorrels; *Life* Chicago send original film to Life HQ in New York; film later damaged at frames 155-6 and 207-212; Stolley told to purchase all rights to film; Secret Service make copies of film in Washington	Trask, 131-2; Stolley; Wainright, "The Great Magazine", 369; Wrone, 35; Mack e-mail to author, May 26, 2010; Zavada e-mail to author, July 9, 2010

Thirteen | The Authenticity of the Zapruder Film

8 pm	16mm film brought from Kodak in Rochester to McMahon and Hunter at NPIC by "Secret Service Agent Bill Smith." Hunter recalls nothing of "Smith" or "Rochester". McMahon says it was original film, but Hunter recalls working on a copy with no intersprocket images. Hunter says film "not high resolution."	Horne, 1222 ff; Bugliosi endnotes, 354; "Murder In Dealey Plaza", 314-322; Thompson, 2001
Nov 25: Afternoon	Stolley and Zapruder agree sale of all rights to film to *Life*. Dan Rather may have been present for part of meeting. Stolley leaves with the last of the first-day copies, which Zapruder retained since Nov. 22.	Horne, 1202; Wrone, 35-6, 283-5; Trask, 146; Mack e-mail to author, May 14, 2010; Zapruder/Time Inc contract, Nov 25, 1963
Unknown time	Multiple copies of film (#0186) generated by FBI Lab in Washington between Nov. 23 and Nov. 25	Trask, 122; Wrone, 30; Murr 1567-8, 1574
8:40 pm	Dallas Secret Service contact Dallas FBI office requesting return of their copy (#0186) of the film. Request passed to Washington HQ	Wrone, 31; Trask, 122
Unknown time	Possible unauthorised copies of film made by FBI personnel	Wrone, 31
Nov 26: 3:21 am	FBI HQ return film to Dallas office on Braniff Airlines flight 543; film picked up by SA Hall and given to SA Bookhout	Wrone, 31; Trask, 122
9 am	Bookhout returns film to Inspector Kelley (Dallas Secret Service)	Wrone, 31; Trask, 122

JFK | Echoes from Elm Street
A Search for Historical Accuracy on the
Assassination of President John F. Kennedy

Dec 3: Unknown time	FBI HQ send one of the two requested copies of the film to Dallas office	Murr, 1569
Dec 5: Unknown time	Dallas Secret Service ask FBI for copy of the film for Dallas Police Dept.	Wrone, 31; Murr, 1569
Dec 6: Unknown time	FBI HQ send copy of film to Dallas office, for transmittal to DPD via Dallas Secret Service	Wrone, 31; Murr, 1569
Dec 9: Unknown time	FBI SA Brown passes copy for DPD, received on Dec 6, to Secret Service Agent Kunkel	Murr, 1569; Wrone, 31; Trask, 359

of research, which is a never-ending process of enlightenment, to which this chapter is hopefully a small but valid contribution.

In consequence, while the reader is left to draw their own conclusions, it is this author's strong personal opinion that the Zapruder film is indeed a truly authentic and priceless historical artifact, and not a technological Hollywood-style special effects creation.

Acknowledgements

I am deeply indebted and forever grateful to authors Richard Trask and David Wrone for their groundbreaking work in documenting the history of the Zapruder film. Gary Murr has also been extremely generous in providing me with a vast amount of his unpublished research material relating to the Zapruder film, and Richard Bartholomew has very kindly made details of his notes from his interview with Erwin Schwartz in 1994 available to me. I am also very grateful to Doug Horne, Gary Mack, Richard Stolley, Josiah Thompson, and Roland Zavada for taking the time to answer my many queries, to Bill Kelly for his assistance, and to Mark Bridger, Debra Conway, Larry Hancock, Barry Keane, and Randy Owen for their encouragement and support.

Many others have also made invaluable contributions to our knowledge of the history of the film, and the reader is referred to the published work of the following authors/researchers, which is referenced here and gratefully acknowledged: David Healy; Doug Horne; David Lifton; Harrison E. Livingstone; Gary Mack; Martin Shackelford; Josiah Thompson; Noel Twyman; David R. Wrone; and Roland Zavada. The Sixth Floor Museum's Oral History Project, which consists of interviews with many of the key people involved in the

Thirteen | The Authenticity of the Zapruder Film

broader story of November 22, 1963, many of whom are mentioned in this chapter, is also an invaluable source of information.[181]

Endnotes

The reader should be aware that Internet links are not 'permanent', and are therefore subject to change or deletion from time to time. However, at the time of writing, all links cited below were correct.

[1.] Warren Commission testimony of Abraham Zapruder, Volume 7, page 570 (hereafter in form WH7, 570); Zapruder interview by FBI Agent Robert M. Barrett, December 4, 1963 in Commission Document (CD) 7, pp. 12-3; Zapruder testimony at Clay Shaw trial, New Orleans, February 13, 1969, Dietrich & Pickett stenographer's transcript, p. 3

[2.] David R. Wrone, "The Zapruder Film – Reframing JFK's Assassination" (Lawrence, Kansas: University Press of Kansas: 2003), hereafter 'Wrone', p. 9; Douglas P. Horne, "Inside the Assassination Records Review Board", Vol. 4, (Self Published/Mary Ferrell Press: 2009), hereafter 'Horne', p. 1194; Richard B. Trask, "National Nightmare on six feet of film" (Yeoman Press, Danvers, Massachusetts: 2005) hereafter 'Trask', p. 29

[3.] Wrone, p. 9; Trask, pp. 29-30

[4.] Mark de Valk has a background in film production, and holds a PhD in Film Practice from Oxford Brookes University. He is a Senior Lecturer in Film Studies at Southampton Solent University, and since January 2011 has been editor of the *Dealey Plaza Echo*, the journal of the UK research group, *Dealey Plaza UK*.

[5.] Much of that presentation later appeared in an article, "*The Zapruder Film Chronology*", in the July 2011 issue of the *Dealey Plaza Echo*.

[6.] Wrone, p. 27; Horne, p 1199; photo at Trask, p. 119

[7.] Trask, p. 21; Martin Shackelford, "A History of the Zapruder Film", at www.jfklancer.com/History-Z.html ; Zapruder's birthday was on May 15, and Shackelford believed the roll of film used on November 22, 1963 was the first one to be exposed in the camera, which raises the possibility that the camera was a gift that Zapruder bought for himself around the time of his birthday.

[8.] Kodak Technical Report 318420P – "Analysis of Selected Motion Picture Photographic Evidence", which dealt primarily with the Zapruder film and camera, for the Assassination Records Review Board (ARRB), hereafter 'Zavada Report'. Definition of "PD" in "414PD" – letter of 18 April 1998 letter to Zavada from Rudolph Hartman in Zavada Report, Attachment A4-30; Harrison E. Livingstone, "The Hoax of the Century: Decoding the Forgery of the Zapruder Film" (Trafford Publishing, Victoria, BC, Canada: 2004), hereafter 'THOTC', p. xxxiii. [The Zavada Report and associated appendices, totalling more than 600 pages, is available from the National Archives (NARA) in printed form, and was also released on CD by the JFK Research Assassination Forum. Much (but not all) of the material is available on-line at http://www.jfk-info.com/zreport.htm and http://karws.gso.uri.edu/Marsh/Zavada/Zavada_Report.html]

[9.] By comparison with modern home-movie/video cameras, the Bell & Howell 414PD is heavy, and the fluidity of Zapruder's panning as he followed the President's car down Elm Street is, in fact, quite remarkable

[10.] Despite the quoted exposure speed of 16 frames per second (fps) for normal use, the FBI subsequently tested Zapruder's camera and found that, when fully wound, it filmed at 18.0 to 18.1 fps for the first ten seconds, and gradually increased to 18.3 to 18.5 fps for the next twenty seconds, resulting in an average of 18.3 fps for the assassination film. (FBI memo from W.D. Griffith to I.W. Conrad dated January 31, 1964. RIF 62-109060-2360); Trask, p. 161; Testimony of FBI photo expert Lyndal Shaneyfelt at WH5, 153

[11.] Bell & Howell Director Series Model 414-414P Instruction Booklet; Trask, pp. 21, 23-5; Harold Weisberg, "Photographic Whitewash: Suppressed Kennedy Assassination pictures" (Frederick, Md: self-published, 1967), pp. 148-150; Zavada Report, Study 4, p. 13; Wrone, pp. 9-10; Horne, pp. 1194-5; Vincent Bugliosi, "Reclaiming History", (New York: W.W. Norton & Co., 2007), hereafter 'Bugliosi',

JFK | ECHOES FROM ELM STREET
A SEARCH FOR HISTORICAL ACCURACY ON THE
ASSASSINATION OF PRESIDENT JOHN F. KENNEDY

endnotes, p. 358. The reader is also referred to Marcel Dehaeseleer's website, http://www.copweb.be/Zapruder%20Camera.htm , which contains a number of photos of the camera from various angles, as well as an excellent colour reproduction of the 18 page Instruction Booklet.

[12.] Author Noel Twyman states that the original film was manufactured by Eastman Kodak in 1961, and was part of a large production roll, according to Roderick Ryan – see Twyman, "Bloody Treason", (Laurel Publishing, Rancho Santa Fe, Calif.: 1997), p 154ff. Also see THOTC pp. 64, 303, referring to Zavada Report Study 1, p. 3; Horne memo to David Marwell, 9 Apr 1997, in Zavada Report as Attachment A1-1 ; see also Martin Shackelford, "Notes on the Zavada Report", 1998, available online at http://www.jfk-info.com/mshack1.htm (hereafter 'Shackelford Notes')

[13.] Trask, pp. 30, 354 (endnote 7)

[14.] Bell & Howell 414-414P Instruction Booklet, p. 3: "The Film Footage Indicator... is automatically set when you load. Press the starting button down and run the camera until the indicator reads "0". This will run off the protective leader film. It takes about 12 seconds (or 31.6 inches of film - CS) for the footage indicator to move from START to "0"; Trask, pp. 30-31

[15.] Trask, 33; Horne 1196; "Assassination Science", J. Fetzer, ed., (Catfeet Press, Chicago: 1998), p. 222; Freelance reporter Marvin Scott's interview with Zapruder, November 22, 1966. Scott's original tapes of this interview, along with an interview with Marilyn Sitzman, were given to The Sixth Floor Museum at Dealey Plaza in 2004; Josiah Thompson interview of Sitzman, November 29, 1966; Zapruder testimony, WH7, 570-1. The Hesters can be seen, still at the bench, in the Bronson still photo taken as the President's car moved down Elm Street moments before the shooting, and the bench is visible in a number of still photos taken in the area after the shooting.

[16.] Time Inc. press release, New York, April 9, 1975 in author's files; NARA Receipt and Memorandum for the Record, June 29, 1978; Wrone 72, 286-8. Richard Lubic, at the time a staffer on *Life*'s sister publication *Time,* told author William Turner that in early 1968 the Zapruder film was unaccountably "missing" for several days from the vault in *Time-Life* headquarters in New York. Despite the apparent involvement of the NYPD, the FBI and the CIA, the film's disappearance was never satisfactorily resolved. ("Farewell America: How French Intelligence Wrote a Book about the Kennedy Assassination", by William Turner, at www.jfk-online.com/farewellturner.html)

[17.] Trask, pp. 222-3, citing NARA's "Background Report Prepared for Ad Hoc SubCommittee on Preservation of the Zapruder Film", June 8, 1999, p. 5

[18.] THOTC, p. 28

[19.] THOTC, p. 297, citing Les Waffen memo to file, 30 Oct 1996

[20.] THOTC, p. 297

[21.] Horne, pp. 1196-7; Trask, pp. 335-6; Zavada Study 1, Attachments A1-1, A1-1C, A1-9 and Addendum dated December 9, 1999; Shackelford 'Notes'

[22.] THOTC, 77; Memo from Doug Horne to David Marwell and Jeremy Gunn, April 9, 1997, pp. 1-2, included in Zavada Report as Attachment A1-1; Trask, p. 357, endnote 43

[23.] Livingstone, "The Zapruder Film: A Study in Deception", a 5-part series of articles in *The Fourth Decade* research journal, starting in Vol. 6 No. 4, May 1999, and ending in Vol. 7 No. 2, January 2000; in Vol. 6, No. 6, September 1999

[24.] Zavada Report, Attachment A1-1D; THOTC, p. 36

[25.] Roland Zavada retired as Standards Director for Imaging Technologies from Eastman Kodak in March 1990. Between August 1997 and September 1998 he researched and wrote Kodak's previously referenced report for the ARRB (the Zavada Report).

[26.] Zavada Report, Study 1, p. 2; Livingstone in *The Fourth Decade*, Vol. 6, No. 4, May 1999

[27.] "The Zapruder Film Controversy", by Dr. David Mantik, in "Murder In Dealey Plaza", James H. Fetzer, ed. (Catfeet Press, Chicago: 2000), hereafter 'MIDP', pp. 348-350

[28.] This copy of the film was given to *Life* by Zapruder on November 25, 1963, and retained by them until 2000. The Zapruder family set up the LMH Company, through which all negotiations regarding the film were handled while it was under their control. The initials "LMH" represented the names of Zapruder's wife, Lillian, daughter Myrna, and son Henry.

[29.] Zavada Report: Corrections to Studies 3 and 4, Addendum to Study 3, February 3, 2000, "Evaluation of LMH Co. 1st gen. copy"

Thirteen | The Authenticity of the Zapruder Film

30. Mantik in MIDP, pp. 348-350; Zavada Study 1, Attachments A1-1C, A1-1G and A1-1F; Zavada Report Addendum, February 3, 2000 - "Evaluation of LMH Co. 1st gen. copy", op. cit.; THOTC, pp. 37-8
31. Zavada Report, Study 3, p. 1
32. NARA, NNSM "Status of Selected JFK Nontextual Assassination Records", p. 5, 13 Dec 1996; THOTC, 97; Livingstone in *The Fourth Decade*, Vol. 6, No. 5, July 1999
33. THOTC, 312; Livingstone in *The Fourth Decade*, Vol. 6, No. 4, May 1999
34. The final report of the ARRB is available online at http://history-matters.com/archive/contents/arrb/contents_arrb_report.htm ; David Lifton, "Pig on a Leash", in "The Great Zapruder Film Hoax", James H. Fetzer, ed. (Catfeet Press, Chicago: 2003), pp. 392, 416.
35. Lifton, "Pig on a Leash", pp. 393-4; Roland Zavada, "Open Letter Response to Doug Horne's Chapter 14", May 26, 2010, pp. 10-11 available at www.jfk-info.com/RJZ-DH-032010.pdf (hereafter 'Zavada 2010')
36. Zavada 2010, p. 8 defines a "Dirty Dupe" in this context as a positive print that was made at the same time as the other two copies of the film, in order to create poor - but easily identifiable – positive images to aid in visualizing the negative frames in Zapruder's film; Zavada e-mail to the author, May 22, 2012
37. This address still had a 'Kodak Premium Processing' sign on the wall, as of December 2008
38. Zavada Study 1, Attachment A1-1A (1); Wrone, p. 23
39. As of August 2011, the old Jamieson plant was the premises of Citywide Mechanical, Inc.
40. Zapruder memo to C.D. Jackson, 25 November, 1963 in Zavada Study 1, Attachment A1-1B; Sloan affidavit of November 22, 1963 in Zavada Study 1, Attachment A1-1A (2); Wrone, p. 25; Trask, pp. 114-5
41. Sloan ARRB interview, March 10, 1997; THOTC, p. 393
42. In his late 1970's personal account, Phil Chamberlain of Kodak (erroneously, I believe) thinks this happened at approximately 5:30 pm. Zavada Study 1, Attachment A1-11, p. 5
43. Trask, pp. 115-6
44. Processing number 0184 was apparently expended while cocking the mechanism to accommodate the new processing, according to Wrone, 26; THOTC, 32, 34, 366; Zavada Study 1, Part 3, p. 27 cites the speculation of Phil Chamberlain that the perforators at the head end could have been used for the Zapruder films, the perforator was tested between the original and prints and because of auto-indexing to the next number, 0184 was lost.
45. Zavada Study 1, Attachments A1-1A (3), (4) and (5); Wrone, p. 26; Trask, p. 117
46. Dick Russell, "On the Trail of the JFK Assassins" (Skyhorse Publishing, New York, 2008), pp. 293-4
47. Schwartz Sixth Floor Museum Oral History interview, December 30, 1997, p. 11. All Sixth Floor Museum Oral History Series interviews referenced hereafter will be referred to as 'Oral History interview'
48. Ibid.
49. Photo of front and back of Kodachrome box in ARRB files of Michelle Combs, obtained by the author from NARA, October 12, 2010; Transcript of Phillips' September 7, 1997 ARRB interview with Michelle Combs, in material made available to the author by Gary Murr (hereafter 'Murr'), p. 2029.
50. Interview of Schwartz by Noel Twyman and Richard Bartholomew (the husband of Schwartz's niece) in Bartholomew e-mail to the author, August 10, 2010 (hereafter 'Schwartz/Bartholomew interview'); Horne p. 1199; Trask pp. 119-120; Wrone, pp. 26-7. Trask, p. 120 says the film was transported by military plane, a claim confirmed by Zapruder in both his Warren Commission testimony (WH7, 575) and his testimony at the Shaw trial (transcript p. 83), both of which referred to the film being sent to Washington that night "by Army plane." In his Oral History interview (p. 11), Schwartz said that while he and Zapruder were in the Secret Service office, "they called somebody, and some messenger came in" to collect the film for transportation to Washington. In his report to Inspector Kelley on January 23, 1964, Sorrels said he "went to Mr. Zapruder's office and he gave to me two copies of this film, one copy of which was immediately airmailed to Chief and one copy was retained by me", a version of the story that was then relayed to *Life* Washington Bureau Chief Henry Suydam on January 27, 1964 by Secret Service Chief, James J. Rowley.
51. Schwartz Oral History interview, p. 11.
52. Wrone, pp. 27, 124; Horne p. 1199.
53. CD87, p. 66, reproduced in Josiah Thompson, "Six Seconds In Dallas", (Bernard Geis Associates, New York: 1967), pp. 311-2; see Sorrels memo of January 22, 1964 and Rowley memo of January 27, 1964 in Wrone pp. 279-280

54. Bugliosi, pp. 167, 169; "No More Silence", by Larry Sneed (1998: University of North Texas Press, Denton, Texas), p. 537; Bugliosi endnotes CD, p. 81 and source note 867 on source notes CD, p. 25
55. "Murder From Within", by Fred Newcomb & Perry Adams (Unpublished manuscript, Santa Barbara, California: 1974), p. 129. This story is included here for completeness, although it is highly unlikely that any such event took place, as the Secret Service did not have a projector with which to view the film, and were relying on Zapruder to show the film for them over the weekend.
56. Phillips' ARRRB interview transcript in Murr, p. 2030
57. Id. at p. 2032
58. Murr, p. 1563; Kelley Warren Commission affidavit WH7, 403; Kelley HSCA testimony, 3HH 325. Although Kelley told the HSCA that he joined Sorrels in DPD HQ where Oswald was being questioned, Murr provides evidence to suggest that Kelley did not attend any interrogations of Oswald until about 10:30 am on Saturday morning – see Murr, pp. 2334-5 fn. 154; WH7, 314; Warren Report, p. 199; and Kelley memo to Chief Rowley dated November 23, 1963, RIF 124-10027-10093.
59. Murr, pp. 1553
60. If Zapruder went home directly from the Secret Service office, it would have taken him approximately 20 minutes to complete the 9-mile journey, leaving him at home by approximately 10:15 pm.
61. Wrone, p. 31; Trask, pp. 126-7; Schwartz Oral History interview, p. 11
62. Zapruder's testimony at WH7, 575
63. Author's Google Maps query, January 19, 2012
64. Myrna Ries Oral History interview, March 4, 1997, p. 10; Trask, p. 127; Wrone, p. 26
65. The shortest flight time from Dallas to Chicago, according to figures obtained from a number of Internet sources, is 1 hour 27 minutes. The average time appears to be in the region of 1 hour 45 minutes, but the author's personal experience on a scheduled United Airlines flight is just over 2 hours 15 minutes. It is unlikely, therefore, that the same journey on a commercial flight in 1963 took anything less than 1 hour 30 minutes.
66. Horne, p. 1240
67. Exchange of e-mails between the author and Richard B. Stolley, November 5, 2012.
68. Zavada 2010, pp. 7-8
69. Zavada 2010, p. 8
70. Horne p. 1199; Trask, p 118; Zavada 2010, pp. 7-8
71. Trask, pp. 117, 358-9; Zavada 2010, pp. 7-8; Zavada research note of June 5, 2007, made available to this author by e-mail, May 31, 2010. The Allied Film Labs box also had a typed label stuck to its side, which provided a tantalising glimpse of a partial address in the Manhattan (NY 10017) area, and a telephone number. Recent calls to the number reveal a recorded message saying the number is 'out of service', although it has been assigned in the recent past to a subscriber on East 42nd Street. Efforts with the help of the New York Public Library (e-mail query ref 7408688) in February 2012 to identify the subscriber in 1963 were unsuccessful.
72. Cook Oral History interview, September 3, 2003, pp. 6, 9
73. Id. at pp. 6, 7; Trask, p. 154
74. According to the author's Google Maps calculations on January 13, 2012, the distance from Allied Film Labs premises at 306 West Jackson to the 53 West Jackson office was 560 yards, or a six-minute walk.
75. Cook Oral History interview, p. 10. It had not, as at the time of writing, been possible to trace and interview any of the individuals named by Cook.
76. Author's e-mail exchange with Chicago Public library, December 27-8, 2011 (CPL e-mail query ref. 7300053).
77. See Will Emaus' biographical details at http://educationforum.ipbhost.com/index.php?showtopic=14996 and his posts on Education Forum thread "Life Magazine, LBJ and the Assassination of JFK", November 13, 2009, at http://educationforum.ipbhost.com/index.php?showtopic=14966&st=15 and also on thread, "The Zapruder Film Provenance", Jan 3, 2010, at http://educationforum.ipbhost.com/index.php?showtopic=15190 . See also http://en.wikipedia.org/wiki/R.R._Donnelley_and_Sons_Co._Calumet_Plant . We know from Joe Cook's Oral History interview, p. 6, that *Life*'s deadline for all necessary work on the story was 6 pm on Sunday.
78. Wrone, 35; Gary Mack/Sixth Floor Museum film chronology, available online at http://jfk.org/go/

Thirteen | The Authenticity of the Zapruder Film

collections/about/zapruder-film-chronology ; Stolley interview in "Image of an Assassination: A New Look at the Zapruder Film", MPI Media Group, released in DVD and Video formats, July 1998.

[79.] "The Scavengers and Critics of the Warren Report", by Richard Warren Lewis and Lawrence Schiller (New York: Dell Publishing Co., 1967), pp. 149-150; Wrone, p. 53

[80.] Roland Zavada e-mail to author, July 9, 2010

[81.] Richard B. Stolley, "The Greatest Home Movie Ever Made: What happened next...", Esquire, November 1973, p. 135 – hereafter, 'Stolley 1973'; Wrone, pp. 35-6; Wainright, p. 323; Trask, p. 132

[82.] Zavada 2010, p. 7

[83.] Id. p. 8

[84.] On March 15, 1968, New Orleans Criminal District Judge Matthew Braniff signed a subpoena ordering *Life* to produce the Zapruder film before District Attorney Jim Garrison's Grand Jury at 9 am on April 4. Garrison subsequently allowed copies to be made, and further copies of these were quickly circulated among the research community [New Orleans DA's office press release, March 15, 1968; Garrison, "On the Trail of the Assassins", (Sheridan Squire Press, New York: 1988), p. 239; Fetzer's "Assassination Science", p. 212]

[85.] A good early example is Chapter 4 of Adams and Newcomb's "Murder From Within", which deals extensively with a range of issues from colour differences between frames to splices, retouching, refilming and deletion of frames.

[86.] The on-going study of high-definition, high-quality logarithmic colour scans of every frame in the film by Sydney Wilkinson [See Horne, p. 1352ff, "Addendum: The Zapruder Film Goes to Hollywood"; "The Two NPIC Zapruder Film Events: Signposts Pointing to the Film's Alteration", by Doug Horne, May 2012, pp. 28-9] is based on a copy of NARA's 35mm copy of NARA's "Forensic Copy" of the Zapruder film, which was only created for NARA by the Monaco Film Laboratory in San Francisco in 2002, according to Trask, p. 340.

[87.] Harrison Livingstone's 2004 book, "The Hoax of the Century", is to be commended for its thoroughness in addressing a significant number of these supposed alterations. Some of the more recent claims of alteration are also discussed in Trask, pp. 273-282.

[88.] Posting by Ian Kerr in thread #8720, "The Other", on the JFK Lancer Forum, at http://www.jfklancerforum.com/dc/dcboard.php?az=show_topic&forum=3&topic_id=8720&mesg_id=8720&listing_type=search on December 30, 2002

[89.] DellaRosa's personal account of what he saw appears as Appendix E in "The Great Zapruder Film Hoax", James H. Fetzer, ed. (Catfeet Press, Chicago: 2003), pp. 463-5; See also DellaRosa's own description of the film at www.youtube.com/watch?v=XrRbkY9gENQ ; See post on the Deep Politics Forum on October 23, 2010, by Bernice Moore in the thread, "The 'Other' Zapruder Film" at https://deeppoliticsforum.com/forums/showthread.php?4703-The-quot-Other-quot-Zapruder-Film/page2

[90.] While noting that DellaRosa has reported that the limousine stopped for "3 to 4 seconds" in 2003, but "2-3 seconds" in 2009, the author does not ascribe any significance to the difference.

[91.] "The 'other' film – FAQs", posted on DellaRosa's www.jfkresearch.com forum on March 15, 2009 – see https://deeppoliticsforum.com/forums/showthread.php?4703-The-quot-Other-quot-Zapruder-Film/page3

[92.] Ibid.

[93.] Posts by Greg Burnham in Education Forum thread, "Is the 'Other' film a hoax?", November 15 and 16, 2010 at http://educationforum.ipbhost.com/index.php?showtopic=16757&st=15 and http://educationforum.ipbhost.com/index.php?showtopic=16757&st=45

[94.] Ibid; Burnham post on March 25, 2010 to Education Forum thread, "Did Zapruder Film 'The Zapruder Film'?", at http://educationforum.ipbhost.com/index.php?showtopic=17516 ; Radio interview with Jim Fetzer on "The Real Deal", April 4, 2011, http://radiofetzer.blogspot.com

[95.] Burnham posts in Education Forum thread, "Is the 'Other' film a hoax?", on November 16, 2010, cited above

[96.] Burnham post on March 24, 2010 to Education Forum thread, "Did Zapruder Film 'The Zapruder Film'?", at http://educationforum.ipbhost.com/index.php?showtopic=17516

[97.] See Reymond / Marrs interview at www.youtube.com.watch?v=hSdyqDBTpeo

[98.] David Healy, "Technical Aspects of Film Alteration", in 'The Great Zapruder Film Hoax', p. 118; Revised

2006 on-line PDF version of article, p. 5
[99.] Livingstone, *The Fourth Decade*, Vol. 6, No. 4, May 1999
[100.] THOTC, p. 129 (footnote 'nnn')
[101.] Truly's Warren Commission testimony at WH6, 195. Truly, the TSBD building superintendent, was the same person who, in the company of Officer M.L. Baker, stopped Oswald in the 2nd floor lunchroom immediately after the shooting.
[102.] Greer HSCA interview by J.P. Kelly and B. Lawson, 28 Feb 1978 (RIF 180-10099-10491); THOTC, p. 326
[103.] Zapruder interview by FBI Agent Robert Barrett, December 4, 1963, at CD 7, pp. 12-3
[104.] Zapruder Warren Commission testimony at WH7, 571
[105.] "Livingstone's Creation Science and the Zapruder Film", by Hal Verb in *The Fourth Decade*, Vol. 7, No. 2, Jan 2000, p. 13
[106.] "59 Witnesses: Delay on Elm Street", by Vincent Palamara in MIDP, pp. 119-128
[107.] "What Happened On Elm Street? The Eyewitnesses Speak", in *Assassination Research*, Vol. 5, No. 1 at http://www.assassinationresearch.com/v5n1/v5n1costella.pdf
[108.] Duke Lane post in Education Forum thread, "Zapruder, Four Questions", on Jan 1, 2006 at http://educationforum.ipbhost.com/index.php?showtopic=5708&st=105
[109.] "The Case for Zapruder film Tampering: The Blink Pattern" by Mike Pincher, J.D., and Roy L. Schaeffer in "Assassination Science", pp. 224-5
[110.] "The Two NPIC Zapruder Film Events: Signposts Pointing to the Film's Alteration", by Doug Horne, May 2012, available on-line at http://www.manuscriptservice.com/NPIC-DougHorne/ as a PDF file, and also at http://lewrockwell.com/orig13/horne-d1.1.1.html The article is hereafter referred to as 'Horne 2012'.
[111.] Doug Horne Black Op Radio interview by Len Osanic, December 10, 2009. Transcript available at http://justiceforkennedy.blogspot.com/2010/01/transcript-of-doug-horne-on-black-op.html
[112.] Horne 2012, p. 20
[113.] Horne, pp. 1231, 1236; Horne 2012, p. 21
[114.] Wrone, pp. 28-29; Horne, p. 1231
[115.] Horne 2012, pp. 4, 20-21
[116.] Horne, pp. 1233, 1236, 1328
[117.] Id. at p. 1231; Horne 2012, p. 10
[118.] Transcript of Phillips' ARRB interview in Murr, pp. 2035-6.
[119.] Horne pp. 1226, 1241; Horne 2012, pp. 11-12, 15, 18-19
[120.] Horne 2012, pp. 13-16
[121.] ARRB interview with McMahon, June 12, 1997; MIDP pp. 311-2
[122.] ARRB interview with McMahon, August 14, 1997; MIDP pp. 322
[123.] Horne, p. 1224; McMahon's recorded interview with the ARRB July 14, 1997, transcript, pp. 8, 21. The 'McMahon interview transcript' referenced in these endnotes was produced by researcher Bill Kelly in January 2010 from the actual interview recording, available from NARA.
[124.] Murr p. 1537; ARRB memo from Doug Horne to David Marwell and Jeremy Gunn, July 16, 1997, ARRB Doug Horne files, Box 4
[125.] Zavada Report, Study 1, "Edge Print Examination of the "Out-Of-Camera" Original 8mm Movie Film", p. 6
[126.] Horne p. 1223; Richard Russell, "On the Trail of the JFK Assassins", op. cit., p. 293
[127.] Genealogy-based research has revealed a Social Security Death Index record and local newspaper obituary notices for one Homer A. McMahon, born on January 6, 1928, who died on May 12, 2006 in Millsboro, Delaware. The author believes this to be the ARRB/NPIC Homer McMahon.
[128.] E-mail exchanges between this author and William Kelly, August 30 and September 2, 2010, and June 17 and August 22, 2011.
[129.] Horne, p. 1236
[130.] McMahon's ARRB July 14, 1997 interview transcript, p. 8
[131.] Horne 2012, p. 21
[132.] McMahon ARRB interview transcript, pp. 21-22, 27

Thirteen | The Authenticity of the Zapruder Film

[133.] Horne 2012, p. 21
[134.] Horne, p. 1280 (Emphasis in original)
[135.] Zavada Report Appendix A1-11, p. 5 (Emphasis in original)
[136.] Id. p. 6
[137.] Zavada Report Appendix A1-8, p. 4
[138.] Zavada Report, Study 1, pp. 26-7. This sequence of events was further refined on pp. 6-10 of Zavada 2010.
[139.] Zavada 2010, pp. 7-8
[140.] Horne, pp. 1232-3
[141.] Id. at p. 1329
[142.] Id. at p. 1281
[143.] Hunter ARRB interview, June 17, 1977, reproduced in MIDP, p. 315
[144.] Zavada Report Appendix A1-11, p. 5
[145.] McMahon ARRB interview, June 12, 1977, in MIDP, p. 312
[146.] McMahon ARRB interview transcript, p. 8
[147.] Trask, p. 26 and Endnote 3, p. 354
[148.] This footage totals 65 seconds, which would use up just over 14 feet of film, rather than the 12 feet estimated by Trask.
[149.] Memo from Doug Horne to David Marwell and Jeremy Gunn, April 9, 1997, pp. 1-2, included in Zavada Report as Attachment A1-1; Trask, pp. 357 (endnote 43), 372 (endnote 251)
[150.] Trask, 30 and Endnote 7, p. 354
[151.] Id. at Endnotes 3 and 7, p. 354; Livingstone Secret Service copy #1 Film Map, THOTC, p. 36
[152.] Fig. 4-9 in Zavada Report, Study 4, p. 13
[153.] FBI Lab report, from W.D. Griffith to I.W. Conrad, Dec 20, 1963 (62-109060-2360); memo dated Feb 3, 1964 from J. E. Hoover to Warren Commission General Counsel, J. Lee Rankin; Trask, p. 161; Weisberg, "Photographic Whitewash", p. 140
[154.] Zavada Report: Corrections to Studies 3 and 4, Addendum to Study 3, February 3, 2000, "Evaluation of LMH Co. 1st gen. copy", p. 16
[155.] At the time of writing the film can be viewed on the Sixth Floor Museum's site by going to http://www.jfk.org/ and choosing 'Collections'. Using the 'Click to explore' link, follow the link for the 'Collections Database', and enter 'Zapruder' in the 'Quick Search' box. Then click on the thumbnail titled 'Abraham Zapruder Film' which appears on page 1 of the search results to view the Rogers scene from Side A of the film.
[156.] The website http://www.travelmath.com/flight-time/from/Dallas, TX/to/Chicago, IL shows the present-day flight time from Dallas to Chicago is 1 hour 36 minutes. The same website also confirms that there is no time difference between Dallas and Chicago.
[157.] While every effort was made to ensure the accuracy of the timing tests, the reader should be aware that they were carried out using a manually-operated stopwatch, so the accuracy of the timings are subject to the accuracy of the stopwatch operator, and any differences between the DVD recording and playback speeds.
[158.] Author's e-mail exchange in February 2012 with Dwayne's Photo, a Kansas-based company that processed Kodachrome film for over 20 years, and was the last company in the world to do so.
[159.] Zavada 2010, p. 8
[160.] *Life* magazine, November 29, 1963, p. 27
[161.] Trask, p. 119
[162.] *Life* magazine, November 29, 1963, p. 27; *Life* magazine, October 2, 1964, p. 46 (photo #8)
[163.] Josiah Thompson in "Six Seconds In Dallas", pp. 217-8; FBI Director J. Edgar Hoover letter to Commission General Counsel J. Lee Rankin, April 21, 1964. The damaged frames were missing from the official Commission Exhibit (CE 885) when it was shown to Zapruder during his testimony on July 22, 1964.
[164.] "Zapruder Fakery 3 – David Healy Part 10", starting at 5:07 into the clip – available on YouTube at http://www.youtube.com/watch?v=ggkOpf6V_Nk
[165.] Healy, "Technical Aspects of Film Alteration", 2006 Internet PDF version, p. 20; 'The Great Zapruder

Film Hoax', p. 134

166. Post #46 by David Healy on February 8, 2011 in Education Forum thread "Math Part 4", at http://educationforum.ipbhost.com/index.php?showtopic=17330&st=45

167. "The Great Zapruder Film Hoax", pp. 208, 220-221

168. Bruce Jamieson letter to Harry Livingstone, May 26, 1999; THOTC, pp. 463-4

169. Bugliosi Endnotes CD pp. 352-3

170. Noel Twyman, "Bloody Treason", pp. 154ff., and e-book version; Horne, p. 1196, says that "Kodachrome II was known as a 'reversal film', which meant that instead of producing a *negative image*, as was normal in the commercial film world, it produced a *positive image* when developed that could be directly viewed in a projector." This avoided the expense and slight degradation of image quality resulting from using a negative film, and copying to a positive, to produce a print for projection – see http://en.wikipedia.org/wiki/Reversal_film Details of the K-14 process used in producing the finished film is available at http://en.wikipedia.org/wiki/K-14_process

171. Twyman, op. cit.

172. THOTC, pp. 102-3

173. Id. at p. 186

174. Zavada letter to Livingstone, March 13, 2004; THOTC, p. 188; Zavada, *"The Zapruder Film, Understanding the Tools Available for Authentication"*, JFK Lancer 'November In Dallas' Conference, Dallas, November 13, 2010

175. Zavada meeting with Livingstone, May 16, 2004; THOTC, pp. 186-7

176. Zavada 2010, pp. 30-2

177. Noel Twyman, "Bloody Treason", pp. 154ff., and e-book version.

178. Copies in author's files. The second memo bears NARA RIF 62-109060-68. The memos are also reproduced in "The Great Zapruder Film Hoax", p. 426 and Trask, p. 121

179. Searches on January 31, 2012 showed that Kansas was the nearest destination, with a flight time of 54 minutes from Dallas (http://www.travelmath.com/flying-time/from/Dallas, TX/to/Kansas City, MO); Chicago was 1 hour 36 minutes away, Los Angeles was 2 hours 29 minutes away, and New York was the furthest, at 2 hours 45 minutes.

180. See http://ereview.org/2010/11/12/kc-production-beginnings-the-calvin-company/ re Calvin Photo Lab, and http://en.wikipedia.org/wiki/Fairfax_Army_Airfield re Fairfax Army Base; Google Map calculations.

181. A full list of interviews can be seen at the Sixth Floor Museum site - http://www.jfk.org/go/collections/oral-histories/interviews-by-name

Fourteen
The Other Side of the Mirror
The Single Bullet Theory as a Necessary Construct

Adrian Morris

> *"When we look into a mirror we think the image that confronts us is accurate. But move a millimetre and the image changes. Sometimes the writer has to smash the mirror for it is on the other side of that mirror that the truth stares at us."*
> – Harold Pinter, 2005.

As always in any form of historical study and debate there is always a structure that runs through it. After all, the historian's job is to *interpret* the past. This is true for the amateur as well as the professional historian, although true levels of expertise will inevitably vary. These structures show that elements such as prevailing ideas, models of analysis and competing theories will develop.

Models of analysis develop that can be applied to areas of historical research to help the historian and researchers build up a probable scenario or likely chain of events and a likely set of actions of those under research. These models, more commonly known as paradigms, will aid historians and researchers develop new theories and avenues of research. They can also dictate the orthodoxy of a given historical view. One might look at the series of events that led up to the First World War for instance, and use available paradigms to develop theories. Of course, paradigms can, and often do, change over time, thus allowing historical interpretation to change. The areas of history where such paradigms can become a matter of debate and be problematic happen where there is no broad consensus on an area or areas of history that have become polarised by irreconcilable and competing interpretations of an historical event. In other words; there is no *ultimate resolution*.

JFK | ECHOES FROM ELM STREET
A SEARCH FOR HISTORICAL ACCURACY ON THE ASSASSINATION OF PRESIDENT JOHN F. KENNEDY

The case under review; the assassination of President John F. Kennedy in Dallas on 22nd November 1963, has yielded no real consensus that has led to ultimate resolution despite various groups of historians and researchers claiming such. We need to look at one area of this debate that has been proffered as a paradigm to aid ultimate resolution; *the single bullet theory*, and see how and why it was constructed and who needed to construct it. Therefore we can assume that the *single bullet theory* was a necessary construct for various reasons. There is a discernible reluctance by many orthodox and professional historians and commentators to embrace conspiracy theories. To some extent this is correct and obvious. The researcher who is unable or willing to reconcile their small area of research with the wider known and accepted events can find themselves marginalised. They can see their work ignored or viewed as outlandish. A good example of this type of conspiracy theory might be seen in those conspiracy theories that have developed concerning the Apollo moon landings of July 1969. The immense body of evidence shows emphatically that Neil Armstrong and 'Buzz' Aldrin set foot on the lunar surface and returned to earth successfully. Yet, there still persists a small – but vociferous – clique of researchers who tender theories that say this was not the case. They then develop theories as to why this might not be the case as part of a wider conspiracy which has a certain motive or end.

The above conspiracy theories, although resilient and popular, nevertheless are treated with scorn by the mainstream media and particularly the academic community who justifiably ignore such works. We see, also, other areas where conspiracy theories have developed that follow the line of the Moon landing conspiracy theories, whether these have looked at areas of supposed alien activity (Roswell) or popular and unsolved crime. Basically, the term 'conspiracy theory' has been used to express distain for an approach to an historical debate that one wishes to denounce or ridicule. But do conspiracies exist? Are they a good model or framework to help explain areas of history?

The simple fact is; conspiracies do exist. History is full of them. The *Gunpowder Plot* of 1605, when a group of radical Catholic insurgents tried to assassinate the English and Scottish King, James I *was* a conspiracy. The assassination of the Archduke Franz Ferdinand in 1914 in Sarajevo which helped contribute to the outbreak of the Great War was a conspiracy. The assassination of President Lincoln at Ford's Theatre in Washington D.C. in 1865 was, to all intents and purposes, a conspiracy. Yet these conspiracies are fully accepted by the public and the academic community as such. Why accept these ones and not the previous marginalised ones?

A simple answer is that there has been some form of *ultimate resolve* to these cases. To solve them one has had to accept that a conspiracy was at play. The framework of a conspiracy, essentially a conspiracy theory, is employed by the historian/researcher to help them interpret the series of events that led up

FOURTEEN | THE OTHER SIDE OF THE MIRROR
THE SINGLE BULLET THEORY AS A NECESSARY CONSTRUCT

to the ultimate act. One might say for the three cases I have just outlined; the conspiracies at play have become the orthodoxy and the broad consensus. One might also add that the main paradigm that has been employed to construct the theory of what happened was a political one. In all the above cases there was a wider political motive at play; 1605 – religious and political; 1914 – nationalist and political; in 1865 – nationalist/separatist.

Another aspect in some of the three cases just outlined was that ultimate resolve was largely gained at the time through a court of law or inquiry by the authorities where fresh evidence was brought before a jury and/or a judge for consideration. Allowing for the prejudices and intense bias there might have been, it was quite clear the singular intention of Guy Fawkes to blow up parliament in 1605 was part of a rapidly uncovered conspiracy that resulted in the pursuit and apprehending of a number of conspirators. In 1914 the Yugoslav nationalist, Gavrilo Princip, who shot Archduke Franz Ferdinand, was tried with other members of his political faction as part of a wider conspiracy that was suspected. And in 1865, despite John Wilkes Booth pulling the trigger that killed President Lincoln, others would hang for an assassination that the authorities felt was a conspiracy.

Conspiracies in history are common and normal and are certainly not rare. It is not correct, as some commentators would claim, that conspiracies are for the outlandish to employ, but it is fair to say that some conspiracy theories are outlandish. The dictum that *"there are conspiracy theories and there are conspiracy theories"* is largely true. It is largely the evidence that is used to support them and how they fit with the wider details and events that is important. They must stand up to intense scrutiny and debate and be allowed to explain the wider understanding of an event of historical incident.

In criminal law much debate surrounds the law that governs most conspiratorial crimes, whether they are minor or serious. The crime of joint enterprise is cited in many jurisdictions and is very commonly used in the prosecution of criminal gangs. So to say, as some commentators might say of the assassination of President Kennedy, that *"these sorts of crimes are nearly always committed by one person"* is grossly misleading when each case needs to be examined to see if it is a single perpetrator or a case of joint enterprise with others involved. Therefore: a conspiracy. The Oxford English dictionary describes a conspiracy as *"a secret plan to carry out an illegal or harmful act; especially with political motivations; plot. The act of making such plans in secret."* One could expand this meaning to mean a criminal endeavour involving more than one participant within a plot.

One has to be careful when dealing with criminal and historical conspiracy theories as can be shown with the terrorist attacks on the World Trade Centre in 2001. Two types of conspiracy theories have developed in this case. The more disputable ones cite that the destruction of the World Trade Centre was

JFK | ECHOES FROM ELM STREET
A SEARCH FOR HISTORICAL ACCURACY ON THE ASSASSINATION OF PRESIDENT JOHN F. KENNEDY

a conspiratorial act perpetrated by the U.S. government for various foreign or security policy reasons. Proponents of these conspiracy theories draw on sceptical opinions and views of modern governments in advanced industrialised nation states as being inherently dishonest and covert. Dishonest and covert they may be, but does this extreme viewpoint meet with the accepted facts?

For even with the accepted facts the terrorist attack on the World Trade Centre *was* a conspiracy and has been universally accepted as such. It is just a different, less grand conspiracy that would have involved governmental collusion, but more a criminal/political conspiracy in nature as the terrorists involved, numbering more than one, plotted covertly the intended outcome for a wider political end. Therefore, even in the hands of officialdom and the orthodox chroniclers of this event, they cannot escape the inevitable conclusion of a conspiracy. It's a case of; what type of conspiracy?

So where does this leave us with our central area of concern: the assassination of President Kennedy in Dallas in 1963? The Kennedy assassination case, despite the claims otherwise from subsequent writers and researchers, has never been resolved – in that a definitive conclusion has not been reached. There was no resultant court case to test the guilt or otherwise of the main suspect; Lee Harvey Oswald and the official inquiry set up to investigate it, the Warren Commission, has not silenced the critics to the degree that it is acceptable as a resolution to the case. Essentially there are two broad models that have been put forward to try and provide ultimate resolution to the case.

On the one level there is the lone assassin theory. This predicates that one gun man – Lee Harvey Oswald – assassinated President Kennedy from his place of work in the Texas School Book Depository. The other model is the conspiracy theory model which argues that Kennedy was assassinated by more than one gunman and that a wider plot to murder him was at play. Unlike the lone assassin theory, the opposing conspiracy theory position encompasses a wider range of scenarios, personalities and reasons. For instance, some of the conspiracy theories surrounding the Kennedy assassination see Lee Harvey Oswald as deeply involved, unknowingly involved, or not involved at all. Some allow for him to fire shots from the window of the Texas School Book Depository in congress with other gunmen or not fire any guns at all. The range of conspiracy theories can vary wildly and conflict – but they do allow for a greater range of evidence to help explain the events in Dealey Plaza that day in 1963.

The lone assassin theory is supported by evidence that has to discount other conflicting evidence such as eyewitness evidence from the grassy knoll adjacent to the murder spot. This theory will also draw on the testimony of those within Lee Harvey Oswald's associates to show he acted alone. However, the main keystone in the lone assassin theory was the development of the *single bullet theory*.

FOURTEEN | THE OTHER SIDE OF THE MIRROR
THE SINGLE BULLET THEORY AS A NECESSARY CONSTRUCT

In the aftermath of the assassination of President Kennedy, the Dallas police authorities rapidly investigated claims that the fatal shots may have come from the Texas School Book Depository. A search would eventually lead to them finding a Mannlicher Carcano rifle on the sixth floor of the building. Eventually, enquiries showed that this belonged to an employee of the Book Depository, Lee Harvey Oswald.

There had been other reports of other shots fired from other locations during the moments surrounding Kennedy's murder. Yet, as Mark Lane[1] would argue, the Dallas police eventually narrowed down their investigation, for they had a clear suspect with a rifle they could prove belonged to Lee Harvey Oswald stowed barely hidden in his place of work. Moreover, some witnesses claimed that they saw and heard the shots or gunman from that location. Problem was, as the injuries to Kennedy and his fellow passenger, Governor Connally began to show, there seemed to be too much damage and injuries for the three bullets that were supposed to have been fired during the assassination from the Book Depository. It must be remembered that due to the positioning and series of shots, including the final fatal shot to Kennedy's head, the first shot (if one takes the lone assassin theory as valid) must have missed.

This would, and still does, pose a serious problem for the proponents of the lone assassin. They have to rely on only two bullets delivering a series of separate injuries to two targets in the limousine Kennedy and Connally were travelling in. This problem faced the Dallas police in the wake of the assassination as it would the resultant governmental commission that would be set up later.

The eventual resolution that was put forward by the official inquiry into the assassination, the Warren Commission, was to accept the lone gunman proposition and therefore hold as valid the single bullet theory. The artefact that was retained from the assassination that was claimed as the single bullet that passed through both Kennedy and Connally became known by critics of the Commission's findings as the 'magic bullet' for it showed very minor – almost negligible - damage. Critics would dispute this artefact as being the actual bullet on a number of points. The pristine condition of the bullet, the confusion over the finding of the bullet on a stretcher in Parkland hospital away from Kennedy's body and the injured Governor Connally and, more specifically, the improbability of a single bullet travelling through two bodies in the time frame the Warren Commission claimed it had.

The Warren Commission, and some historians and researchers since (most notably Gerald Posner[2]), argue that this single bullet theory must be true. In their eyes it has to be true. For if there is to be but one lone gunman firing from a single location and for the time framing to allow up to three shots from the same rifle, it has to be true. Therefore they have set up a paradigm that then has to hold a wider grip on the case. It must hold that only Oswald was the killer, for it was his gun fired from his workplace. It must also hold that he did not gain

JFK | ECHOES FROM ELM STREET
A SEARCH FOR HISTORICAL ACCURACY ON THE
ASSASSINATION OF PRESIDENT JOHN F. KENNEDY

any conspiratorial influence and direction from others; individuals or groups. It must also hold that his movements and contacts prior to the assassination are peripheral and irrelevant. Basically, the single bullet theory is inextricably linked to the lone gunman theory; it has to be in this scenario for it was designed to put Lee Harvey Oswald as the rifleman in the window of the Texas School Book Depository on that fateful day acting entirely on his own. There can be no other conclusion. In the Warren Commission's eyes, and therefore the U.S. government's eyes, it could be saliently argued, the single bullet theory became a necessary construct to eradicate any prospect or discussion of a conspiracy.

There are problems with the single bullet theory. It lacks flexibility to help historians and researchers develop theories of what might have happen in Dealey Plaza on that day. For instance, to believe the single bullet theory as part of the lone gunman scenario, one is restricted to only accepting the eye/ear witness testimony of those who believed the gun shots came from the Texas School Book Depository. This testimony is questionable in itself as it often is a belief that shots originated from behind the Kennedy motorcade which does not exclude the positioning of other gunmen from other locations to the rear. Also, and most importantly, this theory excludes the significant amount of witnesses who felt the shots fired at the motorcade came from the front, or more specifically, the grassy knoll area to the direct front-right of the motorcade. A fair-minded historian, acknowledging the unresolved nature of a case such as this - which is highly disputed - must accept that a significant group of witnesses believed they heard shots from various locations and that it would be ill advised to discount one in favour of the other. Those who accept a conspiracy was at play can at least acknowledge shots coming from separate locations.

By only accepting the witness statements that support shots from the Book Depository the advocates of the single bullet theory are using this selective evidence to underpin their desire to have a lone gunman and are not being guided by the variety of evidence and weighing it up and testing it. This is a case of that dread of historical research and analysis: *confirmation bias*. For balance, conspiracy theorists must also avoid confirmation bias, but the interpretations that allow for a conspiracy are less likely to discount evidence that is problematic which may explain the various different conspiracy scenarios that have been developed over the years to explain this case.

As a model of interpretation, those that embrace the possibility of a conspiracy are at another advantage over those who embrace the single bullet theory. The single bullet theory fails on the technical side from the basic point of timing. In the widely seen Zapruder film, the best filmic evidence available of the shooting, the two incidents of impact that the single bullet theorists claim is the simultaneous injuries to both Kennedy and Governor Connally do not appear to happen at the same time. In fact, a simple watching of the film shows

Fourteen | The Other Side of the Mirror
The Single Bullet theory as a necessary construct

a considerable delay in reaction to the supposed impact of the single bullet from when it hits Kennedy (clasping his throat) and when it hits Connally (visible grimace and puffing out of his cheeks). Single bullet theorists claim delayed reaction, yet the reaction of Connally to the bullet is purely physiological. Allowing for the delay, there is still no possible chance that the lone gunman, for instance, could have fired off a second shot that hits Connally. Besides, the quota of bullets available to do what lone gunman theorists need to be done must only be accomplished by two bullets.

Isn't it more rational to acknowledge that both Kennedy and Connally in this part of the Zapruder film are being hit by two separate bullets from two separate guns? Acknowledging this possibility of another gunman destroys the single bullet theory and by intimation establishes a conspiracy.

The conspiracy – whatever its motivation – was the main target of the Warren Commission. The Warren Commission's raison d'être was to place the lone gunman (Oswald) in the window of the Texas School Book Depository. Yet, even the lone gunman theory, and thus also the single bullet theory, can fall prey to the conspiracy model here. For even if Oswald had shot Kennedy on his own with two bullets, hitting Connally on the way, it does not prime facia exclude a conspiracy. For instance, Oswald could have been encouraged to kill Kennedy due to political or criminal activity with others. In this scenario, even if Oswald acted alone, he would be part of a conspiracy type similar to the earlier ones I cited in this article; Wilkes Booth, Guy Fawkes and Gavrilo Princip, who all acted alone but were part of a joint enterprise.

Lee Harvey Oswald's bizarre and, at times, covert movements and behaviours were such that the Warren Commission and pro-lone gunman/single bullet theory researchers since have had to ignore or significantly downplay Oswald's activities to the point of weakening their findings. An example of this was seen in Gerald Posner's book when he claimed Oswald had never known the shady far-right individual, David Ferrie. Subsequent research showed photographs of Oswald in Ferrie's company years before. Essentially, the problem facing the lone gunman/single bullet theorists is that they have to extrude backwards Oswald's entire life and career so that it excludes problematic and conflicting data.

The problem isn't that a lone gunman thesis has been proposed for the murder of President Kennedy. Lone gunmen have killed celebrities and politicians in the past, such as Mark Chapman murdering John Lennon or the anarchist malcontent Leon Czolgosz murdering President McKinley in 1901. The problem with the lone gunman thesis in the Kennedy assassination is that it doesn't fully explain the complexities of witness, ballistics and medical evidence and is wholly underpinned by the single bullet theory which, as a tool of historical interpretation, is decidedly weak.

A better model of historical interpretation in this case must be the conspiracy model as it shows greater compatibility with the complex evidence and is nuanced to the wider facts related to the case. The conspiracy model may not fully answer the case - which as I said earlier is ultimately unresolved for a variety of reasons already outlined - but it does offer the best prospect of garnering more research and arguments about what happened in Dealey Plaza that day.

Detractors of the conspiracy model tend to fall into two camps; those who criticise conspiracy theories as being outlandish and bizarre. Conspiracy theories can of course be this if they are not grounded in evidence and do not balance streams of data and witness evidence rigidly. Then there is the other camp which criticises conspiracy theorists by virtue of the fact that they already adhere to the lone gunman and single bullet theory for many reasons. For instance the original political proponents of the Warren Commission accepted the findings of this report because it offered a solution that refuted a wider conspiracy. Their reasons were due to political expediency or to cover up wider avenues of investigation.

More sound criticisms of conspiracy theories in the Kennedy case question the historicism employed by some researchers and theorists. These criticisms fairly argue that there is a research bias towards finding a conspiracy and, lo and behold, one duly appears. The temptation is to identify a group that one wishes to be the conspirators and then find supporting evidence for this to be so.

The more sober conspiracy theories must somehow reconcile the difficulty in gaining evidence of a conspiracy and deducing likely scenarios from other supporting sources such as witnesses and balancing the evidence available. In doing this, for this particular confused case, one will fully understand that applying the conspiracy model will always be more successful than restricting oneself to the lone gunman/single bullet theory approach with its improbable conclusions. The conspiracy model is more likely to help us look beyond the other side of the mirror in this case.

Endnotes
[1] Mark Lane – *Rush to Judgement* (Bodley Head-1966) 1st edition. HB Pp478
[2] Gerald Posner – *Case Closed: Lee Harvey Oswald & the Assassination of JFK* (Time Warner - 1993) PB. Pp607. ISBN: 978-0751509243

Fifteen
Why we don't know

Larry Hancock

At the time, there was little doubt that we would get the full story behind the President's assassination. Reporter Merriman Smith had been riding in the press pool car in the motorcade. As the car raced towards Parkland Hospital he had grabbed the mike for the car radiophone and described three "bursts" of gunfire coming into the motorcade (much later, Secret Service Agent Greer, riding security in the President's car, would be adamant in his remarks to the Warren Commission, telling them that he was absolutely certain that there certainly more than three single shots). Local and national media were clearly on the chase in Dallas, during the afternoon and evening there were numerous interviews and viewers heard a Parkland Doctor talk about the President's wounds, indicating a shot to the front of the head.[1]

Local reporters interviewed the Doctor and prepared their stories for print. The Dallas Chief of Police described someone being picked up and driven away from the street in front of the Texas School Book Depository (TSBD); several individuals would later make statements of having witnessed the incident. Home movie footage was located (filmed by Abraham Zapruder in Dealey Plaza), which appeared to clearly show the actual shooting and Life Magazine rushed to purchase first print rights to the frames in the film and the following day returned to obtain full movie rights for the film.

The Dallas Police were aggressive, tracking down and taking a TSBD employee into custody. On camera the suspect, Lee Oswald, was adamant with the media that he had not killed the President and in fact was simply being used as a "patsy" for the crime. Crime scene personnel appeared to be active, taking a variety of evidence into custody, and being photographed while doing so – media coverage of the investigation appeared to be wide open and to some extent even chaotic and uncontrolled. Police prepared lists of individuals parked in the lot behind the TSBD, of individuals in the Texas Theatre where Lee Oswald was arrested. A host of individuals gave statements and some of them were brought back in for further interrogation and polygraph interviews. Both were threatened with arrest and one actually was temporarily taken into custody. The police certainly appeared to be running an open ended investigation, even with a primary suspect in custody. And formal charges were prepared for Lee Oswald, as a participant in a conspiracy to murder the President of the United States.[2]

And then....the phones in Texas began to ring with calls from Washington D.C.

"...any word of a conspiracy – some plot by foreign nations – to kill President Kennedy would shake our nation to its foundation. President Johnson was worried about some conspiracy on part of the Russians...it would hurt foreign relations if I alleged a conspiracy – whether I could prove it or not...I was to charge Oswald with plain murder. -- *Dallas District Attorney Henry Wade*

Others would get similar calls from President Johnson's personal aide, Cliff Carter; the list included Dallas Police Chief Curry and Texas Attorney General Waggoner Carr. The calls directed that there should be no discussion of conspiracy that they should proceed against Lee Oswald and issues of foreign relations and national security were invoked in all the calls. The initial paperwork charges were torn up and replaced.[3]

In an apparent extension of this evening effort to quickly contain the investigation, we now know that when the President's personal physician, Admiral Burkley, arrived at Bethesda Naval Hospital, he instructed the senior officers that their was no need to conduct a formal autopsy, rather they simply needed to obtain the bullets from the President's body – "the police had captured the guy who did this and all we need is a bullet."[4]

Although the commanding officer rejected Burkley's directions, there is now ample evidence that the autopsy Doctors were told that the shooter had fired three shots from the rear at the President. Not only did that set expectations among the Doctors, but there are a variety of other indications that standard autopsy protocols were violated. As an example, Dr. Boswell stated that he was ordered not to inspect the President's clothing, a standard procedure. The actual notes from the autopsy were either burned or lost and based on the work of the ARRB; we now know that at least the first written report was actually destroyed. It very much appears that the official autopsy report seems to have changed and evolved over some 72 hours and ultimately did not match either the original autopsy work sheet or the official certificate of death.[5]

In Dallas, the police investigation was further hamstrung by the fact that, literally within hours, much of the primary evidence had been removed from their possession and from Dallas by the FBI. The removal was so hurried that the head of the DPD crime scene section was unable to complete his studies of the rifle prints and would later have to testify that he could not confirm the prints he observed as being those of Lee Oswald. Clearly the FBI must have been acting under direction of the new President and given the calls to Dallas,

Fifteen | Why we don't know

President Johnson would seem to have been extremely concerned about some matter of national security. Surprisingly the extant historic record confirms neither any specific orders from President Johnson to Director Hoover nor any actions on Johnson's part relating to national security concerns.

What the record shows is that Director Hoover simply left his office at the end of the regular work day and went home to watch television news coverage of the assassination. William Manchester, in *The Death of a President*, reports a call from Johnson to Hoover at approximately 7:30 in the evening. We seem to see corroboration for such a call in the fact that within half an hour after that time, FBI Headquarters issued a Director level communication to all offices on contacting potential informants (security, radical, and criminal) and other sources for information on the assassination. Still, the call no longer shows on the official Johnson call log (which shows other calls only minutes before and minutes after Manchester's stated time of the Hoover call). The record also shows no evidence that Director Hoover informed President Johnson that only weeks before, Lee Oswald had met with Soviet personnel in Mexico City, individuals suspected to be KGB intelligence officers. In fact the FBI was, at the time, running a double agent against one of those officers. The individual was living in the United States and had actually travelled to Mexico City to meet with the KGB officer and discuss the collection of intelligence for sabotage operations in the US. Both the FBI and CIA files contained information on the Soviet agent, his intelligence activities and his contact with Oswald in the Soviet embassy in Mexico City. Yet available records provide no details as to when (or if) the information was communicated to either CIA Director McCone or President Johnson.[6]

Actually the tapes of Johnson's communications while on Air Force One, during the flight back to Washington D.C., reveal no sign of any such topic, beyond that they show no evidence of any Presidential concern over any issue of national security, even though Johnson had raised the possibility of am international conspiracy on at least two occasions while still at Parkland Hospital. Over the ensuing years various individuals would suggest that Johnson was emotional, frightened or even panicked while on Air Force One. The communications tapes reveal nothing of that nature, not even a single attempt by the new President to speak with the Secretary of Defence, the Joint Chiefs or the National Military Command Canter.[7]

Indeed the record suggests that Johnson's primary concern while still in Dallas was in arranging to take the oath of office as President; during the flight back his calls were of a more personal nature, including condolence calls to the Kennedy family. There are also no records of meetings of a national security nature the evening of the assassination and only a brief encounter between CIA Director McCone and Johnson the next morning.[8]

Clearly this leaves us with a mystery. Johnson's aide began calling Dallas

JFK | ECHOES FROM ELM STREET
A SEARCH FOR HISTORICAL ACCURACY ON THE
ASSASSINATION OF PRESIDENT JOHN F. KENNEDY

Friday evening, suppressing any law enforcement pursuit of conspiracy and focusing attention solely on Lee Oswald. International concerns and national security were cited in the calls, yet according to the record Johnson has received no communications that would create any such concern – yet we know from memoranda that the CIA (if not Hoover and the FBI) in both Mexico City and Washington D.C. was already highly agitated in regard to Oswald's contacts in Mexico City, beginning the evening of the assassination. And we have good reason to suspect that Director Hoover was equally concerned, based in the fact that very early the following morning, his agents were evaluating tapes of calls in Mexico City, calls supposedly made by Oswald and involving both the Cuban and Russian embassies.

The calls in question have been interpreted as casting suspicion on Oswald's contacts with both the Russians and Cubans, authors John Newman and Peter Dale Scott have suggested that it was those contacts which were the national security concern that drove Johnson to suppress investigations and later to convene the Warren Commission, with instructions that it put an end to such dangerous rumours.

We now have extensive evidence that Johnson indeed did just that, using Mexico City and the threat of an atomic exchange (and millions of American deaths) to ensure that Lee Oswald would be established as the lone suspect. The evidence is revealed in tapes of Johnson's calls recruiting Commission members but is perhaps most evident in the instructions delivered by Warren himself at the first meeting of the Commission:

"After brief introductions the Chief Justice discussed the circumstances under which he had accepted the chairmanship...the President stated that rumors of the most exaggerated kind were circulating in this country and overseas. Some rumors went as far as attributing the assassination to a faction within the government wishing to see the Presidency assumed by President Johnson. *Others, if not quenched, could conceivably lead the country into a war which could cost 40 million lives.* The Chief Justice discussed the role of the Commission. He placed emphasis on the importance of quenching rumors and precluding speculation such as that which had surrounded the death of Lincoln."[9]

Yet while the Warren Commission's findings have often been greeted with skepticism, many readers will be surprised to learn that the FBI report which formed the basis of conclusions was begun after no more than 48 hours of investigation. We know from FBI memoranda that the Bureau itself was instructed to prepare an investigation report which would present Lee Oswald as the sole participant in the President's murder. We know that on Friday evening (November 22, 1963) the Director's office issued an open ended instruction for all offices to query all informants and sources on the assassination, but by noon on Saturday that instruction was rescinded and efforts were focused strictly on Lee Oswald.

Fifteen | Why we don't know

That Saturday directive was issued within an hour of a conversation between Hoover and Johnson in which Hoover had described the evidence against Oswald as not very, very strong and likely not sufficient to obtain a conviction in court. Yet only 24 hours later, on Sunday November 24, Alan Belmont of the FBI prepared a memo for FBI Deputy Director Clyde Tolson. The memo concluded suggested that the investigation of Oswald was virtually complete and that the next step would be preparation of a report for the Attorney General, one which would set forth the items of evidence which made it clear that Oswald alone had been responsible for the President's murder.[10]

Within two weeks the final FBI report was submitted to the President; however, it appears that much of that time was taken up not with further investigation but with the actual writing of what Belmont himself described as a "difficult report." Elements of the report, maintaining Oswald's guilt, began being leaked to the press (from the Bureau) within only a few days, well before the report itself was complete.

At this point in time it seems clear that the investigation of President Kennedy's murder was constrained and focused on a single individual, a process which began within something like six hours following the shooting. But while Johnson's actions in limiting the investigation are documented, his motives and what was actually going on behind the scenes at the highest levels of government has only begun to reveal itself, several decades after the President's murder in Dallas. With research only available during the past few years, we also find much of that activity was going on not within the FBI or the Secret Service, it was occurring within the Central Intelligence Agency.

To understand why the CIA would be so deeply involved (when officially – and surprisingly – they reportedly played no role in investigating the assassination) we will need to turn to Lee Oswald's time in Mexico City, a bit less than two months before the assassination. A trip which seems to have coincided with one and possibly more intelligence operations centered on Oswald himself, operations never admitted by the Agency and operations, in regard to which the CIA appears to have knowingly destroyed materials, withheld information and mislead even the Warren Commission. In this examination we will find indications that senior officers within the CIA were much more involved in assassination inquiries than they ever admitted and that what they learned may have been intentionally suppressed.

Much of the following dialog is based in primary research performed by Professors John Newman and Peter Dale Scott. Readers are particularly referred to Chapters 18-20 and the Epilogue of Newman's 2008 edition of *Oswald and the CIA*. Unless otherwise noted the following is based in Newman's work. The conclusions offered are strictly this author' analysis, interpretation, and speculation.[11]

JFK | ECHOES FROM ELM STREET
A SEARCH FOR HISTORICAL ACCURACY ON THE
ASSASSINATION OF PRESIDENT JOHN F. KENNEDY

When Lee Oswald appeared at the Cuban and Russian embassies in Mexico City in October of 1963, he was entering one of the most massive intelligence operations run by the United States. The CIA's Mexico City station was well respected, regarded as one of the largest and most active resources for foreign intelligence collection, political action and covert operations – the lynchpin in US activities against Communism and Cuba throughout Latin America.[12]

The station was opened in 1950 when CIA was assigned responsibility for intelligence in Latin America, taking over that role from the FBI. Howard Hunt initially opened the office (in a far less than graceful fashion involving conflicts with the US Ambassador, misunderstandings with CIA headquarters continuing arguments over responsibilities) but in 1951 Chief of Station duties were taken over by a former FBI officer. One of the stations first intelligence collection activities was to establish a telephone tap operation and that was soon extended to telex. Initial focus was on the Russian embassy but after the Castro revolution extensive attention was focused on the Cuban embassy and personnel. Technical intelligence would become one of the primary activities of the station. In addition to phone taps, over time the station established six separate photo safe houses for ongoing surveillance of the Russian and Cuban embassies.

Winston Scott became station chief in 1956 and the station grew dramatically; in 1960 Cuba had become the stations primary intelligence target, taking priority over the Russians. By January of 1963 four secretaries had been added to support the technical collections against both the Soviet and Cuban embassies. Station activities concentrated on recruitment of Cuban embassy staff, placing taps on all lines and assigning case officers to handle informants and penetration agents. Eventually the Mexico City station came to support some 200 indigenous agents. By 1964 the station had 50 agents working specifically on Cuba as a target.

Initially the station had formed an extensive double agent network targeting the Soviets and Cubans. The doubles were especially useful in identification of individuals working in and visiting the embassies but produced little concrete foreign intelligence. Because of that the stations efforts eventually switched recruiting "access" agents who had social or business contacts with the embassies. These individuals produced much more substantive intelligence. By 1966 the double agent effort was totally terminated.

In 1963, when Lee Oswald appeared in Mexico City, CIA station activities included:

LIKAYAK – access to international passenger lists, air shipments, spot photography of travellers, a mobile photo truck, camera installations at the airport and apparently some access government files and mail relating to international travel.

LIFIRE – a travel monitoring operation with focus on all travel to and from

FIFTEEN | WHY WE DON'T KNOW

Cuba; the Cubans had been found to be shipping arms to Latin America through Mexico and also sending cash through Mexico City to support arms buys and transhipment to other Latin American countries.
LIFEAT and **LIENVOV** – extensive telephone taps of the Russian and Cuban embassies.
LIEMBRACE – a physical surveillance capability using multiple teams.

Photographic embassy surveillance – the Soviet and Cuban embassies were constantly monitored with photo surveillance from six different photo safe houses. The camera monitoring the door to the Cuban embassy was also equipped with a circuit that allowed audio monitoring of visitors. The camera and audio circuit was activated as people neared the door.

A comprehensive study of Oswald's visit to Mexico City is far beyond this work; instead we will focus on the contacts and telephone calls which seem to be the source of the "rumours" out of Mexico City, described by President Johnson as having the potential of inciting an atomic exchange, leaving 40 million Americans dead. As we will see, there were no such "rumours", instead there were certain very concrete incidents – and those incidents seem to have been quickly determined "not" to have pointed at Oswald being an agent of either the Russians or Cubans - but rather to something entirely different than the fear that Johnson continued to use as leverage.

Lee Oswald arrived in Mexico City at 10 am on September 27, 1963. By around 11 am he was at the Cuban embassy requesting a transit visa to the Soviet Union. He presented Sylvia Duran with several documents including Fair Play for Cuba materials and reportedly a fake Communist Party USA card. However, Oswald carried no personal endorsement from either the FPCC or CPUSA (which did have an arrangement with Cuba to allow members to immediately get visas). He also had no personal photo, required for all visa applications (a fact known to Oswald who had routinely obtained visas for international travel on prior occasions). Oswald was informed that he must have a photo but more importantly that he would have to have a Soviet endorsement for transit travel.

Oswald responded by going to the Russian embassy, where he met with both embassy officers Kostikov and Nechiporenko. Both men were known to US. Intelligence as being probable Soviet intelligence officers (as was true of virtually all male staff of the embassy) and at the time the FBI was running a double agent against Kostikov. The agent (code name "tumbleweed") had been doubled in Europe, had moved to the United States and was providing information to the FBI in regard to his contacts with Kostikov. He had already made at least one trip to Mexico City to meet with Kostikov and discuss assignments, reportedly including the collection of information for potential sabotage activities in the United States. At the Russian embassy, Oswald made an emotional plea for a transit visa, stating that he had come to Mexico because he was afraid the FBI would arrest him for further contacts with the Russian embassy in Washington. The Russians advised him that they could give him an application form for the visa but that it would still have to go to Washington and would take months for action. Oswald did not accept their offer and neither took nor completed a request form while at the embassy on that Friday afternoon.[13]

Oswald then returned to the Cuban embassy and lied to Sylvia Duran, telling her there was no issue with his Russian visa application. Duran was sceptical as she was well aware of both Russian and Cuban visa protocols; she immediately called the Russian embassy. The call was tapped and taped by the Mexico City CIA station system and the existing transcript reveals that the Russians asked Duran for her name and number and called back shortly, to tell her they could not give him an approval in anything less than four or five months.. Duran mentioned that the applicant (Oswald was not named in the call by either party) had hoped to wait in Cuba for the Russian approval but since he knew nobody in Cuba they could not give him a transit visa. At that point, the afternoon of his first day in Mexico City, it is clear that Oswald's luck had already run out. Indeed Oswald also apparently realized it; reportedly he became excited and quarrelled with one of the senior Cuban embassy staff members.

Oswald never returned to the Cuban embassy after his first day in Mexico City.

Professor Newman notes in his analysis that Oswald's name was not mentioned in the Friday telephone call, so at this point there was no information available to the CIA staff which would have triggered an intelligence response specifically to Oswald. In addition, the call and the overall visit would have, at that point, sounded rather routine.

However, what occurred next was a good deal more interesting. The following day, September 28, 1963, was a Saturday and both the Russian and Cuban embassies were routinely closed on the weekends. But when Russian counsel Nechiporenko arrived at the embassy to play a regular Saturday volleyball game, Oswald was outside waiting. Again he became highly emotional, reportedly even stating that the FBI might kill him if the Russians would not help. This made no impression on the Russians and they simply offered him another chance to complete an application which they would send to Washington for him. Again, he refused.[14]

Matters got even stranger within an hour of Oswald's departure from the Russian embassy. At that point the phone tap system recorded a call, apparently from the Cuban embassy to the Russian embassy. The transcript of that call still exists and reveals a rambling dialog, in which both a female and male spoke to the Russians, the man asking the status of his application (which we now know that Oswald did not actually make, not even accepting a form) and the woman clearly represented herself as a Cuban embassy staff member. During the call, the male mentioned Kostikov by name and remarked that he had not supplied

FIFTEEN | WHY WE DON'T KNOW

his address while with the Russians because he did not know it, the Cubans had that information. Such a remark would seem meaningless unless it was interpreted that Oswald was being housed by the Cubans or they were in some fashion taking special care of him.

In *Oswald and the CIA*, Newman presents a strong case that both the male and the female callers in the dialog were impersonators (Duran denied making the call and indeed she would not have been at the Cuban embassy as it was closed). This is corroborated by the fact that the CIA station staff translators, both very familiar with Duran as the desk person at the Cuban embassy, were unable to identity the woman in this call. The translator report also notes that the male caller spoke very poor, broken Russian yet very good Spanish; of course Oswald's Russian was good, far better than any minimal Spanish he might have picked up.

Newman also points out that this call shows little evidence of being made with knowledge of what either Duran or Oswald had discussed previously. The woman makes no reference to Duran's earlier conversation with the Russian embassy and puts the man on directly with the Russians. The man stated that when he was at the Russian embassy he could not give them an address, because he had to get it from the Cubans. He told them he now has it and agreed to go to the Russian embassy and give it to them (which did not happen). Clearly the call served to register Oswald's name and could be interpreted to imply some special relationship with the Cubans. Newman posits the call is made by someone who had Oswald under surveillance but who was not in direct contact with him.[15]

A second call, which appears to have been another impersonation, was made on October 1 (Tuesday). In that call, Oswald's name was mentioned and recorded. That was the key that the translators had been advised to watch for and indicates the point at which "Oswald" was identified as the person visiting both the Russian and Cuban embassies. Still, it would be several days, until October 9, until Mexico City officially transmitted a cable to CIA headquarters on the Oswald/Russian contact, and even then the cable only described Oswald's contact with the Russian embassy and specifically with Kostikov. The cable mentioned telephone calls and intercepts but provided no further information; at the same time a photograph of an individual who had visited the Russian embassy was sent to headquarters (the individual was not identified as Oswald in the message and in fact was not Oswald). Mexico City requested a current photograph of Oswald but was not actually sent one until after November 22.[16]

In addition to the mystery of the Saturday and Tuesday "impersonation" calls, there is also the question of at least one other Oswald "impersonation" call to the Russian embassy. One of the Mexico City staff translators, Mrs. Tarasof, specifically described another lengthy call, stating that the caller specifically identified himself as Lee Oswald; spoke only English and that Oswald asked for

JFK | ECHOES FROM ELM STREET
A SEARCH FOR HISTORICAL ACCURACY ON THE
ASSASSINATION OF PRESIDENT JOHN F. KENNEDY

financial aid from the Soviets. He stated he had already asked the Cubans for financial aid (it appears that requests for financial aid and offers of information in exchange may have been made only in the recorded telephone calls, not by Oswald in person. Years after the assassination, both David Phillips (head of the CIA's embassy spy operations in Mexico City) and Thomas Kelly of the FBI (which apparently had its own access to the phone taps in Mexico City) both commented that Oswald had offered money and requested assistance in return from both the Cubans and Russians.

Mr. Tarasof, the other CIA translator, also stated that the translators had been superficially asked to try and identify the man who was contacting the Russians, that it was a "hot" topic at the Mexico City station as it had to do with a known defector. He also commented that the "missing" conversation/tape was designated as "Urgent" for priority handling – suggesting the call was an immediate operational priority within the Mexico City station and that Oswald had definitely been a person of interest to the CIA while he was in Mexico City.

On the afternoon of the President's assassination, a check of either the either the headquarters FBI or CIA files on Lee Oswald would have revealed his recent travel to Mexico City and his contact with an Russian embassy officer known to be Soviet intelligence, suspected of being KGB and known to be running agents into the United States. Certainly that information would have been explosive. In Mexico City, a quick scan of the transcripts of purported Oswald telephone calls would have confirmed contact with Kostikov and brought up suggestive information about his relationship with both the Russians and Cubans. Certainly such information should have been immediately transmitted to the CIA Director and to the FBI Director; there is no record that such communications occurred. What is recorded is a host of much lower level communications, communications reflecting considerable confusion and total disconnects about what information (tapes, transcripts, photos) was actually still available. Whether this reflects actual confusion or a developing obfuscation on the part of the CIA is a key question. Another is to what extent any of the information was being shared with President Johnson by the CIA.

What is clear, however, is that the FBI and Director Hoover were in communication with Johnson about events in Mexico City. It is clear that tapes of at least some of the telephone calls were reviewed by FBI agents and compared with Oswald's voice. Hoover and one other senior FBI officer stated that had occurred early on Saturday morning. And later that morning, President Johnson called Director Hoover and asked him for an update on the Mexico City situation. It appears that Hoover and Johnson had discussed events in Mexico City at some earlier and unrecorded point.

We know from the record that on Saturday morning, at which time Hoover told Johnson that *the early morning FBI voice comparisons had revealed that it was not Lee Oswald on the telephone calls to the Russians*, rather it was some

FIFTEEN | WHY WE DON'T KNOW

unknown party – in fact *Hoover told Johnson explicitly that Oswald had been impersonated in Mexico City.*

If Oswald had been impersonated in contacts with the Russians (with a suspected KGB agent and known spy handler) and with the Cubans, the impersonations would not have implicated the Russians or Cubans. Instead, it would have raised major questions about the motives of "parties unknown". And those parties would have to have been very much aware of current intelligence information as well as in the technical intelligence conducted against both the Russians and Cubans in Mexico City. That suspicion would have been equally explosive, suggesting not that Oswald had been manipulated by the Russians or Cubans (as might well have been initially suspected Friday evening) but in something perhaps even more suspicions, even more sinister. Fear of a Communist conspiracy would be replaced by fear of something very different. What seems most amazing, given the implication, is that according to the existing transcript, President Johnson seems to have made no comment at all in regard to the news about Oswald being impersonated!

As it turns out, it may well be that we were never intended to know of the impersonation, that it had been revealed by Hoover to Johnson and that Johnson had apparently shown no interest. Researcher Rex Bradford has given detailed study to both the existing transcript of the Hoover/Johnson call and the tape which still exists. In studying the tape as compared to the transcript, it became apparent that the tape that should have contained the conversation is now blank. After considerable further research and dialog with the Johnson Library, he received confirmation that the tape had been intentionally erased by parties unknown. Apparently either those parties were unaware of the transcript or were unable to get to it. The full story of Bradford's research and his efforts to clarify the issue (along with an official confirmation from the Johnson library that that a section of the tape related to the Hoover call had been intentionally erased) are available on the Mary Ferrell web site at http://www.maryferrell.org/mffweb/archive/viewer/showDoc.do?mode=searchResult&docId=361

Two other examples of tape censorship related to the assassination are known and may be related. The airborne communications from Air Force One, during its flight back from Dallas, was tape recorded. William Manchester learned of that and requested the tape for historical reference in his book on the events of the assassination. That request was initially denied by President Johnson, but after considerable time Manchester was provided with an "edited" version of the recordings. Studies by the Assassination Records Review Board, comparing open Air Force One communications channels (as described by the actual communications personnel on the plane) versus the Air Force One transcript now available, suggests that the tape was heavily edited and that possibly hours of transmissions may not be in the existing transcript.

The third instance involves the CIA telephone tap tapes from Mexico City. A close study of CIA communications between Mexico City and Headquarters during the 48 hours after the assassination suggests that initially there was no doubt that Oswald related tapes and transcripts were still available in Mexico City. However, by the end of the weekend the memoranda suggest (apparently by some unspoken agreement) both locations were speaking of the tape recordings as if they no longer existed. Eventually the FBI would take the same position, totally repudiating Director Hoover's early remarks on the tapes and voice comparisons.

Yet at least two Warren Commission staff members not only knew that the tapes had not been erased but actually listened to at least portions of them months after the CIA and FBI both moved to the official position that the tapes had been erased prior to the assassination. David Slawson and William Coleman have described listening to such tapes during their trip to Mexico City in April of 1964. Slawson and Coleman confirmed that to both authors Peter Dale Scott and Anthony Summers.[17]

The existence of the tapes was also reportedly confirmed "off the record" to the Assassinations Records Review Board and noted in the testimony of Anne Goodpasture, of the Mexico City staff and author of the official CIA Mexico City station history. The following is an excerpt of the relevant portion of Goodpasture's ARRB testimony:

Gunn. *I have spoken with two Warren Commission staff members who went to Mexico City and who both told me that they heard the tape after the assassination obviously. Do you have any knowledge of information regarding tapes that may have been played to those Warren Commission staff members?*
Goodpasture. *No. It may have been a tape that Win Scott had squirreled away in his safe.*[18]

Yet, although the Warren Commission staff members knew of the tapes existence, there is no indication that they performed the same voice comparison that the FBI had the evening of the assassination - or that the knowledge of the tapes was conveyed other than to Chief Counsel J. Lee Rankin. In fact there is no indication that the Warren Commission was aware of the Hoover/Johnson call or the FBI's initial finding that Oswald had been impersonated in Mexico City, obviously a matter that would have been a vital concern in any comprehensive investigation.

Other authors have argued that the impersonation calls and their suggestive association of Oswald with a known KGB agent served as a "poison pill" which almost immediately triggered fears of a Communist conspiracy and suppression of an open investigation. Initially this may well have been the case; however, as soon as the transcripts were studied and especially given

FIFTEEN | WHY WE DON'T KNOW

voice comparisons, it would have become clear (certainly within 24 hours) that Oswald had been impersonated, in a rather clumsy fashion. The conversation in the second call, and especially in the now missing third call, would have clearly shown that some third party was involved, that the Russians and Cubans were not actually associated in a suspicions fashion with Oswald. And we know that the FBI did just that, advising Johnson of the impersonations (and likely much more) on Saturday morning following the assassination. A conversation so explosive the presidential tape of the conversation actually had to be erased – a "true smoking gun" indicating a cover up of some sort. Beyond that both the FBI and CIA were forced into a position of stating that all the Mexico City tapes had been erased, an untruth known even to Warren Commission staff members.

All of which seems to leave us with only two options. The first is that the impersonation calls were official, CIA conducted "pretext" probes of the Russians – perfectly reasonable for intelligence purposes and with precedent.[19]

It is also possible that the Mexico City station conducted a "sting" on the Soviets based on Oswald's visit, not realizing that Oswald was himself being used in a much more elaborate CIA intelligence operation, unknown and compartmentalized from the Mexico City station staff.

The second option is that the calls were indeed made by "parties unknown" but parties with a very good knowledge of current intelligence (such as the importance of Kostikov and the "tumbleweed" operation), a working knowledge of Oswald's own background and recent associations and also inside knowledge of the technical intelligence capabilities of the Mexico City station.

Given the sensitivity of either option, it is likely that matters were discussed only verbally and that even "suggestive" tapes or notes were eliminated after the fact. We do know that President Johnson continued to use the leverage of Mexico City and possible Russian and/or Cuban sponsorship as leverage in driving the cover up, long it should have become a non-issue. Was it because to do anything else would have exposed CIA operations in Mexico City (in particular operations involving prior knowledge or association with Lee Oswald himself) or because, at the highest levels, there was suspicion of a conspiracy against the President involving US intelligence offices?

At present we simply have no answers for these questions. Still, what we have learned is that an open ended investigation of the Kennedy assassination was blocked and constrained beginning as early as the evening of the murder. We know that was ostensibly done over issues of international relations and national security. And we know that the impersonation of Lee Oswald, and his "suspicious" contact with the Russians and Cubans should have been quickly resolved with the tapes, photographs and reports available from Mexico City. That would have revealed that there had been no Russian or Cuban manipulation of Lee Oswald. In short, what we find indicates a US national security issue,

JFK | ECHOES FROM ELM STREET
A SEARCH FOR HISTORICAL ACCURACY ON THE
ASSASSINATION OF PRESIDENT JOHN F. KENNEDY

one significant enough to tightly constrain the murder investigation and ensure that Lee Oswald was presented as a "lone nut".

So, at last, we at least know "why we don't know" ....

Endnotes

[1] Dr. Perry's television interview was broadcast live and the Warren Commission requested a copy for reference. The Secret Service informed them that the footage could not be located; decades later the Assassination Records Review. Board determined that actually the Perry interview had been obtained by the Secret Service and at the time of the Warren Commission's request remained was held in the office of Secret Service Chief Rowley. This other instances of evidence suppression are detailed in the five volume work of Douglas Horne, *Inside the Assassinations Records Review Board*, 2009. The tape incident is detailed on p. 646).

[2] The lists from the parking lot and the Texas Theatre disappeared from the DPD records as did the late night polygraph interview with the young man who had driven Lee Oswald to work that morning.

[3] Oxford, Edward, Destiny in Dallas, *American History Illustrated*, November 1988; also Warren Commission Volume 5, p. 259.

[4] Readers are referred to Horne's detailed work, *Inside the Assassinations Records Review Board, 2009* for detailed descriptions of the activities of all the medical professionals at the Bethesda autopsy. For corroboration, the observations of the FBI agents viewing and reporting on the autopsy are contained in William Law's *In the Eye of History: Disclosures in the JFK Assassination Medical Evidence*, 2005.

[5] A chart detailing the various stages of the evolving autopsy report is provided on page 873 of *Inside the Assassinations Records Review Board*, Douglas Horne, 2009.

[6] *The Man Who Knew Too Much*, Dick Russell, 2003, pp. 314-315.

[7] The author wishes to thank William Kelly who made available a complete transcript of the existing Air Force One tapes for detailed study.

[8] Jack Russell Smith, *The Unknown CIA; My Three Decades with the Agency*, 1989, p. 163.

[9] Other authors have done an excellent job of enumerating the formation, working process and the extent to which the Warren Commission (and the FBI) was involved in preparing a report for the President which focused strictly on Lee Harvey Oswald. Readers are referred to the most comprehensive work on that subject, *Breach of Trust: How the Warren Commission Failed the Nation and Why*, Gerald McKnight, 2009.

[10] FBI Memorandum of November 24, 1963, Tolson to Belmont, Subject: Lee Harvey Oswald Assaulting a Government Officer, FBI 105-82555, Oswald HQ file section 3:13. Available online at www.maryferrell.com.

[11] Readers without access to Newman's book are referred to his JFK Lancer November in Dallas presentation available at JFK Lancer. Materials from Professor Newman's presentation were prepared for posting by Joseph Backes:
http://www.jfklancer.com/backes/newman/newman_1a.html.

[12] Background information on the Mexico City station is taken from *Our Man In Mexico City; Winston Scott and the Hidden History of the CIA*, Jefferson Morley, 2008 and the official CIA station history prepared by Anne Goodpasture, available at www.maryferrell.com.

[13] Since Oswald had written the Russian US embassy early in 1963, and received a reply at that time, with no related FBI contacts for follow up; his remarks – like many of his other statements and activities – are extremely inconsistent. His actual lack of fear of the FBI can be seen in his request to talk to an FBI agent after his arrest during a street protest in New Orleans that summer.

[14] As of Saturday morning when he left the Russian embassy, defeated in his quest, there should have been some ten photos of Oswald entering and leaving the two embassies; later the CIA would go on record as claiming there were none. That claim has proven to be highly questionable.

[15] Sylvia Duran denied both a Saturday visit by Oswald or making a telephone call with him; Nechiporenko denied that the call could have even been received at the Russian embassy since their switchboard closed on Saturday. Newman suggests that may well be true since the supposed purported Russian on the call could easily have just asked "Oswald" for his address while on the telephone call. It is indeed

FIFTEEN | WHY WE DON'T KNOW

possible that the entire call was made by unknown parties.

[16.] On October 10, CIA headquarters sent a cable to FBI, State and Navy describing the Kostikov contact and incorrectly describing the individual (Oswald) as the man pictured in the photo. It identified the man as "Lee Henry Oswald" Newman points out that headquarters was very much aware that information in that cable was incorrect and incomplete and goes into extensive detail in evaluating this as suggestive of another intelligence operation going on around Lee Oswald.

[17.] Peter Dale Scott, *Deep Politics II*, p. 12 and Anthony Summers, *Not in Your Lifetime*, p. 277.

[18.] Goodpasture ARRB testimony, 12-15-1999, p. 147 available on the Mary Ferrell web site: Anne Goodpasture ARRB testimony of 12-15-1995, p.147.

[19.] Earlier in 1963 a caller to the Cuban embassy had offered information in exchange for money; his call had been taped and his identity determined using CIA assets inside the Cuban embassy. Pretext calls and visits were made with him and the resulted in his being jailed back in the United States. This incident involved Eldon Henson and details can be found in a 7/20/73 CIA memo on Eldon Henson and the Cuban Embassy, RIF: 104-10132-10243). The document is available online at the Marry Ferrell site http://www.maryferrell.org/mffweb/archive/viewer/showDoc.do?docId=49131&relPageId=2c

JFK | Echoes From Elm Street
A Search for Historical Accuracy on the
Assassination of President John F. Kennedy

Sixteen
JFK – Relevant Today?
Barry Keane

Plaque commemorating JFK's speech at the American University Washington DC, June 10th 1963.
Photo by Barry Keane

JFK | ECHOES FROM ELM STREET
A SEARCH FOR HISTORICAL ACCURACY ON THE ASSASSINATION OF PRESIDENT JOHN F. KENNEDY

A few days before John F. Kennedy took office his predecessor President Eisenhower, in his farewell address warned the nation of the huge and unwarranted influence on American society by what he described as the Military Industrial Complex. Kennedy when President was to come face to face with this monolithic entity, to his detriment.

It is true of course that major traumatic events always change history, whether it is the death of a world leader or a world war resulting in the death of millions. For many people who remember JFK's assassination it will always be a moment captured like a time capsule. November 22nd 1963, a day to study, a death to be mourned. But it happened 50 years ago, in the last century, two generations have been born since. Surely it should now be confined to the history books, we cannot change what occurred. So why is that event relevant today?

Should we be concerned now, after so many years have passed? What possible relevance does it have to the world we live in today? Of course we will never know for sure what would have happened had President Kennedy not been killed that day, perhaps not knowing is the real tragedy of his death.

What we do know is that during his term of office, January 20th 1961 to November 22nd 1963, Kennedy made decisions that, had he lived, would have had far reaching consequences.

These are a few examples:

1. His decision to withdraw American armed forces from Vietnam by the end of 1965.[1]

2. His intention of removing Lyndon Johnson as his running mate in the 1964 Presidential election, replacing him with Governor Terry Sanford of North Carolina.[2]

3. His attempt to wrest the Federal Reserve's monopoly on the issuing of US currency.[3]

4. His vigorous endorsement of the investigation into government corruption during the 1950's regarding the Stockpiling scandal.[4]

5. His support of his brother Attorney General Robert Kennedy's clampdown on Organised Crime in the United States.

Had Kennedy lived, his ending of America's involvement in Vietnam, in my opinion, would have changed the United States' role as the world's policeman. It certainly would have affected the rest of the world's attitude towards American Imperialism.

Sixteen | JFK – Relevant Today?

On June 4th 1963 Kennedy issued Executive Order 11110,[5] which was designed to strip the Federal Reserve Bank of its power to loan money, with interest, to the United States Federal Government. With this order, President Kennedy declared that the privately owned Federal Reserve Bank would soon be out of business.

Dropping Lyndon Johnson as his running mate in 1964 would have had serious consequences for LBJ's political future. Johnson's connection with his former aides Bobby Baker and Billy Sol Estes, and their criminal activities threatened not only his political but his personal life; possibly meaning a prison term for LBJ. Lyndon Johnson's backers in the Military Industrial Complex would have lost a powerful ally.

At his press conference on January 31st 1962,[6] JFK announced that he had ordered the US Senate to investigate financial corruption in the stockpiling of critical materials, minerals etc, which were to be utilised in the event of a national emergency. Huge amounts of this material, far more than was needed, was bought by the government at inflated prices. The surplus was then sold at a discount back to the companies, the difference going to the conspirators. On November 13th 1963 President John F. Kennedy drew attention to this investigation and made it clear that he would make this an issue in the 1964 presidential campaign.

All of these examples of Kennedy's intended actions were neutralised by his assassination. The Vietnam War was escalated during the Johnson administration. Billions of dollars was made by the arms manufacturers in the United States. Terry Sanford was denied his period in the limelight.

The Federal Reserve still has a stranglehold on the US and by extension the world's economy. No one was ever prosecuted for the billions of dollars that were corruptly acquired during the Stockpiling Scandal. In 1973, President Nixon wrote off four billion Dollars of this money effectively ending any further investigation into the matter.

After JFK's assassination Robert Kennedy's attack on the Mafia became muted due to a lack of support from the new President, Lyndon Johnson and the Director of the FBI, J. Edgar Hoover, both of whom hated Bobby Kennedy. The Mafia had a great deal to lose had JFK lived. President Kennedy's death and corrupt relationships with Hoover and LBJ secured their immediate future at least.

One further example is President Kennedy's handling of the Cuban Missile Crisis. Through his deft use of statesmanship the world was brought back from the brink of nuclear war. Despite his military advisers urging Kennedy to launch air strikes on the missile sites in Cuba, he stood firm. He understood the implications of such action, the inevitable escalation of the crisis to a point where it would become out of control. The devastating consequences were just too bitter to contemplate.

JFK | Echoes from Elm Street
A Search for Historical Accuracy on the Assassination of President John F. Kennedy

In October 1962, mankind reached a point where it very nearly destroyed itself. This was the inevitable point in human history where centuries of war and conflict would reach a decisive moment. The nations of the world now had the choice of a genuine move towards peaceful co-existence or total destruction.

An obvious choice it may seem, but Kennedy was faced with powerful opposition to his softly, softly approach. His advisers in the military saw this crisis as a golden opportunity to rid the world of the scourge of communism. To not only remove Fidel Castro's government from Cuba but also the hated Soviet system itself.

JFK's Commencement Speech at the American University on June 10th 1963[7], where he advocated a softening in America's attitude toward the Soviet Union, was I believe, too much for the Military Industrial Complex to accept. He announced a series of meetings between the Western Powers and the Soviet Union with the intention of reaching agreement on a limited Nuclear Test Ban Treaty. This was to be the first attempt since the beginning of the Nuclear Age, to begin to rid the world of these terrible weapons of mass destruction.

Points of Relevance
One important reason why Kennedy's assassination is still relevant today is that, I believe, the truth should never be negotiable; justice should never have a time limit. In fact there is no Statute of Limitations on murder in the United States.

The assassination of President Kennedy was in my opinion, one link in a chain of events which are continuing today. International terrorism chiefly aimed at the United States is, I believe, one of the main results of JFK's untimely death. In recent years highly dubious wars in Iraq and Afghanistan are examples of the continuing influence of the Military Industrial Complex in the world today. President Kennedy took on big business in 1962 when the steel companies tried to force a price rise which would have had a huge effect on inflation in the USA. He forced them to back down and cancel the increase for which they never forgave him. Fiscal integrity is sadly lacking in today's society, abuses by the discredited banking industry go unpunished if not rewarded. The ramifications of Kennedy's assassination still reverberate today.

"The History of war is written by the victors."
Winston Churchill et al

This quote is so very true of the JFK assassination. The victors wrote the history of JFK's death. The Warren Report with its Lone Assassin conclusion became the official account.

Sixteen | JFK – Relevant Today?

What is Truth?
As with all events there are three "Truths" Which I somewhat simplify as: Indisputable, Perceived and Political.

Indisputable Truth:
An event takes place.

Perceived Truth:
An event takes place with the addition of human interpretation. Doubt and confusion enter the equation.

Political Truth:
An event takes place and the facts are tailored to produce a desired explanation.

This book demonstrates that the official account is a perfect example of political truth. The manner of President Kennedy's death is an indelible stain on the history of the United States of America. The perpetrators have left that country with an appalling legacy. Distrust in government in the United States began with the fallout from the cover-up known as "The President's Commission on the Assassination of President John F. Kennedy", commonly referred to as The Warren Report. One thing is certain, had JFK not been in charge in the White House in October 1962, during the Cuban Missile Crisis, the world may have entered a new Dark Age for which mankind may not have recovered. The way that John F Kennedy handled that dangerous crisis, how he resisted the Military Industrial Complex and all of its evils, ensure that his relevance continues fifty years after his death and indeed for all time.

– Barry Keane.

Endnotes
Note Website addresses correct at time of writing.

[1] John Newman "JFK and Vietnam" (New York-Warner Books 1992) pages 319-325

[2] Evelyn Lincoln " Kennedy and Johnson"(Austin Texas-Holt, Rinehart and Winston; First Edition 1968) pages 204-205

[3] For an excellent history of the Federal Reserve ; G. Edward Griffin "The Creature from Jekyll Island: A Second Look at the Federal Reserve" (Amer Media; 5 edition 2010)

[4] For an account of his investigation of the Stockpile Scandal; Ira Jesse Hemingway " Friendly Fire on Holy Grounds: The Stockpile Conspiracy " (AuthorHouse 2005)

[5] For Text of Executive Order 11130 http://www.presidency.ucsb.edu/ws/index.php?pid=59049

[6] Press Conference Jan 31 1962 "http://www.presidency.ucsb.edu/ws/index.php?pid=8747&st=&st1=

[7] American University Speech June 1963 "http://www.jfklibrary.org/Research/Ready-Reference/JFK-Speeches/Commencement-Address-at-American-University-June-10-1963.aspx

See also:
• John F. Kennedy Library http://www.jfklibrary.org/
• The Mary Ferrell Foundation http://www.maryferrell.org/wiki/index.php/Main_Page is an excellent source of information on The Assassination of President Kennedy.

JFK | ECHOES FROM ELM STREET
A SEARCH FOR HISTORICAL ACCURACY ON THE
ASSASSINATION OF PRESIDENT JOHN F. KENNEDY

INDEX

1026 North Beckley Avenue 46, 49-52, 265
81 minutes 47

ABC (News) 42, 124
ABC of Trauma 74-75
Abrasion Collar 189, 366
Adamcik, John 50
Adams, Perry 11, (28 n 6,) (488 n 15), (489 n 85)
Adams, Victoria 23-26, 258-259
Admission Notes 67
Adrenal Glands 72, 360
Aguilar, Dr Gary L. (97 n 10), 190, (221 n 38)
Air Force One 305-307, 503, 511, (514 n 7)
Aldrin, 'Buzz' 494
Alexander, Bill (William) 313, 316, 395
Allied Film Laboratory, Chicago 451
Alvarez, Luis 111-112, (167 n 224)
American University Commencement Address 2, 517, 520, (521 n 7)
Andrews, James 48, 239
Andrews Air Force Base, Washington 459
Anglin, Bill 237
Angleton, James Jesus 273, 334
Apollo Moon Landing 494
Archduke Franz Ferdinand 494-495
Armed Forces Institute of Pathology 215, 345-346 353,379
Armstrong, John 6, 46, 269, 266, (266 n 11), (267 nn 16,17 & 19), 287, 295, 298, 318, 326-327, 333, 340, (341 n 17)
Armstrong, Neil 494
Aschkenasy, Ernest 106-109, 111-113, 125, 131, 139, (163 n 88), (166 n 189), (167 n 243)

JFK | ECHOES FROM ELM STREET
A SEARCH FOR HISTORICAL ACCURACY ON THE
ASSASSINATION OF PRESIDENT JOHN F. KENNEDY

Assassination Records Review Board (ARRB) 56, 78, (97 n 36), (98 nn 37 & 41), 149, (221 n 36), 347, 351, 353, 355, 366, 373, (380 nn 2, 4, 10, 12, 13, 16, & 22-26), (381 nn 30, 58, 65, 67, & 68), (382 nn 74, 77, & 87), 447-449, 451, 461, 462-463, (486 n 25), (487 nn 34, 42, & 49), (490 nn 118, 121-124, 127, 130, & 132), (491 nn 143, 145 & 166), 502, 512, (515 n 18)
Austin's Barbecue 235-236
Autopsy Photos 57-59, 69, 81-82, 84-86, 362, 380
Autopsy Report 8, 57, 65, 71-73, 75-78, 80, 82, 91, (98 n 44), 177-179, 189, (221 n 32,33 & 45), 345-382, 502, (514 n 5)

Baker, Bobby 3, 519
Baker, Marrion L. 13, 23, 43
Ball, George (342 n 24)
Ball, Joseph 244-245, 249, 262
Banister, W. Guy 301-303, (341 n 21)
Barnes, Dr Joseph K. 374
Barber, Stephen 112, 122, 127-128, 132, 148, 151, (163 n 88), (166 n 190), 201
Barger, James E. 106-108, 111, 113-114, 127, 131, 135, 138-139, 146-48, 152-154, 158-159, (162 n 32),(163 nn 68, 80, 84, & 88), (166 nn 190 & 200), (167 n 239), (170 nn 315, 321 & 322), (171 nn 356 & 390)
Barrett, Robert M. 396, 481, (485 n 1), (490 n 103)
Bartholomew, Richard 482, 484, (487 n 49)
Batchelor, Charles 118, 143-144
Baxter, Dr Charles 95, 357-358
Bay of Pigs 2, 223, 230, 243, 390
Beilharz, Leslie 115-117
Belin, David W. 23, 25-27, 90, 209, 216, 219, 243-244, 250-251, 261, 263-264
Bell & Howell 414pd Camera 443, 446, (485 n 9 & 11), (486 n 14)
Bell, Audrey N. (97 n 9), 182, 185
Belmont, Alan 313-314, 342, 505, (514 n 10)
Benavides, Domingo 240, 242, 250-252, 254, 259-261
"Best Evidence" 77-78, (97 n 20), 350, (380 nn 21, & 70), (383 n 88), 447
Bethesda 62, 64-65, 69-70, 72 76-79, 81, 86, 156, 177, 202, 215, 278, 306, 345-348, 354, 375, 379, (381 n 38), 505, (514 n 4)
Bennett, SSA Glenn 189, (221 n 30)
Bentley, Paul 117
Bernier, Brenda (161 nn 23 & 24), (171 n 378)
Bevelling 366-367, 370-371
Billings, Richard N. (162 n 30), (166 n 202), (168 n 271), (169 nn 295 & 303), (170 n 351), (171 n 353)
Blair, Richard 463

Index

Blakemore, Bill (171 n 377)
Blakey, G. Robert 106, 119, 130, 144-146, 152,) 162 n 30), (163 n 81), (166 n 202), (168 n 271), (169 nn 295 & 303), (170 n 351), (171 nn 353, 357, & 358), 397, 413
Bledsoe, Mary 280
Bolden, Abraham 228, (232 nn 10 & 11)
Bolt, Beranek and Newman (BBN) 104-107, 109, 111-112, 114, 127, 135, 138-139, 145-146, 152-154, 158-159, 162, (167 n 239), (170 nn 315, 318, 322 & 323), (171 n 363), (172 n 394)
Bond, Wilma 124, (156 n 161)
Bonner, Judy 144, (169 n 299)
Bookhout, James W. 481, 483
Booth, John Wilkes 308, 374-375, 495, 499
Boswell, Dr J. Thornton 188, 208, 215, 345-349, 351, 353, 362, 367, 376-377, 502
Bowers, Lee 21, 44, 45
Bowles, James C. 115-119, 121, 123-124, 127-128, 139, 141-143, 145, 147-151, 154-155, (161 n 145, 152, 155, 157, 166 & 167) (166 n 179, 190, 195, 196, & 197) (167 n 221) (168 n 284, 285, 287 & 310) (170 n 345) (171 n 373)
Bowley, Temple Ford 251, 256
Brain 15, 30, 42, 66, 68-69, 74, 348-349, 351, 354-355, 360, 362, 365, 367-369, 377, 379
Braden, Jim (Also Brading, Eugene Hale) 45, 72
Braniff Airlines 483
Braniff, Matthew (489 n 84)
Brehm, Charles 30, 60
Brennan, Howard 46
Brewer, E.D. 130
Brewer, Johnny Calvin 47-48
Bridger, Mark 1, 41, 484
Bringuier, Carlos 301
Bronson, Charles (486 n 15)
Brown, Charles 396, 484
Brown, Earle 12, 133
Brown, Walt 59, 176, 204, (220 n 5), (222 n 66)
Brugioni, Dino 460-464, 482
Bugliosi, Vincent 9, 116-117, 119, (164 n 108), (165 n 146), 175, (220 n 2) 287, 306, 309-310, 313-314, 328, 330-331, 335-337, (342 nn 25,30 & 31), 353, 394, 399, 417-418, 421-422, 424, 437, 474, 480, 483, (485 n 11), (488 n 54), (492 n 169)
Buhk, Marvin 49
Bullet marks 38

Buncombe, Andrew (171 n 377)
Burkley, Admiral George G. 188, 306, 502
Burnham, Greg 455-456, (489 nn 93, 94, 95 & 96)
Buttimer, Anne 149

Cabell, Earl (Mayor of Dallas) 11-12
Callaway, Ted 242, 252, 254, 256
Calvin Laboratories, Kansas 475-476
Cancellare, Frank 124, 127
Carousel Club 205, 231, 383, 385, 388, 395, 400, 402, 432, 434
Carr, Richard Randolph 26, 33, (39 n 25)
Carr, Waggoner (Attorney General of Texas) 275, 502
Carrico, Dr Charles J. 63-64, 67-68, 75
Carter, Cliff 502
"Case Closed" 62, (97 nn 11, 19, 21, 24 & 33), 430, 437, (500 n 2)
Castro, Fidel 2, 227, 230, 265, 301, 312, 389-392, 401, 506, 520
Cat Scan 190
CE387 188, (221 nn 33 & 45), (381 nn 34, 41, & 52), (382 n 73)
CE388 (98 n 48), 348
CE399 (See Magic and Single Bullet Theory) 93-96, 178-180, 184-188, 192-193, 195, 197-199, 202, 206-207, 210-212, 214, (220 n 7), (222 nn 58 & 59), 349
CE567 & CE569 (99 n 84), 199
CE679 196-197, 201, 203, 211
CE680 196, 211
CE842 180-181, 184-187
Cerebellar Tissue 66-69
Cerebellum 66-69, 367
Cerebral Tissue 66
Cerebrum 66-68, 367
Chamberlain, Phil 447, 463-464, (487 nn 42 & 44)
Chambers, G. Paul 135, (167 n 223)
Chaney, James 13, 42
Chapman, Mark 499
Chest Wound 93, 191-194, 218, 358
Chicago Police 228
Chicago Public Library 452, (488 n 76)
Chino 223
Churchill, Winston 520
CIA (Central Intelligence Agency) 6, 36, 229-230, 265-266, (266 n 11) 273, 276-277, 301-302, 323, 330, 333-334, 336, 340, (341 nn 17, 18 & 20), (342 n 32), 387, 389-393, 436, 460-461, 464, 475, 482, (486 n 16), 503-506, 508-

INDEX

509, 513, (514 nn 8, 12 & 14), (515 nn 16 & 19)
Clark Panel Report 190, (221 nn 36 & 38), (381 n 58)
"Classical Mistakes in Forensic Pathology" 366, (382 n 85)
Clark, Dr Kemp 69, 75
Clay Shaw 236
Clay Shaw Trial 33, 79, (166 n 202), (221 nn 24 & 26)
Clemons, Acquilla 257-258
Colburn Photo Laboratory, Chicago 476
Collapsed Lung 356-357
Combs, Michelle (487 n 49)
Commission Document -326 90
Commission Document- 362a 355
Commission Document- 381 91
Connally, Idanell Brill "Nellie" 30, 91, 204, 209, 213, 219
Connally, Governor John Bowden 5, 1, 18, 29-31, 33-34, 43, 55-57, 60-61, 73, 87-96, (98 n 61), 173-175, 177-188, 190-194, 198-199, 202-214, 216-217, 219-220, (221 n 10 & 11), 263-264, 270-271, 349, 497-499
Conrad, I.W. 484 n 10), (491 n 183)
Conway, Debra 484
Cook, Joe 451, (488 n 77)
Cooper, John Sherman (US Senator) (98 n 63), 195, 204
Cornett, Anjii (171 n 376)
Cornwell, Gary 114, 119, 132, 146, (166 n 210)
Costella, John P. 13, 19, 458, 474, 490 n 107)
Couch, Malcolm 124-126, (165 n 161)
Courson, Officer James W. 12, 109, 117, 123-126, 134, (166 nn 177, 178, 180 & 181)
Craig, Roger 26-27, 44, 46, (53 n 24), 250
Cranor, Milicent 190, (221 n 37)
Crouch, Mark 59
Cuban Missile Crisis 2, 519, 521
Cubbage, Roger 139, 155, (168 nn 248 & 249), (171 nn 369 & 372)
Cunningham, E.L. 49-50
Cunningham, Kathy 190, (221 n 38)
Curry, Chief Jesse E. 13-15, (28 n 7), 42, 44, 51, 112, 114-115, 121-123, 126, 133-135, 141-145, 152, 154, (167 n 220), (168 n 277), 175, 186, 224, 2425, 263-264, 307-309, 311, 314-316, 388, 401, 409, 428, 502
Curtain Rods 6, 7, (27 n 3), 230
Cutler, Robert B. 121, 127, (165 n 161), (166 nn 190, 194, 199 & 200)
Cutting Corporation, The 156, (171 n 376)
Czolgosz, Leon 499

JFK | ECHOES FROM ELM STREET
A SEARCH FOR HISTORICAL ACCURACY ON THE
ASSASSINATION OF PRESIDENT JOHN F. KENNEDY

Dale, Bobby Joe 12, 116
Dallas County Records Building 37-38
Dallas Police Department (DPD) 21, 30, 36, 42, 52, 103, 105, 109, 138-139, 142, 146-147, 156, (170 n 342), 186, 233-235, 237, 241, 263, (266 n 2), 326, 383, 386, 388-389, 396, 398-400, 402-411, 414-414, 420-421, 424-427, 429-430, 433, 435-436
Dallas Trade Mart 116-119
Dal-Tex Building 33, 36-38, 45-46, 441, 450
Davis, Barbara 242, 256, 260
Davis, Virginia 242, 256-257, 259
Davis Thomas Eli 390-391
Day, Lt J.C. 311
De Morenschildt, George 271, 282, 319-320, 322, (340 n 1)
De Valk, Mark 442, (485 n 4)
Dealey Plaza 6-7, 9-12, 19-20, 26, 29, 31-32, 34-36, 38, (39 n 28), 42-43, 45-46, 52, (53 n 30), 60, 87, 95, 105-107, 115, 121, 125, 127-128, 130, 132-133, 135, 144, 146, 149, 158, 160-161, (162 n 49), 165, 178, 188, 193, 207, 209, 233, 238, 140-241, 250, 264-265, 269, 271-272, 279, 399. 436, 444-445, 447, 456, 458, 467, 469, 471, 479, 483, 496, 498, 500-501
Dealey Plaza UK (DPUK) 5, 133, 207, 241, 245, (267 n 25) 441-442, (485 n 4)
Dealey Plaza Echo (53 nn 30 & 32), (220 n 8), (222 n 72), 269, 479, (485 nn 4 & 5)
Decker, James E. ('Bill') 26-27, 42, 112-113, 134-135, 160, (167 n 222)
Dehaeseleer, Marcel (486 n 11)
Dellarosa, Rich 454
Deloach, Cartha 475
Dictabelt (Also Belts) 30, 36, 103-104, 107-108, 113, 135-149, 151-153, 155-160, 161 n22), (162 n29), (170 n 343), (171 n 359), (172 n 382)
Transcripts,
    Bowles Transcript – CE 705 142, (168 n 274)
    FBI Transcript – CE 1974 136,147, (167 nn 227 & 231), (171 nn 364, 340)
    Henslee (DPD) Transcript – Sawyer Exhibit B 141, 142, (168 nn 268, 270)
Dictaphone 103, 137, 139, 142, 156-157
DiEugenio, James 78
Dillard, Tom 33
Dolce, Dr Joseph 209-210, 219-220
Donnelley, R.R. & Sons, Calumet Printing Plant, Chicago 452, (488 n 77)
Donovan, John E. 326-329, 339, (343 n 39 & 44)
Dorman, Mrs. Elsie 121, 123-126, (165 nn 161 & 175)
Dox, Ida G. 86
Drain, SA Vincent E. 186
Drenas, Bill (53 nn 44, 45 & 46),(162 n 226)

| INDEX

Dulles, Allen 93, 195, 243, 262, 292-294
Duran, Sylvia 507-509, (514 n 15)
Dwayne's Photo Co., Kansas (491 n 158)
Dzieman, Dr Arthur 210

Eddowes, Michael (341 n 15)
Edgewood Arsenal, Development Laboratory 208-210, 215, 219
Eisenberg, Melvin Aron 207-209, 215-216, 219
Eisenhower, President Dwight 284, (341 n22), 518
Ellis, Stavis ('Steve') 14, 34
Elm Street 5, 7-9, 13-14, 16-20, 22-23, 26-27, 29-35, 37-38, 42-43, 106, 110-111, 113, 120-127, 132-133, 135, 305, 441-443, 454-457, 470-471, 478, (485 n 9), (486 n 9), (190 nn 106 & 107)
Elmer, Robert G. ('Tad') 159
Emaus, Will 452, (488 n 77)
Enberg, Eric 114
Entrance wound 61-65, 67, 70, 78-79, 86-87, 94-95, 177, 189, 192-193, 198, 348, 366-367
Epstein, Edward J. 276, 281-282, 286-287, 326-328, 332-334, 336-337, (340 n 3), (341 n 20), (343 n 39)
Ernest, Barry 26, 258-259
Estes, Billy Sol 3, 519,
Euins, Amos 34, 44
Evans, Mr Julien 280-281, 291
Evans, Myrtle 280-281, 291
Ewing, Michael (169 n 286)
 Exit wound 57, 61-65, 67, 70-71, 79-80, 86-87, 94, 177-179, 189-190, 198, 201, 206, 211, 349, 370-371, 373, 377

Fairfax Army Airfield, Kansas 476, (492 n 180)
Falx Cerebri 367-368
Fawkes, Guy 495, 499
FBI Report 16, 76, 78, (98 n 38), 143, 9161 n 200), (168 nn 278 & 283), (169 n 285), 176-177, 183, (220 n6), (232 n 14), 242, 321, (342 n 35), 374, 386-390, 395-396, 424, 504-505
Federal Bureau of Investigation (FBI) 7, 10, 16, 20-21, 31, (39 nn 19 & 23),76-79, 96, 111, 138-143, 148-152, 154-155, 158, (162 n 34), (168 nn 248, 260, 278 & 283), (169 nn 299 & 301), (170 n331), (171 nn 354 & 369), 175-177, 180, 182-183, 186, 204, 208-209, 212-213, 215, 219, (220 n 6), 224-229, 231-232, (232 nn 3 & 14), 244,252, 259, 275-278, 382, 290, 301-304, 307-314, 321, 326-327, 329, 333, 335-337, (342 n35), (343 nn 39, 40, 41, 42 & 43), 372, 380, 384, 386-391, 394-396, 399, 403-411, 414-415, 417, 420 422-426,

JFK | ECHOES FROM ELM STREET
A SEARCH FOR HISTORICAL ACCURACY ON THE
ASSASSINATION OF PRESIDENT JOHN F. KENNEDY

432-433, 435-436, 457, 462-463, 475, 478, 481-484, (485 nn 1, 10), (486 n16), (490 n103), (491 nn 153 & 163), 502-508, 510, 512-513, (514 nn 4, 9, 10, & 13), (515 n 16), 519
Federal Reserve 518, 519, (521 n 3)
Fensterwald, Bernard (169 n 286)
Fenton, Cliff (167 n 211)
Felde, Allan 285
Ferrell, Mary 51, 136, 144, (162 n 35), (168 n 259), (267 n 15), (485 n 2), 511, (513 n 10 & 12), (515 n 18 & 19), 521
Ferrell, Tom 141, (168 n 263)
Ferrie, David 499
Fetzer, James H. (221 n 39), (484 nn 15 & 27), (487 n 34), (489 nn 84, 89 & 94)
   'Murder In Dealey Plaza' (Also MIDP) 483, (486 n 27), (487 n30), (490 nn 106, 121 & 122), (491 nn 143 & 145), 483, (486 n 27)
Finck, Dr Pierre Antoine (Lt. Col.) 79, (98 n 44), 188, 208, 215, (221 nn 24 & 25), 345-355, 362, 366-367, 373, 375-377, (380 nn 5, 5, 12, 22, 23, 24, 25 & 26), (381 nn 67 & 68)
First World War 493
Florer, Larry 45, 52
Fogel, Jeff (163 n 98)
Folsom, Allison 286, 291, 295-298, 339, (341 n 16)
Foramen Magnum 68
Ford, Gerald 242, 274-275, 324, 338
Ford's Theatre 494
Forensic Pathologist 346-347, 349-351, 354, 362, 377
Fort Worth 10, 16, 45, 104, 140, 236, 262, 274, 277 279, 289-293, 298-299, 319, 337-338, (341 n 7), 357
Fox, SSA James K 58
   "Fox Photos/Set" 59, 81, 83-85
Frazier, SA Robert A. 180, 183, 186
Buell Wesley Frazier (27 n 3)
Fritz, Captain Will J. 260, 306-317, (341 n11), (342 n 30), 400, 430-431
Fulgham, Matt (170 n 341)

Garner, Darrell 236
Garrison, Jim 236, 349, (489 n 84)
Garwin, Richard L. 135, (167 n 224), (171 n 376)
Gauthier, SA Leo J. 208-209, 215, 219
Giancana, Sam 2, 393
Gibson, Mrs Donald 320, 339
Gloco Service Station 238-239

Index

Golz, Earl 115, 133, (163 n 106, 109 & 111), (168 n 272), (170 n 351), 390
Goodpasture, Anne 512, (514 n 12), (515 n 18)
Grant, Dr Patrick M. 188, (221 n 21)
Grassy Knoll 5, 9-11, 17-19, 22, 29, 32, 35-38, 43, 45, 101-102, 106-113, 120-122, 124, 130-132, 258, 444, 446, 496, 498
Gray Audograph Recorder 104
Greer, William 12, 133-134, 16, 454, 456-458, (490 n 102)
Gregory Diagrams 194, 200
Gregory, Dr Charles Francis 87-92, 94-95, (98 n 60), 180-183, 191, 193-196, 198-203, 205, 208-211, 219
Gregory, Dr Peter Paul 274-275, 281, 332-323, 328, 335, 337=339, (343 n 38)
Griffith, W.D. (485 n 10), (491 n 153)
Griggs, Ian 121, (39 n 30), (164 n 118), (170 n 337)
Groden, Robert J. 30-33, 36, (39 n 1, 2, 4, 13, 18, 21 & 36), 81, (220 n 9), (221 nn 28 & 29), 287, 329
Guinn, Dr Vincent Perry 183, 186-188, (221 n 19)
Guinyard, Sam 242, 254-255
Gulf of Tonkin 3
Gun Powder Plot (1605) 494-495
Gunn, Jeremy T. 351-352, 366, (381 n65), (486 n 22), (490 n 124), (491 n 149), 512

Haber, Carl 157, (172 nn 382 & 383)
Hall, C. Ray 407, 425-426, 432, 483
Hamby, Adrian 49, 52
Hancock, Larry 5, 223, (232 n 1, 6, 9 & 14), (267 n 25), 484, 501
Hargis, Officer B.W. ('Bobby') 12-15, 42-43, 109, 121-122, 125, 129-132, (165 n 161), (166 nn 187, 199 & 202)
Harkness, David V. 12, 116
Harley-Davidson 131-132
Harris, Larry 137, (167 n 234)
Harrison, Jack 480
Hartman, Rudolph (484 n 8)
Hauser, Myron 450
Hawkeye Facility, Rochester New York 461
Haygood, Clyde 125
Healy, David 456,473-474, 484, (489 n 98), (491 nn 164 & 165), (492 n 166)
Heart 7, 74, 115, 231, 351, 360, 362, 377, 379, 442
Hemming, Gerald P.
Henchliffe, Margaret M. 64
Henslee, Gerald ('Jerry') 119, 139-141, 144, 148, (164 n 156), (168 nn 254, 267, 268 & 269), (169 n 298), (170 nn 338 & 350), 255

Henslee (DPD) Transcript – Sawyer Exhibit B 141, (168 nn 268 & 279)
Hensley Field Naval Air Station 448, 450, 476
Hester, Beatrice & Charles 444-445, 469, 472, 479, (486 n 15)
Hidell, A. 47
Higginbottom, George 301, (341 n 21)
Higgins, Mr & Mrs Donald 258-259
Higgins, Roy 118
Hill, Gerald D. 144, (169 n 291), 259, (341 n 9)
Hill, Jean 30
Hill, Clinton J. ('Clint') 12, 32, 42-43, 60-61, 121-122, 124-126, 189, (221 n 31)
Hoch, Paul L. 138, 140-141, (167 nn 225 & 236), (168 nn 262 & 265), (169 nn 299 & 300), (170 n 340), (171 n 356)
Hoffa, James R. 2, 394
Hoffman, (Virgil) Ed 10, 19-20, 22, 29, 35, 44, (53 n 19)
Holland, Sam 21, 42
Holmes, Harry D. 311, 449
Hoover, J. Edgar 2, 142, (168 n 276), 175-176, 186, 226, 266, 277,309, 313-314, 475, (491 nn 153& 163), 503-505, 510-512, 519
Horne, Douglas P. 56, 78, 87, (97 nn 4 & 9), (98 nn 41& 43), 352, 369, (381 nn 65 & 71), (382 nn 75& 79), 448, 451, 459-464, 471-472, 475, 479-484, (485 nn 2, 6 & 11), (486 nn 12, 15, 21 & 22), (487 nn 35, 50 & 52), (488 nn 66 & 70), (489 n 86), (490, nn 110-117, 119, 120, 123, 124, 126, 129 & 131), (491 nn 133, 134, 140 & 149), (492 n 170), (514 nn 1, 4 & 5)
Horowitz, Paul 136
Hosty, James 276, 311, 329-330, (342 n 43)
House Judiciary Committee 101-102
House Select Committee on Assassinations (HSCA) 5, 11, (28 n 5), (30, 36, 51, (54 n 61), 55, 69, 85-86, (97 nn 3 & 25), (98 n 49), 101-117, 119-120, 122-125, 127, 129-132, 135, 138-141, 143-148, 152-156, 158-160, (161 n20), (162 nn 30, 31 & 34), (163 nn 88 & 100), (164 n 134), (165 nn 156, 164 & 174), (166 nn 177, 181, 187, 308, 312 & 313), (167 nn 212, 219 & 237), (168 nn 253, 254, 259, 263, 267 & 269), (169 nn 298, 305 & 307), (170 nn 317, 338 & 350), (171 nn 355, 359 & 365), 175, 180, 182-183, 185-187, 199, (220 n 4), (221 nn 16, 18 & 20), (222 n 58), 227-228, (232 nn 8, 9, 11, 12 & 13), 287-288, 318, 322, 333, 347-348, 351, 367, (380 nn 15, 16, & 22), (381 n 69), (382 nn 72, 77 & 87), 391-395-399, 404, 408- 413, 421, 429, 434, 437, 457, (488 n 58), (490 n 162)
House, Donald Wayne 45
Hovland, John 133, (167 n 214)
Howlett, SA John J. 208, 215
Hudson, Emmett J. 19
Hughes, Robert 109, 120, 126,(165 n 161)

INDEX

Hulse, Clifford E. ('Bubba') 254
Humes, Dr James Joseph 76-80, 83, (97 n 36), 177, 188-189, 208, 215, (221nn 25 & 32), 345-351, 354, 356, 358-363, 366-367, 369-379, (380 nn 2 & 10), (381 nn 30 & 65)
Hunt, E. Howard 506
Hunt, H.L. 302, 319
Hunter, Ben 464, 483, (491 n 143)
Hurt, Henry 138, (167 n 235)

Ireland 5

Jackson, C.D. (487 n 40)
Jackson, Douglas L. 13, 109, 133
Jackson, Margo 132, 140-141, 145, (166 n 210), (167 nn 211 & 212), (168 n 263), (170 n 314)
Jackson, Murray 139, 148, (168 n 253), (170 n 350)
Jaggars-Chiles-Stovall Co, 278
Jamieson, Bruce 474, (492 n 168),
Jamieson Film Laboratory, Dallas 447-448, 452, 459-460, 464, 480, (487 n 39)
Janney, Peter 464
Janofsky, Michael (171 n 377)
January, Wayne 229-230
Jaynes, Greg 121-122, (164 nn 116 & 117), (165 nn 154, 165, 169 & 170)
Jenkins, Dr Marion T. 69-74
Jenkins, James 373
Jennifer Juniors 441
Jefferson Boulevard 47-48, 238, 252, 254
Jefferson Library 49
JFK Assassination Records Collection Act, 1992 446
JFK Lancer (28 n 8), (165 n 161), (170 n 337), 442, 475, (489 n 88), (492 n 174), (514 n 11)
Jenner, Albert 285-286, 291-294, 299, 319-320, 231, 323, 339
John Birch Society 3, 301
Johnson, Arthur 50
Johnson, Lyndon Baines (LBJ) 2-3, 13, 32, 176, 224, 242, 249, 264, (267 n 26), 278-279, 304-307, 309, 313, (342 nn 23 & 26), (488 n 77), 502-505, 507, 510-513, 518-519, (521 n 2)
Jones, Dr Ronald 357-358
Jones, J.B. 479-480
Journal of the American Medical Association (JAMA) 352, (380 n 9), (381 n 27), (382 n 89)

Kantor, Seth (169 n 292), 314, 390-400, 413, 437
Karnei, Dr Robert F. 373
Katzenbach, Nicholas Debelleville 175
Keane, Barry 517, 484
Kellerman, Roy 61, 306
Kelley, SSA Thomas J. 87, 90, 141, 208, 215, 311, 449, 481, 483, (487 n 50), (488 n 58)
Kelly, James P. 130, 139, (166 n 219), (490 n 102)
Kelly, William ('Bill') 462, 484, (490 nn 123 & 128), (514 n 7)
Kennedy, Jacqueline 12, 18, 21, 30, 60, 121-122, 124, 126, 204, 302, 305, 319
Kennedy, John Fitzgerald (Frequent References throughout book)
Kennedy, Joseph P. 1
Kennedy, Robert F. 2, 223, 304, 355, 518, 519
Kerr, Ian (488 n 88)
Keuch, Robert L. 156, (167 n 240), (171 nn 357, 359, 361 & 371)
Kilduff, Malcolm 43
Kimbrough, Arch 136, (167 n 225), (169 nn 299 & 300)
    Kimbrough Transcript (164 nn 135 & 139), (166 n 186), (167 nn 226 & 228)
King James I 494
Kodachrome Film 464, (491 n 158)
Kodak 480-481, 483, (486 n 8), (486 nn 12 & 25), (487 nn 37 & 42)
Koenig, Bruce (168 n 248), (170 nn 331 & 369)
Kostikov, Valeriy 507-510, 513, (515 n 16)
Ku Klux Klan 3
Kunkel, Charles 484
Kurtz, Michael 301-302, (341 n 21), (342 n 32)
Kuzmin, Joyce (172 n 394)

Lacerated wound 366
Landis, Paul 43
Lane, Duke 458, (490 n 108)
Lane, Mark 11, 13, 44, (53 n 14, 18, 21 & 34), 258, (267 n 20 & 22), 497, (500 n 1)
Laos 3
Lawson, Belford V. (167 n 219), (490 n 102)
Lawson, Winston G. 13-14, 135
Ledford, Bruce 140, (168 n 258)
Left temple 70-74
Lennon, John 499
Lewis, Richard Warren (459 n 79)
Leavelle, James 255-256, (342 n 27), 430
Liebeler, Wesley J. 17-19, 22, 252-253, 274-275, 284, 321, 339

| INDEX

Lifton, David S. 68, 77-78, 81 (97 n 20), 377, (380 n 21), (381 n 70), (382 n 88), 484, (487 n 34 & 35)
Light, Dr F. W. 208-210, 215, 219-220
Lincoln, Abraham 373, (382 n 81), 494-495, 504
Lincoln, Evelyn (521 n 2)
Linsker, Ralph 149-150
Livingstone, Harrison E. (39 n 16), 81, (97 n 28), (266 n 7), (382 n 83), 456, 474-475, 484, (486 nn 23 & 26), (487 n 32), (490 nn 99 & 106), (492 nn 168, 174 & 175)
   'The Hoax of The Century' (Also 'THOTC') (167 n 219), (485 n 8), (487 n 33), (489 n 87), (490 n 100), (491 n 151)
LMH Co. 445, 447, 465, (486 nn 28 & 29), (487 n 30), (491 n 154)
Lone Gunman/Theories 19, 497-500
Love Field Airport, Dallas 75, 230, 236-237, 305, 307, 447, 451, 459
Lovelady, Billy 6, 23-26
Lumpkin, George 140-141, 152
Lundahl, Arthur 460, 482
Lungs 73, 351, 356, 360, 362, 377, 379
Lyons, Steven 153

Mack, Gary 104, 133, 143-144, 149, 161, (162 n 30), (167 nn 215, 216, 218 & 219), (168 nn 275, 279, 281, & 282), (169 nn 285, 286, 287, 289, 291, 299, 301, & 302), (170 nn 317 & 340), 434, 482-484, (488 n 78)
'Magic Bullet' 29, 177, (220 n 2), 497
Malley, SA James R. 208, 215
Manchester, William 304, (342 n 26), 503, 511
Mannlicher-Carcano 29, 37, 47, (163 n 81), 177, 199
Mantik, Dr David W. 81, 190, (486 n 27), (487 n 30)
Marcello, Carlos 2, 312, 394-395, 397-398
Markham, Helen 241-242, 244-249, 257, 261-262
Marrs, Jim 32, (39 nn 8, 12, 15 & 38), (267 n 23), 437, 456, (459 n 97)
Marsalis Bus 48
Martin, Officer, B.J. 13, 42-43, 109, 133, (166 nn 181 & 202)
Martinez, Jorge Soto 227
Marwell, David (486 nn 12 & 22), (490 n 124), (491 n 149)
Mauser 47,
Mayn, Charles (171 nn 361 & 375)
McBride, Palmer 283-286
McCaghren, Paul 104, 144-147, 152, 154, (162 n 31), (168 nn 271, 272), (169 nn 293, 293, 304, 305, 307 & 308), (170 n 351), (171 nn 355, 359), 427-428)
McClelland, Dr Robert N. 70, 74, 95
McCloy, John J. (98 n 63), 195, 209, 219, 264

535

McCone, John 460, 482, 503
McCormick, Harry 479-480
McIntire, Mel 125, 133-134, (167 n 213)
McKinley, President William 499
McLain, H.B. 109-110, 113-117, 119-126, 131, 133-134, 146,(163 nn 72 & 97), (165 nn 161, 163, 167, 169 & 174), (166 n 184)
McMahon, Homer A. 461-464, 483, (490 nn 121, 122, 123, 127, 130 & 132), (491 nn 145 & 146)
McNamara, Defence Secretary, Robert 305
McWatter, Cecil 48
McWilliams, William ('Bill') 103, (161 n 24), (162 nn 26 & 27)
Medico 192
Medicolegal Autopsy 80, 345, 355, 359, 362, 376-377
Mentzel, Officer, William D. 239
Mercer, Julia Ann 9-10
Mexico City 265, 503-513, (514 nn 12)
Microscope Slides 81, 348
Midway Airport, Chicago 451
Military Industrial Complex 518-521
Miller, Bill (167 n 217)
Milteer, Joseph 225-226
Miron, Murray 138
Mohr, John P. 474
Monaco Film Laboratory, San Francisco (489 n 86)
Mooney, Deputy Sheriff, Luke 47
Moore, Bernice (489 n 89)
Moore, Elmer W. 140
Moorman, Mary Ann 40, 60
Moriarty, Jack 119, 130, 144-146, (162 n 31), (169 n 305 & 307), 421
Morissette, Denis 116, (164 n 115)
Moritz, Dr Alan R. 376, 379, (382 n 85)
Morley, Jefferson (171 377), (514 n 12)
Motorola Radios (162 n 34)
Moyers, Bill 175
Muchmore, Mary 121
Murphy, Sean (166 n 183)
Murphy, William T. (171 n 360)
Murr, Gary 483-484, (487 n 49), (488 n 56), (490 n 118 & 124)
Myers, Dale K. 119-120, 124, 126, 143, 145, (163 n 99), (165 nn 154, 158, 161, 162 & 163), (166 nn 176, 180, 184 & 188), (169 nn 288, 290 & 292), 237, 242, (266 nn 3 & 10), (267 n 24)

National Academy of Science (NAS) 101-102
National Archives 58-59, 81, 130, 136, 140-141, 143, 154-155, 158, 161, (168, n 262,266), (169, n 286), 374, 444, 449, 461, (485, n 8)
National Archives and Records Administration (NARA) (161, n 6), 444
National Photographic Interpretation Center (NPIC) 442, 459-464, 473, 482-483, (489, n 86), (490, n 110, 127)
National Research Council 101
National States Rights Party 225-226
Neck Organs 350, 354-355, 362
Nelson, Ronald C. 137, 238, 240
Neutron Activation Analysis (NAA) 56, 186, (221, n 15, 19)
New Orleans 225-226, 236, 262, 265, 280, 298, 301, 312, 326, 340, (380, n 5, 7), 393-394, 397, 453, (485, n 1), (489, n 84), (514, n 13)
Newcomb, Fred 11, (28, n 6), (488, n 55), (489, n 85)
Newman, Bill 17-18, 42, 60
Newman, William J (DPD) 411-413
Nix, Orville 32, 38, 121
Nixon, Richard 1, 519
Nolan, Bobby 182, 185
Nuclear Test Ban Treaty 520
Nulty, Tom 447, 463

O'Donnell, Ken 306
Oakes, Mark 12, 122, (165, n 173)
Occipital 65-70, 83, 348, 364, 366-367, 369
Occipital, lobes 68
Off record discussion 73, 349
Oglesby, Carl (163, n 83)
Oliver, Beverly 8, 30
Olivier, Dr A. G. 208-210, 219-220
O'Neill, SA Francis X. 76-79, (98 n 37, 40, 42), 372, 374, (380, n 13), (382 n 74)
Operation Mongoose 265
Oppenheimer, Robert (342, n 22)
Orange Bowl 223-224
Ormsby, Mark (161, n 24)
Osanic, Len 400, (490, n 111)
Osborn, C.R. 479-480
Osborne, Mack 336
Osborne, William Dr. 94, 198
Oser, Alvin 349-350
Oswald, Harvey 5, 6, 23, 26, 318, 326, 340, (341, n 18),

JFK | Echoes From Elm Street
A Search for Historical Accuracy on the
Assassination of President John F. Kennedy

Oswald, Lee Harvey (LHO) i, 5-7, 23, 26, 27, 29, 41, 44-47, 49-51, 56, 61, 65, 67, 82, 96, 101-102, 106, (169, n 288, 292), 173, 175, 205, 238, 241-242, 249, 252, 258, 262-265, (266, n 3), (267, n 20), 271, 273-274, 279, 286-288, 301, 306-309, 314, 318, 326, 328, 329-330, 336, 340, (341, n 18), 375, 383, 391, 398, 399, 408, 421, 428, 430, 436-437, 496-499, (514, n 9, 10)
Oswald, Marguerite (LHO's Mother) 289, 295-296, 321, 323
Oswald, Marina (LHO's Wife) 274, 321-323, 337-338, (343, n 47)
Oswald, Robert (LHO's Brother) 279, 290-291, 293, 298-299, 324, 326, 337
Owen, Randy 484
Oxford English Dictionary 495

Paine, Ruth 27, 50, 205, 313, 320-321, 328, 338-339
Palamara, Vincent (39, n 16), (232, n 5), 458, (490, n 106)
Paradigms 493
Parietal 65, 68-70, 83, 357, 364, 365, 369, 371, 373-374
Parkland Hospital 13, 15, 36, 43, 46, (53, n 17), 72, 74, 114-115, 118, 121-123, 133, 219, 235, 270, 278, 283, 306, 383, 399-400, 497, 501, 503
Paraffin test 51
Parrot Jungle 227
Paternostro, Samuel 37
Payne, Darwin 479
Peacock Jewellery Co. 443
Peel, John 317, (343, n 37)
Pein, David Von 314
Penetrating Wound 63, 92, 191, 198-199
Perforating Wound 55, 63, 92, 188, 190-191, 361-362, 374
Permindex 266
Perry, Dr Malcolm Oliver 36, (53, n 17), 61-64, 69, 79-80, 95, (97, n 10), 177, 203, 211, 357-358, 371, 373, 375, (514, n 1)
Peters, Dr Paul 68, 358
Phillips, Max 448-450, 460, 476, 481, (487, n 49), (488, n 56), (490, n 118)
Pic, John (LHO's Half- Brother) 290-291, 297, 323
Picket Fence 19-22, 29, 35, 37, 44, 106
Pincher, Mike 459, (490, n 109)
Pinter, Harold 493
Pleural Sac 92, 191, 358
Pneumothorax 75, 355-358, 360
Poe, Officer J.M. 252, 259-260
Porter, Marina (Oswald) 271
Posner, Gerald 62, 67-69, (97, n 11, 19, 21, 24, 33), 193, 430-431, 497, 499, (500, n 2)
Postal, Julia 48

| INDEX

Post Mortem 75, 77, 190, (220, n 7), (221, n 32), (222, n 64), 355-356, 366-377, (381, n 40, 63)
Potts, Walther E. 49-50
Powers, Daniel 281
Price, J.C. 29, 35, (39, n 34), 44
Price, W. ('Willie') 115-119, (164, n 139, 140, 143)
Princip, Gavrilo 495, 499
Protective Research Service 141, 223
Protective Services 224-226

Queens College, New York 106-107
Quinn, Rosaleen 325-333, 335-337, 339, (343, n 39)

Radius 92, 94-95, 179, 191, 198, 209-210, 220, (221, n 11)
Rader, Charles 118, 139, 149, (168, n 248, 251), (170, n 331, 346), (171, n 369)
Rambler Station Wagon 20-21, 23, 26-27, 44, 46
Ramsey, Norman 101, 115, 135, 139, 141, 148, 151, (163, n 88), (167, n 216, 218), (168, n 246, 248, 265), (170, n 331, 334), (171, n 369)
  Ramsey/NAS Panel 101-102, 111-113, 115, 118, 132-133, 135-136, 139, 141, 145, 147-151, 154-156, 158, 160, (166, n 190), (167, n 245), (168, n 248, 251), (170, n 331, 346), (171, n 369)
  Ramsey Panel Report 102, 115, 139, (163, n 82), (169, n 311)
Randlich, Dr Erik 188
Rankin, J. Lee 60-61, (168, n 276), 209, 212, 216, 219, 276-277, 323, 413, (491, n 153, 163), 512
Rather, Dan 483
Raytheon 158-159, (172, n 392, 394)
Reagan National Airport, Washington 461
"Reclaiming History" 116, (164, n 108, 119), 175, (220, n 2), 287, 328, 336, (342, n 25, 33), 421, 437, (485, n 5)
Redbird Airport 229
Redlich, Norman 208-209, 215-216, 219
Reily Coffee Co 278, 298
Revill, Jack (168, n 271), (170, n 351), 396, 406, 412, 427-428
Reymond, William 456, (489, n 97)
Reynolds, Dr Jack 96, 183, 204
Reynolds, Warren 242, 252-254
Rhyan, Lillian L. 449
Roberdeau, Don 38, (39, n 41)
Roberts, Craig 34, 36-37, (39, n 28, 35, 40)
Roberts, Earlene 47, 49-50, 249, 265

Rodino Jr., Peter W. 102, (161, n 10)
Rogers, Lillian 441, 444-446, 465-466, 468-472, 478-479, (491, n 155)
Rogge, Richard 140, (168, n 260), (171, n 354)
Roll call 47, (53, n 32)
Rooney, Daniel (172, n 387, 395)
Rose, Dr Earl Forrest 59, 75-76, 87, 260, 306, 374
Rose, Guy 50
Rose, Harold 120, 123, 130, 139, (232, n 8)
Rosman, Alaric 5, 179, (220, n 8), (222, n 72), 241, 245, (267, n 15)
Roswell 494
Rowan, Roy (Also Rowen, Roy) 450-451
Rowland, Arnold 33-34, 44
Rowley, James J. 448, 481, (487, n 50, 53), (488, n 58), (514, n 1)
Ruby, Jack 5-6, 10, 23, 46, 141, (169, n 292), 174, 231, 236, 242, 265-266, 326, 383-395, 397-409, 411, 413-417, 419-429, 431- 438
Rusk, Dean 305
Russ, Michael 120, (165, n 154, 158)
Russell, Senator Richard - 264
Ryan, Roderick 474-475, (486, n 12)
Russian Language 273, 285, 318, 324-325, 330, 333-334, 338-339, (343, n 38)
Rydberg, Harold A. 86, 348

Saggital Sinus 367
Sanford, Terry 518-519
Sarajevo 494
Sawyer, J. Herbert 141-142, (168, n 268, 270)
Schaeffer, Roy L. 459, (490, n 109)
Schiller, Lawrence (489, n 79)
Schmidt, Edward C. (170, n 315)
Schmidt, Mary Kay (172, n 395)
Schwartz, Erwin 447-449, 479-482, 484, (487, n 47, 50, 51), (488, n 61)
Schwartz, Mrs. Doris 148-149
Scoggins, 242-244, 255-256
Scott, Marvin (486, n 15)
Sealy, Dr W. C. 374, (382, n 78)
Seaton, Paul 120, 160, (165, n 154, 158)
Secret Service 15, 22-23, 27, 41-42, 44, 49, 59, 62, 67, 75, 90, 140-141, 152, 154, 208, 212, 215, 223-229, 276, 278-280, 306-308, 310-313, 369, 378, 387, 444-446, 448-450, 454-456, 458-463, 465, 475-476, 481-484, 501, (514, n 1)
   Secret Service Copy 1 445-446, 465, (491, n 151)
   Secret Service Copy 2 445, 465

INDEX

Secret Service File 87
  File 969 87, 89-90
Senkel, Bill L. 49-50
Seymour, William 266
Shackelford, Martin 484, (485, n 7), (486, n 12, 21)
Shaneyfelt, SA Lyndal L. 208-209, 215, 219, (485, n 10)
Shanklin, Gordon (342, n 35), 481
Sharp, William 45
Shaw, Clay 33, 79, (166, n 202), (211, n 24, 26, 40), 236, 349, 375, (380, n 5, 7), 453, 474, (485, n 1), (487, n 50)
Shaw, Dr Robert Roeder 87-88, 91-94, (98, n 59, 64, 65), 191-198, 205-206, 209-211, 219
Shearer, Russ (167, n 226)
Shipp, Bert 480
Shirakova, Rima 283, 298, (341, n 13)
Shires, Dr George T. 88, 92, 95-96, (99, n 85), 184, 191, 202-203, 205, 211, (222, n 62)
Shots, Known and Possible Numbers of 10-12, 16-18, 29-30, 32, 36-38, 41-44, 101-102, 105-107, 110-114, 120-121, 123-124, 131-132, 158-160, 497-498
Sibert and O'Neill Report 76-79, (98, n 37, 40, 42), 372, 374, (380, n 13)
Siegal, Evelyn 281
Single Bullet Theory (SBT) 60, 87, 91, 93-96, 174-175, 178-180, 184-185, 188, 191, 193-194, 196-197, 199-212, (220, n 1)
Sitzman, Marilyn 441, 444-445, 457, 469, 472, 479, (486, n 15)
Sixth Floor 23, 29, 32-34, 45, 110, 132, 259, 497
Sixth Floor Museum, Dallas (Also SFM) 143-145, 149, 161, (164, n 140, 143), 443, 445, 447, 451-453, 459, 463, 465-467, 469, 471, 477-478, 484, (487, n 47), (491, n 155), (492, n 181)
Skelton, Royce 16-17, 31-32, 34
Skull Fragments 348, 370
Slawson, David 512
Sloan, Frank 447, (487, n 40, 41)
Slough, Hugh 49-51, (53, n 51)
Smith, Bill 461-462, 483
Smith, Marshall 20-22, 42, 44
Smith, Merriman 501
Smith, William 242
Sneed, Larry A. 12, 121-122, 124, 149, (165, n 168, 172), (166, n 181, 187, 273), (179, n 343), (488, n 54)
Sniper's nest 33-34, 45, 47, 132
Snyder, Richard 300, (341, n 20)
Soldier Field 227

Sorrels, Forrest V. 13-14, 43, 135, 448-449, 479-482, (487, n 50, 53), (488, n 58)
Specter, Arlen J. 9, 11, 64, 67, 69, 71-74, 87, 91, 94-96, (98, n 59), 179, 194-197, 199-201, 203-204, 206, 208-209, 212, 215-216, 218-220, 348, 357-358, 363, 375, 378
Specter, Shanin (164, n 100)
Spengler, Lillian 227
Spiegelman, Dr Cliff 188, (221, n 22)
Spradlin, L.W. 136
Sprague, Richard E. 113-115, (163, n 70, 93, 94, 95, 98), (165, n 154)
Stereo Pair 85
Stevenson, Adlai 224
Stockpiling Scandal 518-519, (521, n 4)
Stolley, Richard B. 450-451, 459, 464, 466-467, 473, 476, 478, 481-484, (488, n 67), (489, n 78, 81)
Stokes, Louis 271
Stout, Zack 281
Stovall, Richard 50
"Strange Conferences" 191, 207-209, 212
Stringer, John Thomas 81
Sturdivan, Larry M. 199, (222, n 58)
Sulci 66
Summers, Malcolm (166, n 187)
Supplementary Autopsy Report - 348
Suydam, Henry (487, n 50)
Swenson, Robert ('Bob') 103, (161, n 24), (162, n 27)

Tague, James Thomas 29, 31, 36, 45, 173, 178, 207, 212
Talbert, E. 263
Tarasof, Mr. and Mrs. 509-510
Taylor, Maxwell 305
Temporal 65, 69-70, 72-74, 83, 364-365, 369
Tenth and Patton (Oak Cliff) 47, 49, 240-241, 244-245, 250, 252
Terminal Annexe Building 44
Texas School Book Depository (TSBD) 5-7, 10-11, 16, 18-19, 21-23, 26-27, 29, 31-34, 36-37, 42-44, 70, 101, 106-108, 110-111, 123, 129-132, 137, 174, 177-179, 199, 231, 240, 250, 258-259, 266, 269-270, 278, 303, 436, 441, 454, 457, (490, n 101), 496-499, 501
Texas Theatre 47-49, 52, 246, 248, 252, 259, 262-265, 398, 501, (514, n 2)
Thigh Wound 95-96, 191, 198, 202-204, 206, 211-213
Third Thoracic Vertebrae 189, 372
Thomas, Donald Byron ('Don') 120, (162, n 35), (163, n 84), (169, n 299),

(171, n 375), (172, n 390)
Thompson, Josiah (167, n 217), 479-484, (486, n 15), (487, n 53), (491, n 163)
Thoracic Organs 356
Thornley, Kerry 279, 285-286
Three tramps 45, 52
Throat Wound 36, 60-64, 70, 76, 79-80, 177, 179, 189-191, 358, 362, 373, 375-376
Time/Life Inc. (also Life) 215, 219, 443-448, 450-454, 459-460, 462-467, 471-473, 476-478, 481-483, (486, n 16, 28), (487, n 50), (488, n 77), (489, n 84), (491, n 160, 162), 501
Tippit, Edgar Lee 233-234
Tippit, J.D. 47-50, 52, (54, n 51), 59, 130, 137-138, 141, 233-242, 244-252, 255-266, 269-270, 279, 315-316, (342, n 27, 28), 374
Tippit Lizzie Mae 233-234
Tobin, Dr William A. 188, (221, n 22)
Tolson, Clyde 505, (514, n 10)
Toney, John Burton 116
Top Ten Record Store 48, (53, n 45), 238
Torbitt, William (A Pseudonym for David Copeland) - 266
Tracheotomy 62-64, 76, 78-80, 177, 189, 350, 357-358, 371, 373, 375
Trafficante Santo 2, 393-394
Transcripts 60-61, 137, 145, 147, 152, 154, 510, 512
Trask, Richard B. (165, n 161), (167, n 213), 464-466, 468, 472, 479-484, (485, n 2, 3, 6, 7, 10, 11), (486, n 13, 14, 15, 17, 21, 22), (487, n 40, 43, 45, 50), (488, n 61, 64, 70, 71, 73), (489, n 81, 86, 87), (491, n 147, 148, 149, 150, 153, 161), (492, n 178)
"Treachery in Dallas" 204
Trulock, Alison (172, n 395)
Truly, Roy 13, 23, 46-47, 51, 457, (490, n 101)
Truman, (341, n 22)
Turner, William (486, n 16)
Twyman, Noel 484, (486, n 12), (487, n 50), (492, n 170, 171, 177)

U.S. Department of Justice (DOJ - Justice Department) 139, 152-153, 156, (163, n 98), (165, n 154), (167, n 240), (170, n 344), (171, n 360, 361, 371, 374)
University of Texas Medical School 92-95, 192, 198, 202
U.S. Army Medical Corp 192
U.S. Military Autopsy Manual 352-356, 359-362, 376, (380, n 11), (381, n 28, 31-37, 39, 43, 49-52, 56-57, 59-61), (382, n 86, 1-3)
Vallee, Thomas Arthur 228, (232, n 9)

Van Noord, Richard (165, n 161)
Vaughan, Todd W. 123-125, 127-128, 153, 158, (166, n 178, 180, 182, 185, 190, 201), (171, n 362), (172, n 389)
Verb, Hal (490, n 105)
Vietnam 3, 518-519, (521, n 1)
Vigilance Committees 234

Wade, Henry 275-277, 316, 401, 413, 502
Waffen, Leslie C. ('Les') 158, 161, (161, n 24), (171, n 360-361, 375), (172, n 384-386), 446, (486, n 19)
Walker, General Edwin 270, 301-302
Walther, Carolyn 33-34, (39, n 23), 44
Walthers, Buddy 31
Ward, Theron 76, 306
Warner, SSA Roger C. 87-91, 140-141, 404
Warren Commission 5, 7-10, 17, 19, 23-27, 29, 31-34, 38, (39, n 9-11, 17, 20, 22-23, 26-27, 39), 46-47, 55, 57, 60-64, 67, 69-74, 78, 80, 84-87, 90-96, (97, n 5), (98, n 38), 102, 106, 111, 128-129, 131, 134-135, 141-143, 146-147, 152, (162, n 25), (168, n 261, 268), (169, n 286, 297), (171, n 354), 175-180, 185, 188-199, 202-209, 212-213, (220, n 6), (221, n 11), (232, n 5), 239-242, 244, 248-249, 252, 254, 256, 258-259, 263-264, (266, n 1), 271, 274, 278, 282, 290, 294, 318, 321, 323, 333, 335, 337, (340, n 2-3), (342, n 25), (343, n 39-40), 345-349, 355-358, 363, 375, 380, 384-392, 394, 398-407, 409-437, 450, 456-457, 472, 474, (485, n 1), (487, n 50), (488, n 58), (490, n 101, 104), (491, n 153, 496-501, 504-505, 512-513, (514, n 1, 3, 9)
Warren Commission Report (WCR) 8, 23, 55, 78, 93, (97, n 1-2), (98, n 39), 102, 175, 192, 197, 208-209, 212, (221, n 23), (222, n 52), 244-245, 307, (380, n 18), (381, n 34, 41, 52), (382, n 73, 4), 384, 410, 439
Warren, Earl 264, 274-275, 380
Washington D.C. 75-76, 186, 207, 339, 476, 517
Weatherford, Harry 42
Weisberg, Harold 33, 81, 203, 208-209, 212, 355
Weiss, Mark 106-109, 111-112, 131, 139, (162, n 58), (163, n 63, 88), (167, n 243)
Weitzman, Seymour 42
Wheeler, Craig L. (168, n 259)
White, Roscoe 265
Wilkinson, Sydney (489, n 86)
Winchester (gun) 36, 46, (222, n 58), 260
Woodward, Dr Joseph Janvier 374
Wolf, Jared J. (179, n 315)
Wolf, William 284

INDEX

World Trade Centre 495-496
Worrell, James 33, 44
Wright, Frank 258
Wright, Mary 258
Wrist wound 94, 185, 191, 198-201, 213, 217, 220
Wrone, David R. 479-484, (485, n 2, 3, 6, 11), (486, n 16), (487, n 38, 40, 44-45, 50, 52-53), (488, n 61, 64, 78), (489, n 79, 81), (490, n 114)

X-Rays 57-59, 81, 84-85, 183-184, 190, 347, 361, 363, 369, 377, 380

Yarborough 11
Yates, Ralph Leon 6-7, 230-231, (232, n 14)
Youngblood, Rufus 307, (342, n 23)

Zapruder, Abraham 17-19, 30, 43, (220, n 3), 441, 443, 464, 473, (485, n 1), 501
Zapruder Film 8, 13, 15, 19, 29-30, 32, 36, 93, 111, 135, 175, 177, 180, 191-192, 195, 197-198, 207-208, 215, 219, 441-492, 498-499
   Black-And-White Unslit (16mm) Copies 448, 450, 458, 460-461, 463, 466, 469, 472-473, 478, 480
   Life/Lmh Copy 445, 447, 465
   Secret Service Copies 444-446, 465, 468, 475, 482
Zapruder, Lillian Mrs. (486, n 28)
Zapruder, Myrna (Also Hauser, Myrna and Reis) 450, (486, n 28)
Zavada, Roland J. 443, 445-446, 451-453, 462-466, 468, 471-472, 474-476, 482, 484, (486, n 25), (487, n 36), (489, n 80, 82), (492, n 174-176)
Zavada/Kodak Report 446, 463, 480, (485, n 8, 11), (486, n 12, 22, 24-26, 29), (487, n 30-31), (490, n 125), (491, n 135-139, 144, 149, 152, 154)

www.ingramcontent.com/pod-product-compliance
Lightning Source LLC
Chambersburg PA
CBHW060311230426
43663CB00009B/1662